# Psychology
# in
# Organizations

## The Social Identity Approach

### S. Alexander Haslam

SAGE Publications

London • Thousand Oaks • New Delhi

First published 2001
Reprinted 2001
Reprinted 2002

SAGE Publications Ltd
6 Bonhill Street
London EC2A 4PU

SAGE Publications Inc
2455 Teller Road
Thousand Oaks, California 91320

SAGE Publications India Pvt Ltd
32, M-Block Market
Greater Kailash - I
New Delhi 110 048

**British Library Cataloguing in Publication data**

A catalogue record for this book is available from the British Library

ISBN 0 7619 6157 7
ISBN 0 7619 6158 5  (pbk)

**Library of Congress catalog card number record available**

Printed in Great Britain by Athenaem Press, Gateshead

# Contents

# Figures

# Tables

# Foreword

Over the last decade or so (following Ashforth & Mael, 1989) there has been a rapid growth of interest in applying social identity ideas to the problems of organizational psychology. In this book Alex Haslam has taken on the huge but important task of surveying the whole field of organizational psychology from the general perspective provided by the social identity approach. In doing this he has produced a quite outstanding book, one which provides original insights at varying levels and serves several purposes.

He has written firstly a wonderful textbook. The book summarizes and reviews research and theory in all the major areas of the field. Moreover, it puts this work in an historical and a systematic theoretical context. There is a unity and coherence of perspective which makes the book, unusually for a textbook, highly readable and thought-provoking. How many textbooks can be read effortlessly from beginning to end with a sense of pleasure and intellectual nourishment? Not many, but this is one. The book is characterized by confident scholarship and a thoughtful consideration of the field's most basic issues and yet is a delight to read.

As one works through the chapters, one not only learns about particular topics, one also gradually becomes aware of a strategic critique, of an argument, constructive rather than destructive, for a major reorientation of thinking, focused on the importance of the social group in organizational life. There is no denial of the importance of individual processes, but there is a recognition of the need to restore balance, to recognize that human beings are *psychological group members* who act in terms of shared social identities as well as individuals who act in terms of individual differences and personal identities, and moreover that psychological group membership can be a positive and productive organizational force. There is a long tradition in organizational and social psychology which construes group influences as a source of irrationality, pathology and primitivism. Think of the idea of 'deindividuation', that to be 'submerged' in the group is to lose one's conscious, rational self and become prey to the dark instincts of the collective unconscious. The social identity approach rejects this slant on the group outright. It sees group actions as regulated by a different level of self, a higher-order, more socially inclusive self, a change of self, not a loss of self. And it also assumes (and explains) that positive and powerful processes of human social life to do with social cohesion, cooperation and influence are made possible only because human beings have the capacity to act as other than purely individual persons. The fact that human beings are able to act as both individuals and as group members is a plus, adding immensely to the sophistication and possibilities of our social relationships. Just as important for this reorientation, there is the related recognition, explicit in the social identity approach, that the functioning of social identity processes always takes place in a social context and is shaped by social structural realities. Organizations are social structures and how people orient and define themselves psychologically in relation to and within these social structures is fundamental to understanding how they will feel, think and act.

Haslam has also produced a superb introduction to the social identity approach, one of the best I have come across. This is no easy task. This approach encompasses two related theories, social identity theory and self-categorization theory, both with a research history stretching back to the 1970s. They have generated a vast amount of empirical work in social psychology (and elsewhere) and are stimulating more work today than they have ever done before, in areas as diverse as intergroup relations, stereotyping, group processes, social influence, language and communication, social cognition and the self-concept. Both theories are unusually complex and well-developed compared to the norm in social psychology. Haslam's summary manages to be wide-ranging, up-to-date, lucid and accurate. He gets the general picture right in an introductory chapter and he gets the details right in his elaboration of specific applications. This is a rare feat. He also adds original twists and insights of his own consistent with the spirit and substance of the theories. This is not surprising given that Haslam himself is a leading researcher in the social identity tradition and has made highly influential contributions to the literature.

Haslam's summary of the social identity approach takes three forms. One emerges from the book as a whole. As the discussion of the field progresses, more light is thrown back onto his particular perspective and the 'feel' of the social identity approach is conveyed. Then there is Chapter 2 where he provides an explicit statement of the basic ideas of social identity and self-categorization theories. And finally, but by no means least, each subsequent chapter contains both a review of an area of organizational psychology and a detailed discussion of how the social identity approach has been applied in the area and what more it can offer. These discussions are full of ideas for contemplation and future research. They provide a further major contribution of the book, a systematic, comprehensive and concrete statement of how social identity ideas can be integrated into organizational psychology and of what both the social identity approach and organizational psychology have to gain from each other. For it is important to note that the traffic is not all one way. It becomes clear that organizational contexts are a natural home for social identity research and that social identity ideas are going to benefit enormously from the work of organizational researchers.

So much for the achievements of this book. It may now be useful to say a few words about the social identity approach more generally. Social identity theory (Tajfel, 1972, 1974; Tajfel & Turner, 1979; Turner, 1975) was developed in the early 1970s and self-categorization theory (Turner, 1978, 1982, 1985; Turner, Hogg, Oakes, Reicher & Wetherell, 1987) emerged in the late 1970s and early 1980s. Both were developed in social psychology. Both also took some years to evolve into their final form (they were given their present names only in 1978 and 1985 respectively), a fact which can still lead reviewers (not Haslam) to ignore later developments in favour of earlier, more truncated versions. To say 'final', however, is not to imply that the theories are 'finished and perfect'. On the contrary, like all theories, both have their lacunae, both contain elements which need elaborating and developing, both are deliberately selective in their explanatory scope. Important ideas have been and are being contributed by subsequent and contemporary research. To say 'final' is rather to indicate the point at which the essential ideas became systematized into a mature and coherent form. The term 'approach' is useful as shorthand for referring to both theories together and the notions which they share, but it is important to note that they are 'theories', that is, that they comprise a set of core, interrelated assumptions and hypotheses which lead to specific, testable and novel predictions. They are much more than merely ways of thinking. This is important to grasp because the danger otherwise is that the current upsurge of research activity will lead only to eclecticism and conceptual vagueness rather than solid cumulative theoretical development.

Because self-categorization theory built upon (but subsequently redefined) some of the ideas in social identity theory and in part was a response to some issues raised by that theory, there is a tendency to confuse them. This is unfortunate because it leads to misinterpretations of the ideas. The theories are complementary and related but they are different, defined by different core hypotheses and different problems. Social identity theory is a theory of intergroup relations. It began as a way of trying to make sense of discrimination between social groups and its fundamental *psychological* idea was that where people make social comparisons between groups, they seek positive distinctiveness for their ingroups compared to outgroups in order to achieve a positive social identity. Self-categorization theory is a theory of the psychological group. It seeks to explain how different individuals are able to become, act, think and feel as a psychological group under particular circumstances. How, from a psychological point of view, are people able to behave collectively rather than as individual personalities? Its core idea is that behind the shift from individual to group psychology and behaviour is a shift from people defining and seeing themselves in terms of their personal identities to people defining and seeing themselves more (it is relative) in terms of their shared social identities. We could say very crudely that the former theory deals with the implications of 'us versus them' distinctions (ingroups versus outgroups), whereas the latter deals with 'I and me' versus 'we and us' distinctions (acting as an individual versus acting as a group member). This contrast helps to illustrate why they are both useful to make sense of group processes and intra- and intergroup relationships. It is too crude because the theories are much richer psychologically than such a condensed picture suggests. They are 'process' theories rather than simple assertions of the effects of just one factor or variable.

A basic idea which both theories have in common is that one cannot make sense of how people are behaving when they are acting in terms of their social identities by extrapolating from their properties as individual persons. There is assumed to be a psychological discontinuity between interpersonal behaviour (people reacting to each other as individuals) and group behaviour. Moving from the 'I' to the 'we' psychologically transforms people and brings into play new processes that could not otherwise exist. Indeed it is to this creative capacity that most organizations owe their success.

Another important point is that both theories take for granted and are absolutely committed to the notion that social structure, social context and society more broadly are fundamental to the way that social identity processes come into being, are experienced and shape cognition and behaviour. There is no psychology in a social vacuum. From a social identity perspective, how people define themselves, make sense of the world and act in relation to each other is always a function of an interaction between their psychology, individual and/or collective, and the socially organized environment within which they exist. Indeed, social identity processes are seen as a means whereby social organization exerts a psychological as well as an external, situational influence on individual and group behaviour. Organizations are not merely 'stimulus settings' which constrain or facilitate behaviour from the outside, which change what we do, they also shape our cognitively represented self, changing our subjective experience of who we are and the psychological meaning of the environment. They change our feelings, goals, values, motives, attitudes and beliefs, the cognitive interpretations and resources which define us as psychological and social actors. And this point is true too of the wider social, political and economic system within which organizations themselves function.

The affinity between this theoretical commitment and the distinctive issues of organizational psychology is well illustrated in the pages to follow. Alex Haslam has done an excellent job of bringing out this particular strength of the social identity approach. One could say more but it would be gilding the lily in light of what is to come. It remains only to commend a book which I am sure will have a significant influence on teaching and research in both organizational and social psychology.

*John C. Turner*
The Australian National University
Canberra, May 2000

# Preface

According to Adair (1983), the most important word in the would-be leader's vocabulary is 'we' and the least important word is 'I'. Yet readers who set themselves the task of trawling through the organizational literature in an endeavour to discover the psychological underpinnings and consequences of 'we-ness' are destined for disappointment. For despite perennial claims that team-work and *esprit de corps* lie at the heart of all successful organizations, to date, the psychology of organizational behaviour has — with some notable exceptions — been written largely in the first person singular. From the popular titles that swamp airport bookstalls to the weightier texts that shape the thinking of young students, organizational psychology is very much about 'I-ness'. Amongst other things, it is about the qualities of individuals that make them good or bad employees, about principles of personal exchange that determine motivation and perception and about the way that these elements combine to predict success or failure in particular environments.

This book challenges this dominant view of organizational psychology by examining and explaining the ability of people to define themselves, and act, not only as 'I' but also as 'we'. More formally, it suggests that people's sense of self can be determined both by *personal identity* (their sense of themselves as unique individuals) and by *social identity* (their sense of themselves as group members who share goals, values and interests with others). Moreover, in line with Adair's observation, it argues that many of the most significant organizational phenomena — from leadership and motivation to communication and commitment to change — are dependent upon this ability to define and promote the self in a way that is inclusive of other people. From this perspective, groups are not merely part of the physical environment that we experience as being 'out there', they are also part of our own psychological make-up. They determine what we feel 'in here' and the way we behave as a consequence.

As the growing body of research that is informed by social identity and self-categorization theories is demonstrating, these ideas have the ability to breathe fresh life into the analysis of topics that are the traditional focus of the discipline of organizational psychology. These range from the very general (How does human psychology make organizational behaviour possible? How does belonging to teams affect the way we think, feel and behave?) to the very specific (What makes individuals willing to work unpaid overtime? What makes negotiators creative?). It is also true, though, that by raising new questions and establishing new frontiers, the organizational field lays down significant challenges for workers in the social identity tradition. Not least, because organizational science is having an increasing impact on all our lives, these researchers must now confront difficult questions about the practical implications of the social identity approach and about the ways in which it might be used to harness organizational potential while at the same time contributing to the well-being of individuals, groups and society.

It is this dual goal — to extend psychological theory and promote its practical application — that this book sets out to achieve. I hope too that it provides readers with a sense that many of the organizational activities and philosophies that they are often encouraged to take for granted can (and should) be re-appraised and revised. For despite appearances and claims to the contrary, the psychology of organizational behaviour is rarely cut-and-dried, inevitable or self-evident. And partly by proving this point, I would like to think that the book will empower readers by making them more informed participants in organizational life and increasing their sense of theoretical and practical *choice*.

At a more basic level, I also hope that in the course of reading the following chapters the reader will share some of the sense of challenge and invigoration that I experienced in writing them. It needs to be said however, that this experience would have been much less positive if I had thought that I was engaging in it alone. In large part the final product is a reflection of the tremendous support (intellectual, social and material) that I have received from friends and colleagues both during and prior to the last two years of writing. At The Australian National University I have benefited enormously from the advice, direction and substantive input of three close colleagues with whom I have been exceptionally fortunate and immensely privileged to work for the past fourteen years: John Turner, Craig McGarty and Penny Oakes. They — and John in particular — have made a major contribution to every stage in the production of this book and their generosity is something for which I will always be extremely grateful.

Others at the ANU and elsewhere have been extraordinarily helpful too. In particular, Kate Reynolds, Rachael Eggins and Kris Veenstra provided invaluable assistance as readers, collaborators, commentators and critics. So too did Agnes Agama, Amanda Fajak, Barbara David, Bob Wood, Clare Powell, Clifford Stott, Daan van Knippenberg, Dick Moreland, Erin Parker, Fabio Sani, Jamie Burton, Jeanine Willson, Jim Cameron, Judy Harackiewicz, Linda Glassop, Mark Nolan, Michael Cook, Mike Smithson, Naomi Ellemers, Natalie Taylor, Nyla Branscombe, Phil Smith, Richard Sorrentino, Rick Kuhn, Robert Gregson, Rolf Dick, Russell Spears, Ruth Wright, Sandra McGahy, Steve Reicher, Tom Postmes, Debbie Terry, Tom Tyler, Tony Warren and Tricia Brown. Michelle Ryan and Mike Platow warrant special mention and thanks for their painstaking reading of the entire text and their role in shaping the final manuscript. Michael Carmichael, Naomi Meredith, Ziyad Marar and Seth Edwards at Sage also deserve credit for their constant encouragement and for having survived the torture of my unremitting e-mails.

Although my name is the only one that appears on the book's spine, its production has therefore been a truly collaborative effort and one that I could never have attempted on my own. It is partly for this reason that the chapters are written in the voice of the first person plural (e.g. suggesting that 'we argue ...' rather than that 'I argue ...'). However, in a book which tries to engage the reader in the idea that much of what is valuable in organizations (and in life in general) flows from the collective self, it would also have made little sense for me to assert my personal identity throughout the text. But this was not just a pragmatic decision. To do otherwise would have been wrong.

Nonetheless, if I could indulge myself in one very personal sentiment, it would be to express my love and gratitude to Cath for her unwavering support and guidance along the road that brought this book to its conclusion. Her ability to sustain and encourage my enthusiasm is the best proof I have that there is much more to what we receive and produce than our individual deserts and capabilities.

*Alex Haslam*
The Australian National University
Canberra, January 2000

# 1   Organizations and their Psychology

Humans are social animals. No-one who reads this book lives entirely alone, remote from the influence of society and other people. We each seek out contact with others, in the knowledge that this has the capacity to enrich our lives in different ways. This contact usually appears to be natural and uncomplicated, but most of it is highly structured. It is regulated, co-ordinated and managed. This is partly because much of our day-to-day activity involves dealing with people who are acting as members of organizations. As well as this, a great deal of our *own* behaviour is determined by our place within an organization. Today you may encounter a shop assistant, a bus driver, a lecturer, a newsreader, a politician, and you may also act, and be treated by others, as a student, a team-mate, or a fellow worker. And precisely because these sorts of interactions are aspects of organizational behaviour, they are — at least to some extent — purposeful, predictable and meaningful.

Understanding the psychological underpinnings of individuals' behaviour in organizations is a particular focus for researchers in two sub-disciplines: organizational psychology and social psychology. Amongst other things, both fields examine and attempt to understand the mental states and processes associated with behaviour in structured social groups and systems. This chapter discusses in more detail what organizations are and how they have been studied by organizational and social psychologists, before going on to outline how the social psychology of organizational life will be examined in this book.

A central question that provides a backdrop to the issues addressed in this chapter, and in the book as a whole, is how we should understand the contribution that groups make both to the psychology of individuals within organizations and to the functioning of organizations as a whole. Do groups detract from individual motivation and performance or do they augment it? Do groups introduce error and bias into judgement and decision-making or are they sources of validation and validity? Are individual products and behaviour superior to group output and collective action? More importantly, *when* and *why* are different answers to these questions correct? This book's goal is to answer questions of this form, and in so doing to come to grips with issues at the heart of both organizational and social psychology. At its core is an assumption that we have to have a satisfactory appreciation of the psychology of group behaviour in order to understand how and why organizations are (or aren't) effective.

## What is an organization?

In their seminal text, Katz and Kahn (1966) note that organizations have classically been defined as 'social device[s] for efficiently accomplishing through group means some stated purpose' (p. 16). However, they note that this definition, like many others, runs into problems because the stated purpose of an organization may be incidental to the function that it actually fulfils. The stated purpose of a religious movement may be to enhance the spiritual well-being of its followers, but it has a number of other functions that may be considered more important: to provide social support, to exercise social control, or to generate revenue for various other purposes.

As an alternative to this definition, Katz and Kahn (1966) prefer to think of organizations as *social systems* that co-ordinate people's behaviour by means of roles, norms and values. *Roles* relate to the particular place and functions of an individual. These are defined within a system that is internally differentiated in ways relevant to the system's operation. These can be thought of as group-based *categories* of position and activity. Thus universities contain academics and administrators who each have different tasks to perform and there are further sub-divisions within these categories (lecturers, accountants, etc.). Roles are categorical in the sense that the individuals who fulfil them are functionally interchangeable and equivalent. *Norms* are attitudinal and behavioural prescriptions associated with these roles or categories. They create expectations about how a person or group of people ought to think, feel and behave. They tend to be defined externally (e.g. in formal job descriptions or informal codes of conduct) but are internalized by individual group members (Sherif, 1936). Thus lecturers are expected by others, and expect themselves, to run courses and mark exams, while accountants are expected and expect to monitor and administer budgets. Finally, *values* are higher-level principles that are intended to guide this behaviour and the organization's activity as a whole (see Peters & Waterman, 1995). Lecturers should be well informed and studious, accountants should be honest and prudent, a university should advance knowledge and reward scholarship.

Partly because of their regulatory function, the precise constellation of roles, norms and values within any particular organization serves to create shared meaning for its members. This provides each organization with a distinct *organizational culture* (e.g. Bate, 1984; Deal & Kennedy, 1982; Freytag, 1990). However, it is still clear that in organizations this system of roles, norms and values exists for some *purpose* and indeed that it generally works to direct and structure individuals' activities in relation to this purpose (Tannenbaum, 1966). Leaving aside the issue of whether this purpose is explicit or implicit (or is manifest or latent — see Merton, 1957), this point is fundamental to most definitions. So, for example, Stogdill (1950) defines an organization as 'a social group in which the members are differentiated as to their responsibilities for the task of achieving a common goal' (p. 2). However, Smith (1995b) elaborates on this type of definition by adding that:

> Awareness of membership, or self-categorization, is critical in that we cannot, from a psychological point of view, attribute the effects of organizational life to the organization unless we can be sure that the organization is psychologically 'real' [for its members]. (p. 425)

It is also important to recognize that internal differentiation exists not only because individuals in organizations have different roles, but also because they belong to different groups *within* organizations. In all organizations there is therefore an *internal* system of social relations between such groups (Alderfer &

Smith, 1982; Levine & Moreland, 1991; Turner & Haslam, 2000). This means that departments or teams within an organization are typically differentiated not only in terms of their own shared roles, norms, values and culture but also in terms of their power and status.

On the basis of observations like those above, Statt (1994) abstracts three core features of organizations from a range of different definitions. He suggests that an organization is: (a) a group with a *social identity*, so that it has psychological meaning for all the individuals who belong to it (resulting, for example, in a shared sense of belonging); (b) characterized by *co-ordination* so that the behaviour of individuals is arranged and structured rather than idiosyncratic; and (c) *goal directed*, so that this structure is oriented towards a particular outcome. Obviously, though, the precise character of these features varies from organization to organization and for this reason careful study of the concrete features of any specific organizational context will always be important (Turner & Haslam, 2000).

When most people think about organizations they think about the places where people work. Indeed, such places are the focus of the present text and most others that have the word 'organization' in their title. However, it is clear that the above characteristics define organizations more generally *as any internally differentiated and purposeful social group that has a psychological impact on its members*. In these terms, sporting teams, clubs, societies, even families, are all organizations. Of course people do perform work in all these groups, but they are also a focus of leisure and recreation. It is the fact that organizations relate to this breadth of experience that gives them such relevance to our lives and that in turn makes attempts to understand their psychological dimensions so important, so complex and ultimately so interesting.

## Studying organizations

Researchers interested in the psychology of organizations study an array of topics and questions, almost as broad as the discipline of psychology itself. Nonetheless, the area has been of particular interest to: (a) social psychologists who study the interplay between social interaction and individuals' thoughts, feelings and behaviour; (b) clinical psychologists who examine the basis and consequences of individuals' dysfunctional processes and states; and (c) cognitive psychologists who look at how people process information in their environment in order to think, perceive, learn and remember.

This breadth of issue coverage is enlarged further by the fact that organizations are not only of interest to psychologists. Sociologists, economists, anthropologists, historians and political scientists are all interested in how organizations work and in their products and impact. People in all these areas make an important contribution to understanding organizations, and the nature of this contribution is important to bear in mind as we progress through this book. This is for two quite different reasons: first, because work in these other fields often provides a distinct way of approaching a particular topic; but also second, because the way psychologists think about organizations is profoundly influenced by work in other disciplines. The study of productivity, for example, is heavily influenced by economic theories which tend to define output in financial rather than social terms.

This book, however, is largely concerned with the social psychology of organizations. What it has to say has relevance to, and draws upon, work in other areas of psychology and in other disciplines, but it is largely concerned with the way in which the psychological processes of individuals contribute to, and are affected by, organizational life. On reflection, we can see that organizational behaviour is quite an amazing accomplishment. But what features of our psychological make-up make this accomplishment possible? And how exactly does membership of organizations affect the way we think, feel and behave?

Given the scope of these questions, it should not be surprising to discover that they have been answered in a number of different ways. Yet since the start of the twentieth century psychologists have tended to answer them using only a few relatively circumscribed forms of answer, or paradigm (Brown, 1954; Pfeffer, 1997, 1998; Viteles, 1932). In the first part of that century these focused on the distinct underpinnings of organizational behaviour in economic motivation, individual differences and human relations, but more recently there has been an upsurge of interest in the cognitive aspects of organizational life (Landy, 1989).

The following sections look in turn at the historical foundations of each of these four paradigms. We will consider these in some detail for a number of reasons. First, because in many respects the ideas and work of pioneers in organizational enquiry represent the bedrock of later work in the field. The studies they conducted are rightly considered classics and all are widely discussed and commented on in just about every organizational text (though sometimes in a rather disjointed and fragmentary way). For that reason it is important to consider closely their methods and ideas, in order to get a clearer picture of 'where they were coming from' and what they were attempting to do. Even though these ideas are now rarely applied in their original form, their impact on the field has been considerable and most will be recognizable in some guise when we deal with specific content areas in later chapters. And finally, this early work is still immensely interesting to read and reflect upon, not least because the researchers had an enthusiasm and vigour that were genuinely infectious.

## Paradigms for studying organizations and their psychology

### The economic paradigm

The economic paradigm is closely associated with the work of Frederick Taylor at the start of the twentieth century. Despite the fact that he had previously passed the entrance examination for Harvard, Taylor entered the Midvale Steel Company as an unskilled yard labourer at the age of 22 in 1878. Six years later, in the process of rising to the position of chief engineer, he had laid the groundwork for a theory of *scientific management* (otherwise known as Taylorism) that revolutionized the industrial workplace and had enormous impact on the study of organizational behaviour.

At the heart of this theory was a rejection of the idea that workers should learn how best to do their jobs through experience, informal training or their own insight. In short, Taylor believed that the management of workers and their work was an exact science and that the job of any manager was to perfect and implement that science — to discover and implement 'the one best way' of doing any particular job. This doctrine was set out in a number of texts, most notably Taylor's (1911) *Principles of Scientific Management* (see also Person, 1911/1972, pp. 5–7). Here the four principal duties of managers, corresponding to the four main principles of the theory, were listed as follows:

*First*    They develop a science for each element of a man's work, which replaces the old rule-of thumb method.
*Second*    They scientifically select and then train, teach and develop the workman, whereas in the past he trained himself as best he could.
*Third*    They heartily co-operate with the men so as to insure all of the work is being done in accordance with the science which has been developed.
*Fourth*    There is an almost equal division of work and the responsibility between the management and the workmen. The management take over all the work for which they are better fitted than the workmen, while in the past almost all of the work and the greater part of the responsibility were thrown upon the men. (Taylor, 1911, pp. 36-7)

Yet over and above these principles, Taylor (1911/1972) considered scientific management to be a psychological enterprise involving 'a complete mental revolution both on the part of management and on the part of men' (p. 29).

On reading Taylor's work, one of its most salient features is the zeal with which his ideas were promoted, a zeal which was shared by other members of the movement that he founded. One quirky illustration of the level of Taylor's commitment is that his 1911 book ends with an invitation for any reader sufficiently interested in scientific management to call in on him at his house in Philadelphia. Such enthusiasm led, amongst other things, to the foundation of the Taylor Society, an organization which vigorously discussed and religiously promoted Taylor's ideas.

Central to this zeal was a disapproval of human and financial waste and a particular (some have argued pathological; e.g. Kakar, 1970, p. 188) dislike of the practice of 'soldiering' or loafing. Taylor believed that this led to collective under-achievement, usually as a deliberate co-ordinated act. He identified this as 'the greatest evil with which the working-people of both England and America are now afflicted' (Taylor, 1911, p. 14) and suggested three roots to the problem. First, he argued that workers were often poorly selected for the jobs they performed, so that a failure to achieve their maximum potential was inevitable. Second, he pointed out that under most existing systems of 'initiative and incentive' it made sense to loaf because workers were discouraged by the fact that targets were continually raised once they had been achieved. Finally, third, Taylor (1911) believed that loafing was a tendency that arose naturally from 'the loss of ambition and initiative ... which takes place in workmen when they are herded into gangs instead of being treated as separate individuals' (p. 72).

Corresponding to each of these problems, Taylor proposed three remedies. First, he argued that workers needed to be systematically selected for any job they were to perform in a manner that weeded out all but the 'first-class men' (as per the second principle of scientific management). Typically this meant going through a process of exhaustive testing that might lead a company to retain only one worker in ten from an existing workforce. Taylor acknowledged that this strategy appeared to be hard on those workers who were not up to scratch, and that, left to their own devices, workers themselves would never enforce or endure decimation of this form. He added, though, that sympathy for those who lost their job was 'entirely wasted', as the strategy was a necessary step towards finding work for which they were properly suited and therefore 'really a kindness' (Taylor, 1911, p. 64).

The second strategy Taylor devised was to introduce a 'piecework incentive system'. This involved rewarding each worker for higher productivity and ensuring that the worker had faith that pay rates would not subsequently be adjusted. Taylor was critical of employers who went back on their word in this regard (citing it as one major contributor to the touted failure of his principles), but he also counselled against increasing workers' pay by much more than 60 per cent — noting that beyond this level of increase many workers 'will work irregularly and tend to become more or less shiftless, extravagant and dissipated' (Taylor, 1911, p. 74).

Finally, third, Taylor emphasized 'the importance of individualizing each workman' (1911, p. 73). From experience he found that groups of workers were extremely resistant to the sorts of changes scientific management necessitated. In some cases he attributed this resistance to stupidity, to the 'almost criminal' tyranny of unions, or to 'an almost universal prejudice in favour of the old' (pp. 82, 116), but he also recognized that bonds of friendship made it unrealistic to expect workers to agree collectively to retrenchments and dramatic changes to their working practices. Taylor thus argued that managers needed to appeal directly and constantly to the economic aspirations of individual workers, as 'personal ambition always has been and will remain a more powerful incentive to exertion than a desire for the general welfare' (p. 95).

Application of the principles of scientific management was not a simple exercise, and Taylor himself berated managers who went in search of quick fixes by instituting radical change over a short time span. Nonetheless, the practices were widely instituted around the industrialized world and a number of seminal interventions are commonly used to illustrate both the manner in which the principles can be applied and the results they can produce. Of these, the most widely cited case study relates to the work of pig iron handlers at the Bethlehem Steel Company.

Taylor began his work with this company in 1898 at which time it had five blast furnaces and 75 pig iron handlers who were part of a total force of around 600 labourers. Their task was simply to pick up pigs weighing 92 pounds, and then to walk up an inclined plank in order to load them onto a railway carriage. At the start of the study each worker was loading an average of 12.5 tons of iron each day. Taylor noted that there was nothing unusual about the gang of handlers who were doing this work and that they were labouring and being supervised about as well as workers anywhere else in the industry. However, after careful study Taylor and his colleagues worked out that a first-class pig iron handler ought to be able to handle 47.5 tonnes — in other words, nearly four times as much as the pre-existing average. The task Taylor set himself was to achieve and maintain this level of handling and in so doing to raise the profitability of the company.

To do this, Taylor had to use the principles of scientific management to develop 'a science of handling pig iron'. The first step was to identify the physical and mental attributes best suited to the job and then select men who possessed these. Physically, the workers had to be incredibly fit and strong. Mentally, the profile was more complex, but not especially flattering: 'one of the very first requirements for a man who is fit to handle pig iron as a regular occupation is that he shall be so stupid and so phlegmatic that he more nearly resembles in his mental make-up the ox than any other type' (Taylor, 1911, p. 47). Taylor also noted that the worker should be someone concerned for financial advancement who might therefore be lured away from 'the herd' by the promise of greater personal remuneration.

The second stage of scientific development involved identifying the set of movements and exact timing of the handling process. In other fields a large amount of work went into the process of tool development so that, for example, the science of shovelling required workers to have access to eight or more shovels depending on the material being lifted. In the case of handling iron this process involved eliminating all superfluous movements of the hand and feet and instructing workers to take precisely timed breaks to minimize muscle fatigue. This type of research established the basis for elaborate time-and-motion studies that are still common-place in all forms of workplace today (after Barnes, 1937).

One common recommendation in such studies, in line with Taylor's views about the deleterious impact of groups on individual performance, was that workers were usually encouraged to work on their own as far as possible. This strategy, for example, was an important component of two major studies into the scientific management of bricklayers and bicycle ball-bearing makers (Gilbreth, 1909; Taylor, 1911). At the Bethlehem Steel works this meant that no more than four workers were allowed to work in a gang without first obtaining a special permit. However, Taylor was proud of the fact that the superintendents responsible for these permits were themselves so busy that they had no time to issue them.

The final part of the process of scientific development involved implementing the above insights. It was here that most difficulty was envisaged and experienced. Again Taylor emphasized the need to deal with workers individually and to engage in one-on-one discussions to ensure that they knew what they were meant to be doing and what they stood to gain (Taylor stated that he was not opposed to the right of workers to bargain collectively, but such rights had no place in his schemes, a point that ultimately led to them being challenged by unions in front of a special House of Representatives committee). Of course, individual-based negotiation and training took a long time, adding to the already extensive process of identifying the single best way of doing each job. Moreover, it also meant that large numbers of supervisors were needed to instruct and monitor workers. For this reason, Taylor argued that companies would often need to have one supervisor for every three workers. This necessitated setting up highly structured lines of command built upon principles of discipline and hierarchical authority. Taylor (1911) pointed out that this also placed a greater burden on management as his system only worked if they '*enforced* standardization of methods, *enforced* adoption of the best implements and working conditions, and *enforced* co-operation' (by discharging those 'who cannot or will not work with the new methods', p. 83, original emphasis).

Astoundingly perhaps, Taylor's work at the Bethlehem plant achieved his aims. In the company as a whole workers' average wages rose from $1.15 to $1.88 a day, each handled about 59 tons of iron a day where previously the average had been 16 tons, and the cost of handling each ton fell from 7.2 cents to 3.3 cents. Similar work served to bring about equally remarkable upturns in profitability through studies of occupations as diverse as shoe manufacture and municipal government (Person, 1929). These improvements flew in the face of belief at the time, and Taylor defied his many critics (including the owners and managers of the companies who employed him) who said he would never be able to achieve, let alone maintain, the high production goals he set himself.

All, however, was not beer and skittles. This is literally true as Taylor noted that only two of the remaining workers at the steel plant were 'drinking men' because alcohol consumption was incompatible with the extreme physical demands of the new regime. More significantly, about 460 of the 600 labourers at the plant lost their jobs. Taylor defended this action by arguing that most workers who were laid off by the company were re-employed in other positions. However, details of this redeployment were not elaborated. There is also indirect evidence that the management of the company were unconvinced by this claim as they complained that the dramatic rise in unemployment had an adverse effect on the profitability of stores and housing that the company also owned in Bethlehem (Copley, 1923). Local economic gains were thus offset by costs to the broader community — costs that were not just economic.

As well as this, it is clear that Taylor himself experienced considerable personal discomfort as a result of his behaviour, which can be likened to that of an economic vigilante. So, despite an emphasis on peaceful co-operation and industrial harmony, his efforts to implement change actually involved conflict and mutual intimidation. Reflecting on his earlier experiences as a foreman he remarked:

> After three years of that fight, three years of never looking a man in the face from morning till night except as a tactical enemy, three years of wondering what that fellow was going to do next and wondering what I could do to him next, I made up my mind that some remedy would have to be devised ... or I would cease to be a foreman or go into some other business. (Taylor, 1911/1972, p. 28)

It is clear too, that the mechanical coldness of Taylor's theorizing and practices was not even to the liking of all his disciples. In a paper reviewing the positive contributions of scientific management, Farquhar (1924) thus mused openly:

> I wonder whether with our admirably proper insistence on considering each individual as an individual we have not obscured the possibility of making that individual and his fellows more productive and more contented through recognizing the psychological benefits to be gained through group dealings? (p. 48)

Such concerns became even more pronounced when it was proposed that the principles of scientific management be extended beyond the bounds of manufacturing industry into areas such as education and public policy making. Particular alarm was raised when the Carnegie Foundation produced a bulletin by Morris Cooke (1911) entitled *Academic and Industrial Efficiency* which proposed that higher education be restructured according to the four principles of scientific management. This suggested, amongst other things, that lecturing and teaching be systematized and monitored, that academics work with greater intensity and purpose, that decision-making be taken out of their hands and centralized in the offices of managers and that students be provided with greater vocational teaching and direction.

Three points are worth making here. The first is that Cooke and his colleagues were justifiably bemused that academics who had enthusiastically embraced scientific management when they and others applied it elsewhere, were so testy at the suggestion that it might be applied to their own work. Second, it is apparent that many of the suggestions made by Cooke served to highlight some of the major limitations of a theory which focuses on economic imperatives to the exclusion of all others. Thus Bartlett (1911/1972) observed that academics' and students' *commitment* to a university, which contributes enormously to its morale and wealth (both intellectual and financial; e.g. in the form of endowments), 'springs little from an appreciation of the economy with which it is managed' (p.12). Webster (1911/1972) similarly wondered:

> Whether there is any resemblance between the purposes of college and university activities and those of business ... [since] the object is not to make money [and] standardization is quite impossible ... and can be attended only with laughable results. (pp. 295-7)

He concluded:

> Nothing can do more to confirm the position of mediocrity in which this country finds itself in the status of learning, than the application of commercial judgements to matters that are essentially concerned with spirits. (1911/1972, p. 298)

Finally, third, it is apparent that these limitations notwithstanding, many of the principles of scientific management *have* been implemented around the world and across the organizational board (e.g. in universities, schools, hospitals and throughout the public and private sectors). These are most apparent in personalized evaluation and reward practices (sometimes called 'incentivation'; Parsons, 1992; Rothe, 1978), individualized work contracts, pursuit of 'best practice', commitment to 'lean production' and over-arching faith in the management's 'right to manage'. Like it or not, the political and practical legacy of scientific management remains an important feature of the contemporary industrial landscape (Locke, 1982; Merkle, 1980; Thompson & Warhurst, 1998; Waring, 1991). Indeed, according to Braverman (1974), 'the importance of the scientific management movement in the shaping of the modern corporation and ... all institutions ... which carry on labor processes' is 'impossible to overestimate' (p. 86; see also Pfeffer, 1998, p. 375).

*The individual differences paradigm*

When Wilhelm Wundt founded the first laboratory of experimental psychology in Leipzig in 1879 he set about the task of identifying principles of psychological functioning associated with human behaviour *in general*. However, two of Wundt's students, J. McKeen Cattell and Hugo Münsterberg, later rebelled against this approach and sought instead to understand the nature and consequences of human *individuality*. Influenced by the pioneering work of Francis Galton, this work involved attempts both to identify core dimensions on which individuals differed and to develop tools for quantifying those individual differences. In order to advance this work both researchers left Germany and settled in the United States where they rose to positions of prominence and exerted considerable impact on the emerging science of psychology.

Münsterberg was particularly interested in applying the experimental method and the study of individual differences to the analysis of organizational behaviour, and as a result is often identified as the founder of industrial psychology (Hothersall, 1984; Viteles, 1932). A keen proponent of the principles of scientific management, he was committed to building upon the theory's second principle by developing psychological tools to help identify workers whose psychological qualities made them suitable for particular tasks. Consistent with Taylorism's tenet of 'the one best way', Münsterberg's (1913) classic text *Psychology and Industrial Efficiency* was divided into three sections: 'The best possible man', 'The best possible work' and 'The best possible effect'.

In outlining how psychologists might contribute to improved personnel selection, Münsterberg argued that researchers needed to do two things. First, they needed to develop precise analyses of the requirements of any job and to identify the key psychological components associated with effective performance of it. Second, they needed to devise tests that could reliably measure a person's aptitude in important areas.

Illustrative of this approach, Münsterberg conducted studies with women who were working as telephone operators for the Bell Telephone Company in New England. Here the key psychological attributes of an effective operator were discovered to be memory, attention to detail, precision, speed and intelligence (as well as nine others). Once these had been identified, workers were then screened in order to establish the extent of their ability in each domain. This involved asking them, respectively, to perform tests of digit recall, to cross out all instances of a particular letter in a newspaper column, to sort sets of cards, to draw as many instances of a specified zig-zag pattern as they could in a given amount of time and to recall lists of logically paired words. The validity of the method was demonstrated by the fact that, unbeknown to the researchers, the phone company included some of their superior existing operators in the study and found that they all performed extremely well in the tests.

Another of Münsterberg's key innovations was the development of 'tasks in miniature' that attempted to assess the extent to which people possessed an integrated set of skills necessary for a particular job. Such tasks were designed to overcome the limitations of procedures which broke work down into such low-level component processes that the measures bore no meaningful relation to the jobs people actually performed. As an example, Münsterberg devised a simulation game to assess the skills of drivers of street railway cars. The game required drivers to make judgements about whether a series of objects were going to cross their path. The objects were pedestrians, horses and cars and these were represented by digits that corresponded to their speed of movement (1 = a pedestrian, 2 = a horse, 3 = a car). These passed through an aperture at a speed determined by the driver being tested and the driver's score on the game was then weighted as a function of speed and accuracy. The apparent validity of this method was demonstrated by the fact that a group of drivers who had been identified as possessing superior driving skills performed better on the task than a comparison group comprising drivers who had been close to dismissal. On the basis of such results, Münsterberg argued that similar tests should be used proactively in a range of trades and professions to select workers for particular jobs.

When it came to getting the best possible work from appropriately selected workers, Münsterberg followed other researchers (e.g. Scott, 1911) in arguing that the challenge of psychologists was to identify motivational principles that would facilitate workers' participation in the process of scientific management. Like many other psychologists after him, he argued repeatedly for the need to conduct experimental research in order to ascertain the impact of specific personality and environmental variables on job performance.

However, empirical data to back up these recommendations was thin on the ground. This was partly because Münsterberg identified a number of complex factors that shaped people's reaction to their work, and which served to thwart attempts at systematization. The first of these was the highly *subjective* nature of workers' reactions to their employment. It was observed that many jobs which seemed objectively to be very dull and intrinsically unmotivating were considered by those that did them to be interesting and varied. One case in point was a woman who worked for a light bulb manufacturer and whose job was to wrap bulbs in tissue paper for safe transportation. Münsterberg noted that the woman had wrapped 13,000 bulbs a day for twelve years and yet still found the job 'really interesting' and full of 'constant variation' (1913, p. 196). On the other hand, he noted that many people who supposedly had very exciting and rewarding jobs (e.g. teachers, doctors and lawyers) actually found the routine nature of their work extremely dull.

A second complicating factor was the role of *group memberships* in determining an individual's satisfaction with, and enthusiasm for, their work. Where Taylor had argued that groups were an impediment to performance and that their influence needed to be minimized, Münsterberg (1913) noted that groups could make a positive psychological contribution to the workplace by 'enhanc[ing] the consciousness of solidarity amongst the labourers and their feelings of security' (p. 234). The practical potential of groups was also revealed in Münsterberg's pioneering experimental studies of group decision-making in which individuals were shown two grey cards each with about 100 white dots on them. When asked to judge which card had the most dots, it was found that individuals picked the correct card 52 per cent of the time, but that after group discussion this figure rose to 78 per cent. Controversially, Münsterberg suggested that these positive effects were confined to the deliberations of men, as a replication involving women indicated that their performance (45 per cent correct) was identical at pre- and post-discussion phases.

Münsterberg (1913) also noted that, because it was often difficult to obtain information about an individual's personality directly, it was sometimes useful and practical to start by obtaining indirect knowledge. Consistent with the idea that group memberships serve to shape (and were therefore a good cue to) individuality, he added that:

> Such indirect knowledge of a man's mental traits may be secured first of all through referring ... to the groups to which he belongs and inquiring into the characteristics of those groups. (p. 129).

At this group level Münsterberg still argued that researchers needed to employ objective scientific methodology as he was aware of the tendency for different managers to develop different theories about the attributes of different groups. This meant, for example, that while one manager regarded Swedes as the most diligent and steady labourers, another considered them unfit for work.    Yet Münsterberg's strategy for dealing with this and all other problems was to recommit himself to the task of identifying the individual differences that he believed were ultimately responsible for job performance.  This was because, as he put it, in the end 'only the subtle psychological individual analysis can overcome the superficial prejudices of group psychology' (Münsterberg, 1913, p. 133).

In mapping out a framework for such analysis, Münsterberg foresaw and promoted the development of a profession that would pursue these goals through psychological testing.   This, he thought, should be available both to the employer who wanted to assess potential or current employees, and to the potential employee who wanted to discover their suitability for a particular profession or trade. Although the extent of Münsterberg's personal contribution to all these developments has been questioned (e.g. by Kuna, 1978), there is little doubting Moskowitz's (1977) conclusion that Münsterberg's writings 'laid the groundwork for every major development' (p. 838) in the psychology of business and industry (see also Hothersall, 1984; Landy, 1992; Spillmann & Spillmann, 1993).   Reflecting this legacy, over the last 80 or so years organizational psychology has retained and developed its methodological commitment to time-and-motion studies, testing-based personnel selection and individualized head-hunting for managers.

*The human relations paradigm*

One common feature of both the economic and the individual difference paradigms is that they place an emphasis on the individual as the proper unit of psychological enquiry and as the prospective source of organizational efficiency and improvement.  Both Taylor and Münsterberg held the view that identifying the right person for a job and fashioning the organizational environment to suit that individual's circumstances and potential is a key part of organizational success.   Yet despite the simplicity and early success of these paradigms, considerable doubt about their appropriateness and utility emerged in the wake of research conducted at the Hawthorne Works of the Western Electric Company in Chicago between 1927 and 1932.   The person most associated with the

Hawthorne studies (as they became known) and the human relations movement as a whole is Elton Mayo, an Australian educated at the University of Adelaide who went on to become professor of industrial research at Harvard. The research he oversaw started off looking at just five workers but went on to study about 20,000 and remains one of the most extensive and important pieces of psychological research ever conducted.

Prior to the major series of studies being conducted, two other significant pieces of research were carried out. The first of these involved attempts by the management at the Hawthorne works to deal with problems of production and worker dissatisfaction by calling in a team of researchers trained in principles of scientific management (Snow, 1927; for a review see Roethlisberger & Dickson, 1939, pp. 14-19). In this research attempts to manipulate the working environment and identify the single set of conditions that would maximize efficiency were a spectacular failure.

In particular, experiments involving changes to the level of illumination in the rooms where women worked assembling telephone components showed that lighting had no predictable or reliable impact on their work. When workers were divided into two groups and one group was exposed to increasing levels of illumination, the performance of *both* groups increased (Experiments 1 and 2) and when one group's lighting was dramatically reduced *both* groups maintained a high level of performance (Experiment 3). The workers also commented and reacted favourably when the experimenters *pretended* to change the light bulbs to give a higher level of illumination, but in fact did not change them at all. Improved performance was even sustained in a final study in which two women were exposed to a level of illumination 'approximately equal to that on an ordinary moonlight night' (Roethlisberger & Dickson, 1939, p. 17).

Totally at odds with the logic of Taylorism, the only conclusion from the 'illumination fiasco' was that 'somehow or other that complex of mutually dependent factors, the human organism, shifted its equilibrium and unintentionally defeated the purpose of the experiment' (Mayo, 1933, pp. 54, 62). Indeed, such was the importance of the pattern of results observed in these studies that the 'Hawthorne effect' has become a widely recognized phenomenon in psychological research — referring to the capacity for people's behaviour to change as a result of their participation in research, rather than as a result of the nature of the research manipulations (e.g. Haslam & McGarty, 1998).

At about the same time as this first Hawthorne investigation, Mayo (1924) himself was conducting studies of mule spinners at a textile mill in Philadelphia. At this time, relative to other departments at the mill, the spinners were experiencing very low levels of production and extraordinarily high levels of turnover. This meant that for every position, approximately 2.5 workers had to be taken on each year (representing a turnover rate of about 250 per cent). This was occurring in spite of the fact that the company had set in place a very attractive incentive system that rewarded the workers for reaching particular targets.

As a first intervention to address these problems, Mayo introduced a series of rest periods throughout the day in an attempt to counteract fatigue. This was a strategy Taylor had recommended and previously perfected with the pig iron handlers at the Bethlehem Steel works. To look at the effects of this innovation, the spinners were divided into two groups, the smaller of which received the new breaks with the remainder carrying on as normal. The effect of the change was felt immediately with levels of satisfaction and production rising dramatically in the experimental group, so that its members now reached production targets and obtained bonuses for the first time ever. But Mayo quickly realized that these effects could not simply be the result of a reduction in fatigue. This point was confirmed by the fact that a very similar pattern of improvement was apparent in the work of the control group. This group had experienced no obvious change in their conditions, yet they too (like the control groups in the Hawthorne illumination studies) were now more happy and more productive. Why?

Not surprisingly, Mayo had no immediate answer to this pressing question. But what he did know was that economic analysis of the type put forward by Taylor afforded no explanation. Mayo also suspected (though he later noted that this was not clear at the time) that a clue to the effects observed in the mule spinning department lay in some seemingly trivial features of the investigation. In particular, he noted that the only time production declined during the study was when a supervisor intervened to eliminate the rest breaks in order to cope with an influx of orders. Even when rest breaks were re-introduced the workers were still disenchanted and distrustful and they remained so until the president of the company intervened to take the side of the workers and fire the supervisor. By doing this, and through the process of talking and listening to the workers to discover their thoughts about the study, Mayo (1949) conjectured that the major contribution of the president lay in the fact that he had inadvertently 'transformed a group of "solitaires" into a social group' (p. 58).

The opportunity to examine this hypothesis in more detail came when Mayo and his colleagues commenced the second series of studies at the Hawthorne works. The company's management encouraged the research because they wanted to know what psychological and environmental factors had been responsible for the marked improvements in performance observed in the illumination studies, so that these principles could be used to inform changes in the plant as a whole. As an initial focus for the research the company isolated a group of six women from the general workforce and placed them in a special room where they worked assembling 35-piece relays and could be observed more closely. The experimenters then set about systematically manipulating various features of the women's working conditions by introducing particular changes that lasted up to 31 weeks. For example, between 1927 and 1929 changes were made to the number and duration of rest periods and the length of working days and weeks. The researchers also fastidiously examined all aspects of the women's work and their reaction to it by monitoring the number of relays assembled and their quality, as well as the women's health, details of their personal history and any comments they made in relation to the study and its findings.

As discussed by Mayo (1949), the impact of the changes made during the first phase of research on the workers and their work was that 'slowly at first, but later with increasing certainty, the output record mounted' (p. 63). Later phases of the study which reproduced conditions in earlier periods also showed marked improvement. So, for example, each woman's average weekly output was less than 2,500 relays in the third period of investigation in mid-1927, but under exactly the same conditions in the twelfth period in late 1928 it was more than 2,900. Once workers had entered the test room, attendance irregularities also fell from an average of 15.2 per person per year to just 3.5. Moreover, as the study continued the women in the room reported less fatigue, greater contentment and more convivial relations with their fellow workers both inside and outside the relay assembly room. The nature of these changes is summarized by Roethlisberger and Dickson (1939) in the following observations:

> No longer were the girls isolated individuals, working together only in the sense of an actual physical proximity. They had become participating members of a working group with all the psychological and social implications peculiar to such a group. In Period X a growing amount of social activity developed among the test room girls outside of the plant. The conversation in the test room became more socialized. In Period XIII the girls began to help one another out for the common good of the group. They became bound to one another by common sentiments and feelings of loyalty. (p. 86)

In order to account for these results, the researchers tested and systematically eliminated a number of potential hypotheses (Roethlisberger & Dickson, 1939, pp. 90-160). The findings appeared not to derive simply from an improvement to material conditions, relief from fatigue or monotony, or economic incentive. The only hypothesis that fitted with the data suggested that experimental interventions had some social impact in communicating information about a changing *state of relations* between the management and the workers. It was not the *content* of change that mattered but the fact that the process of *change itself* redefined managers and workers as collaborative participants in a common venture. In order to examine this hypothesis, in a second phase of investigation the researchers conducted an extensive open-ended interview programme. This confirmed the researchers' views and identified a number of factors that appeared to have contributed to the earlier improvements. These included: (a) the introduction of a less formal and impersonal supervisory style; (b) an increased sense of control on the part of workers; (c) an increased feeling that the management was actually interested in, and shared some concern for, their welfare; and (d) an emerging belief that management and workers were part of a team that was pulling together. The workers also commented favourably on the fact that as a result of the experimental changes they (e) took home more money and (f) worked shorter hours, but these factors appeared to have secondary importance.

So, where previously workers had felt that management was only concerned with their production, they now believed (mistakenly in some instances) that it was taking their feelings seriously and attending to their grievances. They felt that what they did mattered and hence were actively *self-involved* in their work.

Moreover, it was clear that the feeling of being in a team exerted a powerful influence on the workers' actual behaviour, so that where previously their contributions had been more-or-less idiosyncratic, they now became highly uniform. This uniformity was both internally and externally imposed, so that the workers both wanted to conform to the team's expectations and norms (e.g. to produce a certain number of relays — no more, no less) and also encouraged and exerted pressure on each other to do so. In a later phase of investigation carried out in a different area of the Hawthorne works (the Bank Wiring Observation Room) this was sometimes observed to take the form of subjecting those who over- or under-performed to sarcasm or ridicule, as the following exchange illustrates:

> $W_4$: (To $W_6$) How many are you going to turn in?
> $W_6$: I've got to turn in 6,800.
> $W_4$: What's the matter — are you crazy? You work all week and turn in 6,600 for a full day, and now you're away an hour and a quarter and you turn in more than you do the other days.
> $W_6$: I don't care. I'm going to finish these sets tomorrow.
> $W_4$: You're screwy.
> $W_6$: All right, I'll turn in 6,400.
> (Roethlisberger & Dickson, 1939, p. 420)

Occasionally though, male workers also resorted to regulating each others' output physically through a practice known as 'binging' — hitting someone as hard as possible on the upper arm:

> $W_8$: (To $W_6$) Why don't you quit work? Let's see, this is your thirty-fifth row today. What are you going to do with them all? ...
> $W_6$: Don't worry about that. I'll take care of it. You're getting paid by the sets I turn out. That's all you should worry about.
> $W_8$: If you don't quit work I'll bing you.
> $W_8$ struck $W_6$ and finally chased him round the room.
> (Roethlisberger & Dickson, 1939, p. 422)

The influence of the informal work group on performance was subsequently confirmed in a study of the aircraft industry in California conducted by Fox and Scott (1943). This showed quite clearly that levels of absenteeism and turnover were associated with the particular company that a worker was in and with the norms that that company established for its workers in light of the particular circumstances it faced. Mayo observed too that the company with the best record of attendance was the one where the foreman was concerned not only with the technical aspects of his job but also with handling human relationships. One concrete consequence of this was that workers in that company collectively arranged which day of the week they would each take off. Importantly, this meant that if a worker broke with this arrangement, and thereby inconvenienced his colleagues, they would put pressure on him of a form that 'management would never dare to exercise' (Mayo, 1949, p. 90; see also Parker, 1993, p. 267). On this basis, Mayo argued that it was not individual-based incentives but mechanisms that created *group solidarity and appropriate group norms* which were critical to bringing about sustained production.

The Hawthorne programme of research served to make two further points clear for Mayo. The first was that the capacity for the work group to shape the behaviour of the individual suggested that:

The belief that the behaviour of an individual within the factory can be predicted before employment on the basis of a laborious and minute examination of his technical and other capacities is mainly, if not wholly, mistaken. (1949, p. 99)

This conclusion is clearly at odds with the logic of both the economic and individual difference paradigms that place an emphasis on careful analysis of the individual in isolation, and urge employment selection on that basis. For Mayo it was the fact that organizational life *transformed individual differences into group similarities* that was its defining feature, and it was this fact that researchers and practitioners primarily needed to come to terms with.

Building on this insight, the second more general point that Mayo abstracted from his and his colleagues' research was that prevailing economic and organizational theory had contrived to completely misrepresent the nature of natural society. As he saw it, the dominant view (following Hobbes, Rousseau and others) was built on three key assumptions: (a) society is comprised of a horde of disorganized individuals; (b) individuals act purely to further their own personal interests; and (c) individuals act logically to service those interests. Mayo rejected these views — 'the rabble hypothesis' as he termed it — and instead endorsed sentiments similar to those with which this chapter began. That is to say, he argued that organized behaviour shaped by group membership and group interests was the *rule*, not the exception, and that individuals acted in terms of their personal self-interest only when social association failed them. As he quite forcefully put it:

> The economists' presupposition of individual self-preservation ... is not characteristic of the industrial facts as ordinarily encountered. The desire to stand well with one's fellows, the so-called human instinct of association easily outweighs the merely individual interest and the logical reasoning upon which so many spurious principles of management are based. (Mayo, 1949, p. 40)

### The cognitive paradigm

Mayo and his colleagues identified important limitations with existing paradigms in organizational research and underlined the significance of the social dimension to organizational life. Yet despite this, their work afforded little systematic insight into the psychological processes associated with organizational activity. Indeed, the major contribution of this work was simply to call into question the paradigm that sought to couch such analysis in terms of individual differences in people's psychological make-up.

This critique was consistent with a general trend that emerged after the Second World War for social psychologists to look for the basis of social behaviour in universal *group dynamics* rather than processes unique to the individual (e.g. Cartwright & Zander, 1956, 1960). One important reason for this refocusing was that it made little sense to try to explain the commonalities of behaviour displayed in wartime in terms of people's individuality. What was it that led whole nations to support some groups while turning against or vilifying others? Some time later, similar questions initiated a quest to identify *general cognitive processes* that might underpin important aspects of social life — a movement that picked up on a general 'cognitive revolution' in the study of psychology in the 1960s.

Significantly too, this revolution coincided with, and contributed to, a general upsurge of interest in all forms of psychological enquiry. For this reason it is relatively difficult to identify key figures who brought the study of cognition to the organizational arena or who provided it with its distinct character. There are also no single studies whose impact mirrors that of research at the Bethlehem Steel Company or the Hawthorne Electrical Works. It is clear, however, that the study of cognition has had and is still having massive influence on the study of organizations and that it has provided rich and diffuse insights into almost all aspects of organizational enquiry (Landy, 1989). The broad goal of such developments has been to identify mental processes that might account for particular patterns of organizational behaviour — attempting to explain, for example, how a person's *perceptions* of their working environment determine their reaction to it.

A central focus of this work has been the attempt to transpose general principles of cognition (e.g. examining issues of memory, judgement, attention, information processing and perception) to the organizational domain. In this it has mirrored and drawn extensively upon the *social cognition* movement in social psychology (e.g. Fiske & Taylor, 1984). This holds to the view that people's social behaviour is not simply determined by environmental factors but is mediated by their cognitive response to their environment — what they *think* about it. Few social psychologists have ever accepted the argument made by behaviourists like J. B. Watson and B. F. Skinner that behaviour can be explained simply by looking at the stimulus inputs that a person receives. To understand how an employee would respond to a special payment, for example, it would be important to know not just how big the payment was but how it was *understood* by the person concerned — whether it was seen to constitute a bribe, an insult or a justified reward. Such questions cannot be answered without an analysis of cognitive process.

Since the Second World War, social psychologists' study of cognition has been heavily influenced by three basic models (Fiske & Taylor, 1984; Taylor, 1981). These have characterized the social thinker in turn as: (a) a consistency seeker; (b) a naive scientist; and (c) a cognitive miser. The first of these models was particularly influential in the study of attitudes where it was assumed that people strive to manage and make sense of their various attitudes and beliefs by making them mutually consistent (Heider, 1958). Other things being equal, if Anne thinks that her supervisor is stupid, but one of Anne's colleagues, Bob, thinks the supervisor is intelligent, then Anne is going to be more comfortable with the idea that Bob is also stupid than with the idea that he is intelligent. And if Anne actually thinks that Bob *is* intelligent then she will have to do 'cognitive work' (e.g. engage in rationalization that might lead her to conclude that Bob is intelligent except when it comes to assessing supervisors) to allow her different cognitions to coexist.

The conception of people as naive scientists was most influential in the study of *attribution* in the 1960s and 1970s (e.g. Jones & Davis, 1965; Kelley, 1967). This concerns the way that people explain social events in their environment. A key issue here is whether people explain their own and other's behaviour in terms of internal or external factors. For example, a manager might try to understand whether a female employee resigned because the job didn't suit her (perhaps because she was an extrovert — an internal attribution) or as a result of something about the job itself (perhaps it was boring — an external attribution). The view of the manager as a naive scientist asserts that the manager's understanding would be based on a more-or-less rational assessment taking into account features of the environment other than just this employee's actions. So if this worker was the only person to leave the company, the manager would be more likely to make an internal attribution (it didn't suit her) than if everyone else who did the job also resigned.

The model of the social thinker as a cognitive miser developed in the early 1980s from an awareness that people's attributions were generally found not to be as rational or objective as might be expected. For example, studies indicated that people are generally inclined to make internal attributions to explain other people's behaviour (the 'fundamental attribution error'; Ross, 1977) but that people typically explain their own behaviour in terms of external factors (the 'actor-observer effect'; Jones & Nisbett, 1972). We see other people's behaviour — particularly their failings — as a reflection of their true nature and personality, but see our own as a product of the situation in which we find ourselves. A poor workman blames his tools, but other people blame the workman.

One popular explanation of these apparent errors was that they derived from limitations inherent in the cognitive system. People were assumed to make attributional errors because they lacked the mental resources to enable them to take into account all the factors that bore upon a particular behaviour, especially when that behaviour was not their own. In making attributions, as in making other cognitive decisions and judgements, people's actions were seen to be constrained by a need to preserve their precious *limited information-processing capacity* — so that they acted like cognitive misers (Fiske & Taylor, 1984). Under this view, a great deal of human behaviour (including a great deal of human error) can be explained by the fact that people are forced to make decisions that are quick and easy (but often wrong) rather than ones that are time-consuming and onerous (but more likely to be right).

The view that human activity is constrained by cognitive limitations actually goes back to some of the very earliest writings in social psychology (e.g. Lippmann, 1922). However, it is in the last two decades that it has had most impact. In the organizational domain the central challenge has been to identify cognitive short-cuts (otherwise known as heuristics or biases) that might be responsible for errors in areas such as decision-making, judgement and negotiation. Researchers have also tried to suggest strategies for circumventing these errors. However, precisely because the cognitive processes that are identified are seen as normal (or 'natural'), errors are often seen to be inevitable and hence unavoidable.

In fact, though, the influence of the cognitive miser model in social psychology is currently waning, giving way to the model of the perceiver as a 'motivated tactician' (Fiske & Taylor, 1991; Leyens, Yzerbyt & Schadron, 1994). As we will illustrate in upcoming chapters, the view that perceivers are strategic information processors rather than just resource conservers has also found favour in the organizational field, largely because it is consistent with *social exchange* approaches to topics like leadership, motivation, information management and power (e.g. Thibaut & Kelley, 1959). These argue that people's actions are guided by the personal costs and benefits perceived to be associated with the various behavioural choices they face (e.g. to follow a leader, to keep a secret, to obey an order). They suggest that when the personal costs of a course of action appear to outweigh the benefits, it is unlikely to be perceived as equitable or to be pursued. Yet while exchange theories (in particular, equity theory — see Adams, 1965; Walster, Walster & Berscheid, 1978) have had enormous impact on organizational psychology over the last three decades (see Lee & Earley, 1992), there is evidence that their influence has also passed its peak (Tyler, 1993, 1999a).

## The purpose and structure of this book

The above review is far from exhaustive. Nonetheless, by focusing on the origins of key paradigms, it identifies some of the important intellectual and practical currents that have shaped researchers' study of organizations over the last hundred years. The review should also make it clear that each of the existing paradigms has a specific set of strengths and weaknesses. The economic paradigm focuses on the contribution of the individualized worker to overall organizational performance and sets out a clear strategy for practical intervention. The same is true of the individual differences paradigm (with which it is theoretically aligned), although this incorporates a consideration of psychological factors that is generally absent from the economic approach. The cognitive paradigm takes the analysis of psychological process even further by helping researchers understand the grounding of organizational behaviour in normal cognition. However, Pfeffer (1997) identifies a weakness in this model that also applies to the economic and individual difference views:

> Although research on the cognitive model of organizations will sometimes use the phrase 'social cognition' and will frequently invoke the term 'organization', much of the work is actually quite silent on the obvious social and contextual influences on the processes of attribution [and] sensemaking ... that go on. In this sense, the cognitive model of organizations ... downplay[s], empirically, if not in the language used, the social, relational reality of organizational life. (p. 79)

An emphasis on this social dimension, and on the important contribution of groups to organizations, is the primary strength of the human relations paradigm. By pointing to the capacity of group life to *transform* the behaviour and psychology of individuals it also undermines other approaches at the very point where they appear to be strongest. Yet this approach offers little analysis of psychological process in return, and this is one major reason why its impact has not been as dramatic as might be expected. Nonetheless, the lessons of the human relations movement are reflected in trends to involve workers more in organizational activities and decisions — for example, by introducing suggestion boxes, consultative committees, employee-involvement groups (EIGs), participative decision making (PDM), total quality management (TQM), 360-degree feedback, teamworking and enterprise bargaining. However, it is easy to see these as superficial and cynical attempts to appease and co-opt workers (many of which fail — see Harley, 1999) rather than as reflections of deeper theoretical commitment (Hardy & Leiba-O'Sullivan, 1998; Kelly & Kelly, 1991; Milkman, 1998; Parker, 1993, p. 250; Strauss, 1977).

Moreover, where such commitment does emerge — for example, in the contemporary language of human resource management (HRM) — it is often found to be a recasting of Taylorist managerialism in group-based terms. Here the manager's strategy is to achieve economies of scale and to tap the productive potential of groups revealed in Mayo's research but ultimately to control the group in much the same way that Taylor controlled the individual (see Parker, 1993; Sewell, 1998; Warhurst & Thompson, 1998). Baldry, Bain and Taylor (1998) refer to this as 'team-Taylorism' and argue that:

> Contemporary HRM rhetoric counterposes the empowering and collective effort of teamworking to the linear process and individual effort that is historically associated with Taylorism. [However,] the evidence ... demonstrates that, appearances notwithstanding, workers experience such forms of team organization as being no less coercive than classically understood Taylorism. (pp. 168-9)

Along similar lines, Buchanan (1995) notes:

> Human resource management ideology ... at its most basic represents a modified version of th[e] very old doctrine of management's right to run the workplace as it sees fit. While some of the rhetoric may be about participation and devolution, these practices will only be adopted if senior management retains control. (p. 62)

In theoretical terms, this means that organizational psychologists often make a nod in the direction of the Hawthorne studies and the lessons they provide, but then bash on with an individualistic approach regardless (e.g. see Lawler, Mohrman & Ledford, 1992; Levine & Tyson, 1990). It is also worth adding that this decision is often based on arguments (a) that the Hawthorne studies are methodologically flawed and their findings over-interpreted (see Argyle, 1953; Carey, 1967) or (b) that the core message of the human relations approach is that groups can do no wrong (see Whyte, 1960, pp. 36-60).

However, Pfeffer (1997, 1998) points out that decisions to embrace individualism also have deeper-rooted ideological underpinnings. This is because the approach lends itself to models that sit very comfortably with the benign view that organizations are melting-pots of individuals devoid of political division, social tension or group conflict. Managers find this approach more attractive because it does not threaten the status quo and ultimately justifies their own positions of power and control — their 'right to manage' (Levine & Tyson, 1990; Statt, 1994). In the end, then:

> Models of behaviour take on a religious quality, adopted or rejected on the basis of beliefs or aesthetics rather than on the basis of scientific evidence. So, even though organizations are inherently social and relational entities, there is great interest in the economic model of behaviour in spite of the fact that many of its variants proceed from a position of methodological individualism that denies the very reality of the institutions and organizations being explained. (Pfeffer, 1997, p. 80; see also 1998, p. 744)

Bearing these points in mind, the objective of this book is to define a path through the organizational field that outlines a new and fully integrated approach to its investigation. Building upon the strengths of existing paradigms, this attempts to provide an analysis of psychological process that recognizes and explains how group memberships and social relations contribute to organizational life.  This approach is *social psychological*, because it takes both the social and the psychological aspects of organizational life seriously.  Indeed, the approach is concerned to clarify the way in which *social and psychological elements are structured by each other*, rather than — as previous paradigms have tended to do — emphasizing one element at the expense of the other.  In so doing it thus seeks to redress problems which stem from the fact that:

> Social psychology's increasing emphasis on individual cognition on the one hand and personality on the other, with a de-emphasis on groups and social influence ... has left a growing gulf between psychological research and organizational issues and problems. (Pfeffer, 1998, p. 735).

The approach in question derives from a tradition in social psychology that was developed by two European researchers: Henri Tajfel and John Turner.  At the heart of this work is an awareness of the reality of the group and of its contribution to human psychology.  There are thus echoes of Mayo in Tajfel's assertion that:

> In our judgements of other people, ... in our work relations, in our concern with justice, we do not act as isolated individuals but as social beings who derive an important part of our identity from the human groups and social categories we belong to; and we act in accordance with this awareness.  (Tajfel, Jaspars & Fraser, 1984, p. 5; see Turner, 1996, p. 14)

The idea here is that groups are not only external features of the world that people encounter and interact with, but that they are also *internalized* so that they contribute to a person's *sense of self.*  Groups define who we are, what we see, what we think and what we do.

In recognition of these points, Tajfel (1972) coined the term *social identity* to refer to that part of a person's self-concept that derives from his or her group memberships.  With their many colleagues, the body of Tajfel and Turner's work then went on to examine the workings and implications of social identity processes in relation to a broad array of social phenomena.  This work is the basis of two theories that share a range of assumptions and present a number of hypotheses which have been subjected to extensive empirical testing over the past 25 years: *social identity theory* (Tajfel & Turner, 1979, 1986) and *self-categorization theory* (Turner, 1985; Turner, Hogg, Oakes, Reicher & Wetherell, 1987).  Social identity theory is largely concerned with the psychological underpinnings of intergroup relations and social conflict.  Self-categorization theory focuses more broadly on the role of social categorization processes in group formation and action.  It looks at the processes which lead collections of individuals to believe they share (or don't share) group membership, and at how this then affects their perceptions and behaviour.

Early work with these theories addressed key theoretical topics in social psychology.  However, in recent years there has been a growing interest in applying them to the study of organizations.  So after a seminal paper by Ashforth and Mael (1989), an ever-growing and quite diverse body of work has revealed numerous ways in which the analysis of organizational behaviour can be enriched by social identity principles (e.g. as broadly represented in the work of Abrams, Ando & Hinkle, 1998; Bornman & Mynhardt, 1992; Bourhis, 1991;

Brewer, 1995; Dutton, Dukerich & Harquail, 1994; Haslam, Powell & J. Turner, 2000; Haunschild, Moreland & Murrell, 1994; Hogg & Terry, 2000; in press; Hopkins, 1997; Kelly & Kelly, 1994; Kramer, 1993; Lembke & Wilson, 1998; Oaker & Brown, 1986; Ouwerkerk, Ellemers & de Gilder, 1999; Postmes, Spears & Lea, 1998; Terry & Callan, 1998; J. Turner & Haslam, 2000; M. Turner & Pratkanis, 1998a; Suzuki, 1998; Tyler, 1999a; van Knippenberg & van Schie, in press; Wharton, 1992).

A major goal of this book is to clarify the nature and place of this work within the broader canvas of organizational and social psychological research. As Figure 1.1 illustrates, the social identity approach also attempts to fill the significant void that the above review identifies within existing organizational literature.

The chapters in the book address major areas of organizational enquiry that are customarily treated as more or less separate from one another. Each chapter starts by reviewing some of the influential approaches to the topic in question (e.g. those that emerge from economic, individual difference or cognitive paradigms) and discussing illustrative work. Critique of this work is then used to frame an alternative analysis based on the social identity approach. Some of the research that supports and elaborates this analysis is then reviewed in ensuing sections that focus on specific sub-problems in a particular area. In

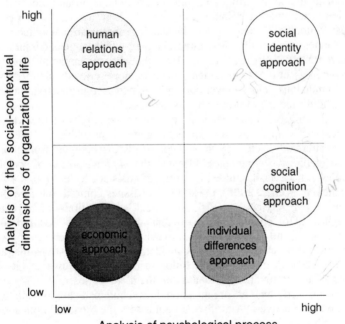

*Figure 1.1* Differences between organizational paradigms in terms of their attention to social and psychological dimensions of organizational life

many instances this research represents an extension of existing theorizing, but on occasion it takes it in radically new directions. Some of this research has already influenced mainstream thinking (particularly that on leadership, negotiation and collective action), but much of it is work-in-progress whose full impact is yet to be felt.

At the very least, our exploration of social identity and self-categorization principles is intended to be interesting and provocative. More ambitiously, though, the book's goal is to provide an *integrated framework* for rethinking core issues in organizational psychology and for making much-needed theoretical, empirical and practical progress. Accordingly, it is hoped that even those who disagree with the approach will find it to be a useful vehicle for interrogating and sharpening their own research and the assumptions that underpin it.

The chapters are organized in a sequence that attempts to unfold the substance and implications of the social identity approach in as logical a manner as possible. The first content-focused chapters examine issues of *leadership* and *motivation*. Previous theorizing in both areas has focused heavily on the importance of individual qualities, but these chapters suggest that both phenomena have important bases in the psychology of group membership. The next three chapters discuss *communication*, *decision-making* and *negotiation*. These are topics in which the role of the group is much more self-evident, but where its psychological impact has tended to be maligned — for example, because it is believed to distort information, polarize opinion or inflame conflict. Against this view, each chapter points to ways in which groups can play a constructive and psychologically creative role in shaping organizational outcomes. These same themes recur in the next three chapters which confront issues of *power*, *productivity* and *collective action*. Here though, it is apparent that analysis of the psychology of these phenomena becomes more seriously clouded by their *political* dimensions. Does power corrupt? Is increased productivity always desirable? Should industrial protest be discouraged?

In reflecting on such questions, one of the strengths of the social identity approach is that in these (and earlier) chapters it provides analytical tools that enable matters of psychology to be theoretically disentangled from those of politics and ideology. Nonetheless, because the *implementation* of social identity principles is necessarily guided by political goals and values (as is all organizational theory; Pfeffer, 1998), these political issues come to the fore in the final chapter which reflects upon the practical ramifications of this and other approaches. This chapter pays particular attention to the *sustainability* of the organizational and social outcomes delivered by different approaches to organizational psychology. These considerations raise questions that are among the most difficult that any psychologist can ask. However, it would be irresponsible not to attempt to answer them. Not least, this is because the professional activities of organizational psychologists are having a growing impact on all our lives. And if we do not assess the broader implications of that impact, who will?

So we have some challenging terrain ahead of us. However, in order to establish a broad theoretical platform for our journey, we need to start by summarizing the main tenets of social identity and self-categorization theories. This is the aim of the next chapter.

## Further reading

At the end of every chapter a small number of references will be identified for further reading. Selection is based on the ability of a reading to supplement points raised in the chapter and to generate enthusiasm for the issues discussed. In relation to the material covered in this chapter, it is hard to go past Taylor's (1911) spirited elaboration of the principles on scientific management and Mayo's (1949) equally engaging account of the Hawthorne studies and their background. Both are genuine classics. McGregor's (1960) book is written in the same engaging manner and it too is a milestone text. The chapter by Pfeffer (1998) is a bit more heavy-going, but it provides a thorough and up-to-date discussion of the strengths and weaknesses of various approaches to the study of organizational behaviour including some that have not been discussed here. Kelly and Kelly's (1991) paper offers a review of apparent innovations in industrial practice and it uses social psychological theory to explain why their impact on manager–worker relations has been less spectacular than one might expect. Like Parker's (1993) highly engaging essay, it also underlines the point that the managerial philosophies criticized by Mayo and McGregor are as prevalent today as they ever were.

Kelly, C. & Kelly, J. (1991). 'Them and us': Social psychology and 'the new industrial relations'. *British Journal of Industrial Relations, 29*, 25-48.

Mayo, E. (1949). *The social problems of an industrial civilization*. London: Routledge & Kegan Paul (especially Chapters 2 to 5, pp. 31-100).

McGregor, D. (1960). *The human side of enterprise*. New York: McGraw-Hill.

Parker, M. (1993). Industrial relations myth and shop floor reality: The team concept in the auto industry. In N. Lichtenstein & J. H. Howell (Eds.), *Industrial democracy in America* (pp. 249-274). Cambridge: Cambridge University Press.

Pfeffer, J. (1998). Understanding organizations: Concepts and controversies. In D. Gilbert, S. Fiske & G. Lindzey (Eds.), *The handbook of social psychology* (4th ed., pp. 733-777). New York: Oxford University Press.

Taylor, F. W. (1911). *Principles of scientific management*. New York: Harper.

# 2   The Social Identity Approach

As we saw in the previous chapter, paradigms for understanding organizational behaviour have tended to take the individual as the primary unit of psychological analysis.   They see groups simply as another context in which individual behaviour takes place.   This is particularly true of work in the individual differences paradigm (after Münsterberg, 1913) where psychological analysis gives no consideration to the way in which people's personal attributes and cognitive processes are affected by the groups to which they belong.  However, it is also true of more recent social cognitive work which has tended to deny the capacity for groups to impact upon and change the cognitive processes of individuals.

In an attempt to lay the foundations for an alternative way of approaching the field, this chapter summarizes those features of the social identity approach that are of potential relevance to the study of organizational psychology.  The chapter's central argument is that in order to understand perception and interaction in organizational contexts we must do more than just study the psychology of individuals *as individuals*. Instead, we need to understand how social interaction is bound up with individuals' *social identities* — their definition of themselves in terms of group memberships.

As Mayo (1949) recognized, groups *change* individuals and this in turn makes groups and organizations more than mere aggregations of their individual inputs.   Consistent with this point, the social identity approach argues that groups are not simply a passive context for individual behaviour.  In contrast to theories which tend to see the individualized person as the fundamental building block for theoretical and practical development, this approach therefore argues that organizational theory needs to give more emphasis to the way in which the psychology of the individual is a product of group life and its *distinct* psychological and social realities.

But in suggesting that the psychology of people in organizations is shaped by group forces, are we suggesting that their behaviour is thereby doomed to be irrational, under-motivated and counterproductive?  This is a pertinent question as most organizational topics can be approached in a way which suggests that groups undermine accurate cognition and useful action.  We saw this clearly in the writings of Taylor (e.g. 1911), but this view also follows from the model of the social perceiver as a cognitive miser which suggests that individuals only cope with group life by relying on cognitive shortcuts that save resources but open up the door to error and poor judgement.  The ideas discussed in this chapter challenge this view by suggesting that it is the ability to think in terms of 'we' and 'us', not just 'I' and 'me', that enables people to engage in meaningful, integrated and collaborative organizational behaviour.  As we will see, amongst other things, this capacity underpins people's ability to achieve social cohesion, to communicate effectively, to influence and persuade each other, to act collectively, and to go beyond the call of duty.  In this way the fact that groups transform the psychology of the individual is seen not as a necessary evil but as an essential good.

At this stage, though, these various points may sound hollow and sloganistic. Organizational theory has had more than its fair share of fashionable mantra and dogma, and is in little need of any more (for assurance on this point, see Micklethwait & Wooldridge, 1997). To have any chance of ensuring that these arguments do not share the same fate as the fashions of the past, and to have something on which to base our arguments in later chapters, we therefore need to go to the trouble of articulating the empirical and theoretical foundations of the social identity approach carefully and in some detail. We need to go in at the deep end.

## Social identity theory

### The minimal group studies

Social identity theory was originally developed in an attempt to understand the psychological basis of intergroup discrimination. Why do group members malign other groups and what makes people so often believe that their own group is better than others? To examine questions of this form, a series of studies was conducted by Tajfel and his colleagues in the early 1970s which sought to identify the *minimal* conditions that would lead members of one group to discriminate in favour of the ingroup to which they belonged and against another outgroup (Tajfel, Flament, Billig & Bundy, 1971). Our treatment of social identity theory needs to start by considering these studies in some detail, as the points that emerge from them are critical to a number of major claims that we will want to make, and these points are easily misunderstood.

As a first step in the research process Tajfel and his colleagues assigned participants to groups that were intended to be as stripped-down and meaningless as possible. The plan was then to start adding meaning to the situation in order to discover at what point discrimination would rear its head (Tajfel, 1978a, pp. 10-11). In the first studies schoolboys were assigned to one of two groups. The boys were led to believe that this assignment was made on the basis of fairly trivial criteria — either their estimation of the number of dots on a screen, or their preference for the abstract painters Klee and Kandinsky. In fact though, assignment to groups was random. Importantly too, this process excluded a range of factors that had previously been considered to play an essential role in intergroup discrimination — factors such as a history of conflict, personal animosity, or interdependence. Individual self-interest and personal economic gain were also ruled out because the task that the boys had to perform involved assigning points (each signifying a small amount of money) to an anonymous member of both their own ingroup and the other outgroup but never to themselves.

Findings from Tajfel et al.'s first experiment indicated that even these most minimal of conditions were sufficient to encourage ingroup-favouring responses. That is, participants tended to deviate from a strategy of fairness by choosing a reward pair that awarded more points to people who were identified as ingroup members. In other words, they displayed *ingroup favouritism*.

To investigate this process more closely, a second study incorporated a range of different matrices in which the boys chose a pair of rewards from a number of alternatives. An example is provided in Figure 2.1 (from Tajfel, 1978c, p.78). This procedure allowed the experimenters to differentiate between all the possible decision strategies that participants might employ. These strategies were: (a) fairness; (b) maximum joint profit (giving the greatest total reward to the two recipients); (c) maximum ingroup profit (giving the greatest total reward to the ingroup member); and (d) maximum difference in favour of an ingroup member (choosing the strategy that led the ingroup member to 'beat' the outgroup member by the largest margin).

The results of this second experiment indicated that participants again departed from a strategy of fairness. Here though, when given reward choices like those in Figure 2.1, they tended to adopt a reward strategy that maximized the difference between groups in a way that favoured the ingroup member. In other words, participants were motivated less by a desire to maximize their own *absolute* gain than by a keenness to enhance their *relative* gain vis-a-vis the outgroup. The authors therefore concluded that:

> In a situation devoid of the usual trappings of ingroup membership and all the vagaries of interacting with an outgroup the subjects still act in terms of their ingroup membership and an intergroup categorization. Their actions are unambiguously directed at favouring the members of their ingroup as against the members of the outgroup. This happens despite the fact that an alternative strategy — acting in terms of the greatest common good — is clearly open to them at a relatively small cost. (Tajfel et al., 1971, p. 172)

Points for member of

| Klee group: | 7 | 8 | 9 | 10 | 11 | 12 | 13 | 14 | 15 | 16 | 17 | 18 | 19 |
|---|---|---|---|---|---|---|---|---|---|---|---|---|---|
| Kandinsky group: | 1 | 3 | 5 | 7 | 9 | 11 | 13 | 15 | 17 | 19 | 21 | 23 | 25 |

MD                                           F                                    MIP
                                                                                 MJP

*Figure 2.1* A typical matrix from a minimal group study (based on Tajfel, 1978c)

*Note*: Participants decide how many points to award to the ingroup and outgroup member by selecting one pair of numbers. In this example a participant in the Klee group would make a choice towards the left-hand end of the matrix to achieve the maximum gain of the ingroup member relative to that of the outgroup member (MD). A choice in the middle of the matrix would achieve fairness (F), and one towards the right-hand end would achieve maximum joint group profit (MJP) and maximum ingroup profit (MIP). The shaded response thus indicates a compromise between strategies of maximum difference and fairness.

The conflict between these findings and those predicted by a model of economic self-interest is striking. Why didn't the participants simply try to get as much money for themselves as they could? Or failing that, why didn't they simply try to obtain as much money as possible for the two recipients combined — thereby extracting the maximum amount of money from the experimenter? In the original minimal group studies the strategy adopted by participants was especially intriguing in view of the fact (a) that the participants had no personal stake in the outcomes and (b) that as a result of the participants' chosen course of action ingroup members actually got *less* than they would have done with any other strategy. What seemed to matter was not *doing well* as such, but *doing better* than the other group.

Lest it be thought that these laboratory findings are of only academic interest, similar findings have emerged in an organizational setting where workers have been asked how they would like wage rises to be structured. Brown's (1978) research with employees at an aircraft engine manufacturing company showed that workers' primary concern was to preserve wage *differentials* between various categories of employee rather than to increase their own absolute earnings. Amongst other things, this research examined the wage levels that groups of workers at three skill levels (Grades 6, 5D and 5) thought were appropriate for people at their own level and the other two. As shown in Figure 2.2, the findings indicated that groups were keen to maximize wage differences between their group and other less skilled workers, but generally minimized differences between their group and others that were more skilled. Particularly noticeable was the fact that this meant that workers with the highest level of skill actually

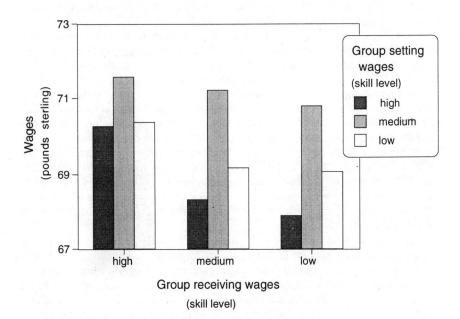

*Figure 2.2*  Wages awarded to their own and other groups by three groups of aircraft engine workers with different skill levels (from Brown, 1978)

ended up awarding themselves *less* pay than they were awarded by the other groups. Significantly though, they awarded the other two groups much less than those groups awarded themselves. However, the highly skilled workers were happier to receive a smaller rise because the level of pay they ended up with preserved their wage superiority relative to other sectors of the workforce. As one highly skilled employee put it: 'the status of the job is more important than the actual wage' (Brown, 1978, p. 421). Discussing the strategies adopted by these skilled workers, Brown (1978) observes:

> Their responses showed almost total unanimity. ... There is no doubt that they were primarily concerned with establishing the largest possible difference over the grade 5 groups, even if this meant a sacrifice of as much as £2 a week in absolute terms. They were highly articulate men and recognized the problems associated with this strategy. As one steward realized:
> > 'Your sectarian point of view is going to cost *you* money and *save* the company money',
> which completely contradicted his duty as a shop steward:
> > '... to extract the maximum from an employer for the labour we sell'. (p. 423)

As later argued by Turner (1975) and Tajfel (1978b), the important finding of the original minimal group studies (as they became known) was that they suggested that the mere act of individuals *categorizing themselves* as group members was sufficient to lead them to display ingroup favouritism. The results also challenged established theories of intergroup conflict (e.g. Dollard, Doob, Miller, Mowrer & Sears, 1939; Sherif, 1966) by pointing to 'the possibility that discriminatory intergroup behaviour cannot be fully understood if it is considered solely in terms of 'objective' conflict of interests or in terms of deep-seated motives that it may serve' (Tajfel et al., 1971, p. 176).

Since Tajfel et al.'s (1971) initial studies, a number of experiments have replicated these findings and clarified the key role that group-based identity plays in the observed results (Tajfel, 1978d). In particular, an experiment by Billig and Tajfel (1973) ruled out the possibility that the results of the original minimal group experiments arose simply from the fact that participants perceived themselves to be similar to ingroup members. This study manipulated social categorization and similarity orthogonally so that in one of four conditions participants assigned points to two people who were (a) either identified or not identified as an ingroup and outgroup member and (b) either identified or not identified as having similar and different artistic tastes. As predicted, patterns of point allocation were affected much more by the presence or absence of social categorization than by the presence or absence of similarity. Indeed, the only necessary and sufficient prerequisite for discrimination was the existence of an ingroup-outgroup division.

Other attempts to reinterpret minimal group findings as the product of methodological artefacts or as the result of implied interdependence between participants have also gained little empirical support (see Bourhis, Turner & Gagnon, 1997, for an extended discussion of this point). There appears to be nothing in the minimal group paradigm which demands discrimination or which leads participants to believe that they are engaging in beneficial social exchange.

Further research has also shown that the minimal group studies have broader relevance to issues of social perception and cognition (for a review see Oakes,

Haslam & Turner, 1994). For example, Doise et al. (1972) found that participants who were assigned to minimal groups described their ingroup more favourably than the outgroup. Without knowing anything about the groups at all, ingroup members were seen, amongst other things, to be more flexible, kind and fair than members of outgroups. Brewer and Silver (1978) also showed that the tendency to represent ingroups more favourably than outgroups was unaffected by attempts to highlight the similarity between all individuals and the arbitrary nature of group membership. In this study participants still displayed ingroup favouritism even after they had been told that their initial responses to paintings 'were too similar to provide a basis for grouping, so they would have to be split into the groups randomly' (pp. 395-396).

Minimal as they were, the group memberships invoked in these sort of studies thus exerted a strong hold over those to whom they were assigned. Not only did they make otherwise fair, decent and normal people act in a way that was transparently unfair, but they did so in the absence of any obvious reason for such behaviour. The researchers were understandably keen to explain these findings, but it was clear that to do so they needed to look beyond the psychological profiles of the individual participants.

## Understanding the minimal group studies

One of the most important points that Tajfel himself saw to emerge from the minimal group studies was that when participants categorized themselves as members of a group this gave their behaviour a *distinct* meaning. As he put it:

> This meaning was found by them in the adoption of a strategy for action based on the *establishment*, through action, of a distinctiveness between their own 'group' and the other, between the two social categories in a truly minimal 'social system'. Distinction from the 'other' category provided ... an identity for their own group, and thus some kind of meaning to an otherwise empty situation. (Tajfel, 1972, pp. 39-40)

As a part of this process Tajfel argued that in the minimal group studies 'social categorization required the establishment of a distinct and positively valued *social identity*' (Tajfel, 1972, p. 37, emphasis added). He defined social identity as 'the individual's knowledge that he [or she] belongs to certain groups together with some emotional and value significance to him [or her] of the group membership' (p. 31). In other words, social identity is part of a person's sense of 'who they are' associated with any *internalized group membership*. This can be distinguished from the notion of *personal identity* which refers to self-knowledge that derives from the individual's unique attributes (e.g. concerning physical appearance, intellectual qualities and idiosyncratic tastes; Turner, 1982).

Noting the distinct psychological contribution that social identity made to 'creat[ing] and defin[ing] the individual's place in society', Tajfel and Turner (1979, pp. 40-41) went on to develop a fuller explanation of the findings from the minimal group studies. In so doing, they formulated the *social identity theory* of intergroup behaviour. This is an 'integrative theory' that attends to both the cognitive and motivational basis of intergroup differentiation. In essence it suggests that after being categorized in terms of a group membership, and having *defined themselves* in terms of that social categorization, individuals seek to achieve positive self-esteem by positively differentiating their ingroup from a comparison outgroup on some valued dimension. This quest for *positive distinctiveness* means that when people's sense of who they are is defined in terms of 'we' rather than 'I', they want to see 'us' as different to, and better than, 'them' in order to feel good about who and what they are. In this way, a company employee who identifies strongly with the department they work for — where the department makes an important contribution to their sense of self — may be motivated to see that department as better than others in order to feel better about themselves (Ashforth & Mael, 1989; Brown, Condor, Mathews, Wade & Williams, 1986). This point is expressed in the following statement by the facility manager of a port authority studied by Dutton et al. (1994, see also Dutton & Dukerich, 1991):

> I've always felt that the Port Authority is ... and part of our self-image is, as I put my fingers on it, that we do things a little better than other public agencies. There's a whole psyche that goes with that ... and that's why, when there's time like now, when times get tough, people get nervous a bit because that goes to their self-image, which is that the Port Authority and therefore we, do things first class. (p. 247)

In the minimal group situation Turner (1975) argued that when participants identified with one of the social categories (e.g. the Klee group), they engaged in a process of *social competition* involving comparison of the ingroup and the outgroup on the only available dimensions (reward allocations or evaluative ratings). Participants then achieved positive distinctiveness for their own group by awarding it more points or representing it more favourably. This interpretation has been supported by a considerable body of subsequent research (for reviews see Brewer, 1979; Hogg & Abrams, 1988; Turner, 1981; van Knippenberg & Ellemers, 1990).

Yet while the findings of minimal group studies have proved highly reliable, social identity theory itself is commonly *mis*interpreted in a number of ways. In particular, the theory is often taken as suggesting that group members have either an automatic or a personal drive to display prejudice (Turner & Oakes, 1997; Turner & Reynolds, in press). A tendency to display ingroup favouritism has therefore mistakenly been seen either as a universal cognitive bias or as an individual difference. In contrast to both interpretations, the theory suggests that ingroup favouritism is not an automatic or a person-specific response, but a reaction to particular social psychological circumstances. Accordingly, it will vary with the social situation in which individuals find themselves and is far from universal. Early field studies that supported this conclusion were reported by Stephenson and Brotherton (1973, 1975; see also Brotherton, 1999, pp. 78-79). Here the level of discrimination between coal mine employees was not constant across groups but depended, amongst other things, on the level of pre-existing disagreement between groups and their size (see also Sachdev & Bourhis, 1984).

Tajfel and Turner (1979, p. 41) identify three variables whose contribution to the emergence of ingroup favouritism is particularly important. These are: (a) the extent to which individuals identify with an ingroup and internalize that group membership as an aspect of their self-concept; (b) the extent to which the prevailing context provides ground for comparison between groups; and (c) the perceived relevance of the comparison outgroup, which itself will be shaped by the relative and absolute status of the ingroup. As we will clarify below, individuals are therefore likely to display favouritism when an ingroup is central to their self-definition and a given comparison is meaningful or the outcome is contestable. However, they may in fact display *out*group favouritism if the outgroup's relative superiority is not contested or the task is irrelevant to the ingroup (Mummendey & Schreiber, 1983, 1984; Reynolds, Turner & Haslam, 2000; Terry & O'Brien, 1999).

A clear illustration of these patterns is provided by Terry and Callan's (1998) extensive study of over 1,000 employees in two hospitals — one high status, one low status — that were about to undergo a merger. As the results presented in Figure 2.3 indicate, employees of the high-status hospital showed ingroup favouritism when evaluating the two hospitals on status-relevant dimensions (prestige in the community, job opportunities and variety in patient type), but outgroup favouritism on status-irrelevant dimensions (e.g. industrial harmony, relaxed work environment, modern accommodation). Members of the low-status hospital, on the other hand, acknowledged the inferiority of the ingroup on status-relevant dimensions, but accentuated their superiority on the status-irrelevant ones. Indeed, as Terry and Callan note, while employees in both hospitals acknowledged the strengths of the other group, the motivation of the low-status group to re-establish its positive distinctiveness (which had been threatened by the merger) led its members to assert their superiority much more strongly on the status-irrelevant dimensions than members of the high-status group had on status-relevant ones.

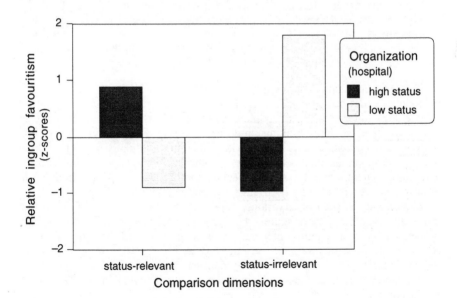

*Figure 2.3* Patterns of relative ingroup favouritism displayed by employees of high- and low-status organizations (from Terry & Callan, 1998)

*Beyond discrimination: The impact of perceived social structure*

Although social identity theory is usually invoked to explain patterns of discrimination like those found in minimal group studies, this is not its only contribution to the analysis of group behaviour. Two other important sets of ideas examine how people's cognitions and behaviour are affected (a) by movement along the interpersonal–intergroup continuum and (b) by perceived social structure. These ideas are quite complex and for that reason it may help to refer to Figures 2.4 and 2.5 as we work through them.

In relation to the first of these themes, Tajfel (1978a) asserted that behaviour in general could be represented in terms of a bipolar *continuum*. At one extreme interaction is determined solely by the character and motivations of the individual *as an individual* (i.e. interpersonal behaviour). At the other, behaviour derives solely from the person's group membership (i.e. intergroup behaviour). In making this distinction, Tajfel suggested that intergroup and interpersonal behaviour were qualitatively distinct from each other. As Mayo (1949) and Asch (1951) had argued, groups are not just collections of individuals and group behaviour cannot be explained in terms of interpersonal principles. Tajfel also noted that while these extremes were hypothetical forms of behaviour, the interpersonal extreme was logically absurd because membership of social categories always plays some role in shaping interaction. In his words:

> It is impossible to imagine a social encounter between two people which will not be affected, at least to some minimal degree, by their assignments of one another to a variety of social categories about which some general expectations concerning their characteristics and behaviour exist in the mind of the interactants. ... This will ... be even more true of professional 'role' encounters, as between patient and doctor, student and teacher, car owner and mechanic, however familiar those people may have become and however close their personal relationships may happen to be. (Tajfel, 1978a, p. 41)

Tajfel argued that social identity processes come into play to the extent that behaviour is defined at the intergroup extreme of this continuum. That is, people think in terms of their group membership when the context in which they find themselves is defined along group-based lines. For example, as conflict between two companies escalates, workers may be more likely to start thinking about themselves as members of one or other company than as individuals. There is a dynamic here too, because social conflict leads to people thinking in terms of their social identity but is also *dependent* upon their doing so.

Elaborating on such observations, Tajfel (1978a, pp. 44-45) formulated two important hypotheses (see Figure 2.4). He suggested that as behaviour became defined in intergroup terms, members of an ingroup would be more likely to react *uniformly* to members of the outgroup and to treat the outgroup as an *undifferentiated* category. Thus during conflict the 'other side' is more likely to be consensually treated as a uniform whole — as if 'we all agree that they're all the same'.

These hypotheses have received a considerable amount of empirical support and are implicated in a range of important social psychological phenomena. In particular, they are consistent with evidence that the heightened salience of group memberships is associated with increases in the perceived homogeneity

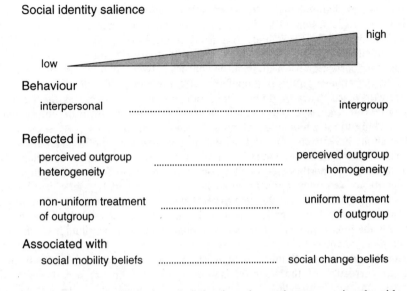

Social identity salience

low ——————————————————————— high

Behaviour

interpersonal ........................................................ intergroup

Reflected in

perceived outgroup heterogeneity ............................................... perceived outgroup homogeneity

non-uniform treatment of outgroup .............................................. uniform treatment of outgroup

Associated with

social mobility beliefs ............................................. social change beliefs

*Figure 2.4* Psychological and behavioural continua associated with the interpersonal–intergroup continuum (after Tajfel, 1978a)

outgroups and in consensus among the ingroup (for reviews see Haslam, Oakes, Turner & McGarty, 1996; Haslam, Turner, Oakes, McGarty & Reynolds, 1998).

Exactly where individuals place themselves on the interpersonal–intergroup continuum was understood by Tajfel to be a consequence of an interplay between social and psychological factors. Social factors have to do with the objective features of the world that an individual confronts and psychological factors are associated with the individual's interpretation of that world. Thus the way we see ourselves depends both on events happening in the world around us and on the perspective we take on those events.

Key elements of this perspective are an individual's *belief structures*. These lie on another continuum between an ideology of *social mobility* and one of *social change* (Tajfel, 1975; see Figure 2.4). Social mobility beliefs are characterized by the view that individuals are free to move between groups in order to improve or maintain their social standing. They are underpinned by an assumption that a given social system is flexible and permeable. In the workplace, a belief in social mobility might lead to an assumption that it is possible for anyone to rise to the top of an organization if they have sufficient personal acumen or gumption. Social change beliefs, on the other hand, are underpinned by an assumption that it is not possible to escape one's group for the purposes of self-advancement. According to this view, the only prospect for improving negative conditions (or maintaining positive ones) lies in action as a group member. In the workplace this might involve participation in the activities of a professional association or union which actively advances the cause of one's ingroup.

Tajfel (1978a) identified a number of conditions which could lead individuals to hold social change beliefs. These included situations in which there is: (a) an objectively rigid system of social stratification which is perceived to be in some sense illegitimate and unstable; (b) a desire to create or intensify the impact of group memberships; (c) a motivation to clarify otherwise vague or non-existent group boundaries; or (d) a division or conflict between two groups that makes movement between groups unthinkable. All these conditions can and do prevail in the workplace. They might be found, for example, where a professional group (of organizational psychologists, say) perceived its treatment to be unjustified, was seeking to raise the collective consciousness of its members, was seeking to differentiate itself from other professional groups, or was in conflict with them.

The location of an individual's beliefs on the continuum of belief structures will therefore be partly determined by objective features of the world that he or she confronts (e.g. whether a given social structure is widely believed to be, or really is, permeable). Yet whatever their basis, to the extent that an individual embraces social change beliefs, this will cause that person's behaviour to lie towards the intergroup end of the interpersonal–intergroup continuum and hence to be dictated more by social identity–related concerns. To help clarify these arguments, the inter-relationships between the various behavioural and psychological correlates of the interpersonal–intergroup continuum are represented schematically in Figure 2.4.

Social identity theory's third strand integrates elements of the two that have already been discussed — analysis of discrimination in the minimal group studies and of movement along the interpersonal–intergroup continuum. It does this by examining how people's shared understanding of status relations leads to different strategies for self-enhancement. How does a person's status, and the perceived basis of that status, affect the way they set about feeling good about themselves?

Amongst other things, social identity theory's answer to this question takes into account the extent to which people perceive (a) group boundaries to be *permeable* and (b) their group's relative position on a dimension of social comparison to be *secure* in the sense of being both *stable* and *legitimate*. These perceptions are argued to impact upon the strategies pursued by members of low- and high-status groups in their attempts to achieve or maintain a positive social identity (see Figures 2.5a and 2.5b). In this, they have particular implications for the way in which people deal with social and *organizational change* (along lines suggested by Terry & Callan's, 1998, hospital merger study, discussed above). For example, the employees in a company that is taking over a smaller competitor may see group boundaries as permeable and status relations as irrelevant, and their means of securing a positive social identity will be quite different to that of employees in the company that is being taken over (who are more likely to see boundaries as impermeable and their company's relative status as insecure).

This point is confirmed in Bachman's (1993; see Anastasio, Bachman, Gaertner & Dovidio, 1997) studies of a bank takeover in which members of a large acquiring bank tended to accept a new superordinate corporate identity and believe this gave them enhanced personal opportunity, while members of the acquired bank collectively resisted this view and were more likely to act in terms of their old pre-acquisition social identity. Very similar patterns were observed by van Knippenberg, van Knippenberg, Monden and de Lima (1998) in a study of merging local government departments. Moreover, these researchers also found that organizational identification was negatively correlated with workers' intention to leave the new organization. Patterns of social identification were thus important predictors of behaviour that was of considerable significance both to the merger itself and to long-term organizational structure.

Elaborating on their earlier work (e.g. Terry & Callan, 1998), Terry and her colleagues examined similar processes in the context of a merger between a high-status international airline and a low-status domestic airline (Terry, Callan & Sartori, 1996; Terry, Carey & Callan, 1997). Here, as long as they perceived the status relations to be legitimate, members of the low-status airline more readily accepted the new superordinate structure (believing it offered them better prospects as individuals), while the high-status group members (who believed their group as a whole stood to lose status) resisted change and were more likely to seek to act collectively in terms of their pre-merger identity. This pattern was subsequently replicated by Terry and O'Brien (1999) in a study of the merger between high- and low-status scientific organizations.

Similar patterns of status protection and enhancement were observed by Skevington (1980) among groups of nurses who were undergoing organizational change. When high-status nurses were told they would be merged with a lower status group they exhibited greater ingroup favouritism than the low-status group (who actually showed outgroup favouritism) as a way of emphasizing their perceived superiority and distinctiveness. These patterns were also reproduced in experimental research conducted by Haunschild et al. (1994; see also van Leeuwen, van Knippenberg & Ellemers, 2000). Here when task groups were forced to merge, members of groups that had a history of superior task performance were much more resistant to change and showed much more ingroup favouritism than did members of groups that had performed less well.

However, the above patterns do not exhaust the forms of response that workers can have to organizational change. Yet another strategy was observed by Breakwell (1983) in a study of social workers whose social identity was increasingly threatened by lowering status. In response to this threat, these low-status workers became more likely to *dis*identify with social workers as a class and sought instead to define themselves in terms of *other* readily available group memberships (e.g. as health workers).

The above research reveals a range of quite different ways in which employees can respond to diverse forms of organizational change. But how can these various responses be systematized? In an attempt to address this question, Tajfel and Turner (1979) identified three basic strategies of self-enhancement: *individual mobility*, *social creativity* and *social competition*. Individual mobility is seen to be associated with a general belief in the possibility of *social mobility*, while social creativity and social competition are conceptualized as aspects of a *social change* belief system. The latter belief system is likely to dictate behaviour when an individual is locked into their membership of a group and must act either to improve or to defend its status. Some of the key premises of Tajfel and Turner's arguments are represented schematically in Figures 2.5a and 2.5b. These figures summarize aspects of social mobility and social change belief systems associated with membership of low- and high-status groups, respectively.

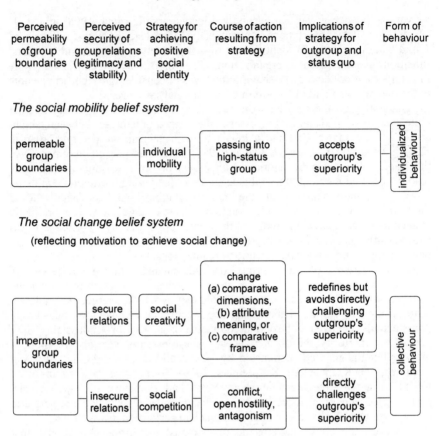

| Perceived permeability of group boundaries | Perceived security of group relations (legitimacy and stability) | Strategy for achieving positive social identity | Course of action resulting from strategy | Implications of strategy for outgroup and status quo | Form of behaviour |
| --- | --- | --- | --- | --- | --- |

*The social mobility belief system*

permeable group boundaries — individual mobility — passing into high-status group — accepts outgroup's superiority — individualized behaviour

*The social change belief system*

(reflecting motivation to achieve social change)

impermeable group boundaries

secure relations — social creativity — change (a) comparative dimensions, (b) attribute meaning, or (c) comparative frame — redefines but avoids directly challenging outgroup's superioirity

insecure relations — social competition — conflict, open hostility, antagonism — directly challenges outgroup's superiority

collective behaviour

*Figure 2.5a* The relationship between belief structure and strategies for achieving positive social identity for members of low-status groups

Considering each of the three strategies for self-enhancement in turn, Tajfel and Turner (1979) argued that individual mobility is most likely to be pursued when a group has relatively low status and group boundaries are perceived to be permeable — as it was for employees of the domestic airline in Terry et al.'s (1997) research. Here group members disassociate from the group and pursue individual goals designed to improve their personal lot rather than that of their ingroup. In the workplace, for example, women who perceive there to be no 'glass ceiling' may believe that their best strategy for advancement is to try to get on as an individual (e.g. by working hard or acting like 'one of the boys') rather than trying to engage in collective action designed to improve the treatment and status of women as a whole (Fajak & Haslam, 1998).

Social creativity and social competition, on the other hand, are strategies associated with a social change belief system that are intended to improve the negative or maintain the positive conditions of one's ingroup. These are likely to arise when people believe group boundaries to be impermeable and hence they

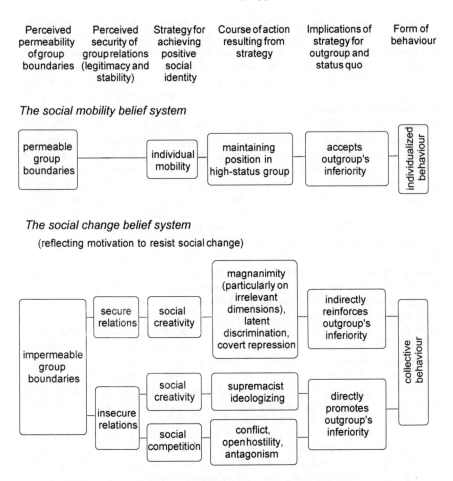

*Figure 2.5b*   The relationship between belief structure and strategies for maintaining positive social identity for members of high-status groups

are unable to better themselves by moving between groups. Here individuals are forced to deal with the group-based reality that confronts them (Tajfel, 1974).

Under these conditions, members of low-status groups are most likely to resort to social creativity when their ingroup's status is secure — as was the case for the social workers studied by Breakwell (1983). This can take a number of forms including: (a) finding a new dimension on which to compare ingroup and outgroup; (b) changing the values assigned to the attributes of the ingroup; and (c) engaging in comparison with a different outgroup.   So, for example, representatives of a company with a small market share may seek to compare themselves with a larger company on a new dimension ('we may not be big, but we're friendly'), they may redefine the meaning of market size ('less is more') or they may change the frame of reference ('we have the largest share of the high-tech market').

Different forms of social creativity are likely to be displayed by members of a high-status group. If their status is secure this may take the form of magnanimity towards the outgroup (Platow et al., 1999) or relatively covert, seemingly benign forms of discrimination. Members of high-status groups may, for example, show favouritism towards the outgroup on irrelevant dimensions in a manner that mirrors the social creativity of low-status group members (e.g. by conceding that 'we're bigger but they're more friendly'; Ellemers, Doosje, van Knippenberg & Wilke, 1992; Ellemers & van Knippenberg, 1997; Ellemers, van Rijswijk, Roefs & Simons, 1997; Terry & Callan, 1998). They may also engage in behind-the-scenes censorship or repression of the outgroup (so as to ensure its continued low status) while publicly denying such activity. However, if their status is insecure (particularly because it is illegitimate) the social creativity of high status groups is likely to take a more sinister form and be reflected in ideologies (e.g. racism and sexism) which attempt to justify and rationalize the ingroup's superiority and the outgroup's inferiority.

As noted above, social competition is also likely to arise when boundaries are impermeable. This typically occurs in reaction to the perceived insecurity of relative status — for example, when a group's low status is perceived to be illegitimate or a group's high status appears unstable. In such situations individuals also conceive of some *cognitive alternative* to the status quo. In this way, members of any group who perceive there to be real and unfair barriers to their progress at work (e.g. women or the disabled) and can imagine an improved situation may act collectively to change their circumstances by confronting the relevant outgroup. Even more aggressively, members of a high-status group who feel their relative advantage is under threat may band together to resist change — as employees of the high-status international airline did in Terry et al.'s (1997) study and members of successful groups did in Haunschild et al.'s (1994) research (see also Turner & Brown, 1978). Because this strategy sets the ingroup directly against the interests and values of the outgroup, it is also much more likely to involve some form of social conflict and open hostility than strategies of individual mobility or social creativity (which either accept or avoid directly challenging the high status group's interests and values). In this way social competition represents a direct and overt attempt to challenge or maintain the status quo in a way that other strategies are not.

The above outline gives some indication of the intricate way in which psychological and social factors combine to dictate the particular courses of action that individuals pursue in order to achieve positive social identity. For this reason the application of social identity principles to organizational settings clearly needs to be sensitive to features of social psychological context (Ashforth & Mael, 1989; Bornman & Mynhardt, 1992; Bourhis et al., 1997; Brown et al., 1986; Ellemers, 1993; George & Chattopadhyay, 1999; O'Brien & Terry, 1999; Turner & Haslam, 2000; Turner & Oakes, 1997). In particular, this is because social competition of the form displayed in the minimal group studies is only one possible response that group members can make to the social reality they confront. So although vulgarized versions of social identity theory suggest that 'social identification leads automatically to discrimination and bias', in fact this is not true. On the contrary, discrimination and conflict are anticipated only in a limited set of circumstances — where intergroup relations are in some way insecure and the prevailing definition of social reality is seen to be contestable.

*Understanding the theory's impact*

Social identity theory has had, and continues to have, considerable impact on the field of social psychology. Developed in Europe and initially used to address quite tightly defined issues of group antagonism and social competition (e.g. Turner, 1975), it was soon applied to a broad array of topics including prejudice, stereotyping, negotiation and language use (Turner & Giles, 1981). In the past decade its international profile and breadth of application has increased further, with the result that the theory is now influential around the world not only in organizational psychology but also in areas of clinical and health psychology, linguistics and political science.

This success can be attributed to at least three factors. First and most straightforwardly, the core tenets of the theory have proved remarkably valuable in helping researchers explain and understand important aspects of social behaviour. Compared to other theories whose explanatory potential is quickly compromised by boundary conditions and caveats, a strength of social identity theory is that the hypotheses it puts forward are testable in a wide range of fields and settings. And although they have often been adapted to address the particular problems faced in any area, these hypotheses have generally received strong support. For this reason the theory has simply been an expedient option for researchers interested in doing research that 'works'.

Moreover, second, in the areas where it has been applied, the theory has provided a novel and refreshing alternative to established theorizing. As exemplified by the research reviewed in Chapter 1, social psychologists have often fallen foul of a tendency to explain social behaviour in terms of purely interpersonal principles, thereby seeing groups as a psychological inconvenience or irrelevance (Steiner, 1974). In this way researchers have followed Floyd Allport's (1924) assertion that 'if we take care of the individuals, psychologically speaking, the groups will be found to take care of themselves' (p. 9; see Asch, 1952; Turner, 1987b). By actively countering such injunctions, social identity theory has been an important resource for researchers who contend that there is more to the psychology of groups than just the sum of their individual parts (Ashforth & Mael, 1989; Lembke & Wilson, 1998; Turner & Oakes, 1986). Moreover, once this social dimension of the theory is embraced, it proves to be a highly versatile intellectual resource which can be used to develop a coherent and integrated understanding of diverse topics. In this it serves as a tonic to the general tendency for social and organizational psychologists to develop unique and highly localized mini-theories that remain specific to the particular phenomenon (or effect) in which they are interested (see Aronson, 1997, p. 29; Mone & McKinley, 1993; Smith & Mackie, 1997; Smith, Murphy & Coats, 1999).

Associated with this point, third, the theory is also aligned with a more sophisticated *political* analysis of social behaviour than is afforded by many competing models. Many social psychological analyses are premised upon a model of society in which individuals are the primary agents and their fate is determined either (a) by various forms of individual competence (or lack of it) or (b) generalized psychological forces. This is true, for example, of social exchange approaches like equity theory (Adams, 1965; Walster et al., 1978). As we noted in Chapter 1, these assert that people will be satisfied with any relationship or course of action to the extent that the personal benefits they receive are consistent with their personal costs. However, approaches of this form overlook the fact that in society individuals belong to groups that are meaningfully differentiated on a range of potentially important dimensions (e.g. class, power, material wealth) and that this social structuring has important psychological consequences (Kelly & Breinlinger, 1996; Platow, Hoar, Reid, Harley & Morrison, 1997; Pfeffer, 1998; Nkomo & Cox, 1996; Tyler, 1993). This means, for example, that 'costs' and 'benefits' cannot be appreciated independently of the status-based values and interests of the groups that incur and receive them (Tajfel, 1982a; van Knippenberg & van Oers, 1984). Along the lines of the minimal group findings, a powerful airline may be happy to bear and actively encourage the 'cost' of a downturn in passenger demand if that downturn hurts a weaker competitor more. Managers may prefer a poorly performing workforce in which workers are 'kept in their place' to a more productive one in which workers are treated as equals. Part of the appeal of social identity theory is not only that it accounts for such phenomena, but that it does so by appreciating rather than denying social and political forces (Oakes et al., 1994; Turner & Reynolds, in press).

## Self-categorization theory

Curiously perhaps, one important limitation of social identity theory is that it offers a relatively underdeveloped analysis of the cognitive processes associated with social identity salience. What is the relationship between personal and social identity? What makes people define themselves in terms of one group membership rather than another? How exactly is a person's psychology transformed by his or her group ties? How does social identification produce ingroup consensus and co-ordinated social action? Despite the fact that the construct of social identity is obviously central to social identity theory, the theory itself provides no real answers to questions like these. Thus after reviewing the relevance of the social identity concept to the study of organizations, Wharton (1992) comments:

> Social identity plays an important role in shaping organizational members' evaluations of and responses to situations. It provides a basis for distinguishing between similar and dissimilar others and thus supplies the criteria that underlie perceptions of the self and the social environment. (p. 67)

But she then adds:

> Much more needs to be done with respect to understanding how particular social identities become salient, and the consequences of salience for organizations and their members. (p. 67)

It was partly to address such issues that self-categorization theory was developed by Turner and his colleagues in the 1980s (Turner, 1982, 1985; Turner et al., 1987; Turner, Oakes, Haslam & McGarty, 1994).

Self-categorization theory has a broader cognitive agenda than social identity theory and has greater explanatory scope, largely because its core hypotheses are not targeted specifically to issues of social structure and intergroup relations (Turner & Oakes, 1997; a point represented schematically in Figure 2.6). In fact though, self-categorization principles can be elaborated to encompass most of the social structural phenomena addressed within social identity theory. Nonetheless, as we will see in upcoming chapters, the two theories have typically been used to tackle slightly different problems. So, as Turner points out in this book's foreword (p. xiii), although we can use the epithet *the social identity approach* as shorthand to refer to the full range of arguments and hypotheses that are generated by the two theories, it is still important — intellectually and practically — to continue to distinguish between them. In particular, retaining the distinction avoids the misunderstandings that arise when self-categorization theory is crudely subsumed within social identity theory.

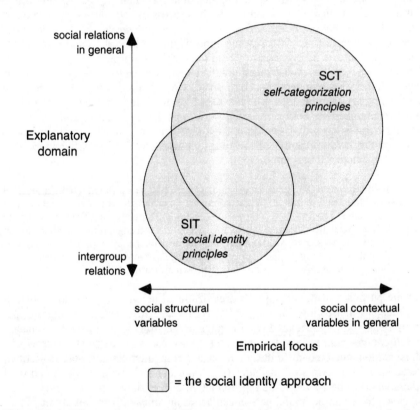

*Figure 2.6* The explanatory profiles of social identity and self-categorization theories

### Depersonalization and self-stereotyping

Formative work on self-categorization theory focused on the theoretical implications of the notion of social identity itself. In particular, Turner (1982) sought to provide a more complete explanation of individuals' movement along

Tajfel's interpersonal–intergroup continuum (as depicted in Figure 2.4). As a part of this development he hypothesized (Brown & Turner, 1981; Turner, 1982) that an individual's self-concept could itself be defined along a continuum ranging from definition of the self in terms of personal identity to definition in terms of social identity. Moreover, he proposed that the functionin*f*g of the self-concept *is the cognitive mechanism that underpins* the behavioural continuum described by Tajfel (1978a). Thus interpersonal behaviour is associated with a salient personal identity and intergroup behaviour with a salient social identity. Turner (1982) also argued that the 'switching on' of social identity actually *allowed* intergroup behaviour to take place. As he put it, 'social identity is the cognitive mechanism that makes group behaviour possible' (p. 21).

A further important part of this development was to specify a *psychological process* associated with this 'switching on' of social identity. Turner referred to this as *depersonalization*. This refers to the process of *self-stereotyping* through which *the self comes to be perceived as categorically interchangeable with other ingroup members*. So, elaborating upon Tajfel's (1978a) hypothesis that in intergroup contexts individuals will tend to perceive outgroups as homogeneous, Turner predicted that social identity salience should lead to the *ingroup* being seen as similarly homogeneous. Employees who are parties to conflict between their company and another should therefore tend to emphasize similarities amongst members of *both* companies — not just the rival one. In this way they will tend to see both that rival company and their own in stereotypic terms — although the favourableness of the two stereotypes will often differ markedly. Here, then, when self-stereotyping:

> Individuals react to themselves and others not as differentiated, individual persons but as exemplars of the common characteristics of their group. It is through this process that salient or functioning social identifications help to regulate social behaviour; they do so directly by causing group members to act in terms of the shared needs, goals and norms which they assign to themselves, and indirectly through the perceptual homogenization of others which elicits uniform reactions from the perceivers. (Brown & Turner, 1981, p. 39)

For the purposes of the analysis of organizational behaviour to be developed in the chapters that follow, this argument is crucial. In essence, it suggests that group behaviour is associated with change in the structure of the self — change in *self-categorization*. As an individual, 'who one is' is defined in terms of idiosyncratic personal attributes, but as a group member the self is defined stereotypically in terms of attributes (e.g. values and goals) that are shared with others who are perceived to be representative of the same social category. This suggests, for example, that a person can act as an army officer only to the extent that they define themselves less as a unique individual (e.g. as the conservationist who likes animals and works for children's charities) and more as someone who is categorically interchangeable with other officers and whose behaviour is regulated by norms associated with that category (e.g. to wear a uniform, follow orders, and distrust the enemy). These ideas are represented schematically in Figure 2.7.

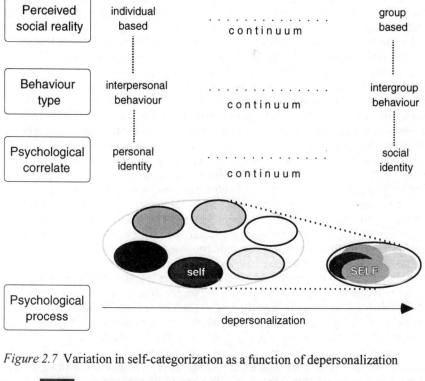

*Figure 2.7* Variation in self-categorization as a function of depersonalization

*Note*:  **self** = self as unique individual with personal identity salient.

SELF = self as interchangeable group member with social identity salient.

The shift from **self** to SELF is produced by depersonalization (self-stereo-typing).

## The self-categorization process: Some assumptions and hypotheses

In suggesting that group behaviour follows from an act of self-stereotyping, the above arguments point to the role which *categorization* — and more specifically *self*-categorization — plays in social perception and behaviour. The key contribution of early work with self-categorization theory was to elaborate upon the workings and implications of this self-categorization process. This elaboration is formalized in a number of core assumptions and related hypotheses of which five are the most important (Turner, 1985; Turner et al., 1987).

First, cognitive representations of the self take the form of *self-categorizations*. That is, the self is seen as a member of a particular class or category of stimuli. As such it is perceived to be (a) more or less equivalent to other stimuli in that category, and (b) more or less distinct from stimuli in other categories. So, for example, when a person categorizes themselves as a psychologist they acknowledge their equivalence to other psychologists and their difference from, say, sociologists or economists.

Second, self- and other categories exist at different levels of abstraction with higher levels being more inclusive (cf. Rosch's, 1978, analysis of the structure of natural categories). Lower level categories (e.g. biologist, physicist) can be subsumed within higher ones (e.g. scientist) and are defined in relation to comparisons made at that higher level. To help illustrate various theoretical arguments it is also useful to consider three important levels of the social self-concept: self-categorization (a) at the superordinate *human* level as a human being (in contrast to other species), (b) at the intermediate *social* level as an in-group member (as distinct from outgroups), and (c) at the subordinate *personal* level as a unique individual (different from other relevant ingroup members). Importantly, level of category abstraction is a relative concept and so for any one person more than one level of social self-category will be available (Nkomo & Cox, 1996). For example, someone who works in a biology departmfent may define themselves in terms of social self-categories varying from the more to the less abstract — as a scientist, life scientist, biologist, or molecular biologist. However, an assumption of *functional antagonism* (Turner, 1985, p. 98) suggests that as one of these levels of self-categorization becomes more salient, so self-categorization at other levels should become less salient. Other things being equal (and depending on the actual *content* of the identity; see Chapter 7 below), the more a woman defines herself as a biologist the less she should see herself (at a lower level) as an individual or (at a higher level) as a scientist, and the more she sees herself as an individual the less she should see herself (at a higher level) as either a biologist or as a scientist. Moreover, self-categories at all levels of abstraction are seen to be equally 'real' and just as much a reflection of a person's 'true' self. No one level of self-categorization is inherently more appropriate or useful than another and hence none is in any sense more fundamental to who or what the person is. This proposition is at odds with a general tendency for psychological theorizing to give privileged status to personal identity — believing that a person's *true* self is defined by their individuality (see Asch, 1952; Oakes & Turner, 1990). To illustrate some of these points, a hypothetical hierarchy relevant to a person's self-definition in an organizational context is presented in Figure 2.8.

Third, the formation and salience (i.e. cognitive activation) of any self-category is partly determined by comparisons between stimuli at a more inclusive *level of abstraction*. Biologists are therefore distinguished from chemists only with reference to a higher order category such as scientists, and in this way the perception of difference at one level of abstraction is premised upon similarity at a higher level (Medin, 1988; Oakes, 1996). More specifically, the formation of self-categories is a function of the *meta-contrast* between inter-class and intra-class differences. This means that within a frame of reference comprised of salient stimuli, any given collection of stimuli will be perceived as a categorical entity to the extent that their difference from each other is seen to be less than the difference between them and all other stimuli. So, for example, a physicist and a biologist are more likely to be seen to share a higher level social identity as scientists when they are encountered in a context that includes non-scientists. This is because here the differences between them are small relative to those between them and the non-scientists. Meta-contrast thus *contextualizes*

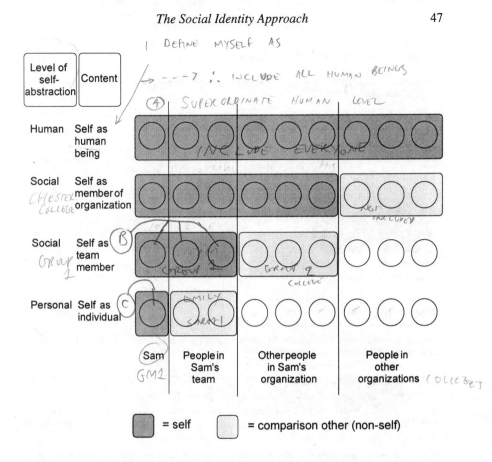

*Figure 2.8* A hypothetical self-categorical hierarchy for a person in an organization

*Note*: The darkly shaded regions indicate those others who are included in Sam's definition of self at different levels of abstraction. Thus self-definition becomes more inclusive at higher levels of abstraction. The lightly shaded regions indicate others who are compared with self at different levels of abstraction. These are the people who are part of the self at the next highest level of abstraction. Intermediate social identities could exist between those presented here (e.g. self as member of a department, self as worker).

categorization by tying it to an on-the-spot judgement of *relative differences*. This point is illustrated in Figure 2.9, which shows how categorical representation of *exactly the same* social stimuli can vary as a function of comparative context.

Fourth, just as the meta-contrast principle is a partial determinant of *which* categories perceivers use to represent a given stimulus array, so too it is a partial determinant of the *internal structure* of those categories. Following cognitive theorizing (e.g. Barsalou, 1987; Rosch, 1978) categories are assumed to have an

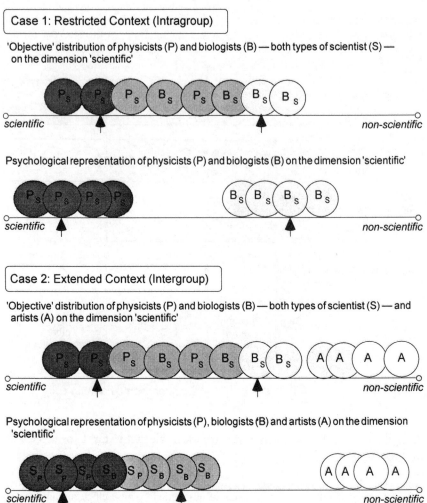

*Figure 2.9* A schematic representation of the role of comparative context in defining the self-categorical relationship between people

*Note*: The important point to abstract from this figure is the way in which the representation of physicists and biologists changes as a function of comparative context — for example, how, amongst other things, context changes the relationship between the individual biologist and the individual physicist denoted by arrows. When only physicists and biologists are present (Case 1), these groups are perceived as distinct lower-level social categories, so that the similarities within the categories are accentuated as well as the differences between them. However, when the comparative context also includes artists (Case 2), physicists and biologists are represented in terms of a shared higher level social category membership as scientists. In this extended context the similarities between these two groups of scientists are accentuated as well as their difference from artists.

internally *graded structure* so that some features of a category (i.e. particular behaviours, attributes or individuals) define it better than others. This means that people differ in the extent to which they are perceived to be representative or *prototypical* of groups in the same way that a sparrow is generally more representative of the category 'bird' than a penguin. In this way all category members share a certain degree of *prototypicality*, while at the same time the extent of their relative prototypicality varies. All academics may be perceived as to some extent intelligent, but some are perceived as more intelligent than others. Similarly, a manager may perceive all union members as recalcitrant but some members (often the union leaders) will be perceived to embody this recalcitrance more than others.

More specifically, it follows from the meta-contrast principle that any particular category member will be perceived to be more prototypical of a category to the extent that it is less different from other members of that category than from other social stimuli that are salient in a given context. In a comparison with physicists, a relatively non-scientific psychologist (Freud, say) may be quite prototypical of the category 'psychologist' because that person partly embodies the *difference* between psychologists and physicists, but in a comparison with artists that person's prototypicality will tend to decrease relative to someone who is more scientific (who embodies the difference between psychologists and artists — e.g. Skinner). Self-categorization theory therefore predicts that the prototypicality of exactly the same exemplar for exactly the same category will vary lawfully as a function of the social context within which categorization takes place.

Finally, fifth, the salience of a categorization at a particular level of abstraction leads to the accentuation of perceived intra-class similarities and inter-class differences between people as defined by their category membership at the same level. In this way patterns of accentuation reflect the extent of people's categorical interchangeability. For example, if a woman's social self-category 'scientist' becomes salient, other scientists will be perceived to be more similar to each other (and her) and more different from other non-scientists (whose similarity to each other will also be accentuated) on dimensions that are seen to define membership of those categories (e.g. commitment to the scientific method). This point is also illustrated in Figure 2.9.

*Perceiver readiness and fit as determinants of social identity salience*

From the quite complex ideas outlined in the above section, it can be seen that self-categorization theory recasts some of the important insights of earlier social identity research within a broader explanatory scheme. Moreover, the above arguments put us in a position to understand exactly what factors dispose people to act in terms of a particular social self-categorization. When will an employee in an organization see and act in terms of the organization as a whole, or in terms of the department or team to which they belong, or as an individual? Answering this question is extremely important, because — as we will see — it is apparent that people are capable of acting at *all* these levels, but that the *particular* level at which they define themselves has distinctive implications both for their own behaviour and for the functioning of the organization as a whole.

To address this issue, the principles of self-categorization theory outlined above have been formally applied to the analysis of social identity salience and ingroup–outgroup categorization (Oakes, 1987; Oakes, Turner & Haslam, 1991; Turner, 1985).   Following the work of Bruner (e.g. 1957), one crucial determinant of social category salience is *fit*. This is the degree to which a social categorization matches subjectively relevant features of reality — so that the category appears to be a sensible way of organizing and making sense of social stimuli (i.e. people and things associated with them).   It has two components: comparative and normative.

*Comparative fit* is defined by the principle of meta-contrast that we discussed in the previous section.  As illustrated in Figure 2.9, this leads us to expect that a person will define themselves in terms of a particular self-category to the extent that the differences between members of that category on a given dimension of judgement are perceived to be smaller than the differences between members of that category and others that are salient in a particular context.  If a (female) economist was surrounded by psychologists and other economists, she would tend to define herself as an economist only if the differences between the two groups appeared to be larger than the differences within them.  This is more likely to be the case at a social science conference than at a football match, which is one reason why people are more likely to classify the people at an inter-disciplinary conference in terms of their occupational category than the people in a sporting crowd.  To see people as economists and psychologists will be fitting at a social science conference in a way that it won't be at a football match.

*Normative fit* arises from the *content* of the match between category specifica-tions and the stimuli being represented.  In order to represent sets of people as members of distinct categories, the differences between those sets must not only appear to be larger than the differences within them (comparative fit), but the *nature* of these differences must also be consistent with the perceiver's expecta-tions about the categories.  If these content-related expectations are not met, the social categorization will not be invoked to make sense of events and define the person's own action.  Our economist at the social science conference will be unlikely to classify participants as economists and psychologists (or to act as an economist herself) if the members of these two groups are seen to differ from each other in ways that are unexpected — perhaps if the economists are concerned only with people's well-being and the psychologists only with profit.

One important implication of the comparative fit hypothesis is that as the comparative context that a perceiver confronts is extended so that it includes a range of more different stimuli, salient self-categories will be more inclusive and will be defined at a higher level of abstraction (see Figure 2.9). A male worker who compares himself with another worker will tend to categorize himself in terms of personal identity and accentuate individual differences between himself and that other person.  However, as the context is extended to include different others — for example, managers — he is more likely to categorize both himself and the other in terms of a higher level social identity, as 'us workers' who are similar to each other and different from 'those managers' (Haslam & Turner, 1992).

Empirical support for this argument is provided by a study reported by Hogg and Turner (1987a) in which individuals were organized either into four-person groups comprising two males and two females or into same-sex pairs.  Here participants were more likely to define themselves in terms of gender and to accentuate their similarity with other members of the same sex when men *and* women were present rather than just another person of their own gender (i.e. in an intergroup rather than an interpersonal context).

A study by Gaertner, Mann, Murrell and Dovidio (1989; see also Gaertner, Mann, Dovidio, Murrell & Pomare, 1990) also demonstrates the way in which a person's perception and treatment of other people is dependent upon their categorical relationship to the self. In this study all participants were initially defined as members of one of two groups each comprising three members. As in the minimal group studies (Tajfel et al., 1971), this categorization led to intergroup discrimination. After this, however, some participants were induced to *re*categorize the people as either one group of six or as six individuals. As predicted, intergroup discrimination was reduced by both these 'recategorization' strategies. Specifically, the 'one group' manipulation increased the perceived attractiveness of former outgroup members by redefining them as members of an ingroup at a higher level of abstraction, and the 'six individuals' redefinition reduced the perceived attractiveness of former ingroup members, by redefining them as different individuals at a lower level of abstraction (i.e. members of non-self personal categories).

Providing further support for self-categorization theory, researchers have shown that as a perceiver's frame of reference is extended, the extent to which a target person is seen to share a common categorical identity with the perceiver varies in a manner predicted by the meta-contrast principle (Haslam & Turner, 1992, 1995, 1998; Wilder & Thompson, 1988). As in Gaertner's studies, this in turn impacts on a host of other very important variables — including how positively the other person is described and how willing the perceiver is to communicate and co-operate with them (Morrison, 1998).

Similar manipulations of comparative context have also been shown to impact upon the prototypicality of individual category members. Such changes will redefine the group's overall normative structure because they change who or what most represents its position, values, and goals. For example, as comparative context is extended, extreme members of a group become more representative of its position and this makes the group as a whole more extreme (Haslam, Oakes, McGarty, Turner & Onorato, 1995; Hogg, Turner & David, 1990; Mackie & Cooper, 1984; McGarty, Turner, Hogg, David & Wetherell, 1992; van Knippenberg, de Vries & van Knippenberg, 1990).

In all these various studies the status of individuals and groups as representative of self- or nonself-categories — upon which the perception of similarity is based — is shown to vary with context. There are thus no inherent, stable differences between representations labelled 'ingroup' and 'outgroup' and no pre-defined, universal identity in terms of which a person will define themselves. This point is recognized by Wharton (1992) in an extended discussion of the way in which employees' self-definition in terms of gender and race can change across different workplace settings (see also Fajak & Haslam, 1998; Jackson, 1992; Ridgeway, 1991).

Such research suggests that the very same people can be defined as an ingroup or an outgroup in different contexts. The colleague who is seen as a rival in the context of intra-organizational competition for funds and resources, may be redefined as an ally when the organization is in competition with another. Two managers who are at loggerheads over a plan to restructure their company may enjoy each others' company at a promotional event which draws attention to their similarities rather than their differences.

This is one way in which changes in context can have a profound impact on the *meaning* of any particular self-category. Psychologists, for example, will define themselves and the world very differently when they compare themselves with physicists rather than dramatists, or within a Science rather than an Arts community (a point confirmed empirically by Doosje, Haslam, Spears, Oakes & Koomen, 1998). *Organizational culture*, and the way in which this informs employees' behaviour, will change in a similar way. For example, the norms, values and goals espoused by a prestigious university will change depending on whether it compares itself with prestigious businesses on dimensions of economic performance or whether it compares itself with non-prestigious universities on dimensions of scholarship and learning. As contexts change, employees and the organization as a whole redefine what they are 'about' and where they are going.

Importantly too, the principles of fit also determine category salience in interaction with *perceiver readiness* (or *accessibility*; Oakes et al., 1994; Turner et al., 1994; see also McGarty, 1999b, p. 192; Appendix 1 below, Figure A1.1). Individuals do not participate in social encounters by mechanically processing information in a dispassionate, uninvolved manner that leads them to decide matter-of-factly whether or not a particular person should be seen as a member of a particular category. As Mowday and Sutton (1993) put it, it is wrong to 'portray organization members as cognitive stick figures whose behaviour is unaffected by emotions or interactions' (p. 197). So as well as being determined by the subjectively perceived features of a stimulus array, categorization also depends on the *prior* expectations, goals and theories of perceivers — many of which derive from their group membership and group encounters. People organize and construe the world in ways that reflect the groups to which they belong and in this way their *social histories* lend stability and predictability to experience (Bar-Tal, 1990; Cinnirella, 1998; Oakes et al., 1994; Reicher, 1996; Sherif & Cantril, 1947; Turner & Giles, 1981).

*Identification* with a group — the extent to which the group is valued and self-involving — is therefore one particularly important factor which affects a person's readiness to use a given social category in order to define themselves (e.g. Doosje & Ellemers, 1997; Doosje, Ellemers & Spears, 1995; Ellemers, Spears & Doosje, 1997; Kramer, 1993; Spears, Doosje & Ellemers, 1997; Turner, 1999). Amongst other things, when a person identifies strongly with a given organization, he or she may more readily interpret the world, and their own place within it, in a manner consistent with that organization's values, ideology and culture (Kramer, Brewer & Hanna, 1996; Mael & Ashforth, 1992; Rousseau, 1998). For this reason alone, identification has proved to be an important construct in both social and organizational psychology and a number of researchers have developed scales that attempt to measure both its nature and strength. Some of these measures are presented and discussed in Appendix 1.

*Social influence as a determinant of organized behaviour*

Self-categorization theory's analysis of social identity salience is directed to the explanation of social psychological phenomena that are often studied by looking at the responses and perceptions of non-interacting individuals. Significant as it is, such analysis therefore makes only a partial contribution to an understanding of organizational behaviour that involves *structured social interaction*. Importantly though, the dynamic processes of self-categorization described above do not just affect the perception of individuals in the abstract. They are also assumed to have ongoing consequences for the *active co-ordination* of individuals' perception and behaviour.

In this respect, a key assertion of self-categorization theory is that social self-categorizations serve to regulate individual cognitive activity not only by providing a shared perspective on social reality and a common set of experiences but also by *providing a basis for mutual social influence* (Turner, 1987a, 1991; see also Turner & Oakes, 1989). That is, when people perceive themselves to share category membership with another person in a given context they not only *expect to agree* with that person on issues relevant to their shared identity but are also motivated to *strive actively to reach agreement* on those issues. Where only physicists and biologists are present (e.g. Case 1 in Figure 2.9), a single biologist and a single physicist may define themselves in terms of distinct social self-categories and expect to have different views, intentions, and goals. But if they meet in a context that also includes people from very different backgrounds (e.g. artists, as in Case 2) they should redefine themselves in terms of a higher-order *shared* social self-categorization that provides them with a relatively common perspective and which motivates them to co-ordinate that perspective further. They should attempt to achieve such co-ordination through, amongst other things, identifying shared beliefs, specifying frames of reference, articulating background knowledge, clarifying points of disagreement, and exchanging relevant information — in short, through communication, persuasion, negotiation and argument (all processes that we will examine in detail in upcoming chapters).

Self-categorization theory argues that social influence of this form is *necessary* because it is not possible for a person to establish the subjective validity and correctness of their beliefs simply through 'independent' activity. Social reality testing — which involves testing and validating one's views in collaboration with others who are categorized as similar to self in a given context — is therefore a necessary accompaniment to personal reality testing (Turner, 1991). In this way, other members of the groups to which we see ourselves as belonging (those who contribute to our sense of 'we-ness' — i.e. ingroup members) serve as essential reference points for our own perception.

An example of these points might be found in the case of an individual who is working as part of a team on a particular project (see Ibarra & Andrews, 1993; Lembke & Wilson, 1998). As an individual, the person will necessarily reflect privately on the team's operation and its output. But if that person sees themselves as part of the team they will also attempt to sound out and refine their ideas in collaboration with other team members — whose inputs are perceived to be relevant to the project and the individual's own participation in it as a group member. As the interaction of workers in the Hawthorne plant showed, groups members also exert influence over each other by suggesting appropriate forms of behaviour and, if necessary, acting to enforce group norms.

As Turner (1991) puts it, these two forms of intellectual activity — individual and social — are equally important interdependent phases of social cognition. In order to function adequately, we need input from fellow ingroup members just as much as we need independent sensory input because these work *in tandem* to give structure and direction to our behaviour. Moreover, it is precisely through individuals' identification of, and conformity to, norms that are perceived to be shared with others in a particular context that their potentially idiosyncratic views become socially organized and consensual. It is through this process that individual views are co-ordinated and transformed into *shared* values, beliefs and behaviours. These values and beliefs also have particular force because they are no longer experienced as subjective but instead articulate a common, as-if-objective view (Bar-Tal, 1998; Hardin & Higgins, 1996; Haslam, Turner, Oakes, McGarty et al., 1998; Moscovici, 1984). In this way, what had been simply *personal opinion* now becomes *social fact*. '*I think* it is important to be polite to customers' becomes '*it is* important to be polite to customers'; '*I think* we are the best', becomes '*we are* the best'.

The importance of social influence processes is well documented in relation to a number of social psychological topics and dates back to famous studies by Sherif (1936) and Asch (1951) which highlighted the power of ingroups to regulate and structure individual cognitive activity. Because these processes play such an important role in organizational behaviour we will return to examine their role in a number of the specific phenomena that we discuss in upcoming chapters. However, at the most general level, we will see that it is through categorization-based processes of influence that low-level individual inputs are transformed into higher-order group products.

In organizations, then, when combined with motivations to achieve positive distinctiveness for the collective self, influence processes have the capacity to focus and energize employees by providing them with a shared sense of purpose — a mission — that is distinct from those of other organizations (Peters & Waterman, 1995) and which contributes a synergic organizational culture (Deal & Kennedy, 1982; Hofstede, Neuijen, Ohayv & Sanders, 1990; Weick, 1985). In the words of Deal and Kennedy (1982):

> For those who hold them, shared values define the fundamental character of their organization, the attitude that distinguishes it from all others. In this way, they create a sense of identity for those in the organization, making employees feel special. Moreover, values are a reality in the minds of most people in the company, not just the senior executives. It is this sense of pulling together that makes shared values so effective. (p. 23)

## Conclusion

The principles outlined in the foregoing sections accord with a large body of evidence which suggests that context is a key determinant of organizational behaviour (for major reviews see Mowday & Sutton, 1993; O'Reilly, 1991). Moreover, many researchers agree that context is a variable that researchers neglect at their cost. In an influential review in the *Annual Review of*

*Psychology* O'Reilly (1991) argues for 'the importance of context' by noting that:

> Group demography and dynamics affect both the members and functioning of groups with respect to communication, social interaction and group development... The very composition of the group may have important effects on individual outcomes, beyond what is normally captured in measures of individual attributes. (p. 447)

This point is consistent with points raised in discussing the individual difference paradigm in the previous chapter (see also Kramer, 1993; Salancik & Pfeffer, 1978). Elaborating on this argument, Mowday and Sutton (1993) note, as we also did in Chapter 1, that the study of organizational behaviour has 'relied more heavily on cognitive approaches in recent years'. However, they warn that:

> Because social context is rarely considered in such work ... much research published in organizational behaviour journals no longer reflects the field's distinctive competence. We agree with Cappelli and Sherer's (1991, p. 97) assertion that 'what is unique about behaviour in organizations is presumably that being in the organization — the context of the organization — somehow shapes behaviour, and it is impossible to explore that uniqueness without an explicit consideration of the context'. (pp. 196-7)

Pfeffer (1998) too bemoans the fact that:

> Although we know that organizations are, fundamentally, relational entities and that the environment of an organization consists of other organizations, many theories and analyses fail to incorporate ideas or measures of social · ·cture into research ... which is invariably a weakness in the analysis. (p. 746)

Significantly, then, a key feature of the social identity approach is that its analysis points to the *interdependence* of individual cognition and a social context with structural, comparative and normative dimensions (Turner et al., 1994). Indeed, the approach is explicitly *interactionist*, in arguing that self-categorization processes serve to represent — and are shaped by — various forms of social reality in the world that confronts the perceiver (Asch, 1952; Haslam, Oakes, Turner & McGarty, 1996; Turner & Oakes, 1986). This reality encompasses human behaviour that occurs at many different levels: individual, group, organizational, societal and cultural.

Developing this point and applying it to the organizational domain, a core hypothesis to be explored in the remainder of this book is that *self-categorization processes are a critical mediator between organizational contexts and organizational behaviour*. Put slightly differently, we suggest that the way in which characteristics of organizational life affect behaviour will depend upon the *self-categorical meaning* of those characteristics for organizational members. Where features of context lead a person to react to a situation in terms of a social identity that is shared with specific others, behaviour will be qualitatively different from that which results where this identity is not shared. This means, for example, that the relationship between a biologist and a physicist should differ markedly across restricted and extended comparative contexts (e.g. a meeting of the science faculty rather than a meeting of the university council; see

CRUCIAL

Cases 1 and 2 in Figure 2.9). Primarily, changes in context should affect the extent to which people see themselves as categorically interchangeable and hence similar. This is because perceptions of similarity and difference are the single most important *outcome* of the categorization process (McGarty, 1999b; Medin, 1989; Medin, Goldstone & Gentner, 1993; Oakes, 1996). However, flowing from these perceptions, context should impact, amongst other things, on the degree to which people: (a) like and trust each other; (b) communicate effectively; (c) are able to persuade and influence each other; (d) seek to co-operate; and (e) are able to act collectively. These points are summarized in Table 2.1.

In sum, *self-categorization is a fundamental basis of our social orientation towards others* (Turner & Haslam, 2000). Moreover, many of the disparate psychological and demographic variables that are the focus of research in a broad range of organizational and social areas can be seen to achieve much of their force through their capacity to impact upon self-categorization. This is true, for example, of variables like leadership, power, control, interdependence, group heterogeneity and size. Clearly these claims suggest that the self-categorization process is relevant to a broad range of significant organizational behaviours. Our task in the upcoming chapters will be to tease out the above arguments in relation to issues that arise in key areas of organizational functioning and to establish the implications and utility of the social identity approach for these domains of enquiry.

*Table 2.1* Some predicted effects of variation in the context-based self-categorical relations between two or more people

| Self-Categorization | Perceived similarity | Trust | Ability (and desire) to communicate | Mutual influence | Ability (and desire) to co-operate and act collectively |
|---|---|---|---|---|---|
| shared | high | high | high | high | high |
| non-shared | low | low | low | low | low |

### Further reading

The references below provide good introductions to the social identity approach. For a solid grounding in social identity and self-categorization theories, and to gain a sense of how these developed, it makes sense to read Tajfel and Turner (1979), Turner (1982) and Turner et al. (1987). Brown's (1978) chapter and Terry and Callan's (1998) paper both provide a clear indication of the way in which social identity processes impact upon behaviour in the workplace and of how these can be investigated — points which are amplified and tied much more explicitly to the organizational literature in the seminal paper by Ashforth and Mael (1989; see also Dutton et al., 1994). There are, however, plenty of more recent publications that it is also useful to read in order to find out how both theories have been developed, tested and applied (e.g. Hogg, 1992; Oakes et al., 1994; Turner et al., 1994).

Ashforth, B. E. & Mael, F. (1989). Social identity theory and the organization. *Academy of Management Review, 14*, 20-39.

Brown, R. J. (1978). Divided we fall: Analysis of relations between different sections of a factory workforce. In H. Tajfel (Ed.), *Differentiation between social groups: Studies in the social psychology of intergroup relations* (pp. 395-429). London: Academic Press.

Tajfel, H. & Turner, J. C. (1979). An integrative theory of intergroup conflict. In W. G. Austin & S. Worchel (Eds.), *The social psychology of intergroup relations* (pp. 33-47). Monterey, CA: Brooks/Cole.

Terry, D. J. & Callan, V. J. (1998). Ingroup bias in response to an organizational merger. *Group Dynamics: Theory, Research and Practice, 2*, 67-81.

Turner, J. C. (1982). Towards a cognitive redefinition of the social group. In H. Tajfel (Ed.), *Social identity and intergroup relations* (pp. 15-40). Cambridge: Cambridge University Press & Paris: Editions de la Maison des Sciences de l'Homme.

Turner, J. C., Hogg, M. A., Oakes, P. J., Reicher, S. D. & Wetherell, M. S. (1987). *Rediscovering the social group: A self-categorization theory*. Oxford: Blackwell.

# 3  Leadership

DEF
Leadership is commonly defined as the process of influencing others in a manner that enhances their contribution to the realization of group goals (e.g. Hollander, 1985; Smith, 1995a). This process is widely seen to involve the positive impact of one person on the behaviour of many others, and for this reason it is often viewed as the key to effective and efficient organizations. If one exceptional person is capable of marshalling the energies of all others, logic dictates that effort expended in recruiting, retaining and understanding such a person is effort well spent. For this reason 'leadership training is big business' (Pfeffer, 1998, p. 736). It should also be no surprise to find both that leadership is widely considered 'the most important topic in the realm of organizational behaviour' and is probably the most researched (Lord & Maher, 1991, p. 129). Testament to this fact, enquiry into the topic dates back at least as far as the writings of Plato over 2,000 years ago and a recently updated handbook of leadership includes more than 9,000 references (Bass, 1990).

In this chapter it is therefore clearly impossible to do justice to the detail and scope of leadership research. Rather more modestly, its aim is to identify some key assumptions that tend to underpin work in this area and to subject them to theoretical and empirical scrutiny. However, in the process we also apply ourselves to what can be considered the 'master problem' in the leadership literature — the question of how exactly leadership is achieved (Haslam & Platow, in press; McGregor, 1966). How do individuals come to wield so much influence over a group that their vision is able to provide a blueprint for group action?

As we will see, established answers to this question have tended to see leadership as an attribute of an individual that manifests itself either generally or in particular contexts. In this way the study of leaders and leadership is divorced from the broader social context within which these roles and qualities emerge and which give them meaning. Yet while this approach mirrors the lay person's understanding of leadership, we argue that it is empirically and theoretically unsatisfactory. In contrast, the social identity approach suggests that leadership is much more *a property of the group* than it is a property of the individual in isolation (see also Alderfer & Smith, 1982, p. 63; Hollander, 1995; McGregor, 1966, p. 73; Meindl, 1993).

This assertion calls into question the greater body of leadership research which is based on the identification of individual characteristics and which provides the rationale for strategies of leader selection, training and reward that proliferate in the organizational field. However, it also opens up the study of leadership by integrating it with broader issues in the organizational domain and within an encompassing theoretical framework. In this way leadership turns out to be important not only because it is an avenue to group accomplishment, but also because it provides a window on to social psychological processes of general and far-reaching significance.

## An overview of leadership research

*Single factor approaches*

Broadly speaking, approaches to leadership have sought to examine the extent to which successful leadership is a product of either: (a) specific characteristics of the leader; (b) features of the situation in which those qualities (or others) come to the fore; or (c) some combination of these elements. The very first trait-based approaches argued that leaders were set apart from followers by their possession of distinctive intellectual and social characteristics (e.g. intelligence, good judgement, insight and imagination) which led to them being inherently more adept at directing, managing and inspiring others. This approach was exemplified by the 'great man' theory which, as the name suggests, argued that (male) leaders were set apart from their followers (and all women) by virtue of their inherent greatness. According to this view, leaders are simply people who are made of 'the right stuff' — a belief that was firmly cemented in place during the nineteenth century as the élites of many nations (especially Britain) nurtured a passion for portraits, statues and biographies of the worthy and heroic (Pears, 1992).

A slight variant on this perspective is offered by researchers who have sought to identify leaders not on the basis of their character, but on the basis of their actions. The logic here is that because it proves hard to select leaders on the basis of their personal qualities, one might instead be able to do so on the basis of what they actually *do* (and make prescriptions for effective leadership on this basis; see Vroom & Yetton, 1973; Chapter 6 below). The most famous enquiries of this form were the Ohio State studies (Fleishman, 1953; Fleishman & Peters, 1962). In the first phase of this research, nearly 2,000 descriptions of effective leader behaviour were collected from people who were working in different spheres (industrial, military and educational). These were then reduced and transformed into 150 questions which became part of a questionnaire (the leadership behaviour description questionnaire; LBDQ) that was then administered to employees in a range of organizational contexts with a view to identifying the behaviours associated with both effective and non-effective leaders.

As one might expect, the questionnaire identified a broad range of potentially relevant leader behaviours. However, two categories of behaviour emerged as being particularly important: consideration and initiation of structure. *Consideration* relates to a leader's willingness to look after the interests and welfare of those they lead and also to trust and respect them. *Initiation of structure* relates to the leader's capacity to define and structure their own and their followers' roles with a view to achieving relevant goals. A similar factor structure also emerged from research subsequently conducted at the University of Michigan (Bowers & Seashore, 1966). Although this actually identified four categories of effective leader behaviour: support, interaction facilitation, goal emphasis and work facilitation, the first two of these behaviours can be subsumed within the concept of consideration and the last two relate to aspects of initiation of structure (Mitchell, Dowling, Kabanoff & Larson, 1988).

In contrast to approaches which look for the key to leadership in the nature or behaviour of the leader, *situationalist* approaches argue that effective leadership is largely determined by features of the context in which leaders operate (see Cooper & McGaugh, 1963). In particular, leaders are seen as displaying leadership to the extent that they are able to satisfy the task demands of a particular group at a particular point in time — for example, helping to win a war, or to maintain peace (Hemphill, 1949). According to this view, successful leaders are distinguished more by being in 'the right place at the right time' than by their personal qualities.

Although single factor theories continue to have considerable currency in lay accounts of leadership, a range of theoretical and empirical problems have meant that in recent times they have attracted few academic adherents. Most tellingly, these problems include a failure to find evidence of any constant element which reliably distinguishes leaders from non-leaders and a general lack of predictive power (e.g. Jenkins, 1947; Mann, 1959; Stogdill, 1948; see also Steiner, 1972, pp. 173-176). These problems derive from the fact that each approach over-compensates for the inadequacies of the other: one by denying the role of context, the other by denying the agency of the individual. Having said that, it is generally agreed that consideration and initiation of structure have *some* role to play in leader effectiveness and the durability of these constructs is one lasting legacy of this work.

*Contingency approaches*

In light of the clear limitations of situationalist and great man theories, more recent theories of leadership have generally argued that it is an interactive product of *both* personal and situational characteristics (Gibb, 1958). It is worth noting that this view is also shared by most business leaders. For example, in Sarros and Butchatsky's (1996) survey of Australian CEOs, almost all generated an answer of the following form when asked if leaders were born or made:

> I have to say there's a lot of circumstance in the way things turn out. There's actually a theory that it's all random. I don't think it's totally random, but I think there's a lot of circumstance. You have to be in the right place at the right time, which to a certain extent you manage. ... I've sought out leadership, so to a certain extent it's in my make-up. There are others who will shy away from high-profile positions. They're the analysts, or the thinkers, who don't particularly want to be leaders and so don't push themselves, and retire away from that. (Tony Berg, CEO Boral Ltd, p. 221)

Most contemporary approaches to leadership are of this type, a point confirmed by the number of recent attempts to integrate different approaches (e.g. Fiedler & House, 1994; Hollander, 1993; House & Shamir, 1993). As Fiedler and House observe, of the dozen or so theories of leadership which have widespread currency 'there has been a notable complementarity and convergence in recent years' (p. 107). Yet probably the most prominent approach to leadership over the past forty or so years has been Fiedler's *contingency model* (e.g. Fiedler, 1964, 1978; Fiedler & Garcia, 1987). This considers successful leadership to be a product of the match between the characteristics of the leader (specifically, whether they are relationship- or task-motivated) and features of the situation (specifically, the quality of relations between the leader and other group members, the degree to which the leader has power, and the extent to which the group task is structured). A person's leadership style is established by asking them to identify characteristics of their *least preferred co-worker* (LPC) on a number of dimensions (e.g. rejecting–accepting, tense–relaxed, boring–interesting). Scores on this measure are used to differentiate between people who generally describe this co-worker relatively negatively and those who describe the co-worker more positively — those with low and high LPC scores, respectively. A sample LPC inventory is presented in Figure 3.1.

*Instructions:*
Think of a person with whom you can work least well. He or she may be someone you work with now or someone you knew in the past. He or she does not have to be the person you like least well, but should be the person with whom you have had the most difficulty in getting a job done. Describe this person by circling one of the numbers between each pair of adjectives.

| | | | | | | | | | |
|---|---|---|---|---|---|---|---|---|---|
| pleasant | 8 | 7 | 6 | 5 | 4 | 3 | 2 | 1 | unpleasant |
| friendly | 8 | 7 | 6 | 5 | 4 | 3 | 2 | 1 | unfriendly |
| rejecting | 1 | 2 | 3 | 4 | 5 | 6 | 7 | 8 | accepting |
| tense | 1 | 2 | 3 | 4 | 5 | 6 | 7 | 8 | relaxed |
| distant | 1 | 2 | 3 | 4 | 5 | 6 | 7 | 8 | close |
| cold | 1 | 2 | 3 | 4 | 5 | 6 | 7 | 8 | warm |
| supportive | 8 | 7 | 6 | 5 | 4 | 3 | 2 | 1 | hostile |
| boring | 1 | 2 | 3 | 4 | 5 | 6 | 7 | 8 | interesting |
| quarrelsome | 1 | 2 | 3 | 4 | 5 | 6 | 7 | 8 | harmonious |
| gloomy | 1 | 2 | 3 | 4 | 5 | 6 | 7 | 8 | cheerful |
| open | 8 | 7 | 6 | 5 | 4 | 3 | 2 | 1 | guarded |
| backbiting | 1 | 2 | 3 | 4 | 5 | 6 | 7 | 8 | loyal |
| untrustworthy | 1 | 2 | 3 | 4 | 5 | 6 | 7 | 8 | trustworthy |
| considerate | 8 | 7 | 6 | 5 | 4 | 3 | 2 | 1 | inconsiderate |
| nasty | 1 | 2 | 3 | 4 | 5 | 6 | 7 | 8 | nice |
| agreeable | 8 | 7 | 6 | 5 | 4 | 3 | 2 | 1 | disagreeable |
| insincere | 1 | 2 | 3 | 4 | 5 | 6 | 7 | 8 | sincere |
| kind | 8 | 7 | 6 | 5 | 4 | 3 | 2 | 1 | unkind |

*Scoring:*
Add up the numbers you have circled on each of the above scales. Normative data (obtained from a sample of first-year psychology students in 1997) indicates that the median score on this scale is approximately 68 (25th percentile = 53; 75th percentile = 83). A score of 68 or below thus suggests low LPC (i.e. a task orientation) and a score above 68 suggests high LPC (i.e. a relationship orientation).

*Figure 3.1* A typical LPC inventory (after Fiedler, 1964)

Exactly what the LPC scale actually measures is unclear (Brotherton, 1999; Landy, 1989). It might, for example, be a measure of a person's generosity of spirit, their sensitivity to norms of social desirability, or their breadth of experience. Generally though, high LPC individuals (who rate least preferred co-workers relatively positively) are considered to be more relationship-oriented and those with low LPC scores are considered more task-oriented. In this regard, the poles of the LPC scale also approximate to the two dimensions that emerged from the Ohio studies. That is, a high LPC person should be primarily concerned with consideration and a low LPC person with initiation of structure.

Building on this personality distinction, Fiedler's theory predicts that different types of leader will be most effective in different types of situation. Stated most simply, task-oriented leaders are most effective when features of the situation are all favourable (i.e. when relations are good, the task is structured, and the leader has power) or all unfavourable. On the other hand, relationship-oriented leaders are considered more effective in situations of intermediate favourableness. The core predictions of this approach are summarized in Table 3.1.

Views about the correspondence between these predictions and the success of leaders in the field vary enormously. Fiedler and his colleagues have produced evidence consistent with the model and he remains a staunch defender of it (e.g. Fiedler, 1978). Others are less convinced by the empirical evidence and continue to question the validity of its core constructs and their capacity to capture the dynamic essence of the leadership process (e.g. Brown, 1988; Turner, 1991). Nevertheless, at least in part because it formalizes lay thinking on the topic, the model continues to appeal to students of leadership (and writers of organizational textbooks).

*Table 3.1* Performance of high LPC and low LPC leaders predicted by Fiedler's contingency model (after Fiedler, 1964)

| Leader–Member Relations: | good | | | | bad | | | |
|---|---|---|---|---|---|---|---|---|
| Task Structure: | high | | low | | high | | low | |
| Leader's Position Power: | strong | weak | strong | weak | strong | weak | strong | weak |
| *Leader Style* | | | | | | | | |
| relationship-oriented (high LPC) | ✗ | ✗ | ✗ | ✓ | ✓ | ✓ | ✗ | ✗ |
| task-oriented (low LPC) | ✓ | ✓ | ✓ | ✗ | ✗ | ✗ | ✓ | ✓ |

*Note*: ✓ = situation in which this leader style is associated with superior performance

✗ = situation in which this leader style is associated with inferior performance

*Transformational and transactional approaches*

As the above comments suggest, one common criticism of contingency theories is that they reduce the energy of leadership to a mundane and mechanical matching process. Something appears to be lost between the textbook and the boardroom, between the training course and the battlefield. As part of attempts to reintroduce some of the vigour that appears to be missing from recipe-like contingency models, one concept that has been of particular interest to researchers is that of *charismatic leadership* (after Weber, 1921, but recently re-vitalized by, amongst others, Burns, 1978). In many ways a throwback to the early trait-based approaches, this concept has been incorporated into theorizing which suggests that effective leaders are those whose personal qualities enable them to articulate a vision for a given (typically large) group. A considerable part of this charisma is believed to derive from the leader's ability to set an example which provides a behavioural model for others, enabling them to contribute to the vision's realization and an associated group mission.

Lending some credibility to the underlying construct of charisma, studies find reasonable agreement between raters in assigning leaders to charismatic and non-charismatic categories (e.g. amongst historians describing US presidents; Donley & Winter, 1970; see also Kinder, 1986). Nonetheless, the precise nature of charisma has proved rather difficult to specify. Moreover, a person's possession of charismatic characteristics appears to have little predictive value. For this reason, Nadler and Tushman (1990) note that, 'unfortunately, in real time, it is unclear who will be known as visionaries and who will be known as failures' (p. 80). Nonetheless, the argument is made that, whatever their exact nature, charismatic leaders (e.g. Mahatma Gandhi, Martin Luther King, Nelson Mandela) achieve their success through an ability to impact upon the self-concept and self-esteem of followers and thereby *re*define group norms and objectives (House & Shamir, 1993; Shamir, House & Arthur, 1993; see also Haslam, Platow et al., 2000). Under this model, leaders achieve results not merely by making the best of the people they have to work with, but by actively transforming those followers' behaviour (Burns, 1978; Peters & Waterman, 1995).

*Transactional* approaches to leadership arrive at similar conclusions, but from a different starting point. These set out from an assumption that the basis of leadership lies not in the qualities of the individual per se but rather in the quality of *relations* between leaders and other group members. This argument incorporates principles of social exchange (e.g. Thibaut & Kelley, 1959) by suggesting that effective leadership flows from a maximization of the mutual benefits which leaders and followers potentially afford each other. This approach is most associated with the work of Hollander (1958, 1995) which points, amongst other things, to the role that the group plays in validating and empowering the leader and to the importance of followers in the leadership process.

Hollander makes the simple — but largely neglected — point that without dedicated followers there is no prospect of successful leadership and that it is therefore as important to understand the psychology of effective *followership* as it is to study the behaviour and psychology of leaders. Leaders cannot simply barge into a group and expect its members to embrace them and their plans immediately. Instead, they must first build up a support base and win the respect of followers. Hollander (1958) argues that they do this by accumulating *idiosyncrasy credits* — psychological 'brownie points' which licence the leader to take the group in new directions. Support for these arguments is provided by studies which show that elected leaders (i.e. those who have the explicit backing of group members) are more likely to challenge poor group decisions than appointed leaders (those with no direct mandate from the group; Hollander & Julian, 1970). It thus appears that unless they have the backing of followers, leaders are unable to display genuine leadership in their management of the group's interests and that the group as a whole will suffer.

Some of the above ideas concerning leader charisma and active followership are also echoed in House's (1971) path–goal theory. Presented as a *transformational* approach to leadership, this asserts that the key to leaders' success lies in their ability to identify and ultimately provide the path for satisfaction of subordinates' goals, while at the same time ensuring that those goals are compatible with those of the group or organization as a whole. Here, then, a leader is someone who engages followers' wills by reconciling their personal goals with those of the collective. Despite differences in complexity and emphasis in Hollander's and House's treatments, both suggest that leaders and followers engage in reward-based transactions which are ultimately for the greater good:

> In sum, transformational leadership can be seen as an extension of transactional leadership, in which there is greater leader intensity and follower arousal. This amounts to having a large fund of credits accorded to the leader by followers, thereby granting esteem and more sway in being influential. (Hollander, 1995, p. 79; see also Bass, 1985)

A significant elaboration of these approaches is also provided by work which argues that, because the effectiveness of leadership is not entirely under the control of leaders, a range of factors can act as leadership *substitutes* and as leader *neutralizers*. Leader substitutes make leadership unnecessary and include high group cohesiveness, a professional orientation among followers and an intrinsically motivating task (Howell, Dorfman & Kerr, 1986; Kerr & Jermier, 1978). Leader neutralizers undermine leadership effectiveness and include organizational indifference and low leader power (Yukl, 1981). A major contribution of this work is therefore to re-emphasise the point that there is more to leadership than the behaviour and character of leaders alone. The temptation to explain group performance solely with reference to these factors is immense but evidence suggests that this is romantic folly at best (Meindl, 1993) and dangerous propaganda at worst (Gemmill & Oakley, 1992).

### The leadership categorization approach

One comparatively new development in leadership research is provided by Lord's *leadership categorization theory* (Lord, Foti & De Vader, 1984; Lord, Foti & Phillips, 1982; Lord & Maher, 1990, 1991). Derived from cognitive theories of categorization (e.g. Rosch, 1978), this argues that a leader's effectiveness is determined in large part by others' *perceptions* of him or her, and that these are based primarily on fixed, pre-formed leadership prototypes. These prototypes are hierarchically organized, with prototypes at lower levels being more specific. Like stereotypes, prototypes are believed to provide perceivers with a set of expectations regarding a person's appropriate traits and behaviours.

*Def* In these terms, leadership itself is defined as 'the process of being perceived by others as a leader' (Lord & Maher, 1990, p. 11) and its success depends upon the ability of leaders to embody their followers' expectations. One important problem noted by advocates of the model arises when leaders attempt to move from one behavioural domain to another (e.g. from sport into politics). Lord and Maher argue that because different expectations are typically associated with different domains (depending on their degree of overlap or 'family resemblance'), leader mobility is restricted and leadership is necessarily context-specific (as argued by Fiedler and others).

As with Hollander's work, the leadership categorization approach recognizes that leadership is something that followers *confer* on leaders rather than something that leaders exhibit in the abstract. Moreover, the distinctive contribution of the approach is that it also recognizes the role that categorization plays in this process. In arguing that leadership is underpinned by an act of categorization, the work of Lord and his colleagues allows researchers to treat leadership as an aspect of a general (rather than an unusual) psychological process and therefore integrate it within mainstream social cognitive theorizing. However, one key problem of the approach is that it again falls back on the view that leaders are individuals who have specific and invariant characteristics that equip them to succeed in particular tasks. The lessons of transformational and transactional research thus suggest that the insights of Lord and his colleagues might have greater power if they married analysis of the leadership categorization process with sensitivity to the ongoing dynamics of the group and its interests (for recent evidence to this effect, see Lord, Brown & Freiberg, 1999). As we will see in the next section, achieving this union is one of the major goals of the social identity approach.

## Social identity and leadership

A number of the themes noted above are consistent with important ideas in social identity and self-categorization theories. In particular, Turner (1987a, 1991) has argued against trait-based approaches which suggest that particular personality characteristics determine a person's suitability for leadership. Like Fiedler, self-categorization theory suggests that different types of leaders will be better suited for different tasks, but it suggests that the reasons for this lie not so much in the variable match between the leader's characteristics and structural features of the leadership context as in the variable definition of the group *per se*. As an example, it would attribute the common observation that different types of national leader fare better in different international climates primarily to the fact that war and peace change the overall definition and *meaning* of a group, rather than to the fact that they impact on leader-follower relations, leader power and task structure (although the latter are undoubtedly affected by changes in intergroup relations and group identity; see Chapter 8 below).

In this regard, the theory has most in common with work on followership which suggests that the analysis of leaders cannot be divorced from consideration of the group of which they are part and which they need to represent:

> It is therefore important that the leader, by his [or her] behaviour, manifest a loyalty to the needs and aspirations of group members. These things must matter to him [or her] in ways that are accessible to view because such evidences of good faith and sincere interest serve to elicit greater acceptance of influence. (Hollander, 1964, p. 231; see also 1995).

Hollander (1995) therefore argues that in order for groups to function as effectively as possible 'the leader needs to be attuned to the needs of followers, their perceptions and expectancies' (1995, p. 75). Likewise, Kanter (1979) argues:

> For top executives, the problem is not to fit in among peers; rather the question is whether the public at large and other organization members perceive a common interest which they see the executives as promoting. (p. 70)

In essence, it can be seen that if a group is to function *as* a group rather than just an aggregate of individuals, its leaders must represent the interests of the collective as a whole rather than just their personal interests or those of a power elite (see also Brown, 1954, p. 242; McGregor, 1960, p. 239).

In this sense, leadership is intimately bound up with the shared concerns of followers. This point was expressed succinctly when the nineteenth century French politician Ledru-Rollin remarked of his political supporters during the 1848 Revolution 'I must follow them; I am their leader' (an observation so profound it was recycled sixty years later by Andrew Bonar Law, leader of the British Conservative Party). A similar sentiment is apparent in Bergen Evans's observation that 'for the most part our leaders are but followers out in front; they do but marshal us in the way we are going'. Von Cranach (1986) also points to the higher-order nature of leadership as a group phenomenon, in noting that the behaviour of leaders and the perceptions of their behaviour by other group members are necessarily bound up with issues relating to the social identity that they share, and which leaders play a central role in defining:

> Groups have an identity that originates from the members' cognitions and emotions as a system of mutual feedback on the group level. It serves as a source of unity and stability and forms an important part, in turn, of members' social identity ... The leader is likely to form the nucleus of this structure. (p. 128)

Consistent with this perspective, one important way in which self-categorization theory conceptualizes the leader (the group member who is likely to exercise most influence in any given instance) is as the *ingroup prototype*. As the (most) prototypical group member the leader best epitomizes (in the dual sense of both *defining* and *being defined by*) the social category of which he or she is a member. This means that to be seen as displaying leadership in a given context a person needs to be maximally representative of the shared social identity and consensual position of the group (Turner, 1987a, 1991; see also

(Duck & Fielding, 1999; Foddy & Hogg, 1999; Hains, Hogg & Duck, 1997; Hogg, 1996, p. 80; Hogg, Hains & Mason, 1998).

Clearly there are significant points of contact between this analysis and that proposed by Lord and his colleagues (e.g. Lord & Maher, 1991). Both see leadership as the outcome of an act of categorization and both develop and apply ideas from cognitive literature. However, an important point of divergence between this idea and the early work of Lord and his colleagues is that prototypicality is not considered to be a fixed property of a given stimulus category, but rather is a variable feature of the definition of the social category in context. As Turner (1987a) puts it:

> The relative prototypicality of an individual varies with the dimension(s) of comparison and the categories employed. The latter too will vary with the frame of reference (the psychologically salient pool of people compared) and the comparative dimension(s) selected. These phenomena are relative and situation-specific, not absolute, static and constant. Also, unlike in Rosch (1978), categories are not defined simply by 'prototypes' or 'best exemplars' ... prototypes are [also] defined by the given categories, in turn a function of the relevant dimensions selected for comparison. (p. 80)

The variability of relative prototypicality follows from the principle of meta-contrast that we introduced in the previous chapter. To recap, meta-contrast predicts that any particular stimulus will be perceived as more prototypical of a category to the extent that it is less different from other members of that category than from other stimuli that are salient in a given context (Haslam & Turner, 1992, 1995; Turner & Oakes, 1989). A critical implication is that *the prototypicality of exactly the same exemplar for exactly the same category will vary as a function of the social context within which categorization takes place.*

As a schematized example, one can think of the most extreme left- and right-wing members (L and R) as well as the most moderate member (M) of a hypothetical political group that occupies a central position on the political spectrum. This is the situation depicted in Figure 3.2.

On the basis of the meta-contrast principle, self-categorization theory predicts that where this centrist group is considered in context of the broad political spectrum (i.e. Case 1), L and R would tend to be equally prototypical of the group as a whole but that M would clearly be most prototypical. However, the prototypicality of L relative to R would increase (making this person almost as prototypical as M) where the group is compared with a right-wing group (Case 2) and decrease if the group is compared with a left-wing group (Case 3). This is because in Case 2 the left-winger is associated with a greater interclass difference than the right-winger, while this pattern is reversed in Case 3. Thus if the extent of a person's relative influence and hence their ability to lead, or at least be perceived as a leader, is determined by relative prototypicality, then the moderate's authority should be most secure when the group is defined relative to groups occupying the full political spectrum (as in Case 1). However, the same person would be more open to challenge from a left-winger if the party confronted only right-wing opponents (Case 2), while they would be more likely to face a challenge from a right-winger in the context of conflict with a left-wing group (Case 3).

*EMILYS OWN ADMISSION*

*FACTORING*
*NEED*
*TO*
*GET*
*GOING*

*PANIC*
*WHEN*
*LOOK*
*AT*
*OUTGROUP*

*MOVE*
*TOWARDS*

*NEED TO*
*WORK*
*DAMN IT*

*WHY LEADER*

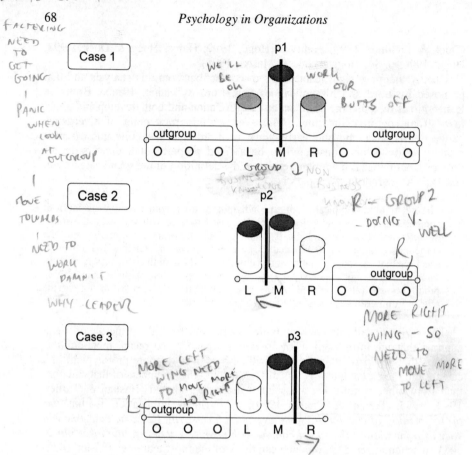

*WE'LL BE OK*   *WORK OUR BUTTS OFF*

*GROUP 1 NON business know*

*R = GROUP 2 — DOING V. WELL R,*

*MORE RIGHT WING - SO NEED TO MOVE MORE TO LEFT*

*MORE LEFT WING NEED TO MOVE MORE TO RIGHT*

*Figure 3.2* Prototypicality of group members (L, M and R) as a function of a comparative frame of reference comprising other individuals or groups (the O's)

*Note*: The height of each cylinder indicates the extent to which the individual is pro-totypical (i.e. representative) of the group. pN represents the most prototypical ingroup position. This is displaced away from the outgroup in Cases 1 and 3.

It needs to be re-emphasised that meta-contrast is only a partial determinant of *which* categories perceivers use to represent a given stimulus array. Norma-tive fit and a perceiver's readiness to use a category always contribute to this process too. Social structural issues of legitimate power and formal authority also have a role to play (see Chapter 8 below). Similarly, meta-contrast is only one determinant of the *internal structure* of those categories (Haslam, Oakes, McGarty et al., 1995, pp. 510-512). So, as with contingency theories (e.g. Fiedler, 1964), this analysis is intended to provide only a partial explanation of the fact that different leaders (or different leadership styles) are appropriate for dif-ferent situations. Yet unlike most of the accounts presented in mainstream lead-ership theory, the properties of the individual associated with the variation we have described derive not from qualities inherent in the person *as an individual* (e.g. their personality or personal style) but from features of the individual *as a representative of a contextually defined social category*.

As an example of this process at work one can reflect on the emergence of General Eisenhower as an American leader during the Second World War. This, we would argue, arose not from the fact that his personality equipped him for the task, but from the fact that in the context of the specific set of intergroup relations that prevailed at this time, the particular values and goals he espoused and the facets of American identity he projected epitomized Americans' feelings, intentions and strategic aims in relation to Fascist Germany. These were reflected, for example, in his commitment to democratic 'Midwestern' values rather than to autocratic practices and policies (unlike General Patton, say). The same factors also explain his continued success after the war when the United States defined itself in opposition to the Stalinist Soviet Union. In this sense, Eisenhower's emerging and continued authority as a leader derived not from his individuality, but from the group whose values he came to represent.

All this is not to suggest that the emergence of a leader is an entirely passive process, dictated purely by the whims of the group and the tides of changing circumstance. Under the above conceptualization, the leader is an *active* constituent of the group, who is simultaneously defining of and defined by the group (see Kelley & Thibaut, 1969, p. 43). In this role, in order to be successful, leaders need to be 'entrepreneurs of identity' (a term coined by Reicher & Hopkins, 1996b; see also Peters & Waterman, 1995; Reicher, Drury, Hopkins & Stott, in press). So where would-be leaders espouse views that are not representative of their group (e.g. L's views in Case 1), one strategy they might pursue is to seek to restructure the social context that defines the group, as a way of increasing the prototypicality of their own candidature. They might do this by, for example, arguing for the appropriateness of particular categorizations — especially those that distinguish between 'us' and 'them' in a manner that defines the leader and the ingroup positively and as distinct from the outgroup. Vivid examples of such rhetoric are provided in Reicher and Hopkins' (1996b) examination of the contributions of political leaders to debate about the 1984-5 British miners' strike.

Moreover, the position of a leader in power can clearly be strengthened by backing up the rhetoric of 'them and us' with actual hostility towards an outgroup. This strategy of *approval-seeking outgroup violation* (Haslam & Platow, 1999) is much favoured by political leaders who face dissent from their constituents and can be seen to have played a role in any number of major international conflicts (e.g. Brown, 1988; see also Worchel, Coutant-Sassic & Wong, 1993, p. 82). Supporting this idea, three empirical studies reported by Rabbie and Bekkers (1978) revealed that leaders whose positions within their group were unstable were more likely to choose to engage in intergroup conflict than leaders whose positions were secure.

Along similar lines, Hogg (1996; Fielding & Hogg, 1997) notes that as individuals identify more strongly with a group they increasingly confer leadership on those who are perceived to be prototypical of the ingroup's position. In this way, a dynamic can develop so that as *attributions* of leadership escalate, so does the capacity of the leader to influence the group as a whole:

> Having acquired power in these ways, the person occupying the leader position will be able to adopt the more active aspects of being a leader, including the power to maintain his/her leadership position by influencing the social comparative context and thus his/her prototypicality. (Hogg, 1996, p. 81)

Fielding and Hogg (1997) tested some of these ideas in a field study which examined developing attributions of leadership during a week-long Outward Bound Course. As predicted, members became more attracted to the group, identified with it more strongly and perceived the group's leadership to be more effective as the course progressed. These patterns were also enhanced amongst those who identified most strongly with the group.

The emerging perception of effective leadership can thus be seen as the hallmark of an increasingly effective and cohesive group — the same also being true of heightened perceptions of intragroup homogeneity (Oakes, Haslam, Morrison & Grace, 1995). It is customary for researchers and laypeople alike to attribute the group's success under these circumstances to its leadership (for supporting data see Larson, Lingle & Scerbo, 1984; Nye & Simonetta, 1996; Pillai & Meindl, 1991). Indeed, the tendency for people to make attributions of this form is symptomatic of what Meindl and colleagues (Meindl, 1993; Meindl & Ehrlich, 1987; Meindl, Ehrlich & Dukerich, 1985) refer to as the 'romance of leadership'. It is an aspect too of what Gemmill and Oakley (1992) characterize as 'an alienating social myth' which serves to reinforce the cult of the individual and to preserve the status quo by leading followers to believe that: (a) they are ruled out of contention for high office due to their lack of a suitable psychological profile; (b) high office is potentially open to them if they work hard to develop the requisite profile; and (c) it is by those individuals who possess this profile (rather than social groups) that all forms of worthwhile progress and social change are brought about.

For a number of reasons, then, attributions to leadership typically represent a very limited (though very popular) interpretation of a correlation that arises from a complex interplay between multiple organizational elements. Without a cohesive and purposeful group there can be no effective leadership and, as we will see in later chapters, these group properties are themselves largely a product of shared social identity (Hogg, 1992). In seeking to discover the secret of any group's success, it is therefore often quite misleading to do so with primary reference to the distinctive character of its leader (Meindl, 1993; Pfeffer, 1977).

The arguments developed in the preceding paragraphs do not deny the reality of charismatic leadership. However, in contrast to the dominant view that charisma is inherent in particular leaders' personality, we suggest that these individuals achieve their impact largely through an ability to define (or, more typically, *re*define) a group's objectives in a way that enhances both the shared self-concept of its members and their own relative influence (as proposed by House & Shamir, 1993). Here charisma is an *emergent product* of the self-categorization process and the associated definition of the group and its leader in context (Haslam, Platow et al., 2000). As Nye and Simonetta (1996) put it, 'leadership is in the eye of the follower' (p. 153; see also Kouzes & Posner, 1988, 1990; Meindl, 1993, p. 107). Leadership is thus *conferred* by followers and charisma is an *expression* of the leader–group dynamic as perceived by those followers in a specific social context.

Accordingly, we argue that charisma is essentially the product of a social relationship not a personal trait. The quality of this relationship depends, of course, on what the leader actually *does* (or does not do) but his or her behaviour cannot be reduced an abstract shopping list of attributes or styles. Indeed, amongst other things, such a view helps to explain why the death of a leader (particularly at the hands of an outgroup) often powerfully *augments* rather detracts from his or her charismatic appeal.

## Some empirical tests of the social identity approach

### *Prototypicality and leader emergence*

We noted above that Lord and his colleagues suggest that leader prototypicality is based on 'a match of the characteristics of the person to abstractions or features common to category members' so that 'perceivers use degree of match to this *ready-made* structure to form leadership perceptions' (Lord & Maher, 1991, p. 132, emphasis added). Our own arguments, however, suggest that this idea of the leader as an off-the-peg commodity is implausible. In large part this is because research into other topics suggests that judgements of prototypicality are context-sensitive and structured on-the-spot by, amongst other things, the intergroup realities of the situation (Oakes, Haslam & Turner, 1998). This implies that prototypical 'leadership material' in any sphere is unlikely simply to reflect the matching of a given candidate with a stored set of requisite attributes, and is more likely to reflect the extent to which the candidate is representative of the group as it is currently defined in a given social context.

Lord and Maher (1991) use the domain of politics to illustrate their argument, stating that here 'someone seen as wanting peace, having strong convictions, being charismatic, and a good administrator would be labelled as a leader' (p. 132). Yet such a rigid and prescriptive approach seems incompatible with on-the-ground realities where the demand for particular qualities clearly varies with social context. This point is illustrated in the response of the South African leader Steve Biko when asked in 1977 (just before his death in detention) if he was going to lead his supporters down a path of conflict or of non-violence:

> It is only, I think when black people are so dedicated and united in their cause that we can effect the greatest results. And whether this is going to be through the form of conflict or not will be dictated by the future. I don't believe for a moment we are going willingly to drop our belief in the non-violent stance — as of now. But I can't predict what will happen in the future, inasmuch as I can't predict what the enemy is going to do in the future. (Biko, 1988, p. 168)

An empirical illustration of this point is provided by a study in which Australian students were asked to identify the desirable characteristics of sporting, business and national leaders (Haslam, Turner & Oakes, 1999, Experiment 1; Turner & Haslam, 2000). Half of the students completed this task under standard conditions (conceptually similar to those used by Lord et al., 1984) but half were asked to reflect first on their own national identity as Australians. Amongst other things, this simple manipulation greatly affected the extent to which patriotism was perceived to be an important quality for different types of leader.  In standard conditions patriotism was seen to be much more important for national leaders than for sports or business leaders.  However, where participants' national identity had been made salient this attribute was seen to be equally appropriate for all three groups.

A second study employed a slightly different design in which participants had to vote for one of seven different types of business leader, each of whom had a different mix of dedication, intelligence and consideration.  This task was completed either in a control condition or in one of six other conditions which suggested that the leader of a rival group had either an abundance or a lack of these three qualities.  The findings of the study were complex, but there was considerable variation in the pattern of voting as a function of the presumed qualities of the rival leader.  Most notably, when this outgroup leader was extremely intelligent, 68 per cent of participants voted for a leader who was *un*intelligent (but dedicated and considerate), yet when the outgroup leader was also unintelligent this same candidate was endorsed by only 20 per cent of participants.  Such findings support the general prediction that group members' preference for leaders is not a function of those leaders' qualities in the abstract, but of their capacity to positively differentiate between the ingroup and outgroup and to make their group 'special' (Duck, 1998; Turner, 1998).

A key theoretical point made by these studies is that there appears to be no absolute level of a given trait which is inherently fitting for a given leadership category.  Accordingly, the idea that to become an effective national leader, for example, a person should simply aim to be seen by others as extremely patriotic and quite unaggressive (cf. Lord & Maher, 1991, p. 132) might well prove problematic if he or she were perceived in a sporting context or in a context where Australian norms (of perhaps greater aggressiveness and less patriotism) were salient.  The point is more significant because the above studies all involved relatively weak manipulations of judgemental context.  It seems highly likely that the perceived appropriateness of given attributes would change much more dramatically in the context of real-world fluctuations in the character of intergroup relations.

Evidence that leader prototypes vary with context thus suggests that the cognitive aspects of leadership are more dynamic than envisaged by leadership categorization theory.  Nonetheless, one might well ask whether social categorical processes of the sort we have described have any impact on leader emergence in a more interactive setting.  To this end, an experiment by Burton (1993) examined how group members' choice of a leader varied in the face of different intergroup tasks.

At the start of Burton's study undergraduate students (who participated in groups of four) completed a bogus inventory which served to identify them as either 'idealistic' or 'pragmatic'.  Participants were informed that they were going to take part in a debate with another group.  In some cases this outgroup was identified as extremely pro-authority and pragmatic and, in others, as anti-authority and idealistic.  The participants then watched a video in which this outgroup discussed a range of issues related to crime and punishment.  After having seen the video, participants were informed that before they took part in the debate they needed to elect a leader for their own group and that the best way to do this was to find out what each other's views were and make a decision on that basis.  The participants were ushered into separate cubicles to perform this task. Each completed items constructed so that he or she tended to give idealistic responses (where participants had been assigned to an idealistic group) or pragmatic responses (where participants had been assigned to a pragmatic group). They then received feedback supposedly emanating from the other three group members. In fact, the feedback was false and had been manipulated by the experimenter to suggest that the group members differed in the extent to which they were idealistic or pragmatic. Thus, for participants assigned to the pragmatic group, one other group member espoused extremely pragmatic views, one espoused moderately pragmatic views and one espoused only slightly pragmatic views (with a similar pattern for members of the idealistic group).

After receiving this feedback, participants were asked to divide ten votes amongst the three other group members, being told that the person who obtained the most votes would be appointed group leader. The chief prediction here was that leadership selection would vary depending on the specific group which participants expected to face, due to the role that this outgroup would play in redefining ingroup prototypicality (as per the example in Figure 3.2 above). Variation in leader choice was thus expected across conditions where the characteristics of the ingroup (its internal relations and structure) remained constant and hence where standard contingency theories would predict no variation (e.g. Fiedler, 1964).

The pattern of results revealed an interaction between participants' assigned identity and that of their opponents which supported this hypothesis and supported key predictions derived from self-categorization theory. In particular, participants assigned to the idealistic group cast more votes for the extremely idealistic candidate when they believed they were going to encounter a pragmatic group rather than an idealistic one. Indeed, when their group was set to confront pragmatists, these idealistic participants gave most votes to the extreme idealist, but when set to confront other idealists they allocated most votes to the moderate and *fewest* to the extremist. In other words, when they faced a clearly different outgroup, those participants who identified with their group were more likely to vote for the candidate who maximized intercategory difference — this being the candidate who was most representative of the group's distinctive qualities in the anticipated intergroup encounter (see also Hogg et al., 1998).

It is worth noting that as well as being incompatible with contingency theories which accord no status to the intergroup dimensions of a given context, the results from this study are also inconsistent with situationalist accounts which seek to explain leadership emergence in terms of the demands of the task at hand (cf. Cooper & McGaugh, 1963). Following this model one might argue that participants' interpretation of the upcoming task varied as a function of the outgroup they were due to debate, seeing the encounter with the like-minded group as co-operative and that with the very different group as competitive. However, as Burton (1993) remarks, if that were the case, one would actually expect participants to have selected the most hard-nosed candidate (i.e. the *least* idealistic group member) to lead the group through the competitive task. Again, then, it appears that the leader emerges as someone qualified for the job not by virtue of their purely personal qualities (qualities that could be appreciated in isolation from the group) but by virtue of being contextually representative of the essence of the group and of what differentiates 'us' from 'them'.

*Shared social identification as the link between a leader's vision and followers' actions*

The above studies reveal preference for leaders whose abstract credentials represent the contextually defined interests of a group, but the analysis we have offered would clearly be strengthened if it were shown that social context affected followers' reactions to actual leader *behaviour*. This link has been explored in an imaginative programme of research conducted by Platow and his colleagues (Platow et al., 1997). This looks at how group members respond to leaders who dispense justice in different ways. In effect, it serves to unpack the riddle first alluded to by Homans (1951) when he reflected:

> The leader must live up to the norms of the group — all the norms — better than any follower. At the same time he is the member of the group who is most in danger of violating the norms. In disputes between two followers, he is expected to do justice, as the group understands justice, but what man can always be just? (p. 427)

This work takes as its starting point research by Tyler (e.g. 1994; Tyler & Degoey, 1995) which shows that in interpersonal (intragroup) contexts group members prefer leaders who are procedurally and distributively fair. In disputes between employees, for example, leaders should not be observed to 'take sides' either in the rules they set in place for making decisions or in the decisions they ultimately make (cf. Homans, 1951, p. 427). Tyler argues that, amongst other things, this is because such fairness communicates information about the followers' standing as worthy group members. At the same time, by treating people who have different positions even-handedly, leaders demonstrates their place at the maximally prototypical centre of the group (see Figure 3.3).

However, elaborating upon this point, Platow et al. (1997; see also Tyler, Lind, Ohbuchi, Sugawara & Huo, 1998) argue that in *intergroup* contexts this concern for across-the-board fairness should be attenuated, if not reversed. In particular, this is because when group members are motivated by a concern for a positive social identity they should be more supportive of leaders who explicitly favour the ingroup over an outgroup and who are therefore procedurally and distributively *un*fair.

This idea was tested in an initial study in which group members had to indicate their support for a leader who was observed distributing tasks to other people. Some of these tasks were easy and interesting (making word associations) and others were difficult and boring (counting vowels in a matrix of random letters). Fair allocations involved the leader giving two easy and two difficult tasks to two other people, and unfair allocation involved one person receiving four easy tasks and the other person receiving four dull tasks. To preclude decisions made on the basis of personal self-interest, in this (and all subsequent) studies participants were never personally affected by the leader's decision.

On the basis of social identity theory, the authors predicted that when the two recipients were ingroup members participants would be more likely to support the leader when she allocated tasks fairly rather than unfairly. However, this concern for fairness was expected to diminish when one of the recipients was an outgroup member and this person was allocated four hard tasks. These predictions were supported, so that while fairness was much preferred when both recipients were ingroup members (the interpersonal setting), there was no significant preference for fairness in the intergroup context.

This pattern of results was replicated in a second study in which participants made judgements of leaders who had distributed funds to attend a conference among ingroup members (student delegates), or an ingroup member and an outgroup member (a government delegate). Importantly too, this study also included conditions in which participants belonged to neither of the groups affected by the allocation of rewards. Here, when participants had no group-based stake in the leader's decision there was no evidence that a concern for fairness declined in intergroup contexts (i.e. when a leader displayed ingroup favouritism). This suggests that when participants did endorse ingroup favouring leaders, this was not simply the product of a general preference for leaders who show loyalty to their own group. What mattered was that loyalty was displayed to the *participants'* group.

As with the research discussed in the previous section, the above two studies address issues relating to the *emergence* of group leaders, but social identity processes should also impact upon a person's capacity to *demonstrate* leadership once they have assumed the mantle of leader. This point was examined in Platow et al.'s (1997) third experiment, which looked at the extent to which distributively fair and unfair leaders were capable of exerting *positive influence* over group members. The cover story to the study suggested that a hospital CEO in New Zealand had been faced with a decision about how to allocate time on a kidney dialysis machine. He either had to allocate time to two ingroup members (long-time New Zealanders) or to an ingroup member and an outgroup member (a recent immigrant). A rationale for this decision was provided, but as well as this, in the course of indicating how the time would be allocated, the leader also stated his views about the appropriateness of internal memoranda as a means of informing employees about hospital policy.

Findings on the leader endorsement measures replicated those of the previous two studies. Indeed, here there was evidence that in the intergroup setting participants actually favoured a leader who was distributively unfair over one who was fair. Significantly though, there was also evidence that these patterns of leader endorsement extended to the internalization of the CEO's views about the appropriateness of internal memoranda. Specifically, participants were more likely to align their personal views on this issue with those of the CEO when he was fair in the interpersonal context and unfair in the intergroup context.

Research by Haslam and Platow (1999) has also extended the above findings by examining how followers' endorsement of a leader varies as a function of that leader's treatment of different members of an ingroup. In an initial study, participants were told about a student leader, Chris, who had had to make a decision about who to reward amongst members of the student council who had endorsed or challenged the government's decision to cut university funding. In different conditions they were told that Chris had either rewarded more people who challenged the government, more who had supported the government, or an equal number of pro- and anti-government students. As predicted, participants were more likely to perceive the leader as fair when his reward policy had been even-handed, but they also saw him as more fair when this policy favoured ingroup members who had taken a normative (anti-government) line than when it favoured ingroup members who had taken an anti-normative (pro-government) line. However, students were most likely to *support* the leader to the extent that he favoured ingroup members who took the normative line.

This is all well and good, but under what conditions does leader behaviour translate into *long-term* commitment from followers? Under what circumstances are followers willing to exert effort in order to ensure that a leader's aspirations are collectively realized? As we suggested at the start of this chapter, this is a fundamental question but it is not one that researchers have been able to answer convincingly. To test hypotheses derived from self-categorization theory that relate directly to this issue, Haslam and Platow (1999) replicated their first study but now also looked at how information about the leader's treatment of ingroup members affected followers' reaction to his leadership on a *new* issue. In this study participants were told about which ingroup members Chris had rewarded, but also that he had come up with a new plan to lobby the university to make it erect permanent billboard sites on campus.

Results from this study are presented in Table 3.2. As well as replicating earlier findings, the novel contribution of this experiment was to demonstrate that the history of the leader's behaviour towards the ingroup played a significant role in followers' decision to support his new vision for billboards on campus. Specifically, those who had been told that Chris had previously favoured anti-government ingroup members supported the idea much more than those who were told he had supported pro-government members. Significantly too, participants were also given an opportunity to write down points and arguments that they considered relevant to Chris's decision to lobby for permanent billboard sites. Here participants generated many more arguments that backed up Chris's billboard policy when he had previously rewarded normative ingroup members, than they did when he had been even-handed or had rewarded anti-normative members.

*Table 3.2* The impact of leader strategy on follower perceptions and support (from Haslam & Platow, 1999)

|  | Leader's Reward Policy | | |
| --- | --- | --- | --- |
| Measure | Anti-normative | Even-handed | Pro-normative |
| Perceived fairness of leader's reward policy | 3.47 | 4.69 | 3.88 |
| Perceived sensibleness of leader's reward policy | 3.13 | 4.56 | 4.19 |
| Support for leader's reward policy | 3.00 | 4.03 | 4.13 |
| Support for leader on billboard issue | 2.72 | 3.66 | 3.72 |
| Number of arguments supporting leader on billboard issue | 0.25 | 0.44 | 1.03 |

In other words, support for the even-handed leader was short-lived and half-hearted, but support for the pro-normative leader was stronger and much more enduring. As well as this, the leader's ability to represent the group-based interests of followers also bore upon his capacity to make them engage in the intellectual activities of justification and rationalization necessary to ensure that the structure he had initiated was taken forward. In other words, only when the leader had a history of standing up for the group was the group prepared to stand up for him and *do the work* necessary for his vision to be realized.

Here, then, as in Platow et al.'s (1997) third experiment, we can see that embodiment of ingroup norms impacted directly on the leader's capacity to *show true leadership* — that is, his capacity to enhance followers' contribution to group goals. Moreover, Platow's research as a whole shows that this capacity for leadership is contingent not on the leader's characteristics per se (i.e. whether he is fair or unfair) but on a match between behaviour and group demands that *varies with context* — a point illustrated in Figure 3.3. In the authors' words 'what makes a leader in an intragroup or interpersonal context is not what makes a leader in an intergroup context' (Platow et al., 1997, p. 487; see also Sherif & Sherif, 1969). Reflecting on the leadership qualities revealed by the Ohio State studies (Fleishman, 1953; see above), it is thus clear that 'consideration' must take different forms in different settings, and that only where it is aligned with the social-identity based needs of followers will those followers work to translate the leader's 'initiation of structure' into group action (Haslam, 1998; Haslam & Platow, in press).

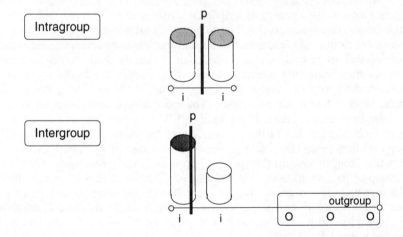

*Figure 3.3* Variation in a leader's approved distribution of resources among followers as a function of comparative context

*Note*: The height of the cylinders indicates the quantity of resources distributed by the leader to group members. i's and O's represent the positions of ingroup and outgroup members, respectively. p represents the most prototypical ingroup position (i.e. that of the leader). In the intergroup context, it is perceived to be fair to give more resources to the group member who maximizes intergroup difference (i.e. the difference between the i's and O's) because he or she is more prototypical of the group-in-context.

## Leader–follower differentiation and group performance

Throughout this chapter we have remarked that a leader's capacity to lead will depend upon their ability to embody those norms and values that the group they lead *shares* in any given context. One implication of this analysis is that if group activities and interaction serve to emphasize what makes the leader *different* from other ingroup members, their leadership may be undermined and rendered less effective (Vanderslice, 1988). Along these lines, Worchel (1994, 1998; Worchel, Coutant-Sassic & Grossman, 1992) presents a model of group formation and development which examines the dynamic interplay between perceived ingroup homogeneity, social identity salience and group functioning. Amongst other things, this describes a process whereby group identification leads to group productivity but is in turn followed by individuation and ultimately group decay. Worchel (1994) describes this process as follows:

> As the group achieves its goals and gains resources, members turn their attention from the group needs to their individual needs. ... Members magnify the differences between themselves and other group members. ... Solutions to social dilemmas become individually based, and, consequently, less group oriented. The group remains a focal point, but the nature of this focus now involves the individual's relation with the group. The group next enters a period of decay as increasing attention is paid to personal needs and the group becomes less salient. (p. 213)

It follows from this analysis that if a group process draws attention away from the group as a whole towards its individual constituents, then it may precipitate a shift from group-based productivity to group disintegration. This may be one reason why democratic leadership styles and participatory leadership practices which appeal to shared interests and goals generally lead to better group outcomes than leadership practices which either impose the leader's personal values on the group or impose no values (Lippitt & White, 1943; Preston & Heintz, 1956; White & Lippitt, 1956). The most famous demonstration of this point was in studies conducted by Lippitt and White where leaders of groups at a boys club adopted one of three leadership styles: *democratic* (involving all group members in decision making, welcoming a range of contributions), *autocratic* (dictating orders, making personal criticisms) and *laissez-faire* (leaving the group to its own devices, with no unsolicited input from the leader). Here the democratically led groups were more cohesive and more harmonious than groups with the other two styles of leader. Interestingly too, the democratic group was also more likely to continue with the group task of its own free will when the leader left the room.

A related activity that might draw attention to interpersonal differences between group members is *systematic leader selection* in which individual group members vie competitively for the role of leader. Although it is customary to view this process as one that enhances group performance, it is possible that it might actually have the opposite effect to the extent that it invokes a state of heightened interpersonal rivalry. In part this is because when a group member vies competitively for the role of leader, consideration for the group as a whole (revealed to be so important in the Ohio State studies; Fleishman, 1953) may give way to consideration for the personal self.

This hypothesis was examined in a series of studies reported by Haslam, McGarty et al. (1998) which examined the impact of systematic and random leader selection on the two main indices of group productivity identified by Cartwright and Zander (1960, p. 496), namely (a) the achievement of some specific group goal and (b) the maintenance or strengthening of the group itself. Our objective was not to demonstrate that the process of systematically selecting group leaders is *generally* counter-productive. Instead we hypothesised that this could be the case under a specific and restricted set of conditions — in particular, where, in the absence of a leader being chosen, the group *already has* a salient social identity and is already oriented to a well-defined shared goal.

In an initial study, small groups of participants containing between three and five members were asked to complete a task which involved ranking items to be rescued in a survival situation. Either their plane had crashed in a frozen wilderness, or their bus had overturned in the desert (the 'winter survival task', and the 'stranded in the desert task' developed by Johnson & Johnson, 1991). Groups were asked to arrive at their decision collectively and after they had done this individuals indicated what their personal ranking of rescuable items would be.

The experiment manipulated the method of *leadership selection* across three levels. In a *random* condition the leader was simply the person whose last name came first in the alphabet. In an *informal* condition groups decided amongst themselves who should be group leader. In a formal condition the leader was selected after all group members had completed a 'leadership selection inventory' in which they rated their own ability in areas which Ritchie and Moses (1983) have identified as being positively correlated with long-term managerial success. This meant that here the people selected as leaders were those who, amongst other things, perceived themselves to be tolerant of uncertainty, verbally skilled and aware of their social environment.

Two dependent measures corresponded to the goal achievement and group maintenance functions identified by Cartwright and Zander (1960). The first was simply the quality of the survival strategy that groups decided upon (as measured relative to expert ratings). A second measure was obtained by looking at how much the strategy which individuals eventually decided upon deviated from the earlier decision of their group. Less deviation was taken to provide evidence of greater group maintenance, suggesting that individuals were more bound to the group and its original decision.

Our main prediction was that groups would make better decisions where their leader was randomly rather than systematically selected. Although there was no variation in group maintenance, the pattern of results on the primary performance measure supported these predictions. This basic pattern of results was also replicated in a second study which involved a slightly different survival task and which replaced the informal selection condition with a control condition in which no group leader was appointed. This served to ensure that the results obtained in the first study were not due to the fact that the task was actually one for which *no* leadership was required. In this study there was again clear evidence that groups with a randomly selected leader performed better than groups with no leader or a systematically selected one. As well as this, individuals from the groups with a randomly selected leader also showed greater group maintenance in deviating less from the group decision when given an opportunity to do so.

While these results provided clear support for our predictions, another interesting feature of the studies was that post-test measures indicated that both leaders and followers tended to perceive the process of randomly selecting group leaders to be relatively unsatisfactory, ineffective and illegitimate. This finding was obviously puzzling in view of evidence that the random procedure was actually associated with *superior* outcomes. One way of explaining this pattern is to suggest that it was a product of stereotypic expectations about how leaders *ought* to be selected and how they *ought* to behave. The existence of such stereotypes was confirmed in a third experiment where naive participants were asked to speculate as to the results that would be likely to be obtained from a study with the same design as our second experiment. Here there was general agreement that groups with a systematically selected leader would perform better than ones with a random leader and that systematic leader selection would engender greater loyalty and be perceived as more legitimate.

Results from this final study confirm the counter-intuitive nature of our original predictions, but they also suggest that *stereotypes* about leadership are an important *resource* which inform people's expectations about group productivity and performance. These beliefs appear to possess many of the key properties of other stereotypes, not least because they can be seen to serve a range of social *functions* (Meindl, 1993; Tajfel, 1981a). So, amongst other things, they serve (a) to *differentiate* between supposedly expert leaders and their followers, (b) to *explain* the differential treatment and respect accorded to leaders, and (c) to *justify* that special treatment. Like other stereotypes, they also exert a powerful grip on those who hold them, while at the same time being highly contestable at an empirical level (Oakes et al., 1994; Thierry, in press). Accordingly, one might muse that even where leadership does not exist, there are pressures to invent it — at least in cultures where leadership is a prized commodity.

Taken as a whole, the findings from these studies serve to question the belief that the process of systematic leadership selection is *always* in the interest of better group performance (for related evidence see also Durham, Knight, & Locke, 1997). This assumption is more-or-less implicit in many organizational settings and in a great deal of organizational literature (as well as in the self-justificatory pronouncements of senior executives like those of Tony Berg that we presented at the start of this chapter; see Hollander, 1995; Sarros & Butchatsky, 1996). Yet, as we have seen, there are strong theoretical grounds for believing that the procedure can be counter-productive. If, as researchers like Worchel (1994) imply, a group can realistically assert that 'united we stand, divided we fall', then it follows that where leadership selection brings to light and even engenders intragroup division, it may presage poor group performance and ultimately group disintegration.

It is important to note, however, that in presenting these arguments it is not claimed either that the process of seeking to select the best leader always reduces group performance, or that random leader selection always enhances it. The pattern of findings obtained in the above studies is likely to hold only for particular groups performing particular tasks. Broadly speaking, random leader selection might only ever be advantageous where the group (a) has a clearly defined shared goal, (b) is disposed or *able* to behave in a relatively democratic and egalitarian manner (involving collective decision-making, sharing of labour and responsibility, etc.), and (c) already has a strong sense of shared social identity *without a leader being appointed*. Clearly these circumstances are not ubiquitous and may only prevail when small groups perform well-defined and relatively mechanical tasks (cf. Howell et al., 1986). Having said that, many important groups in the workplace (and elsewhere) have exactly these qualities and in such situations it is often the case that leadership is sought purely in the interests of personal self-advancement (Kanter, 1979; Mulder, 1977).

While under such circumstances random leadership selection might engender greater identity-based group cohesiveness, it is also not necessarily the case that this will manifest itself in performance that is considered universally superior. A large body of research on the phenomenon of 'groupthink' (Janis, 1972; see Chapter 6 below) testifies to this point, as does other research showing that there is no simple relationship between group cohesiveness and group productivity or performance (Hogg, 1992; Mullen, Anthony, Salas & Driscoll, 1994; Seashore, 1954). In part this is because what actually *counts* as productivity is negotiable (Pritchard, 1990; see Chapter 9 below). As we intimated in the previous chapter, a key issue here is the extent to which the judged value of the group product is aligned with the contextually defined goals and values of the group itself: only where such alignment exists would greater cohesiveness be expected to enhance performance.

These points notwithstanding, one of the important conclusions that can be drawn from the above analysis is that attributions of leadership appear to be contingent upon followers perceiving that they and their leaders are 'in the same boat'. As an instructional manual for organizational leaders might put it, the difference between a boss and a leader is that a boss says 'go' while a leader says 'let's go' (Sarros & Butchatsky, 1996, p. 4).

As we have seen, this sense of shared identity can be eroded by a number of factors of the type investigated in our 'random leader' studies. However, more routinely, it also seems likely that shared identity — and hence group productivity — can be undermined where leaders are perceived to receive rewards (financial or otherwise) that differentiate them from their followers. A pattern consistent with this argument was evident in a series of famous field experiments conducted at summer Boys' Camps by Sherif and his colleagues between 1949 and 1954 (Sherif 1956; Sherif, Harvey, White, Hood and Sherif, 1961). In one phase of the studies two teams of boys engaged in competition for valued prizes and at the 1949 camp the researchers used sociograms to map the patterns of interaction within the two teams. These revealed that the differentiation between leaders and followers was much lower in the winning group (the 'Bulldogs') than it was amongst the losers (the 'Red Devils'). In Sherif's (1956) words:

> Bulldogs had a close-knit organization with good team sprit. Low ranking members participated less in the life of the group but were not rejected. Red Devils ... had less group unity and were sharply stratified. (p. 57)

A similar observation is made by Hollander (1995) in relation to evidence that the difference between the highest and lowest paid members of an organization may be *negatively* correlated with organizational performance (see also Cowherd & Levine, 1992; Drucker, 1986; Pfeffer & Langton, 1988; Robinson, 1995; Vanderslice, 1988). For example, in highly productive countries like 1980s

Japan and Germany CEO's salaries were only about 20 times the wages of average employees, but in countries with lower industrial performance the disparity was much greater. Thus 'super-bosses' in Britain earned about 40 times as much and in the USA about 100 times as much as normal workers (Hollander, 1995). Despite companies' own assertions to the contrary, a growing body of research indicates that executive remuneration is rarely associated with an organization's performance, it is much more likely simply to reflect its size (Carr, 1997; Gomez-Mejia & Wiseman, 1997; Grossman & Hoskisson, 1998; Lambert, Larcker & Weigelt, 1991; Thierry, 1998, in press; Tosi, Katz & Gomez-Mejia, 1997). To receive fat pay cheques, executives don't need to contribute to productive organizations — they just need to work for big ones.

In an attempt to provide some experimental evidence that would speak directly to this argument and address the limitations of correlational data of the form obtained by Sherif (1956) and Hollander (1995), Haslam, Brown, McGarty and Reynolds (1998) conducted a study which manipulated the *position* of individuals as leaders or followers and also the *rewards* that group members were led to expect as a result of their contribution to a group task. This latter variable was manipulated across three levels with followers always receiving the same reward (3 points), but with leaders being given either 3, 6 or 9 points (where each point entitled the participant to a ticket in a $100 draw). Having been told about a particular reward structure, all participants were asked to indicate their commitment to the group and its upcoming task on a number of measures. Subsequent analysis of these measures suggested that they tapped two key factors: (a) how individuals felt about the group's leadership (how important leaders and leadership selection were perceived to be) and (b) how they felt about their group (how much effort they were willing to make to help achieve the group goal and how much they looked forward to the upcoming task).

Consistent with the view that beliefs about leadership are often self-justificatory, leaders were generally more likely than followers to consider leadership of the group to be important. However, in light of arguments derived from the social identity approach, our central prediction was that followers would be less favourably disposed to the group and less willing to make an effort on its behalf, to the extent that the reward structure differentiated (for no obvious or fair reason) between themselves and their leaders. As can be seen from Figure 3.4, this prediction was confirmed. Indeed, the pattern of results suggested that although followers received the same absolute reward in each condition, their feelings towards the group and its tasks changed considerably in response to variation in the reward structure. In contrast, leaders' rewards changed markedly across conditions but their feelings changed very little.

This pattern of results is in direct contrast to the assertion (commonly voiced by employer bodies) that leaders need to be provided with personal incentives to attract and motivate them. Instead it appears that the primary impact of such incentives may be to *de*motivate followers. This argument concords with Pfeffer and Davis-Blake's (1992) finding that greater pay differentiation between academic administrators was associated with higher staff turnover — especially among those administrators that were relatively lowly paid. As Drucker (1986)

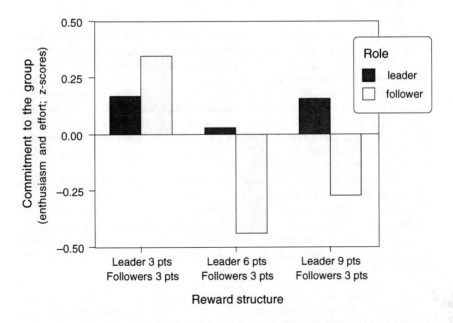

*Figure 3.4* Leaders' and followers' commitment to the group as a function of reward structure (from Haslam, Brown et al., 1998)

notes, it also accords with observations made by J. P. Morgan at the start of the twentieth century that the only feature shared by Morgan's poorly performing clients was a tendency to overpay those at the top of the company:

> Very high salaries at the top, concluded Morgan — who was hardly contemptuous of big money or an 'anticapitalist' — disrupt the team. They make even high-ranking people in the company see their own top management as adversaries rather than as colleagues. ... And that quenches any willingness to say 'we' and to exert oneself except in one's own immediate self-interest. (p. 14)

Significantly, then, and as with the findings from the minimal group studies that we discussed in the previous chapter (Tajfel et al., 1971), these patterns appear paradoxical if looked at from a perspective which sees individuals' behaviour as being guided purely by their personal outcomes. However, they make perfect sense once it is recognized that organizational behaviour is determined by a higher-order rationality that takes into account group-level realities and relativities (Tyler, 1999a). Because leadership is a product of the *relationship* between leader and follower, it is this relationship that needs to be nurtured by those concerned to engender followership. Accordingly, to the extent that resources are directed at the leader in isolation, they may not only be wasted but prove downright counterproductive.

## Conclusion

The major theoretical point to emerge from leadership research conducted from a social identity perspective is that the functioning of leaders and the emergence of leadership cannot be appreciated independently of the social context which gives these roles and qualities expression. This itself is not a new point. Indeed, Fiedler and House (1994) are scathing of Tsui's (1984) suggestion that leadership research fails to attend to environmental factors and that its focus on managers' personal characteristics has retarded practical and theoretical progress. 'What,' they ask, 'has Tsui been reading?', pointing to the fact that almost all contemporary theories of leadership acknowledge the capacity of the environment to determine the impact of specific leaders.

In fact though, Tsui's (1984; see also Tsui & O'Reilly, 1989) point is more subtle than this, and likewise our argument is not simply that the suitability of particular individuals for offices of leadership will change as a function of their circumstances. Rather it is that individuals are *transformed* by features of the context they confront, so that models which are founded upon an appreciation of individuals *in their individuality* are necessarily limited. As Vanderslice (1988) observes:

> The problem, then, is not the concept of leadership *per se*, but the operationalization of leadership in individualistic, static and exclusive position-roles that are supposedly achieved or assigned on the basis of expertise. (p. 683)

In these terms, the problem with Fiedler's contingency theory, for example, is not primarily that its conceptualization of context is limited or that the meaning of the LPC construct is poorly specified (as argued by Landy, 1989). Rather it is that the theory neglects the dynamic relationship between these variables, and the capacity for each to *redefine* the other. The character of individuals and the meaning of their behaviour is changed by the groups that impinge upon them, just as the character and meaning of groups and intergroup relations is changed by individuals (Reicher & Hopkins, 1996a, 1996b). Importantly too, this is true for both leaders *and* followers. Thus while ideological and metatheoretical imperatives lead researchers to neglect issues of followership, they do so at their peril.

In line with these arguments, we have suggested that effective leaders are those whose individuality is *transformed* by group membership in such a way that they come to articulate, embody and direct the social identity-based interests that they share with other group members. These higher order, group-level attributes of the leader cannot be reduced to enduring personality characteristics. Neither can the collective interests of the group that the leader represents be equated with his or her personal self-interest.

Successful leaders of organizations are therefore rarely, if ever, mavericks — set apart from those they lead by virtue of superior intellect, personality or heroism. This is for the simple reason that successful organizations are *collective achievements* that have little use for personal indulgence (Weick & Roberts, 1993, p. 378). In this way, accomplished leaders have much in common with effective stand-up comedians. Success in both spheres depends upon an ability to adapt to the tastes and prejudices of a particular audience in order to establish a mutually sustaining rapport that allows for the collaborative exploration of new territory. Performance in both domains is also notoriously hard to dissect or to recreate mechanically. In focusing on the parts, one always loses sight of the greater whole.

This analysis does not deny the distinctiveness and importance of charismatic leadership. What it does suggest, however, is that to discover its source, researchers need to look not only to the personal qualities of the individual but also to the character and demands of the groups to which they appeal. This is because, while leadership is traditionally seen to revolve solely around the impact of the individual on the group (and is sometimes explicitly defined in these terms; e.g. Mitchell et al., 1988, p. 385), the influence of group on the individual is just as important (Steiner, 1972, p. 175).

Leadership, then, is a process of *mutual influence* that centres around a partnership in a social self-categorical relationship. It is about the creation, coordination and control of a shared sense of 'we-ness'. Within this relationship neither the individual nor the group is static. What 'we' means is negotiable, and so too is the contribution that leaders and followers make to any particular group's self-definition. But it is only because they are partners in a relationship of this form that leaders and followers have the capacity to empower and energize each other. And it is in this group-based synergy that the essence of leadership lies.

## Further reading

The challenge facing someone who wants to come to terms with the literature on leadership is a daunting one. Indeed, there are almost as many reviews of this literature as there are papers to review in other organizational areas. Nonetheless, Smith's encyclopaedia entry offers a straightforward and concise introduction to the area. The chapter by Fiedler and House (1994) is written by two of the most influential researchers in this area and offers a short and readable overview of current trends in this field. The same is true of the chapters by Hollander (1995) and Meindl (1993), but both provide provocative and compelling antidotes to more conventional approaches. Hogg (1996) and Platow et al. (1997) provide more detailed elaboration of the social identity approach to aspects of leadership. The latter is a particularly good example of empirical ingenuity and of the capacity for programmatic experimental research to advance theoretical understanding.

Fiedler, F. E. & House, R. J. (1994). Leadership theory and research: A report of progress. In C. L. Cooper & I. T. Robertson (Eds.), *Key reviews in managerial psychology* (pp. 97-116).. New York: Wiley.

Hogg, M. A. (1996). Intragroup processes, group structure and social identity. In W. P. Robinson (Ed.), *Social groups and identities: The developing legacy of Henri Tajfel* (pp. 65-93). Oxford: Butterworth-Heineman.

Hollander, E. P. (1995). Organizational leadership and followership. In P. Collett & A. Furnam (Eds.), *Social psychology at work* (pp. 69-87). London: Routledge.

Meindl, J. R. (1993). Reinventing leadership: A radical, social psychological approach. In J. K. Murnigham (Ed.), *Social psychology in organizations: Advances in theory and research*. Engelwood Cliffs, NJ: Prentice Hall.

Platow, M. J., Hoar, S., Reid, S. Harley, K. & Morrison, D. (1997). Endorsement of distributively fair and unfair leaders in interpersonal and intergroup situations. *European Journal of Social Psychology, 27*, 465-494.

Smith, P. M. (1995) Leadership. In A. S. R. Manstead & M. Hewstone (Eds.), *The Blackwell encyclopedia of social psychology* (pp. 358-362). Oxford: Blackwell.

# 4  Motivation and Commitment

Take a few moments to ponder the following question: why did you start reading this chapter? For you to do this a certain level of motivation was clearly required on your part — motivation that some other people (e.g. other students, other researchers) may not have, and that you yourself may not have again at some point in the future. Perhaps your reading satisfies a thirst for knowledge and is a manifestation of a particular intellectual need that currently presses upon you. Perhaps you are simply a very motivated person, someone who differs from others in being dedicated and committed or in having a strong need for achievement. Perhaps you enjoy reading and so find the task intrinsically motivating. Perhaps you have engaged in a form of cognitive accounting and think the rewards associated with reading this chapter (e.g. increased knowledge, better performance in exams) outweigh the costs (e.g. expenditure of time and effort, loss of leisure time). Or perhaps you have decided that reading this chapter is a reasonable use of your time in light of your personal goals and the competing demands on your time. If you had something better to do, you'd be doing it.

This is a relatively trivial example, but it obviously bears upon the much more important question of why people work hard to achieve particular objectives. Why do they make an effort to contribute to organizational activities and goals? And why do they do this when many activities are not ones that they themselves have chosen to participate in, but rather relate to goals considered important by other people (e.g. their employers)?

In looking at the way in which these questions have been answered by organizational psychologists, a number of points can be made by thinking about this chapter's opening question. First, all of the listed reasons for reading this chapter were quite plausible, and so it is not surprising that all bear more than a passing resemblance to different accounts of motivation that have been generated in the research literature. Second, it is apparent that the accounts are all quite different — one appeals to features of context, one to individual differences, another to a universal cognitive process. In light of this disunity, a number of researchers have argued that a unified theoretical analysis of motivation in organizations would be highly desirable, but that it is difficult, perhaps impossible, to achieve (e.g. Kanfer, 1994; Nuttin, 1984).

In an attempt to rise to the challenge of providing an integrated approach to this topic, this chapter briefly reviews some of the major approaches to motivation in the workplace, and points to a common (but largely overlooked) thread which runs through most theorizing in this field — the importance of *self-definition*. In light of this point, it is proposed that a full understanding of motivation must be based on an adequate model of self. Our review also suggests that one common limitation of motivational theories is their tendency to neglect or to over-simplify the role of a person's *social* self-definition.

An account which acknowledges the role of social self-definition would suggest that you have read this far because you have internalized a particular self-categorization (e.g. as a psychology student or academic). In these terms, social motivation arises from commitment to norms associated with a salient social category (in this case a norm to read category-relevant material). In the cliché of the cowboy bracing himself for one more fight: 'A man's gotta do what a man's gotta do' — a canon that can be tailored to any social identity. Such an analysis suggests that a large component of work motivation derives not from the unique qualities of individuals but from their collective sense of who they are and what they feel compelled to do in order to maintain and promote that identity.

### An overview of motivation research

*The economic approach*

One of the very clearest analyses of people's motivation to work is contained within the principles of scientific management that we outlined in Chapter 1. According to Taylor (1911), the natural state of the worker in an organization is one of indolence and slothfulness and the individual is coaxed out of this only by the prospect of personal financial gain. This analysis assumes that whenever people are forced to work in groups or for a fixed wage, they will be under-motivated and reluctant to exert themselves. The remedy for this is simple: select only the very best workers, ensure that they are treated and work as individuals, and pay them only for what they produce.

Partly because of its simplicity, but also because it fitted with managerial ideology, this view of motivation was very influential in the first half of the twentieth century (see McGregor, 1957, 1960). Even now it is still influential in management circles. In fact, as we discussed in the previous chapter, executives themselves often appeal to this logic when they justify their own high salaries and fringe benefits by arguing that these are needed for motivational and recruitment purposes. Thus the chairman of the Australian Investment Management Association recently defended multi-million dollar share options given to CEOs as 'a useful way to reward executives, as long as they are issued with some kind of performance hurdle' (Carr, 1997, p. 28).

The extremity of this example highlights some of the key problems inherent in the economic approach. Most straightforwardly, it is improbable that someone would work a great deal harder if they were paid ten million dollars a year rather than two million. And yet there are some things that people would never do however much they were paid. As well as this there are large numbers of people (e.g. aid workers) who work extremely hard for almost no financial reward at all (Landy, 1989). These examples point to the fact that there is no straightforward relationship between pay and effort. Empirical support for the idea that pay-based incentives enhance motivation is thus mixed (see Pfeffer, 1997, pp. 111-112). Reviews also indicate that, when asked, people generally perceive financial reward to be a much less important aspect of employment than things like security and enjoyment (Blackler & Williams, 1971; Lawler, 1973; Stagner, 1950).

*Needs and interest approaches*

Aside from some straightforward empirical problems, a more fundamental limitation of the economic approach is that it presents a thoroughly inhuman model of human behaviour (see Brown, 1954; Griesinger, 1990). This is not to say that pay is a trivial or inconsequential feature of people's work (Lawler, 1973). However, its contribution to motivation is far from uniform and can be seen as an indirect consequence of its capacity to satisfy other needs, like a need for respect and self-esteem.

These arguments were fleshed out by McGregor (1957, 1960) in his assertion that conventional Taylorist wisdom was underpinned by a profoundly pessimistic theory of motivation. McGregor referred to this traditional view as *Theory X*. Core assumptions of the theory were: (a) that the average person dislikes work and wants, if possible, to avoid it, (b) that, as a result, most people must be coerced or bullied into working hard, and (c) that most workers are looking for little more out of employment than an easy life devoid of interest, challenge or responsibility.

While acknowledging that these assumptions may hold true under a limited set of conditions (e.g. in a feudal master-slave relationship), McGregor argued that the assumptions of Theory X were not only limited, but that motivation was better understood in terms of *exactly the opposite* set of assumptions. These he referred to as *Theory Y*. This theory included assumptions: (a) that expenditure of effort is as natural as play or rest; (b) that people will generally tend to exercise self-direction and self-control to reach objectives to which they are committed; (c) that commitment to goals is a function of self-relevant rewards associated with their achievement; (d) that humans learn to seek and accept responsibility; (e) that most people are capable of ingenuity, imagination and creativity; but (f) that under the standard conditions of modern organizational life the intellectual potential of humans is generally under-explored and under-developed.

McGregor gave the theories the names X and Y largely in recognition of the fact that they represented sets of beliefs that were extreme and largely hypothetical. Accordingly, he noted that it would be rare to encounter a manager who endorsed either theory in an unadulterated form. Nevertheless, he argued that in many sectors of industry managers were disposed to base their treatment of employees on an implicit view of human motivation that was more akin to Theory X than Theory Y. In so doing, problems arose because this strategy tended to thwart the higher-order needs of workers:

> Many studies have demonstrated that the tightly knit, cohesive work group may, under proper conditions, be far more effective than an equal number of separate individuals in achieving organizational goals. Yet management, fearing group hostility to its own objectives, often goes to considerable lengths to control and direct human efforts in ways that are inimical to the natural groupiness of human beings. When man's social needs ... are thus thwarted, he tends to behave in ways which seek to defeat organizational objectives. He becomes resistant, antagonistic, unco-operative. (McGregor, 1960, pp. 37-38)

This analysis was partly informed by previous theorizing which had noted the contribution of needs to human motivation. In particular, Maslow (1943) argued that humans have a hierarchy of needs that range from the low level and basic (like a need to eat and sleep) to the high level and complex (like a need for self-fulfilment). This five-level hierarchy of needs is presented in Figure 4.1.

Maslow proposed that the most important motivator of people's behaviour in any given context is their lowest level of unsatisfied need. Thus a person who has no food, security or affection, will be driven more by the need to eat than by the need to feel secure or loved. Applying these arguments to organizational behaviour (see also Maslow, 1972), McGregor argued that a Theory X approach placed too much emphasis on the role of lower-order needs as motivators of worker's beliefs. In contemporary Western society the physiological and safety needs of most workers *are* satisfied and this means that their behaviour is more commonly motivated by higher-order needs. Here McGregor (1960) differentiated between two kinds of 'egoistic needs':

> [Type I]  Those needs that relate to one's self-esteem — needs for self-confidence, for independence, for achievement, for competence, for knowledge.
> [Type II]  Those needs that relate to one's reputation — needs for status, for recognition, for appreciation, for the deserved respect of one's fellows. (p. 38)

McGregor argued that much of the malaise in industrial organizations arose from the fact that they typically offered no avenue for the realization of these needs. Moreover, he noted that 'if the practices of scientific management were deliberately calculated to thwart these needs ... they could hardly accomplish this purpose better than they do' (McGregor, 1960, pp. 38-39).

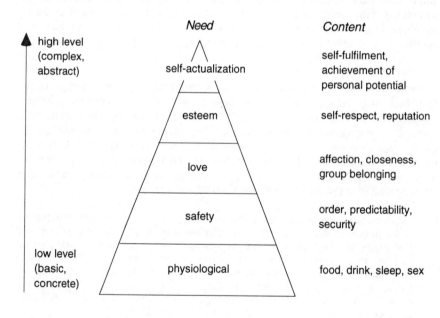

*Figure 4. 1* Maslow's (1943) hierarchy of needs

Similar ideas to these are also central to Herzberg's (1966, 1968; Herzberg, Mausner & Snyderman, 1959) motivation–hygiene theory. In 12 different studies Herzberg and his colleagues interviewed a total of 1,685 workers from a variety of occupations and with a range of skill levels and responsibilities. All were asked to reflect on times when they had felt exceptionally good or exceptionally bad about their work (a so-called 'critical incidents' approach). On the basis of the responses, the researchers identified two sets of needs. Animal needs are associated with 'hygiene factors' and relate to the context in which work is performed. These include work relationships, working conditions, status and security. On the other hand, human needs are associated with 'motivator factors' and are related to things involved in actually doing the job. These include achievement, recognition, work itself, responsibility, advancement and growth.

The researchers argue that each set of needs is rendered salient in different organizational contexts. Specifically, when workers are dissatisfied they tend to refer to an *absence* of hygiene factors (e.g. poor pay, company inefficiency, bad relationships with supervisors). However, when they are satisfied, workers tend to link this to the *presence* of motivator factors (e.g. a sense of personal satisfaction and achievement, the opportunity to do creative work). Accordingly, hygiene factors can be thought of as 'dissatisfiers', while motivator factors can be thought of as 'satisfiers' (Herzberg et al., 1959, p. 82).

On this basis Herzberg (e.g. 1968) suggests that if employers really want to motivate workers, they need to stop doing this through hygiene-related interventions (e.g. improving working conditions, punishing under-performance) and should instead attend to motivator factors. The primary strategy envisaged here is one of *job enrichment*. Amongst other things, this involves attempts to increase individuals' accountability for their own work, to increase their control over discrete and varied elements of a particular job, and to allow workers the opportunity to become authorities and experts in relation to those elements (Hackman & Oldham, 1980).

The results of such interventions are generally quite positive. To investigate their effects, one early study divided people employed to correspond with the stockholders of a large corporation into a control group and an experimental group (Herzberg et al., 1959). The experimental group's jobs were enriched by giving them control, autonomy and the opportunity to develop expertise. Here, despite an initial drop in the performance and satisfaction of the experimental group arising from the increased demands of the new work regime, in due course members of the experimental group were more productive and more satisfied than members of the control group.

The general utility of this type of approach to motivation is well documented (e.g. see Hackman & Oldham, 1976, 1980; Murrell, 1976). Indeed, there is evidence that researchers and industrial innovators had developed similar approaches to Herzberg's well before he proposed his motivation–hygiene model (Ernst Abbé in the 1890s and Henri De Man in the 1920s). However, as *theories* of motivation, needs accounts still leave something to be desired (Landy, 1989; Murrell, 1976). Most simply, while there is general agreement that needs are hierarchically organized with higher-level needs being more abstract, there is debate about the number of different types of motivation between which it is appropriate to distinguish. Maslow (1943) suggests five, Alderfer (1969, 1972) three (existence, relatedness and growth) and Herzberg (1966) two. Moreover, the *process* through which particular needs come into play is rather unclear. Thus while Maslow argues that it is the most basic unsatisfied need which determines motivation, Alderfer suggests that attention to a higher-order need is contingent upon satisfaction of lower-level needs but that individuals regress to a previously satisfied level of need if a more abstract need is frustrated. Finally, although the needs approach has led to important organizational innovation, the underlying theoretical principles on which such innovation is based remain poorly specified and quite difficult to test (Chell, 1993, p. 64). In the words of Salancik and Pfeffer (1978) 'they take as given much of what ought to be explained' (p. 250). In a similar vein, Landy (1989) concludes that:

> There are too many elements that are left open to question. Under what conditions will a difficult task be attempted? What will occur if one *fails* the task? How do individuals differ with respect to their willingness to approach difficult tasks? Why are needs arranged in one hierarchy rather than another? ... In order to justify the title 'theory', there should be a tight set of interrelated propositions that can be empirically tested. This is where most of the need approaches have fallen short. (p. 379)

### Individual difference approaches

An individual difference approach to motivation suggests that whether or not people work hard is largely a function of their personality. Some people will go to great lengths to achieve great things whatever barriers are placed in their way, but others will loaf at every opportunity (Smither, 1992). The work that has been most influential in advancing this view over the past forty or so years is that of McClelland (e.g. 1985, 1987; McClelland & Winter, 1969). As a variation on the position of theorists like Maslow, McClelland has argued that everyone shares lower-level physical and security needs but that motivation to work reflects a higher-order, more specialized *need for achievement* (nAch for short) which only a limited subset of the population develop. Within McClelland's work nAch is differentiated from two other lower-order needs: the need for affiliation (nAff) and the need for power (nPow). This variable also has a lot in common with other personality variables which have recently been identified as predictors of work performance — in particular, *conscientiousness* or *will to achieve* (Digman & Takemoto-Chock, 1981) and *achievement orientation* (McCrae & Costa, 1990; see Kanfer, 1994).

People who are high in need for achievement are said to have high levels of personal motivation associated with a preference for working alone under conditions of moderate risk (i.e. where the likelihood of success is not too high or too low). Such needs are established early in childhood and are shaped both by the culture to which the individual belongs and, more especially, by his or her parents. In particular, in order to develop high nAch, McClelland (1955, p. 275, 1961; McClelland, Atkinson, Clark & Lowell, 1976) insists that children need to perform competitive tasks as individuals and learn the appropriate emotional reactions to their performance with reference to 'standards of excellence'. Children should learn to feel positive about success and negative about failure.

This model of motivation has been tested in both laboratory and large-scale field studies. For example, an early study by French (1955) showed that people with high *n*Ach worked much harder than low *n*Ach individuals when given a competitive task to perform. In a relaxed setting both groups worked equally hard, and if participants were told they would be allowed to leave the experiment after completing the task, those with low *n*Ach actually worked harder. On this basis McClelland suggested that the prime motivator for people with low *n*Ach is the prospect of *avoiding* work. Consistent with the status of *n*Ach as a long-term predictor of motivation and performance, a study reported by McClelland (1961) also found that 83 per cent of entrepreneurs had had high *n*Ach as students 14 years previously, compared to only 21 per cent of the non-entrepreneurs. At the opposite end of the employment spectrum, research by Sheppard and Belintsky (1966) found that after retrenchment, workers with high *n*Ach were much more likely to find new work.

Rather more ambitiously, a number of cross-organizational and cross-cultural studies have also been taken as providing evidence for this model. In particular, a study conducted by Andrews (1967) suggested that the difference in performance of two large Mexican firms, A and P, could be explained by the fact that the executives of one firm (A) had higher levels of need for achievement. This difference was also used to account for the fact that executives in Firm A were more likely to get promotions and pay rises. On a broader canvas, McClelland and Winter (1969, after LeVine, 1966) argued that differences in the economic productivity of two Nigerian tribes — the Ibo and Hausa — could be attributed to the generally higher levels of *n*Ach among the Ibo.

In all this work, McClelland and his colleagues appeal to an individual difference analysis in light of the fact that their studies reveal different patterns of motivation within a broadly uniform social context. In particular, they argue convincingly against an economic approach to motivation, noting that the general economic climate of incentives and rewards was similar for Firm A and Firm P, and for the Hausa and Ibo. Their response to the question 'Why is it that different groups respond differently to similar situations?' (McClelland & Winter, 1969, p. 20) also reflects post-Second World War desperation with the so-called 'United Nations decade' where politicians and economists were perceived to have tried to solve all foreign aid problems simply by appealing to a common desire for financial gain (McClelland & Winter, 1969; Wilhelm, 1966).

A case in point was a ten-year aid project devised by the American Friends Service Committee which set out to improve living conditions in an Indian community by spending $1 million on infrastructure and education projects (e.g. improving sewerage and teaching farming techniques). At the end of the project the technology was abandoned and none of the training was put into practice, leaving little to show for the investment. To prove the value of his own approach, in perhaps his most famous study, McClelland (1978) attempted to deal with this issue by means of an aid package that put a small number of businessmen through an entrepreneurial training programme designed to enhance their need for achievement. The programme lasted six months, cost $25,000 and ended up creating jobs for 5,000 local people.

Significantly though, despite its apparent success, this study actually presents a theoretical challenge to McClelland's own analysis. Specifically, if need for achievement is set firmly in place at childhood so that it becomes a feature of a person's personality, how can it be acquired in adulthood? And if it can be acquired, the explanatory force of the *n*Ach construct is diminished because the source of entrepreneurial success lies in training and experience not personality. At the very least, then, this research implies that a person's need for achievement is a psychological *outcome* not just an input variable (for additional evidence, see Atkinson, 1964, pp. 225-227; Sorrentino, 1973; Sorrentino & Field, 1986).

Moreover, while it may be the case that broad features of context are similar across groups whose levels of motivation and *n*Ach vary, it is clear that there are a number of more local contextual factors that may impact upon both variables. The Ibo, for example, place much more value on personal advancement and provide greater opportunity for upward mobility than the Hausa, and this may be the primary determinant of both their motivation to work and their need for achievement (Parker, 1997). It is also worth adding that personality-based explanations of human behaviour lose much of their explanatory power when they are invoked to explain the behaviour of large groups of people. This is because here the variables in question look much less like individual differences and much more like widely shared social norms (Oakes et al., 1994).

Attempts to refine McClelland's model have therefore suggested that people's approach to a task is dictated by their achievement orientation in interaction with contextual factors such as the probability of success and the perceived value of success (Atkinson & Feather, 1966; Sorrentino & Field, 1986). Although quite popular, it is important to recognize that these hybrid models are still founded upon the questionable view that motivation has its psychological basis in the enduring character of the individual as an autonomous social agent.

*Cognitive approaches*

Cognitive work on organizational motivation is dominated by two main approaches, each represented in a large body of research. The first reflects the influence of social exchange theories, the second a more specialized interest in issues of intrinsic motivation. Both bodies of work are compatible with the view that workers are motivated tacticians (Fiske & Taylor, 1991) who base decisions about how to act on an appraisal of the personal meaning and implications of the rewards (and costs) associated with any behavioural strategy.

In the exchange theory tradition, three distinct approaches are particularly influential: expectancy theory, goal-setting theory and equity theory. *Expectancy theory* (Vroom, 1964; also developed by Lawler, 1973; Naylor, Pritchard & Ilgen, 1980) argues that people act with a view to maximizing their personal outcomes. In other words, people are motivated by the prospect of achieving the largest possible payoff for any work they perform. The nature of this payoff is subjectively defined so that people will not necessarily agree about what is the best course of action to pursue. Behaviour is also seen to be guided by the likelihood of a particular outcome occurring ('expectancy', relative to other outcomes — 'instrumentality') and the amount of personal satisfaction associated with that outcome ('valence'). Under this theory, the overall force of a person's motivation is seen to be a mathematical product of these three elements: valence (V), instrumentality (I) and expectancy (E) — the so-called VIE model.

Amongst other things, this formulation implies that a person may opt to pursue a less rewarding outcome if there is a greater probability that they will achieve it. This means that a student may enrol in an undemanding course they are likely to pass rather than a prestigious one they may fail — especially if they place a greater value on the prospect of letters after their name than on intellectual development. Similarly, an employee may decide not to work hard if they have no expectation of reward (low E), do not value the reward associated with performance (low V), or if the value of the reward is offset by negative outcomes associated with their endeavour (e.g. fatigue; low I).

*Goal-setting theory* has a lot in common with expectancy theory, but differs in emphasizing the overriding importance of goals in a person's cognitive evaluation of their behavioural options. In particular, Locke and Latham (1990; Locke, Shaw, Saari & Latham, 1981; see also Zander, 1985) have proposed that individuals are more likely to be motivated by concrete, specific and challenging goals (e.g. 'Reach a sales target of $7 million by June') than by abstract, vague and undemanding ones (e.g. 'Do the best you can'). It is argued that this is because — as long as a goal is realistic and reachable — the more concrete and challenging it is the greater its capacity to focus a person's attention, to demand effort, to encourage persistence and to allow for goal-directed strategic planning (Kanfer, 1994).

Empirical evidence appears to be broadly consistent with this approach, and accordingly goal-setting is a motivational strategy that has been eagerly integrated into organizational practice. However, an unresolved question in this area relates to the effects of *involving* employees in the goal-setting process. It appears that worker participation generally improves satisfaction with the emerging goals, but does not necessarily make them any more likely to be achieved (Latham, Mitchell & Dossett, 1978; Mitchell et al., 1988) — although Wegge (1999, in press) argues that one reason for this is that participation is typically superficial and short-lived (see also Kelly & Kelly, 1991). More recent research also suggests that different types of goals are associated with different motivations and that the desire to demonstrate competence is most associated with tasks that are self-involving (Dweck & Leggett, 1988; Nicholls, 1984).

*Equity theory* is also similar to expectancy theory, but it differs in emphasizing the role that perceived costs, not just rewards, play in motivational processes. The theory is founded upon an assumption that people are likely to be motivated to perform particular behaviours to the extent that they are perceived to be just. As Vroom (1969) puts it:

> The individual's decision to participate in the system is determined by the relative magnitude of inducements and contributions. ... The attractiveness of a social system to a person and the probability that he will withdraw from participation in it, are related to the consequences of organizational membership, specifically the rewards and punishments, or satisfactions and privations incurred as a result of organizational membership. (p. 200; see also Katz, 1964b; Lawler, 1973, pp. 72-74, 1995, p. 8)

According to this analysis, justice or fairness is achieved when a person's inputs match their outcomes and a similar balance exists in the inputs and outputs observed for others with whom the individual compares themselves. Indeed, under the theory, equality between individuals in the *ratio* of inputs to outputs is more important than equality of inputs and outputs per se as in most instances what is a fair return on one's investment of energy can only be established by looking at the returns of others. Inputs include all costs associated with a behaviour (e.g. expended effort, qualifications, expertise) and outcomes include all things that contribute to the gratification of a person's salient needs (e.g. self-actualization, esteem, security).

Two particular forms of justice are also identified as important: distributive and procedural (Thibaut & Walker, 1975, 1978). Distributive justice relates to the fairness of a given outcome (e.g. whether one worker gets promoted at the same time as another who they perceive to be of equal merit) and procedural justice relates to the fairness of the processes which lead to that outcome (e.g. whether both workers had the same opportunity to apply for promotion). People thus seek fairness not only in the rewards they receive, but also in the way they are treated — a point which applies in the workplace, in courts and in the home (Tyler, 1989, 1998).

The key prediction of equity theory is that when an outcome or process is perceived to be inequitable, this creates a state of psychological tension which the individual is motivated to reduce. This varies as a function of the size of the perceived inequity, so that the larger it is the more the individual is motivated to reduce it. The theory also predicts that motivation will vary in response to inequity that is both positive (over-reward inequity, where rewards outweigh costs) and negative (under-reward inequity, where costs outweigh rewards; Mowday, 1978). Thus a person who is overpaid or receives an undeserved promotion should be motivated to work harder to restore equity, but to achieve the same end a person who is underpaid or fails to receive a deserved promotion should want to work less.

Although it may be intuitively appealing, a number of reservations about equity theory have been voiced in the research literature. At a theoretical level, the inherent 'rubberyness' of the concepts that are central to the theory means that any behaviour can be explained in terms of cost–benefit analysis (a point that applies to all exchange theories). For example, if a person's behaviour appears inconsistent with equity theory because he or she works harder after being refused a promotion, it can be argued either that they are trying to restore equity by ensuring that they get promoted in the future or that they are a masochist for whom being treated badly is a valued reward. Part of the problem here is that exactly what constitutes a reward, a cost, an appropriate comparison 'other', and an appropriate strategy for equity-restoration is actually as much an *outcome* of social-motivational processes as an *input* (Tajfel, 1982a; van Knippenberg & van Oers, 1984). The theory is correct in acknowledging that each of these elements is subjective, but it loses its explanatory edge if the appeal to subjectivity is used to conceal a lack of predictive power.

The importance of this point at an empirical level is demonstrated by evidence that in fact people are generally much more sensitive to, and keen to redress, under-reward inequity than to over-reward inequity (Caddick, 1981, 1982; Landy, 1989; Tajfel, 1981a, 1982a). In other words, there is often self-favouring motivational asymmetry, so that injustice is felt more keenly when one loses rather than gains. This point was shown clearly in Platow's research examining the reactions of followers to fair or unfair leaders that we reviewed in the previous chapter (e.g. Haslam & Platow, in press; Platow et al., 1997).

A final social cognitive influence in the motivational literature relates to the concept of *intrinsic motivation*. An activity that is intrinsically motivated is one that is engaged in for its own sake because it is enjoyable or interesting, rather than because it is associated with an extrinsic factor like monetary reward (Harackiewicz & Sansone, 1991; Lepper, Greene & Nisbett, 1973). Popular theories of intrinsic motivation argue that people perform intrinsically motivating tasks because they offer the opportunity to gratify higher-order need for personal development and achievement (deCharms, 1968; Deci, 1975). On the other hand, extrinsic rewards are seen to achieve results through their capacity to gratify lower-level needs. For this reason the intrinsic-extrinsic distinction corresponds closely to Herzberg's (1966) distinction between motivator and hygiene factors, discussed above (see Herzberg, 1968, p. 56).

One of the major points of debate in this literature concerns how intrinsic and extrinsic factors combine to motivate individuals as they set about particular tasks. A pioneering piece of research in the field was conducted by Lepper et al. (1973). They found that young children's willingness to play with colouring pens — a task which they found enjoyable and intrinsically motivating — was reduced when they were given an extrinsic reward (a certificate) for engaging in this activity.

Two explanations of this type of result have been proposed. One suggests that extrinsic motivators can undermine motivation because they detract from individuals' sense of control over their behaviour (cognitive evaluation theory; deCharms & Muir, 1978), the other that they detract from individuals' need to justify to themselves why they are engaging in a task (overjustification theory; Lepper & Greene, 1975). For example, according to these theories, if academics were paid a lot of money for doing their job, they might enjoy their work less and consequently work less hard (a) because they would perhaps feel uncomfortable with the sense that they were being paid a lot of money in return for being controlled by a university or government (which would violate their sense of academic and personal freedom) or (b) because they would perhaps no longer have to convince themselves that academic work was intrinsically interesting ('I must enjoy this — why else would I be doing it for so little pay?').

Research suggests that people's sense of control and their self-justification both have a role to play in the motivation process (e.g. Harackiewicz & Larson, 1986). Again though, as with much of the other research we have reviewed, there are some residual empirical and theoretical problems in this field. Most pressingly, it is not clear what actually makes a particular motivator intrinsic or extrinsic. Indeed, one of the implications of over-justification theory is that under certain circumstances people are motivated to, and can, *redefine* an intrinsically motivating task as one that is extrinsically motivated (and vice-versa). Again, then, the status of a motivator as intrinsic or extrinsic can be seen as the *outcome* of a cognitive process as well as a cognitive input. This is one reason why there is considerable disagreement about the classification of motivators in terms of the intrinsic–extrinsic dichotomy. This point was confirmed in a study conducted by Dyer and Parker (1975) in which organizational psychologists classified a range of outcomes as intrinsic or extrinsic. In classifying 'recognition', for example, 28% indicated it was an intrinsic factor, 41% that it was extrinsic, 30% indicated it could be either and 1% were unsure. Respondents were similarly divided on the classification of outcomes such as 'opportunity to develop friendships' (21% intrinsic, 47% extrinsic), 'variety in job' (47%, 31%), 'stress or pressure' (20%, 31%) and 'more authority' (17%, 40%). In his review of this work, Landy (1989) thus comes to a conclusion that is similar in tone and content to that offered in his treatment of needs theories:

> It seems that there is a good deal more here than meets the eye. ... Whether something called 'extrinsic motivation', actually exists, and if it does, whether it is a property of a person or a task, has not been decided. *Why* the effects are found is also open to question. (p. 434)

## Social identity, motivation and commitment

From the above review it is clear that the general patterning of research into work motivation corresponds quite closely to that outlined in Chapter 1, with considerable bodies of research exploring economic, individual difference and social cognitive approaches to this topic. Here though, group-based human relations approaches have had little impact and partly for this reason, the field appears to have little in common with, and leave little room for, the social identity approach. Indeed, this is probably one reason why issues of motivation have been relatively underexplored by researchers in this tradition.

Having said that, we observed in Chapter 2 that social identity theory is actually founded upon motivational assumptions in arguing that intergroup behaviour is partly motivated by the esteem-related need to achieve or maintain a positive social identity. Moreover, self-categorization theory has the potential to provide a broader and more integrated model of (work) motivation than social identity theory by virtue of the fact that it incorporates self-esteem-related needs within a *process model of self* (Haslam, Powell et al., 2000). The starting point for such an approach can simply be to ask 'who am I?' (for related arguments see Leonard, Beauvais & Scholl, 1999; Handy, 1976, p. 47; Oyserman & Packer, 1996, p. 201; Shamir, 1991). As we noted in Chapter 2, self-categorization theory suggests that a question of this form can be answered at varying *levels of abstraction* (see Figure 2.7). These range from conceptions of the self in terms of one's personal identity as a unique individual, through group-based self-definitions in terms of a salient social identity, to more abstract representations of self as a human being (or at an even higher level as an animal).

Importantly too, each of these different levels of self-definition should be associated with a distinct set of needs. In particular, when people categorize themselves at a personal level they should be motivated to do those things which promote their personal identity as individuals, but when they categorize themselves at a social level they should be motivated to do those things which promote their social identity as group members. In this way, needs associated with a salient personal identity should be more specialized and idiosyncratic than those associated with a social identity, which in turn should be more specialized and idiosyncratic than those associated with a human or animal identity.

As Table 4.1 shows, the actual content of the needs associated with each of these levels of self-definition should correspond closely to the different categories of needs identified within established needs hierarchies (e.g. those of Maslow, Alderfer, McClelland, McGregor and Herzberg). So, when personal identity is salient this should be associated with needs to self-actualize and to enhance personal self-esteem through personal advancement and growth. On the other hand, when social identity is salient this should be associated with the need to enhance social self-esteem through a sense of relatedness, respect, peer recognition and the achievement of group goals (see Hogg & Abrams, 1990, 1993; Zander, 1971). Yet when human or animal identities are salient, needs should be more existence-, security- and safety-related. Indeed, it seems reasonable to suggest that one reason why there is such a high degree of correspondence amongst needs hierarchies is that they all map onto this underlying hierarchy of self.

Although the above analysis goes some way to explaining why there is such a strong resemblance between various needs hierarchies and why hierarchies have

*Table 4.1* The relationship between level of self-categorization and the different categories of need identified by major theorists

| Level of Self-Categorization | Content | Associated Needs as Identified by Key Theorists | | | | |
|---|---|---|---|---|---|---|
| | | Maslow | Alderfer | McClelland | McGregor | Herzberg |
| personal | self as individual (in contrast to ingroup members) | self-actualization | growth | nAch | Theory Y [Type I] | motivators |
| social | self as group member (in contrast to outgroup members) | esteem / love | relatedness | nAff | Theory Y [Type II] | hygienes |
| human | self as human (in contrast to other animals) | safety | existence | nPow | Theory X | |
| animal | self as animal (in contrast to non-animals) | physiological | | | | |

the structure they do, self-categorization theory would still offer the field of motivation rather little if it simply provided a new hierarchy of needs as an alternative to those already developed by other theorists. Its primary contribution, however, is that it presents a framework for understanding when and why particular levels of self-categorization become salient. This in turn leads to predictions about when and why a given class of need will play a role in motivating organizational behaviour. And because these ideas are testable and conceptually interrelated, they offer the prospect for genuine theoretical advance in the sense implied by Landy (1989, p. 379).

The principal difference between this analysis and that of other needs theories is that it suggests that the key process determining which category of needs guides a person's behaviour is *self-category salience*. We are motivated to live up to norms and to achieve goals that are relevant to our self-definition. But, as we discussed in Chapter 2, the way in which we define ourselves varies as a function of context. If I define myself as a man, I will be motivated to embody male-related norms and achieve male-related goals (if you like, 'to do what a man's gotta do'), but if I define myself as an individual, I will be motivated to achieve personal standards and personal goals. Importantly too, it follows from the fact that no level of self is any more real or essential than any other that 'higher level' needs are in the abstract no more important, superior, valuable or valid than 'lower level' needs. Contrary to the assertions of many needs theorists, there is nothing special about personal self-actualization that makes it an inherently better motivator than the need to stand well with one's peers or to *collectively* self-actualize (e.g. see Leavitt, 1995, p. 386).

As outlined in Chapter 2, social identity and self-categorization theories discuss a large number of social structural and psychological factors which determine whether a person defines themselves in terms of their idiosyncratic characteristics or in terms of shared group membership. In particular, social identity theory suggests that whether individuals think of themselves in terms of a given social identity — and hence are guided by self-esteem and other needs related to that identity — depends, amongst other things, upon the status of their ingroup, the perceived permeability of group boundaries, and the individual's belief system. Thus a member of a low-status group will be more likely to think and act as a group member to the extent that intergroup boundaries are seen as impermeable and they embrace a social change belief system. And such a person is more likely to be motivated by the prospect of enhancing the status of their group as a whole and their social self-esteem than by the prospect of personal achievement and self-actualization. However, the opposite will tend to be the case when individuals perceive boundaries to be permeable and see social mobility as a viable means of enhancing their personal status (although even here, some members of the group may still pursue group-based interests if they remain identified with it; e.g. if they are 'die-hard' group members; Branscombe & Wann, 1994; Ouwerkerk et al., 1999; Wann & Branscombe, 1990, 1993).

Interestingly, when one thinks of the groups of workers that are likely to fit these examples, this analysis provides an important insight into McGregor's Theory X–Theory Y distinction. Specifically, we can see that the predictions of Theory X (the view that workers seek to avoid work) will generally be borne out to the extent that people define themselves in terms of membership of low-status social categories whose social identity-based needs can only be satisfied by *rejecting* the values and goals of the high-status outgroup. Examples might be provided where union workers are locked into conflict with an employer, or where employees of small companies are subjected to an aggressive takeover by larger organizations (Bachman, 1993; van Knippenberg & van Schie, in press). In both cases workers have little *personal* motivation to work hard in a manner consistent with the goals of the dominant group. On the other hand, Theory Y should apply where individuals are convinced of the possibility of personal self-advancement. This might apply where a low-status group is subjected to a benign merger (Terry et al., 1997) or more generally within a culture that embraces an ideology of individual mobility — as do most of the latterday Western societies to which McGregor addressed himself (e.g. see Triandis, 1990, 1994).

As we saw in Chapter 2, ideas about category salience are also formalized within self-categorization theory. This argues that the salience of self-categories at any level of abstraction (personal, social, human) is determined by perceiver readiness in interaction with category fit. The extent to which a person acts in terms of a particular social self-category depends on both the prior meaning and the contextual meaning of that category. As an example, a person is more likely to act as a member of a workteam if they have prior experience of that team (so that the concept is psychologically accessible) and if the team is positively distinguished from others in the workplace.

Significantly, these arguments about category salience can be elaborated in a way that helps us reconceptualize the psychological basis of Herzberg's observation that motivator factors tend to be associated with organizational satisfaction and hygiene factors with organizational dissatisfaction (e.g. Herzberg et al., 1959). A preliminary observation is methodological and relates to the structure of the items Herzberg and his colleagues used to assess participants' reactions to motivator and hygiene factors. Close inspection of these items indicates that they differ in terms of their fit with positive and negative responses (for related ideas see Eiser & Stroebe, 1972; Reynolds et al., 2000). More specifically, it is clear that when answering questions of the form 'Are these a source of satisfaction?' or 'Are these a source of dissatisfaction?', items classed as motivators (e.g. achievement, recognition, responsibility, advancement) fit more highly with a positive reaction. Indeed, when you think about it, it's very hard to respond in the affirmative to a question like 'Were your achievements a source of dissatisfaction?'. Motivator factors therefore tend to be perceived as sources of satisfaction rather than dissatisfaction (e.g. see Figure 4.2). In contrast, items classed as hygienes (e.g. working conditions, interpersonal relationships, status) are equally fitting for positive and negative responses and therefore are likely to be sources of either satisfaction or dissatisfaction. Accordingly, it can be argued that methodological bias, not a basic discontinuity of needs, could account for workers' tendency to associate motivator factors more strongly with satisfaction than hygiene factors.

Yet, beyond this, self-categorization theory also leads us to predict that the basic pattern of responses to motivator and hygiene factors should change as a function of a person's salient level of self-abstraction. Following the arguments presented above, we would expect that motivator factors would be the primary source of satisfaction when an individual's sense of self is defined in terms of personal identity.  For example, personal achievement and recognition are more important to someone who thinks of themselves as an individual because they are working solo on a project.  However, 'lower-level' needs (i.e. those typically associated with 'hygiene') should become more important as motivators when a person defines themselves in terms of social identity.  For example, good working relationships with colleagues may be very important to someone working in a team.   Here social relations and other features of the group environment should play a much greater role in work satisfaction, because in this context they are *a part of* the social self, not *set apart from* the personal self.

The basic truth of this assertion seems to be affirmed by people's experiences when they are acting as group members in organizations.  It is clear, for example, that trade union meetings are oriented more to the satisfaction of the economic and security-based needs of the group as a whole than to the personal goals of individuals.  Likewise, when members of the armed forces, the police force or sporting teams act in terms of a shared of social identity (e.g. as soldiers, strike-breakers or defenders) their behaviour is motivated by group goals as much as (or even to the exclusion of) personal ones.  In other words, what functions as a motivating factor depends on 'who you are' in any given context: someone who is going it alone or someone who is part of a team.

As a more formal test of this hypothesis, Haslam (1999b) conducted a study in which employees in a university psychology department were asked to respond to the six motivator and ten hygiene factors identified by Herzberg et al. (1959).  Half the participants had to indicate whether these factors were a source of work satisfaction, the other half whether they were a source of dissatisfaction.  As well as this, in a variation on the 'critical incidents' methodology used by Herzberg and his colleagues, half the participants were asked to think about times when they had worked alone and half thought about times when they had worked in a team.   It was expected that when participants thought about themselves as individuals their responses would be underpinned by a salient personal identity.  Responses in these conditions were thus expected to replicate those obtained by Herzberg, with motivator factors being associated primarily with work satisfaction and hygiene factors being associated with work dissatisfaction.  However, when participants thought of themselves as team members it was expected that responses would be underpinned by a salient social identity and hence that hygiene factors — to do with the character and functioning of the group — would also become a source of satisfaction.  As can be seen from the results presented in Figure 4.2, both predictions were supported.  Motivator factors were always associated more with satisfaction than with dissatisfaction, but only when people thought of themselves working alone were hygiene factors primarily associated with occupational dissatisfaction.  In contrast to the motivation–hygiene model, when employees thought about working in teams, hygiene factors were more a source of satisfaction than dissatisfaction.

The findings from this study lend weight to the argument that the role which hygiene factors play in determining work motivation is not a static or predetermined one as implied by Herzberg (e.g. 1968).  On the contrary, the status of factors as motivators appears to be an outcome of the self-categorization process.  So, while groups may play a background role in motivating workers in

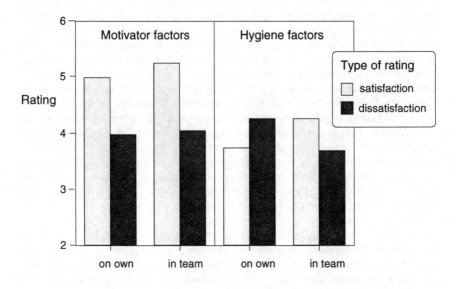

*Figure 4.2*   Ratings of satisfaction and dissatisfaction with motivator and hygiene factors as a function of working conditions (from Haslam, 1999b)

conditions where their personal identity is salient (as it typically is in organizational research into motivation), these factors should come to the fore when their behaviour is dictated by membership in a social group.   This argument is consistent with Murrell's (1976) observation that:

> Herzberg's ... motivators apply far more to management than they do to supervisors, and ... they apply even less to the shop floor.  Since it is on the shop floor that most of the action is, the idea that you can ignore the so-called 'hygiene' factors could be quite dangerous.  (p. 74)

This general analysis has two further important implications for the field of work motivation.   First, it allows the role of social cognitive processes in motivation to be reconceptualized.   In particular, the argument that the nature and content of motivation is underpinned by an act of social categorization allows us to predict when equity will be a source of social motivation and when it will not (as well as who individuals will compare themselves with in a given context; see Figure 2.8).   Along the lines of research by Platow and his colleagues (Bruins, Platow & Ng, 1995; Platow et al., 1997), we would broadly suggest that equity will play an important motivational role in contexts where individuals' personal identity is salient and they are involved in interpersonal exchanges.   In this regard it is worth noting that equity theory is explicitly founded upon a cosy assumption that group boundaries are permeable and that workers all embrace individual mobility beliefs — conditions generally associated with personal identity salience (see Vroom, 1964, 1969, p. 200; also Caddick, 1981; Tajfel, 1981a, p. 52).

But what happens when these conditions are not met — for example, when boundaries are impermeable and group status is insecure (e.g. during industrial conflict)? In intergroup contexts like these, where workers' *social identity* is likely to be salient, we would expect that the very same people who were previously motivated by equity principles will often strive for, and be motivated by the prospect of, ingroup favouring *in*equity. This point was demonstrated in the original minimal group studies and the research of Brown (1978; see Chapter 2 above). Caddick (1982) has also shown that a desire for ingroup favouring inequity increases in the minimal group paradigm when participants are illegitimately assigned to low-status groups. As well as this, related research has shown both that intergroup discrimination can be motivated by the need to enhance group-based self-esteem (Hogg & Sunderland, 1991) and that when individuals engage in such discrimination it does indeed achieve this end (Branscombe & Wann, 1994; Lemyre & Smith, 1985; Oakes & Turner, 1980; for a review see Long & Spears, 1997).

It also follows from these arguments that where shared social identity becomes psychologically meaningful for an individual it should be a powerful determinant of his or her motivation (James & Cropanzano, 1994; Ouwerkerk et al., 1999). As one very basic demonstration of this point, Haslam (1999b) conducted a study examining the willingness of students enrolled in an introductory statistics class to attend an additional lecture. The lecturer had previously discussed the importance of this lecture with students but it had been cancelled as part of ongoing industrial action. All participants in the study were given a questionnaire in which they were asked to indicate how willing they would be to come to the lecture and had to select from a list all the possible times that they would be able to attend (information needed by the lecturer in order to schedule the class). Importantly, however, half of the students were given a questionnaire which introduced the additional lecture as something the lecturer had told the students about himself ('As I told you the other day I need to schedule an additional lecture ...'), and for the remaining students the questionnaire introduced the lecture as something that the class as a whole had discussed ('As we discussed the other day we need to schedule an additional lecture ...'). As predicted, it was found that students were more willing to attend the lecture and listed more times that they could attend when attendance was framed in terms of an inclusive social category ('we'), than when it was framed in terms of a category exclusive to the lecturer 'I'). As well as placing it in some theoretical framework, this data is consistent with the spirit of Adair's (1983) 'short course on leadership' in which he asserts that the most important word in the leader's vocabulary is 'we' and that the least most important word is 'I'.

Along similar lines, self-categorization processes can be seen to play a crucial role in determining whether particular motivators are perceived to be either internal to the self and intrinsic or external to the self and extrinsic. Because the self is defined at different levels of abstraction, this means that a motivator that is perceived to be extrinsic when a person's personal identity is salient, may be redefined as intrinsic when they define themselves in terms of a more inclusive identity (e.g. in terms of team or organizational membership; Ashforth & Mael, 1989, p. 27). This point was recognized by Katz (1964b) when he observed:

The pattern of motivation associated with value expression and self-identification [with the organization as a whole] has great potentialities for the internalization of the goals of the subsystems and of the total system. ... Where this pattern prevails individuals take over organizational objectives as part of their own personal goals. (p. 142; see also Katz & Kahn, 1966, p. 346; Shamir, 1991; Thompson & McHugh, 1995, pp. 309-310)

The status of supervisor feedback provides an important illustration of this argument (see Hopkins, 1997). In contexts where the supervisor and supervisee are acting in terms of distinct social (or personal) identities (as will often be the case in intra-organizational contexts), the feedback of the supervisor may be associated with a non-self category and hence will have no role (or a negative one) in validating and motivating the behaviour of the worker. On the other hand, where the supervisor is instructed to take the perspective of the supervisee (or in any other context where their interaction is dictated by common social category membership), this should enhance the fit of a shared social identity in terms of which the supervisor's feedback will be seen as self-relevant and intrinsic. Accordingly, in such circumstances feedback should play a more positive motivational role. This analysis fits with data reported by Harackiewicz and her colleagues in an extensive programme of studies looking at the role that contextual factors play in mediating between supervisor feedback and the motivation and perceptions of the work supervisee (e.g. Harackiewicz & Larson, 1986; Harackiewicz, Manderlink & Sansone, 1984; for a review see Harackiewicz & Sansone, 1991; see also Ellemers, van Rijswijk, Bruins & de Gilder, 1998; discussed in Chapter 8 below). On this basis we can again assert that work *in general* is motivated in a manner consistent with neither Theory X nor Theory Y (nor by some hybrid set of motivations; e.g. as suggested by Ouchi's Theory Z, 1981; Ouchi & Jaeger, 1978). Instead Theory Y assumptions will tend to apply when supervisor and worker share the same social identity, but Theory X assumptions will tend to apply when they don't.

Moreover, this appreciation of the variable status of feedback leads to the second important implication of the social identity approach for the analysis of work motivation. It points to the role that *social influence* plays in this process. Evidence that group interaction has an important motivational influence in the workplace goes back to the Hawthorne studies that we discussed in Chapter 1. There members of the informal workteams provided verbal and occasionally physical feedback (in the form of 'binging') aimed at maintaining uniform output across group members. Thus under these circumstances, even if individuals had very high or very low *personal* need for achievement, social factors ultimately played a defining role in shaping and standardizing the motivations and behaviour of individual workers.

Of course in cases where workers are physically restrained from working harder, or where the threat of such intervention exists, it is easy to see why workers might forsake their personal motivations and comply with those of the group. Yet as Mayo (1949) made clear in his own research, such cases were the exception rather than the rule and most of the time seasoned workers sought and happily conformed to group norms (see also Salancik & Pfeffer, 1978; Tannenbaum, 1966, pp. 65-69; Zander, 1985, p. 6). Why? This question becomes even more intriguing in light of arguments that most people are driven by higher-order goals of self-actualization and personal growth (as suggested by

McGregor, Herzberg and others). One obvious answer is that factory workers are naturally sluggish and have low need for achievement (along lines suggested by McClelland, e.g. 1985; McClelland & Winter, 1969). Perhaps they come from that section of the community that Murrell (1976, p. 78; after Maslow) identifies as being permanently adolescent and unwilling to accept responsibility or take advantage of opportunities.

This argument certainly fits with views that many managers want to believe, along the lines of McGregor's Theory X. However, it is inconsistent with evidence that groups also bring under-performers (referred to as 'chiselers' at the Hawthorne plant) back into the fold, and that under certain circumstances extremely high levels of group performance are demanded and achieved (e.g. as part of a war effort or in concerted teamwork; Sewell, 1998; see Chapter 9 below). An alternative answer, consistent with the approach we outlined in Chapter 2, is that under conditions where workers come to define themselves in terms of a common social identity, they are motivated to identify and live up to shared group norms, because those norms — not the individual's idiosyncratic personal goals or values — are self-defining. Here, then, because the worker's sense of self — who they are — is defined by a *social* category, mutual social influence with others who are perceived to be interchangeable representatives of that category is an important means of self-validation and self-regulation. As Zander (1971) puts it:

> The fact that members have accepted one another's beliefs toward a common end causes each participant to accept the shared ideas of colleagues as a prime basis of truth. As a result of such events, a group's purpose tends to be approved by members, and each expects to act in accord with that purpose. Because all feel it is proper to accept the group's purpose, they give that objective common support. (p. 6)

Importantly though, this influence is confined to members of the relevant social self-category ('us') and does not extend across category boundaries (to 'them'). So workers do not have free-floating needs for relatedness, cohesiveness, solidarity, and respect (as needs theories tend to suggest). Instead these needs are associated with a *specific* group membership which is internalized and serves as a guide and motivator for behaviour in a *specific* working context. However, it is worth noting that despite the fact that social influence played such a pivotal role in determining workers' collaborative efforts at the Hawthorne plant and in other follow-up studies (Coch & French, 1948; Mayo, 1949; Roethlisberger & Dickson, 1939; Seashore, 1954), its impact on work motivation has been subjected to very little direct investigation since (see Salancik & Pfeffer, 1978). Moreover, in what can only be seen as a major oversight, consideration of the influence process is conspicuously absent from almost all contemporary theorizing in this area. As Moreland, Argote and Krishnan (1996) lament, 'what's so surprising is not that such collaboration occurs, but that so few psychologists (who claim social influence as their area) acknowledge or investigate it' (p. 84).

## Some empirical tests of the social identity approach

*Need for achievement as a socially mediated outcome*

The above analysis argues strongly that the social dimensions of motivation are a product of the group's definition in context. So, for example, a person locked into membership of a low-status group is more likely to be motivated by 'lower-level' needs and interests associated with that group membership than someone who believes it is possible to leave such a group. Consistent with this argument, a large body of work from a social identity perspective has shown that factors of organizational stratification, perceived permeability and legitimacy all serve to influence both a person's awareness of their identity as a group member and their identification with the group (Ellemers, van Knippenberg, De Vries & Wilke, 1988; Ellemers, van Knippenberg & Wilke, 1990; Ellemers, Wilke & van Knippenberg, 1993; Lalonde & Silverman, 1994; Taylor, Moghaddam, Gamble & Zellerer, 1987; Turner & Brown, 1978). Illustrative of such work, Ellemers et al. (1993) found that members of low-status minimal groups were more likely to identify with that group when they believed it was impossible to leave it. Moreover, identification with the group and a concern to achieve group-based goals was heightened for members of *all* low-status groups (permeable and impermeable alike) when the group's status was unstable and its members thought there was an opportunity to improve its fortunes collectively.

An important corollary to these arguments is that these same factors should also impact upon an individual's higher-order needs. In other words, to the extent that individuals set about collectively pursuing group goals, they should display correspondingly less interest in their own individual advancement. So, as suggested by Sorrentino (1973; Sorrentino & Field, 1986), personal need for achievement (like social need for achievement) could be the *outcome of a social process* rather than a hard-wired individual difference. In the words of Crockett (1966, p. 201): 'it can be argued ... that the experience of upward mobility may produce an increase in the strength of the achievement motive' (see also Crockett, 1964; Hyman, 1953).

Indeed, armed with this analysis, most of the evidence put forward by individual difference theorists can be reinterpreted in a manner that supports predictions derived from the social identity approach (Parker, 1997). The fact that in Andrews's research, workers at Firm A had higher levels of need for achievement than those at Firm B can thus be seen to be a *product* of the fact that Firm A was experiencing greater growth and was therefore in a position to offer its workers greater prospects for promotion and pay rises (see McClelland & Winter, 1969, p. 12). In other words, in this company the boundaries between groups of different status were highly permeable, making personal identity-based advancement a much more realistic prospect. Similarly, it is apparent from descriptions of the Ibo and Hausa, that differences in need for achievement between the members of these tribes could be attributed to cultural differences (McClelland & Winter, 1969, pp. 8-9). Specifically, the Ibo were far more Westernized and had largely abandoned the rigid intra-tribal stratification which represented an obstacle to individual progress. Accordingly, for them a strategy for advancement based on their personal identity made much more sense.

Clearly though, this re-analysis is inconclusive and merely indicates that it is possible to put a very different spin on research that has been used to sustain an individual difference approach. Indeed, because most of the data relating to need for achievement is correlational, the causal role of both personality and social structural factors is impossible to establish from studies of this form (a point acknowledged by Crockett, 1966, p. 201; see also Pfeffer, 1998, p. 740). In order to provide a more telling test of the above arguments, Parker (1997) conducted an experimental study which investigated the impact of two theoretically important social structural variables (group status and boundary permeability) on individuals' need for achievement.

The participants in the research were school leavers who were all shown a video presenting information about the graduate training programme supposedly being run by a fictional organization ('Delta Micro-Systems'). They were also presented with a diagram which represented the three-tier structure of this company: Level A (high status), Level B (intermediate status) and Level C (low status). The students were told that they would be randomly assigned to one of the three levels because the management did not have enough time to assign them to these levels systematically. As well as this, half the students were presented with a video in which the company was described as forward-looking, flexible and fair so that 'if you have been placed at a lower level in the company it will only take a little hard work and perseverance to gain entrance to the higher more demanding and responsible positions'. However, the remainder of the students were told that Delta Micro-Systems was old-fashioned, contemptuous of its employees and set in its ways. As a result, these school leavers could not expect 'to move or advance at all in the company' and had to be prepared to stay at the level they were assigned.

After being given this information all the students completed a questionnaire. This measured their identification with the group to which they had been assigned, their level of ingroup favouritism (using matrices similar to those in Tajfel et al., 1971), and their need for achievement (based on relevant items from the Manifest Needs Questionnaire developed by Steers & Braunstein, 1976). Results from the first measures indicated that all participants identified with their assigned identity and that they tended to favour groups to the extent that they had high status. This finding is consistent with arguments that ingroup favouritism is not a universal cognitive bias, but a response to perceived social structure (Mummendey & Simon, 1989; Reynolds et al., 2000; Skevington, 1980; Tajfel & Turner, 1979). Yet most importantly for the present discussion, results on the need for achievement measure indicated that this too was dramatically affected by these same structural factors. These results are presented in Figure 4.3.

From this figure it is clear that students had significantly greater need for achievement to the extent that they were assigned to a high-status group and group boundaries were permeable. Indeed, while most students actually showed quite high levels of need for achievement, those assigned to the fixed low-status group exhibited need for achievement below the scale midpoint and more than two scale-points lower on a 7-point scale than the group with the highest need for achievement. Yet the process of randomly assigning participants to experimental groups ensures that students in this fixed low-status group did not have inherently different personal needs to those assigned to other groups.

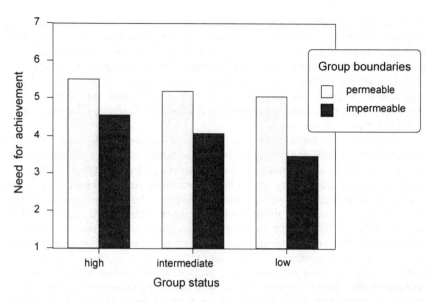

*Figure 4.3* Group members' need for achievement as a function of group status and the permeability of group boundaries (from Parker, 1997)

Accordingly, we can only conclude that the divergent needs displayed by the various groups in this study were an emergent product of the particular social environment they confronted. Parker's study therefore provides strong support for the proposition that individual differences in need for achievement are in substantial part the *outcome* of a general social psychological process of the form envisaged by social identity and self-categorization theorists (e.g. see Turner & Onorato, 1999). These emergent differences will obviously have an ongoing and dynamic impact on people's work motivation, but for theoretical and practical purposes it is important to recognize that their origins lie as much (if not substantially more) in social and organizational structure as in the individual's unique psychological make-up.

### Social identification as a basis for organizational commitment and citizenship

When Ashforth and Mael (1989) first outlined the possible applications of social identity theory to organizational settings, their discussion focused on the role of *organizational identification* — 'a specific form of social identification' associated with definition of the self in terms of the organization as a whole (Ashforth & Mael, 1989, p. 22). In particular, this was because they noted the correspondence (and confusion) between this construct and that of *organizational commitment* — commitment to the goals and values of the organization as a whole and a willingness to exert effort on its behalf (see also Dutton et al., 1994, p. 242; Mowday, Steers & Porter, 1979; Salancik, 1977). Organizational commitment occupies an important place in the research literature because it has been shown to be a very good predictor of a range of important behaviours, including employee turnover, employees' adherence to organizational values and their willingness to perform extra-role duties (i.e. to do more than is formally asked of them). However, Ashforth and Mael argued that identification may also be a useful construct in this regard, because it relies upon *internalization* of the organization's goals, whereas some forms of commitment can simply reflect attraction to the *resources* the organization offers (O'Reilly & Chatman, 1986; Tyler, 1999a).

Consistent with these claims, a number of studies have shown that the concepts of organizational commitment and organizational identification can be empirically distinguished (Mael & Ashforth, 1992; Mael & Tetrick, 1992). As suggested by social identity and self-categorization theories, research has also shown that organizational identification is likely to be increased to the extent that the ingroup is positively distinct from other groups. For example, Mael and Ashforth (1992) found that alumni of a religious college were more likely to identify with that college to the extent that they perceived it to be prestigious and to expound a distinct educational and religious philosophy. Moreover, this identification was also an important predictor of those alumni's behaviour in relation to their former college. Those who identified more strongly were more willing to contribute funds to the college, to send their children there, and to attend college functions.

As a slight variant on this position, van Knippenberg and van Schie (in press) note that for a range of reasons employees' primary identification will often not be with the organization as a whole but with their specific work-group or team (see also Barker & Tomkins, 1994; Brewer, 1995; Kramer, 1993; Lembke & Wilson, 1998). Indeed, this prediction follows from the principles of (a) comparative fit and (b) positive distinctiveness that we discussed in Chapter 2 (Brewer, 1991; Deschamps & Brown, 1983; Tajfel & Turner, 1979; Turner, 1985). These principles suggest that social identities are likely to become salient at a level below that of the organizational category as a whole (e.g. at a departmental, divisional or work-team level) because in an intra-organizational context (a) people should be more likely to make comparisons between different work groups than between different organizations and (b) sub-organizational identities allow employees to feel that their ingroup is in some way 'special' and distinct from others. Consistent with these assertions, van Knippenberg and van Schie (in press) found that in two organizational samples (local government workers and university employees) individuals' identification with their immediate work-group was higher than with the organization as a whole. As well as this, identification with this lower-level self-category was a much better predictor of a range of key work-related variables, including job satisfaction, job involvement, and intention to continue working for the organization. Moreover, work-group identification was also a better predictor of work motivation and job involvement (as measured by items like 'I am always prepared to do my best'). Similar patterns have also been predicted and observed by a number of other researchers who note that workers are often committed to different organizational *constituencies* rather than to an organization as a whole (Becker, 1992; Becker & Billings, 1993; Hunt & Morgan, 1994; Reichers, 1986; see Ouwerkerk et al., 1999).

But, as van Knippenberg and van Schie (in press, p. 12) note, these findings do not imply that work-group identification will *always* be a better predictor of organizational behaviour than identification with the organization as a whole. The principle of comparative fit would lead one to predict, for example, that the importance of organizational identification as a predictor of behaviour would increase to the extent that people make inter-organizational comparisons — as they might be more inclined to do in multi-organizational comparative contexts. Indeed, an extended frame of reference of this form was very likely to have been salient for the college alumni studied by Mael and Ashforth (1982).

The contribution of different forms of social identification to organizational behaviour has also been examined in an extensive programme of experimental research conducted by Ouwerkerk and his colleagues (1999). Based on work by Ellemers, Kortekaas and Ouwerkerk (1999), and consistent with claims made by Ashforth and Mael (1989; Mael & Tetrick, 1992) and Tajfel and Turner (1979), these researchers distinguish between two components of social identification and argue that these may have distinct implications for organizational behaviour. The *cognitive/perceptual* aspects correspond closely to the concept of organizational identification as defined by Ashforth and Mael (1989). Ouwerkerk et al. (1999) propose that these can be distinguished conceptually from the emotional or *affective* aspects of social identification, which are more consistent with the notion of organizational commitment. They argue that these aspects are particularly likely to come to the fore when a group is under threat — for example, as a consequence of intergroup competition or an overt challenge to its status.

Moreover, Ouwerkerk et al. (1999) argue that this team-oriented affective commitment can be usefully differentiated from an individual's commitment to his or her *personal* goals (referred to as *career commitment*). This claim was supported in two large studies conducted by Ellemers, de Gilder and van den Heuvel (1998). In both of these studies affective commitment to the work-group emerged as a much better predictor of a person's willingness to engage in extra-role helping behaviour and so-called *organizational citizenship behaviour* (Organ, 1988, 1990, 1997; a core component of *contextual performance*; Borman & Motowidlo, 1997; see Figure 4.4 below) than career commitment. In the first study these patterns were also supported by reports of actual behaviour in a one-year follow-up questionnaire, and in the second study they were supported by supervisors' independent ratings of employee performance. However, in both studies career commitment was a much better predictor of behaviours that fostered individual mobility (e.g. willingness to attend training courses) than commitment to the team.

In line with the arguments presented earlier in this chapter, it thus appears that when people's work behaviour is determined by a salient personal identity they are likely to engage in activities that advance their personal status (e.g. to obtain additional qualifications). On the other hand, when they act in terms of a salient social identity they are likely to work hard to promote the interests of the group with which that identity is associated (e.g. by helping out new employees and performing other 'thankless' tasks). As Lembke and Wilson (1998, p. 931) argue 'teamwork needs to be motivated by more than individualistic (personal) benefits and is intimately linked to the social identity of the team' (see also Dutton et al., 1994; Haslam, Powell et al., 2000; van Knippenberg, 2000).

To the extent that organizational researchers are interested in predicting and encouraging collective forms of behaviour (as they often are), they may therefore need to focus less on motivation associated with personal identity (e.g. need for achievement) and more on motivation rooted in social identification. This approach appears to be justified further by evidence that the utility of individual-based motivators is likely to be confined to relatively weak interpersonal situations (see Kanfer, 1994, p. 11; Weiss & Adler, 1984) and of little help in predicting who will get going when the going gets tough (e.g. in intergroup settings; Ouwerkerk et al., 1999).

### The importance of identity-based pride and respect

The work discussed so far all suggests that social identification will play a key motivational role in relation to a range of important organizational behaviours. Three that are particularly important are *compliance* (a willingness to conform to group norms and follow rules), *extra-role pro-organizational behaviour* (helping out beyond the call of duty) and *loyalty*. In an effort to explore the social psychological underpinnings of these three behaviours in more detail, Tyler and his colleagues (Smith & Tyler, 1997; Tyler, 1999a, 1999b; Tyler, Degoey & Smith, 1996) have conducted a major programme of research that explicitly compares accounts of their origins put forward by social identity and social exchange theories.

In his review of the field, Tyler (1999a) points to the sheer impracticality of seeking to obtain positive organizational outcomes through an approach based on principles of social exchange. As one example, he raises the case of a company attempting to retain an employee who has received a better job offer from another firm. Dealing with this by matching the offer may succeed in retaining the employee, but it is a costly and demanding process. Moreover, it may create more problems than it resolves, because domino-like it creates new inequities for other members of the organization. How are these to be dealt with? An additional problem is that the concern with social exchange may itself communicate to employees that the work they are engaged in only has extrinsic worth and is not something to be engaged in for its own intrinsic sake. As we saw earlier, this may have a further de-motivating impact (Harackiewicz & Sansone, 1991; Lepper et al., 1973). As well as this, managers' beliefs that they can (and must) deal with staff through systems of rewards and punishment can lead to an 'ideology of control', rather like that envisaged under McGregor's Theory X (Pfeffer, 1997; Tyler & Blader, in press). The basic problem with an exchange-based strategy, then, is that it leads to a downward spiral of 'What's in it for me?' behaviour, which works against the 'What's in it for us?' perspective of the organization.

Along the lines of the arguments put forward earlier in this chapter, Tyler (1998, 1999a, Tyler & Blader, in press) argues that the rational alternative to this approach is one where the individual *internalizes* the values and goals of the organization by defining them as part of self. Indeed, this process would seem to play a major role in the success of goal-setting strategies which allow goals to become *self-involving* (Locke, 1968; see also Brown & Leigh, 1996; Nicholls, 1984). As Wegge (in press) has shown, goal setting is also likely to be particularly effective where group members' *participation* in the goal setting process makes social identity salient and thereby encourages individuals to define a group's goal as relevant to their sense of collective self. Here 'after values are internalized people want to follow rules and live up to values, even when they are not being monitored and reward or punishment are unlikely' (Tyler & Blader, in press, p. 19).

In order to test this hypothesis, Tyler (1999a) conducted a multi-national study of nearly 650 employees. As predicted, internalized values were a significant predictor of the three types of co-operative organizational behaviour identified above (rule-following, extra-role activities, loyalty). More strikingly, variance in internalized values accounted for about 14 per cent of the variance in these behaviours, but only about 3 per cent was associated with variance in the perceived utility of outcomes associated with organizational membership.

Extending this analysis, Tyler (1999a, 1999b) has gone on to investigate how organizational *pride* and *respect* contribute to pro-organizational behaviour. Pride reflects an individual's positive feelings about their group and respect is associated with the group's positive feelings about the individual. Pride is therefore derived from the relative status (and state) of an organization as a whole, while respect derives from the status of an individual within it (i.e. his or her prototypicality in relation to that social category).

Again Tyler argues that these two status-based constructs achieve their impact by enhancing social identification with the organization rather than the conditions of social exchange. This argument is supported by the findings of two studies, one using the same sample as the above study and the second an additional 409 workers from Chicago (for further support see Smith & Tyler, 1997). Here workers' perceptions of outcome utility (i.e. their judgements of whether work afforded them appreciable benefits), accounted on average for less than 1 per cent of variance employees' in organizational rule following, helping behaviour and loyalty over-and-above that of their organizationally based sense of respect and pride. On the other hand, respect and pride accounted on average for about 18 per cent of the variance over-and-above that associated with outcome utility. On this basis Tyler (1999a) concludes:

> To some extent, people are more likely to act on behalf of organizations which provide them with desired resources. However, these resource-based influences are small in magnitude when compared to the influence of status-based judgements of pride and respect. (p. 208)

As an interesting but important nuance to these findings, another pattern also emerges consistently from the research of Tyler and his colleagues. This indicates that individuals' sense of pride is linked more strongly to organizational rule-following while respect is associated more with a tendency to engage in extra-role helping behaviour. As Tyler points out, this finding fits perfectly with the social identity approach, since pride derives from the high status of the organization as a whole which individuals are motivated to preserve *collectively* through adherence to *shared* norms and rules. Respect, however, is conferred on certain individuals within the organization, and gives them license to act creatively — as trusted members of the group — to pursue group interests.

In this regard, pride and respect correspond closely to the interrelated concepts of followership and leadership that we discussed in the previous chapter. Pride in the group as a whole motivates group members to act in a uniform manner as followers, while prototypicality-based respect empowers individuals to act in a leadership role on behalf of the group. Importantly too, both appear to be aspects of a shared sense of self rather than to derive from a crude exchange of resources.

## Conclusion

This chapter has covered a lot of ground. Yet despite the plethora of seemingly distinct theoretical approaches to motivation, a unity of process can be detected within them all. At heart, this unity arises from the fact that the nature of work motivation is bound up with workers' sense of who they are. Figure 4.4 attempts to summarize this argument and draws on a number of research programmes informed by social identity theory (e.g. those of Dutton et al., 1994; Ouwerkerk et al., 1999; Tyler, 1999a; van Knippenberg and van Schie, in press).

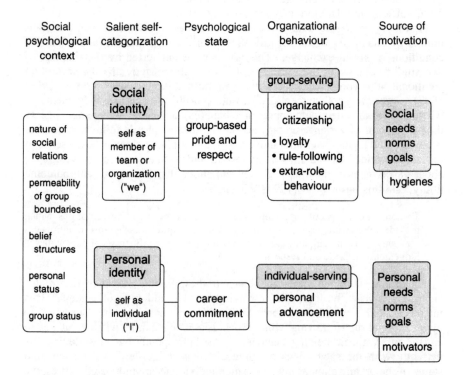

*Figure 4.4* Two dimensions of motivation: A schematic representation of the relationship between level of self-categorization, organizational behaviour and different classes of motivator

*PART of GROUP Different Levels of Abstraction* [handwritten annotation]

From this figure, and from the considerable body of research which speaks to this point, it can be seen that where the self is defined in terms of personal identity, individuals are motivated to enhance themselves as individuals. This can typically be detected in measures of need for achievement and career commitment and manifests itself through, amongst other things, a desire for personal self-actualization, personal growth and the acquisition of personal skills and resources.

But this is only part of the story. A great deal of organizational behaviour is actually structured not by personal identity but by a sense of shared group membership and a salient social identity. This can be defined at different levels of abstraction and reflects the impact of a range of variables that combine to define workers' psychological and social structural environment. These include the status of their work-team and organization, the permeability of group and organizational boundaries, the salient dimensions of social comparison and the comparative frame of reference. When these serve to make an individual's social identity salient, he or she will be motivated less by purely personal gain and more by the prospect of contributing to group goals and thereby achieving *collective* self-actualization. Here the worker displays greater sensitivity to the quality of social relations, is more responsive to the views of other ingroup members and conforms more to group norms. Importantly too, where this form of motivation has traditionally been seen as inferior or second-rate, it is actually uniquely associated with a range of potentially positive organizational behaviours including rule-following, helping behaviour, and loyalty. Under conditions of social identity salience workers are also more likely to provide, receive, and benefit from social support (Schmidt & Haslam, 1999; Terry, Neilsen & Perchard, 1993).

Exactly how positive the products of social motivation are perceived to be will depend on the goals and interests of the group with which the individual identifies. Certainly, the fact that employees often identify with groups that do not share the interests and perspective of management (and hence may be motivated to reach goals of *under*-performance; see Chapter 9 below) is one reason why the motivational influence of groups has often been maligned in the past. Yet from the arguments presented in this chapter we can see that researchers are doing the field of motivation a disservice to the extent that they overlook its social dimensions. In part this is because such oversight neglects aspects of motivation that make a large (and in many instances the largest) contribution to what people seek to achieve through work. More importantly, by focusing only on the personal dimensions of this topic, the field as a whole loses the opportunity to integrate the wealth of existing knowledge within a unified theoretical understanding of the motivation process.

## Further Reading

Early research into work motivation by Maslow, Herzberg, McGregor and others makes fascinating reading for psychologists and non-psychologists alike. In this regard, the volume by Vroom and Deci (1970) is an excellent sourcebook that contains chapters by a range of influential theorists. The reviews by Harackiewicz and Sansone (1991) and Kanfer (1994) provide comprehensive and detailed coverage of more recent progress in this field. For additional insights into the role of social identification in organizational behaviour and motivation it is also well worth reading the review papers by Ouwerkerk et al. (1999), Tyler (1999a) and van Knippenberg (2000).

Harackiewicz, J. & Sansone, C. (1991). Goals and intrinsic motivation: You can get there from here. *Advances in Motivation and Achievement, 7,* 21-49.

Kanfer, R. (1994). Work motivation: New directions in theory and research. In C. L. Cooper & I. T. Robertson (Eds.), *Key reviews in managerial psychology* (pp. 1-53). New York: Wiley.

Ouwerkerk, J. W., Ellemers, N. & de Gilder, D. (1999). Social identification, affective commitment and individual effort on behalf of the group. In N. Ellemers, R. Spears & B. J. Doosje (Eds), *Social identity: Context, commitment, content.* Oxford: Blackwell.

Tyler, T. R. (1999a). Why people co-operate with organizations: An identity-based perspective. In B. M. Staw & R. Sutton (Eds.), *Research in organizational behaviour* (vol. 21, pp. 201-246). Greenwich, CT: JAI Press.

van Knippenberg, D. (2000). Work motivation and performance: A social identity perspective. *Applied Psychology: An International Review, 49,* 357-371.

Vroom, V. H. & Deci, E. L. (1970). *Management and motivation.* Harmondsworth: Penguin.

# 5 Communication and Information Management

If you asked a sample of managers the question 'What did you do at work today?', the answers you are likely to receive would probably indicate that most spent the greater proportion of their time engaging in some form of communication. Phoning clients, e-mailing colleagues, discussing projects with team members, faxing customers, advising employees, chatting with friends — this is the stuff of day-to-day organizational life. Accordingly, estimates suggest that around three-quarters of managers' time is taken up with various acts of communication (Klemmer & Snyder, 1972; Mintzberg, 1973). Indeed, having completed a series of detailed observational studies in a relatively technical research laboratory, Klemmer and Snyder were able to sum up their findings in one sentence:

> The conclusion of all studies is that communication with people, not equipment, is the principal focus of activity for the professional [person] as well as the administrator, clerk, secretary and technician. (1972, p. 157)

Moreover, the significance of this topic is revealed by the fact that communication is integral to each of the various content areas addressed in the chapters of this book. Without communication there could be no leadership, no motivation, no decision-making, no negotiation, no power. There could be no productivity or collective action either, because in the absence of communication people would have no notion of *what* to produce and do, or of *why* they should. For this reason, when we come across organizational failure in any of these areas, it is common to perceive communication problems to lie at its root. Thus poor leadership, low motivation, faulty negotiation and under-performance are often seen to result from a 'failure to get a message across' or from a general paucity of information. 'No-one knew what was going on', 'Our wires were crossed', 'I'm not sure we're speaking the same language', 'Why wasn't I told?' — these are common complaints of exasperated employers and employees alike.

Yet precisely because it relates to so many different activities and takes so many different forms, communication itself is not an easy concept to define (Krauss & Fussell, 1996). Testament to this, in surveying the different definitions put forward by researchers, Dance (1970; see also Putnam, Phillips & Chapman, 1996) identified fifteen discrete meanings of the term. These range from those which define communication as activity pertaining to any form of interaction to those which see it as the means by which any discontinuous parts of the living world are united. Broadly speaking, however, most researchers agree that communication is characterized by (a) the transfer of information from one party to another, and (b) the transfer of meaning (e.g. Katz & Kahn, 1966, p. 223; Roberts, O'Reilly, Bretton & Porter, 1974, p. 501).

The significance of the distinction between information and meaning arises from the fact that the transfer of information alone does not ensure effective communication. For example, if by making the statement 'The mail has arrived' a person intends that the person to whom they are speaking should come and pick up a parcel, it is clear that the potential exists for this to be misunderstood as implying something else (perhaps that the speaker is very busy, or that a long-standing industrial dispute has been resolved; Grice, 1975; Semin, 1997). In order to be effective and useful, the recipient must therefore imbue the message with the same significance and purpose as is intended by its source.

Essentially, then, communication is the process of sharing information within a shared interpretative framework that allows that information to be meaningful and useful (see Krauss & Fussell, 1996). But how does this occur and what makes it possible? The broad goal of this chapter is to attempt to answer these questions and explain how social and psychological factors combine in different ways to render organizational communication both effective and ineffective. Following from the above points, it looks at the factors which dictate (a) whether information is shared, and (b) whether that sharing is conducive to the emergence of shared meaning.

In doing this, the chapter moves towards an integrated analysis of the nature of information and meaning that sheds light on a number of long-standing conundrums in the field — in particular, the question of how communication of the same message between the same parties can have very different impact as a function of apparently subtle changes in social psychological context. The argument we put forward suggests that the key to resolving such issues lies in an appreciation of the way in which subjectively apprehended features of any communicative context are able to redefine the *self-categorical relationship* between participants in the communication process, and hence to change their psychological orientation towards each other. Communication is viewed both as a determinant and as a product of this categorical relationship (O'Reilly, Chatman & Anderson, 1987; Roberts et al., 1974) and this role as *both cause and effect* underlines its status as a core organizational activity and as a pivotal feature of organizational dynamics.

## An overview of communication research

### The structural approach

In an influential review of research into organizational communication, Roberts et al. (1974) identify a number of approaches that correspond closely to those which we discussed in Chapter 1. We saw in that chapter that Taylor's economic approach suggested that management functions in organizations should be concentrated in the hands of managers and hence that they should be the source of most organizational communication. Within this scheme it was recommended that information flow downwards through an organization from those qualified to instruct to those destined to be instructed. Thus:

> Almost every act of the workman should be preceded by one or more preparatory acts of management which enable him to do his work better and quicker than he otherwise could. And each man should daily be taught by and receive the most

friendly help from those who are over him. (Taylor, 1911, p. 26; see also pp. 37-39, 44-46)

The approach that has most clearly built upon this line of thinking is a *structural* (or mechanistic) one. Work in this tradition attempts to discover 'the one best way' in which communication networks and channels might be arranged in order to optimize organizational outcomes. Yet researchers who adopt this approach have tended to discover that there are *many different ways* in which information can flow effectively through an organization (Bavelas & Barrett, 1951). Accordingly, they have redefined their task as being to identify which of these are *most* appropriate for different situations. Typical research involves arranging research participants in different communicative configurations (like those presented in Figure 5.1) and then examining how these affect the flow of information, the accuracy with which it is transmitted, and the extent to which it facilitates group performance. The result is a contingency solution (like those favoured in much leadership research; e.g. Fiedler, 1964; see Chapter 3 above), that matches particular forms of communication network to particular group outcomes.

Illustrative of such work, Smith (1956; cited in Bavelas, 1956, pp. 499-501) presented each member of a five-person group with a card on which there were six different symbols. As a group their task was to identify which of these symbols appeared on every member's card on the basis of written messages that could only be passed through slots in a cubicle wall to particular group members. In this way the experimenter controlled exactly who each person was able to communicate with. Smith found that when the communication

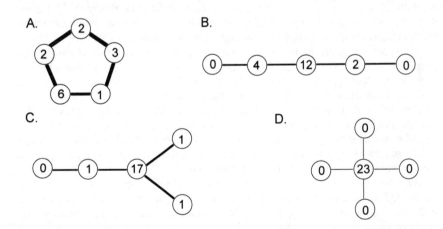

*Figure 5.1* Some communication configurations for five-person groups (following Bavelas, 1956, p. 501)

*Note*: The numbers in the circles indicate the number of times that a person in that position was seen to be fulfilling the role of leader; the thicker the line between circles the higher the overall level of group member satisfaction (based on data reported by Leavitt, 1949; cited in Bavelas, 1960). The leader role is more distributed and satisfaction is higher the more decentralized the structure.

configuration was linear (e.g. configuration B in Figure 5.1) rather than circular (configuration A), solutions were arrived at with fewer errors and that the group could adapt to meet particular task demands more quickly. In the interests of efficiency, decentralized communicative networks (like that in configuration A) were therefore not recommended for simple tasks of this nature.

However, this and other research suggested that participants were generally more satisfied with decentralized communicative arrangements (e.g. configuration A rather than B, C or D) and with the group's performance under these circumstances (e.g. Bavelas & Barrett, 1951). One reason for this is that in centralized networks leadership roles tend to be concentrated in the hands of the person who occupies one particular position, while decentralized networks encourage distributed leadership (see Figure 5.1). Research also suggests that, partly for this reason, decentralized arrangements may lead to more effective communication on complex tasks (Burgess, 1969; Shaw, 1964, 1978; Stohl & Redding, 1987).

## The human relations approach

As Bavelas & Barrett (1951) and Leavitt (1972) observed, a major problem with work that seeks to identify and prescribe the 'one best way' of communicating is that organizational communication is rarely an end in itself. Moreover, even if it is seen as such, it is not clear on what dimensions the *quality* of communication should be judged. In particular, because communication is necessarily a collaborative process, there are clearly problems with an approach that judges the efficacy of communication simply in terms of information transfer. When we greet colleagues on a Monday morning with the question 'Did you have a good weekend?', the answer we receive may be incidental to our ability to do a good day's work, but few people would suggest that organizations would function more effectively if these routine pleasantries were avoided.

Thus, reflecting on the results of the above studies, we can ask which is to be preferred — a network that generates few errors but which is associated with low morale (e.g. configuration D) or a network with high morale but more errors (e.g. configuration A)? This is a dilemma that we are all aware of in the workplace — managers with very direct and controlling communicative styles may succeed in achieving relatively well-defined organizational objectives (e.g. to make sure that everyone is aware of a new management policy), but as a result fail to secure other less well-defined, but nonetheless crucial, outcomes (e.g. to ensure that the new policy is willingly followed).

Sensitive to this issue, most of those researchers whose work might have been used to further the goals of scientific management, actually rejected this path in favour of an approach that championed the social functions and requirements of communication. Indeed, the study of communication is probably the area of organizational studies in which the human relations approach has had the most impact, precisely because the social dimensions of this phenomenon prove hard to deny. Much of this impact followed directly from Mayo's own conviction that many of the organizational problems he identified in his own research at the Hawthorne plant and elsewhere flowed directly from poor communication. He thus argued that:

Failure of free communication between management and workers in modern large-scale industry leads inevitably to the exercise of caution by the working group until such time as it knows clearly the range and meaning of changes imposed from above. (Mayo, 1949, pp. 70-71; see also pp. 89-90).

Indeed, generalizing beyond research contexts, Mayo (1949) argued that lack of communication 'is beyond reasonable doubt the outstanding deficit that civilization is facing today' (pp. 20-21).

Within the human relations framework, a core argument of researchers was that the social aspects of communication must be attended to in order for communication within organizations to be useful or even to be said to have occurred. Along these lines, Leavitt (1972) argued that effective communication was much more a two-way than a one-way process of the form envisaged by Taylor (1911). Moreover, his own research showed that when individuals approached a communicative task as if it were a two-way rather than a one-way exercise, the nature of their communication changed dramatically:

The [one-way] system is like a phonograph record. Once it starts it must be played through. Hence it must be planned very carefully. Two-way communication is a very different strategy, a kind of 'local' strategy in which the sender starts down one path, goes a little way and then discovers he is on the wrong track, makes a turn, discovers he is off a little again, makes another turn and so on. He doesn't need to plan so much as he needs to listen, and be sensitive to the feedback he is getting. ... Two-way communication makes for more valid communication, and it appears now that more valid communication results not only in more accurate transmission of facts but also in *re-organized perceptions of relationships*. (Leavitt, 1972, pp. 120-121; emphasis added)

As these statements suggest, the central message of the human relations approach was that effective organizational communication was characterized by the flow of information *both* downwards and upwards through an organization and that, where this occurred, such communication was fundamentally different to one-way downward communication and led to fundamentally different outcomes. In effect, this difference mirrors that between Theory X and Theory Y, between control and mutual participation, between dictatorship and democracy (McGregor, 1960).

Although this approach gained widespread currency in the organizational field, it had two core problems. The first was that, like advocates of the structural approach, human relations researchers tended to assume that the features of communication networks were internal to the organization and immune to external influences (e.g. the gender or class of employees).

In order to address this problem, one significant development of human relations work was *open systems theory* (also known as *natural systems theory* or just *systems theory*; Katz & Kahn, 1966) This was based on the argument that:

Communication needs to be seen not as a process occurring between any sender of messages and any potential recipient, but in relation to the system in which it occurs and the particular function it performs in that system. (Katz & Kahn, 1966, p. 225)

Open systems theory also challenged the view that communication is achieved through the free and frequent transfer of information within an organization, suggesting that this is in fact a recipe for Babel-like pandemonium. Instead, Katz and Kahn (1966, p. 227) suggest that the key to understanding communication is to appreciate how information-processing is constrained and shaped by 'coding categories' that serve as boundaries between different sub-systems within the organization. These system-based categories, they argue, operate like stereotypes to 'impose omission, selection, refinement, elaboration, distortion, and transformation upon the incoming information' (p. 227). In this way:

> All members of an organization are affected by the fact that they occupy a common organizational space in contrast to those who are not members. By passing the boundary and becoming a functioning member of the organization, the person takes on some of the coding system of the organization, since he accepts some of its norms and values, absorbs some of its subculture, and develops shared expectations and values with other members. The boundary condition is thus responsible for the dilemma that the person within the system cannot perceive things and communicate about them in the same way that an outsider would. (Katz & Kahn, 1966, p. 228)

Yet although these theoretical developments provided important new insights into the on-the-ground complexities of organizational communication (and organizational functioning in general), open systems theory still shared a second problem with earlier structural work — namely, that it did not lend itself to concrete empirical advance and offered no detailed insights into psychological process. Roberts et al. (1974) thus bemoaned the fact that Katz and Kahn's theory 'is constructed at such an abstract level that it is difficult to reduce its principles to testable hypotheses' (p. 511). As we argued in Chapter 1, what human relations approaches offer in critical insight they tend to lack in theoretical specificity.

### The cognitive approach

In pointing to some of the links between the communication process and processes of categorization and stereotyping, one of the significant legacies of Katz and Kahn's work was to lead researchers to focus on the way in which the normal cognitive activities of communicators open the door to communication error and misunderstanding (see also Campbell, 1958). In particular, this was because, as we have seen, open systems theory argues that subsystems within an organization help to reduce 'information overload' but in the process also perturb and distort communication in various ways (Katz & Kahn, 1966, pp. 231, 257). Following Miller (1960), Katz and Kahn argued that the maladaptive consequences of this overload for organizations included: (a) *omission* of key information; (b) *error* in information transmission; (c) *delay* in transmission; (d) *filtering* of information; (e) *simplification* of messages; (f) use of *multiple communication channels*; or, most drastically (g) *escape* through communication avoidance.

This analysis provided researchers with ample scope for experimentation and examination of psychological process. Indeed, in this regard, developments in the communication literature closely parallel those in the mainstream social psychological literature on stereotyping in which the idea of the information processor as 'cognitive miser' held sway through much of the 1970s and 1980s (Fiske & Taylor, 1984; Oakes et al., 1994; see Chapter 1 above). In both fields of enquiry researchers have been concerned to identify cognitive biases associated with people's membership in groups and their segmentation of the world along group-based lines. These biases are assumed to save information-processing energy but to introduce certain forms of error as an unavoidable and unfortunate by-product (see Oakes & Turner, 1990; Spears & Haslam, 1997).

One commonly cited illustration of such bias is provided by Snyder's (1981a, 1981b) work into confirmatory hypothesis-testing. In this, participants are typically given information, or asked to test a hypothesis, about a target person with whom they believe they are going to interact. For example, as part of a personality assessment exercise they might be set the task of finding out whether someone is introverted (Snyder & Swann, 1978). In studies of this form it is usually found that participants ask questions in a way that serves naturally to confirm the primed hypothesis or relevant stereotype. So, if asked to find out whether or not a woman is an extrovert, participants tend to want to ask her 'What is it about these situations that makes you like to talk?' rather than 'What factors make it hard for you to really open up to people?' Similar processes of hypothesis confirmation have also been found to play an important role both in the interrogation of applicants during job interviews and in the interpretation of their responses (Binning, Goldstein, Garcia & Scatteregia, 1988; Macan & Dipboye, 1994; Phillips & Dipboye, 1989). Indeed, because of such findings, Stohl and Redding (1987, p. 479; after Campbell, 1958) suggest that the tendency to distort information in order to make it fit with expectations and pre-existing stereotypic beliefs is probably the most prevalent cognitive bias in organizational communication.

This confirmatory approach to hypothesis testing obviously saves time (compared to a more even-handed strategy), but Snyder (1981b, 1984) argues that it is likely to create problems when the primed hypothesis is wrong. He also argues that this is especially true in light of empirical evidence of a 'self-fulfilling prophecy' such that, as a result of biased hypothesis testing, targets actually come to *behave* in a manner consistent with participants' expectations. Illustrative of this tendency, Snyder, Tanke and Berscheid (1977) found that targets believed by their interrogators to be attractive subsequently responded in a more pleasant and amiable way to the interrogators' communications than those believed to be unattractive.

A great deal of communication research has been of this general form, but one particularly large body of work has focused on the cognitive processes associated with *information management* (e.g. Larson, Christensen, Abbott & Franz, 1996; Larson, Foster-Fishman & Keys, 1994; Schittekatte & Van Hiel, 1996; Stasser & Stewart, 1992; Stasser & Titus, 1985, 1987; Stewart, Billings & Stasser, 1998; Winquist & Larson, 1998; for a review see Wittenbaum & Stasser, 1996). This research has addressed the question of how people pool information when they tackle collective tasks and what processes may lead this pooling astray.

At the heart of this literature is a widespread observation that when groups collectively handle information they have a strong preference for exchanging material that is common to all group members rather than that to which only a minority of members have access. This preference is typically revealed through a 'biased sampling paradigm' in which all group members are given a different body of information that pertains to a particular activity in which they are engaged. For example, Stasser and Titus (1985; also 1987; Stasser, Taylor & Hanna, 1989) gave students different pieces of biographical information about various candidates for a job as president of a student organization. What the researchers found was that, in appointing a person to this position, the students' decision was primarily influenced by the information that all of them had access to. Moreover, because this shared information was unrepresentative of the total body of information available, this meant that groups failed to select the candidate who had the best *overall* profile. Related research also suggests that groups have a preference for sharing information that they already know and which is in line with the dominant group sentiment rather than that which is novel and potentially disturbing (e.g. Stasser & Titus, 1985, 1987). Such tendencies also seem to increase as groups get larger, so that larger groups benefit least from the potential to access new knowledge (Stasser, 1992). In this way an expert group often finds itself 'swimming against a strong current in collective information sampling that floods group discussions with already shared information' (Wittenbaum & Stasser, 1996, p. 8).

Findings such as these have been replicated in a number of organizational settings, including those of medical patient diagnosis (Larson et al., 1996) and jury decision-making (Tindale, Smith, Thomas, Filkins & Sheffey, 1996). Reviewing these findings, Wittenbaum and Stasser (1996, p. 11) note that in a benign world where everyone has access to representative subsets of information, a group's over-sampling of shared information can have beneficial consequences — especially in helping to generate confidence and commitment. However, they consider these basic cognitive tendencies to have 'dire implications' when this is not the case because superior outcomes are concealed by *hidden information profiles* of the type illustrated in Figure 5.2.

Considerable research attention has thus been devoted to the discovery of ways in which these biases can be avoided. These include the encouragement of critical leadership (Larson et al, 1996), assignment of group members to expert roles (Stewart & Stasser, 1995), and making a group aware of which members have access to unique information (Stasser, Stewart & Wittenbaum, 1995). However, researchers also note that because the various factors associated with information sharing tend to arise together and are typically embedded in a group-centred syndrome, the prospects of avoiding such problems are often bleak.

By exploring the impact that social context has upon tendencies towards information sharing, the work of Stasser, Larson and others advances beyond early cognitive theorizing which tended to suggest that various information-processing biases were hard-wired and well-nigh impossible to overcome (e.g. Hamilton, 1981). For example, initial presentations of Snyder's hypothesis-testing research (e.g. Snyder, 1981a, 1981b) suggested that communicators *inevitably* used communication to solicit information that confirmed their stereotypic preconceptions. However, later research indicated that this was not always the case. Communicators were likely to test hypotheses in a more even-handed

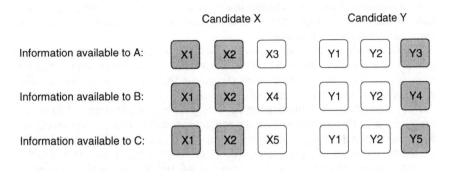

*Figure 5.2* An example of a hidden profile

*Note*: The figure represents information about two job candidates X and Y that is available to members of a three-person selection panel, A, B and C. Shaded boxes denote negative information, unshaded denote positive information. Each number refers to a unique piece of information.

    In this example, if panel members focus on information that they all have access to (i.e. X1, X2, Y1, Y2) they will favour Candidate Y over Candidate X, although in fact there is more positive information about Candidate X (3 positive pieces of information: X3, X4, X5 and 2 negative X1, X2) than Candidate Y (3 negative pieces of information: Y3, Y4, Y5 and 2 positive Y1, Y2).

manner when the task was defined as one of hypothesis-falsification (Snyder and White; 1981) or when they were asked to reflect on whether their behaviour would appear biased to another person (Snyder, Campbell and Preston; 1982, Investigation 2).

    In the final analysis, however, evidence that cognitive biases (e.g. those towards hypothesis confirmation and information sharing) actually respond to context only highlights the need for *an integrated theory of psychological process that is capable of accounting for this contextual variation*. This is something that cognitive (and human relations) theorizing typically fails to provide. However, it is a task to which the social identity approach appears well suited.

## Social identity and communication

An appropriate way to introduce the social identity analysis of organizational communication is to ask the question '*Why* do people in organizations communicate?' Given that this is what most managers spend most of their time doing, this is not a trivial question. In line with previous researchers (e.g. Mitchell et al., 1988, pp. 292-296), we can point to at least five key functions of organizational communication: (a) to *exert influence* over other people; (b) to *reduce uncertainty* on the part of either the communicator or the recipient; (c) to *obtain feedback* relevant to task performance; (d) to *co-ordinate* group performance; and (e) to serve *affiliative needs*. In this way we may be motivated to communicate with colleagues in order to tell them what to do, to clarify whether we or they have understood something appropriately, to see whether we have performed a task adequately, to ensure that we are working towards a common goal, or to enjoy some sociable interaction.

Looked at closely, we can see that the first four of these functions all relate to aspects of the social influence process that we have discussed at some length in each of the three previous chapters (functions that Wiemann & Giles, 1996, group together as issues of *control*). Moreover, it follows from our discussion that the capacity for communication between people to achieve any of these five functions is itself contingent upon the self-categorization process and associated perceptions of shared social category membership (Turner, 1991). Specifically, empirical evidence suggests that: (a) it is only possible to exert positive influence over other people to the extent that we and they are acting in terms of common social category membership (McGarty, Haslam, Hutchinson & Turner, 1994; Mackie, Worth & Asuncion, 1990; Wilder, 1977); (b) only those with whom we share social category membership will be seen as qualified to inform us about relevant aspects of social reality and hence to reduce our uncertainty (McGarty, Turner, Oakes & Haslam, 1993); (c) the impact of feedback from another person on our perceptions and behaviour will depend on the nature of our social categorical relationship with them (Balaam & Haslam, 1998; Brewer & Kramer, 1985; David & Turner, 1996, 1999; Haslam, Oakes, McGarty et al., 1996); (d) expectations of an ability to co-ordinate behaviour, and the motivation to do so, are contingent upon perceptions of shared social category membership (Haslam, Turner, Oakes, McGarty et al., 1998); and (e) desire for affiliation and positive construal of interaction also depend on a sense of common identity (Hogg & Turner, 1985).

Expressed in the way they are, the foregoing statements may appear hard to integrate schematically. However, we can clarify the common theoretical logic that underpins them by stating more simply that *perceptions of shared social identity provide people with multiple motivations for communicating and also with a shared cognitive framework which allows that communication to be mutually beneficial and productive.* Yet as a corollary, it can be seen that where individuals do *not* perceive themselves to share social category membership they will have fewer reasons to communicate with each other and much greater scope for mutual miscommunication and misunderstanding.

Spelling these points out further, the motivations to communicate associated with shared social identity include all five of those listed above (influence, uncertainty reduction, feedback, co-ordination, and affiliation). Moreover, because they are associated with a relevant *self*-categorization, individuals themselves should be oriented towards these functions and hence the activities to which they relate should be engaged in freely. Where two or more people share a common social identity they should *want* to communicate for all these reasons (to reduce uncertainty, to co-ordinate their action, to affiliate; see Donnellon, 1996).

On the other hand, where identity is *not* shared (e.g. perhaps between people in different departments or of different rank; Wilensky, 1967; or between long-term employees of a failing organization and new recruits; Levine & Moreland, 1991), these same motivations should be much weaker (see Daft, 1995, p. 449). Thus even where formal organizational arrangements and policies necessitate communication (e.g. as part of performance appraisal or in formal strategy meetings), the individuals' collaboration in such activities should be less willing and ultimately be less productive in regard to relevant organizational objectives. In particular, this is because attempts at influence are likely to be based on a coercive *power* relationship and to be perceived as such (Harackiewicz & Larson, 1986; Spears & Lea, 1994, p. 442; Turner, 1991, 1998; see Chapter 4 & 8 below). Here people will communicate because they must, not necessarily because they want to.

However, aside from the motivation of the individuals concerned, a further significant impediment to communication across social category boundaries is the fact that communication is not just a *medium* of information exchange but also an emergent group-specific *property*. This much is apparent from early structural studies (e.g. Bavelas, 1956; Leavitt, 1972; see Figure 5.1), where particular communication networks led the individuals in particular positions to assume particular roles and also produced a particular form of intragroup relations. Indeed, consistent with arguments we developed in Chapter 3, it is apparent that: (a) leadership is typically conferred on the person who is, on average, nearest to all other group members in a communication network (i.e. the person who minimizes intraclass differences in a manner suggested by the meta-contrast principle); and (b) intragroup relations are generally more positive to the extent that communication networks do not create arbitrary interpersonal inequalities (cf. Haslam, McGarty et al., 1998).

It is also the case that where social identities become an ongoing and relatively stable part of people's self-definition, the groups to which those identities relate develop *shared and distinctive* forms of communication. Perhaps the most extreme example of this arises where people who live in different countries cannot understand each other for the simple reason that they speak different languages. This is true in organizational settings too, where people often have a language and manner of communicating specific to their profession, their department, or their team. As with Katz and Kahn's (1966) notion of a coding category, this communication takes the form of an *ingroup code* and can be reflected in technical jargon, recognized ways of expressing particular ideas, as well as in pet-phrases, in-jokes, slang and argot (e.g. see Zurcher, 1965).

These coded forms of communication can serve as convenient way of summarizing information (e.g. where reference to a 'UB40' saves someone in Britain from having to refer to the enrolment form for receipt of unemployment benefit), but they also serve as important *identity markers* (Levine & Moreland, 1991, p. 264; Montgomery, 1986). Thus when communicators use such language they: (a) demonstrate their own membership of a particular social group; (b) make potential recipients aware of their own status as a member of the communicator's ingroup or outgroup; and (c) potentially restrict access to the meaning of the communication to other ingroup members. For example, if administrators send e-mails to members of an organization inviting them to apply for 'ASA funding', they demonstrate their own membership of a group that knows what ASA funding is (e.g. people who have attended a relevant briefing), they make people in the organization who are not members of this group aware of the fact and also limit the capacity of those people to make sense of the message. Clearly these effects can be either intentional or inadvertent, but this fact itself will not necessarily matter. The point is that all communication is associated with *contours* of access to meaning (Postmes et al., 1998). Those who share a communicator's social identity will always have most access to his or her meaning, but such access — and the likelihood of mutually beneficial interaction — will tend to decline dramatically when communication occurs across a social categorical divide (although this will depend on the state of intergroup relations and the over-arching *theory* of intergroup relations which guides the parties' interaction). This point is represented schematically in Figure 5.3.

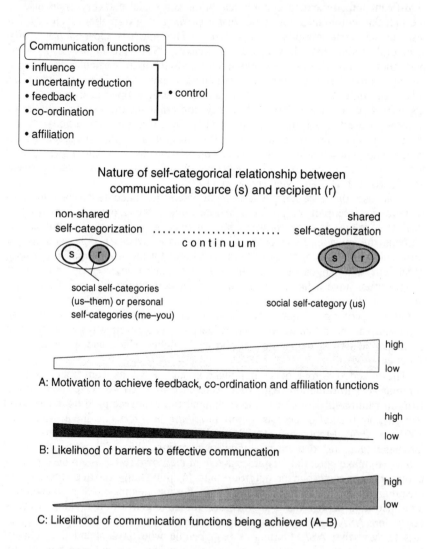

*Figure 5.3* Schematic representation of the manner in which the realization of communication functions is affected by the social categorical relationship between participants in the communication process

There is a clear correspondence between the above claims and Katz and Kahn's (1966, p. 228) observation that communication and its effects are structured by intra-organizational group boundaries. However, as in previous chapters, a critical feature of our analysis is that the self-categorization process which underpins these effects is understood to be dynamic and context-sensitive. As we have noted at various points in the previous chapters, people in organizations are capable of defining themselves in terms of very many different social identities defined at different levels of abstraction and with different levels of inclusiveness — for example, as a member of a particular work group, a particular department, a particular organization or a particular industry (e.g. see Figure 2.8). Moreover, to the extent that people have the experience of defining themselves and acting in terms of a particular social identity, the specific communication codes associated with that identity should become part of their communication *repertoire*. Clinical psychologists, for example, may have repertoires that include codes specific to their clinical interactions with clients, to professional meetings with other clinical practitioners and to academic discourse with other psychologists.

Nonetheless, exactly how people define themselves — and hence which communication codes they draw upon from the repertoire of those available to them — will depend on features of the organizational context that they confront at any point in time (Lazega, 1990). Along lines suggested in Chapter 2, it will depend, amongst other things, on the accessibility of a particular group-based self-definition (e.g. whether one has prior experience of defining oneself in a particular way), and on features of comparative context (e.g. who is present at a particular point in time), normative context (e.g. expectations about appropriate ways to define oneself), and social structure (e.g. the status relations between groups and the security of those relations).

In this way, the quality and efficacy of communication between *the same two people* should vary considerably as a function of these contextual factors. For control and affiliative purposes, a clinical and a social psychologist may be motivated to communicate and may achieve effective communication when they act in terms of a shared identity as psychologists (e.g. in a context where they are both drawing on the same professional communication codes to discuss the merits of psychology compared to economics), but those motivations and the efficacy of communication will tend to diminish when they act in terms of distinct identities (e.g. in a context where they are drawing on different sub-discipline communication codes to discuss the relative merits of clinical and social psychology). Only in the former context will they be psychologically aligned and hence motivated to speak and hear 'the same language'. And clearly, the former context will be conducive to collaborative endeavour in a way that the latter will not.

Significantly too, the processes described above should operate in whatever form and medium communication takes place: whether it is formal or informal, verbal or non-verbal, face-to-face or remote. This is a point emphasised by Spears and Lea (1994; see also Postmes et al., 1998) in their investigations of the social psychology of computer-mediated communication (CMC) — a medium that has been claimed to contribute to an emerging 'global village' transcending all forms of political and social boundary (e.g. Hiltz & Turoff, 1992). The work of Spears, Lea and Postmes suggests that such claims are ill-founded. Indeed, far from releasing individuals from their ties to the group, anonymous communication via computer appears to make those ties *stronger* (e.g. to induce greater conformity to group norms; Postmes & Spears, 1998). In part this is because in this medium social identification is not offset by individuating information relating to participants' personal identities. The researchers thus conclude that:

> Although concurring that CMC offers interesting possibilities, and highlights fundamental questions of self and identity, there are also dangers of romanticizing the effects of CMC by viewing it as a sort of virtual reality where the individual can escape from the strictures of ordinary identity and interaction. ... While recognizing these new possibilities, we argue that identity and interaction in CMC will often be grounded in the realities of identities and relations beyond CMC that pervade the rest of our social lives. (Spears & Lea, 1994, p. 449, see also Postmes et al., 1998; Spears & Lea, 1992)

In short, no form of communication is immune to the influence and consequences of self-categorization. This is for the simple reason that communication is necessarily *oriented towards* and *structured by* our social self-definition in any given context. It is about *who we are* and serves to express and develop the self at both personal and collective levels by allowing us to engage in the full range of activities (co-operative and conflictual) that are necessary to advance our interests as individuals and as group members.

## Some empirical tests of the social identity approach

### Self-categorization as a basis for information management

One of the most basic implications of the foregoing analysis is that individuals should generally be most motivated to communicate with other people that are perceived to be members of a salient social self-category. Moreover, where such communication occurs, it should tend to be focused on matters related to that identity. Where the behaviour of two members of an organization is structured by a shared self-definition (e.g. as members of the same department), they should be motivated to talk to each other and with particular reference to things that pertain to that common identity (e.g. departmental issues).

In many respects this prediction might seem rather obvious and something of a necessity in organizational life. However, it is clear that colleagues do not always talk to each other about seemingly essential matters, and that the experience of being 'left in the dark' is relatively prevalent. As Feldman (1988, p. 87; see also Bellman, 1981) observes, *secrecy* is a pervasive feature of managerial behaviour and is the source of regular complaints from disempowered workers. Along lines intimated by Fine and Holyfield (1996) and McGregor (1966, p. 237), we suggest that this arises from (and reinforces) a perceived lack of common identity between employees that is often encouraged by particular social-structural arrangements and organizational practices.

Evidence that supports such arguments is provided by Agama (1997; Haslam, 1999a) in research that involved employees of 'AirSafe' — a government agency responsible for issues of air safety. There had been a long-standing history of inter-departmental conflict in the agency and consultants had recently been called in to address a recognized lack of communication within the workforce as a whole. In the study employees were given a description of a hypothetical organization, similar in structure to their own, and were assigned to a position as a member of one of two teams (A or B). This was thus what might be termed a 'minimax' study: the groupings were minimal in having no prior meaning or history (as in Tajfel et al., 1971), but the prior experience of the participants was maximally relevant to the topic in question.

In the study half of the participants were instructed that the teams were working in collaboration (one was responsible for computer software, one was responsible for hardware), the other half that both were working in competition (both were trying to design the best software). Participants were then given 12 pieces of work-related information that pertained to (a) the organization as a whole, (b) their team, or (c) themselves personally. Their task was to indicate how willing they would be to pass information to other workers from their own and the other team. The results are presented in Figure 5.4.

As predicted, these results revealed two main effects. First, employees were generally much more willing to disseminate information that pertained to the organization as a whole than that which pertained to their team, but more willing to pass on team-related information than personal information. Second, they were much more willing to pass on information to members of their own team than to members of the other team.

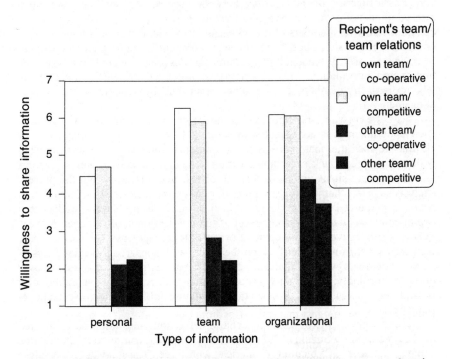

*Figure 5.4* Willingness to share information with another person as a function of that person's team membership and the nature of inter-team relations (from Agama, 1997)

However, these effects were qualified by two highly significant interactions. One indicated that the greater willingness of participants to pass on information to members of their own team was particularly pronounced in the case of team-related information.   As self-categorization theory would predict, ingroup-outgroup differences in information flow were most marked where information was directly relevant to the team-level ingroup–outgroup division.  On the other hand, there was evidence that when information was relevant to the organization as a whole, employees were more willing to pass it on to members of the other team, but that when it was personal they were much less willing to pass it on to members of their own team.

In this way, the pattern of information flow closely followed the contours of self-categorization.  When dealing with organization-relevant material this was communicated to members of the other team because they were categorized as ingroup members at this organizational level, but when dealing with personal material this was not communicated to members of participants' own team because its members were categorized as different individuals at a personal level (thereby mirroring patterns observed by Gaertner et al., 1989; see Chapter 2 above).  Moreover, the fact that the teams in this study had no prior meaning but that participants had relevant organizational experience allows us to be confident that these patterns do not simply reflect the nature of pre-existing intergroup relations or the inherent naivety of the communicators.

Beyond this though, a second interaction indicated that the above pattern also varied as a function of the *relations* between groups.  As predicted, the most marked impact of competitive relations was to increase participants' reluctance to communicate with members of the opposing team.  However, it is interesting to note that when relations between teams were competitive rather than co-operative there was an *overall* tendency to communicate less team-related and organiza-tion-related information.  Thus participants responded to conflict not only by talking less to members of the other team but by tending to 'clam up' altogether.

This pattern (which reflected the communication problems that AirSafe was itself experiencing) is consistent with some of Mayo's original observations at Hawthorne and other factories, where intra-organizational conflict was associated with a widespread lack of communication.  Mayo's inclination was to explain this secrecy and silence as an expression of fear and insecurity, but the present analysis suggests that it may arise more routinely from a generalized reduction in people's perceived 'need to know'.  In this study, as in Mayo's studies, co-operation clearly *demanded* some level of communication in order for employees to rise collaboratively to the creative organizational challenge with which they were newly confronted.  Conflict, on the other hand, appeared to demand less of all team members — possibly because it was what they had become used to over time.  Accordingly, we might expect a different pattern amongst members of a workforce with a history of co-operation for whom conflict would present a novel challenge.

Results from this experimental scenario-based study are also complemented by data reported by Suzuki (1998) in a survey of actual communication patterns amongst members of a bicultural American workforce.  The study asked Japanese and American employees of four banks and four trading companies around Chicago to indicate which members of their organization they communicated with when it came to discussing (a) general task-related matters, (b) specific task-related matters, and (c) non-task matters. On the basis of social identity theory, Suzuki reasoned that workers would communicate more with members of their national ingroup than with outgroup members, but that this difference would be more pronounced to the extent that information was not directly related to the task at hand. This prediction was confirmed and the pattern was found to be particularly strong in the responses of American employees (members of the high-status group) who identified strongly with their national ingroup. These high identifiers thus restricted their communication with the outgroup to what was strictly necessary in order to get the job done, while their communication with ingroup members was much less circumscribed.

Evidence that effects such as these are underpinned by a flexible categorization process of the form envisaged by self-categorization theorists emerges from a study conducted by Dovidio et al. (1997). This elaborated upon the authors' earlier work investigating the impact of recategorization on people's perception and treatment of others (e.g. Gaertner et al., 1989, 1990; see Chapter 2 above). As in earlier studies, in this experiment participants were first assigned to one of two three-person discussion groups and were subsequently informed that they would be interacting with a member of their own or the opposing group. Amongst other things, they were to discuss the question 'What are you most afraid of?' as a means of finding out 'how people become acquainted and get to know each other'. At this phase of the study structural features of the setting such as seating arrangements (segregated or integrated), labelling (the groups were given separate or common names) and dress (different or common uniform) were manipulated so as to maintain a two-group categorization or to suggest an overarching common identity.

One of the key variables in which the researchers were interested was the extent to which these different arrangements would impact upon individuals' *self-disclosure*. How much information about themselves would they give a person from their own or the other group, and how intimate would this information be? Consistent with the authors' predictions, when structural arrangements promoted a one-group categorical representation, participants were much more willing to reveal intimate facts about themselves to members of the other three-person group than they were when the two-group categorization was reinforced. Indeed, while in the two-group situation participants communicated much more intimate information to ingroup than to outgroup members, in the one-group situation this pattern was reversed. This reversal was largely attributable to an extremely high level of self-disclosure to former outgroup members. Here, then, the priority was to get to know those people who had just become part of the participants' salient self-category.

As this study suggests, a fundamental reason for sharing information with other people is to find out more about the self. If the self is understood to be defined purely at an individual level this point appears paradoxical or even slightly flaky. However, if we accept the possibility of a social definition of self such that in some contexts others are seen to be categorically interchangeable with us (i.e. where 'you' and 'I' are defined by a sense of common 'we-ness'), then communication with those others may become necessary to define and co-ordinate the content and form of that social categorical self. In this way, *communication is an essential path to social self-knowledge and to self-oriented collective   behaviour* (Haslam, 1999a).  For this reason, as Dovidio et al.'s (1997) study suggests, motivation to share information should be particularly strong where uncertainty about the self is great (e.g. where people have had no prior interaction with people who have only recently been defined as members of a salient self-category).  It is no accident that on our first day at university or in a new job we speak to more people and work harder to establish common ground with them, than we do when our position in the organization is well established (Worchel, 1994).   Similarly, it is not surprising that formal channels of information transmission are also supplemented by informal ones (e.g. unofficial 'leaks', the rumour mill, the grapevine).  These informal channels are often more sensitive to the social motivations and strategic aims of employees and are likely to be increasingly important under conditions of uncertainty and change (Davis, 1981; Jaeger, Anthony & Rosnow, 1980; Rosnow, 1991; Sutton & Porter, 1968).

Extensive evidence of precisely these motivations is provided in the cognitive research of Stasser, Larson and others that we discussed above.  The only additional issue that their research raises is whether the tendency for group members to share common information should be construed as a cognitive bias that constitutes a basic source of social and organizational deficiency.  As we have seen, this is the position adopted by Wittenbaum and Stasser (1996) on the basis of evidence that in the informationally malign scenarios they create (where group members all have access to an unrepresentative sample of the total information pool; see Figure 5.2), the commonly available 'error' is preferred to the idiosyncratically available 'truth'.

However, the social identity approach suggests a rather different reading of this research.  In the first instance, this is because, as Wittenbaum and Stasser (1996, p. 11) note, the sharing of information to which all group members have access may have a positive motivational impact upon groups — making them feel committed and self-assured.  More fundamentally, at least in the initial stages of group formation, the process of sharing common information is essential for a shared sense of self to emerge amongst group members.  Finding out and demonstrating publicly what 'we' have in common is essential to putting some content-related flesh onto the bone of psychological group membership.  As research by Worchel (1994, 1998) demonstrates, it is thus at an early stage in their development that 'groups often adopt a dress code or uniform, a special language and other symbols that identify the group and mark people as group members' (1998, p., 59).  In this way, the process of sharing common information derives from and instantiates a sense of 'we-ness' — what Levine and Moreland (1991; see also Kim, 1997) refer to as a *shared mental model* of 'us'.  Without this shared understanding of the collective self no group can continue as a psychological (and hence organizational) force.

It also follows, however, that once group members have established some shared and relatively secure basis for action, the demand to focus exclusively on shared information will be relaxed.  This point is confirmed in Larson et al.'s (1996) study of medical practitioner groups in which members were willing to share more unique information as their discussion progressed over time.  Moreover, research by Postmes and Spears (1999) also suggests that it is possible for groups to develop and internalize norms of critical thinking in which the demand for creative and original contributions overrides the tendency to pool only shared information (see also Janis, 1982; Chapter 6 below). When this is the case, groups prove quite adept at uncovering hidden profiles.

However, even if this were not the case, at an even more basic level, we can question whether the truth in biased sampling paradigms necessarily lies in the hidden profiles they conceal. The argument that it does rests on an assumption that all pieces of social information are of equivalent objective value (e.g. that in Figure 5.2, X1 is just as informative as X5). Yet it does not seem unreasonable to suppose that in such scenarios the fact that one piece of information is known to all group members while another is known to only one *is itself* real and important information that needs to be taken into account. If six people have evidence that a person is honest, and only one has information that he or she is corrupt, the sensible course of action is to try to *resolve the inconsistency*, not simply to see these pieces of information as cancelling each other out. And in such a situation it will generally be more rational to conclude that the one consensually available piece of evidence constitutes information and that the discrepant evidence is actually noise, rather than the other way round. A key point here, then, is that *what constitutes information* in any organizational setting is actually an *outcome* of a social process not simply an objective 'given' as cognitive theorists have tended to suggest (for a related argument see Feldman, 1988).

## Social identity and speech accommodation

We noted above that there is a lot more to organizational communication than what people actually tell or say to each other. In particular, *the way* information is communicated says a lot about the relationship between the parties involved and contributes a lot to both the future of that relationship and the fate of the information. A person who responds to the question 'Can I use the photocopier?' by saying 'That is not permitted under departmental regulations' is saying something quite different about themselves and their relationship with the person making the request than someone who responds 'I'm sorry, but it's more than my job's worth' — even though, in the abstract, the responses may appear to communicate much the same information (i.e. 'No').

This example highlights the fact that a range of features of any particular communication convey social information about the communicator's own identity and about his or her relationship to the person or people with whom he or she is attempting to communicate. As another example we could think about a consultation between a male doctor and a patient in the doctor's surgery. Here the doctor's own social identity (as a doctor) might be conveyed by a standardized, formal and direct speech style, his use of medical language, and interrogative utterances. Moreover, his social relationship with the patient could be conveyed by the extent to which these aspects of communication were accentuated or down-played during the interaction. Accentuation of these characteristics would be associated with his desire to maintain or enhance the social distance associated with a professional doctor–patient differentiation. On the other hand, a desire to show sympathy with the patient or to break down the doctor-patient division would be conveyed by a relaxation of these features and adoption of a less formal, less interrogative style and use of everyday language (Bourhis, Roth & MacQueen, 1989; Fisher & Todd, 1983).

The dynamics of this process have been the focus of a large body of research informed by the social identity approach. In particular, such work has been integrated by Giles and his colleagues within *speech accommodation theory* as part of a thorough examination of the way in which language use reflects and creates social structure (Giles, Coupland & Coupland, 1991; Giles & Johnson, 1981; Giles, Mulac, Bradac & Johnson, 1987). The theory focuses on the two features of communication style alluded to above: *convergence* — the tendency for speakers to modify their communication (e.g. vocabulary, accent, rate of speech) so that its features are *more similar* to those perceived to be characteristic of the recipient — and *divergence* — the tendency for a speakers to modify their communication so that its features are *more different* from those perceived to be characteristic of the recipient. As in our doctor–patient example, convergence is assumed to signify some desire on the part of the communicator to break down any intergroup division and affiliate with the recipient at an interpersonal level, while divergence is assumed to signify a desire to maintain or reinforce such division.

In this way, speech accommodation can be thought of as a form of *linguistic self-stereotyping* (Giles et al., 1987, p. 29; Turner, 1982). Significantly though, accommodation is not restricted to verbal interaction but can be reflected in non-verbal communication as well — encompassing, amongst other things, the communicator's dress, body language and use of space. As Figure 5.5 suggests, in all communicative domains convergence reflects the existence of, or the desire for the recipient to be encompassed within, a shared social self-categorization, but divergence reflects a desire to maintain social self-categorical division (Sachdev & Bourhis, 1990, p. 227).

Even from this cursory overview, it is apparent that these arguments elaborate upon key ideas contained within social identity and self-categorization theories. In the first instance, we can see that accommodation processes (convergence and divergence) are an ongoing component of any perceiver's self-categorical world. Where we see others (or want to be seen by them) as part of a shared social self-category we align our communication with theirs. This is a practical consequence of perceived social categorical interchangeability (Turner, 1982) and will often (but not always) contribute to the emergence of a shared perspective on the world and access to common meaning.

Moreover, these arguments can be fleshed out to predict *when* people will display particular forms of accommodation and what the effects of such accommodation will be. For example, following self-categorization theory's principle of comparative fit (and in a manner suggested by Figure 2.9), the communication styles of members of different departments in the same organization would be expected to converge under conditions of extended inter-organizational comparison where they categorize themselves in terms of a common organizational identity. However, the same two groups would be expected to diverge in a narrower intra-organizational context which encouraged categorization in terms of distinct lower-level identities.

Following key tenets of social identity theory (Tajfel & Turner, 1979; see Chapter 2 above) the tendency to converge or diverge should also vary as a function of the array of social structural features that impinge upon the perceiver

Social self-categorical
relationship A has, or
desires to have, with B

shared

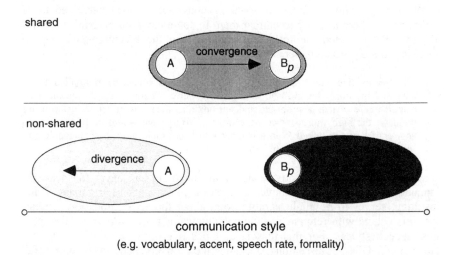

non-shared

communication style
(e.g. vocabulary, accent, speech rate, formality)

*Figure 5.5* Speech accommodation as self-categorization in action

*Note*: A's communication style converges or diverges from that *perceived* to be
characteristic of B (i.e. B*p*). Convergence reflects and contributes to shared
social self-categorization and communicates a desire to identify and affiliate with
B; divergence reflects and contributes to social self-categorical division.

in any given context. In particular (and following arguments represented in
Figure 2.5a), members of low-status groups should tend to display individual
mobility by converging towards the perceived communication patterns of a target
from a high-status group when they perceive intergroup boundaries to be
permeable, while the same people should tend to diverge in order to challenge
the position of the same target when boundaries are seen as impermeable and
intergroup relations as insecure (Bourhis & Giles, 1977). In this way, factory
workers might speak the language of their bosses if they believe they have
prospects of personal promotion, but speak the language of other workers when
they are planning industrial action to collectively improve their plight (see also
Chapter 10 below).

Note, too, that this last example serves to make a number of other points.
First, we can see that a person's patterns of accommodation provide cues that
allow other perceivers to make inferences about his or her psychological
orientation towards themselves and others. Over-and-above the information a
person communicates, accommodation patterns are thus critical features of the
social and organizational landscape. Secondly though, it is apparent that speech
accommodation does not only reflect perceived social reality, but that it can also

serve to further perceivers' personal and collective interests in relation to that reality. For a factory worker, speaking like one's boss might help to promote personal interests in a way that speaking like a worker would not; and speaking like other workers might help give collective voice and meaning to industrial action in a way that speaking like bosses would not. The same is true of course, for a manager whose manner of speaking converges on that perceived to be typical of workers in order to entreat them to some common enterprise. Thus Taylor (1911) passed the following comment on the recommended way of speaking to a pig-iron handler:

> This seems like rather rough talk. And indeed it would be if applied to an educated mechanic, or even an intelligent labourer. With a man of the mentally sluggish type ... it is appropriate and not unkind, since it is effective in fixing his mind on the high wages which he wants. ... [But] what would be [the worker's] answer if he were talked to in a manner which is usual under the management of 'initiative and incentive'? (p. 46)

The fact that Taylor's advice about the need for managers to speak the language of workers (i.e. to converge) comes across as rather patronizing, if not insulting, serves to highlight another point about the accommodation process: that this occurs with reference to the communicator's *perceptions* of other parties' speech styles. For this reason, as Giles (e.g. Giles et al., 1987, p. 18; Hewstone & Giles, 1986) emphasizes, attempted convergence can sometimes fail to achieve its desired effects and may foster *mis*understanding because these perceptions are inaccurate. Along similar lines, it may also fail when a person's convergence is interpreted as a cynical attempt at manipulation. A CEO who writes to employees informing them that they are soon to be retrenched may evoke a particularly negative reaction if the letter appeals to a sense of friendship and shared understanding that is perceived by its recipients to be conspicuously false.

The above arguments have received broad support in a large number of studies and a range of applied contexts (for reviews see Giles et al., 1987, 1991; Giles & Johnson, 1981; Sachdev & Bourhis, 1990). However, such research has typically examined accommodation as a function of a social identity defined in national or regional terms (e.g. Abrams & Hogg, 1987; Bourhis & Giles, 1977; Bourhis, Giles, Leyens & Tajfel, 1979) rather than occupational ones. Nonetheless, several studies have explored issues related to speech accommodation in work-related settings and demonstrated the relevance of the above theoretical principles to the understanding of organizational dynamics.

Studies of this kind have typically shown that the way a person speaks affects judgements of them and the response that their communication elicits. Thus British-based research by Giles, Wilson and Conway (1981) found that the accent of job candidates was a key determinant of their perceived suitability for particular jobs (see also Gallois, Callan & McKenzie-Palmer, 1992; Willemyns, Gallois & Callan, in press; Willemyns, Gallois, Callan & Pittam, 1997). Candidates who spoke with a standard accent were considered more suitable applicants for high-status positions (e.g. as an accounts manger) than low-status ones (e.g. as a cleaner), but the opposite was true when they spoke with a non-standard regional accent. Less obviously, Giles and Farrar (1979) found that when women were asked to respond verbally to questions about the economic situation, those approached by an interviewer who spoke with a standard (i.e. non-regional) British accent produced responses that were on average 51 per cent longer than those given to the same interviewer when she spoke in a non-standard dialect. Street (1984; Putman & Street, 1984) also found that a professional interviewer perceived interviewees to be more attractive and more competent to the extent that those interviewees converged to the interviewer's own speech rate. As social identity principles would predict, convergence either (a) to recipients' communication styles or (b) to styles associated with what is for those recipients a prototypical ingroup, thus communicates and encourages affiliation, approval and influence.

However, the most extensive examination of speech accommodation theory's relevance to workplace communication is provided by Bourhis (1991). Building upon a review which clarifies how enquiry into all facets of organizational communication might be enriched by application of social identity and speech accommodation principles, Bourhis (1994a) adds substance to his case by considering results from a study of bilingual workers in the Canadian Federal Administration. This research focused on the extent to which workers' use of English and French in the workplace was affected (a) by the consensually perceived status of each language and (b) the perceivers' own fluency in their second language.

Consistent with social identity theory, an initial finding was that workers whose mother tongue was English (the language of the dominant high-status group) were much less likely to converge towards French-speaking co-workers (by speaking in French) than were workers whose mother tongue was French (who were much more likely to speak English to English-speaking co-workers). Interestingly too, although the tendency of English-speaking workers to converge towards their French-speaking counterparts was enhanced when all workers had received special training to achieve proficiency in their second language, this training had no impact on the willingness of French-speakers to converge towards English speakers. French speakers almost always converged regardless of whether they were fluent in English or not. Accordingly, these findings suggest that when it comes to speaking another worker's language, issues of competence are secondary to the communicator's motivation to identify with the group to which that other worker belongs — especially for members of low-status groups.

Bourhis (1991, 1994a) followed up this analysis by examining the extent to which these patterns of convergence were also constrained by the *linguistic climate* within which organizational communication took place. The central finding to emerge from this analysis was that workers were much more likely to converge by speaking their second language to the extent that that second language was spoken by a high proportion of workers in the immediate working environment. So, for example, when French speakers constituted less than one-fifth of the workers in a particular workplace, only 13 per cent of English speakers converged by speaking French to their colleagues, but this figure rose to 48 per cent when more than three-quarters of the workers were French.

There is clearly a functional dimension to these findings (reflecting the fact that convergence becomes less necessary to the extent that one's own language is dominant), but over-and-above this, they point to the way in which structural and identity-based motivational factors *interact* to dictate patterns of organizational communication. In Bourhis's research, these processes are brought into clear relief by the bilingual nature of the workforce he investigated. However, once we understand that 'the language a person speaks' relates to far more than just their mother tongue, it seems likely that similar processes impact upon all aspects of the communication culture within the workplace.

### Social identity as a determinant of information processing

We have seen from the previous two sections that *whether* a person communicates with another person, and *how* they do so, both vary as a function of the recipient's social self-categorical status for the communicator — whether he or she is perceived to be an ingroup or an outgroup member. The next obvious issue concerns the recipient's *reaction* to any such communication. Is this affected by the social categorical relationship between the parties? And if so, how? Building on the platform of self-categorization theory, these questions have been addressed in a number of interrelated research programmes, in particular, those of Mackie (Mackie et al., 1990; Mackie, Gastardo-Conaco & Skelly, 1992), Wilder (1977, 1990), van Knippenberg (van Knippenberg, Lossie & Wilke, 1994; van Knippenberg & van Knippenberg, 1996; van Knippenberg & Wilke, 1992) and McGarty (Haslam, McGarty & Turner, 1996; McGarty et al., 1994).

Mackie et al.'s (1990) research demonstrates clearly that a source's ingroup–outgroup status does indeed have a profound impact on the way in which any message he or she delivers is received. In the first of two studies, students at the University of California, Santa Barbara (UCSB) were exposed to messages about the relative merits of standardized university testing. Some were presented with relatively weak arguments, others with relatively strong ones. As well as this, half of the participants were told that the arguments had been developed by UCSB students, while the other half were told they had been generated by students at the University of New Hampshire (UNH). Results suggested that this latter manipulation was a major determinant of whether or not the participants attended to the content of the message. Specifically, as one might expect, students were more persuaded by strong arguments from the ingroup than by weak ones. However, the quality of arguments had little bearing on the persuasive impact of arguments from members of the UNH outgroup — all their messages (both weak and strong) were singularly unpersuasive. Moreover, Mackie's argument that these effects were underpinned by a failure to attend to the content of the outgroup messages was supported by evidence that students generally had far superior recall of ingroup messages. It thus appears that students did not listen to what the outgroup had to say and then make up their mind about whether or not they agreed with it. Instead, they concluded that because it was an outgroup, its message was not worth listening to in the first place.

These effects were replicated in a second study, but this also showed that processing of ingroup messages depended on whether or not the arguments they contained pertained to an issue that was relevant to the students' own group membership. When the issue was relevant (the merits of drilling for oil off the Californian coast), students were more convinced by strong than weak ingroup arguments (as in Experiment 1), but they were equally persuaded by strong and weak arguments on an issue that was irrelevant to their group membership (the imposition of controls to minimize acid rain). In all cases outgroup messages were still unpersuasive and given little attention. These data thus suggest that in order to be seen as warranting close attention, arguments need to be presented by an ingroup member and to be relevant to the issue on which their ingroup status is defined.

Such insights have been elaborated further by Wilder (1990) in a series of studies examining the association between the relative persuasiveness of ingroup messages and the organization and judgement of the information those messages contain. Wilder's core hypothesis is that the persuasiveness of ingroup messages is derived in part from the assumed *independence* of the various ingroup members who provide information. This independence is seen to reflect the fact that ingroup members are often perceived to be individuals, while outgroup members are generally seen to be categorically interchangeable — a pattern of asymmetric judgement that can be explained in terms of the categorization principles that we discussed in Chapter 2. Specifically, it follows from the meta-contrast principle that outgroups should generally be perceived in social categorical terms because they are always judged in the context of an ingroup-outgroup comparison, but that ingroup members may be perceived in terms of personal (or lower-level social) categories because they are often judged without reference to a comparison group (an asymmetry that contributes to the 'outgroup homogeneity effect'; see Haslam, Oakes, Turner & McGarty, 1996; Oakes et al., 1994).

Wilder's basic idea, then, is that exposure to the same message from lots of different outgroup members is unconvincing because the similarity of their messages is understood to reflect a group-based bias, while the similarity of ingroup messages is seen to provide multiple-source validation of a common truth. In other words, perceivers are believed to find ingroup messages more persuasive because they hold a view of the form 'you lot say the same thing because you all share the same biased view of the world, but we say the same thing because we have each worked out the truth for ourselves'.

To examine this hypothesis, participants in Wilder's first study were assigned to four-person groups whose task was to decide upon the appropriate treatment for an employee accused of selling information about some new company products to a rival firm. Each participant was led to believe that they would control the flow of information between ingroup and outgroup members as they worked on the task. As an initial stage in this process they were then given information that supposedly came (a) from the other three ingroup members, (b) from three of the four outgroup members, or (c) from three people whose group membership was undisclosed (a control group). The information that appeared to have come from these three people was all slightly different, but it always indicated that the employee was guilty of industrial espionage and should be treated leniently.

The results of the study are presented in Table 5.1. Consistent with the experimental hypotheses, it is clear that participants were much more likely to endorse this verdict and opt for leniency themselves when this recommendation was made by other ingroup members. Under these conditions they also made relatively few errors in their recollection of which person had made specific

*Table 5.1* Influence, recall error and judgements of similarity and independence associated with messages from different sources (from Wilder, 1990, Experiment 1)

| | Source of Communication | | |
| | Ingroup | Outgroup | Control |
| --- | --- | --- | --- |
| Measure | | | |
| Social influence | 3.37 | 2.21 | 2.83 |
| Recall errors | 2.02 | 3.11 | 1.96 |
| Perceived similarity among information sources | 4.84 | 5.49 | 5.33 |
| Perceived independence of information sources | 5.47 | 4.53 | 5.58 |

recommendations and were more likely to see the three other people as different from each other and to have made independent contributions to the task. Similar results were obtained in a study where ingroup–outgroup status was based not on *ad hoc* group memberships, but on real-life identities (as members of the participants' own university, Rutgers, or a rival institution, Princeton; Wilder, 1990; Experiment 2).

However, the sensitivity of these effects to features of the overall categorical context was revealed by additional studies in which some participants were encouraged to perceive all information sources not as group members but as individuals (Wilder, 1990; Experiments 3 & 4). This was achieved through the provision of extensive biographical information about each person which effectively overrode the ingroup–outgroup categorization. In these conditions outgroup members were effectively recategorized as members of a common ingroup (cf. Gaertner et al., 1989) and their influence and perceived independence increased accordingly — to a level equal to that of other ingroup members.

These latter results reinforce the point that the categorical status of a source for any perceiver is not fixed and immutable but rather depends upon features of the prevailing social landscape. Thus the same person who is categorized as an ingroup member in one context and perceived as an independent and valid source of influence, can be recategorized as an outgroup member in another setting and be perceived as biased and unreliable. This point is confirmed in research by David and Turner (1996, 1999) which shows that the same moderate feminist who is definitely not influenced by a message from a radical feminist in a context that only includes feminists, is much more influenced by such a person in a context that also includes anti-feminists (see also Haslam & Turner, 1992; Chapter 2 above, Figure 2.9).

Further appreciation of the contribution that the social categorization process makes to the impact of communication is provided by van Knippenberg and Wilke (1992). These researchers elaborated on the earlier work of Mackie and Wilder by showing that messages from an ingroup were more influential than those from outgroups, and that this increased to the extent that they were said to be *prototypical* of an ingroup position. Law students told in advance that a message came from another law student who opposed time restrictions on university entrance exams (the prototypical ingroup position) were more influenced by that person's message than those told the source was a law student who favoured time restrictions.

In a subsequent study van Knippenberg et al. (1994) went on to demonstrate that when cues about the source of a message were available before its presentation, the influence of a prototypical ingroup message was associated with more *detailed and elaborate processing* of its content. A message from a prototypical ingroup member was thus not only more influential than one from an aprototypical member, but it also led participants to provide more message-relevant information when they were asked to write down their reactions to the message in a thought-listing task. A very similar pattern of findings was observed by McGarty et al. (1994, Experiment 2) in a study examining the capacity of an ingroup speaker to change students' attitudes to road safety.

The effects revealed by the above studies are important not only because they confirm the point that persuasion is contingent on the self-categorical status of a message source, but also because they show that such persuasion is based on *active* message processing. This finding conflicts with the widely held belief that where ingroups produce a change in their members' attitudes and behaviour this arises from laziness or fear on the part of those constituents. The layperson's idea of 'peer group pressure' suggests, for example, that group members 'go along' with others because they are too indolent, too scared or too stupid to do anything else (an idea formalized in Deutsch & Gerard's, 1955, view that groups produce normative rather than informational influence and Petty & Cacioppo's, 1981, 1986, suggestion that they induce heuristic rather than systematic message processing; see Turner, 1991). However, like Haslam and Platow's studies of leadership (in press; see Chapter 3 above), van Knippenberg and McGarty's work suggests that cognitive effort and true influence are not subverted by group membership. Indeed, very much to the contrary, it is shared group membership that provides people with the motivation to work hard in order to achieve shared meaning.

## Conclusion

In their review of research into organizational communication, Thompson and McHugh (1995) note that this field has tended to be dominated by work which examines *stages* of the communication process and which identifies factors that contribute to successful message transmission or communication breakdown. Based on such an approach, researchers commonly describe a range of relatively simple interventions designed to remedy communication breakdowns when they occur. In this vein, prior to Agama's (1997) research at AirSafe, communication consultants had recommended that strife-torn departments (a) ensure that members from each department were placed on a shared e-mail bulletin board, (b) contribute to a joint newsletter, and (c) participate in more cross-departmental social events. At a more general level, Handy (1976, p. 356) provides the following recommendations for effective organizational communication: (a) use as many communication channels as possible (or at least do not rely on one alone); (b) encourage two-way rather than one-way communication; and (c) use as few linkages as possible in any communication chain.

Yet a clear problem with remedies like those which Handy (1976) offers is that they fail to appreciate the psychological processes that contribute to communication difficulties. As he himself observes, 'communications are symptoms' (p. 356). Thus, the perceived appropriateness of multiple channels, the capacity for two-way communication, and the possibility of direct communication are all partly *outcomes* of organizational dynamics. They are therefore far easier to recommend than to bring about. Accordingly, Thompson and McHugh (1995) observe that despite the intuitive appeal of an approach like Handy's, its contribution is ultimately limited by the fact that:

> It tends to view communication as a step-by-step, rather than a simultaneous process and consequently tends to ignore the interpersonal dynamics of communication. (p. 283)

The broad recommendation of these authors is that:

> This type of model needs to be augmented by sensitivity to the perceptions of the sender and recipient that give rise to the shared meanings that allow communication to take place. (p. 283)

Krauss and Fussell (1996) arrive at a similar conclusion in a review which identifies the need for 'a fully dialogic' model of communication. As they see it:

> This would start from the assumption that ... meaning is inherently social — that it does not reside solely in the mind of individual speakers and hearers. ... External dialogues take place in an intersubjective context (a state of *mutual orientation* toward the other). (p. 691, emphasis in original)

This chapter has attempted to flesh out a process-based analysis of organizational communication compatible with the difficult task that Thompson and McHugh (1995) and Krauss and Fussell (1996) correctly identify as being of paramount importance to the field. However, it may appear that we too have tended to compartmentalize various features of the communication process and have failed to elaborate in full the dynamics that are at play in any act of attempted communication (e.g. as set out by Levine & Moreland, 1991). Importantly though, this has been a pragmatic or stylistic choice rather than a reflection of our underlying conceptualization of the issues at hand. Processes affecting (a) the desire to pass on information, (b) how that information is communicated, and (c) how it is received, have therefore been discussed in separate sections only to make our theoretical analysis easier to follow and supporting evidence easier to appreciate. There is no sense in which these (or other related) processes are considered to be independent of each other. On the contrary, all are interwoven features of the ongoing dynamic which *reflects and creates* people's social identities in any particular organizational context.

The main goal of this chapter, then, has been to show how the social identity approach might provide a parsimonious and unifying framework for understanding the complex intersubjective achievement of organizational communication. At heart, this analysis suggests that the ability of any communication to contribute to shared understanding rests upon a psychological alignment of participants in the communication process arising from the internalization of a social self-categorization that they share. Only when individuals define themselves in terms of a common sense of 'we-ness' will their motivation and attempts to communicate ultimately ensure a full transfer of information and meaning. In this way, communication *produces and is produced by* a shared cognitive framework that has the capacity to transform potentially idiosyncratic inputs into co-ordinated action. This process is social cognitive in the fullest sense (see Ickes & Gonzalez, 1994; Moreland et al., 1996; Weick & Roberts, 1993) and is fundamental to our ability to share experience and organize collective activity.

But precisely because it is contingent upon an internalized psychological orientation, mutual understanding between members of an organization is hard to feign and impossible to impose by decree. Indeed, attempts to 'get one's message through' by force are usually doomed precisely because the use of force is made necessary by a lack of identity-based influence (see Chapter 8 below). For this reason, as a great many organizational theorists have recognized, the capacity for productive communication is one of the clearest indicators of the state of any set of organizational relations (e.g. McGregor, 1966; Mayo, 1949). In particular, and as a line of research dating back to Sherif's famous Boys Camp studies has shown, effective communication is almost impossible to obtain across the boundaries of intergroup conflict (see Sherif, 1966). It is therefore in those circumstances where 'quick fixes' to communication problems are most commonly sought that they are likely to prove least effective.

## Further Reading

Narrowing down the literature on communication to a recommended list of no more than half-a dozen papers is no easy task. Accordingly, the reader who is seriously interested in this topic is advised to take the following list simply as a point of departure. Nonetheless, Porter and Roberts' (1977) edited volume is recommended for its compactness and the fact that it contains a number of classic papers. The chapter by Katz and Kahn (1966) provides insight into system theory's development of human relations ideas and reveals further important points of contact between this tradition of research and the social identity approach. Krauss and Fussell's (196) chapter does not deal directly with social identity research, but it provides much more up-to-date coverage of communication research from a social psychological perspective and points to the as-yet-unfulfilled need for a 'fully dialogic' analysis of the form we have outlined. The papers by Bourhis (1991), Postmes, Spears and Lee (1998) Suzuki (1998) elaborate on the social identity principles that have been addressed in this chapter, but others (in particular, those by Mackie et al., 1992, van Knippenberg et al., 1994, and Wilder, 1990) are also well worth reading.

Bourhis, R. Y. (1991). Organizational communication and accommodation: Toward some conceptual and empirical links. In H. Giles, J. Coupland & N. Coupland (Eds.), *Contexts of accommodation: Developments in applied sociolinguistics. Studies in emotion and social interaction* (pp. 270-303). Cambridge: Cambridge University Press.

Katz, D. & Kahn, R. L. (1966). *The social psychology of organizations*. New York: Wiley (especially Chapter 9, pp. 223-258).

Krauss, R. M. & Fussell, S. R. (1996). Social psychological models of interpersonal communication. In E. T. Higgins & A. W. Kruglanski (Eds.), *Social psychology: Handbook of basic principles* (pp. 655-701). New York: Guilford Press.

Porter, L. W. & Roberts, K. (Eds.) (1977). *Communication in organizations*. Harmondsworth: Penguin.

Postmes, T., Spears, R., & Lea, M. (1998). Breaching or building social boundaries? SIDE-effects of computer-mediated communication. *Communication Research, 25,* 689-715.

Suzuki, S. (1998). In-group and out-group communication patterns in international organizations: Implications for social identity theory. *Communication Research, 25,* 154-182.

# 6   Group Decision-making

17 April 1961, was a dark day in American history. Early in the morning the US Navy, US Air Force and CIA helped a brigade of around 1,500 Cuban exiles invade the swampy coast of Cuba at the Bay of Pigs. On day one, four crucial supply ships failed to arrive on time, then two were sunk by Cuban planes and the other two fled. On day two the invasion force came up against about 20,000 members of the well-trained Cuban army. By day three, most of the 1,200 invaders still alive were captured and imprisoned. As described by Janis (1982, pp. 14-47) and other commentators, the invasion was 'a perfect failure'. Moreover, its repercussions were enormously damaging to the United States government, not least because it had to give $53 million worth of aid in exchange for the prisoners' release and the incident as a whole contributed to a strengthening of relations between Cuba and the Soviet Union with the result that Cuba went on to become a military stronghold for Soviet troops and home to a sizeable arsenal of nuclear weapons targeted at America.

Disastrous as it was, the Bay of Pigs invasion appeared all the more remarkable because it had been masterminded by a group of advisers in the White House administration of John Kennedy, a president widely perceived to be level-headed, peace-loving and intelligent. As well as this, all members of the advisory group were senior policy-makers, with expert qualifications and experience at the highest levels of a range of prestigious organizations — the Rockefeller Foundation, Harvard Business School, the Ford Motor Company and the US Air Force. According to Janis (1972, p. 43) the group represented 'one of the greatest arrays of intellectual talent in the history of American government'.

Not surprisingly, then, insider accounts of Kennedy's reaction to events suggest that as the news of failure reached him he was shocked and felt sick at heart. Unsurprisingly too, he also asked himself 'how could I have been so stupid to let them go ahead?' (Sorensen, 1966; cited in Janis, 1982, p. 16). The same question was asked formally by Janis (1971, 1972, 1982) and his answers have become part of the lore of the decision-making literature in organizational and political studies.

Janis's answers to the question centred on his characterization of the Bay of Pigs invasion as a perfect illustration of a phenomenon he termed *groupthink*. Groupthink is seen to occur where:

> Members of any small cohesive group tend to maintain esprit de corps by unconsciously developing a number of shared illusions and related norms that interfere with critical thinking and reality testing. (Janis, 1982, p. 35)

The term is therefore:

> A quick and easy way to refer to a mode of thinking that people engage in when they are deeply involved in a cohesive ingroup, when the members' strivings for unanimity override their motivation to realistically appraise alternative courses of action. (Janis, 1982, p. 9)

Significantly too, Janis argued that groupthink was not an isolated phenomenon confined to one decision-making group at a particular point in time and within a particular culture (a point previously made by Wilensky, 1967). On the contrary, he identified its symptoms in a variety of situations and within a number of very different groups. For example, amongst President Johnson's administration prior to the escalation of the Vietnam War in the 1960s; amongst President Nixon's administration as it created and then dealt with the Watergate scandal; amongst senior military officers prior to the Japanese invasion of Pearl Harbour in 1941; and amongst British Prime Minister Chamberlain's inner circle prior to the declaration of the Second World War. More recently too, the same analysis has been used to explain, amongst other things, decisions such as those which led to the marketing of the drug thalidomide in 1957 (Raven & Rubin, 1976), to the Carter administration's scheme to rescue hostages from Iran in 1980 (Smith, 1984) and to the explosion of the Space Shuttle Challenger in January 1986 (Moorhead, Ference & Neck, 1991; see Turner & Pratkanis, 1998c).

Indeed, such is the popularity of the groupthink account, that it has come to represent a major conceptualization of the group decision-making process in general, and the predominant conceptualization of the process of collectively arriving at faulty decisions. For this reason Janis's (1971) original *Psychology Today* article is religiously reproduced in collections of seminal organizational readings (e.g. Kolb, Rubin & McIntyre, 1979; Organ, 1978; Staw, 1995) and his model typically receives coverage in textbooks that is uncharacteristically lavish relative to the treatment accorded other social psychological theories (Fuller & Aldag, 1998; Paulus, 1998).

This chapter is thus one of a very large number on the topic of group decision-making that begins by recounting details of the Bay of Pigs fiasco, and for this reason the above introduction is really rather hackneyed. Yet, building upon growing criticism of Janis's formulation (see M. Turner & Pratkanis, 1998b), what is distinctive about this chapter is that it attempts to reconceptualize the groupthink model of faulty decision-making within a broader theoretical framework suggested by the social identity approach. This analysis focuses on two features of group decision-making that are apparent in groupthink — the tendency for groups to have both a *polarizing* and a *consensualizing* impact on individuals. In relation to these processes, and in direct contrast to Janis's assertions, it is argued that group decisions do not subvert the wisdom of individuals but actually express the group's collective meaning and purpose in important and creative ways. Viewed in this light, the decisions leading to the Bay of Pigs invasion and other similar fiascoes are seen not as the flawed manifestations of inevitably deficient group processes, but as outcomes of *rational processes played out in groups whose decisions we object to.*

## An overview of research into group decision-making

### The groupthink model

When Janis set himself the task of identifying the basis of the Kennedy administration's stupidity, the first possibility he considered was that its members were actually stupid. This was an option that he quickly dismissed. On the basis of the obvious qualifications of the personnel involved, the second paragraph of Janis's (1971) article concluded abruptly 'stupidity certainly is not the explanation' ( p. 43).

The groupthink analysis proposed by Janis was based on extensive analysis of historical accounts produced by participants in the various fiascoes he considered. In the case of the Bay of Pigs invasion, this information was provided in two key texts written by observers of the Kennedy administration: Arthur Schlesinger's *A Thousand Days* and Theodore Sorensen's *Kennedy*. Indeed, it was on reading the account put forward by Schlesinger — himself a member of the key advisory circle — that the seeds of Janis's analysis were sown. Specifically, after reading Schlesinger's book Janis (1982) 'began to wonder whether some form of psychological contagion, similar to social conformity phenomena observed in studies of small groups had interfered with their mental alertness' (p. vii). Later, on re-reading the same volume, Janis (1982) was struck that:

> Observations began to fit a specific pattern of concurrence-seeking behaviour that had impressed me time and time again in my research on other kinds of face-to-face groups, particularly when a 'we-feeling' of solidarity is running high. Additional accounts ... [led] me to conclude that group processes had been subtly at work, preventing the members of Kennedy's team from debating the real issues posed by the CIA's plan and from carefully appraising its serious risks. (p. vii)

As we have already suggested, the formal theorizing that developed out of these observations suggested that the decision to land troops at the Bay of Pigs arose from the groupthink syndrome. Janis expounded this analysis in terms of a number of key symptoms, a range of decision-making characteristics, and a set of antecedent conditions (see Figure 6.1). As well as this, he also identified a number of remedial interventions that could prevent groupthink occurring. And in view of the seriousness of the problem that the phenomenon was seen to pose for organizations (from those making sensitive commercial judgements to those considering issues of national importance), the need for these interventions was seen to be self-evident.

The core symptoms of groupthink fall into three classes: overestimations of the power and morality of the group, closed-mindedness and pressures towards uniformity. A group that has fallen prey to the syndrome thus tends to believe it is better, more powerful and more invulnerable than it really is and has unquestioning faith in its own moral authority. It is also very effective at explaining away warnings from outsiders and tends to underestimate the competence and strength of the relevant outgroups with which it is competing. Within-group consensus is also highly prized, so that individual group members who have doubts fail to voice them (i.e. they engage in self-censorship) and the group as a whole puts pressure on members who deviate from the group position. Here too group members collectively overestimate the degree to which group consensus actually exists and 'mindguards' emerge from within the group to shield it from information that might destroy its illusions.

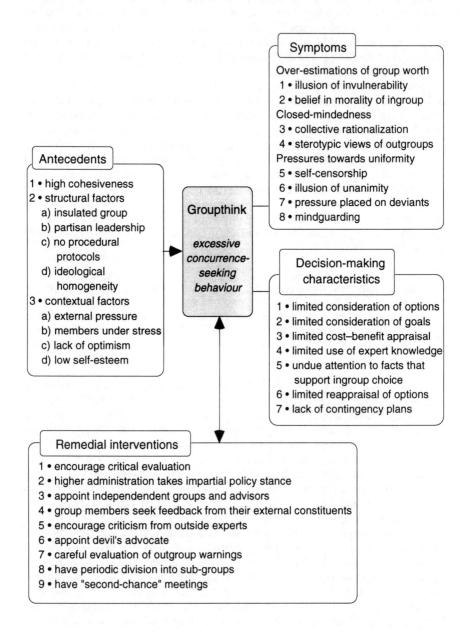

*Figure 6.1* Janis's model of groupthink (following Janis, 1971; Janis & Mann, 1977, p. 132)

All of these features were readily apparent in accounts of the Bay of Pigs invasion. Kennedy and his advisers clearly subscribed to the view that the Cubans were morally and politically inferior, ill-equipped and incompetent. Schlesinger also wrote that he himself kept silent while harbouring grave doubts about the invasion plan in order to preserve the unanimity of the group. Indeed, his doubts were so considerable that he apparently kept hoping that someone else would reveal the foolhardiness of the plan — though of course no one did. On top of this, Schlesinger admitted to playing the role of mindguard in having kept vital pieces of information from other members of the group.

In this case, as elsewhere, the consequences of groupthink are most apparent in patterns of concurrence-seeking decision-making. In order to preserve the sanctity of the group decision, and their faith in it, group members: (a) restrict the options and goals they consider and then fail to reappraise them later; (b) focus on the benefits rather than the risks associated with their decision; (c) fail to solicit as much information as they might and then process the information they do obtain in a manner that favours their decision; and, finally, (d) fail to set in place any safety nets or contingency plans to protect against adverse outcomes. Janis (1982) conceded that on rare occasions such strategies could lead to positive outcomes (e.g. renewed morale after defeat), but argued that:

> The positive effects are generally outweighed by the poor quality of the group's decision-making. My assumption is that the more frequently a group displays the symptoms, the worse will be the quality of its decisions, on average. (p. 175)

Having summarized the nature of groupthink, the key task that Janis set himself was to identify its causes and remedies. What leads groups to collectively 'lose their mind', and how can they be helped? The short answer to this question is that for Janis the causes of error lay in pressure for mutual support amongst members of very 'groupy' groups. At least moderate levels of cohesiveness are therefore seen as essential for the phenomenon to occur. However, full-blown groupthink is considered unlikely unless other structural and contextual conditions are in place. Specifically, it is more likely to eventuate when the group is insulated from outsiders, does not have a history of impartial leadership, and has no norms or protocols for making decisions methodically and carefully. Finally, a pattern of 'defensive avoidance' within the group is also believed to precipitate groupthink (Janis & Mann, 1977, p. 131). That is, the syndrome is more likely to occur where group members experience stress and low self-esteem in the face of threat from external agencies and perceive there to be little prospect of arriving at a better decision than the one under consideration.

As a corollary to these arguments, the means by which the errors of groupthink could be avoided are seen to lie in interventions which break down the group's status as a social and psychological entity. These include: (a) encouragement of group members to act autonomously, as critical agents and vigilant problem-solvers (e.g. through impartial leadership and appointment of devil's advocates; see Janis, 1982, 1989, pp. 231-264); (b) appointment of external experts and close attention to outgroup information and sources; and (c) periodic changes in group membership and division into sub-groups. Janis based his advocacy of these arrangements partly on evidence that such practices were associated with successful decision-making by the Kennedy administration

18 months after the Bay of Pigs invasion during the Cuban missile crisis. This crisis was brought about when Soviet ships suspected of bringing nuclear weapons to Cuba were subjected to a blockade by the US Navy. Here Kennedy is reported to have encouraged people with divergent views to participate in the decision-making process, to have encouraged new norms for vigilance, to have resisted the temptation to state his own preferences at the outset, and to have deliberately absented himself from key meetings. For Janis, these actions suggested that Kennedy had learned his lessons the hard way — a fact that enabled him to steer the world back from the brink of all-out nuclear war.

In setting out these various propositions, Janis deliberately presented his ideas about groupthink in the form of hypotheses, arguing that it would be for future researchers to test and develop his analysis. Yet, as Turner and Pratkanis (1998c) observe, upon surveying the history of empirical research into groupthink, one of the most striking features is the fact that there is very little of it. Indeed, these reviewers note that Janis's formulation has been the subject of less than two dozen empirical investigations. This is very much at odds with the prominence of the theory that we noted earlier (see Paulus, 1998). What is even more alarming is that of these studies, almost none provide unequivocal support for Janis's original arguments.

As an illustration of this point, a study by Peterson, Owens, Tetlock, Fan and Martorana (1998) examined archival information relating to successful and unsuccessful decision-making regimes within senior management groups in seven top American companies (e.g. CBS News, Chrysler, Coca-Cola). Amongst other things, aspects of decision-making practice were sorted on the basis of whether or not they were characteristic of the groupthink syndrome. The researchers then examined the extent to which the display of groupthink was associated with decisions of different quality. In contrast to Janis's hypothesis, groupthink symptoms appeared to be apparent in *all* group decision-making, and no more characteristic of the unsuccessful regimes than the successful ones. In one particularly interesting departure from Janis's predictions, Peterson et al. also found that successful decision-making groups did not have impartial leaders who refrained from informing other group members of their views at the outset, but rather had strong leaders who made their preferences clear and actively sought to persuade other group members that these were justified (see also Flowers, 1977; Leana, 1985).

It is interesting to note too, that Janis (1982, p. ix) recognized that his own reading of the political fiascoes that were the focus of his original investigations would have to be carefully checked as further evidence came to light due to the 'imperfect historical materials' he was working with. However, re-examination and checks of newly declassified documents by Kramer (1998) fail to provide the support for which Janis would have hoped. Indeed, Kramer's conclusion is that the process of decision-making that led Kennedy to sanction invasion of the Bay of Pigs and Johnson to approve escalation of United States involvement in the Vietnam War was utterly unremarkable, and characteristic of standard patterns of political behaviour:

> If anything, [Kennedy and Johnson] tended to ruminate intensely about their decisions, and always with a careful appraisal of the political consequences of action or inaction on a given issue. Consistently, their decisions as president

reflected the same sort of pragmatic appraisal that had helped them reach the highest pinnacles of power. (Kramer, 1998, p. 263)

## Group polarization research

Although most researchers believe that there are serious problems with Janis's groupthink hypothesis, its endurance is partly attributable to the fact that most also concede that it captures important features of the group decision-making process. In particular, it is apparent that there are significant points of contact between the features of groupthink described by Janis and the outcomes observed more generally in studies of the effect of group interaction on individuals' attitudes and beliefs. These have consistently shown that groups play a key role in both extremitizing and galvanizing individual inputs.

The history of research into such effects predates Janis's work and goes back to ground-breaking work conducted by Stoner (1961) and later replicated by Wallach, Kogan and Bem (1962; see also Kogan and Wallach, 1964). Stoner was a masters student in the school of Industrial Management at MIT and his thesis investigated the impact of discussion on people's willingness to endorse risky strategies as a means of resolving dilemmas. In a typical task participants were asked to consider the circumstances under which a young graduate should leave a secure but dull job with Company A in favour of an exciting but potentially insecure position at Company B. Stoner found that if individuals were predisposed to select risky options then group discussion had the effect of making their decisions even more risky. So, for example, if individuals initially thought that the graduate should join Company B only if the chance of that company succeeding were better than 3 in 10, then after discussion they might agree that the graduate should move so long as the company's chances of succeeding were better than 2 in 10.

Stoner coined the term *risky shift* to describe this effect and his results caused something of a stir amongst decision-making researchers because previous wisdom had suggested that group decisions simply reflected an *averaging* of individual responses (e.g. Allport, 1962; Kelley & Thibaut, 1954). This received view was based on famous studies by Sherif (1936) which showed that when making judgements about the apparent movement of a point of light in a darkened room (the so-called *autokinetic effect*), group members simply converged on the group mean. Thus if three people initially estimated that the light moved 7, 3 and 2 inches, as a group they might converge on a judgement that it moved 4 inches (see Sherif, 1936, p. 103).

In fact though, subsequent research by Moscovici and Zavalloni (1969) advanced upon Stoner's findings by showing that group interaction did not have a uni-directional impact upon individual preferences. Instead, the group served to extremitize the initial views of its individual members *in whichever direction they were already tending.* So in studies of French students with a positive view of President de Gaulle, group discussion led to even more positive views, but the same form of interaction tended to make their negative views of Americans even more negative. Similarly, Fraser, Gouge and Billig (1971) showed that when individuals shared an initial inclination towards caution, group discussion led them to become more cautious not more risky.

On the basis of such findings, Moscovici and Zavalloni (1969) argued that what Stoner had called the risky shift was better understood as *group polarization*. This term was preferred, and has been widely adopted, in recognition of the fact that after group discussion individuals' views become polarized (i.e. more extreme) in whichever direction they are already tending. Reconceptualizing the effect of group discussion in this way also helps to make sense of earlier findings of convergence under conditions where there was no tendency towards a particular pole in individuals' pre-discussion views (e.g. as reported by Sherif, 1936).

In the period of research immediately after Moscovici and Zavalloni had clarified the precise impact of group discussion on individual views, two explanations of the polarization effect came to dominate the literature: *persuasive arguments theory* and *social comparison theory* (see Myers & Lamm, 1976; Wetherell, 1987; Whyte, 1993). Persuasive arguments theory proposes that polarization arises from information sharing within a group that exposes individuals to novel and persuasive arguments (Burnstein & Vinokur, 1973, 1975, 1977). For example, if we think about the Kennedy administration in early 1961, it is easy to imagine that each of its members initially had slightly different reasons for wanting to invade the Bay of Pigs (to bolster morale, to teach the Cubans a lesson, to score a decisive victory against communism, etc.). Advocates of persuasive arguments theory would suggest that polarization is likely to occur under these circumstances (of the form that led to the decision to invade) because after group interaction each individual would now have access to *all* these arguments and hence their initial predispositions would be strengthened.

Although empirical research lends some support to these ideas, in its raw form persuasive arguments theory is seriously challenged by evidence that polarization can occur without the exchange of arguments at all. In this vein, Cotton and Baron (1980) found that simply making individuals aware of the *positions* of other ingroup members (without reference to *why* they held those positions) was sufficient to bring about a polarizing shift in the group as a whole. The idea that polarization results from a mechanistic aggregation of information is also inconsistent with evidence that polarization is typically accompanied by some convergence of the form identified by Sherif (1936). Thus while moderate group members become more extreme in their views, extreme members generally become slightly more moderate (Turner, 1991; Wetherell, 1987).

Evidence of convergence is also damaging to the analysis of group polarization advanced by social comparison theorists (e.g. Lamm & Myers, 1978; Myers, Bruggink, Kersting & Schlosser, 1980). This theory suggests that polarization results from a desire amongst group members to vie competitively with each other for the opportunity to express values and beliefs that are held dear in society at large. Versions of this theory also suggest that prior to group discussion individuals are subject to *pluralistic ignorance*, believing that they alone hold strong views about a given topic (Levinger & Schneider, 1969). The discovery that colleagues in fact share their views is thought to release group members from this misconception, so that extremitization results.

According to such an analysis, members of Kennedy's team might have arrived at a polarized decision because they sought to outdo each other in displaying anti-Cuban and pro-American credentials having previously been oblivious to the strength of other team members' views. Again though, the evidence presented by Janis and in other empirical studies (e.g. Whyte, 1993, pp. 434-5; see also Chapter 5 above), suggests that individual contributions to group decisions are characterized more by a desire for consensus than by a desire to be different. Evidence therefore indicates that in making their contribution to a group decision, individuals do not want to stand out as deviants but want to be embraced as prototypical group members. Moreover, it is worth noting that Janis (1982, p. 175) believed pluralistic ignorance was not ameliorated but exacerbated (albeit in a different form) by groupthink. So while social comparison theorists argue that prior to group interaction individuals are unaware of how much their colleagues *support* a particular stance, Janis argued that as group members individuals are unaware of how much their colleagues share their *misgivings*.

Taken together, these views point to a fundamental discontinuity between individual inputs and group output — a point recognized in different ways by both Sherif (1936) and Janis (1971, 1982). In this they suggest that any analysis of the group decision-making process that is based on a consideration of inputs or values that exist independently of the group in question, is likely to be limited. It is the character of a particular group in a particular context that *makes* particular arguments persuasive and that *leads* to particular positions being valued. In essence, then, the core problem with both persuasive arguments and social comparison theories is that their individualistic assumptions encourage researchers to neglect the distinct psychological properties of group decisions as social products (see Turner, 1991; Wetherell, 1987).

However, as well as this, it is clear that differences in locating the source of pluralistic ignorance point to complex problems with attempts to identify the nature of error in the decision-making process. Do groups produce stupidity, or do they reduce it? Do they distort intentions or do they clarify them? The arguments we have reviewed offer no satisfactory resolution to these questions, but they make a good case for the need to go beyond the very one-sided answers originally provided by Janis (see Miller & Prentice, 1994).

### Decision-tree and other prescriptive approaches

Before attempting to provide an analysis of psychological process that addresses some of the difficult questions thrown up by groupthink and group polarization research, it is worth pausing to consider (a) why organizations bother making group decisions at all and (b) various prescriptions for the *form* of group discussion that have been generated by organizational researchers. In light of the research we have already discussed, the first question seems entirely pertinent. If groups routinely produce only faulty and extremitized decisions, why aren't organizational decisions simply made by suitably qualified individuals? Wouldn't organizational goals be better served if the decisions of experts and leaders were simply communicated in an appropriate fashion to relevant parties?

Leaving aside the fact that groups can sometimes make better decisions than individuals (e.g. as in the handling of the Cuban missile crisis), one of the key reasons why group decisions are important to organizations was revealed in seminal research by Lewin and his colleagues conducted immediately after the Second World War (Lewin, 1960). In a series of studies designed to change the health and dietary habits of Americans, these researchers looked at the impact of procedures which involved either (a) giving people relevant information in the form of public lectures or private instruction or (b) inviting them to discuss the information in small groups and make decisions about the appropriate form of action.   All these studies indicated that participants' acceptance of the information was greatly enhanced where they had the opportunity to discuss ideas amongst themselves and decide what to do.   For example, Radke and Klisurich (1947) found that when new mothers attended a lecture on the benefits of giving their children orange juice and cod liver oil only 19 per cent were following this advice two weeks later, compared to 47 per cent of those who had come to a group decision on the basis of the same information. In an industrial context, Levine and Butler (1956) also found that foremen who discussed and decided upon a policy of non-prejudiced worker evaluation were much more likely to implement this policy than those given the same information in a lecture.   Lewin (1956) himself explained such effects in terms of the difference between the individualized and social character of the two situations:

> Both the mass approach and the individual approach place the individual in a quasi-private, psychologically isolated situation with himself and his own ideas.  Although he may, physically, be part of a group listening to a lecture, he finds himself in an 'individual situation', psychologically speaking.  (p. 290)

In individual situations like this:

> The degree of eagerness [to go along with the message] varie[s] greatly with the personal preference. ...  [But] in the case of the group decision the eagerness seems to be relatively independent of personal preference; the individual seems mainly to act as a 'group member'.  (p. 300)

The significance of group decisions for organizations thus derives from the fact that individuals are generally quite willing to internalize and abide by a collective decision because they are *self-involved* in it as group members (e.g. see Katz & Kahn, 1966, p. 380).   On the other hand, as non-involved individuals, their commitment to any decision is much more idiosyncratic and tenuous.  These observations are consistent with arguments about the distinct contributions of the personal and social self to work motivation that we developed in Chapter 4.

In light of all the above evidence, organizational theorists making recommendations about how to handle group decisions have had to tread a fine line that balances (a) recognition of the group's contribution to increased compliance with (b) awareness of the fact that groups can also be more extreme than the organization desires or demands.   One way of dealing with this dilemma has been to argue that group decisions should only be made when they are absolutely necessary.  This position has been justified on grounds not only that group decisions can be deficient in key ways, but also that they are costly and time-consuming to generate (Jewell, 1998; Maier, 1967).

To help managers ascertain whether or not they need to involve other people in the decision-making process, a number of decision-tree models identify feasible forms of participation as a function of specific features of the decision to be made. The models 'attempt to come to grips with the complexities [of leadership]' (Vroom, 1974, p. 67), but in effect they provide prescriptive strategies similar to others that we discussed in Chapter 3.

The best known contribution of this form was presented by Vroom and Yetton (1973; Vroom, 1974; updated by Vroom & Jago, 1988) but others sharing similar assumptions have also been developed and tested by Hackman and Morris (1975), Nutt (1976), and Stumpf, Zand and Freedman (1979). Vroom and Yetton's model outlines appropriate participation options for managers as a function of seven decision features: whether (a) the decision requires a high quality solution; (b) the manager has sufficient information to make a high quality decision on his or her own; (c) the problem is structured; (d) subordinates' acceptance of the decision is critical; (e) subordinates' acceptance of the decision is likely if they are not involved; (f) subordinates share the manager's and organization's goals; and (g) subordinates are likely to disagree about the solution. As can be seen from Figure 6.2, of the fourteen possible combinations of responses to these various questions, in only three cases is a group meeting and accompanying group decision the preferred option. One of these (problem type 3 in Figure 6.2) is when a quality decision is not required, acceptance by subordinates is essential for implementation and those subordinates would not accept a solo decision by the manager. The second (problem type 6) is when a quality decision is required, the problem is structured, acceptance by subordinates is essential for implementation and those subordinates would not accept a solo decision by the manager but they share the organization's goals. The third (problem type 12) is when a quality decision is required, the manager lacks sufficient information, the problem is unstructured, acceptance by subordinates is essential for implementation and those subordinates would not accept a solo decision by the manager but they share the organization's goals. In essence, then, the model suggests that group decisions are only essential when a manager faces mutiny over something trivial, or when the involvement of subordinates cannot be avoided (e.g. because the manager knows nothing).

Prescriptive as they are, normative models of this form are not the only way in which researchers have attempted to carefully script and stage-manage the contribution of personnel to organizational decision-making. Another way in which this issue has been approached is through the development of different *types* of decision-making and employee-involvement group, each tailored to achieve particular objectives. The features of some of the more prominent types are summarized in Table 6.1, together with their primary purpose.

Evidence as to exactly how well each of these groups perform their function is generally quite mixed and depends upon the criteria upon which such a judgement is based (Guzzo, 1982; Mitchell et al., 1988). Moreover, models which reduce the management of group decision making to a mechanistic set of prescriptions meet with similarly mixed support (for reviews see Field & House, 1990; Horgan & Simeon, 1990; Tetrault, Schriesheim & Neider, 1988).

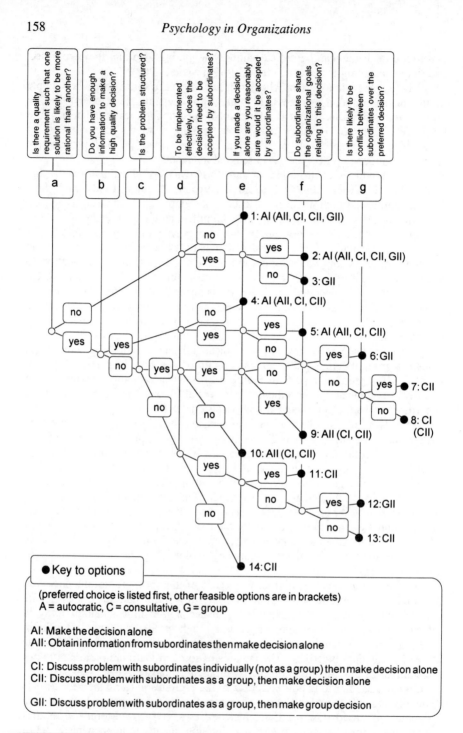

*Figure 6.2* Vroom and Yetton's normative model of participation in decision-making (Vroom & Yetton, 1973; Vroom, 1974)

*Table 6.1* Prominent types of organizational decision-making and employee-involvement group

| Group Type | Features | Primary Purpose |
| --- | --- | --- |
| Brainstorming | • ideas are generated regardless of quality<br>• individuals elaborate and augment ideas<br>• evaluation occurs after all ideas have been generated | generating new ideas |
| Committee | • hold regular meetings of formally selected or eligible individuals<br>• group discusses formal agenda and keeps record of discussion and any decisions | exchanging information and views, evaluating options |
| Delphi | • individuals respond privately to questionnaires<br>• responses are collated and returned to individuals along with a second questionnaire<br>• responses are collated again and an executive decision is made | generating and evaluating options |
| Nominal | • individuals generate ideas alone<br>• individuals present their ideas to the group<br>• group discusses ideas<br>• individuals vote privately on options | generating and evaluating options |
| Quality circle | • hold regular, frequent and voluntary meetings of small groups of employees working in similar area but with different personal characteristics<br>• groups discuss problems affecting quality of work<br>• group has no power to implement ideas or decisions | monitoring and improving quality and productivity |

One potential source of these problems is that most prescribed forms of collective decision-making impose major strictures and controls on the group and its place in the organization. In particular, most decision-making and employee-involvement groups are designed with a 'safety-first' principle in mind which serves to protect the organization as a whole from radical decisions of the form discussed by Janis (1982) and Moscovici and Zavalloni (1969). Innovations in this area are therefore designed to create groups that are non-threatening both to the participants and to the organization as a whole. This is achieved either by minimizing evaluation and criticism of options (in brainstorming groups), by making the group exist in name only (in nominal and delphi groups), by isolating individual participants (in delphi groups), or by giving the group no formal power (in quality circles and on many consultative committees; e.g. Harley, 1999; Kelly & Kelly, 1991).

At the same time, though, group activities have become increasingly fashionable in recent years and there has also been a general move in the organizational field to recommend *participative decision-making* (PDM; e.g. see Harvey-Jones, 1994; Jewell, 1998; Miller & Monge, 1986; Sagie, 1995). This partly reflects attempts to maximize employees' involvement with a view to increasing their acceptance of organizational decisions and their faith in procedural justice (along lines suggested by Coch & French, 1948; Lewin, 1956; Tyler, 1997; Tyler, Rasinski & Spoddock, 1985). Managers are thus given the challenging task of creating groups that are visible and abundant but superficial and emasculated. Stein (1982) therefore counsels that:

> Managers need ... to be aware that their subordinates might well profit from the facilitating effects of group membership. At the same time, however, they need to be aware of steamroller tactics, in which the group may become overstimulated and oversell itself. (p. 146)

As we intimated in Chapter 1, a common way to respond to this challenge is to allow the rhetoric of group participation to part company with organizational reality. In this way, groups and teams become hollow slogans used primarily to pacify workers rather than to empower them (Harley, 1999; Kelly & Kelly, 1991). Although this approach often proves to be politically expedient (because it protects the status quo), we will see in upcoming sections that its psychological validity is somewhat suspect.

## Social identity and group decision-making

META — CONTRAST PRINCIPLE

The theoretical principles that have been expounded in previous chapters establish a clear platform for an explanation of the potential for group interaction to polarize and consensualize group decisions in the manner described by Janis (1982). Indeed, in many ways examination of the properties of group decisions allows us to synthesize a range of points that arise from the social identity approach to issues of leadership, motivation and information management.

In the first instance, the capacity for social interaction to polarize a group's position can be seen to follow straightforwardly from self-categorization principles that were developed in Chapters 2 and 3 (see Turner, 1991; Turner & Oakes, 1986, 1989; Wetherell, 1987). A core idea presented in those chapters was that the process of social categorization reflects the capacity of any category to allow the perceiver to make sense of a particular stimulus array. One aspect of this argument is that categorization is partly dependent on the perception of *relative differences* between stimuli, in a manner specified by the principle of meta-contrast (Turner, 1985).

According to the principle of meta-contrast, any collection of people (or things) is more likely to be seen as a categorical entity (as a common group) to the extent that the differences between those people are smaller than the differences between them and others that are salient in a particular context. As well as this, any particular group member (Alan, say) will become more prototypical of the group to the extent that the average difference between him and other ingroup members is smaller than the difference between him and outgroup members. In this way meta-contrast determines both the extent to which a given category becomes salient and the extent to which particular category members are representative of it (e.g. see Figures 2.9 and 3.2).

To revisit these ideas in terms of an example, we could think of three senior policy-makers working on a project to promote the fortunes of an incumbent conservative-leaning government. All are sympathetic to the government in power, but they also differ in the extent to which they support its goals and values. Let's imagine that Alan (a) is very right wing, Beth (b) is moderately right wing and Clive (c) is slightly right wing, as in Figure 6.3.

Now, in a situation in which these three people are formulating policy on their own and with little reference to external events and forces, the meta-contrast principle suggests that they should be relatively unlikely to define themselves as members of a common social category in terms of a shared social identity (Case 1 in Figure 6.3). In this setting, then, because the differences between them should be relatively pronounced, the individuals are more likely to categorize themselves and each other in terms of distinct personal or lower-level social identities (perhaps as members of different party factions). To the extent that any member of the group represented what they had in common, this should also tend to be the person whose views are most representative of a compromise between all three's views (i.e. Beth). At the same time the other two individuals (Alan and Clive) should be equally and minimally representative of what the group has in common.

We can extend this example to think of situations in which this same group of people is acting in a context where events lead them to make comparisons with other people who are (a) more left wing (Case 2 in Figure 6.3), (b) more right wing or (c) both more left and more right wing. Perhaps the group is entering an election campaign in which it faces opposition from a left-wing party, a more right-wing party, or both. In all of these situations the meta-contrast principle suggests that the three policy makers should be more likely to define themselves in terms of a shared social identity as 'us conservatives' different from 'those ultra-conservatives' or 'those lefties'. In this situation, then, their personal differences should be transformed into group similarities and their ingroup as a whole should be seen as more homogeneous. Along lines suggested in Chapter 2, evidence from a large number of empirical studies supports precisely such predictions: social identity salience and perceptions of ingroup homogeneity (i.e. of similarity amongst members of the ingroup) are heightened dramatically as the context of individuals' judgement changes from being intragroup to intergroup in nature (e.g. Doosje et al., 1998; Haslam, Oakes, Turner & McGarty, 1995; Simon, Pantaleo & Mummendey, 1995).

However, in these intergroup settings, the meta-contrast principle predicts not only that Alan, Beth and Clive should be more likely to categorize themselves as members of a common social category, but also that the extent to which each is representative (i.e. prototypical) of that category will vary as a function of who they compare themselves with. If the group compares itself with ultra-conservatives, Clive (the least conservative of the three) should gain in prototypicality relative to Alan because he is more different to this particular outgroup and thus serves to maximize the inter-class component of meta-contrast. For the same reasons, Alan (the most conservative group member) should become more prototypical than Clive if the group compares itself with a

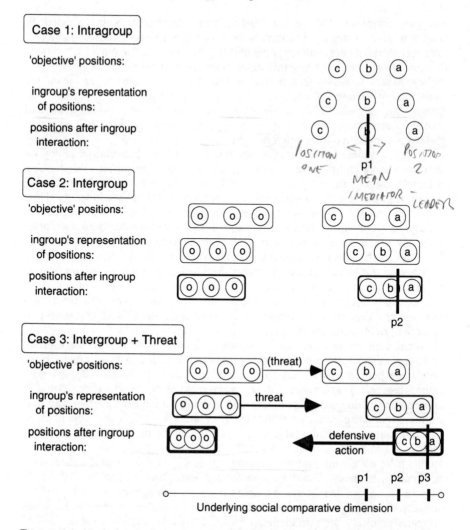

*Figure 6.3* Variation in intragroup homogeneity, consensus and the position of an ingroup prototype as a function of social comparative context

*Note*: a, b, c = ingroup members, o = outgroup member (as defined in Cases 2 and 3), pN = position of ingroup prototype.  Boxes indicate salience of social category (ingroup and outgroup), with greater thickness indicating heightened salience. In Case 1 a, b and c are defined in terms of personal (or low-level social) identity and differentiated from each other, but in Cases 2 and 3 they (and the o's) are defined in terms of a shared category membership and represented as more interchangeable with each other.  As the intergroup context becomes more salient (especially when associated with the perception of threat to the ingroup) the ingroup prototype becomes more polarized, perceived intragroup homogeneity is increased and is further enhanced by the consensualizing effects of social interaction.  In these cases social reality is defined in terms of a much more sharply differentiated sense of 'us' and 'them'.   When the collective self is threatened (as in Case 3) this may also lead to social identity-maintaining defensive action.

left-wing outgroup (Case 2 in Figure 6.3). However, in the context of comparisons with both left- and right-wing outgroups, Beth should be more prototypical (as she was in the intragroup context), because she is maximally different from these two outgroups, but also least different to the other two ingroup members.

In this way, and as we argued in relation to the emergence of group leaders in Chapter 3 (see Figure 3.2; Turner, 1991), we can see that the position that is prototypical of the group as a whole will shift as a function of social comparative context. In particular, this ingroup norm (or prototype) will become extremitized to the extent that an ingroup compares itself to an outgroup that advocates a different position on an issue that is relevant to the ingroup members' social self-categorization. When 'us' is opposed to 'them', what 'us' means will be less 'them-like' than it would if 'you' and 'I' are considered alone.

Support for these arguments has been provided by Hogg et al. (1990) in research which looked, amongst other things, at variation in participants' perceptions of the position of an ingroup norm (i.e. the prototypical ingroup position) as a function of changes to the comparative frame of reference. As predicted, when participants were presented with information about a more cautious outgroup they perceived the prototypical ingroup position to be more risky; when presented with information about a more risky outgroup they perceived the prototypical ingroup position to be more cautious; and when presented with information about both risky and cautious outgroups they saw the prototype as lying close to the mean ingroup position. Along similar lines, computer simulations and empirical studies reported by McGarty et al. (1992) have found that as an ingroup becomes more extreme within a given frame of reference, the relative prototypicality of extreme members is increased and thus the normative position of the group as a whole becomes more polarized.

This analysis therefore goes some way to explaining how the norms of a group can change in response to changes in the social environment. But how do the arguments bear upon processes of social interaction and the impact of such interaction on group decisions? Here again the answer lies in arguments introduced in Chapters 2 and 4 concerning the manner in which social influence is structured by the self-categorization process (see Abrams & Hogg, 1990; Hogg & Turner, 1987b; Turner, 1991; Turner & Oakes, 1986, 1989).

At the heart of our earlier discussion was an assertion that the perceived importance of another person's view of the world — and the motivation to ascertain and act upon his or her view — depends upon how that person is categorized relative to self. When others are seen as sharing social self-category membership with a perceiver, they are perceived to be qualified to inform him or her about aspects of social reality relevant to the ingroup. As well as this, the perceiver *expects* them to hold similar views to him or herself and so he or she is motivated to *appropriately resolve* any differences of opinion (Turner, 1987a). This process therefore sets the scene for *mutual social influence*, whereby individuals who categorize themselves in terms of a common social identity discuss and negotiate their differences with an expectation, and motivational pressure, to reach agreement. To help them do this, they exchange information relevant to their shared identity, clarify points of disagreement, identify and build upon common ground (along lines discussed in Chapter 5; see Haslam, Turner,

Oakes, McGarty et al., 1998; Postmes & Spears, 1998). Moreover, the position that serves to guide such interaction, and towards which it should lead, is that of the ingroup prototype. This is because it is this position that defines what they have in common in this particular setting (e.g. as found by Stasser & Titus, 1985, 1987).

Accordingly, *under conditions of shared social identity salience, group discussion should generally lead to convergence upon a prototypical ingroup position.* Moreover, in light of the foregoing discussion about the manner in which the ingroup prototype varies with context, we can see that these arguments lead to a prediction that in particular social settings, group decisions should be both consensual and polarized. In particular, this outcome is predicted when an ingroup compares itself with a highly salient outgroup — for example, under conditions of social competition (Cases 2 and 3 in Figure 6.3). On the other hand, convergence without polarization is anticipated when a group compares itself with multiple outgroups that are both more and less extreme than itself, and *div*ergence without polarization is predicted when decisions are made in an intragroup (or interpersonal) context (Case 1). This latter prediction follows from the argument that in intragroup contexts, individuals should be more inclined to categorize themselves in terms of personal or lower-level social identities and in these circumstances — as members of different self-categories — they should not perceive one another to be qualified to inform, validate and correct their various views of the world (see Abrams, Wetherell, Cochrane, Hogg & Turner, 1990).

Applied to the example of our political decision-making group, we would therefore predict that Alan, Beth and Clive should be most likely to disagree about what form the project to promote the government should take in a situation where they are making their decisions alone and are very inwardly focused (e.g. because they are competing with each other). Of course factors other than comparative context (e.g. a history of prior association as members of the group) might serve to increase their awareness of a shared social identity and these would make convergence on a common solution more likely. The same is true in a situation where the group defines itself in relation to multiple groups (or social positions) both more and less extreme. Here a salient social identity should increase mutual influence and convergence on an ingroup norm, but because that norm is unlikely to be polarized, no group polarization should ensue. In effect, this situation corresponds to situations like those confronted by participants in Sherif's (1936) classic studies, where circumstances serve to make a shared identity meaningful but the group compares itself with no clear outgroup and no specific set of alternative positions (Turner, 1987a).

However, both polarization and convergence would be expected when our three decision-makers explicitly compare themselves with a specific outgroup (or the situation dictates that they consider alternative social positions of a particular type). Based on the principle of meta-contrast, we would expect that they would converge on a position more aligned with Alan than with Clive if they were confronted by a left-wing group (Case 2 in Figure 6.3), but that they would converge on a position more aligned with Clive than with Alan if they were confronted by an ultra right-wing group.

Support for predictions of this form was generated in the research by Hogg et al. (1990) that we referred to above. Here manipulations of comparative context led to the prototypical ingroup position being perceived as more polarized when the ingroup was compared with a single different outgroup, and under these (and only these) circumstances group discussion also led to individual views converging on that polarized position. These conditions also correspond closely to those that are observed to lead to polarization elsewhere in the research literature (e.g. Fraser et al., 1971; Moscovici & Zavalloni, 1969; Stephenson & Brotherton, 1975; Stoner, 1961; for reviews see Myers & Lamm, 1976; Turner, 1987a; Wetherell, 1987).

The above account proves an elegant, parsimonious and empirically powerful explanation of key effects reported in the decision-making literature (a point confirmed in recent studies of organizational decision making reported by Abrams, 1999). But how does it lead to an explanation of full-blown groupthink of the type discussed by Janis (1971, 1982)? In fact, if we look closely at the picture that is emerging under conditions of intergroup comparison, we can see that this is already starting to resemble the one portrayed by Janis in his original work. The group is polarized, its views are consensually shared, its members are sharing information that is relevant to their shared identity (but not that which is of a more idiosyncratic nature and irrelevant to that identity), they are supporting ideas which are in line with the ingroup norm and rejecting (or not raising) those aligned with the outgroup. As well as this, they have a well-developed sense of 'us' and 'them', and social identity theory's esteem-related principles suggest that they should be motivated to develop a relatively positive view of their ingroup and a correspondingly negative view of the outgroup.

Moreover, while all these features of the group may be relatively unexceptional in standard conditions of intergroup comparison (of the form created in most empirical studies), they should become notably more pronounced under conditions of heightened social identification. This in fact is the basis of arguments developed by M. Turner and Pratkanis (1994, 1998a) in their social identity model of groupthink. In particular, these authors highlight the role that perceived or actual threat from an outgroup can play in accentuating all of the above tendencies. This, they argue, heightens pressure on the ingroup to maintain its positive self-image 'at all costs', and will be felt particularly keenly when the threat is associated with negative outcomes for individuals who are highly identified with, and 'locked in' to their membership of the particular group in question (i.e. the die-hards; see Branscombe & Wann, 1994).

So, to elaborate our example further, we could think of a situation in which Alan, Beth and Clive are devising a policy to help the government respond to a left-wing group that has been highly critical of the policy-making group and its activities (Case 3 in Figure 6.3). Here Turner and Pratkanis's arguments would lead us to anticipate that the threat that such an attack was perceived to pose for the ingroup might precipitate a decision to retaliate with which all members would agree. In the process of arriving at this decision we would also expect the group members to be highly motivated to protect a positive sense of shared social identity. Accordingly, they are likely to express indignation at the effrontery of the attack while at the same time interpreting their own actions as morally and intellectually superior to those of the outgroup.

And here, of course, if we think of Alan, Beth and Clive not as members of a fictional group, but as members of the Kennedy, Johnson or Nixon administration, then we can see that these outcomes correspond closely to those observed in the acts of political decision making discussed by Janis (1982). Moreover, we see that while we may very well judge such outcomes to be foolhardy, unjustified or stupid, they are not themselves a manifestation of irrationality or mindlessness. On the contrary, they flow from processes that are, in important ways, normal, rational and unremarkable (Fuller & Aldag, 1998; Hogg, 1992; Kramer, 1998; Whyte, 1989). Accordingly, where they exist, the problems of groupthink can be seen to lie not in the *way* the group thinks but in *what* it thinks.

## Some empirical tests of the social identity approach

### Group polarization as conformity to an extremitized norm

The analysis of group polarization presented above has been tested in several extensive programmes of empirical research (for detailed reviews see Turner, 1991; Wetherell, 1987, pp. 159-170). A central goal of this work has been to show how polarization, and factors that contribute to it, are shaped by features of social context. In particular, researchers have sought to show that polarization of any particular form is underpinned by an act of social identification on the part of group members, and that it is this transformation of the self that is responsible for the distinctive features of group decisions.

In an early study of this form, Mackie and Cooper (1984) asked students to listen to a tape-recording of a discussion between members of a group that the students were led to believe they would either be joining or against which they thought their own group would have to compete. The discussion either favoured the retention of standardized university tests or their abolition. As expected, exposure to the arguments on the tape had some general effect on participants, so that those who heard arguments for retention were more disposed to the tests than those who heard arguments for abolition. However, along lines discussed in Chapter 5 (e.g. McGarty et al., 1994; Mackie et al., 1990), this effect was completely conditioned by the presumed source of the arguments. Only when the discussion supposedly emanated from an ingroup were the arguments it contained influential in shaping the participants' own views.

In a second study that extended these findings, participants listened to a tape advocating or opposing test abolition under conditions where they were either given no information about their relationship to the group on the tape (the uncategorized condition) or were told that they were going to join it (the categorized condition). Before stating their own position, participants had to estimate the position of the group on the tape. As predicted, those in the categorized condition perceived this position to be much more extreme than did those in the uncategorized condition. When they expressed their own views, the judgements of categorized participants then showed conformity to this normative position in the manner anticipated by self-categorization theory. There was no extension beyond the norm as would be predicted on the basis of a desire for interpersonal differentiation of the form suggested by social comparison theorists (e.g. Jellison & Arkin, 1977).

Support for self-categorization and social identity principles is also provided by a number of studies which explore the relationship between polarization and depersonalization (i.e. change in the level of self-categorization from a personal to a social level; see Figure 2.7). In a study explicitly designed to examine this relationship, Turner, Wetherell and Hogg (1989) looked at the behaviour of individuals who were randomly identified as having either a risky or a cautious 'decision-making style'. Half the participants were told that decision-making style was a factor specific to particular *individuals*, while the other half were told it was characteristic of particular *groups*. Consistent with the social identity approach, the authors found that group polarization was only displayed by groups of individuals who thought that their decision making style was a *group-based norm*. When they thought riskiness or caution was a personal attribute, groups of risky individuals moved to caution and groups of cautious individuals moved to risk.

Along similar lines, in an extension of her earlier work, Mackie (1986) found that in conditions of intergroup competition for a prize, individuals' views were only extremitized after exposure to group discussion where participants focused on the performance of the group as a whole rather than their own performance as individuals. When the winning group was to be given a monetary prize, individuals conformed to an extremitized group norm, but when the best group member was to receive a prize, no such conformity occurred. As in Turner et al.'s (1989) study, polarization and mutual co-ordination were thus contingent on shared social identification, while the salience of personal identity was associated with a desire for interpersonal differentiation.

Similar effects to these were also obtained in a study reported by Spears, Lea and Lee (1990) which examined computer-mediated group decision-making in relation to a number of social, economic and organizational issues (ranging from the selling off of nationalized industries to support for affirmative action). The study manipulated social identity salience and also the physical presence of other group members. In some conditions group members were individuated in the sense that they were physically present and visible to other group members, but in other conditions they were de-individuated (i.e. isolated and anonymous). Following previous work by Reicher (1984; Reicher, Spears & Postmes, 1995), the authors reasoned that conformity to ingroup norms, and hence polarization, would be greater where participants' social identity was salient and no individuating information was available to conflict with this social categorization. This prediction was confirmed, and in this respect supported other findings (e.g. Kiesler, Siegel & McGuire, 1984) suggesting that the anonymity of computer-based interaction does not always temper group decisions in the manner generally assumed by proponents of Delphi groups. Instead, when it is predicated on a common social identity, such interaction can actually make those decisions more extreme.

Presenting a more elaborate analysis of these data, Lea and Spears (1991, see also Spears & Lea, 1992) sought to test between a social identity-based analysis of their findings and arguments that extremitized computer-mediated communication (e.g. flaming — the sending of hostile or abusive messages) is an example of disinhibition and anti-normative behaviour. This alternative explanation follows from popular views of the deindividuation process which suggest that the behaviour of anonymous group members (e.g. prison guards and prisoners) reflects a loss of self and an associated loss of accountability, responsibility and decency (Zimbardo, 1969; see Chapter 10 below; Reicher, 1987; Reicher et al., 1995). Supporting the social identity analysis, the authors found that the enhanced polarization produced in the condition where social identity was salient and participants were de-individuated was actually associated with the exchange of by far the greatest number of 'socially orientated' remarks (i.e. those with group maintenance functions). Polarization thus arose out of mutual support and encouragement, not hostility and enmity.

As discussed by Turner and Oakes (1986) and Wetherell (1987), the results of all the above studies suggest that many of the informational and social factors that are deemed by theorists to be *explanations* of polarization are themselves *outcomes* of the self-categorization process. Thus, the value of any position lies not in its correspondence to abstract ideals or norms (as proposed by Brown, 1965; Myers & Lamm, 1976), rather it is a function of the position's capacity to define the ingroup — and hence the self — in context. Similarly, arguments themselves are not inherently valid and persuasive (as suggested by Burnstein, 1982), instead it is the fact that they are associated with other people whom one categorizes as similar to self that *makes* them self-referentially informative and hence worth heeding (McLachlan, 1986; see Chapter 5 above). Ingroup arguments invite individuals to do the intellectual and creative work necessary to produce influence in a way that those from an outgroup do not (David & Turner, 1996, 1999; Turner, 1991).

Moreover, this same social identity-based motivation can be seen to endow groups with the ability to generate the *novel collaborative products* that polarized decisions are. This is a critical observation, because it alerts us to two fundamental points (see Asch, 1952; Turner & Oakes, 1986). The first of these is that polarization provides clear evidence of the Gestalt theorists' argument that group decisions (like group products generally) are genuinely more than the sum of their individual parts. The second is that this psychological creativity cannot be explained with reference to individualistic principles such as information aggregation or interpersonal competition. Just as the phenomenon of polarization takes individuals beyond their individuality, so its explanation demands that decision-making theorists move beyond their individualism.

*The contribution of shared social identity to consensual group decisions*

As well as noting that groupthink is associated with radical and polarized decisions, a prominent feature of Janis's model is the assertion that it will also be associated with highly stereotyped views of outgroups and pressures towards consensus in these and all other judgements. A similar constellation of effects is also implicated in the social identity analysis of group decision-making (see Figure 6.3). Accordingly, it is pertinent to consider more closely exactly how (and whether) group members collectively decide upon definitions of their ingroup and relevant outgroups in the process of developing a shared construal of social reality. What processes lead to shared beliefs that 'we're superior' and 'they're inferior'?

In reflecting on this question, it is interesting to note that although Janis garnered evidence of consensual outgroup stereotypes in each of his own case studies, social psychologists have generally been much less successful in attempts to uncover similar effects. Indeed, after extensive reviews of the literature some researchers have concluded that traditional studies of stereotype content (e.g. Gilbert, 1951; Karlins, Coffman & Walters, 1969; Katz & Braly, 1933) actually reveal very little evidence of stereotype consensus. Condor (1990) thus concludes that 'ideas about shared stereotypes ... are often nothing more than a priori assumptions which may function to preclude any further analysis of a contentious issue' (p. 237; see also Gardner, 1993). How, then, can these views be reconciled with those of Janis? Is it really the case that certain forms of group decision are associated with shared stereotypes of outgroups, or is the phenomenon of stereotype consensus illusory?

Such questions are of interest not just to decision-making theorists, but also to a wide range of researchers who have sought to understand the causes and consequences of stereotyping. This debate has also fed into organizational literature which has been concerned (a) to understand how groups in the workplace develop pejorative and potentially damaging views of each other and (b) to work out how these might be changed (e.g. Falkenberg, 1990; Fiske & Glick, 1995; Heilman, 1995; Noe, 1988). Amongst such researchers, two distinct views are readily apparent. On the one hand, many cognitive theorists have argued that the study of stereotype consensus is methodologically inconvenient and theoretically irrelevant. Hamilton, Stroessner and Driscoll (1994) thus suggest that:

> Stereotypes are belief systems that reside in the minds of individuals. ... In this view, therefore, neither the definition nor the measurement of stereotypes should be constrained by the necessity of consensual agreement. (p. 298; see also Judd & Park, 1993, p. 110).

However, this position has been countered by those who argue that consensus is the *defining feature* of properly social stereotypes and that this should be the primary focus of psychological enquiry. In this vein, Tajfel (1981b) argued that:

> Stereotypes can become *social* only when they are *shared* by large numbers of people within social groups or entities — the sharing implying a process of effective diffusion. (p. 147)

For advocates of this view it is the fact that certain stereotypes are widely shared that makes them worth studying in the first place. So, in an industrial dispute, if only a few managers and only a few striking workers held negative views of each other, these perceptions would scarcely merit attention. The same would be true if only a few male managers doubted women's capacity to manage and lead. However, it is the fact that such views are *widely shared* among members of relevant groups that makes them powerful and important (Fiske & Glick, 1995; Heilman, 1995).

The critical question is therefore whether it is possible to develop an analysis of stereotyping that accommodates both social and cognitive considerations and that accounts for the generally low levels of consensus obtained in empirical research but also for the very high levels occasionally observed in the field. Just such a model has been proposed by Haslam and his colleagues (e.g. Haslam, Turner, Oakes, McGarty & Reynolds, 1998) as part of an application of self-categorization and social identity principles to the study of stereotyping in general (for a comprehensive account of this programme see Oakes et al., 1994).

As with the model of decision-making outlined above, and following arguments presented in Chapter 2, the core of this analysis suggests that consensus in stereotypes of both ingroup and outgroup flows from the depersonalization process. Specifically, social identity salience is argued to lead to heightened perceptions of ingroup and outgroup homogeneity, and these perceptions are expected to be further accentuated by processes of identity-based social influence. The broad implication of this analysis, then, is that stereotype consensus should be enhanced (a) by factors that increase the salience of the shared social identity of a group of perceivers (Bar-Tal, 1998; Tajfel, 1978a; see Figure 2.4) and (b) by group interaction *to the extent that* such interaction is premised upon that shared social identity and relevant to the stereotype.

As we noted previously (e.g. after Oakes et al., 1994; Turner et al., 1994), factors that should increase social identity salience include: (a) comparative fit (e.g. whether a situation is defined in intergroup rather than intragroup terms); (b) normative fit (e.g. whether the ingroup is, or can be, defined positively); and (c) perceiver readiness (e.g. prior experience of acting as a member of the particular ingroup in question). It is clear that these factors were generally at play in the political decision-making groups studied by Janis (1971, 1982). All the situations that the various groups faced were intergroup in nature, all the groups had a very well-defined sense of a shared positive identity and their interaction was structured around that identity. As noted at the start of this chapter, all were therefore groups in which 'the "we" feeling of solidarity was running high' (Janis, 1982, p. vii). On the other hand, in most experimental studies of stereotype content any shared identity amongst participants is, at best, implicit and interaction based around shared identity is very rare indeed. Such methodological disparities therefore account for the very different levels of consensus which these two forms of enquiry typically reveal.

Yet like Janis's own work, this interpretation of effects is retrospective and post hoc. Accordingly, a more formal programme of research has been conducted with a view to showing how stereotype consensus emerges as a joint product of social context and social interaction. Particularly relevant are three studies reported by Haslam, Turner, Oakes, Reynolds et al. (1998). Following the same procedure as classic work by Katz and Braly (1933), in all the studies participants had to make a decision about which five traits from a checklist of 84 they would use to describe particular national groups. In the first study, Australian students selected traits to describe both Australians and Americans. Importantly though, some participants judged Americans *and then* Australians while others described Australians *and then* Americans. It was predicted that stereotypes of the American outgroup would generally be more consensual than those of the ingroup because judgements of Americans would always be intergroup in nature (i.e. involving an implicit comparison between Americans and Australians) and hence should be informed by a salient social identity. However, it was predicted that stereotypes of Australians would be more consensual when this ingroup was judged *after* rather than *before* Americans. This is because in the 'after' conditions judgements of the ingroup would be informed by an intergroup comparison, but in the 'before' conditions they would be based on intragroup comparison.

These predictions were confirmed. In particular, when Australians were judged first the five most commonly selected traits were, on average, selected by 38 per cent of participants, but when Australians were judged second these traits were selected by 48 per cent of participants. On the other hand, when describing Americans the most commonly selected traits were assigned by just under 50 per cent of participants regardless of the order of judgement.

Despite confirming predictions, it is clear that the overall levels of stereotype consensus in this first study were quite low. However, it is also important to note that the study contained no group-based interaction of the form predicted to consensualize group perceptions and decisions. With this point in mind, a second study was conducted in which participants individually selected traits to describe either Americans or Australians, and then made the same decision as members of a three- or four-person group. In the individual phase of this study the pattern of findings mirrored those obtained when Australians were judged before Americans in Experiment 1. However, in the group phase, stereotype consensus was enhanced by interaction and this effect was particularly strong when groups judged Americans. This pattern was consistent with the prediction that interaction amongst participants would consensualize decisions to the extent that they were made in the context of a salient social identity (as Australians). Significantly too, in the group phase of this study levels of consensus in the traits selected to describe the American outgroup were generally much higher. On average, the top five traits were assigned by 58 per cent of groups and the vast majority described Americans as extremely nationalistic, materialistic and ostentatious.

As can be seen from Figure 6.4, very similar patterns to these were obtained in a third study (Haslam, Turner, Oakes, Reynolds et al., 1998, Experiment 3). This also demonstrated that it is possible to obtain very high levels of consensus in *in*group stereotypes when an ingroup (in this case Australians) is judged in an intergroup rather than an intragroup context (being judged in contrast to Americans rather than alone). These patterns have also been replicated by Sani and Thomson (1999) in a study where Scottish students were asked individually and then in groups to report their dress-related stereotypes of (a) students, (b) students in contrast to managers, or (c) managers. When their social identity was salient (i.e. in conditions (b) and (c)), groups of students exhibited very high levels of agreement in characterizing their ingroup as dressing 'originally' and 'for comfort' and the apparel of the managerial outgroup as 'smart', 'tailored', and 'conservative'.

Such results confirm the point that while most cognitive accounts of stereo-typing focus on the processes involved in the development and expression of beliefs about *out*groups, the same processes also shape individuals' perceptions of their ingroup. Again, this can be seen in Janis's studies of groupthink, where shared perceptions of the inferiority of relevant outgroups went hand-in-hand with universal beliefs about the superiority of the ingroup. Sani and Thomson's (1999) research into stereotypes of organizational dress also supports the argument that these processes play a key role in the development of a consensual *organizational culture* that provides people with a common framework for inter-preting and acting within their work environment (as argued in Chapter 2 above; see also Deal & Kennedy, 1982; Guimond, 2000; Pratt & Rafaeli, 1997).

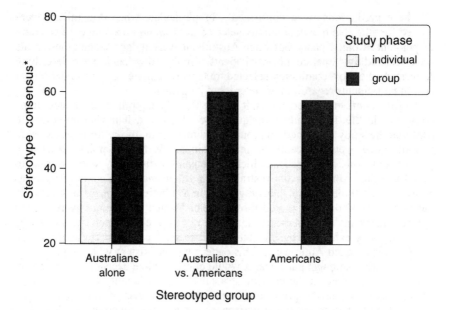

*Figure 6.4* Levels of stereotype consensus as a function of experimental phase and stereotyped group (from Haslam, Turner, Oakes, Reynolds et al., 1998)

*Note*: * Stereotype consensus = percentage of individuals or groups assigning five most commonly selected traits.

To provide final theoretical closure on the foregoing arguments, Haslam, Oakes, Reynolds & Turner (1999) investigated stereotype consensus in the context of a direct (rather than an indirect) manipulation of social identity salience (details of the manipulation are presented in Appendix 2). Here when Australian students were instructed to think about themselves as individuals, levels of stereotype consensus were comparatively low at both individual and group phases of a trait selection task. However, when participants thought of themselves as Australians, levels of consensus were generally much higher and were especially high after group interaction. In the group phase of this condition stereotype content was also extremely positive — with most groups describing the Australian ingroup as happy-go-lucky, sportsmanlike and pleasure-loving.

Considered together, the findings of the above studies make a number of points directly relevant to the group decision-making literature. First, they indicate that, despite allegations to the contrary (e.g. Condor, 1990; Gardner, 1993), stereotype consensus of the form and extent discussed by Janis is not illusory. But, as well as this, they also suggest that such consensus will only eventuate where perceptions and social interaction are structured by a shared social identity. Thus, if individuals do not communicate with each other or such interaction is informed by different social perspectives (conditions that prevail in most empirical studies), consensus is unlikely to be a naturally occurring feature of their stereotypes or their collective decisions in general.

This argument is also consistent with the suggestion that many of the reme-dies for groupthink identified by Janis achieve their impact through their capacity to reduce social identity salience (e.g. by undermining social category fit and accessibility). However, it also follows that *unless* interventions have this effect they are liable to exacerbate any problems with which the phenomenon is perceived to be associated. For example, as Turner and Pratkanis (1998a) observe, this is likely to be the case if the monitors or devil's advocates intro-duced into a group are perceived by its members as outgroup agents. The criti-cal point, then, is that the impact of any changes to group dynamics will always be mediated by the *self-categorical meaning* of those changes for those on whom they impact, and interventions designed without attention to this fact are liable to have unintended consequences. This, we would suggest, is one reason why prescriptive approaches to group decision-making of the form discussed earlier in this chapter (e.g. Vroom & Yetton, 1973; see also Chapter 3 above) have met with only mixed success.

### Groupthink as a form of social identity maintenance

While the research reviewed in the previous two sections relates to key components of the groupthink syndrome, a growing body of research has examined social identity processes as they relate to this phenomenon directly. Dietz-Uhler (1996) reports one such study which examined the relationship between identification with a group and commitment to the group's cause when the enterprise in which it was engaged began to fail. In the study participants role-played the jobs of town councillors collectively working on a project to construct a city playground.

The task was designed to be as realistic as possible and started out with groups being given a package of briefing information about the project. The package included blueprints of the playground, budgetary information and a letter from a benevolent resident donating land. After this, groups were given a second package of information in which a few alarm bells were sounded. Despite a predominance of positive news, the project had started running over budget, there were construction problems and letters of complaint from local residents. By the time the participants were given a third package, things had got seriously out of hand. There was still some positive information in the form of feedback and letters of encouragement, but the contractor was having sewerage problems, a child had been injured and there was a threat of legal proceedings.

Over the course of these developments, Dietz-Uhler was interested in how councillors' reactions to events would be affected by their sense of common identity. This was manipulated across two conditions. Participants in a high-salience condition spent time getting to know each other, wore identical name tags saying 'North Starr Town Council' and were always referred to as 'your group'. On the other hand, those in a low-salience condition had no introduction to each other, had their own names on their name tags and were referred to individually.

Statistical analysis of group decisions, member perceptions and independent ratings of discussion content revealed a number of effects consistent with a social identity approach. In particular, escalation in the amount of money that groups were willing to commit to the project at Stage 3 and the number of arguments in its favour were greater to the extent that members identified with their group. A more complex pattern also suggested that high identifiers became more emotional when the project started to fail, but that this led to more cautious investment behaviour. As Dietz-Uhler (1996, p. 624) notes, the generally positive relationship between identification and commitment to the project was thus not a product of emotionality (or related forms of irrationality) per se. Instead it seems more likely to have been a product of high levels of group cohesiveness and perceived mutual support.

Closer inspection of this relationship between cohesiveness and groupthink is provided in a study reported by Hogg and Hains (1998). Following social identity and self-categorization theories, the authors sought to demonstrate that the cohesiveness associated with group decisions like those studied by Janis (1982) and Dietz-Uhler (1996) was social rather than personal in nature — reflecting attraction amongst people *as group members* rather than as individuals (Hogg, 1987; Hogg & Hardie, 1991, 1992; Turner, 1982; Turner, Sachdev & Hogg, 1983). To test this idea the authors set up conditions that were conducive to groupthink and then looked at whether or not aspects of the syndrome eventuated in groups where membership was either (a) based on personal friendship, (b) based on shared social identification, or was (c) random. In the second of these conditions, social identity was invoked by asking groups to imagine they were part of a student union executive and to develop a name that reflected their shared policies. All groups then had to make a decision about whether to close down a cinema (the Schonell) that specialized in showing 'progressive, non-commercial, classic and avant garde movies' in a situation where each member had access to different information about the cinema's viability.

Consistent with the researchers' hypothesis, within the study as a whole, statistical analysis indicated that symptoms of groupthink — in particular, greater desire for consensus and increased verbal pressure on group members to conform — were generally predicted more by social identification than by personal friendship. As Hogg and Hains (1998) note, such an observation accords with the argument that groupthink is a phenomenon derived from a group-based definition of self, rather than from the personal characteristics and relations of participants. On this basis they argue that the key to groupthink avoidance lies not in breaking down ties of friendship within groups (noting that the existence of such ties might actually work against the syndrome's emergence), but in breaking down shared social identification.

Similar conclusions about the contribution of social identification to groupthink emerge even more strongly from work by Marlene Turner and her colleagues (Turner & Pratkanis, 1994, 1998a; Turner, Pratkanis, Probasco & Leve, 1992). This represents the most extensive coverage of groupthink-related issues from a social identity perspective and includes several tests of the authors' own social identity maintenance model. Aspects of this model were discussed above, but its primary focus is on the way in which groupthink symptoms arise from defensive attempts to restore collective self-esteem in the face of group-based threat.

In an initial test of their ideas, Turner et al. (1992) examined performance on the Parasol Subassembly Task (Maier, 1952) in which groups have to decide how to deal with the dwindling performance of workers producing car instrument panels on an assembly line — problems that centre on an ageing worker no longer able to work efficiently. Social identity salience (operationalized as group cohesiveness) was manipulated using a strategy similar to that adopted by Dietz-Uhler (1996) and Hogg and Hains (1998). As well as this though, the study also incorporated a manipulation of threat. High-threat groups were informed that if the group made a poor decision a video-recording of its deliberations would be used to train other students how *not* to make decisions; low-threat groups were told that the exercise was being conducted for pre-testing purposes only.

Results of the study showed that decision quality was *interactively* determined by social identity salience and threat. Poor quality decisions were particularly likely to be made where groups' social identity was salient and they were under threat. Similar poor quality decisions emanated from groups whose social identity was not salient and who were not under threat, but, significantly, these groups had much less confidence in their own performance. Display of the groupthink syndrome — marrying poor performance with perceptions of high self-worth — thus appeared to be contingent on high identification and high threat.

As an intriguing elaboration of these ideas, in a subsequent study Turner et al. (1992, Experiment 3) replicated the two high-cohesion (i.e. high social identity salience) conditions of their first experiment, but also added a third in which the presence of high threat was accompanied by information that poor performance under these conditions could be attributed to the presence of background noise. The authors reasoned that if the defensive maintenance of group-based self-esteem underpinned the emergence of groupthink in the high-threat condition of Experiment 1, groups in this high-threat condition could attribute any failure to the presence of this noise, and hence would not need to fall prey to the syndrome. The results replicated those of Experiment 1, but also provided support for this additional prediction. Thus group performance was much poorer under conditions of high threat alone than it was when high threat was accompanied by an excuse for failure (where performance was equal to that of groups under no threat).

Like the research of Dietz-Uhler (1996) and Hogg and Hains (1998), Turner and Pratkanis's work clearly points to the capacity for a salient sense of shared group membership to engender decision-making problems under certain circumstances. As Whyte (1993) puts it, 'groups may perform better than individuals on some tasks, but decision making in escalation situations is apparently not one of them' (p. 446). Moreover, the dependent variables in all of the above studies are highly pertinent to organizational settings, and for that reason the gravity of this message appears all the more strong. Organizations are generally keen to avoid throwing good money after bad (the problem for the North Starr council), to avoid backing losers rather than winners (the problem for management of the Schonell Theatre), and to avoid propping up ailing workers (the basis of the Parasol Subassembly problem). To steer clear of these problems, managers in general might therefore be well advised to heed Janis's advice and implement policies that break up the shared sense of self that seems to be implicated in their development.

Having said that, it is apparent that in all of the above studies evaluation of the group product involves a value-judgement on the part of the researchers and the reader. While many would agree that in all these cases the groupthink-style decisions were faulty and foolhardy, it is not hard to see that in other circumstances decisions of a similar form could be construed as courageous and enlightened (Haslam, in press; Haslam, Ryan, Postmes, Spears & Smithson, 1999). In particular, we can see that it would be a very brave and creative group indeed that went against the orthodoxy of 'economic rationalism' and backed a policy that was socially progressive but appeared to be financially perilous. This is an important point that we will return to in Chapters 9 and 11. For now, though, we would note only that 'designing out' of organizations the social identity processes that are associated with groupthink may not always be in those organizations' best interests (as the data reported by Peterson et al., 1998, suggest; see also Suedfeld, 1988) or those of society as a whole.

## Conclusion

In a review of groupthink research in which they explicitly play the role of devil's advocate urged by the groupthink model, Fuller and Aldag (1998; see also Aldag & Fuller, 1993) challenge Janis's (1971, 1982) ideas in an instructive but highly provocative way. Central among these researchers' charges are claims that groupthink research is itself a fiasco of similar proportions to those that Janis himself studied. Thus, it is argued, researchers have conspired to maintain a unanimous fiction about the phenomenon through the practices of stereotyping, rationalization and mindguarding that the model itself criticized. Ultimately, the seductive mythologization of Janis's theory is seen to have led to an 'unnecessary and inappropriate narrowing' of the focus of research into group decision making and to have had a stultifying effect on the field as a whole:

> This reframing of 'group decision making research' as 'groupthink research' represent[s] an evolutionary dead-end to that research branch and one which [has] left few useful fossils. ... Even the most passionately presented and optimistically interpreted findings on groupthink suggest that the phenomenon is, at best, irrelevant. (Fuller & Aldag, 1998, pp. 171, 172, 177)

The arguments presented in this chapter lend credence to many of Fuller and Aldag's contentions, while at the same time leading us to resile from such a withering conclusion. Foremost among the problems with Janis's model are its limitations as a generalized theory of group decision-making. Fuller and Aldag are almost certainly right therefore when they argue that this research area would be much more fertile and rich had it not been dominated by a single model that focused researchers' minds and labour on such a limited set of variables and then encouraged them to interpret their findings in such a restricted way.

On the other hand, for all its flaws, Janis's model *does* identify important and significant features of group decision making that are not routinely captured within experimental studies performed on ad hoc groups with little collective history or purpose (Raven, 1998). The fact that researchers have not obtained groupthink-like levels of polarization and consensualization in such studies need not necessarily mean that these properties of group decisions are irrelevant or of only peripheral interest. On the contrary, they can be seen to point to the failure of experimentalists to conduct research in which participants' perceptions and interactions are informed by membership in meaningful social groups (see Haslam, Turner, Oakes, Reynolds et al., 1998, p. 773; also Brown, 1988; Harkins & Szymanski, 1989; Chapter 9 below). In this regard, Janis's work is a timely reminder of the need to ensure that any gaps between the laboratory and the field are spanned by integrative psychological theory. Moreover, having suggested such a theory, we can see that this has the capacity to incorporate Janis's insights within a broader understanding of decision-making of the form recommended by Fuller and Aldag (1998).

Significantly too, this exercise also highlights one major difference of interpretation between the social identity approach and that of Janis and most of the researchers who have followed in his footsteps. Janis (1982) originally coined the term groupthink to align it with other Orwellian concepts such as 'doublethink' and 'crimethink', adding:

> By putting groupthink with those Orwellian words, I realize that groupthink takes on an invidious connotation. The invidiousness is intentional: Group-think refers to a deterioration of mental efficiency, reality testing and moral judgement. (p. 9; see also Janis, 1971, p. 44)

But in sharp contrast to this interpretation, a social identity analysis suggests that groupthink, like many other collective products, harnesses and builds upon the essence of the group in ways that (a) are psychologically efficient and creative, (b) are grounded in group members' social reality, and (c) have the potential to be socially enriching.

This line of argument has generally been very hard for researchers to consider (let alone concede) when reflecting on the decision-making of White House administrations under Johnson, Nixon or Kennedy. This is for the obvious reason that from where researchers and observers now stand, there is very little to find laudable or socially enriching about the Vietnam War, Watergate or the invasion of the Bay of Pigs. Here though, we must be careful to avoid the pitfalls of psychologization and strive to disentangle our social, historical and political prejudices from our psychological analysis. When we do, we can see that these prejudices led Janis to frame his research in terms of the wrong questions. To understand the destructive dimensions of groupthink we should ask not 'What psychological failings led rational administrations astray?', but 'What social and political failings do the rational psychological processes reveal?'

## Further Reading

For all its shortcomings, Janis's (1982) presentation of the groupthink hypothesis is still a very enjoyable read — especially for those with an interest in modern political history. The special issue of *Organizational Behaviour and Human Decision Processes* edited by Turner and Pratkanis (1998b) is a good tonic to accompany Janis's book and contains a number of articles that are unusually readable, provocative and scholarly. Many of these papers have been referred to in this chapter (e.g. those by

Fuller & Aldag; Kramer; Paulus; Peterson et al.), but the editors' own presentation of a social identity approach to groupthink is especially relevant. Turner's (1991) treatment of social influence is worth reading not only because it provides details of self-categorization theory's analysis of group polarization, but also because it ties this in with a range of other phenomena that we have discussed in previous chapters (e.g. leadership and information management).

Janis, I. L. (1982). *Groupthink: Psychological studies of policy decisions and fiascoes* (2nd ed.). Boston: Houghton Mifflin.

Turner, M. E. & Pratkanis, A. R. (Eds.) (1998b). Theoretical perspectives on groupthink: A twenty-fifth anniversary appraisal. *Organizational Behaviour and Human Decision Processes, 2/3* (whole issues).

Turner, J. C. (1991). *Social influence*. Milton Keynes: Open University Press.

# 7 Intergroup Negotiation and Conflict Management

The previous chapter dealt with processes of decision-making that occur *within* particular groups. However, it is clear that many organizational decisions actually involve *different* groups and that these groups often have sharply diverging agendas, values, perspectives and goals. For example, in wage negotiations between union and management the union's goal will typically be to maximize the gains for its members, while that of management will be to minimize costs to the organization. Likewise, in negotiations between representatives of different nations (e.g. over territorial claims or access to consumer markets) those representatives will generally strive to preserve and promote the distinct interests of their own nation. A key issue is therefore whether and how the conflict of interest between such groups can be managed constructively and in a way that minimizes harm and maximizes benefit to the participants and to the organization or society as a whole. The gravity of this issue — and the possibility of either enormous loss or considerable gain — leads to negotiation being a major topic in both social and organizational psychology.

If we consider the possible outcomes of wage negotiations (as represented schematically in Figure 7.1), it is apparent that many can be construed as quite negative. On the one hand, a management 'win' and a union 'loss' (e.g. where employees get only a 2 per cent pay rise — as in Quadrant B of Figure 7.1) might represent a drop in employees' real (inflation-adjusted) wages with the result that they become demoralized or seek to leave the organization. On the other hand, a union 'win' and a management 'loss' (e.g. where employees get a flat 10 per cent pay rise — Quadrant C) might be financially unsustainable for the organization with the result that it goes into liquidation. Alternatively, the prospect of reaching no agreement (Quadrant A), could be even more damaging as the grievances and frustrations of management and employees fester and a fundamental organizational issue is left unresolved.

For this reason, the goal of negotiations is typically to reach so-called 'win-win' or *integrative* agreements which satisfy the minimum requirements of *both* parties. Such solutions fall into the *bargaining zone* represented by Quadrant D in Figure 7.1 (e.g. where employees get a 3 per cent pay rise but a 4 per cent productivity bonus, or a 9 per cent rise but lose overtime entitlements). The larger this quadrant is, the more *integrative potential* any negotiation has. Importantly though, as these examples illustrate, integrative agreements generally require some degree of *flexibility* and *creativity* on the part of negotiators. A central task for researchers has therefore been to understand the processes that promote this lateral thinking and to identify the psychological and material conditions that lead to integrative solutions.

In response to this issue, one common recommendation is for organizations to implement strategies that serve to downplay the psychological salience of group membership for the parties involved in conflict. This follows from

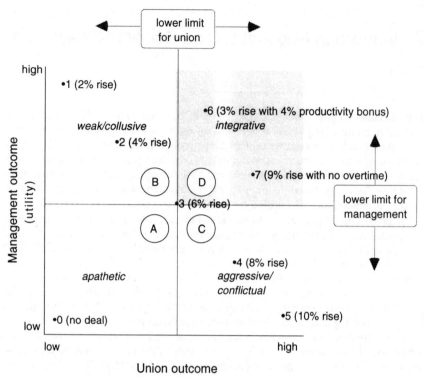

*Figure 7.1* Representation of the joint utility space for wage negotiations between union and management

*Note*: The quadrant labels in italics characterize the union's role in the negotiation. The arrows indicate the fact that negotiators' limits are variable (and this variation will affect the size of the quadrants). The shaded area represents the bargaining zone (quadrant D) that contains all integrative (i.e. win–win) solutions.

readings of mainstream social psychological literature which suggest that groups are a chief cause of social conflict and misunderstanding (e.g. Tajfel et al.'s minimal group research; see Chapter 2 above). It is also compatible with Taylor's (1911) view that industrial accord is best achieved by individualizing the workforce and Mayo's (1949) belief that the path to harmony lies in uniting workers under a single organizational affiliation. However, in contrast to both views, this chapter follows the thinking of a number of social identity and self-categorization theorists in suggesting that the most problematic forms of negotiation are those which do *not* address the concerns of individuals *as group members* (Brown & Wade, 1987; Eggins, 1999; Eggins & Haslam, 1999a, 1999b; Gaertner, Dovidio & Bachman, 1996; Hornsey & Hogg, 1999, 2000; Stephenson, 1981, 1984). Precisely because conflict is grounded in *real* group differences, it is argued that these must be dealt with en route to integrative agreements, and that, if such agreements are possible, the most satisfactory and enduring outcomes will be those that *make sense* of group differences within the framework of a shared superordinate social identity.

## An overview of negotiation research

### Individual difference approaches

One of the obvious solutions to the conundrum of how to achieve integrative solutions is to suggest that this will be a product of the personalities or management style of the individuals involved in negotiation (e.g. see Rubin & Brown, 1975, pp. 157-196). Along these lines, a range of individual differences have been used as a basis for predicting which of the four quadrants in Figure 7.1 a particular negotiator's behaviour will fall into. Most notably, Deutsch (1958, 1973; see also Messick & McClintock, 1968) distinguished between four types of *motivational orientation* that individuals might have towards a particular conflict: individualistic, altruistic, competitive, or co-operative. These orientations differ in the degree to which individuals are assumed to show concern for their own and others' outcomes. *Individualists* are assumed to be concerned primarily with maximizing their own gain with no regard to others, *altruists* with maximizing others' gain with no regard to themselves, *competitors* with maximizing their own gain at the expense of others, and *co-operators* with maximizing their own gain as well as that of others. Such dispositions map, respectively, on to Quadrants C, B, C and D of Figure 7.1 (with individualists in the top half and competitors in the bottom half of Quadrant C). Accordingly, it is individuals with a co-operative orientation that are seen to hold the key to the discovery of integrative solutions, *providing that* their opponents also have the same orientation.

This point is often demonstrated using *prisoner's dilemma games*. These get their name from the quandary faced by criminals who must decide whether or not to betray their partners after having been captured: they will receive a much lighter sentence if they incriminate their partners but their partners don't incriminate them, but if both betray each other they will receive much heavier penalties than if they had kept quiet. As anyone who has held up their side of a deal only to be let down by their partner would probably be aware, research in this paradigm illustrates very clearly that co-operators who have to deal with competitors tend to fair particularly poorly in the negotiation process (e.g. see Brewer & Schneider, 1990; Foddy, Smithson, Schneider & Hogg, 1999).

Along very similar lines, Blake & Mouton (1964; see also Pruitt & Rubin, 1986; Ruble & Thomas, 1976; Thomas, 1976; van de Vliert, 1990) developed a *dual-concern* model that differentiates between individuals on the basis of their *conflict style*. This style is seen to be the product of two more-or-less independent personality variables: concern for self and concern for others. As Figure 7.2 illustrates, concern for neither the self nor for others is seen to be associated with *inaction* (Quadrant A), concern for others but not the self with concession-making (Quadrant B), concern for self but not others with *contending* (Quadrant C), and concern for both the self and others (i.e. dual concern) with *problem-*

*solving* (Quadrant D).  One important purpose of this model is to provide managers with a tool that allows them to know (a) which styles to use in their dealings with other negotiators who have a particular style and (b) what outcomes to expect as a result of any negotiation.  For example, the approach suggests that a concession making style would help achieve integrative outcomes if one was negotiating with someone who was themselves prone to concession-making, but that it would be much less advantageous in negotiations with someone disposed to contending.

These various styles are readily identifiable in different negotiation settings and do indeed appear to be associated with outcomes of the form predicted by Deutsch (1973) and Blake and Mouton (1964).  Nevertheless, a major problem with the individual difference approach is that negotiation styles appear to be the *products* of the particular context in which negotiation takes place rather than fixed and invariant inputs.  This much is clear from the famous Boys Camp studies conducted by Sherif and his colleagues (Sherif, 1956; Sherif et al., 1961; see Chapter 3 above) in which boys who had contended furiously in the context of intergroup competition for scarce resources (e.g. in games where only one team could win a desirable prize) went on to co-operate gainfully when a different set of conditions prevailed (e.g. when both teams needed to pool their finances to rent a movie).  Moreover, the fact that the individuals who behaved competitively in both this research and Tajfel et al.'s (1971) minimal group studies were normal well-adjusted schoolboys suggests that *anyone* is liable to engage in contentious behaviour if the circumstances appear to demand it.

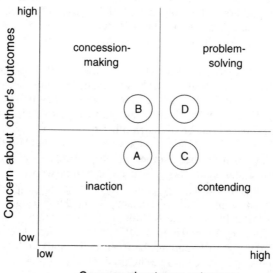

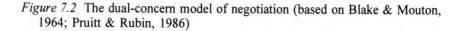

*Figure 7.2* The dual-concern model of negotiation (based on Blake & Mouton, 1964; Pruitt & Rubin, 1986)

## Cognitive approaches

With the above points in mind, the task most researchers have set themselves is to understand why individuals adopt a particular negotiation style and, in particular, what factors induce them to behave co-operatively rather than competitively. One very common class of answers to this question follows from interpretations of research by Sherif (e.g. 1956) and Tajfel (e.g. 1970) which suggest that discrimination, conflict and injustice are natural products of intergroup division. As Horwitz and Berkowitz (1990) put it:

> Perceiving others as group members rather than as unaffiliated individuals calls up a special set of factors that can impel the parties towards relational conflicts. ... Perceiving others as group members opens up a variety of rich possibilities for accounting for their deviations from what is appropriate behaviour, including such attributions as the nature of their socialization within their group, their group loyalty, their conformity to group and leadership pressures, and their group's animus against other groups. (pp. 182-3)

This analysis asserts that intergroup negotiations are particularly prone to conflict as a result of the perceptual and judgmental error that are introduced by the need for participants to *stereotype* their opponents in order to conserve limited cognitive resources. In line with the cognitive miser model that we discussed in Chapter 1 (e.g. Fiske & Taylor, 1984), Bazerman, Mannix, Sondak and Thompson (1990) thus assert:

> Group decision-making processes place greater information-processing demands on negotiations than do dyadic processes. ... Members ... may not have the time or resources necessary to obtain information about each members' interests and alternatives to a negotiated agreement. As such, they may falsely conclude that the other members' interests are more similar than they really are. (pp. 25-26)

The general view here, then, is that social categorization is made necessary by a requirement to render social reality manageable, but that this inevitably introduces error into the negotiation process by over-simplifying the true nature of one's opponents.

Following early work by Tajfel (1969; Tajfel & Wilkes, 1963; see also Judd & Park, 1993; Oakes et al., 1994; Oakes & Reynolds, 1997), the two key forms in which this error is believed to manifest itself are in tendencies to see members of outgroups as (a) more similar and (b) more extreme than they really are. According to Bazerman and his co-workers (Bazerman et al., 1990; Neale & Bazerman, 1991, pp. 104-109), errors of this form are responsible for a plethora of difficulties that can obstruct or de-rail the negotiation process. These include: (a) negative *framing* that leads negotiators to 'expect the worst' from their opponent; (b) inappropriate *anchoring* such that negotiators set out from a starting point that restricts their potential to develop integrative solutions; (c) *availability* bias that leads negotiators to focus on prominent features of the outgroup that may be unrepresentative or misleading; (d) *overconfidence* that leads to illusions of ingroup superiority and invincibility (along lines argued by Janis, 1982; see Chapter 6 above); (e) *mythical fixed-pie* beliefs whereby negotiators mistakenly believe that no integrative possibilities exist and that outgroup gains are always ingroup losses; (f) *stereotyped views* of others' cognitions and motives; and (g) *reactive devaluation* that leads negotiators to devalue any concessions made by their opponents.

Faced with this catalogue of deficit, it is hardly surprising that advocates of the cognitive approach generally recommend that negotiators take steps to eliminate or minimize the intergroup dimension of the negotiations in which they are involved (Grant, 1990). These can be thought of as '*decategorization*' strategies because they are informed by a belief that the process of perceiving individuals *as individuals* avoids categorization and thereby provides the most accurate and informative representation of social reality. For example, Bazerman et al. (1990, p. 31) suggest that negotiators should prepare extensively for negotiations by finding out as much individuating information as possible about the other party to avoid 'falsely conclud[ing] that other parties' interests are more narrow or more similar than they actually are'. Similarly, evidence that conflict can escalate if negotiators use ingroup values as a basis for negotiation, leads to a recommendation that references to ingroup values be set apart from major aspects of the negotiation process in order to ensure smooth and amicable interaction (Druckman, Broome & Korper, 1988). As summarized by Carnevale and Pruitt (1992, p. 537; see also Kolb & Rubin, 1991), the primary lesson here is that negotiators should put 'pragmatics before principles'.

The logic of this analysis has proved to have widespread appeal and for that reason it is routinely reproduced in organizational textbooks. Nonetheless, there are a number of grounds on which it can be challenged (Eggins, 1999). As argued in Chapter 2, a fundamental objection relates to the assumption that individualized social perception is necessarily more valid than that which is based on an appreciation of people's group membership (Oakes & Turner, 1990). Intergroup negotiation occurs precisely because the groups involved *are real* and their members have concerns and grievances that centre around *shared* values and principles. Accordingly, to deny that reality by treating people as if they were individuals, runs the risk of sidestepping the core issues that negotiation is intended to address (Stephenson, 1981). Turning Kolb and Rubin's (1991) advice on its head, it would therefore appear that negotiating *without* attending to principles is itself decidedly *un*pragmatic. Consistent with this argument, longitudinal studies have found that the long-term success of integrative solutions increases to the extent that negotiation addresses substantive group-based issues (Douglas, 1957; Morley & Stephenson, 1979; Pruitt, Pierce, Zubek, McGillicuddy & Welton, 1993). Resolutions to group differences which tackle only inter*personal* issues tend to be short-lived.

As well as this though, it is becoming increasingly clear from experimental research that perceiving people as individuals is just as much an act of categorization as is perceiving them as group members (Asch, 1952; Bruner, 1957; Reynolds & Oakes, 2000). Evidence also suggests that when groups contribute to social reality (e.g. because people are behaving as group members) adding to a person's cognitive load can *reduce* stereotyping rather than increase it (Nolan, Haslam, Spears & Oakes, 1999; Spears, Haslam & Jansen, 1999). Such evidence is consistent with the general claims of self-categorization theorists that stereotyping is not an exercise in cognitive load reduction but rather one of *meaning enhancement*, and that rather than introducing error this process *adds* information that would not otherwise be provided by individuated perception (Oakes et al., 1994; Oakes & Haslam, in press; Oakes & Turner, 1990; Spears & Haslam, 1997). In the case of wage negotiations between union and management, for example, the fact that features of the negotiation process can encourage the individual participants to *categorize themselves* as members of the respective groups and behave accordingly, implies that the situation will contain important social categorical information that a perceiver *needs* to detect if he or she is to understand what is going on and behave appropriately. Similarly, in negotiations between Palestinians and Israelis, one might expect that a negotiator who perceived and treated the participants as if they were individuals would be at a loss to understand proceedings and would — putting it mildly — display enormous historical, political, and cultural insensitivity (Bar-Tal, 1990). For this reason any integrative solutions that he or she proposed would be unlikely to find favour with either party.

### Motivational approaches

One of the limitations shared by both individual difference and cognitive approaches is that both tend to imply that negotiations in which the parties' perceptions and actions are grounded in their group membership are destined to be unproductive. However, the fact that this is not always the case has led other researchers to suggest that a more appropriate goal for research is to try to understand what features of the negotiation process enable groups to 'rise above' their differences and reach integrative solutions. In effect, such research often promotes the view that the path to successful conflict resolution involves 'recategorization' rather than 'decategorization' — serving to unite warring groups under the umbrella of a new all-encompassing identity (along lines envisioned by Mayo, 1949; see also Anastasio et al., 1997; Gaertner et al., 1996; Sherif et al., 1961).

Although they draw on quite disparate bodies of psychological theory, motivational approaches are united by an interest in the way in which the parameters and outcomes of negotiation are shaped by the *motivations* of participants (Carnevale & Pruitt, 1992). This research has demonstrated that negotiated outcomes depend, amongst other things, on the extent to which participants (a) establish high or low outcome *limits,* (b) take the *perspective* of their opponents into account, and (c) *frame* negotiation as a process in which they are likely to win or lose.

Findings from the study of limits suggest, not surprisingly, that integrative outcomes are more likely to be reached when negotiators impose reasonable and realistic limits. As is clear from Figure 7.1, this is because as negotiators set their limits higher the bargaining zone shrinks proportionately. Nonetheless, if limits are set too low sub-optimal outcomes can result because parties reach agreement too quickly and fail to explore the range of possibilities within the bargaining zone (e.g. those in the top right hand corner of Quadrant D in Figure 7.1). Empirical evidence suggests that reasonable limits are more likely to be set when negotiators share a common set of values or the issue itself suggests an obvious solution (Pruitt & Syna, 1985), but that limits generally increase when either side is motivated by principles specific to an ingroup or if they are under surveillance from constituents (i.e. other ingroup members; Druckman et al., 1988; Druckman, Solomon & Zechmeister, 1972).

Research into the process of perspective-taking builds upon the distinction between various motivational orientations outlined by Deutsch (1973). Here though, negotiators' concern for their own and others' outcomes are seen as context-dependent and variable, rather than as fixed personality variables. Consistent with this claim, studies have shown that a person's concern with their own outcomes can be increased by giving them a difficult goal or by making them accountable to powerful constituents (Ben-Yoav & Pruitt, 1984a; Pruitt, Carnevale, Ben-Yoav, Nochajski & van Slyck, 1983). On the other hand, concern with others' outcomes increases when participants are instructed to care about that person or are told that they will have to co-operate with them on a future task (Ben-Yoav & Pruitt, 1984a, 1984b). Results from these studies also support the dual-concern model in suggesting that high concern for one's own outcomes coupled with low concern for others generally leads to contentious negotiating, while high concern for both self and other is more likely to encourage problem-solving.

One other factor which has been found to impact reliably upon negotiated outcomes is the framing of negotiation — whether participants are attuned to the gains or to the losses that it might produce (Kahneman & Tversky, 1979). In part, this is because outcome framing is believed to impact upon perspective-taking so that negotiators who adopt a loss frame are more focused on their own outcomes (i.e. Quadrants A and C in Figure 7.2) than those with a gain frame. Consistent with this view and the argument that negotiators are more sensitive to loss than gain (Kahneman, 1992), research suggests that negotiators who adopt a loss frame (a) demand more, (b) concede less, and (c) settle less easily than those with a gain frame (e.g. Carnevale & Pruitt, 1992; de Dreu, Carnevale, Emans & van de Vliert, 1995). Work by de Dreu and his colleagues (e.g. de Dreu et al., 1995) also suggests that when a loss frame is combined with a high concern for one's own outcomes this tends to exacerbate contentious behaviour and foreshadow an escalation of conflict.

However, contrary to the view that a gain frame is necessarily preferable to a loss frame, de Dreu and his colleagues have found that integrative solutions are most likely to be reached when a loss frame is combined with a high concern for others. This is because concern for others steers participants away from the twin perils of apathy and contentious behaviour (Quadrants A and C) while the loss frame steers them away from concession-making (Quadrant B). For these authors and advocates of the dual-concern model (e.g. Ben Yoav & Pruitt, 1984b), successful negotiation is thus seen to hinge around a process in which participants are encouraged to see beyond the limits of their own perspective but do not forego that perspective altogether.

The major achievement of motivational approaches has been to demonstrate that negotiators' *orientation* to the negotiation process and hence the *outcomes* of that process are structured by features of the social context that the parties confront (Larrick & Blount, 1995). The body of this research also suggests that the dual-concern model provides a useful conceptual framework for thinking about the negotiation process as a whole. Yet, having said that, it is nonetheless true that the mechanics of that process are still underspecified and undertheorized. It is not clear, for example, why changes in context should induce a person to take another's perspective or to adopt a gain frame and why exactly these variables have the impact that they do. It is unclear too, why orientations and motivations often *change* over the course of negotiation (as demonstrated by Douglas, 1957; Morley & Stephenson, 1979; Olekalns, Smith & Walsh, 1996) and why such change plays a particularly important role in outcomes. One way to answer these questions is to see negotiators' orientations as reflections of initially conflicting social identities but negotiation itself as a process that can provide both the forum and the motivation for those identities to be restructured and rendered compatible. It is this possibility (and its ramifications) that we explore in the next section.

## Social identity and negotiation

It is clear that many of the core concepts in the negotiation literature relate to issues of social identity that we have discussed in previous chapters. In particular, the fact that the negotiation process is commonly conceptualized as a process that centres around the dual concerns (and perspectives) of self and other is consistent with the general claim of social identity and self-categorization theorists that the self is a major referent for social action and that the nature of this action is typically determined by the nature of the relations between the self and others (e.g. Tajfel & Turner, 1979). Moreover, many prescribed strategies for negotiation and conflict management incorporate insights from social identity research in suggesting that a primary problem in negotiation is the existence of distinct social groups whose members are prone both to ingroup favouritism and outgroup derogation. As we have seen, these arguments are often based on readings of Tajfel et al.'s (e.g. 1971) minimal group studies which propose that the *mere fact* of social categorization leads inevitably to conflict and tension.

In line with such readings, some early applications of social identity principles argued that the most appropriate method for dealing with social conflict was to implement procedures that served to reduce the salience of the social categories implicated in the conflict. Mirroring the cognitive approach outlined above, Brewer and Miller (1984) proposed a *decategorized contact model* which suggested that contact between members of conflicting groups would be effective in reducing intergroup hostility to the extent that it encouraged differentiated and personalized representations of group members. These researchers argued that because individualized views would be inconsistent with the stereotypic beliefs that perpetuated conflict, they would cause perceivers to abandon those stereotypes and precipitate more harmonious relations. However, mirroring the motivational approach, Gaertner and his colleagues (e.g. Anastasio et al., 1997; Gaertner, Dovidio, Anastasio, Bachman & Rust, 1993; Gaertner, Rust, Dovidio, Bachman & Anastasio, 1994, 1996) argued that a superior strategy was one of *recategorization* which 'transformed members' cognitive representations ... from "us" and "them" to a more inclusive "we"' (Gaertner, Rust et al., 1996, p. 232). This idea is central to these researchers' *common ingroup identity model* which is based, amongst other things, on experimental evidence (especially Gaertner et al., 1989; see Chapter 2 above) that recategorization achieves positive effects by increasing the attractiveness of former outgroup members, while decategorization does so by decreasing the attractiveness of former ingroup members. Mindful of this pattern, the authors' preference for their model was partly dictated by the fact that it involved upgrading the erstwhile outgroup rather than downgrading the erstwhile ingroup.

Both these models have received empirical support that is consistent with self-categorization principles as set out in Chapter 2. However, as recipes for negotiation both also have a number of problems akin to those discussed in previous sections. First amongst these is the fact that both models advocate strategies of conflict management that do violence to the *social reality* that negotiation is designed to address. For example, in the case of conflict between union and management, to suggest that negotiators treat each other as if they were individuals or members of 'one happy family' denies the *real* clash of group-based interests that make negotiation necessary in the first place. It is therefore unsurprising that when either of these recommendations is put in place, the satisfaction than can be achieved around the negotiating table often dissipates when negotiators re-connect with their constituents (Pruitt et al., 1993; Stephenson, 1984).

Moreover, a particular problem of recategorization models is that they tend to overlook the power-related implications of imposing a superordinate social identity on the parties to negotiation. Because the power of those parties is rarely balanced, it is often the case that the superordinate identity is crafted so that it suits the interests of the powerful group while denying the legitimacy of the other group's claims (Berry, 1984; Mummendey & Wenzel, 1999). This much is apparent from dialogue taken from union-management negotiations reported by Stephenson (1984; after Morley & Stephenson, 1979). Here a senior management representative (M1) construes differences with the union over pay and working conditions as a problem for the organization as a whole that the union representative (U1) therefore has an obligation to help resolve:

> M1: How would you suggest then that we deal with this now, as a company? I mean, you're part of the community in this respect.

He then identifies the union's reluctance to do so as an unjust violation of this superordinate ingroup:

> M1: ... the issue is you don't want to be disturbed on that particular day ...
> U1: Yes.
> M1: ... for any reason. Now this leaves us holding the baby in fact. We have in fact positively to do something, but how are we to do this? How in fact are we to cover this? Can you suggest to me some way out? Or, in fact, are we saying, 'Well that's your bloody problem?' [Very long pause] And if you feel that, then, let's say so, I mean, if you say 'Well that's your bloody problem', you say it. (Stephenson, 1984, p. 656)

In this case, then, management's pursuit of a recategorization strategy makes perfect sense and, if that recategorization were accepted by the union, it would clearly lead to more harmonious industrial relations. Nevertheless, it is clear that in this case harmony would have been reached at the expense of the union and its members' interests and also undermines the positive distinctiveness of its identity (Deschamps & Brown, 1983; van Leeuwen, van Knippenberg &

Wilke, 1999; van Leeuwen et al., 2000). And, again, because from those members' perspective such an outcome is likely to be seen as procedurally (and distributively) unjust, they are unlikely to embrace it with any enthusiasm (Tyler, 1999b).

Elaborating on this point, another limitation of both decategorization and recategorization models is that both are explicitly premised upon an assumption that intergroup conflict is *by definition* bad and hence something to be avoided at all costs (Eggins, 1999; see also Worchel, Coutant-Sassic & Wong, 1993). In both cases, conflict reduction or conflict avoidance are seen as preferable to conflict itself or conflict escalation. This reflects the judgement of most contemporary managers and organizational theorists that conflict management is best understood as an exercise in conflict *resolution* (e.g. Daft, 1985). However, as Eggins (1999) argues, there are in fact a number of theoretical and practical grounds for questioning this assumption. Most importantly, she notes that early social theorists like Cooley (1918), Simmel (1955), and Coser (1956) saw conflict and co-operation as two sides of the same coin that *combined* to give structure, meaning and direction to social life. At a practical level it is also apparent that conflict is often a force for *creativity* where co-operation is enfeebling (Douglas, 1957; Tannenbaum, 1965). This point was made whimsically in the film of Graham Greene's novel *The Third Man*, where the mysterious central character, Harry Lime, observes:

> In Italy for thirty years under the Borgias they had warfare, terror, murder, bloodshed — they produced Michaelangelo, Leonardo da Vinci and the Renaissance. In Switzerland they had brotherly love, five hundred years of democracy and peace, and what did they produce? The cuckoo clock. (Greene & Reed, 1968, p. 114)

In light of such observations, it is important to recognize that strategies of conflict management should not be confined only to those that involve conflict resolution. Moreover, it is also clear that where conflict resolution *is* attempted, strategies that do not address conflict *at the level at which it exists* are of questionable merit (Eggins & Haslam, 1999b). Where individuals feel aggrieved as a result of their membership in a particular group, attempts to address that grievance need to allow them to define themselves and act in terms of that group membership. Conflict between Catholics and Protestants or Jews and Muslims cannot be resolved simply by pretending that religion does not exist. On the contrary, religious conflict is given its force by the fact that religion does exist and is *internalized* by large groups of people as part of their social history and as a shared framework for their current feelings, thoughts and actions (Tajfel, 1981b). And because social identification of this form is an essential ingredient of *all* social conflict it must be recognized and allowed expression at some stage in any remedial process.

Clearly though, if the participants to any social conflict continue to act in terms of their initially divergent social identities, any resolution to those differences is unlikely to be achieved. Indeed, as we argued in the previous chapter, in an intergroup context the continued salience of a particular group membership often contributes to an *accentuation* of group differences and an escalation of conflict (e.g. see Figure 6.3). Although such escalation is often maligned by practitioners, in itself it may be no bad thing. If conflict is between forces of good and forces of evil (and it often appears this way to the protagonists) it is not clear that the cause of good is advanced either by blurring the boundaries between the two, or by unduly limiting the exploration and expression of what is good.

Nevertheless, it is generally (but not always) the case that negotiations take place and strategies of conflict resolution (e.g. involving intergroup contact; Amir, 1969; Hewstone & Brown, 1986) are implemented precisely because the parties *desire* some resolution. For example, in the case of wage-bargaining between union and management, both parties typically have an interest not only in prosecuting their respective cases (e.g. for more pay or more productivity) but also in resolving their differences so that, amongst other things, the groups they represent continue to have a future within the same organization. That being the case, genuine negotiation usually only occurs because those who participate in it acknowledge the existence of, or potential for, a superordinate identity. Indeed, it is this identity that provides both a rationale and a motivation for negotiation to proceed 'in good faith'.

Viewed in this light, the process of intergroup negotiation — like conflict itself (Oakes et al., 1994; Turner, 1985) — can be seen to revolve around counterposed social identities defined at subgroup and superordinate levels (Eggins, 1999). Recognizing this, researchers have recently argued that the key to satisfactory conflict resolution lies not in increasing the salience of social identity *at the expense* of subgroup identity (i.e. recategorization; Gaertner, Rust et al., 1996) but in acknowledging and allowing expression of both superordinate *and* subgroup identities (Berry, 1984, 1991; Eggins, 1999; Gonzalez & Brown, 1999; Hornsey & Hogg, 2000; Huo, Smith, Tyler & Lind, 1996; van Leeuwen et al., 2000). Indeed, this thesis lies at the core of Gaertner and Dovidio's (1999; Gaertner, Rust et al.) *dual-identity model* of conflict resolution. This model and its recommendations (as well as the decategorization and recategorization models discussed above) are represented schematically in Figure 7.3.

As we will discuss in more detail below, support for a dual-identity approach to conflict management is quite strong. For example, field research by Gaertner, Rust et al. (1994, 1996) found that levels of inter-ethnic prejudice displayed by North American high school students were lower among students who identified strongly with their ethnic ingroup (e.g. Black, Hispanic) *and* the superordinate national category (American) than among students who tended to identify only with their ethnic ingroup *or* the superordinate category. These researchers also found that one of the best predictors of positive feelings towards different outgroups was students' endorsement of the statement 'although there are different groups of students at this school, it feels as though we are playing on the same team' (Gaertner et al., 1996, p. 249).

Although an approach to conflict management that encourages individuals to maintain identification at both subgroup and superordinate levels appears to have some merit, it is important to reflect on its relationship both (a) to the core premises of self-categorization theory (e.g. Turner, 1985; Turner et al., 1987) and (b) to the dual-concern model of negotiation (e.g. Pruitt & Carnevale, 1993). The first of these points is relevant, because, at first blush, the very notion of dual identification could be seen to violate self-categorization theory's assumption of *functional antagonism* (Turner, 1985, p. 98). As we noted in

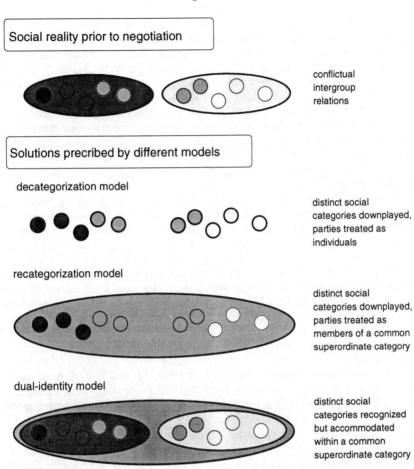

*Figure 7.3* Category-based solutions to intergroup conflict

Chapter 2, this refers to the idea that as the salience of one level of self-categorization increases, that of other levels decreases — primarily because the salience of a particular level of self-categorization transforms lower-level difference into higher-order similarity (so that, for example, the salience of a particular group membership reconfigures individual differences between group members into intra-ingroup similarities). Importantly though, the similarities and differences here are primarily in perspective and motivation ('shared needs, norms and goals'; Brown & Turner, 1981, p. 39). Social identity salience need not suppress individuality or subgroup specialization — it can simply harness these things toward a common goal (Turner et al., 1994; see also Cinnirella, 1997; Mlicki & Ellemers, 1997; p. 111). Accordingly, the notion of dual identification can be reconciled with the assumption of functional antagonism because the process described within dual-identity accounts is one in which the *content* of the emerging superordinate identity *requires* lower-level differentiation and is therefore *sustained by* lower-level identification.

A similar point to this was made by Durkheim (1933) in his seminal analysis of the division of labour in society. Durkheim distinguished between two forms of social group, each of which achieved solidarity by a different means. On the one hand, he identified groups whose strength lay in the fact that their members all had similar roles and similar characteristics — an attribute he called *mechanical solidarity*. On the other hand, though, he identified groups that achieved their strength by virtue of internal differentiation and the capacity for different members (or sub-units) to perform different roles — an attribute he termed *organic solidarity*. Building on this terminology, we can see that while conflict itself can be played out in terms of subgroup identities that have a mechanical or organic form, the superordinate identities that are implicated in conflict resolution must be organic.

Broadly speaking, then, we can hypothesize that the process of successful negotiation requires parties who have different lower-level theories of the self (i.e. conflicting mechanical or organic social identities) to develop and internalize an integrated theory of the self (a superordinate *organic social identity*) that incorporates, makes sense of, and utilizes those differences (Eggins & Haslam, 1999a). Importantly though, *both aspects of this process are essential*. As noted above, the *salience of subgroup identity* is necessary to ensure that the basis of conflict is actually addressed, and, along lines argued in Chapter 4, the emerging *salience of superordinate identity* is necessary for the parties to share a common motivation to do the creative intellectual work that is needed for social differences to be reconstrued as sources of strength rather than bones of contention.

But how do these arguments fit with the tried-and-tested analysis presented in the dual-concern model? Actually, very well. In particular, this is because, as Figure 7.4 attempts to demonstrate, if the two axes of the dual-concern model ('concern for self' and 'concern for other') are reconceptualized in self-categorization terms (as 'salience of subgroup identity' and 'salience of superordinate identity') then the above arguments correspond closely to the predictions and observations of motivational theorists that were outlined in the previous section. This reconceptualization seems appropriate because, as we argued in Chapter 2, concern for the self (at either a personal or social level) arises from the salience of a relevant self-category (a personal or social identity) and concern for others — together with a willingness and ability to take their perspective — arises once those others are categorized as members of a higher-order social self-category (e.g. as demonstrated by Gaertner et al., 1989; Kramer, Pommerenke & Newton, 1993; see also Larrick & Blount, 1995, pp. 272-273). Once the dual-concern model is recast in this way, it is also clear that the quadrants of the resultant repertory grid (as presented in Figure 7.4) make perfect theoretical sense. In the first instance, we can see that negotiation is unlikely to get off the ground or to be pursued with any enthusiasm under conditions where the parties are motivated neither by subgroup nor by superordinate identity (Quadrant A). If, for example, negotiators are only concerned with their personal outcomes then it follows from the arguments presented in Chapter 4 (e.g. see Figure 4.4) that they should have little inclination to engage in a process that involves either working *on behalf of* others or working *with* others.

If negotiators are motivated only by a superordinate identity (i.e. Quadrant B) this may also create problems. These will not necessarily be experienced

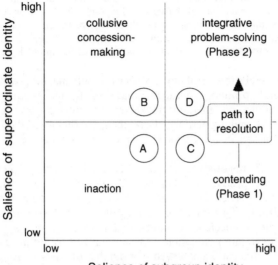

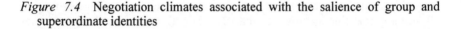

*Figure 7.4* Negotiation climates associated with the salience of group and superordinate identities

*Note*: The path to successful conflict resolution leads from an initial phase of *contending* associated with distinct sub-group identities to a secondary phase of *integrative problem-solving* that makes sense of those distinct identities in terms of a superordinate social identity.

during negotiation itself, but should become more pronounced once negotiators present negotiated outcomes back to their constituents. This is because those outcomes have not been informed by — and therefore do not incorporate — the constituents' concerns. Accusations of having 'sold out' should therefore abound, particularly if the ingroup is perceived to be relatively powerless and to have been co-opted by a superordinate identity that reflects the interests of the powerful (Stephenson, 1984). Moreover, because the solutions in this quadrant do not harness the intellectual and structural potential associated with differentiated group memberships they should also be of an inherently inferior quality (de Dreu et al., 1995; Durkheim, 1933; see Pruitt & Carnevale, 1993, pp. 28-30).

However, consistent with preceding arguments, it is apparent that more positive outcomes can be achieved under conditions where negotiation is informed by a salient subgroup identity. Specifically, we can see that conflict itself is initially played out in contentious behaviour where parties' divergent social identities are salient but they are not accommodated within a superordinate identity (Quadrant C). As Douglas (1957) notes, here:

> The parties ultimately serve their interests best by taking time at this stage for a thorough and exhaustive determination of the *outer limits* of the range within which they will have to do business with each other.   This calls in other words, for preliminary *emphasis* of the disagreement factors.   The more that the contenders can entrench their seeming disparity in this period, the more they enhance their chances for a good and stable settlement at the end.  (pp. 73-74)

Again, it seems likely that in many instances it will not be possible to move beyond this point, primarily because a lack of fit means that no organic superordinate identity can emerge to make sense of inter-party differences or to motivate such sense-making activity.  Here, then, conflict *escalation* is predicted (along lines discussed in the previous chapter; see Stephenson & Brotherton, 1975).

   Nonetheless, if negotiation *is* to proceed successfully, then this will necessarily involve problem-solving activity as lower-level social identities remain salient but parties now endeavour to reconcile them with a salient superordinate identity (Quadrant D).  And again, it is this *synthesizing process* that mobilizes the intellectual resources that help to unlock any integrative potential in the negotiation situation.  As summarized by Pruitt and Carnevale (1993, pp. 36-41), this can be achieved in a number of ways — for example, by (a) *expanding the pie* (looking for new possibilities beyond the original negotiation agenda), (b) *log-rolling* (making concessions to the other party that it considers important but which are relatively unimportant to the ingroup), or (c) *bridging* (developing solutions that provide each party with those outcomes that it sees as a priority).  Importantly though, it is clear that these activities will be compromised by a lack of relevant information unless each party has *first* used social identity-based contending to explore both what its members want and what the other party's members want.  Once more, we can see that, as with effective bridge-building, the foundation of successful negotiation is a thorough survey of the different masses that it is intended to unite.

### Some empirical tests of the social identity approach

*Social identity as a determinant of negotiation tactics and their efficacy*

The above analysis outlines the idealized form that intergroup negotiations should take if they are to be successful.  It is clear, however, that negotiations do not (and cannot) always take this form and therefore that they are not always successful.  Indeed, it follows from the above analysis that integrative solutions are unlikely to be reached where one or more parties is unwilling either to pursue their own subgroup's concerns or to embrace a superordinate identity.  In the latter case it is also likely that the parties will themselves pursue negotiating tactics that serve to exacerbate rather than ameliorate conflict.  In such settings the process of negotiation can thus prove counterproductive — at least in terms of its ostensible goals.

   This point emerges very clearly from research conducted by Rothbart and Hallmark (1988) and Kramer, Shah and Woerner (1995).   Rothbart and Hallmark's research examined variation in negotiators' choice of tactics as a function of the assumed target of those tactics.  In these researchers' first study participants were presented with a scenario in which two fictional nations, Takonia and Navalia, were in conflict and asked to play the role of the defence minister of one or other nation. The stated nature of the conflict paralleled that of the arms race between the United States and Soviet Union in the 1970s and 1980s, and participants were presented with five policies that might be employed in an attempt to resolve conflict and bring the arms race to an end. These policies ranged from one that was highly coercive (building up new weapons and threatening to use them unless the other country backed down) to one that was very conciliatory (unilaterally halting weapons production and reducing stockpiles by 20 per cent in the expectation that the other country would do the same). The participants' task was then to estimate how effective these strategies would be in making either their own nation or the other nation reduce its arsenal.

The study produced a very clear pattern of results. When asked which strategies would encourage their own country to downgrade its weapons pile, participants opted for those that were more conciliatory. However, when they identified strategies that would influence the other nation they chose much more aggressive tactics. Very similar results also emerged from a second study designed to weaken participants' identification with their own nation by informing them that they were simply a citizen of one of the nations rather than a defence minister.

In both these studies, the underlying logic of participants' responses was thus consistent with a belief that 'we listen to reason, but they respond only to force'. Rothbart and Hallmark (1988) note the similarity between this reasoning and that of the protagonists in the latter stages of the Cold War. In particular, they point to the Reagan administration's belief that brute force was the only language that their Soviet counterparts would understand. This is revealed in the following exchange between President Reagan and Paul Nitze (his chief negotiator in weapons talks):

> [Nitze argued that] ... it was inconceivable that the Soviets would ever accept a proposal that required them to dismantle every last one of their most modern intermediate-range missiles [... in exchange for the United States not deploying a system under development]; that was simply asking, and hoping, for too much. The President was unconvinced. 'Well Paul', he said, 'you just tell the Soviets that you're working for one tough son-of-a-bitch'. (Talbott, 1984, p. 144; cited in Rothbart & Hallmark, 1988, p. 144)

Rothbart and Hallmark's research provides some insight into the way in which negotiators tactics can vary as a function of the ingroup–outgroup status of their target. Following on from this research, an obvious question is how these tactics in turn affect the perceptions and behaviour of those targets. This question has been addressed by Kramer and his colleagues in studies of group members' reaction to ultimatums.

As Kramer et al. (1995) note, ultimatums are a reasonably common negotiation tactic in which demands are made of opponents and are accompanied by a threat that some form of punishment will be meted out to them unless they comply within a specified time. As such, they represent a form of coercion of the form that Rothbart and Hallmark's (1988) participants saw fit to use selectively on outgroups. Kramer et al.'s research reveals, however, that when used on an outgroup ultimatums can often have the opposite impact to that which is desired, largely because they communicate to the recipients a pattern of intergroup (us vs. you) hostility and then lock them into an escalation of that conflict.

Support for this argument was provided by an initial experiment in which Kramer et al. (1995) presented business students with an ultimatum about how to divide up $25.00. The ultimatum was said to emanate from an ingroup (another person in the student's class) or an outgroup (a student in another class) and was either fair (both parties would receive $12.50) or unfair (the ultimatum-maker would receive $17.50 and the participant $7.50). When the ultimatum was fair it was accompanied by the message that 'I am offering $12.50 because splitting the money is the fairest thing to do', and when it was unfair participants received a note which stated 'I am offering $7.50 because something is better than nothing'. As the results presented in Table 7.1 indicate, participants' reactions to this ultimatum varied as an interactive function of its fairness of source. When the ultimatum was fair, participants reacted favourably whoever had delivered it. Moreover, in these cases the ultimatum was always accepted. When the ultimatum was unfair reactions were (unsurprisingly) less favourable, but this pattern was much more pronounced when the ultimatum emanated from an outgroup. Significantly, this meant that the ingroup's unfair ultimatum was accepted on 75 per cent of occasions, but the outgroup's on only 43 per cent. Consistent with patterns reported by Tyler (1999b; Tyler et al., 1998; see also Chapter 8 below), it thus appears that people react in a particularly adverse fashion to the distributive unfairness of an outgroup.

These basic dispositions were examined in a subsequent study (Kramer et al., 1995, Experiment 2) which attempted to discern more about the attributional underpinnings of the above experiment. What expectations do negotiators have of an outgroup, and how do these expectations affect reactions to it? To answer

*Table 7.1*  Reactions to an ultimatum as a function of its fairness and source (from Kramer et al., 1995)

| Source of Ultimatum: | Ingroup | | Outgroup | |
|---|---|---|---|---|
| Fairness of Ultimatum: | Fair | Unfair | Fair | Unfair |
| **Measure** | | | | |
| Rationality of ultimatum | 6.58 | 4.48 | 6.43 | 3.98 |
| Selfishness of ultimatum | 1.46 | 4.81 | 1.69 | 5.60 |
| Exploitativeness of ultimatum | 1.13 | 4.44 | 1.50 | 5.57 |
| Fairness of ultimatum | 6.88 | 3.59 | 6.98 | 2.33 |
| Happy with ultimatum | 6.79 | 4.59 | 6.76 | 2.88 |
| Irritated by ultimatum | 1.13 | 3.19 | 1.67 | 4.54 |
| Acceptance of ultimatum | 100% | 75% | 100% | 43% |

this question participants were led to believe that they would be entering into negotiation with another person about how to divide up $25 but that their offers to each other would be channelled through the experimenter who would add or subtract an undisclosed amount to each offer. Participants were told that the amount added or subtracted would vary randomly between 0 per cent and 100 per cent. In other words, the offer that each person received could be anywhere from 0 per cent to 200 per cent of the amount originally intended by the other negotiator.

Kramer and his colleagues were interested in participants' pre-bargaining expectations, and how they would explain the particular outcomes that they actually received. Results supported the prediction that the opponents' group membership would play a major role in these expectations and attributions. Specifically, participants generally expected to receive more from a classmate than from someone in another class and also thought that it was more sensible for a classmate to give them more. Furthermore, when participants received a high offer (between $11.81 and $12.63) they were more likely and more confident that it came from an ingroup member than an outgroup member, but the opposite pattern emerged when they received a low offer (between $5.81 and $6.63).

Considered together, the results of these studies suggest that under conditions where their activity is informed only by opposed identities, negotiators are inclined to expect and believe the worst of an outgroup while having an altogether more generous disposition towards representatives of an ingroup. Moreover, in reaction to outgroup behaviour that is (or is perceived to be) unfair, they display an intense negative reaction that Kramer and his colleagues refer to as *moralistic aggression* (after Brewer, 1981; Campbell, 1975; Trivers, 1971). As Kramer et al. (1995) note, this reaction is likely to play a very prominent role in the failure of the unfair and coercive tactics that negotiators choose to deploy against outgroups (as demonstrated by Rothbart and Hallmark, 1988), explaining 'why conflicts involving ultimatums so often escalate through a series of destructive action-reaction spirals'. Here:

> Each side views the other as more susceptible to coercive strategies, while at the same time resenting the use of those same strategies against themselves. If, on top of such perceptual asymmetries we add individuals' tendency to be preoffended by the offers they receive from outgroup members, the escalatory potential in such situations becomes even more stark. (Kramer et al., 1995, p. 306)

## *The marriage of subgroup and superordinate identities*

Like much of the cognitive research that we discussed earlier in this chapter, the picture that emerges in the foregoing section is very bleak. In part, this is because the research conducted by Rothbart and Hallmark (1988) and Kramer et al. (1995) can be taken to imply that conflict escalation is an inevitable consequence of social identification. Yet against this view, we argued earlier that social identity salience can also be a precursor to more productive negotiation. However, along lines argued by dual-identity models (e.g. Gaertner, Rust et al., 1996), we suggested that this would only be the case where parties to any dispute are able to acknowledge and act on the basis of a shared superordinate identity that makes sense of, and builds upon, their differences.

In the work reviewed in the previous section we can see that these conditions were not met. Indeed, it seems likely that in Rothbart and Hallmark's (1988) and Kramer et al.'s (1995) research participants defined the experiments as games in which their goal was essentially to beat the opposition with no thought for a future in which they would both have to collaborate. The same could also be said of the examples of negotiation alluded to by these researchers. For example, in the context of arms race negotiations between the United States and the Soviet Union, one can see the grandstanding of the parties as *political and ideological behaviour* that was designed solely for ingroup constituents and which explicitly *precluded* any common understanding or motivation. It is clear, however, that when the political climate in the Soviet Union changed to become more aligned with the broader goals of capitalism, it negotiated successfully with the United States on the issue of arms reduction with the result that an intermediate-range nuclear forces (INF) treaty was co-signed by Presidents Reagan and Gorbachev in December 1987.

Consistent with these arguments, a growing body of research suggests that conflict between groups can be assuaged by processes and interventions that allow for both subgroup and superordinate identification. Illustrative of such work, Gonzalez and Brown (1999) conducted an elaborate and ingenious study designed to examine the impact of (a) recategorization, (b) intergroup differentiation, (c) decategorization, and (d) dual identification on the experience of intergroup contact and the generalization of this experience to intergroup perceptions in general. In the study University of Kent students were first assigned to one of two 2-person minimal groups, supposedly on the basis of their capacity for 'analytic' or 'synthetic' thinking. Identification with these groups was reinforced in a number of ways (e.g. through the wearing of badges) and each separately performed the 'winter survival task' (Johnson & Johnson, 1991; see Chapter 3 above). After this, the groups came together to perform a new task (the successful leader-profile task) under conditions that represented one of four contact experiences.

In a *one-group* (i.e. recategorization) condition the two subgroups were brought together and told that the experimenter was interested in how students from the University of Kent could work together to tackle the leader-profile task. To reinforce this identity a team photograph was taken of the four students each wearing the same University of Kent t-shirt and standing in front of a University of Kent poster. The group then performed the leader-profile task by selecting six traits from a list of twelve that best described a successful leader. The only nuance to this task was that each group was told that it had to select two cognitive and two socio-emotional traits and that two members would work on each sub-task before pooling their solutions and having them judged by a leadership expert.

In the *two-groups* condition, students went through a similar procedure but here were told that the study was examining how groups of analytic and synthetic thinkers could work together to perform the leader-profile task. Identification with these two groups was reinforced throughout (e.g. by the wearing of team badges and different coloured t-shirts, and by taking separate photographs of the two subgroups).

In the *separate individuals* (i.e. decategorization) condition, all group labels were removed and participants were told that the study was intended to examine how people individually could tackle the leader-profile task. Here only the students' personal identities were made salient (e.g. by each wearing a different coloured t-shirt, having a personal name badge and a separate photograph).

Finally, in the *dual-identity* condition, students retained their original group name badges and were told that the experimenter was interested in how analytic and synthetic students from the University of Kent could combine to tackle the leader-profile task. Both of these identities were then reinforced in subsequent interaction (e.g. by having the groups wear different-coloured t-shirts that all had a University of Kent logo on them and taking a photograph in which the students held up their team's name standing in front of a large University of Kent sign).

After the leader-profile task had been completed, the participants were asked to evaluate the analytic and synthetic subgroups and allocate points (from a pool of 100) to reward each group for its performance. Participants also watched a video-tape of another analytic group and another synthetic group separately performing the same profile task and were asked to evaluate and assign points to them. This procedure was designed to examine the generalization of feelings towards specific groups to groups of analytic and synthetic thinkers in general.

Evaluation and reward of the actual groups in the study did not vary much across the experimental conditions with all participants tending to show small levels of ingroup favouritism. However, evaluation and reward of the *new* groups was dramatically affected by the nature of participants' contact experience. As Figure 7.5 indicates, on both measures participants showed a strong tendency to favour their ingroup over the outgroup when their experience of the groups had been as members of two groups or as individuals. As a recategorization perspective would predict, this pattern was attenuated when activities had been organized under the banner of a single identity. However, it was in the dual identity condition that the most positive feelings towards the outgroup were apparent. Indeed, far from being adversarial, the participants here showed some inclination to favour the outgroup over their ingroup.

Gonzalez and Brown's (1999) findings support the view that the most positive way to manage conflict does not necessarily involve dissolving the social identities that give rise to that conflict. Instead, it suggests that the most successful strategies *build upon* those identities and the *real* differences between them (e.g. in roles, competencies and perspectives; see also Berry, 1991, Eggins & Haslam, 1999b; Hornsey & Hogg, 2000). Clearly though, one might question the utility of a dual-identity strategy in the management of real groups that have a clearer cause for conflict than those studied by Gonzalez and Brown (1999). Evidence that the dual-identity model *is* applicable to such contexts comes from research by Huo and her colleagues (Huo et al., 1996). This examined the reaction of 221 workers to conflict in the workplace, focusing on the way in which patterns of identification mediated workers' feelings about the way in which that conflict had been managed.

The participants in Huo et al.'s (1996) study were members of unions that had clear ethnic affiliations (e.g. Asian Americans, Latino Americans, European Americans). Following previous work by Berry (1991, 1994), the researchers distinguished between these workers on the basis of their identification with both

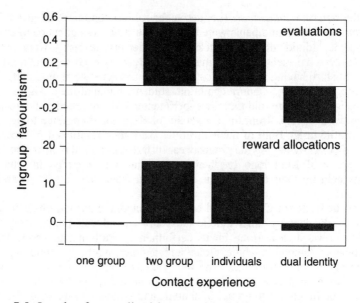

*Figure 7.5* Levels of generalized ingroup favouritism as a function of contact experience (from Gonzalez & Brown, 1999)

*Note*: * Ingroup favouritism = difference in evaluation of, or rewards allocated to, ingroup and outgroup

an ethnic subgroup and their work organization as a whole. Three groups were distinguished in this way: *separatists* (who had high identification with their ethnic ingroup, but low identification with the organization as a whole), *assimilationists* (who had low identification with their ethnic ingroup, but high identification with the organization as a whole), and *biculturalists* (who had high identification with both their ethnic ingroup and the organization as a whole).

In the research respondents had to describe a recent conflict that they had had with a work supervisor. The study then focused on those respondents who described conflicts with a supervisor from a different ethnic background to their own. In relation to the conflict that was brought to mind, participants had to indicate (a) how willing they had been to accept the supervisor's decision, (b) how fairly they felt treated (i.e. their perceptions of procedural justice), and (c) how fair they felt the outcome was (i.e. their perceptions of distributive justice). They also provided *relational* evaluations of the supervisor (e.g. rating his or her honesty and politeness) and *instrumental* evaluations (e.g. rating the favourableness of the outcome).

At a general level the study revealed that relational evaluations predicted decision acceptance, procedural justice, and distributive justice. In other words, the more the participants felt they had a good relationship with their supervisors the more likely they were to accept their decisions and to perceive them as procedurally and distributively just. More subtly, however, separate analysis of participants with different patterns of identification, supported the hypothesis that the reactions of separatists (who defined themselves in terms of an ethnic identity not shared with their supervisor) were largely dictated by instrumental concerns while those of assimilators (who defined themselves in terms of an organizational identity shared with their supervisor) were largely dictated by relational concerns (for related findings from studies of Japanese workers, see Tyler et al., 1998). Identification with the organization thus led workers to base their feelings about conflict on the quality of treatment they received from their supervisor, but identification with an ethnic subgroup led to a focus on outcomes alone. This meant that assimilators were willing to cope with a bad outcome so long as they felt they had been treated fairly by their boss, but separatists were only happy if they got what they wanted. Huo et al. (1996) argue that the latter response poses problems for the general management of work disputes, for the simple reason that workers do not and cannot always get what they want. In dealing with separatists there is therefore the distinct prospect that delivery of poor outcomes will escalate conflict.

Importantly though, the biculturalists in this study (who defined themselves in terms of ethnic *and* organizational identity) behaved in much the same way as assimilators. Huo and her colleagues interpret this finding with optimism, noting that it implies that in order to avoid the potential for conflict escalation, employees need not seek to eliminate subgroup identification altogether (e.g. either through recruitment or training). As they put it:

> The good news is that the promise of superordinate identification as a mechanism for cohesion does not hinge on people feeling less loyal to subgroups. The bad news is that people who do not have a strong attachment to the superordinate group will pose a threat to the functioning of authorities if they are not satisfied with their outcomes. For social cohesion to be maintained and for authorities to function effectively, people do not have to relinquish their ties to the subgroup, but they do have to care about their ties to the superordinate group. (Huo et al., 1996, p. 45)

There is clearly a political dimension to this conclusion and we will consider this in more detail below (see also Chapter 11 below). However, for the time being, the important point is that these findings provide strong support for the view that dual identification (as enshrined in notions of biculturalism or multiculturalism) offers an important path to conflict resolution that steers a delicate course between the twin prospects of conflict escalation (produced by separatism) and conflict avoidance (produced by assimilation).

## *The temporal sequencing of subgroup and superordinate identification*

The research discussed in the previous sections gives an insight into the role that social identity processes play in people's experience and reaction to conflict. However, most of this research hones in on participants' behaviour at one point in time and hence the research allows little opportunity to examine negotiation and conflict processes as they unfold. As Stephenson (1981) and Olekalns et al. (1996) remark, in the case of negotiation this is a particular problem because the process is one in which participants' orientations and their behaviour are predicted to *change* over time. Moreover, the arguments presented earlier in this chapter suggest that the patterning of this change should have major implications for the process and its outcomes. In particular, we argued that if negotiation is to resolve conflict successfully, it needs to proceed from a phase of social identity-based contending to one in which problem-solving behaviour is encouraged by the need to reconcile subgroup identities with an organic superordinate identity.

As we intimated above, this argument is highly consistent with the framework for successful negotiation presented by Douglas (1957) and subsequently elaborated by Morley and Stephenson (1979; Morley, 1992; Stephenson; 1981, 1984). In her own studies of industrial disputation, Douglas noted that successful negotiation evolved through distinct phases that were distinguished by the degree to which the participants' roles as representatives of one side or another were discernible. Specifically, the first phase of negotiation was marked by a high degree of *role indentifiability*, such that naive judges found it easy to tell from unlabelled transcripts of proceedings which side any particular negotiator belonged to. However, by the end of negotiation, role identifiability was much less pronounced. These patterns were subsequently confirmed in extensive formal investigations by Morley and Stephenson (1979; Stephenson, 1981, 1984) of wage and contractual disputes in chemical and food processing industries. Summarizing the findings of this research, Stephenson (1981) observes:

> The allegiance of the negotiators is not first and foremost to the negotiation group, but to their respective parties. Nevertheless, ... successful negotiators do in time come to speak with indistinguishable voices; at this stage it becomes appropriate to think of the group as in some sense an individual entity. This stage, however, is achieved not by masking differences, nor by avoiding conflict. Rather it is a consequence of having explored the differences and fought over them. The implications of the first 'distributive' phase are subsequently explored in an increasingly 'integrative', or problem-solving manner. (p. 187)

Results of a number of other studies support this argument that in order to succeed, negotiation must encourage conflict before attempting to resolve it. For example, from simulated disputes between employers and employees over wages, Olekalns et al. (1996) found that optimal (integrative) outcomes tended to be achieved if early stages of negotiation involved the use of contentious tactics and subsequent phases involved restructuring (i.e. the tabling of new ideas in a flexible and open manner). However, a reversal of this sequencing led to suboptimal solutions. These researchers thus conclude:

> Achieving optimum outcomes is a cognitively complex task that requires dyads both to *differentiate*, recognizing multiple perspectives on a problem, and *integrate*, building relations between these perspectives. ... Suboptimum negotiators focus increasingly on the task of differentiation over time, whereas optimum negotiators focus increasingly on the task of integration over time. (Olekalns et al., 1996, p. 76)

Experimental research by Keenan and Carnevale (1989) also shows that allowing groups the opportunity to develop a sense of positive social identity prior to negotiation can have a positive impact on the direction that those negotiations subsequently take. In this study participants were assigned to fictional roles in a three-person management team and were initially presented with a situation which encouraged them either to co-operate or compete over the distribution of resources among the distinct parts of the organization that each team member represented (the accounting, finance and stock analysis departments of Bolt Industries). They then went on to negotiate as a group with what they believed was another company (International Acme) over a part sale of Bolt. Analysis of this negotiation indicated that groups that had had the experience of working co-operatively — and hence were more likely to have developed a shared sense of positive social identity — were more likely to behave in a constructive manner towards the outgroup (making more offers and behaving less aggressively) than those who had had a competitive prior experience or who had not worked together at all.

Although the results of the research by Olekalns et al. (1996) and Keenan and Carnevale (1989) are consistent with the arguments outlined above (e.g. see Figure 7.4), it is apparent that neither team of researchers frames its arguments in terms of social identity principles or tests the assumptions of this approach directly. Moreover, in common with most other research in this field (see Stephenson, 1981, p. 180), neither team of researchers examines *actual intergroup negotiation*. Partly to address these issues, two interactive studies were conducted by Eggins (1999; Eggins & Haslam, 1999a) within a larger programme that investigated the contribution of social identity processes to the shaping and negotiation of conflict.

Both of Eggins and Haslam's (1999a) studies examined conflict over how to tackle the issue of males' underperformance at university. Each study involved groups of four students (two males, two females) deciding how to deal with this issue by selecting four strategies from a list containing suggestions that ranged from those that were highly inclusive (e.g. raise the profile of the counselling service) to those that were very partisan (e.g. restrict female entry to some courses). Each study had three phases. In the first phase the four participants decided individually which strategies to deploy; in the second they did this in two separate subgroups (each containing two people), and in the final phase the two subgroups came together in an attempt to reach a negotiated agreement over strategy selection. The critical feature of both studies was that in the second phase the subgroups were either comprised of same-sex or opposite-sex students. The primary intention of this manipulation was to vary the extent to which the negotiation process provided students with an opportunity to develop a perspective on this topic which was based upon, and reflected the concerns of, a relevant social identity. It was expected that this identity would be reinforced when subgroups had a same-sex composition but suppressed when they involved opposite-sex students.

In line with the arguments outlined above, the studies' core prediction was that students would be more satisfied with the negotiation process and see it as more worthwhile (key predictors of the long-term success of negotiation; Pruitt et al., 1993; Tyler et al., 1996) if final outcomes were preceded by a phase in which group-based conflict was dealt with in terms of the social identities implicated in that conflict. As illustrated by the data in Table 7.2, this prediction was supported in both studies. So, although very similar strategies were ultimately endorsed in both conditions, participants' sense of procedural and distributive justice was much higher where the subgroup structure had been identity-reinforcing.

*Table 7.2*  Percentage of participants agreeing with statements about negotiation as a function of subgroup structure (from Eggins & Haslam, 1999a, Experiment 1)

|  | Subgroup Structure | |
| --- | --- | --- |
|  | Identity reinforcing (same-sex) | Identity suppressing (mixed-sex) |
| *Positive statements* | | |
| Both groups seemed to move towards a compromise | 100 | 75 |
| There was a mood of co-operation throughout negotiation | 100 | 69 |
| I was looking forward to each stage of discussing the issue | 88 | 38 |
| There was a feeling of conflicting ideas | 81 | 69 |
| There was a sense that this issue affected us all equally | 81 | 25 |
| *Negative statements* | | |
| Negotiation became progressively more difficult | 31 | 50 |
| Negotiation became progressively more tense | 25 | 44 |

Moreover, results from the second (larger) study indicated that incorporating same-sex subgroups led participants to identify more strongly with their sex and that this social identification mediated positive feelings about the negotiation process as a whole. When negotiators had the opportunity to caucus their feelings with similarly identified others, they thus felt better *because* that caucusing allowed them to voice and explore the group-based feelings at the heart of the issue they confronted. Contrary to the injunctions of decategorization and recategorization perspectives, Eggins and Haslam (1999a) thus conclude:

> Encouraging social group representation in negotiation is not necessarily detrimental to the process of conflict resolution and may in fact be beneficial. This is because (a) denying group members access to representation in negotiation will not be acceptable to them and may lead to a rejection of the negotiation process or outcomes [along lines argued by Tyler et al., 1996] and (b) issues of social identification and group definition typically underlie the development of social conflict and must therefore be addressed if the conflict is to be adequately addressed. (p. 24)

Again, then, the effective management of intergroup conflict appears to demand more than merely sweeping the group under the organizational carpet. Yet the fact that this is often the preferred strategy in organizational contexts leaves us with one final question to ponder in concluding this chapter. If subgroup social identification can prove so fruitful in the management of conflict, why is it so frequently suppressed?

## Conclusion

In an essay on the social psychology of conflict, Worchel tells the story of having just delivered a paper on this topic to officials in Greece and being stopped in his tracks by a question from a local man in the audience. After noting that psychologists (Western psychologists, in particular) have been pre-occupied with the *elimination* of conflict, the man simply asked 'Why haven't social scientists devoted more attention to identifying the functions of conflict and developing programmes to manage conflict to a positive end?' (Worchel et al., 1993, pp. 76-77). Upon reviewing the organizational literature, it seems appropriate to ask the same question. This is because, as we have already noted, the consensus in this domain is very much that conflict management should take the form of conflict resolution. Daft (1995) summarizes this well:

> Conflict is natural and inevitable. Yet an emerging view is that co-operation — not conflict or competition — is the way to achieve high performance. The new trends in management ... all assume employee co-operation is a good thing. This means that successful organizations must find healthy ways to confront and re-solve conflict. Managers champion a *co-operative model* of organization, mean-ing they foster co-operation and don't stimulate competition or conflict, which work against the achievement of overall company goals. (p. 457)

Moreover, when it comes to the study and practice of negotiation, the question asked of Worchel seems all the more pertinent because in this area it appears that conflict *can* be harnessed effectively at the same time that the co-operative model runs into serious problems. A range of studies thus suggest that negotiations in which participants' first priority is to co-operate or concede stand less chance of ultimate success than those in which participants stand their ground and are prepared to fight for what they and their constituents believe (e.g. Douglas, 1957; Stephenson, 1984). Amongst other things, the benefits of having conflict 'out in the open' appear to derive from: (a) full exploration of the issues that negotiation is intended to address (a sense of 'clearing the air' and not 'papering over the cracks'); (b) identification of parties' real concerns (information which is needed if integrative solutions are to be developed later); (c) consideration of more options; (d) a lack of false optimism; and (e) enhanced feelings of empowerment and procedural justice.

However, despite the benefits that can flow from encouraging (or at least not suppressing) conflict, it seems likely that one reason why this strategy is not endorsed more widely is that it does not *guarantee* integrative (win–win) outcomes. Instead, the social identity approach we have outlined suggests that these outcomes will only materialize if a superordinate social identity serves to frame subgroup differences and to provide negotiators with the social motivation to do the creative intellectual work upon which integrative solutions depend. In the absence of this superordinate identity, conflict would generally be expected to escalate and this may clearly run counter to the wishes of those who establish and control the negotiation process.

As with the design of group decision-making procedures discussed in the previous chapter, managers may thus be guided by a 'safety-first' principle which deters them from mobilizing group interests and embracing group conflict. Yet the fact that these same people are often prepared to take risks in other domains and that a willingness to take chances is frequently heralded as the supreme managerial virtue (e.g. see Dando-Collins, 1998, p. 363), suggests that this is not the whole story. Indeed, even where the salience of a superordinate identity virtually assures positive outcomes, it is clear that negotiations are often designed in a manner that explicitly downgrades participants' group membership. For example, in Western countries, it is increasingly the case that legislation *demands* that collective bargaining over wages and conditions be replaced by individual bargaining. Such legislation is often justified on grounds that it reduces the likelihood of industrial protest (which it does; see Chapter 10 below), but it is not hard to see that for those who own and control organizations it achieves much more. Most importantly, it denies their opponents (or potential opponents) any collective voice and serves to delegitimize group-based opposition to the organization's existing power structure.

In practice, then, effective conflict management is never simply a question of identifying the psychological and structural arrangements that deliver the best outcomes and attempting to implement them. If that were the case, the man from Greece would never have needed to ask Worchel his question. He did need to, however, because strategies of conflict management are typically selected by those in power and the preservation of that power is often their first priority (see Smyth, 1994). This means that the benefits of what we might term *organic pluralism* — promoting an organic superordinate identity that feeds upon self-generated lower-level subgroup identities (Haslam, Powell et al., 2000) — are often passed over in favour of a strategy that seeks unilaterally to impose a superordinate identity on members of low power groups (e.g. see Stephenson, 1984).

As with many other areas of organizational behaviour, understanding conflict management therefore requires an appreciation of *power* and *politics*, not just psychology. In an attempt to develop this appreciation, it is on these topics that the next chapter focuses.

## Further reading

The article by Pruitt and Carnevale (1993) provides a very good summary of mainstream negotiation research. De Dreu et al.'s (1995) chapter offers an overview of interesting research developments that challenge the assumption that clashing perspectives necessarily detract from negotiation. The other four papers are more directly aligned with a social identity analysis and offer a range of important theoretical, methodological and practical insights into the way that social conflict can be resolved and exacerbated.

De Dreu, C. K. W., Carnevale, P. J. D., Emans, B. J. M. & van de Vliert, E. (1995). Outcome frames in bilateral negotiation: Resistance to concession making and frame adoption. *European Review of Social Psychology*, *6*, 97-125.

Eggins, R. A. & Haslam, S. A. (1999). *Social identity and negotiation: Giving voice to the group*. Unpublished manuscript: The Australian National University.

Huo, Y. J., Smith, H. J., Tyler, T. R. & Lind, E. A. (1996). Superordinate identification, subgroup identification, and justice concerns: Is separatism the problem? Is assimilation the answer? *Psychological Science*, *7*, 40-45.

Kramer, R. M., Shah, P. P. & Woerner, S. L. (1995). Why ultimatums fail: Social identity and moralistic aggression in coercive bargaining. In R. M. Kramer & D. M. Messick (Eds.), *Negotiation as a social process* (pp. 285-308). Thousand Oaks, CA: Sage.

Pruitt, D. G. & Carnevale, P. J. (1993). *Negotiation in social conflict*. Milton Keynes: Open University Press.

Stephenson, G. M. (1984). Interpersonal and intergroup dimensions of bargaining and negotiation. In H. Tajfel (Ed.), *The social dimension: European developments in social psychology* (pp. 646-667). Cambridge: Cambridge University Press.

# 8 Power

Life is a search after power; and this is an element with which the world is so saturated — there is no chink or crevice in which it is not lodged — that no honest seeking goes unrewarded. (Emerson)

There is a universal need to exercise some kind of power, or to create for one's self the appearance of some power. (Nietzsche)

Power tends to corrupt and absolute power corrupts absolutely. (Acton)

Power, like a desolating pestilence pollutes whate'er it touches. (Shelley)

Power, whether exercised over matter or over man, is partial to simplification. (Hoffer)

The wise become as the unwise in the enchanted chambers of power, whose lamps make every face the same colour. (Landor)

An honest man can feel no pleasure in the exercise of power over his fellow citizens. (Jefferson)

A friend in power is a friend lost. (Adams)

The above observations provide a representative overview of popular and influential beliefs about power. If their various sentiments are rolled into one summary statement this might suggest that power is all around us, that we all want it, but that if we acquire it we will lose our sense of judgement and decency in the process, along with all our friends. Although bleak, this conclusion is not seriously at odds with the picture of power that emerges from social and organizational research into this topic. Moreover, it needs to be added, it is a picture that few of us have much difficulty confirming in our everyday experience at work. Most of us could tell plenty of tales of power-hungry tyrants who have mercilessly exploited and perverted the efforts of those they control in order to promote their own self-interests at the expense of the organization as a whole.

When we confront these organizational tyrants, we often ask ourselves how it is that such people are able to acquire their power and why it is that the forces of decency and civility seem powerless to stop them. Do you have to be psychologically maladjusted to be given power? Or is it simply that power produces psychopathology? While our answers to these questions may vary, it is also the case that the remedy we typically identify for these problems is one in which we ourselves assume the mantle power. If power were given to us, we would surely be impervious to its temptations and to moral and intellectual dissolution. Or would we?

In seeking to address these questions, this chapter focuses on three key features of power in organizational life: how people perceive power, how they acquire it and what they do with it. As we will see in the following section, received analyses of these issues have tended to see all aspects of power as flowing largely from individualistic motivations and goals (Ng, 1980). Consistent with the thrust of many of the above quotations, established theories suggest that individuals routinely pursue power to promote their own personal interests at the expense of others and that these motivations inevitably colour and distort their own perceptions and behaviour along the way. In this analysis power in organizations is seen very much as a dog-eat-dog affair — with the striving of individual employees tending naturally to disadvantage everyone but themselves. This is a very ugly picture of both human nature and organizational life. Moreover, this ugliness is one reason why power is something that many managers (and many organizational theorists) would rather not discuss — leading to a situation where, in Kanter's (1979, p. 65) words, 'it is easier to talk about money — and much easier to talk about sex — than it is to talk about power' (see also Bacharach & Lawler, 1980; Ng, 1996; Pfeffer, 1981, 1992).

The analysis offered in this chapter does not deny that such strivings exist or that their consequences are an important and prevalent feature of organizational behaviour. Indeed, it is argued that they are key contributors to, and derivatives of, structural arrangements that promote employees' self-definitions in terms of personal identity. However, as we have seen in a number of earlier chapters, psychologically speaking, these personal aspects of organizational life — and the beliefs in personal mobility that underpin them — are not the whole story. Importantly, then, a great deal of power-related activity is motivated not by employees' personal self-interest but rather (or also) by their *collective* self-interest as members of particular organizational and social groups: as men or women, management or workers, members of this or that department, this or that team (Kanter, 1979).

And as we delve into the psychology of group power, it becomes clear that interpretation of its status and consequences is much more moot than that of personal power. In large part this is because while at a personal level other people's power cannot be working for us (and hence is likely to be seen by us as corrupt or malevolent), this need not be the case at a group level. We can wield group power in the interests of our peers and they can do the same for us. Moreover, while personal power is generally accepting of (and contributory to) the status quo, group power is much more likely to be a vehicle for social and organizational change. Indeed, in many ways, group power is *the* critical ingredient of organizational change and so unless it is achieved and wielded, organizations are doomed to stultification and inertia (Pfeffer, 1992). Although the psychology of personal power is interesting and complex in its own right, this property makes the study of power *in all its aspects* even more intriguing and important.

### An overview of research into power

*Taxonomic and contingency approaches*

In introducing the concept of power, Bierstedt (1950, p. 730; see also Fiske & Dépret, 1996, p. 54) makes the interesting observation that this is similar to the concept of time: we all know perfectly well what it is until we are asked to define it. On this issue there is therefore a great deal of disagreement among theorists and practitioners, and most propose a definition that is tailored to their own objectives and approach. Most definitions, however, embrace the view that power is embedded in a social relationship where one party (an individual or group) has (or is perceived to have) the ability to impose its will on another by virtue of the resources at its disposal (e.g. Blau, 1964; Dahl, 1957; Kaplan, 1964; Weber, 1947). We have power if we are able to make others do what we want and the extent of our power can be gauged by the probability that we will succeed. In saying this, two further issues are raised. The first concerns the various *means* by which power can be achieved, the second relates to the *overlap* between this concept and others in the organizational arena.

The most influential framework for thinking about the different ways in which power can be realized is provided by French and Raven's (1959) identification of five (and later six; Raven, 1965) distinct *bases* of power (see also Raven, 1992). As Table 8.1 indicates, according to this taxonomy, people can achieve power over others through a number of channels each related to their possession of particular material and psychological *resources*. These resources are associated with (a) rewards, (b) coercion, (c) expertise, (d) legitimacy, (e) likeableness, and (f) information.

The ideas here are all reasonably self-explanatory. If, for example, we take the case of a manager who wants her subordinates to participate in a company open day (that takes place on a Saturday but for which employees are not paid) we can see that her ability to ensure their participation may be attributable to a variety of factors. In the first instance, employees may participate on the understanding that the manager has the ability to reward them for their labour (e.g. by granting them time off in lieu, or recommending them for promotion; *reward power*). On the other hand, participation may be encouraged for exactly the opposite reasons, with employees knowing that unless they participate they will be punished in some way (e.g. by being passed over for promotion, or being given more onerous duties in future; *coercive power*). Less instrumentally, the staff may participate because they recognize the manager's expertise and her ability to manage both their interests and those of the department (*expert power*) or because the manager is able to present a logical and persuasive case for participating (*informational power*). And finally, of course, they may participate because they acknowledge the manager's right to tell them when to work and what to do (*legitimate power*) or because they like, respect and look up to her (*referent power*).

If this list covers the main means by which people *can* achieve power in organizations, the next question is obviously 'Which of these do they *actually* select?'. Like a number of other researchers, Bacharach and Lawler (1980) argue that the answer lies in the interaction between structural elements and individual differences. Specifically, they suggest that the use of various forms of power

*Table 8.1* French and Raven's (1959; Raven, 1965) typology of power and employees' ability to use some of the different forms in organizational settings (based on Kahn et al., 1964)

| Form of Power | Examples | Ability to Use on supervisors | on peers | on subordinates |
|---|---|---|---|---|
| Reward | Ability to promote, award pay rise or assign desirable duties | ✗✗ | ✗ | ✓ |
| Coercive | Ability to demote, impose financial penalties or assign undesirable duties | ✗✗ | ✗✗ | ✓ |
| Legitimate | Role-related responsibilities (e.g. as a head of department or a supervisor) | ✗✗ | ✗ | ✓✓ |
| Expert | Access to specialized knowledge in a particular domain | ✓✓ | ✓✓ | ✓✓ |
| Informational | Ability to present logical and persuasive arguments | n/a | n/a | n/a |
| Referent | Capacity to be admired or respected | n/a | n/a | n/a |

*Note*:  ✓✓  = high ability to use power
  ✓  = moderate ability to use power
  ✗  = low ability to use power
  ✗✗  = minimal ability to use power
  n/a  = data not provided by Kahn et al.'s research (although patterns should be similar to those for expert power)

depends on the person's (a) office or structural position, (b) personal characteristics (especially charisma and leadership potential), (c) expertise, and (d) opportunity. So, in order to get staff to attend the open day, our manager may decide to rely on legitimate power rather than coercive power if her position carries with it no authority to punish and she is personally opposed to this tactic, but if, at the same time, she has relevant status (e.g. responsibility for organizing public relations activities) and this is an opportunity to draw on it.

Consistent with such an approach, a large body of research supports the view that multiple factors dictate how and when people use power in organizations. For example, Kahn, Wolfe, Quinn, Snoek and Rosenthal (1964) conducted a survey of managers' perceived ability to use different forms of power and found that which they felt able to use depended on the status of the person whose behaviour they were attempting to control. As Table 8.1 indicates, respondents felt that expert power could be used on any co-worker regardless of his or her status, but that other forms of power could really only be used on subordinates. Other studies also suggest that the ability to use different types of power depends, amongst other things, on the norms of the organization and the personal style and background of the would-be user (e.g. see Ashforth, 1994).

This process of thinking about power use as a multi-faceted phenomenon that is contingent on multiple factors opens our eyes to the breadth and complexity of the topic as a whole. Nevertheless, the approach has a number of shortcomings (e.g. see Bacharach & Lawler, 1980). In the first instance, it is apparent that simply cataloguing the various bases of power and the factors which predict their use does not provide an integrated theoretical understanding of the psychological processes underlying power use. Why do managers resort to one form of power than another, and what is it about a particular power base that makes it appealing or appropriate in any given setting? These are critical questions, but they can never be answered simply by devising better inventories.

Related to this problem, a second limitation of power taxonomies is that they typically confuse power with other concepts in the organizational literature. In particular, most of the more benign forms of power that are catalogued in taxonomies like French and Raven's (1959) might more appropriately be considered as manifestations of *social influence*. This is important because definitions of power typically imply that the power user imposes his or her will *against* the wishes of those that they attempt to control and yet, as we saw in Chapters 2 and 3, the very opposite is true of influence processes. This point is especially relevant to an appreciation of referent power. This concept bears a strong resemblance to notions of charismatic leadership, but such leadership only emerges and is only successful to the extent that followers *willingly* embrace a leader's goal. Leadership, then, is not a power process (Turner, 1991, 1999). Similarly, notions of expert and legitimate power also suggest some implicit acceptance of the user's right to control, and so their status as bases of power is equally questionable (Tyler, 1993). In the interests of making theoretical progress it is therefore on the seemingly more malign, coercive forms of power use that most theorists have focused.

### Individual difference approaches

Although the contingency approach discussed above suggests that the processes underlying power use might be complex, researchers initially set about the process of explaining the use of coercive power in organizations by developing single-factor theories — much as they had in many other areas (e.g. the study of leadership and motivation; see Chapters 3 and 4 above). And as in those other areas, these tended to be couched in terms of either (a) the underlying personality of the power user or (b) motivations common to all employees.

Unsurprisingly perhaps, the personality profile considered to be characteristic of the person prone to the use of coercive power is not especially flattering. Indeed, many of the ideas here were borrowed directly from Adorno, Frenkel-Brunswik Levinson and Sanford's (1950) depiction of the person prone to extreme prejudice and fascism in their influential text *The Authoritarian Personality*. These researchers administered a range of psychometric tests and interview schedules to people and identified a number of distinctive patterns of thinking that appeared to differentiate between those who were potentially prejudiced (authoritarians) and others who were more tolerant. In particular, the thought processes of the prejudiced person were characterized by (a) intolerance of ambiguity, (b) rigidity, (c) concreteness (poor abstract reasoning), and (d) over-generalization.

It is not hard to see how this analysis can be directly applied to the organizational setting. Here authoritarians are expected to display all the hallmarks of pathology in their dealings with fellow workers. Most particularly, within a syndrome of *petty tyranny* or *bureaupathy* (Thompson, 1961), they should behave in a fawning and sycophantic manner towards their superiors while abusing the power those superiors give them by treating subordinates with utter disdain. According to Ashforth (1994), the six defining dimensions of this syndrome are: (a) arbitrariness and self-aggrandizement; (b) belittling of subordinates; (c) lack of consideration for others; (d) a forcing style of conflict resolution; (e) discouragement of initiative; and (f) non-contingent use of punishment. It is unlikely, of course, that in self-reports or interviews of the type used by Adorno and his colleagues, managers would be likely to own up to such behaviour. Accordingly, the primary means of identifying petty tyrants is through subordinates' ratings of managers' behaviour (e.g. using the LBDQ; see Chapter 3 above).

There is no doubt that, for those of us who believe that we have fallen victim to regimes of petty tyranny in the workplace (and most of us have, or will, at one time or another), this analysis is very appealing. Certainly, it is comforting to think that the managers who give us grief are by their very nature socially dysfunctional and mentally deficient. By the same token, it is not hard to imagine that reports of aggrieved workers would support this analysis.

Unfortunately though, the empirical evidence that might back these reports up is uncompelling (for a general critique of the literature on authoritarianism, see Billig, 1978; Brown, 1965; Oakes et al., 1994). Possibly the best illustration of this fact comes from a study conducted by Kipnis (1972). The participants in this research were university business majors who were each told they would be given the task of supervising a group of four high-school students who were said to be working on an administrative task in an adjacent building. In performing this role half of the participants were told that they could exercise a range of powers customarily available to managers, including the ability to reward and penalize the workers financially, to transfer them to another job, or to fire them. On the other hand, the remaining participants had no such power and were simply told that in order to get the most out of the workers they must use their legitimate powers as appointed leaders and their personal powers of persuasion.

In fact the high-school students did not exist, and feedback indicative of their performance was contrived by the experimenter and controlled so as to be identical across the two conditions. In this way, Kipnis (1972) was able to see how granting reward and coercive powers to some of the participants affected their treatment of, and reactions to, the workers independently of actual variation in that performance. The results were very clear and generally supported Kipnis's view that the provision of these powers had a corrupting influence on the student managers. Specifically, participants who were given power were: (a) twice as likely to try to interfere with the workers (e.g. by urging them on or making threats); (b) more likely to underrate the workers' ability and their worth to the company; (c) less willing to want to rehire the workers in future; and (d) less likely to recommend workers for promotion. Even more interestingly, after the experiment had been completed, the participants were asked if they would now like to 'meet with the workers and talk with them while sharing a cup of coffee' (Kipnis, 1972, p. 38). This invitation was accepted by 79 per cent of the participants in the low-power condition but by only 35 per cent of those who had been given a high amount of power.

Because the participants in this study were normal healthy adults who had been randomly assigned to experimental conditions, these findings deal a severe blow to arguments that the corrupting potential of power is confined to individuals with pathological personalities. Instead, on the basis of his findings, Kipnis (1972) concluded that at a much more general level:

> Inequity in power is disruptive of harmonious social relations and drastically limits the possibilities that the power holder can maintain close and friendly relations with the less powerful. (p. 39)

In seeking to apportion blame for abuses of power, it thus appears that we have to look beyond individual differences in personality.

### Motivational approaches

If the corrupting potential of power is not confined to particular power holders, one alternative is that it is the manifestation of universal human drives. This view was developed long before the formal study of organizational psychology, particularly in the philosophical writings of Hobbes and Nietzsche (for an excellent review, see Ng, 1980). For Hobbes (1651/1968), the attainment of power was the primary means by which individuals could satisfy egoistic goals and for Nietzsche (1888/1968) 'the will to power' was a fundamental human drive. Significantly, neither writer saw these drives as inherently wrong or immoral. Both recognized that conflicts of interests between powerful individuals and groups could give rise to discord and hostility, but for Hobbes the achievement of power was also a necessary path to future good and for Nietzsche *powerlessness* was more to blame for tyranny than power per se. Contemporary statements of similar views are presented by Kanter (1979), Ashforth (1989) and Pfeffer (1992).

Nevertheless, the dominant view of power-related motivation is less positive. This is particularly true of Mulder's (1977) *power distance reduction theory* in which power is characterized as a psychological addiction which — like a drug — inevitably makes victims of those who are given even the smallest quantity. Two basic motivations underlie this analysis. The first is *power distance reduction* (PDR): individuals' desire to reduce the psychological distance between themselves and more powerful others. The second is *power distance enlargement* (PDE): the desire to enhance the distance between oneself and powerless others. As Figure 8.1 suggests, these two motivations are assumed to work in tandem to ensure that individuals always gravitate towards more powerful others. This applies (a) as long as a person does not have complete power (so that there

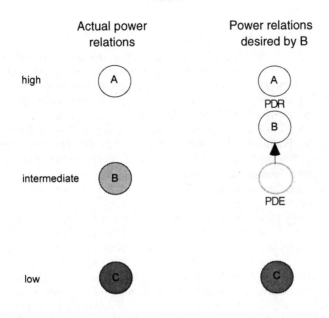

Actual power relations | Power relations desired by B

high — A

PDR

B

PDE

intermediate — B

low — C

*Figure 8.1* Mulder's (1977) principles of power distance reduction (PDR) and power distance enlargement (PDE)

is some distance to reduce) and (b) to the extent that he or she already has some power (so there is some distance to enhance).

The predictions of this model appear to be consistent with observations that the attainment and use of power in organizations is of more concern to those who already have some control over others (i.e. managers) than to those who do not (e.g. Pfeffer, 1992; see also Bruins & Wilke, 1992, 1993). They also accord with the patterns of interaction reported by Kipnis (1972) where the refusal of managers who had been given power to go for a drink with their subordinates can be interpreted as a manifestation of a power distance enhancement motive. The analysis also provides a simple explanation for the 'dog-eat-dog' dimensions of the contemporary corporate world — where the mean get meaner and the lean get leaner.

It is less clear, however, that Mulder's (1977) model is equipped to account for behaviour in less individualistic environments or where structural factors (e.g. rules governing interaction and advancement) impede (and may ultimately redirect) workers' motivations. How does it explain the behaviour of a department head who joins his subordinates on a picket line? Or that of a promising doctor who gives away her career to do overseas aid work? By wedding individuals only to incremental step-by-step changes in power, the model also buys heavily into an assumption that the status quo of existing power relations is an enduring feature of organizational life. As Ng (1980, pp. 224-229) notes, this is a very pessimistic message for those without power, but it is also one that denies the possibility of organizational change that might overturn any given power structure and in which the powerless might play (or at least try to play) a role.

*Social exchange approaches*

Bearing in mind the rather dismal view that many of the above images of power-related behaviour convey, one obvious question is 'Why do people put up with it?'. Why do workers continue to play their part in power games in which, more often than not, they turn out to be the losers? As with topics of leadership and motivation discussed in Chapters 3 and 4, one very popular answer to this question is in terms of social exchange principles (after Thibaut & Kelley, 1959; in particular see Bacharach & Lawler, 1980, pp. 19-26). The idea here is that when workers enter organizations they voluntarily forgo certain powers (e.g. to do as they please, to say exactly what they think) in return for certain rewards (e.g. pay, security, training). Moreover, because workers with less power in an organization are usually dependent on those with more power for the provision of rewards and punishment, this dependence is assumed to foster compliance with the power-holder and tolerance of their whims and foibles. However, if the costs associated with staying in a subordinate power relationship become too high, it is assumed that the individual will either (a) exit the relationship if a more attractive alternative is available or (b) attempt to restructure the relationship through political behaviour, possibly in coalition with like-minded others.

According to the social exchange perspective, *dependency* is therefore the key to power (e.g. Bacharach & Lawler, 1980, p. 20; Robbins, Millett, Cacioppe & Waters-Marsh, 1998, p. 440). As a result, for many researchers (e.g. Pfeffer, 1992), the secret of effective power use is to exploit relationships of dependence appropriately, while poor management is seen to result from neglect or abuse of such relations. In Pfeffer's (1992) words:

> When interdependence exists, our ability to get things done requires us to develop power and the capacity to influence those on whom we depend. If we fail in this effort — either because we don't recognize we need to do it or because we don't know — we fail to accomplish our goals. (p. 38)

In the broadest terms, this approach suggests that success (or even survival) in organizational life is a function of a person's ability to make others dependent on them through control and management of resources. This is best achieved by ensuring that those resources are important, scarce, and non-substitutable (Mintzberg, 1983). Consistent with this view, a number of studies suggest that within organizations it is those departments and officers who allocate key resources, who devise company policy and who promote company activity to outsiders who are perceived to have most power (Gandz & Murray, 1980; Madison, Allen, Porter, Renwick & Mayes, 1980).

The dependence approach has widespread appeal, not least because it opens the door to the study and appreciation of various forms of political behaviour in organizations. In the true spirit of Machiavelli (see Grint, 1997; Ng, 1980, pp. 18-21) it thus points to the use of power as a skill and art, rather than as a blunt and sinister instrument. Nevertheless, the approach has a number of interrelated limitations (see Ng, 1980, pp. 173-185; Turner, 1991, pp. 118-122). The first is that the principles of cost and benefit (and indeed of power and dependency) which lie at its heart, are much less tangible than the approach suggests. Whenever a person submits to coercion we can argue that they perceive the costs of resistance to be too high, and whenever they resist coercion it can be argued that the costs of submission are too high. But, much as we argued in Chapter 4, what actually *makes* a cost too high to bear cannot be specified in advance of the behaviour that it is used to predict. It is certainly the case that perceptions of cost and benefit are *correlates* of the power process (and are a general feature of organizational life), but this may only be as rationalizations of behaviour that actually has *other* causes. Furthermore, even if the full specification of perceived costs and benefits were possible, it is not obvious that people always seek to exit or change what they acknowledge to be a non-beneficial power relationship when options to do so are available. Data presented by Tyler (1988, 1998, 1999a) and Smith and Tyler (1996) suggest, for example, that responses to injustice are best predicted by identification with particular groups and associated feelings of respect and pride (see also Chapter 10 below). Amongst other things, this means that people sometimes stay in highly unrewarding relationships with particular managers because they have a sense of pride in the organization as a whole and leave highly rewarding ones because they have no such sentiments.

Yet probably the most significant problem with the social exchange approach lies in its assumption that power can work as a basis or substitute for social influence. The view that managers should acquire resources and then use them to control others' behaviour through reward and punishment, neglects the fact that such actions can seriously backfire — precisely because they are seen as coercive (Brehm, 1966). Thus attempting to buy the affections of one's subordinates can lead to resentment as can attempts to ingratiate oneself with superiors through acquiescence. This much was recognized by Machiavelli (1513/1984) when he observed:

> If a prince holds on to his state by means of mercenary armies, he will never be stable or secure; for they are disunited, ambitious, without discipline, disloyal; they are brave among friends; among enemies they are cowards ... and your downfall is deferred only so long as the attack is deferred. ... The reason for this is that they have no other love nor other motive to keep them in the field than a meagre wage, which is not enough to make them want to die for you. (pp. 77-78)

Consistent with this point, the evidence that people's attitudes and behaviour are easily manipulated via reward and punishment is much more scant than commonly supposed (Turner, 1991).

## *The cognitive miser approach*

As outlined above, a social exchange approach provides one explanation of powerless individuals' willingness to put themselves at the mercy of those with power. It is still unclear, however, exactly why the powerful so often abuse that relationship by appearing to behave in an insensitive or cavalier manner towards their subordinates. Social exchange principles can be used to explain why people put up with petty tyranny, but why do people behave like petty tyrants in the first place?

One answer to this question is provided by the work of Fiske and Dépret (1996; Dépret & Fiske, 1993; Fiske, 1993) which portrays power holders as victims of insufficient cognitive resources. This builds upon the cognitive miser model of social perception which argues, amongst other things, that people are only inclined to form detailed, individuated impressions of others under conditions where they are dependent on them for important resources (Fiske & Neuberg, 1989; Fiske & Taylor, 1984; see Chapter 1 above).  Under other conditions, where a person does not explicitly need to invest the time required to form such impressions it is argued that he or she is liable to fall back on stereotypes.  In line with arguments that dominate the social psychological literature (e.g. as observed in Chapters 5 and 7 above), these stereotypes are seen as 'necessary evils' — necessary because they allow perceivers to conserve valuable cognitive resources, but evil because they are tools of repression that deliberately or inadvertently maintain the status quo (Jost & Banaji, 1994; Operario & Fiske, 1998) and are liable to prove misleading as guides to the behaviour of any particular individual (Allport, 1954).

To elaborate this argument, Fiske (1993, p. 622) cites the case of Ann Hopkins, a top manager with Price Waterhouse (one of the 'Big Eight' accounting firms in the United States) who, despite her impressive performance in accumulating more billable hours than other applicants and attracting $25 million in business, was denied a partnership on grounds that she was not 'feminine enough'.  Why did this happen?  For Fiske (1993), the answer is that 'the powerful managers simply had no need to attend to the relatively powerless women as unique individual subordinates' (p. 625).  Because the men who controlled the organization were too busy doing other things, they 'took the easy way out' and fell into the trap of stereotyping — a trap that on this occasion proved particularly costly because Price Waterhouse was found guilty of sexual discrimination both at an initial trial brought by Hopkins and on appeal at the Supreme Court (for details of the case and the expert testimony of psychologists, see Fiske, Bersoff, Borgida, Deaux & Heilman, 1991).

Empirical support for these arguments is provided by studies which examine patterns of attention deployment and stereotyping in interpersonal judgement contexts (e.g. Fiske & Dépret, 1993; Goodwin, Fiske & Yzerbyt, 1995).  These typically find that those who are dependent on others for resource outcomes (i.e. the powerless) pay more attention to those others and are more likely to detect stereotype-inconsistent details about them than those who are not outcome-dependent (i.e. the powerful).  In this way, attention is seen to be directed *up* the power hierarchy, while error flows the other way.

As with Mulder's power distance research, this analysis seems to capture some of the motivations that come into play in situations where employees' behaviour is informed by a desire to get ahead *as individuals*.  Even here though, there are reasons to doubt whether the behaviour of the powerful is as thoughtless as the cognitive miser analysis suggests.  In the case of Ann Hopkins, for example, was it the case that the male partners at Price Waterhouse overlooked or failed to accept her individuality because they were too busy or simply couldn't be bothered to treat her as an individual?  Or was it perhaps the case that this was an *intergroup* strategy, knowingly and *carefully* designed to maintain womens' low status?  If it was, we might argue that the treatment meted out to her was a *psychologically rational* response to intergroup reality *as perceived from the vantage point of the male partners* (cf. Oakes et al., 1994; Oakes & Turner, 1990).  Most of us disagree with what the partners did and see things from a different vantage point entirely, but we can still recognize that they did it not because they couldn't have cared less, but because they *couldn't have cared more.* Moreover, recognition of this intergroup dimension to power also alerts us to the possibility that under certain circumstances individuals in positions of low or threatened power (e.g. employees tired of exploitation or managers fearful of worker revolt) might adopt a similar strategy in which they band together *collectively* in order to improve their lot. Such a possibility clearly takes us beyond most of the scenarios that we have considered so far. Accordingly, to understand the dynamics and consequences of such action we need to move beyond the restrictive concepts of economic exchange and cognitive capacity and instead embrace a much more social view of power.

## Social identity and power

The argument that there is a social dimension to power is not new. Working from a social exchange perspective, Bacharach and Lawler (1980) thus start out from the premise that:

> We hold to the sociological adage that is maintained by Marx, Weber and Durkheim: that individuals become political in groups and that groups are capable of affecting and often do affect structure. In turn, if we are to understand organizations as political systems we must come to grips with how, when, and why groups mobilize power. (p.77)

Having reviewed the field, they dismiss individualistic perspectives that accentuate 'the chaotic nature of action in organizations' and 'depoliticize cognition', and settle as a final alternative upon:

> An organizational model that is based on the group as the unit of analysis. ... This perspective affords an empirical middle ground between concentrations on aggregate and on individual data. (Bacharach & Lawler, 1980, p.212).

They add, though, that:

> To date, the potential of the group model has not been fully realized. ... Realization of the full potential of the group perspective requires that the dynamics of group interrelationships become a focal point for future research. (Bacharach & Lawler, 1980, p.212).

As we have seen in previous chapters, a key feature of the social identity approach is that it takes this conclusion very much as a starting point for its analysis — recognizing that people's actions in organizations are shaped by the social and structural realities which impinge upon them and which, amongst other things, lead to them defining themselves either as individuals or as members of social groups. In both cases it suggests that they will be motivated to engage in self-enhancing behaviour and, where appropriate, will use power to that end. However, it follows from arguments presented in previous chapters that *the forms of power available to people and the uses to which they seek to put them will vary as a function of (a) the self-categorization of the power user and (b) his or her self-categorical relationship with those on whom power is used*. In order to expound the social identity approach to power we can therefore start by examining the basis and implications of this statement.

One of the statement's most important features is that it suggests that power is not an invariant property of a particular individual or group, but rather that its form and extent are an *outcome* of the self-categorization process. This is most apparent in the case of referent power — the ability of a person to exert influence because they are admired and respected by others. As we argued in Chapters 2 and 3, this form of influence is heavily structured by the categorical relations between parties. Thus those who are representative of the same social self-category as a perceiver (i.e. prototypical ingroup members) will have considerably more referent power than non-representative members or members of a non-self-category (outgroup members; Hogg, 1996; Turner, 1991; Tyler, 1998). This point emerges clearly from findings discussed in Chapter 3 which show that leadership is conferred upon, and attributed to, those who represent a group and its interests in context (e.g. Burton, 1993; Hogg et al., 1998; see also Lippitt, Polansky, Redl & Rosen, 1956) and that only leaders who act in this way are capable of commanding followership (Haslam & Platow, in press; Platow et al., 1997).

The same argument also applies to expert power. Traditionally, expertise is regarded as an absolute characteristic that any individual either possesses or lacks and something that can be assessed simply by physical reality testing. If a person is an expert carpenter this should be obvious from the quality of the cabinets they make, and if a person is an expert economist they should make insightful economic forecasts — or so the argument goes. However, on closer inspection, this power — and the attributions that lie at its heart — are found to be heavily dependent on social categorization processes (Hewstone & Jaspars, 1982, 1984; Kramer et al., 1995). Nowhere is this more obvious than in the attributions of expertise made by sporting fans (Mann, 1974; Mullen & Riordan, 1988). Here the failures of one's own team are typically forgiven as products of unfortunate circumstance, while the successes of the opposition are explained away as freak events or lucky breaks. Only an ingroup's victory over the outgroup is lauded as a true reflection of skill and talent. Thus, in Turner's (1991) words:

> The influence of experts is not due to the fact that they possess demonstrably correct information. Their information is perceived as valid because they are socially designated as 'experts', the legitimate representatives of normative cultural institutions and values. (p. 151)

In short, experts have power because we assign them that role in recognition of their capacity to reflect the things that *we* hold dear — our values, beliefs, norms and ideals. An expert who starts undermining these things (one who is perceived to be 'batting for the other team') will soon find their expert status revoked and their power rapidly dwindling.

The same arguments are also pertinent to matters of legitimate power and informational power. As we have seen, following French and Raven (1959), it is traditionally argued that the power to influence can reside simply in the fact that a person occupies a particular organizational position or is particularly persuasive. In this vein, standard interpretations of Milgram's famous obedience studies (in which participants were willing to obey the instructions of a malevolent experimenter even when this seemed to involve the administration of life-threatening electric shocks to an innocent person; Milgram, 1963, 1974), suggest that participants' behaviour reflected deference to the experimenter's inherent authority in the experimental situation. Along similar lines, informational power is seen to reside in the intrinsic and non-negotiable quality of any knowledge or information to which a given person has access. Here a person 'in the know' is a person worth knowing, and it is this fact that is seen to make him or her influential.

Again though, it is possible to see that in both these cases the persuasive impact of any given power source will be affected by the identity relations that prevail in a given context. In particular, a person should only be inclined to accept that another person's authority or knowledge is *legitimate* and *relevant* to the extent they internalize and act in terms of a social category which gives the authority and knowledge its meaning. Organizations usually go to a lot of trouble to ensure this is the case — for example, by developing procedures that draw attention to the norms and values that its members share (Tyler, 1990, 1993). Nonetheless, it is clear that people *can* reject any given authority and *can* perceive any particular body of knowledge to be invalid and useless, particularly if they identify with an alternative social category. Industrial spies, for example, are unlikely to be influenced by the authority or knowledge that is vested in the officers of the organizations against whom their espionage is perpetrated. As we saw in Chapter 5, it is also the case that information is much more likely to be withheld from another person — and therefore be perceived as an instrument of power — when he or she is an outgroup member (Agama, 1997; Dovidio et al., 1997; Suzuki, 1998).

The above discussion summarizes ideas from the large body of research which suggests that social influence is a self-categorization process (see Turner, 1987a, 1991). However, bearing in mind that self-categorization theorists draw a clear distinction between influence and power, the next obvious question is whether forms of power that are not influence-based also vary as a function of the user's self-categorical status. The answer is that they do, and in quite interesting ways.

From an objective standpoint, 'power proper' — that which is based on recognition of a person's capacity to control one's behaviour through domination, forced compliance, and submission (i.e. coercive power) — can be held by both ingroup and outgroup members. However, a number of attributional and judgmental processes combine to ensure that, while ingroups are recognized to have some coercive power at their disposal, this form of power is typically seen to be concentrated in the hands of outgroups (Taylor & McGarty, 1999). In the first instance, this is because this representation of the world is consistent with stereotypic views about the difference between ingroups and outgroups that serve to create or maintain positive intergroup distinctiveness (Tajfel & Turner, 1979). Even when little is known about the groups in question, the groups to which we belong are typically seen as fair, just, honest and decent in comparison to outgroups that are unfair, unjust, dishonest and treacherous (e.g. Doise et al., 1972). That being the case, it is clearly more fitting for repressive power to be seen as an instrument of control that is resorted to by outgroups rather than by ingroups.

As well as this, people generally find it less threatening to their self-image and sense of personal control to explain their own adherence to group norms as a product of free will rather than as a response to threat or pressure (Perloff & Fetzer, 1986).  On the other hand, they are less charitable in explaining the behaviour of others.  In this vein, studies into the 'third-person effect' show that, in situations where susceptibility to influence might be characterized negatively (e.g. because it connotes gullibility or weakness), people generally perceive themselves to be relatively unaffected by influence attempts (e.g. media campaigns and advertising) while believing that unspecified third parties will be easily swayed (Davison, 1983).

Importantly though, an extensive programme of research by Duck and her colleagues has also revealed an intergroup dimension to this effect (Duck, Hogg & Terry, 1995, 1997; Duck & Mullin, 1997; Duck, Terry & Hogg, 1999).  More specifically, the effect is found to vary as a function of the third person's social self-categorical status and is largely confined to judgements of *out*group members.  As an example, Duck et al.'s (1995) study of an Australian election campaign revealed that when supporters of a particular party were asked to explain the behaviour of a third person who was a member of the same political party, that other person was believed to have been persuaded by the validity of the ingroup's arguments rather than to have succumbed to propaganda.  However, the opposite pattern was observed in accounting for the behaviour of members of other parties.  These attributions were also enhanced to the extent that respondents identified strongly with their political ingroup.

The general view that emerges from this and related research is that people tend to account for behaviour in a way which suggests that ingroup members behave the way they do 'because it's right' but that outgroup members act for much more instrumental reasons — because they were forced to, because they were paid to, because they are naive (Taylor & McGarty, 1999).  Accordingly, whatever the actual power structure that prevails within a particular organization (i.e. the ability of individuals or groups to administer rewards and punishment), one would expect that there will be a range of situations in which its members are inclined to *downplay* both (a) their self-power (at either a personal or a social level) and (b) the extent to which their dealings with other members of a salient ingroup are affected by power.  On the other hand, they will often be expected to *emphasise* both (a) the power of non-self others (i.e. outgroups or, when personal identity is salient, other ingroup members) and (b) the extent to which dealings involving those others are affected by power.  Support for these predictions is provided by the research of Rothbart and Hallmark (1988) that we discussed in the previous chapter.

The above discussion deals with the way in which individuals' *perceptions* of power vary as a function of the self-categorization process, but it is reasonable to ask whether these perceptions bear any relationship to people's *actual* power use.  Group members may believe that they are more likely to be the victims of an outgroup's power than an ingroup's, but is there any evidence to support this view?  As with most of the early research into intergroup discrimination that we discussed in Chapter 2, a key problem with all of the naturalistic evidence that would support this view is that it is contaminated by a range of confounding variables.  When a group has power its members might use this against members of another group for any number of reasons specific to the intergroup relationship in question: to redress past injustices, because the other group has a history of using power itself, or because that treatment has been formally sanctioned. However, following the rationale of Tajfel et al.'s (1971) original minimal group studies, these confounds can be bypassed by assigning participants to groups that have no prior meaning and seeing whether and how the treatment of ingroup and outgroup is affected by the infusion of power. This was the goal of research conducted by Sachdev and Bourhis (1985; see also Bourhis, 1994b; Sachdev & Bourhis, 1987, 1991).

In Sachdev and Bourhis's (1985) study students were randomly assigned to minimal groups (Group W or Group Z) and asked to allocate points to members of their own group and the other using matrices like those in Figure 2.1. The experimenters explained that the group which ultimately received the most points would gain course credit that would excuse its members from having to write an additional course essay. However, as a variant on Tajfel et al.'s (1971) study, participants were told that a specified amount of weight would be given to the allocations made by members of each group in deciding how many points the groups received. Across five conditions, the weighting given to the participants' allocations and those of other members of their ingroup was 100%, 70%, 50%, 30% or 0%.

The question, then, was whether variation in the ingroup's power to dictate the outcome of the study would impact upon the pattern of intergroup discrimination revealed in the standard minimal group studies. It did. As the results in Figure 8.2 indicate, the more power that the students' ingroup had, the more likely they were to use that as a means of ensuring that outgroup members did not receive the additional course credit. In other words, to the

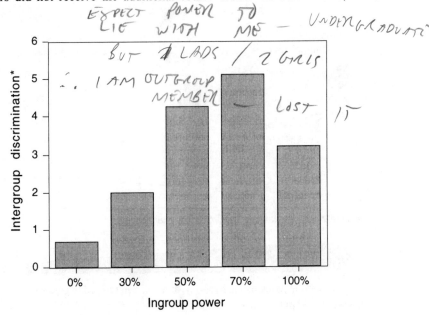

*Figure 8.2* Intergroup discrimination on a minimal group task as a function of the power of the ingroup (from Sachdev & Bourhis, 1985)

*Note:* * This measure of discrimination is based on responses to MD vs. MIP/MJP matrices like those in Figure 2.1 (where max. = 12, min. = –12)

extent that it was available, power was used differentially to disadvantage the outgroup. As a corollary to this point, the results also demonstrate that intergroup discrimination is confined to situations where power relations between groups allow discrimination to occur. So, in the case of the minimal group studies, groups can only discriminate when they have a relatively big say in the distribution of resources (Bourhis, 1994b, p. 200; de Dreu, 1995; Ng 1982, p. 189). Consistent with this point, the only departure from the strong linear correlation between power and discrimination occurred when groups that were given total (100%) power chose to discriminate slightly less than those given 50% or 70%. Where there was no need to fear the outgroup (because it had no reciprocal power at all), participants tempered their use of power, magnanimous in the knowledge that even a small amount of ingroup favouritism would secure them the extra course credit.

This study confirms the point that, as with susceptibility to influence and perceptions of power, when a person or group has access to power its *use* will vary as a function of the self-categorical relations between the parties involved — a point that is represented schematically in Figure 8.3. However, as this figure indicates, influence *increases* to the extent that the parties are perceived to be members of the same self-category, while the use (and perceived use) of coercive power are expected to *decrease*.

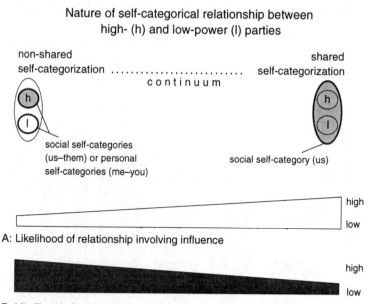

Nature of self-categorical relationship between high- (h) and low-power (l) parties

non-shared self-categorization ......................... shared self-categorization

continuum

social self-categories (us–them) or personal self-categories (me–you)

social self-category (us)

high
low

A: Likelihood of relationship involving influence

high
low

B: Likelihood of relationship involving (and being perceived to involve) coercive power

*Figure 8.3* Schematic representation of the manner in which power and influence are affected by the social categorical relationship between high- and low-power parties

However, as the findings from Sachdev and Bourhis's (1985) study suggest, it is also true that perceptions and the actual use of power will depend on the power-related *social reality* that confronts the perceiver. Moreover, while the coercive power of ingroups will usually be underplayed (because of its negative connotations for the self), there should be some situations in which it will be accentuated or 'talked up'. This is particularly likely to occur at times of intergroup conflict where power (or power-related threat) is used strategically both to ensure the compliance of ingroup members and to win concessions from the outgroup (McGarty, Taylor & Douglas, in press). A general's message that 'We are very powerful' could be used to intimidate both the opposition and those members of his or her own side who may have been thinking of deserting. But precisely because it contravenes the norms alluded to above (and constitutes what Kramer et al., 1995, refer to as *ingroup violation*), such a strategy is most likely to be used (and only likely to prove effective) when those towards whom it is directed are unlikely to respond to identity-based influence attempts. If you are a general, your friends will be upset if you threaten them with a gun and they are unlikely to remain your friends for long.

Having dealt with the question of how self-categorization determines both the likelihood of power being used and of influence being achieved, a final question is how this analysis relates to the existing literature on power use in organizations. This is a particularly significant issue because, on the face of it, the foregoing arguments bear little resemblance to the literature that we reviewed in the previous sections. We have suggested that group membership and social categorization processes play an important role in power-related organizational behaviour, yet, as Bacharach and Lawler (1980) note, such considerations are conspicuously absent from mainstream organizational theorizing. What accounts for this discrepancy, and how can it be resolved?

One of the primary differences between the social identity approach to power and that which informs most other work in the area is that where research has previously tended only to uncover the darker side of power use, the above analysis sees it as a basic feature of intergroup and interpersonal relations. It is clear, though, that many of the darker features of traditional analyses can still be discovered in the arguments we have provided. In particular, if we confine our analysis to interaction that occurs either (a) between groups whose members are acting in terms of distinct social identities or (b) between individuals who are acting in terms of distinct personal identities (i.e. as represented towards the left-hand end of Figure 8.3) then the processes we have discussed account for many of the patterns observed in motivational, cognitive and personality research.

A major reason for this is that in both of these situations the individuals or groups concerned should be striving to enhance the positive distinctiveness of their salient self-category relative to the salient non-self-category. However, because (by definition) they do not share identity with non-self-category members, their dealings with members of those categories will necessarily involve (and be perceived to involve) the use of power rather than the exercise of influence. The patterns observed in power distance research (e.g. Mulder, 1977) can thus be seen to reflect the behaviour of individuals attempting to get ahead of other individuals, just as the patterns observed in Kipnis's (1972) study reflect attempts by ingroup members to get ahead of outgroups. In both cases, the participants' lack of concern for other low-status participants can thus be seen to derive from the fact that they were perceived to be members of a nonself-category.

But is it the case that this action reflects mental deficiency or, more specifically, a lack of cognitive resources on the part of the participants (e.g. as argued by Fiske, 1993)? In line with arguments presented in previous chapters, we think not (Nolan et al., 1999; Oakes & Reynolds, 1997; Oakes & Turner, 1990; Spears et al., 1999; Spears & Haslam, 1997; Turner & Oakes, 1997). Instead, the behaviour of the participants here can be seen to reflect salient inter-group realities as perceived from *their particular* vantage point. For the partici-pants in this study, as for the managers in many organizations, behaviour was dictated by the subjectively important difference between 'us' and 'them' and the need to maintain that difference using the tools at their disposal — stereotypes, discrimination, power. It was political behaviour in the raw.

But political behaviour need not always be this inimical. Indeed, the flip-side of many of the above scenarios comes into play where members of organiza-tions act in terms of a *shared* self-categorization, and it is this possibility (i.e. as represented towards the right hand end of Figure 8.3) that is typically overlooked in received accounts of power use in organizations. This point has particular bearing on the analysis that is implicit in Mulder's (e.g. 1977) power distance theory. As Ng (1980) notes, most of Mulder's theorizing is framed by research in which individuals respond to organizational scenarios in which the possibility of personal advancement is real and salient. However, along lines argued in Chapters 2 and 4, it seems highly likely that this structural reality *constrains* participants' motivations and behaviour in important ways. In particular, it follows from social identity theory that when individuals with low or moderate power are *un*able to advance individually, they should be more likely to embrace a social change belief system that would lead them to join together with others of low power in order to improve their lot *collectively*. As Figure 8.4 illustrates, this would involve a *reversal* of the patterns of power distance reduction and power distance enlargement predicted by Mulder (1977) as middle-managers joined ranks with those beneath them to challenge their superiors and the organizational status quo. Here those managers would seek to empower rather than disempower those beneath them, and interaction between superior and subordinate would be much more likely to involve (and be seen to involve) mutual influence rather than coercion (Ellemers, van Rijswijk et al., 1998).

One domain of organizational life to which these arguments are particularly relevant is the power-related behaviour of women in the workplace (e.g. see Ghiloni, 1987; Kanter, 1979; Ragins & Sundstrom, 1989). Here it is apparent that having traditionally been denied access to the higher echelons of management (e.g. through the existence of a 'glass ceiling'; Dominguez, 1991), one significant response of women (at least those who reject conservative beliefs in social mobility; Hogg & Abrams, 1988) has been to act collectively to change organizational practice (Skevington & Baker, 1989). This has been achieved, for example, through political lobby groups that have fought for legislative changes in areas of sex discrimination, pay equity, access to child-care, and the provision of maternity leave. Indeed, it was just such activity that made possible the prosecution of Price Waterhouse in the case discussed by Fiske (1993, Fiske et al., 1991).

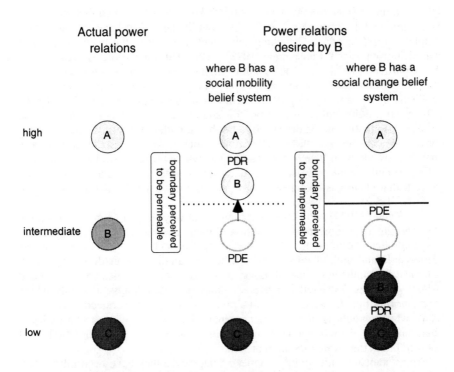

*Figure 8.4* Predicted variation in power distance reduction (PDR) and power distance enlargement (PDE) as a function of the perceived permeability of group boundaries and associated belief systems

Experimental evidence of this process at work has been provided by a study of public servants' promotion-related decisions in different organizational scenarios (Fajak & Haslam, 1998, Experiment 2). In these scenarios the participants were told that they personally occupied either a senior or a junior position and that the senior positions in the organization as a whole were either male- or female-dominated. Key issues in the study were the extent to which the participants would identify with other members of their sex and show ingroup solidarity by preferring to promote a same-sex person to a vacant middle-management position.

The findings of the study revealed that when participants occupied junior positions in organizations women showed no greater identification with their sex than men and no greater preference for promoting a same-sex person to the vacant position. Here both women and men appear to have had little interest in enhancing the status of their group and to have preferred individual mobility as an option. Interestingly though, women who were in more senior positions *did* identify more strongly with other members of their sex than did men, and there was some evidence that they were more likely to support the promotion of another woman than men were to support the promotion of another man.

A number of factors may have contributed to this pattern, including a sense of guilt among high-status men and their *un*willingness to behave in a way that might suggest to others that their own success was also the result of gender-based ingroup bias (Branscombe, 1998). Yet whatever the precise reasons for these particular results, it appears that women were much more conscious of their status *as women* and saw this as an opportunity to improve their circumstances collectively by empowering other members of their sex (see also Ely, 1994). The general point that emerges from this and related research is that the salience of a social identity that is perceived to be shared with other people can serve as a basis for using power *on behalf of* those others. And, as in this case, this is particularly likely to be evident in situations where power is wielded in order to effect social *change*. Indeed, *unless* power is used in this manner it would appear that change is destined either to be slow in coming or not to come at all (Pfeffer, 1992).

As Kanter (1979) argues, one very important way for people in the workforce to increase their power is therefore for them to *share* it. Yet without the psychological substrate of a shared social identity such activity is likely to prove impossible and unthinkable. This will be due, amongst other things, to a lack of the communication, co-ordination and trust that is predicated upon social identity (e.g. as discussed in Chapter 5 above). Accordingly, it is only where the sharing of power *makes sense* in terms of a theory of the collective self — so that 'what is yours is ours' — that its many benefits are likely to be realized. Paradoxically, then, empowerment has its basis not in the redistribution of power, but in the recategorization of self.

Consistent with this point, it appears that, where they have been introduced, changes to organizational practice of the form urged by Kanter (1979) have often served to *reinforce* separations of power rather than to remove them (for a review see Hardy & Leiba-O'Sullivan, 1998). In this vein, Kelly and Kelly (1991) draw the following conclusion from a review of the nature and impact of so-called new industrial relations (NIR) techniques in Britain and America:

> It is impossible to avoid the conclusion that institutional, i.e. management, support for NIR is both instrumental and superficial. Management are willing to implement and support NIR initiatives only so long as they yield profitable results and do not impinge on their own power and status. Yet these are the very constraints that limit the impact of NIR techniques. (p. 41)

Such observations also suggest that merely pointing to the massive organizational dividends that flow from the empowerment of others (e.g. Kanter, 1979; Vanek, 1975) is simply wishful thinking if people are inclined only to see the world in terms of opposed social or personal identities. For under these circumstances another's gain *is* one's own loss (Ng, 1982). Similarly, empowerment programmes must fail if they are conceptualized as a process of 'us' giving power to 'them' — as they are by Foy (1994; see Harley, 1999, p. 61) who asks 'Who manages the empowering?' and answers 'Managers do, that's who. Empowering people must *not* mean disempowering managers' (p. xv). To really empower workers, then, managers need to reject the bifurcated view of the world that is implicit in the managerial prerogative — not use that prerogative simply to reaffirm pre-existing power divisions (Buchanan, 1995; Parker, 1993; Sennett, 1998).

## Some empirical tests of the social identity approach

*Self-categorization and perceptions of power*

One of the key predictions that emerges from the above arguments is that the *meaning* of power should change dramatically as a function of the social categorical relationship between any perceiver and any power holder. Indeed, we argued that power itself should generally be seen as very much an outgroup phenomenon by virtue of its negative connotations and its threatening implications for the self.

Evidence that supports this prediction was obtained in a study conducted by Taylor and McGarty (1999). In this, nearly 200 university employees were asked to indicate how much power the union and management sides had in an ongoing industrial dispute that was taking place on campus. Respondents were categorized into three groups: those who identified with the university management, those who identified strongly with the union and those who identified weakly with the union. Consistent with arguments presented above, the authors found that employees who identified with the union tended to see the university management as powerful but the union as relatively powerless. Moreover, this effect was much stronger for those union members who identified strongly with the union. However, exactly the reverse pattern was displayed by management sympathisers. For these respondents it was the university management that was in a position of powerlessness and the union who were powerful.

These data support the view that perceptions of power do not simply reflect objective features of social reality, but rather are highly structured by the ingroup–outgroup status of the judged entity. However, in relation to Taylor and McGarty's (1999) findings, one might argue that the various parties' representations of each other were simply strategic. That is, they may have been intended to communicate the fact the ingroup was at the mercy of a bullying outgroup rather than to reflect reality per se. Moreover, these representations could clearly be seen as responses to a particular industrial context in which relations between groups were very antagonistic rather than a reflection of power-related representations in general.

We would therefore be in a clearer position to establish that social categorization impacts upon perceptions of power if both the actual power and the meaning of the groups in question were experimentally controlled. This possibility was recently explored in four studies conducted by Dépret (1995; Fiske & Dépret, 1996) as part of a programme of research that extends Fiske's earlier work by acknowledging the distinct implications of group membership for the experience and expression of power. In all four studies participants were led to believe that their performance on a task would be graded by other people. In one experiment participants were assigned to a minimal group (Group A) and told that their task performance would be assessed by other Group A members or by members of Group B. In another study they were told that performance would be assessed by a supervisor who was a member of either the ingroup or the outgroup. As expected, results from both studies indicated that when asked to what extent they felt in control of their own outcomes, those whose be was to be assessed by ingroup members responded more positively.

power (whether wielded by peers or supervisors) was thus perceived to be empowering for the self in a way that outgroup power was not.

However, one potential problem with this conclusion relates to the fact that participants who expected to be assessed by ingroup members also expected to receive better treatment than those assessed by outgroup members. Increased feelings of personal control could thus result from expectations of more generous treatment rather than empowerment per se. To address this issue, Dépret (1995) conducted another study that controlled for expectations of reward by making participants believe that the evaluators were unaware of their group membership. Here participants still felt more in control at the hands of ingroup evaluators, even though they did not expect to receive better treatment from them.

Fiske and Dépret (1996) also note that in these studies participants may have felt more comfortable with an ingroup supervisor simply because they believed that it would be possible to counteract the supervisor's power by exerting personal influence over him or her. If this were the only factor responsible for feelings of personal control, then one would expect feelings of control to decline to the extent that the ingroup supervisor had greater power.

This idea was examined in a final study in which participants anticipated evaluation by an ingroup or outgroup supervisor who was said to have either a high or a low amount of control over their outcomes. Not surprisingly, participants felt less in control when an outgroup supervisor had a high rather than a low amount of control over their fate. However, this variable had no effect on ratings of an ingroup supervisor. These findings are therefore consistent with the argument that positive reactions to ingroup supervisors reflect their social categorical status rather than their power alone. Because they are representative of our shared interests and perspective, we trust ingroup members however much power they have. On the other hand, our distrust of outgroup members grows as they acquire more power because that power simply gives them the capacity to undermine our interests more effectively.

*Organizational context as a determinant of responses to power use*

The research discussed in the previous section deals with perceptions of power in the abstract, rather than responses to actual power use. So although these studies show that people tend to represent ingroups favourably and expect better treatment from them, one might well argue that such reactions would change in the face of power-related behaviour. Indeed, if it is the case that power use is inherently pernicious then one might expect that people would start to turn against powerful ingroup members once they started flexing their muscles. However, contrary to this view, a study conducted by Haslam, McGarty and Reynolds (1999) indicates that people do not react adversely to all forms of power use. Instead it suggests that, like power holding, power use is viewed very much through the lens of one's own group membership (see Chapter 7 above; Kramer et al., 1995; Tyler, 1993, 1998, Tyler et al., 1996).

In this study Australian students were asked to make judgements of the power-related behaviour of immigration officials. Participants were given information about students who had had their passports stolen overseas and needed help from the authorities in the countries they were visiting. They were told either (a) that the students were Australian and the authorities American or (b) that the students were American and the authorities Australian. As well as this, the participants were told that when the students had presented themselves to consulate officials their problems had been dealt with either very fast (a good outcome) or so slowly that they would miss their return flights home (a bad outcome). In each condition participants had to indicate how much power the officials had, how legitimate their power was, and how much they were using that power to punish the students.

Across the study as a whole, there was no difference in the amount of power that the embassy officials were perceived to have. However, as the patterns displayed in Figure 8.5 reveal, the perceived legitimacy and punitiveness of the officials varied considerably as a function of their nationality and their actions. As one might expect, the decision to deal with the students quickly was generally interpreted more as the exercise of legitimate power (and less as an act of punishment) than the decision to deal with them slowly. However, the decision to deal with the students quickly was seen as a slightly more legitimate (and less punitive) act when it was performed by Australian officials rather than Americans. On the other hand, the decision to deal slowly with the students was seen as much more punitive (and much less legitimate) when it was performed by American officials rather than Australians. When Australian officials made Americans miss their plane this was considered quite appropriate, but when the situation was reversed the treatment was much more likely to be seen as unreasonable. So, when commentators like Lord Acton allude to the corrupting influence of power (as in the quotations at the start of this chapter) it thus appears that they have in mind the behaviour of outgroup members rather than those who are authorized to exercise power on behalf of an ingroup.

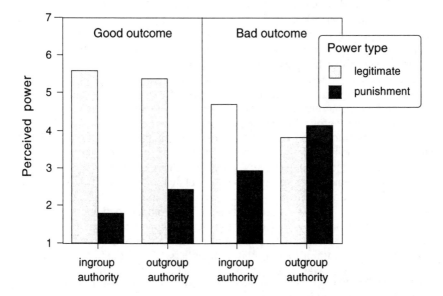

*Figure 8.5* Responses to power use as a function of the power user's identity and action (from Haslam, McGarty & Reynolds, 1999)

Having examined the issue of how group members *perceive* the power use of ingroup and outgroup members, the next obvious question is how those perceptions affect the perceiver's behaviour. As Ellemers, van Rijswijk et al. (1998; see also Bruins, Ellemers & de Gilder, 1999) note, this issue is critical because people's responses to power use will generally have a much more critical impact on organizational outcomes than the power use itself. For example, a supervisor whose attempts at influence serve only to annoy or demoralize subordinates may undermine the goals that he or she seeks to achieve by engendering widespread disaffection or hostility (e.g. see Chapters 3 and 4 above; Harackiewicz & Sansone, 1991; Hollander, 1985).

To investigate the psychological processes underpinning such reactions, Ellemers and her colleagues conducted a study in which science and literature students engaged in a stock trading task and were exposed to high or low levels of power use from an ingroup (i.e. same-discipline) or outgroup (opposite-discipline) member who had been assigned to a superior position in a fictitious organization (Ellemers, van Rijswijk et al., 1998). High-power use involved the superior overriding the participants' decision to buy or sell stock on six of ten possible occasions and low-power use involved just two such interventions.

The study's dependent measures included participants' satisfaction with their trading experience, their evaluation of the superior and the perceived legitimacy of his or her behaviour. Participants were also asked to explain the superior's power use with reference to scales that differed in their *locus* (did they behave as they did due to personal disposition or due to situational circumstances?) and their *level* (did they behave as they did due to their individual characteristic or due to group membership?). Having completed these responses, participants also performed a series of six activities designed to assess their willingness to collaborate with the superior. In each case they were given the choice of engaging in work that would be credited to them alone or to their team (i.e. them and their superior).

Not surprisingly, results indicated that participants generally felt that they had much less power and were much less satisfied to the extent that their superior used his or her power excessively. However, a more complex pattern indicated that explanations of superiors' behaviour varied as a function of their ingroup-outgroup status. In terms of the *locus* of explanation, results indicated that superiors' behaviour was generally attributed to situational factors, with the exception of the *in*group frequent power user whose behaviour was attributed to personal disposition, particularly by those participants who did not identify strongly with their discipline. In terms of *level* of attribution, behaviour was generally attributed to the person's individual character, with the exception of the *out*group frequent power user whose behaviour was attributed to group membership. Considered together, then, these patterns indicate that the behaviour of the intrusive ingroup superior was understood by low ingroup identifiers to be an individual characteristic peculiar to that person, while the behaviour of the intrusive outgroup member was generally seen to be a product of the situation common to all outgroup members. The tyrannical behaviour of the ingroup member was thus seen as a personal deficit (e.g. 'he's just a control freak') while that of the outgroup member was seen as indicative of a situationally induced shared pathology (e.g. 'studying science turns people into control freaks').

However, the big question here was whether these different attribution patterns would be associated with variation in participants' willingness to collaborate with the superior on a team task. When push came to shove, would ingroup members forgive the personal foibles of the ingroup tyrant and/or the situationally induced pathology of the outgroup tyrant? As the results presented in Figure 8.6 indicate, participants' behavioural reactions to power use depended on its intensity in interaction with the identity of the user. When the superior was an ingroup member the amount of his or her interference had little bearing on subordinates' willingness to collaborate on a team task. However, when he or she was an outgroup member it had considerable impact — participants were as willing to collaborate with an outgroup superior who was a low power user as they were to collaborate with an ingroup superior, but they were much more reluctant to work with an outgroup superior who used power excessively. In this context at least, the perceived deficiencies of the ingroup superior were therefore overlooked in the interests of the group as a whole, while those of the outgroup superior seriously undermined participants' commitment to the greater good.

At a theoretical level, the above results underscore the distinction between power and leadership (Turner, 1991, 1999). At a practical level, they also suggest that attempts to impose leadership through power are imprudent. In situations where leaders and followers do not share identity this is because such attempts are liable to elicit a backlash; in situations where they do share identity this is because they are simply unnecessary.

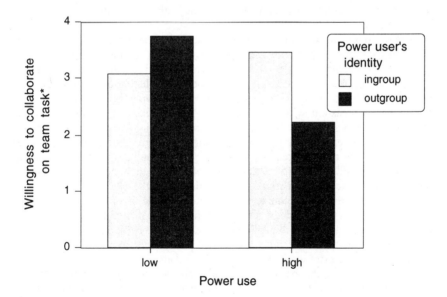

*Figure 8.6* Responses to power use as a function of its intensity and the power user's identity (from Ellemers, van Rijswijk et al., 1998)

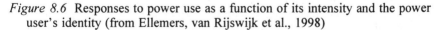

*Note:* * The number of sub-tasks on which participants chose to collaborate (max. = 6)

Although participants in Ellemers, van Rijswijk et al.'s (1998) study showed some tolerance in their reactions to the behaviour of the ingroup member who was a high power user, there are, however, theoretical reasons for expecting that such behaviour would vary with context. One reason for this is that it follows from the principles of fit outlined in Chapters 2 and 4 that in intergroup contexts superiors should be more likely to be seen as sharing social self-category membership with a subordinate than they would in an interpersonal context (Oakes, 1987; Turner, 1985). The intergroup aspects of Ellemers et al.'s study may thus have led participants to put up with the interference of superiors because it was seen as something those superiors were 'doing for us', while in an interpersonal context it would be seen as something they were 'doing for themselves'. As Ellemers found, any such difference in construal should have a significant bearing on subordinates' willingness to respond positively to the superior's injunctions.

Hypotheses related to the above arguments were recently tested in research by Uzubalis (1999). In this, sales assistants in a department store were presented with scenarios in which another member of staff asked them (a) to attend a lunchtime course on sales techniques and (b) to do three hours of unpaid overtime for three successive weeks. For half of the participants the request was made by a very senior member of staff and for the other half it was made by their immediate superior. As well as this, half of the participants were presented with the requests alone (an *interpersonal* context) while half were presented with the requests after having completed items designed to make *intergroup* comparison salient. Amongst other things, these items asked them to identify the store's main competitor and to indicate which store they felt had a better reputation (see Appendix 2 below).

The optional nature of the additional work was emphasized in both cases and so willingness to comply with the superiors' requests served as an indicator of employees' organization citizenship behaviour (Organ, 1988; see Chapter 4 above). Other measures also assessed the perceived legitimacy of the requests and the degree to which compliance with them would be of benefit to the employee. Consistent with the arguments presented above, responses on all these measures varied as a function of the requester's power and the response context. In interpersonal contexts participants were generally reluctant to comply with the requests regardless of their source and generally thought that compliance would not be of benefit to themselves (although there was a tendency for participants to respond more enthusiastically to the superior's request for them to go on the training course). The same was true in an intergroup context when the requests were made by a relatively junior member of staff. However, in this context participants were much more responsive to overtures from the senior staff member to work overtime and much more likely to see this request as legitimate and the extra work to be of benefit to themselves.

As predicted on the basis of self-categorization theory, a request from a powerful superior that was seen as legitimate and elicited an enthusiastic response in an intergroup context was thus seen as unreasonable and met with indifference in an interpersonal setting. Supporting arguments presented in Chapter 4, it thus appears that by translating extrinsic interests into intrinsic ones, context-sensitive change in the self-categorical relationship between supervisor and subordinate has the capacity to transform the supervisors' raw power into social influence and the subordinates' detached apathy into organizational citizenship. Although Uzubalis's (1999) demonstration of this point may appear quite straightforward, in organizational terms this feat is equivalent to the alchemist's ability to turn base metal into gold (Beatty & Ulrich, 1991; Conger & Kanungo, 1988; Velthouse, 1990).

*Power and stereotyping*

Earlier in the chapter it was noted that a number of researchers have argued that in organizations with differentiated power structures, the aspirations and attention of individuals tend to be directed *up* the power hierarchy (e.g. Fiske, 1993; Mulder, 1977). In order to save their cognitive resources for this task, it is suggested that employees have a tendency to stereotype those who are less powerful than themselves and that, as a result, powerless employees receive less personalized and more repressive treatment than they should (Jost & Banaji, 1994). However, using social identity principles to respond to these arguments, it was suggested that the received analysis of the relationship between power and stereotyping takes for granted important structural and psychological features of organizational life (Reynolds et al., 1997; Reynolds, Oakes & Haslam, 1999). In particular, we argued that while powerless individuals may be motivated to reduce the power distance between themselves and their superiors under conditions where they perceive there to be prospects for personal mobility, this will be less evident when they embrace social change beliefs. Indeed, we argued that under conditions where structural barriers are perceived to present obstacles to personal advancement (as in Figure 8.4), individuals may be motivated to distance themselves from powerful others and subject them to intergroup stereotyping of the form discussed by Fiske (1993).

In an attempt to investigate this hypothesis, Reynolds, Oakes, Haslam, Nolan and Dolnik (in press) conducted a study modelled closely on previous research by Wright and his colleagues (e.g. Wright, Taylor & Moghaddam, 1990; discussed in more detail in Chapter 10 below). In this, participants were initially assigned to a low-status 'unsophisticated' group but led to believe that they could gain entry to a more powerful 'sophisticated' group if they performed satisfactorily on an ability test administered by representatives of the powerful group. The situation confronted by participants was thus similar to that which is faced by employees whenever they apply for promotion.

The study had three independent conditions, with participants being told: (a) that they had narrowly failed to make the grade for admission to the sophisticated group (the *open* condition); (b) that they had made the grade but that the powerful group had imposed a quota so that only 10 per cent of the candidates who passed the test would gain entry to their group (the *quota* condition); or (c) that they had made the grade but that the powerful group had decided not to let any of the candidates who passed the test become members of their group because they did not 'want to be swamped' by new members (the *closed* condition).

Amongst other things, the study was designed to investigate patterns of stereotyping across these three conditions. In line with Fiske's (e.g. 1993) previous work, it was predicted that in the open and quota conditions — where the possibility of personal mobility was still present — stereotypes would reproduce the existing power structure and reveal images of the powerful group as relatively benign and favourable. This is what was found. Indeed, as can be seen from Table 8.2, in the open condition stereotypes of the sophisticated group (e.g. as 'analytical' and 'conscientious') were slightly more favourable than those of the unsophisticated group. However, in the closed condition — where an impermeable boundary eliminated all possibility of personal progress — it was predicted that stereotypes of the powerful group would be far less favourable and in fact would pave the way for strategies of social change. This prediction was supported and now members of the low-power group qualified their description of the sophisticated group as 'analytical' with the additional traits 'mean', 'cold' and 'rude'. Additional statistical analysis also indicated that participants' unfavourable stereotypes of the outgroup played a mediating role in decisions to collectively protest against its behaviour (see Chapter 10 below; Taylor et al., 1987). Significantly too, while in the open condition participants had been quite keen to join the sophisticated group, now they were quite reluctant to do so.

The above findings clearly challenge the view that individuals without power are universally motivated both to lessen the distance between themselves and their superiors and to individuate those superiors in an effort to form accurate impressions of them. On the contrary, and as social identity theory predicts, when the structural relations between groups encourage powerless individuals to band together to mount a *collective* challenge against the powerful, they enlist stereotypes as weapons in that conflict and actively enhance power distance. Here they stop 'sucking up' as individuals and start 'getting stuck in' as a group.

*Table 8.2*  Outgroup stereotypes and desire for intergroup mobility as a function of boundary permeability (from Reynolds et al., in press)

Condition

| Measure | Open | | Quota | | Closed | |
|---|---|---|---|---|---|---|
| | | % | | % | | % |
| Stereotype of | analytical | 71 | analytical | 73 | analytical | 43 |
| sophisticated | complex | 35 | rule-bound | 33 | mean | 36 |
| group* | conscientious | 35 | rigorous | 33 | cold | 36 |
| | creative | 35 | conscientious | 26 | rude | 36 |
| Stereotype favourableness (−5 to +5) | 2.00 | | 1.38 | | −0.85 | |
| Desire to join sophisticated group (1–7) | 4.29 | | 3.44 | | 3.00 | |

*Note*: * Percentage of participants who selected traits in each condition. This table only includes traits assigned by more than 25% of participants

Support for similar arguments is again provided by the recent work of Dépret and Fiske. This accompanies an analysis of stereotyping in interpersonal situations (as provided by Fiske, 1993) with an examination of its contribution to intergroup behaviour. Dépret and Fiske (1999) conducted a study which involved psychology students forming impressions of three observers who had high or low power over them, under conditions where those observers were said to be drawn either from a range of disciplines (creating an interpersonal context) or all from the same discipline (creating an intergroup context). The manipulation of power in the study related to the capacity of the three observers to distract the participants while they performed a concentration task: in low-power conditions the distractors simply talked loudly amongst themselves, in high-power conditions they had the ability to make participants start the task again whenever they were successfully distracted.

Consistent with Fiske's previous work, in the interpersonal conditions participants formed more individuated impressions of observers who had high power than they did of those with only low power. When asked to describe one of the high-power observers (e.g. an art student), participants spent much more time reflecting on traits that were stereotype-inconsistent (e.g. 'conventional') than those that were stereotype-consistent (e.g. 'creative'), but there was no such effect in judgements of the low-power observer. Participants also made more dispositional (i.e. individuating) inferences in describing the behaviour of a high-power person than they did in describing that of a low-power observer.

However, none of these patterns were apparent in intergroup conditions (see also Reynolds & Oakes, 1999, 2000). If anything, participants now attended more to the stereotype-*consistent* behaviour of the high-power observer and made fewer dispositional inferences than they did when attending to the low-power observer. In these conditions participants also showed more ingroup solidarity when confronted with the high-power outgroup than they did when dealing with the low-power group.

Although the findings in the interpersonal conditions of this study provide some support for interdependence principles and the cognitive miser model, Dépret and Fiske (1999) thus conclude:

> The lack of individuation in the intergroup condition imposes some restrictions on the model. ... The lack of individuation of outgroup members cannot be explained by the fact that participants' limited information resources would have been drained by attention to ingroup members. (p. 476)

And they continue:

> Because the reproduction or change of power structures depends, in part, on the reactions of the powerless, it [is] important to understand when the powerless will accept or challenge the current partition of power. ... Our results suggest that social categorization of powerful others plays a critical role. On the one hand, when those in power are seen as unrelated to each other, they become intriguing individuals. Indeed, people in power are often described as 'personalities'. ... On the other hand, when those in

power are perceived as an outgroup, power becomes threatening, and intergroup partition of power becomes an issue. (pp. 477-478)

To link the analysis of power-related stereotyping to the availability of cognitive resources or to principles of social exchange is therefore to miss the point behind a great deal of power-related behaviour. In particular, this is because power use is as much about change as it is about stability. Accordingly, in many instances it is explicitly premised upon collective rejection of existing exchange practices and dependence structures. And in this process individuals (including the self) are stereotyped as members of social groups not because this is a cognitive economy but because it is a response to social (i.e. group-based) reality and is a prerequisite for collective action (Oakes et al., 1994; Reynolds et al., 1997, in press; see Chapter 10 below).

## Conclusion

From the review in the first half of this chapter it is clear that existing organizational theory provides a reasonably coherent picture of how power is perceived, achieved and used. Certainly the main strategy that is envisioned here is one in which individuals climb the corporate ladder on their own, aided in their ascent by strategic alliances with the powerful as, all the while, a growing distance develops between themselves and the concerns and problems of those beneath them. It is a climb motivated by a growing hunger for more power, but one that places an increasing strain on the cognitive resources of the corporate mountaineer. As a result, by the end of their climb they are scarcely able to tell black from white, good from bad, right from wrong.

Our own experience, together with much of the empirical research in the field, suggests that the above picture is an accurate representation of some of the key features of contemporary corporate life (e.g. see Micklethwait & Wooldridge, 1997; Thompson & Warhurst, 1998). However, there is also reason to believe both (a) that some of its key features are misleading and (b) that it is incomplete. The root of both problems is the widespread failure of researchers to recognize that in addition to — and in many ways at odds with — its interpersonal manifestations, power also has an intergroup dimension (Deschamps, 1982). As Figure 8.7 attempts to summarize schematically, the existence of this dimension accounts for much of the power-related organizational behaviour that is attributed to individual-based malevolence or cognitive overload and allows that behaviour to be appreciated in a new light. In particular, this is because many of those organizational behaviours that are routinely explained as symptoms of petty tyranny can be understood to reflect general processes of stereotyping and intergroup conflict. Along lines suggested by Oakes et al. (1994; after Tajfel, 1969, 1981b), they therefore appear to reflect normal processes of social categorization and intergroup differentiation rather than pathology or dysfunction.

Accordingly, where we do detect error in the use of power — and we often do — there are grounds for believing that the basis of that error is not psychological but social and organizational (Oakes & Reynolds, 1997). For example, in the case of *Price Waterhouse v. Hopkins* we can argue that the partners at Price Waterhouse were not victims of dysfunctional personality or an over-burdened information-processing system, they were simply pursuing inappropriate goals. The problem, then, was not that having power led the partners to make the wrong decisions, but that having particular political and social values led them to use power for the wrong ends (at least from society's broader perspective as reflected in the verdict ultimately handed down by the Supreme Court).

But as much as it is true that group power can be used for malevolent ends, so it is also true that it can be pressed into service as a force for good. Indeed, Pfeffer (1992) makes the point that, on their own, individuals who are simply 'in the right' are of little use — either to an organization or to society. The archives of most failed companies would provide testimony to the existence of good men and women who did little to counteract the negative forces that brought about the organization's demise. In order for good to be done, it therefore needs to be mobilized through the effective use of power. Pfeffer (1992) makes this point well:

> It is easy and often comfortable to feel powerless. ... Such a response excuses us from trying to do things; in not trying to overcome the opposition, we will make fewer enemies and are less likely to embarrass ourselves. It is, however, a prescription for both organizational and personal failure. This is why power and influence are not the organization's last dirty secret, but the secret of success for both individuals and their organizations. Innovation and change in almost any area require the skill to develop power, and the willingness to use it to get things accomplished. (pp. 343-345)

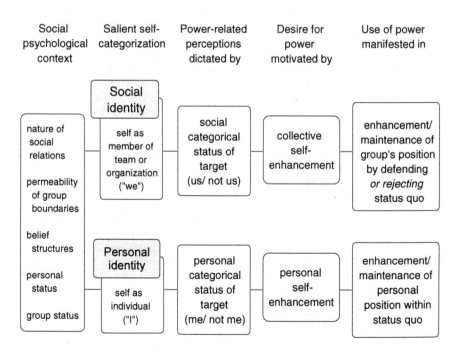

*Figure 8.7* Two dimensions of power: A schematic representation of the relationship between level of self-categorization and power-related behaviour and perceptions

Yet while agreeing with Pfeffer's basic point, in this chapter we have challenged the view that effective power use is simply a personal skill that can be learned and then applied by managers as they go about their daily business. On the contrary, we have argued that the most positive forms of power use are usually the creative outgrowth of shared social identification. As with the discussion of leadership in Chapter 3, we have also suggested that these forms of power express, and are made possible by, a collective sense of self that is created and mobilized in pursuit of a particular common interest. They are not a set of all-weather principles ready for quick implementation by executives on the go.

In response to these claims, the person who is in the process of scaling the corporate cliff-face single-handedly might be inclined to ask what it is about group power that makes it so important and so special. In what way does it differ from the exercise in which he or she is engaged? Isn't it the case that both personal and social power involve strategies of resource deployment that are oriented towards the achievement of self-relevant goals? Aren't both essentially conflictual and quite ugly?

These observations may be correct and it is certainly the case that power use in general is not for the squeamish (Pfeffer, 1992). Nonetheless, group power is distinguished from purely personal power because (a) it benefits and mobilizes others, not just the individual self, and (b) as a result, it can be used to achieve comprehensive organizational and social change, while the pursuit of power in one's personal interests generally lends itself only to incremental change or simply to preservation of the status quo (Ng, 1980). For this reason when power is used for personal purposes it will generally contribute to the repetition of history, but when it is used to achieve collective goals it stands a far greater chance of *making* history (Reicher, in press). To the extent that change is desirable (a political and historical judgement itself), group power thus has the potential to transform tyranny into collective achievement in a way that individualized power hardly ever can.

## Further Reading

Bacharach and Lawler (1980) provide a comprehensive introduction to interdependence theory and other influential approaches to the study of power in organizations. Ng's (1980) book also contains excellent reviews of the field — especially from philosophical and political perspectives. Turner's (1991) book again provides the platform for many of the ideas in this chapter (in particular, see Chapter 5). The chapter by Fiske and Dépret (1996) surveys important developments in social psychological approaches to power and introduces a social identity analysis that is elaborated in greater depth in Ellemers, van Rijswijk et al.'s (1998) very broad-ranging research. Finally, Kanter's (1979) article presents a seminal and highly readable discussion of the many positive organizational consequences that flow from effective power sharing.

Bacharach, S. B. & Lawler, E. J. (1980). *Power and politics in organizations*. San Francisco, CA: Jossey-Bass Publishers.

Ellemers, N., van Rijswijk, W., Bruins, J. & de Gilder, D. (1998). Group commitment as a moderator of attributional and behavioural responses to power use. *European Journal of Social Psychology, 28*, 555-573.

Fiske, S. T. & Dépret, E. (1996). Control, interdependence and power: Understanding social cognition in its social context. *European Review of Social Psychology, 7,* 31-61.

Kanter, R. (1979). Power failure in management circuits. *Harvard Business Review,* July – August, 65-75.

Ng, S. H. (1980). *The social psychology of power.* New York: Academic Press.

Turner, J. C. (1991). *Social influence.* Milton Keynes: Open University Press.

# 9    Group Productivity and Performance

> Most business decisions are already far beyond the capability of single minds and single individuals. Business ... is increasingly a collective operation in which the ability to play as a team member, to listen, to build on the ideas of others and to make two and two equal five rather than three and a half is the key to success.

The above statement by John Harvey-Jones — well-known business commentator and former industry chief — is taken from *The Penguin Book of Business Wisdom* (Dando-Collins, 1998, p. 61). Although it is indexed under the heading 'decision making', the statement is broadly relevant to business operations as a whole. This is because it raises a series of questions about the group as a basis for organizational output. Primary amongst these is the question of *whether* groups really do produce more than the sum of their individual parts. Does two plus two really equal five, or is the truth a much more disappointing three and a half? If we assume that both of these outcomes are possible (an assumption many consider unwarranted), the pertinent questions then become '*When* will two plus two equal five rather than three and a half?' and — even more critically — '*Why?*'

The literature that addresses these questions focuses on two key forms of organizational behaviour: *performance* (raw output or output relative to expectations) and *productivity* (output relative to goals — *effectiveness*; or output relative to input — *efficiency*). There are important differences between these constructs, especially for economists and accountants (see Pritchard, 1992). However, like most other psychologists, we will deal with productivity and performance in the same analysis because both have *behavioural output* as a core component and it is on this that most psychological research has focused.

This research has provided a broad range of answers to the above questions. Over time, though, empirical evidence has led the majority of researchers to believe that despite the big billing groups are sometimes accorded by management gurus like Harvey-Jones, they rarely deliver on their promise. Accordingly, most subscribe to the view that 'two plus two equals three and a half', and tend to be unenthusiastic about the potential for group involvement to enhance organizational output.

On the basis of an array of data that appears to support this conclusion, group researchers therefore argue that organizational psychologists and management theorists — like group members themselves — routinely fall prey to the 'illusion of group effectivity' (Diehl & Stroebe, 1991; Paulus & Dzindolet; 1993; Plous, 1995; Stroebe, Diehl & Abakoumkin, 1992). In addition to (a) explaining why groups consistently perform worse than individuals in experimental research, core tasks for researchers often include (b) explaining why people's faith in group productivity proves so resistant to contrary evidence and (c) attempting to disabuse managers and workers of any pro-group prejudices.

The first two of these goals are central to this chapter. However, our answers are rather different from those offered by the mainstream literature in this field. This is because they suggest that the key to understanding the apparent under-performance of individuals in groups lies in a failure to create or study groups that are psychologically meaningful and self-defining for their members (Brown, 1988; Hogg, 1992; Karau & Williams , 1993; Worchel, Rothgerber, Day, Hart & Butemeyer, 1998). Thus while researchers generally *believe* that they are studying group behaviour it is rare for the tasks they create to encourage action in terms of a salient *social* identity. In this way studies tend actually only to shed light on various forms of *personal* under-productivity.

Elaborating on this analysis, it is argued that under conditions where tasks *do* encourage participants to define themselves in terms of a shared sense of self, group productivity can match that of isolated individuals and may also exceed it. However, it is argued that because measures of group productivity are often insensitive to the goals and values of participants, this productivity is often undetected or undetectable. For this reason the chapter moves towards the conclusion that the key practices and prejudices that need to be re-examined in this field are not those of groups themselves but of those who study them.

## An overview of research into group productivity

### Early research and basic findings

We noted in Chapter 1 that the pioneering studies of Taylor and Mayo led them to very different conclusions about the contribution that groups could be expected to make to workplace productivity. For Taylor (1911) 'loss of ambition and initiative' was an inevitable consequence of team work:

> Careful analysis ... demonstrated the fact that when workmen are herded together in gangs, each man in the gang becomes far less efficient than when his personal ambition is stimulated; that when men work in gangs their efficiency falls almost invariably down to or below the level of the worst man in the gang; and that they are all pulled down instead of being elevated by being herded together. (p. 72)

Taylor's remedy for 'soldiering' of this form was therefore to remove the individual from the group. The best results were to be achieved by 'individualizing ... workmen and stimulating each man to do his best' (p. 81).

Mayo shared a similar belief that groups *could* be a source of inefficiency and that internal pressures to conform to low productivity norms would serve to ensure that 'bad groups' were 'very bad' (1949, p. 93). However, he also believed that groups had the potential to be the source of greatest organizational output. Consistent with this view, his studies of aircraft workers in Southern California showed that some departments were phenomenally productive, leading to output that was typically 25 per cent higher than industry averages. Moreover, his interviews with personnel in these departments led him to endorse the view that 'the achievement of group solidarity is of first importance in a plant, and is actually necessary for sustained production' (Mayo, 1949, p. 96). This claim was backed up by observations that 'when conversing with us [groups of productive workers] tended to say "we" whereas workers elsewhere in the plant said "I"' (p. 98). Far from being a source of industrial sloth, Mayo thus saw appropriate management of groups as the key to organizational success.

Different as Taylor's and Mayo's views are, it is interesting to note that each received support from some of the very earliest experimental research in the emerging discipline of social psychology. Evidence consistent with some of Mayo's claims in fact emerged from what are widely credited as being the very first social psychology experiments ever conducted (though this claim in fact seems unjustified; see Haines & Vaughan, 1979). Carried out by Triplett (1898), these were inspired by the informal observation that racing cyclists generally completed laps of a circuit faster when they had other cyclists accompanying them. Triplett's laboratory-based experiments studied the speed with which children wound fishing reels and obtained evidence of an equivalent phenomenon such that children wound faster when other children were also winding reels in the same room than they did when winding on their own. This general finding that the presence of co-actors can enhance performance is typically referred to as *social facilitation.*

Yet, as suggested at the start of the chapter, signs that the presence of co-workers might enhance performance were soon swamped by evidence that it had the very opposite effect. Evidence of this form dates back to unpublished research conducted by Ringelmann in Germany at the end of the nineteenth century (reported by Moede, 1927; see Kravitz & Martin, 1986). This examined the performance of agricultural students on a rope-pulling task that they performed alone and in groups containing up to eight members. As one would expect, the total pull exerted was greater the more students there were in the group. However, as group size increased, the amount of pull exerted by each participant *decreased*. Thus when individuals pulled on a rope alone they were able to exert 63kg of pull, but when they collaborated with one other person each achieved only 93 per cent of this pull. This figure dropped to 85 per cent in groups of three and to just 49 per cent in groups of eight.

It is possible of course that Ringelmann's results reflected the sheer difficulty of attempting to co-ordinate rope pulling among groups of increasingly larger size: in larger groups it was presumably more difficulty to ensure that everyone pulled at exactly the same time and in exactly the same direction. However, the possibility that such problems were entirely responsible for Ringelmann's findings was ruled out in a study conducted by Ingham, Levinger, Graves and Peckham (1974, Study 2). In this, participants were all blindfolded and led to believe that they were pulling alone or in groups of different size. The study did not reveal the linear decrease in performance as groups became larger, but nonetheless Ringelmann's basic finding was replicated: on average individuals who believed they were pulling with one other person exerted only about 90 per cent of the pull exerted by individuals on their own, and this fell to about 84 per cent in groups that supposedly contained three or more people.

Significantly too, the decline in individual exertion that appears to flow from group membership is not restricted to rope pulling tasks. Instead, Ringelmann's findings are seen to illustrate a much more widespread phenomenon, generally referred to as *social loafing* — the tendency for individuals' performance to diminish when they work in a group. This has been observed on other physical tasks such as shouting and clapping (Latané,

Williams & Harkins, 1979; Williams, Harkins & Latané, 1981) as well as cognitive tasks that require concentration and vigilance (e.g. Harkins, 1987, Experiment 2; Harkins & Szymanski, 1989).

Moreover, social loafing also occurs on intellectual tasks where group participation has become accepted practice. As early research by Taylor, Berry and Block (1958) showed, this is even true in the case of 'brainstorming' — a strategy devised by Osborn (1953; see Chapter 6 above) to *maximize* group creativity and the generation of new ideas. Contrary to Osborn's claims, the evidence surveyed meta-analytically by Mullen, Johnson and Salas (1991) thus suggests that:

> For both quantitative and qualitative operations, productivity loss is highly significant and of strong magnitude. ... [Furthermore,] the quantitative productivity loss engendered by brainstorming groups is not trivially small [and] ... is not compensated for by an increase in the quality of productivity in brainstorming groups. (p. 18; see also Stroebe & Diehl, 1994, p. 273)

### Facilitation theories

Faced with what appear to be enormous differences between Triplett's and Ringelmann's findings, the obvious question is whether they can be theoretically reconciled. Is it possible to use the same principles to explain why in some circumstances groups encourage exertion but in others they suppress it? Certainly this is no easy task, and it is one that many researchers have preferred to shy away from. As Harkins (1987, p. 3) observes, one common way of dealing with the problem has therefore been to develop *unrelated* explanations of facilitation and loafing — discussing the latter as a group process but the former as an example of 'co-action' (i.e. behaviour associated with workers' independent contributions to the same task).

In reflecting on his own observations of male cyclists, Triplett (1898) considered seven potential explanations for the faster times achieved by accompanied riders. These made reference to purely mechanical factors (associated with the accompanied rider's ability to shelter behind and slipstream the other person), to factors associated with the behaviour of the other rider (in particular, his capacity to provide encouragement), and to factors associated with individual physiology, cognition and motivation. The latter included suggestions: (a) that cyclists became hypnotized by the rotating wheels of their partner's bicycle; (b) that the company of another person reduced the cognitive burden on riders so that more of their behaviour became automatic; (c) that the pacing released more of the rider's nervous energy (or 'brain worry') so that 'his nervous system is generally strung up, and at concert pitch' (p. 515); and (d) that the presence of another rider aroused more of the rider's competitive instinct (the so-called 'dynamogenic factor').

Triplett (1898) interpreted his subsequent research as supporting the last of these explanations, attributing the improved performance of accompanied reelers to 'an intense desire to win ... often resulting in over-stimulation' (p. 523). In fact though, the next major attempt to develop a theory of social facilitation owed much more to the notion of 'brain worry'. Developed by Zajonc (1965), this argued that social facilitation results from the capacity for the *mere presence* of others to increase a person's *drive* or arousal. As indicated in Figure 9.1, the theory proposed that this arousal leads to greater expression of a *dominant* response (i.e. one that is habitual or well-learned). The result of this is that on tasks where a person is predisposed to do well (e.g. because the task is simple or rehearsed) enhanced performance should result.

In something of a novelty for the *Journal of Personality and Social Psychology*, evidence to support this idea was gathered not only from humans but also from cockroaches. In Zajonc's laboratory these insects were found to run down a simple maze towards a darkened goal (away from the light) about 20 per cent faster when they ran in pairs than when they ran alone (Zajonc, Heingartner & Herman, 1969). Significantly though, because a person's dominant response is not always to do well on a task, Zajonc argued that facilitation can sometimes take the form of *impaired* performance. Cockroaches thus ran down complex mazes slower when they were accompanied by another cockroach than they did when alone, and people were found to perform complex cognitive tasks faster but less accurately in the presence of a co-actor (Allport, 1924).

However, subsequent research suggests that, on its own, the mere presence of others is not sufficient to induce either of these forms of social facilitation: much depends on *who* those others are. Early research by Dashiell (1930) thus showed that people's performance on mathematical and logical tasks varied depending on whether co-actors were collaborators, rivals or observers. Participants generally performed faster when co-actors were observers or rivals (though less accurately in the former case). Consistent with these findings, the body of more recent work reviewed by Geen (1989) suggests that accompanied performance tends to facilitated by the presence of others when those others are perceived to be evaluating output and to be experts.

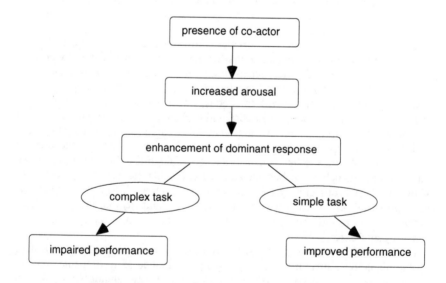

*Figure 9.1* Zajonc's (1965) drive theory of social facilitation

In a twist on Zajonc's arousal model, Cottrell (1972) has argued that these effects are products of *evaluation apprehension* — anxiety that flows from the perceived capacity of the person who accompanies the performer to provide various forms of incentive or reward. In this way, facilitation (often resulting in impaired performance) is seen to result from a person's belief that when his or her work can be monitored by a significant other (e.g. a peer or expert) it *matters more* because it is likely meet with some form of approval or disapproval. As Jones and Gerard (1967, p. 603) note, it is therefore the psychological rather than the physical presence of others that is crucial for facilitation to occur.

In ways foreshadowed by Triplett's (1898) discussion of the role of peer encouragement, these ideas have also been developed in research suggesting that the increase in arousal associated with the presence of others is clearly targeted rather than diffuse (Geen, 1989). Arousal is thus *goal oriented* so that the individual worker is enjoined (implicitly or explicitly) to live up to the norms that significant others appear to endorse (Guerin, 1986). The presence and actions of a fellow cyclist therefore encourage the individual not to be a better person in general, but to be a better cyclist. Accordingly, social facilitation is generally understood to reflect *both* drive and direction, rather than either element alone.

## Loafing theories

Although some of the above work points to the potential for groups to improve individual performance, we have already noted that the prospect of such outcomes has generally been downplayed in the research literature. One event that made a major contribution to this mindset was the publication of Steiner's (1972) *Group Process and Productivity*. This book provided the widely used typology of group tasks set out in Table 9.1, but it also defined group productivity as equal to 'potential productivity minus losses due to faulty process' (p. 79). As Brown (1988, p. 132) observes, by defining group output as inherently sub-optimal and ruling out the possibility that group processes could *enhance* potential productivity, this definition makes collective under-performance inevitable.

Steiner's analysis differentiated between two contributors to faulty process: *co-ordination loss* and *motivation loss*. As we have already seen, it is clear that in physical tasks an inability to co-ordinate individual inputs can detract from even the most efficient group. There is no way in the world that ten people can dig a one-foot square hole ten times faster than one person alone. And if they only have one saucepan, too many cooks must spoil the broth.

However, research has shown that similar problems can also beleaguer group performance on cognitive tasks. In particular, Stroebe and Diehl (1994; after Lamm & Trommsdorff, 1973) note that under-performance on brainstorming tasks can arise from *blocking*. In groups individuals are not always able to express their ideas as they arise and they may forget them when the opportunity finally presents itself. The contributions of others may also distract individuals or interfere with their thinking. Moreover, the amount of time allocated to each individual in a group setting is usually smaller than that afforded individuals, but it is not clear that this can easily be compensated for. If one person is given

*Table 9.1* Steiner's (1972) typology of group tasks

|  | Feature of Task | Example* |
|---|---|---|
| **Task structure** | | |
| divisible | can be broken down into sub-tasks | building a house |
| unitary | cannot be broken down into sub-tasks | pulling on a rope |
| **Task goal** | | |
| maximizing | goal is not absolute or fixed but involves performing as well as possible | writing a report; designing a building |
| optimizing | goal is to reach an absolute, fixed standard | solving a mathematical problem |
| **Task contributions** | | |
| disjunctive | contribution from the best individual group member(s) determines outcome | submitting multiple tenders for a contract |
| conjunctive | contribution from the worst individual group member(s) determines outcome | climbing a mountain with climbers roped together |
| additive | outcome is sum of individual contributions | running a relay race |
| discretionary | contribution of group members to outcome is at the group's discretion | organizing a Christmas party |

*Note*: * The features of most tasks vary with context and are negotiable. For example, building a house might typically be divisible, optimizing and additive (because different people do the plumbing, electrical work, roofing, etc. with the goal of building the house to a specific standard and where the final product is the sum of all their labour). However, it could also be unitary (if a family were building their own house), maximizing (if the objective was to build the house as fast as possible) and conjunctive (if faulty electrical work meant that the completed house failed to gain council approval).

30 minutes to come up with ideas for a project, giving eight people four hours to do the same task will not necessarily achieve the same result. It may simply leave all members of the group tired and frustrated.

Consistent with these arguments, some elaborate research by Diehl and Stroebe (1987) has shown that when attempts are made to eliminate the effects of blocking, production losses on brainstorming tasks can be completely eliminated. In one of their studies, participants were seated in separate cubicles but red lights indicated when another group member was speaking and the person's contribution could also be heard over headphones. Group members who could only contribute suggestions when no-one else was speaking produced fewer ideas than did individual controls, but this difference disappeared when group members could contribute freely (because the headphones were disconnected and participants had been told to ignore the red lights).

Nonetheless, studies of group shouting indicate that motivation losses *do* occur in experimentally created groups (e.g. Latané et al., 1979). In the early stage of their research Latané and his colleagues took such findings as support for *social impact theory* (Latané, 1981), arguing that adding more people to a group reduces the impact of the experimenter's message by an inverse power function (of the form: impact $= f\{1/n\}$) and then decreases the input of each member by a corresponding amount. In this way when there is one person in a group he or she receives the full impact of the experimenter's injunction to work hard and so is maximally influenced to heed it, but as more people are added each is less likely to see the instructions as applying to them.

Refinements to these ideas have suggested that loafing can arise from an increasing feeling amongst group members that their input is not personally *identifiable* (Steiner, 1972; Thelen, 1949). Support for this argument comes from studies conducted by Williams et al. (1981) in which the unwillingness of individuals in groups to cheer as loudly as individuals who were on their own abated once group members were made aware that a computer could work out their individual contribution to the group effort. By the same token, telling individuals who cheered alone that their contribution could not be measured led them to loaf as much as group members in the standard task.

Akin to these ideas, one further factor that has been thought to contribute to social loafing is an increased feeling of *dispensability* among members of larger groups (Kerr & Bruun, 1983; Stroebe & Diehl, 1994). If one person works alone on a task, it is clear that unless he or she does some work the job won't get done; however, as a group becomes larger group members may start to wonder if their input is really needed. This should be especially true if the task is disjunctive and optimizing so that successful performance only requires input from one highly competent group member. Under these conditions group members may also become more cynical and feel that they can 'get away' with a reduced effort and therefore start *free-riding*. Such perceptions have been used to account for standard loafing effects, but also for the finding reported by Collaros and Anderson (1969) that group members loafed more on a brainstorming task when they perceived other group members to be experts (with prior experience of brainstorming) rather than novices.

All of the above arguments are consistent with the broader view that social loafing is 'a kind of social disease' resulting from the diminished responsibility of deindividuated workers (Latané et al., 1979, p. 831). Thus while researchers disagree about the specific mechanism that encourages group members to be indolent, most agree that loafing is a significant social and organizational problem rooted firmly in the simple fact that groups exist. But given that groups are a necessary feature of organizational life and that most tasks could not be completed without them, researchers are left with a major dilemma. This, however, is the inevitable consequence of an analysis which defines the whole notion of 'group productivity' as oxymoronic.

### Integrated theories

From the discussion of Zajonc's (1965) drive theory above, it is clear that although this is primarily a theory of facilitation, the analysis can also accommodate evidence of loafing when this is seen as the enhancement of a dominant response to perform poorly (Jackson & Williams, 1985). In this way the theory is bi-directional and not inherently incompatible with evidence that groups can either improve or reduce individual performance. The same is true of extensions to Zajonc's work which focus on the capacity for groups to engender evaluation apprehension (e.g. Cottrell, 1972). As Stroebe and Diehl (1994) note, fear that one's own contribution was being evaluated by others could explain both under- and over-performance. On the one hand, a person might inhibit output if it was felt that his or her contribution (e.g. to a brainstorming session) might be disapproved of by the group, but on the other, he or she might increase output if it was felt that the contribution would be valued.

Insights of this form have contributed to two lines of research promising integrative analyses of loafing and facilitation. One of these focuses on *evaluation potential* as a determinant of group productivity, the other examines the role played by *social influence and group norms*. The link between performance and capacity for evaluation of performance is central to Harkins' (1987) attempts to reconcile loafing and facilitation effects. He argues that whenever individuals work co-actively their performance will improve but that it will also improve whenever their work can be evaluated. This, of course, explains standard facilitation effects (e.g. Triplett, 1898), but how does it explain loafing? According to Harkins, the problem with most loafing research (e.g. Latané et al., 1979) is that this typically confounds potential for evaluation with potential for co-action. This is because it compares output under conditions where (a) individual contributions to an individual task can be evaluated and (b) individual contributions to a group task cannot be evaluated. Consistent with this argument, in studies that independently manipulated evaluation and co-action both factors led to improved output on cognitive tasks (e.g. Harkins & Jackson, 1985; Harkins & Szymanski, 1989).

In focusing on the contribution that potential for evaluation might make to group performance, Harkins's work also raises another important issue, namely 'evaluation by whom?' (1987, p. 16). Harkins notes that performance might be expected to vary considerably depending upon whether it is evaluated by the actor him- or herself, by fellow ingroup members or by external sources (e.g. the experimenter). Moreover, the *standards* that these different evaluators set for performance should be particularly important.

In this vein, research suggests that group members' production levels are sensitive to norms established by those with whom they co-act and against whom they are compared. Jackson and Harkins (1985) thus found that loafing could be induced or eliminated by lowering or raising participants' expectations about other people's performance on a shouting task — a process referred to as *performance matching*. Along similar lines, Paulus and Dzindolet (1993, Experiments 1 to 3) found that on brainstorming tasks the productivity levels of the various members of interacting groups were much more similar to each other than those of members of nominal groups (i.e. aggregates of individuals). A final study also showed that the productivity of both real and nominal groups could be substantially raised by providing participants with bogus information about the performance of previous groups. When given a very high productivity norm (two and a half times greater than actual performance) interacting groups generated about 50 per cent more new ideas than under standard conditions and their performance was very similar to that of standard nominal groups.

Following up on findings from the original Hawthorne studies (Mayo, 1933; Roethlisberger & Dickson, 1939; see Chapter 1 above), this research therefore confirms the point that workers' output is highly sensitive to the normative structure of the work environment (an argument that is also central to goal-setting theory; Locke & Latham, 1990; see Chapter 4 above). In particular, productivity in groups appears to be sensitive both to localized ingroup standards and to those that prevail within the work culture at large.

Yet while Paulus and Dzindolet's work acknowledges the *possibility* that social influence processes could contribute to *enhanced* productivity in groups, this is not an outcome on which the authors dwell. Consistent with a general emphasis on group deficiency, Paulus and Dzindolet (1993) instead draw attention to evidence that despite the fact that members of real groups generally perform worse than individuals in nominal groups, those in the real groups generally rate their contributions more highly (both in terms of quantity and quality). How could they be so mistaken? Stroebe and Diehl (1994) suggest that one explanation for this apparent self-delusion is that individuals tend to make faulty attributions and mistakenly claim the group's productivity (which is always higher than that of individuals) as their own. This argument is supported by other research which shows that when individuals work in groups they tend both (a) to overestimate their personal contribution to collective products (Williams, Karau & Bourgeois, 1991) and, in brainstorming tasks, (b) to over-report the extent to which other people's ideas had also occurred to themselves (Stroebe et al., 1992).

As Figure 9.2 shows, Paulus and Dzindolet (1993) argue that self-delusion of this form is the consequence of processes of social comparison and social influence that act upon different forms of process loss. Here poor performance and a lack of insight are seen to result from the fact individuals contrive to bring their own performance into line with that of other group members, unaware that this performance has itself been compromised in a variety of ways.

This view that an inflated sense of self-worth is a natural consequence of group activity accords with other research suggesting that groups are prone to think more highly of themselves than they should. Indeed, as we saw in Chapter 6, such arguments are a prominent feature of Janis's (1982) groupthink model. Moreover, we can see that while the focus of Paulus and Dzindolet's

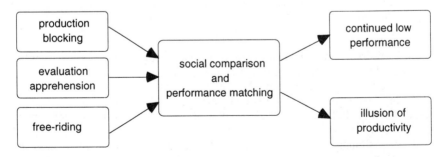

*Figure 9.2*   Paulus and Dzindolet's (1993) model of influence-mediated performance on brainstorming tasks

work is very different to that of Janis, their model shares with his an unflattering characterization of the group as the progenitor of opposing evils: over-statement and under-performance.


## Social identity and group productivity

As the above review suggests, for the majority of researchers who are interested in issues of group productivity, a key question has been 'Why do individuals loaf in groups?' Their answers generally point to a range of factors that contribute to various forms of co-ordination and motivation loss, with an implicit recommendation that the only sure-fire way of eliminating loafing is to do away with the group itself. As with needs theories of old (see Chapter 4 above) the remedy for collective sloth is seen to lie in stripping back the organizational context to its most reliable source of motivation: the individual *as an individual*.

In light of the arguments presented in previous chapters, this view, and the empirical evidence on which it is based, would seem to be highly problematic for the social identity approach. At heart, this proposes that *one significant determinant of task productivity is the congruity between a person's self-definition and features of the task environment* (hereafter referred to as the *congruity hypothesis*). In this way individuals who define themselves in terms of their unique personal identities should be best equipped to perform tasks that appear to demand and reward personalized and independent input, but those who define themselves in terms of a shared sense of social identity should do best on tasks that encourage collaborative participation. Yet if groups are capable of contributing to individuals' sense of self and their collective achievements can become an important vehicle for self-expression and enhancement, it seems prudent to ask why it is that the empirical evidence for positive group outcomes is so thin on the ground.

Some clues to help solve this riddle are provided by Harkins and Szymanski (1989) in their summary of the typical features of studies in this area:

> It could be argued that, despite its billing, there is little that is 'groupy' about the social loafing paradigm. ... In the paradigm, strangers come together for a brief period of time with no promise of future interaction. There is little in the procedure itself to make participants feel that they are part of a group. There is no interaction during the experiment; they are not invited to compete with other groups, or even to try to outdo their own group's last effort. (p. 941)

Similar observations by Brown (1988, p. 141) and Hogg (1992) suggest that the key to understanding social loafing lies in the *mismatch* between task demands and participants' self-definition. If group tasks are to be meaningful and self-involving, participants need to define themselves, and act, in terms of a relevant social identity, but there is precious little in the standard loafing paradigm to make social identity salient.

Clearly though, these arguments need to be fleshed out to encompass the array of phenomena that are discussed in the productivity literature — not just loafing but also facilitation, performance matching and illusions of effectivity. And not for the first time, we can embark on this exercise by locating the self firmly at the centre of the productivity process. In effect, we can think of productivity as being contingent upon a satisfactory answer to the participant's question 'Why is this task important for me?'

The research paradigms that are used to compare individual and group performance typically provide data that reflect two very different answers to this question. The first response is that of individuals alone, whose performance is usually aggregated to provide the nominal group scores against which the performance of participants in other conditions is gauged. Because the standard research environment defines tasks in highly personalized terms — with the capacity for personal identification and evaluation (e.g. Harkins, 1987; Williams et al., 1981) — there should be a high level of congruence between the level at which the task is meaningful and the *personally self-enhancing* activities in which participants are asked to engage. They should therefore be happy to engage in what we can refer to as *personal labouring*. This response should also be facilitated under conditions of interpersonal competition which increase the salience of personal identity and ultimately enhance individual performance (as in Triplett's, 1898, reel-winding tasks). The reasonably high expected output in baseline conditions of this form is represented in cell A of Figure 9.3.

However, tasks which encourage personal self-categorization should generally elicit a much less enthusiastic response when they are defined as group activities. For if participants define themselves in terms of their personal identities it

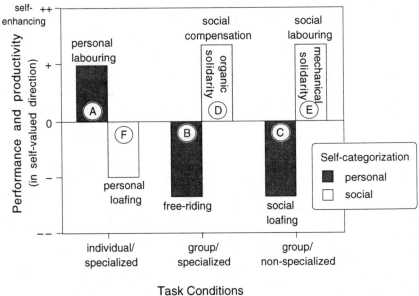

*Figure 9.3* Hypothesized performance (in the direction valued by participants) as a function of level of self-categorization and task conditions

should be much less obvious to them why it is important that they contribute to endeavours that promote the group as a whole. This reaction is therefore much the same as that of the individual with a high level of personal career commitment who is generally unwilling to participate in citizenship activities that enhance organizational well-being (Ouwerkerk et al., 1999, Tyler, 1999a; see Chapter 4 above). Accordingly, if they have to make a specialized contribution (e.g. in an idea-generating task) such participants should tend to *free-ride* — resulting in the low output represented in cell B of Figure 9.3. And if they have to contribute as part of a non-specialized collective (e.g. in a rope-pulling task) they should tend to *loaf* — resulting in the low output represented in cell C of Figure 9.3. In this way, as Harkins and others suggest, free-riding and loafing (like a reluctance to be a good organizational citizen) can be seen as phenomena that are firmly grounded in personal identity salience.

But what will happen if the task context is one that encourages participants to define themselves in terms of a shared social identity — for example, if there is meaningful intergroup competition or membership of a particular group is highly accessible? Again, the first point to note here is that because such contexts are rare in the empirical literature, evidence that might help provide answers to this question is relatively scant. Nonetheless, the social identity approach clearly suggests that when individuals participate in what are perceived to be group tasks and define themselves in terms of a shared, group-based sense of self their performance should at least match that observed in standard control conditions. In this context individuals' behaviour should be *socially self-enhancing*, so that where their contribution is specialized they are motivated to provide mutually supportive co-ordinated contributions and also make up for any other group members' limitations or shortcomings (e.g. by helping them out, providing them with social support, or doing extra work; Schmidt & Haslam, 1999; Tyler, 1999a). Williams et al. (1991) refer to this phenomenon as *social compensation* and this should lead to the high output represented in cell D of Figure 9.3. When input is collective and non-specialized and can be encouraged through identity-based mutual influence, group members should also engage in full-blown *social labouring*, striving collectively to improve the fortunes of the group as a whole — resulting in the high output represented in cell E of Figure 9.3.

In regard to this distinction between social compensation and social labouring, a significant feature of the foregoing arguments is that they suggest the key to productivity is not whether the contribution (and ability) of individuals is specialized or non-specialized, but whether either form of contribution is premised upon shared social identity (Donnellon, 1996). Both the division and the sharing of labour can help to promote group productivity where social identity is salient, but both can also inhibit it where it is not. In part this is because the perception and meaning of similarity and difference is itself an *outcome* of the categorization process (Brown, 1999; Jackson, 1992; McGarty, 1999b; Mummendey & Wenzel, 1999; Turner, 1985). This is one reason, we would suggest, why studies examining the relationship between workforce diversity and group productivity generate mixed results (for relevant discussions see Brotherton, 1999; Northcraft, Polzer, Neale & Kramer, 1995; Jackson, 1992; Jackson et al., 1991).

The issue for organizations is therefore not whether they have heterogeneous or homogeneous workforces, but whether *a socially shared theory of the collective self* allows workers to make sense of, have faith in, and utilize either heterogeneity or homogeneity. As suggested in Chapter 7, this point resonates with Durkheim's (1933) argument that both organic (i.e. role-differentiated) and mechanical (role-undifferentiated) solidarity can contribute to a productive society — though each is suited to different tasks and different conditions. More specifically, the above arguments fit with our earlier suggestions that organic solidarity is premised upon a group-level theory of the self (an *organic social identity*) that acknowledges and utilizes lower-level role (and other) differences between the self and others (e.g. sub-group or individual specialization; Moreland, 1999), while mechanical solidarity is premised upon a group-level theory of the self (a *mechanical social identity*) that acknowledges and utilizes lower-level similarities.

One other quite intriguing implication of the above analysis is that it suggests that under conditions of social identity salience individuals who are asked to engage in tasks that promote their personal self-interests should perform them more reluctantly (and less well) than they would in those (standard) conditions where their personal identity is salient — resulting in the low output represented in cell F of Figure 9.3. This form of personally self-retarding behaviour parallels that observed in standard loafing paradigms but, because it occurs at an individual rather than a group level, it can be referred to as *personal loafing*. Where social loafing reflects the under-productivity on group tasks of the individual whose personal identity is salient, personal loafing therefore refers to the under-productivity on individual tasks of the group member whose social identity is salient.

Again though, largely because standard research settings countermand self-definition in group-based terms, experimental evidence of personal loafing is thin on the ground. Nonetheless, it seems likely that in organizational contexts, this form of behaviour would be much more common. It would appear to be evident, for example, in the actions of the team member who puts the welfare of others before him- or herself and who constitutes what Organ (1988) refers to as a 'good soldier'. It is instructive to note, however, that when such behaviour is observed in these settings it is generally identified by a label with more positive connotations than those of 'loafing' — primarily because it is generally of benefit to the organization. Indeed, just such relabelling can be seen to underpin Organ's (1988) notion of organizational citizenship and its attendant features of altruism, conscientiousness, courtesy, sportsmanship and civic virtue. These are all forms of behaviour through which the group prospers but the individual *as an individual* may suffer. As Muchinsky (1997) notes:

> Civic virtue is the most admiral [sic] manifestation of organizational citizenship behaviour because it often entails some sacrifice of individual productive efficiency. (p. 281)

However, while the research literature affords little direct examination of the impact of social identity salience on group performance, at a rudimentary level the broad predictions of the social identity approach are consistent with a number of the patterns that emerge from meta-analyses conducted by Karau and Williams (1993) and Mullen et al. (1991). In particular, both sets of researchers found that social loafing was reduced to the extent that groups were real and had prior meaning or value for their members. Karau and Williams also found that loafing was reduced to the extent that tasks were intrinsically meaningful, self-involving or relevant to the group — a point confirmed in experimental research conducted by Brickner, Harkins and Ostrom (1986) and Erez and Somech (1996). Under such conditions group members were also more likely to compensate for any perceived deficiencies in their co-workers.

The impact of these variables was also confirmed in a study conducted by Holt (1987; cited in Brown, 1988). This replicated Ringelmann's rope-pulling experiment under different conditions that heightened social identity salience by (a) allowing prior interaction between team members, (b) asking team members to devise a name for their group, or (c) forming teams along the lines of pre-existing groups (of flatmates). There was no difference in the performance of these three types of group, but Brown notes that group productivity was lower than potential productivity in only four of thirty cases. Indeed, on average, groups performed 19 per cent better than individuals. In contrast to the pattern of social loafing observed by Ringelmann and Ingham et al. (1974), this study thus suggests that if they share a salient social identity, people participating collectively in group tasks will engage in social labouring.

Social identity predictions also accord with much of the more sophisticated experimental data presented by Harkins and Szymanski (1989). Their evidence that loafing was eliminated when participants were provided with information about the performance of other groups can be seen to result from the heightened sense of social identity that should flow from redefinition of the task context along intergroup rather than interpersonal lines (Oakes et al., 1994; Turner, 1985). The finding that there is much greater homogeneity in productivity levels amongst members of real groups than nominal ones is also consistent with the argument that social identity salience enhances conformity to group norms. The same principle also accounts for evidence that productivity can be dramatically affected by the provision of fake norms (e.g. Paulus & Dzindolet, 1993).

Although these arguments can be used to make sense of much of the empirical literature, they still leave two important issues unresolved. The first relates to the fact that in some contexts social identity appears to be highly salient and yet group productivity remains stubbornly low (as was the case in a number of the workgroups at the Hawthorne plant; Roethlisberger & Dickson, 1939; see also Seashore, 1954). The second relates to evidence that in these and many other situations of apparent under-productivity, group members remain firmly convinced of the merit and utility of their collective efforts.

Observing that social identity salience does not always guarantee improved group performance takes us back to some important points that were first raised in the early chapters of this book — namely (a) that what constitutes productivity is always in part a *social judgement* on the part of participants and those who judge them (e.g. Pritchard, 1990, 1992; see Chapter 3 above), and (b) that while personal identity salience is often associated with tacit acceptance of the status quo, social identity salience is much more likely to serve as a vehicle for *social change* (Reicher, 1987; Tajfel & Turner, 1979; e.g. see Chapters 2 and 8 above). One of the significant implications of these two points is that when participants have views about the value of tasks that differ from those held by the people who require and evaluate their performance, this difference of perspective is much more likely to be voiced and acted upon if participants are interacting in terms of a shared social identity. If a supervisor (or experimenter) asks an individual to perform an unpleasant or apparently unreasonable task, that person should be much more likely to carry it out than would a group of people given the same instructions (a point that we pursue further in the next chapter). In this way, the social identity-based productivity of low-status groups is much more likely to be perceived as counter-normative and seditious than is the productivity of individuals whose discrete personal identities are salient. One reason for this is that in particular contexts (e.g. where intergroup boundaries are perceived to be impermeable) the group may explicitly be formed as a means of *challenging* the authority of those with power and status. However, this opposition may also emerge meta-contrastively as a way of making sense of perceived intergroup differences and, once it does, it should tend to be reinforced through processes of mutual influence.

Yet in this regard, one recurring problem in the social and organizational literature is that by accepting dominant organizational goals (i.e. those of productivity assessors) as the *single* benchmark for judgements of effectiveness it makes almost no allowance for productivity of this form (see Pritchard, 1992, pp. 451, 466). To illustrate this point, one could think of a hypothetical scenario in which groups of prisoners-of-war are asked to cheer as loudly as they can to mark the arrival of a new camp commandant. The social identity approach predicts that those groups with the strongest sense of shared identification and who are most aware of the difference between their captors and themselves would cheer least loudly. Yet although the prisoners themselves would presumably perceive such inaction to be worthwhile and highly productive (because it is defined as such within their shared *normative framework*; McGarty, 1999b), this might well be perceived as a serious case of under-performance by their captors. Moreover, while the social identity approach would endorse the prisoners' characterization of their actions as productive, this view is unlikely to emerge from orthodox interpretations of their behaviour.

As an example of how this argument applies to the interpretation of productivity research, we can reflect on key features of a study reported by Diehl and Stroebe (1987, Experiment 2). This was one of a series of studies designed to examine the contribution of evaluation apprehension to under-performance on a brainstorming task. In the study participants had to generate ideas that would promote either relatively innocuous schemes or more controversial ones. One of the latter schemes was also one with which the participants themselves disagreed — they had to think of ways of reducing the number of foreign guest-workers (i.e. temporary immigrants) to Germany. Evaluation apprehension was manipulated by informing participants that their contributions either would or would not be evaluated by their peers, with apprehension presumed to be highest on the guest-worker topic where participants might fear that their fellow students would suspect them of holding racist views. Consistent with this argument, the researchers found that by far the smallest number of ideas were generated for the guest-worker topic where contributions were to be evaluated by peers. On this basis the authors concluded that 'evaluation apprehension might be responsible for part of the productivity loss observed in brainstorming groups' (Diehl & Stroebe, 1987, p. 504).

But was this really a case of under-productivity? If one takes the perspective of the experimenters and endorses the received rules of brainstorming tasks (where more suggestions are indicative of a better outcome), then it certainly was. However, looked at from the perspective of the participants — who were opposed to guest-worker policies they perceived to be racist — this conclusion seems questionable. Indeed, it could be argued that the very small number of suggestions that were generated on this task under conditions of ingroup surveillance was a *highly productive* outcome as it allowed participants to collectively express their true feelings about the obnoxious nature of the experimental task (albeit by withdrawing rather than contributing effort). And given the parameters within which they working, how else could these legitimate feelings have been expressed?

The essential point here, then, is that although the social identity approach predicts that performance on group tasks will be enhanced where participants' social identity is salient, this productivity will be displayed in a form and direction *perceived to be appropriate by the group itself.* However, productivity of this form will tend to go undetected when the values of the group are unaligned with those of its judges. One obvious reason for this is that it is almost always the values of the judges — not of the performers — that are instantiated in the performance indicators on a particular task.

This point applies to the body of group productivity research in which participants are typically asked to engage in relatively trivial or frivolous tasks (e.g. to cheer or shout loudly, to think of as many uses as possible for a knife or an extra thumb, to count dots on a screen). However, the point is perhaps even more relevant to the interpretation of organizational behaviour like that displayed by groups at the Bethlehem Steel Plant. From a managerial perspective, this behaviour is routinely maligned and scoffed at (as it was by Taylor in his definition of it as 'soldiering'). Yet amongst the workers themselves it often appears to be a source of some pride — not least because it is a mark of their collective resistance to authority. It is clear too, that prescriptions for enhancing organizational performance by disbanding groups are firmly anchored in the same managerial definition of performance.

This same line of argument also provides one avenue for coming to terms with the disparity between group members' perceptions of their productivity on collaborative tasks and the standard pattern of research findings. Clearly if group members are productive in a way that is counter-normative for those who design tasks and monitor performance, those designers and monitors are likely to perceive the group members' performance as misguided and their perceptions of productivity as deluded.

It is apparent that group members' perceptions under these (and other) circumstances can also reflect feelings of satisfaction associated with the opportunity that the group provides for positive and rewarding social interaction. Working collaboratively can simply be more fun than working alone. Amongst other things, this is because it can fulfil a need for a sense of belonging (Baumeister & Leary, 1995; Manstead, 1997). More tangibly, such feelings can contribute to enhanced *group maintenance* — ensuring that the group has a continued existence and 'lives to fight another day'. As noted in Chapter 3, Cartwright and Zander (1960) considered this function just as important for the group itself as goal achievement, and yet it is a positive outcome that latterly researchers have tended to overlook or downplay (see Jackson et al., 1991; Schneider, 1987).

More generally, though, the 'illusion of group effectivity' can be seen to arise from differences of perspective associated with the interpersonal–intergroup continuum. A key point here relates to the perceived validity of the thesis that any group product can be no more than the sum of its parts. If, like most researchers in the field, one takes the view that groups can be no more than the sum of their individual constituents, then any perceptions to the contrary must be seen as delusional. This would be the case if members of a group are asked to estimate their individual contributions to a group product and the sum of these estimations is greater than 100 per cent (Williams et al., 1991), or if group members are more likely to take credit for having the same ideas as their colleagues than non-group members (Stroebe et al., 1992). However, from the perspective of the group members, both of these effects can be seen to arise from *depersonalized* perception whereby the group becomes a part of self. When a person's social identity is salient 'what is ours' *is* 'mine'. 'Illusions' of group productivity together with genuine obfuscation of 'who did what' are thus a natural outgrowth of social identity salience.

Rather than being a source of weakness, it is, then, *precisely because* groups have the potential be more productive than the sum of their parts that they play such a key role in organization life. And while researchers tend to be disparaging of group members' inflated beliefs about their own productivity, as we saw in Chapter 6, it is the fact that group decisions and activities tend to engender a shared and more concentrated sense of involvement and commitment on the part of their members that makes them an indispensable organizational tool (e.g. Katz & Kahn, 1966). Four people who enthusiastically promote the 30 units of productivity that they have collaboratively crafted will often be much more useful to an organization than four people devoted only to the 10 different units that they have each individually produced — even though the latter may have no 'delusions' about their productivity and may, by standard reckoning, be seen as more productive. Freed from the impositions of individualistic algebra, less *is* more.

## Some empirical tests of the social identity approach

### Social identity, group training and transactive memory

Most of the research discussed above involves performance where the goal towards which people work and the means by which they reach that goal are well understood before embarking on the task. Everyone knows how to shout and clap, and has an idea of how to count dots or think of uses for a knife. But such tasks are not particularly representative of the activities in which people engage when they enter the workforce. In this environment most people have to learn new and often quite complex skills and for this purpose customarily receive on-the-job *training*. Analogous to the debate about whether group productivity exceeds that of individuals, a pertinent question here is whether training people in groups is more beneficial than training them individually.

As Liang, Moreland and Argote (1995) note, evidence for the general efficacy of group training is mixed. However, these authors also point out that very little of the research in this area has been informed by a theoretical account of how group training might achieve positive results, and that findings are difficult to interpret because no attempt is made to monitor the impact of relevant theoretical variables. To fill this breach, the authors draw on Wegner's (1987) notion of *transactive memory*, proposing that in the process of group training individuals collaboratively code, store and retrieve information in a way that allows them to optimize performance. More specifically, Moreland et al. (1996) suggest that group training is associated with the development of a *transactive memory system* — a *shared* understanding of the distinct competencies and knowledge-base of each group member and of the contribution each makes to performance of a group task.

When it comes to performing complex group tasks, the key advantage of such a system is that it eliminates the need for every group member to know everything about all facets of the task. So rather than each group member duplicating the knowledge and skills of others, a transactive memory system allows group members to put greater energy into developing *complementary specializations* that are for the greater good of the group a whole. In effect, the system thus serves as a mechanism that allows a group to orchestrate the processes of social compensation described by Williams et al. (1991).

Significantly though, it is clear that these systems are a property of the group rather than of individuals per se and represent *socially shared cognitions* of the type that underpin effective organizational communication (e.g. Weick & Roberts, 1993; see Chapter 5 above). They are reliant too, on the development of *trust* between group members since it is clear that an individual who fails to make the expected contribution to any collaborative product would have a more devastating impact than they might if their knowledge and skills were non-unique. This impact is revealed in research by Argote, Insko, Yovetich and Romero (1995) which shows that turnover in group membership leads to lowered productivity, particularly for well-established groups.

From a social identity perspective, these various observations would lead one to expect that transactive memory systems should develop in conjunction with a common sense of social identity. Amongst other things, this is because common social identification amongst group members should (a) encourage free and effective knowledge sharing, (b) ensure better co-ordination of their efforts, and (c) enhance mutual trust (e.g. Suzuki, 1998; Tyler, 1993; see Chapters 2 and 5 above). Along lines argued in Chapter 5, individuals will therefore only have the motivation and ability to develop socially shared cognitions when they define themselves as a members of a common group.

Evidence that supports these arguments — particularly in pointing to the role of transactive memory in mediating between group training and productivity — emerges from an inventive programme of research conducted by Moreland and his colleagues (e.g. Liang et al., 1995; Moreland et al., 1996). The goal in this research was for groups to work together on the complex task of assembling a radio kit that contained a large number of mechanical and electrical components. In the first of the researchers' studies all participants were given the same basic training in radio assembly but half received this training individually and half received it in three-person groups. Training involved demonstration of how the components fitted together as well as half an hour of practice at the full assembly task. All participants knew that their ability to assemble the radio would be tested one week after training. However, while those who received individual training did not know who they would be collaborating with during the testing phase, those who received group training were informed that groups would have the same composition during training and testing.

The performance measures in which the researchers were interested included (a) the speed of radio assembly, (b) errors in assembly and (c) procedural knowledge about assembly. Results revealed no differences in the speed of construction; however, as predicted, groups who had previously been trained together made fewer errors and demonstrated superior knowledge of the radio construction process. Analysis of assembly also revealed a number of other interesting effects that pointed to differences in the extent to which groups in the two conditions had developed transactive memory systems. In particular, it showed that amongst groups who trained together there was (a) greater memory differentiation, so that different individuals remembered how to perform different aspects of the task, (b) better task co-ordination and (c) greater trust. Statistical analysis also indicated that it was the improved performance in these areas that accounted for the relationship between type of training and reduced assembly errors.

As well as this, videotaped evidence suggested that the groups who had received group training had a more salient sense of shared social identity, as measured by the tendency for individuals to use collective pronouns (e.g. 'us', 'we', 'our'), rather than personal ones ('I', 'me', 'mine'). Just as Mayo (1949) had observed amongst teams of aircraft workers in the 1940s, productivity thus appeared to go hand-in-hand with the existence of a strong 'we-feeling' — what Donnellon (1996) refers to as 'team-talk'. Here, however, social identification appears not to have impacted directly upon group productivity, but to have achieved its impact through a capacity to engender a shared and mutually supportive understanding of a particular task environment.

Some of these arguments were explored further in a second experiment (Moreland et al., 1996) which replicated key features of the above study but attempted to show that the effects of group training were not attributable simply to the opportunities for group development it provides. In this regard, one possible criticism of Liang et al.'s (1995) study is that the effects it revealed could be attributed to the greater experience that participants in the group training conditions had of working with one another — experience that may have reduced any initial sense of anxiety, uncertainty or awkwardness. To deal with this issue, two additional conditions were included in this second experiment. In one participants received individual training but also participated in an additional *team-building* exercise before testing; in the other, groups that were trained together were scrambled with all their members being *reassigned* to new groups before the testing phase.

The authors predicted that in both of these new conditions group performance would be no better than in the individual training condition because neither provided an opportunity for groups to develop a transactive memory system *relevant* to performance at the testing phase. In the team-building condition any system that developed would be relevant to the group but not to the task, and in the reassignment condition any system would be relevant to the task but not to the group.

The experiment's results provided strong support for these predictions. As Table 9.2 indicates, groups who were trained and tested together had better procedural knowledge and made fewer assembly errors than those in any of the three other conditions. Moreover, statistical analysis again indicated that it was the existence of a group- and task-specific transactive memory system that accounted for this superior performance.

Developing on points raised by Liang et al.'s (1995) first experiment, one of the additional lessons provided by this follow-up study was that social identity salience alone was not sufficient to improve group performance. Thus groups who received task-specific training or irrelevant team-building both showed signs of stronger identification than other groups (this time on measures of attraction to the group and perceived group cohesion rather than pronoun counts), but only those in the first of these conditions showed evidence of greater productivity. Significantly, then, groups who participated in team-building may have trusted each other and *wanted* to share information in a way that would contribute to the development of a relevant transactive memory system, but they clearly lacked the task-specific experience that would allow them to do so. A general point that emerges from this research is thus that both *opportunity and experience* are required to translate motivation into productivity, and that where these are denied the productive potential of any group will inevitably be thwarted (see also Shaw & Barrett-Power, 1998, p. 1323).

*Table 9.2* Scores on productivity and process measures as a function of training and testing conditions (from Moreland et al., 1996)

|  | Condition | | | |
| --- | --- | --- | --- | --- |
| *Measure* | Individual | Reassignment | Team-building | Group |
| Procedural recall | 12.07 | 12.62 | 14.29 | 22.07 |
| Assembly errors | 22.27 | 27.23 | 20.93 | 11.29 |
| Transactive memory | 3.51 | 3.13 | 3.64 | 5.05 |
| Social identity salience | 3.87 | 3.83 | 4.59 | 4.93 |

*Purposive social identity salience as a determinant of group productivity*

The research conducted by Moreland and his colleagues is important in bringing to light some of the psychological processes that contribute to performance-enhancing social compensation in which individualized inputs into a collective product are complementary and mutually sustaining. However, for psychologists interested in issues of productivity, the 'holy grail' has always been to identify conditions that lead to *social labouring* in which inputs are not individualized and where increased effort cannot be attributed to the personal identifiability of contributors. We noted above that some unpublished work by Holt (cited in Brown, 1988) provided preliminary evidence that output of this form might be associated with increases in social identity salience. However, more thoroughgoing and nuanced examination of this hypothesis has subsequently been provided by James and Greenberg (1989) and Worchel et al. (1998; see also Pilegge & Holtz, 1997; van Knippenberg, 2000).

In James and Greenberg's (1989) first experiment students from the University of Arizona were told that they were participating in an anagram-solving task in which their performance would be compared with that of students from the University of Washington. For half of the participants the salience of their university affiliation was heightened by decorating a mirror in the experimental cubicle with University of Arizona colours (red and blue), while for the other half this decoration was neutral (white). On the basis of social identity and self-categorization principles the authors predicted that performance would be greater when decoration was pertinent to the participants' ingroup membership as this would establish more strongly the social self-relevance of task performance. This prediction was confirmed: participants in the red and blue-decorated room solved 55 per cent of the anagrams but those in the white room solved only 42 per cent.

The authors noted, though, that this first study provided no check for the effectiveness of the experimental manipulation and that its findings might not be a product of social identity processes but of greater levels of arousal resulting from vivid room decorations. Though improbable, superior performance may have been brought about by the red and blue banners and had nothing to do with the University of Arizona. These problems were addressed in a second study in which social identity salience was manipulated by starting the experiment with a task where some students solved an anagram that spelled the university's mascot ('wildcats') but others solved an irrelevant anagram ('beavers'). As well as this, the study also involved a manipulation of intergroup comparison (present or absent) such that one set of conditions replicated those of the first study by referring to competition with the University of Washington, while a second set made no such reference. Having performed the anagram-solving task, participants also completed a 'Who am I?' inventory in which they had to write down 20 self-descriptive statements (Kuhn & McPartland, 1954).

The results of this study replicated those of the first experiment with participants in the conditions that referred to intergroup competition solving more anagrams when their university identity was salient than when it was not (89% vs. 80%, respectively). Interestingly though, when no reference was made to competition, this pattern was reversed. Participants whose university affiliation was made salient solved *fewer* anagrams than those whose affiliation was not salient (63% vs. 78%, respectively).

Clues to the basis of this second effect were provided by responses on the 'Who am I?' measure. These indicated that participants in the low-performing social identity/no comparison condition tended to provide by far the greatest number of positive self-descriptions (e.g. I am a good cook, I am intelligent). These responses might indicate that in this 'no comparison' context the comparative fit of a university-based social identity was low and that participants were therefore inclined to assert their personal uniqueness (Brewer, 1988, 1991; Turner, 1985). In any event, as James and Greenberg (1989) comment:

> These results [are relevant] for organizational theories and applied work in
> organizations [where it is common] for businesses to use group and subgroup
> uniforms and other group-related symbols.   If these serve to heighten ingroup
> salience ... they might have either positive or negative effects depending on the
> circumstances.    Therefore, applied uses of group-focusing interventions should
> be approached with caution.  (p. 614)

More specifically, it follows from self-categorization theory that problems may
result from attempts to make group membership salient in situations where the
group has little apparent meaning or purpose. Getting group members 'dressed
up' may backfire unless they have somewhere to go.

Evidence that supports and extends these arguments is provided by the
research of Worchel and his colleagues (1998). As well as teasing out a number
of the effects obtained by James and Greenberg (1989) these researchers' studies
also compared the performance of groups with group members working on their
own, thereby allowing them to examine whether social identity salience
contributes to social labouring rather than simply to reduced social loafing.

In the first of Worchel et al.'s (1998) studies the participants' task was to
construct paper chains with as many links as possible in a ten-minute period. In
one phase of the experiment all participants performed this task alone. However,
on another occasion participants performed the same task in groups that were
constructed in one of three different ways. In a *collective* condition designed to
mimic the structure of groups in standard loafing experiments, individuals were
simply placed in a group and told that they experimenter was interested in the
performance of the group as a whole and that they should therefore endeavour to
do their best.  In a *future interaction* condition, the group was referred to by the
experimenter as a 'work-team' and its members were led to believe that they
would be working together again in the future. These instructions were intended
to satisfy some of the basic conditions necessary for individuals to categorize
themselves as members of a group, and 'dispel the perception that they are
simply a convenient collection of people' (Worchel et al., 1998, p. 392).
Finally, in a third *group reward* condition individuals were told that the group
would be given a $20 bonus if the group exceeded the average level of
performance on the task.  This condition — which mimics the organizational
practice of *gainsharing* — was intended to enhance the meaningfulness of the
group even further.  However, this manipulation also allowed the researchers to
examine predictions derived from expectancy-value theories which argue that
individuals' contribution to group tasks is instrumentally motivated by their
expectation of personal benefit (e.g. Karau & Williams, 1993; Lawler, 1973;
Naylor et al. 1980; Vroom, 1964; see Chapter 4 above).

Comparison of results from the two phases of the study revealed evidence of a
substantial social loafing effect amongst participants in the collective condition.
However, consistent with social identity predictions, loafing was significantly
attenuated in both of the other conditions.  Performance in the group reward
condition was also greater than that in the future interaction condition and indeed
participants here provided some (non-significant) evidence of social labouring.

Although these results provided clear support for the social identity approach,
this first study left two important issues unresolved.  The first was whether the
enhanced productivity of participants in the group reward condition was a result
of enhanced social identification or of economic motivations.  Potentially even

more damaging to the social identity position, a second question was whether the performance of individuals in the future interaction condition was attributable simply to *perceived interdependence* rather than a sense of shared group membership (e.g. as proposed by Shea & Guzzo, 1987).

To address these questions, Worchel and his colleagues (1998) conducted a second study. In this the reward structure of the chain building task was manipulated across four independent conditions. The first of these replicated the collective condition of Experiment 1, the only change being that participants were told they would receive a *personal reward* of $3.90 if their personal contribution to the group task exceeded a set criterion. In the other three *group-reward* conditions task contributions varied so that, according to Steiner's (1972) typography (see Table 9.1), they were either *disjunctive, conjunctive* or *additive*. Specifically, participants were told, respectively, that each group member would receive a $3.90 bonus if the *best* person's contribution exceeded a set criterion, if the *worst* person's contribution exceeded the criterion, or if the group members' *average* contribution exceeded the criterion.

The researchers reasoned that if productivity was sensitive to the interdependence and economic structure of the task, participants should work harder where task contributions were disjunctive and conjunctive because in these conditions there was a clear link between individual performance and reward — if the individual was industrious the group would receive the reward in the disjunctive condition, but if he or she was lazy the group would not receive the reward in conjunctive condition. On the other hand, they argued that if the existence of the group reward served simply to increase the salience of group members' shared social identity and it is this that is responsible for social labouring, then productivity should not vary as a function of task contributions but simply be higher than when the reward was personal.

Findings from the study supported the latter position. Thus although the existence of a reward led to group performance exceeding individual performance in all four conditions, productivity in the personal-reward condition was lower than in the three group-reward conditions (between which there were no differences in output). There were thus general productivity benefits associated with the provision of a reward, but this had far greater impact upon a group that was psychologically real for its members. And as long as the was group real, the nature of task contributions was relatively unimportant.

Participants' responses on a post-exercise questionnaire added further weight to such conclusions. These revealed differences between the three group-reward conditions on measures of perceived interdependence but not on those pertaining to shared social identity. They also indicated that participants in the three group-reward conditions all had a stronger sense of shared social identity than those in the personal-reward condition. This meant, for example, that the former participants perceived themselves as more of a group, liked each other more, and had a stronger desire to continue working together in the future. Accordingly, improved group productivity appeared to be associated with these perceptions of shared social identity not those of interdependence.

In the final study of their empirical programme, Worchel et al. (1998) attempted to use their chain-making paradigm to address some of the questions left unresolved by earlier research. The study incorporated the same two variables as James and Greenberg's (1989) second experiment: group salience (high or low) and intergroup competition (present or absent). In high-salience conditions participants were assigned to groups that were clearly identified by name (alpha or beta) and all members of the group wore lab-coats of the same colour with markings that identified them as members of this group. In low-salience conditions groups had no uniforms or names. The groups performed the chain-making task in the same room as another group in conditions of intergroup competition, but no other group was present in the no competition condition. Participants in all conditions also completed a detailed post-test questionnaire that allowed the researchers to examine the contribution of social identity salience to productivity on primary measures.

On these primary measures, Worchel et al. (1998) predicted and obtained the same pattern of results as James and Greenberg (1989). As Table 9.3 indicates, group productivity was again at its highest where participants' group membership was salient and they were competing with another group. However, productivity was at its lowest where group membership was salient and there was no such competition. Here though, the fact that Worchel et al.'s paradigm incorporated individual and group phases allowed them to conclude that while the latter pattern was an example of social loafing, the former was indicative of social labouring. Importantly too, results on post-test measures indicated that the labouring of participants in the group salient/competition condition was accounted for by their very strong identification with their group, while the loafing of those in the group salient/no competition condition was accounted for by their low social identification.

Consistent with the congruity hypothesis outlined above, Worchel et al.'s (1998) research thus indicates that productivity is contingent on a match between participants' self-categorization and task conditions. Under conditions of intergroup competition, factors that increase the salience of a relevant social identity (e.g. common uniform and treatment) contribute to group productivity because that identity can serve as a meaningful and purposeful vehicle for self-expression and self-enhancement. However, where a group has no clear meaning or purpose and it offers no such opportunities for the self, factors that make a person's membership of it salient will reduce productivity. In such situations, because the avenues to self-enhancement are largely personal, individual productivity will be optimized by factors that make personal identity salient (e.g. personalized dress and treatment).

*Table 9.3*  Scores on productivity and process measures as a function of group salience and intergroup competition (from Worchel et al., 1998)

| Measure | Group Salience: Low (no uniforms) | | High (uniforms) | |
| --- | --- | --- | --- | --- |
| | Competition: Absent | Present | Absent | Present |
| Productivity* | −1.26 | 1.43 | −4.02 | 4.60 |
| Identification with group | 3.75 | 4.10 | 3.14 | 4.49 |

*Note*: * Scores indicate change between individual and group phases; a positive score reflects social labouring, a negative score reflects social loafing

*The importance of self-valued goals*

The research reported by Worchel and his colleagues (1998) provides strong support for the argument that congruity between self-categorization and task conditions is an essential pre-condition of group productivity. Yet in outlining the social identity approach to this topic, it was also argued that many instances of group productivity that satisfy these conditions may go unrecognized and unacknowledged. This is because the *form* of productivity can often be incompatible with the prescriptions of those who evaluate performance (e.g. managers or researchers; Pritchard, 1990, 1992; Zander, 1997).

Some early evidence that speaks to this possibility was reported by Seashore (1954). Conducted in a company that manufactured heavy machinery, this research examined the way in which group productivity varied as a function of feelings of group solidarity and group norms. Consistent with the earlier findings of Mayo (1949) and the later research of Paulus and Dzindolet (1993), Seashore (1954) found much greater within-group similarity in the productivity of groups that had high levels of solidarity. At the same time there was much greater between-group variation in the performance of these groups than there was amongst those with low solidarity. The reason for this was readily apparent and lay in the capacity for those factors that increased group solidarity to *polarize* the productivity-related norms of the group. Thus while there was not much difference in the productivity of low-solidarity groups that accepted or rejected the productivity goals of the company, high-solidarity groups that accepted the company's goals were much more productive, while those that rejected its goals were much less productive.

As it does with other social attitudes and behaviours, social identity salience therefore has a polarizing impact on productivity (see Chapter 6 above). The research discussed in the previous section supports the view that under conditions where groups' self-definitions and goals are aligned with those of evaluators, productivity will be uniformly increased. However, it should also be the case that where the group and its goals are opposed to those of the evaluators, productivity (as measured by the evaluators) will be uniformly reduced. Very similar points to these were acknowledged by Likert (1954) when he observed:

> Work groups which have high peer-group loyalty and common goals appear to be effective in achieving their goals. If their goals are the achievement of high productivity and low waste, these are the goals they will accomplish. If, on the other hand, [they] ... reject the objectives of the organization and set goals at variance with these objectives, the goals they establish can have strikingly adverse effects upon productivity. (1961, p. 30; see also Katz & Kahn, 1966, p. 378)

Significantly though, it is the *uniformity* of the behaviour that produces these 'strikingly adverse effects' that distinguishes it from loafing. Because loafing is grounded in personal identity it should be non-orchestrated and idiosyncratic. However, because group-based under-performance is grounded in social identity it should be consensualized by processes of mutual influence and take the form of soldiering.

Although this line of argument offers a new take on some very significant forms of organizational behaviour, the issues it raises have remained largely unexplored, because most researchers have been locked into an experimenter-centric operationalization of productivity.    One notable exception is an experiment conducted by Wallace (1998) which sought to test social identity predictions in a setting peculiarly relevant to the topic of soldiering: amongst army cadets going about their basic training.  The study's design allowed for a fairly straightforward examination of the congruity hypothesis examined in Worchel et al.'s (1998) research.  At the start of the study participants engaged in activities designed to make salient either their personal identities as individuals or their social identity as soldiers.  Amongst other things, those in the personal identity condition watched extracts from a Hollywood movie in which the hero disobeyed orders and went out on a limb, while those in the social identity condition watched segments from the same movie in which the hero and his comrades rallied round to help each other.  Following this, the cadets completed a number of tasks either on their own or in groups of four.

In line with the congruity hypothesis, the study's main prediction was that productivity would be greatest in those conditions where the context in which the cadets worked (alone or in groups) was consistent with their salient self-categorization.  Those whose personal identity was salient were thus expected to work hard when they worked alone, but to loaf when they worked in groups.  On the other hand, cadets whose social identity was salient were expected to work hard when they worked in groups, but to loaf when they worked in alone.  Thus participants whose personal identity was salient were expected to show signs of the standard social loafing effect when they worked in groups, but those whose social identity was salient were expected to exhibit personal loafing when they worked alone.

In one further twist to the study, Wallace (1998) also conducted pre-testing to identify tasks that differed in their intrinsic appeal to the cadets.  From a battery of such tasks, the most enjoyable proved to be an idea-generating exercise in which they had to generate written lists of things that would prove useful if they were going to live for a year on a desert island in the Caribbean.  The least enjoyable was an activity with which they were all too familiar — tying and untying bootlaces as many times as possible in a 16-minute period.

In light of the arguments presented above, it was anticipated that productivity on the pleasant task would be reflected in conventional ways, so that the more productive individuals and groups would simply generate more ideas.    In relation to the unpleasant bootlacing task, however, the opposite pattern was predicted.  Given participants' own definition of the task as dreary and pointless, it was expected that productivity would here be displayed in the form of stubborn *under*-performance.  Most significantly, cadets whose social identity was salient and who performed the task in groups were expected to display soldiering of the form described by Taylor (1911) and to conspire collectively to tie as few bootlaces as they could.

The results of the study are presented in Figure 9.4.  From this it can be seen that there was support for all of the above predictions.  On the idea-generating task participants generated most ideas where their salient self-categorization was congruent with the task conditions (i.e. where personal identity was salient and they performed the task alone, or where social identity was salient and they

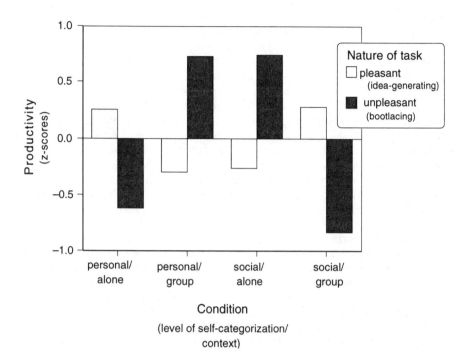

*Figure 9.4* Productivity on pleasant and unpleasant tasks as a function of level of self-categorization and context (from Wallace, 1998)

*Note*: Performance of the two tasks is not directly comparable, so it is variation in productivity on the same task across conditions that is most informative

performed the task in groups), but performance was significantly lower when this was not the case. However, the very opposite pattern emerged on the bootlacing task. Here participants tied *fewer* laces where self-categorization and task conditions were congruent, and this was particularly pronounced when participants' social identity was salient and they performed the task in groups. Supportive of the idea that this under-performance was associated with a heightened sense of ingroup solidarity, evidence on post-test measures also indicated that these participants perceived themselves to have more support from their fellow cadets than participants in other conditions.

The overall pattern of results from this study thus points to the complex interplay of factors that impact upon the display of productivity and its detection. From the point of view of the participants themselves, it was always the case that performance *in a self-valued direction* was enhanced where self-categorization and task conditions were congruent. Yet under conditions where the experimental index of productivity was not aligned with the cadets' values — as was the case with the bootlacing task — this actually manifested itself not as labouring but as soldiering.

From both a theoretical and applied point of view, the message that emerges from this study is one to which Taylor himself appears to have been acutely sensitive in his original research with labourers at the Bethlehem Steel Plant. For while Taylor (1911) believed that soldiering emanated partly from a level of laziness endemic to all labourers, he also recognized that it also arose 'second, from more *intricate second thought and reasoning* caused by their relations with other men' (p. 19; emphasis added). Far from seeing soldiering as mindless and purposeless (as loafing researchers have tended to do), he thus realized that the rational forces of social cognition and social interaction had the power to translate individual disaffection into collective inaction. And because that inaction was so damaging to employers' interests, it was this that Taylor sought to diffuse with his prescriptions for individualization of the workforce.

Of course, the other strategy for improving productivity that is suggested by Wallace's (1998) data would lead employers to harness the collective energies of workers by re-engineering features of the task environment in order to make them more attractive to workers. As we saw in Chapters 1 and 4, such insights lay at the heart of theorizing by workers in the human relations movement (e.g. McGregor, 1960; Mayo, 1949). However, in the absence of a commitment to really improving workers' conditions, the most widely implemented alternative has been to develop strategies of attitude change that induce workers to construe the unrewarding aspects of their work — including their relations with management — more positively. Again though, because these generally fail to address the social and structural realities that lie at the heart of workers' perceptions, they have met with only limited success (for a review see Kelly & Kelly, 1991).

**Conclusion**

As we have noted on several previous occasions in this book, one of the most confusing features of traditional texts is the contradictory manner in which they discuss the contribution of groups to organizations. In discussions of group productivity these contradictions assume centre stage. Thus, on the one hand, sections on team-building and teamwork emphasize the indispensability of groups to the organization but, on the other, treatments of process loss and counterproductive behaviour portray groups as a basis for either indolence or delinquency. Two plus two can equal anything from zero to six. Faced with this awkward scientific fact — which appears to seriously threaten psychology's status as an exact science — one common response of textbook authors has been to locate the various solutions to the equation (e.g. 0, 3.5, 4, 5, 6) in different sections of the text, possibly in the hope that this compartmentalization will go unnoticed (Harkins, 1987).

In contrast to this strategy, the main goal of this chapter has been to account for various forms of group performance — free-riding, loafing and soldiering, facilitation, compensation and labouring — in terms of a unified model of psychological process. This analysis has two core components. The first of these sees productivity as the outcome of a fit between features of task context and participants' self-categorization. In this way, productivity on individualized tasks is expected to be maximized where participants define themselves in terms of their personal identity, but productivity on group tasks (where contributions can be specialized or non-specialized) is expected to be optimal where participants define themselves in terms of a shared social identity. Conditions that allow for social identity-based interaction should also allow group productivity to *exceed* that of individuals working in isolation through its capacity to foster, amongst other things, information exchange, transactive memory systems and mutual influence.

Yet for all this, the second string to the social identity approach emphasizes the fact that, aside from what groups actually *do*, the *appraisal* of productivity and performance is itself a highly contestable act grounded in a particular social perspective. What *counts* as productivity, and judgements of what form it ought to take, will thus vary as a function of the relationship between performers and evaluators. The setting of objectives and the evaluation of productivity with respect to them is therefore 'a highly political process' in what is often a *multiple-constituency* environment (Pritchard, 1992, p. 456). The seriousness of this point is reflected in the final paragraph of Steiner's (1972) book, where he concludes:

> Though our knowledge of collective processes is still rather primitive, the most troublesome unanswered questions concern the goals toward which group productivity *should* be directed rather than the manner in which it *can* be directed. Achieving productivity will probably be easier than deciding what should be produced. (p. 186)

As an extreme illustration of this point, one could reflect on the labour of prisoners who worked on the notorious Burma–Thailand railway during the Second World War and their attempts to thwart the enemy through various acts of sabotage and subversion (e.g. see Dunlop, 1986; McCormack & Nelson, 1993). Were these instances of under-productive, counter-productive or hyper-productive behaviour? The answer, of course, is that it depends on whose goals and whose definition of productivity one sees as valid.

Having made these theoretical arguments, it becomes clear that the interpretation of previous research into group productivity has been hampered by two significant failings, both relating to issues of perspective. The first is simply that in most of the situations where researchers have drawn inferences about the behaviour of individuals in groups, their research has failed to study groups that are psychologically real and engaging for those individuals. This is particularly true in studies of social loafing and free-riding — phenomena that both appear to reflect the motivations and strategies of individuals who define themselves *as individuals* rather than as committed group members. Thus, as Harkins and Szymanski (1989) conclude, this research 'appears to have contributed little to the group literature' (p. 941).

The second problem arises from a tendency to define productivity in terms of the goals and values of researchers (or the interests they represent; e.g. those of managers and employers) rather than those of the research participants themselves. It is not hard to understand why this occurs, but it has at least three adverse consequences. The first is that it leads to group behaviour being dismissed as unproductive on all those occasions where the groups in question have goals and values that are discrepant from those of researchers. This leads researchers to over-emphasize the incidence of unproductive group behaviour, but it has the secondary effect of mystifying the processes that contribute to organizational productivity. The third and possibly most serious consequence, though, is that it leads researchers to belittle the perceptions and endeavours of those who work in groups.

This last tendency is most evident in research into the so-called 'illusion of group effectivity'. Faced with this phenomenon, one is invited by researchers to ponder how it is that group members can be so ignorant of their own shortcomings and so audacious in their self-belief. Based on the counter-arguments that have been presented in this chapter, it is tempting to turn this criticism back onto the researchers themselves. To do so may be harsh, but it may also help restore some balance to a debate in which the terms of reference perpetuate the interests of those with the power to demand and monitor performance, largely at the expense of those who are required to deliver it.

## Further Reading

One of the main features of the literature on group productivity is that while most of it is easy and interesting to read, the various strands of enquiry prove hard to integrate conceptually. This is largely because the array of subtly different paradigms, measures, technical terms and assumptions make it hard to make comparisons and connections between different research programmes and theories. Nonetheless, Steiner's (1972) text remains a landmark contribution because it attempts both to systematize research and to identify process-based links between the study of group productivity and research into other topics such as leadership and communication. Pritchard's (1992) chapter also offers a provocative but convincing discussion of the difficulties inherent in the productivity construct and organizational theorists' attempts to operationalize it.

At an empirical level the review by Williams et al. (1991) provides a very readable introduction to more recent work in the area and also incorporates some insights from the social identity approach. The same is true of the work reported by Harkins and Szymanski (1989) and Moreland et al. (1996). The latter also underscores the importance of a properly *social* cognitive approach to issues of group process along lines advocated in previous chapters. The research by Worchel et al. (1998) is equally imaginative and offers a thorough experimental exposition of key features of the social identity approach to group productivity.

Harkins, S. G. & Szymanski, K. (1989). Social loafing and group evaluation. *Journal of Personality and Social Psychology*, 56, 934-941.

Moreland, R. L., Argote, L. & Krishnan, R. (1996). Socially shared cognition at work: Transactive memory and group performance. In J. Nye & A. Brower (Eds.), *What's social about social cognition? Research on socially shared cognition in small groups* (pp. 57-84). Newbury Park, CA: Sage.

Pritchard, R. D. (1992). Organizational productivity. In M. D. Dunnette & L. M. Hough (Eds.), *Handbook of industrial and organizational psychology* (vol. 3, pp. 443-471). Palo Alto, CA: Consulting Psychologists Press.

Steiner, I. D. (1972). *Group process and productivity*. New York: Academic Press.

Williams, K., Karau, S. & Bourgeois, M. (1991). Working on collective tasks: Social loafing and social compensation. In M. A. Hogg & D. Abrams (Eds.), *Group motivation: Social psychological perspectives* (pp. 130-148). London: Harvester Wheatsheaf.

Worchel, S., Rothgerber, H., Day, A., Hart, D & Butemeyer, J. (1998). Social identity and individual productivity within groups. *British Journal of Social Psychology*, *37*, 389-413.

# 10 Collective Action and Industrial Protest

'One of these days mate, you're going to be sick, and you're going to need us. And when you do, I'll remember, mate. I'll know your face and you'll die'. (Neale, 1983, pp. 91-92)

These are strong words and, for the person to whom they were spoken, no doubt very disturbing. They were delivered through a loud-hailer by a worker on a picket line into the ear of a passing driver who had just told the assembled strikers to 'go back to work'. Significantly, this was not the sort of protester routinely identified in the media as a good-for-nothing troublemaker. She was a qualified nurse, otherwise softly spoken, caring and attentive to duty.

The incompatibility between the nurse's statement here and her professional role is striking. Nurses' job descriptions require them to save people's lives not to take them away. Thus we can assume that if the nurse had shown any trace of her picket-line sentiments in an initial job interview or during standardized personality testing she would have had to pursue another career. So how can we explain her behaviour and the obvious discontinuity between her actions here and what she might otherwise say and do in the course of her duty? What psychological processes have brought her to this point?

These questions are important because few things have as much impact on organizations as the mass dissent of employees. Indeed, if workers are seeking organizational change of some form, this can often *only* be achieved through collective action. This is especially true if negotiation to reduce conflict (as discussed in Chapter 7) has failed to reach a satisfactory outcome. For this reason, those who run organizations, or who are interested in maintaining the industrial status quo, have always been keen to understand the behaviour of collectives in order to keep it in check. Collective action was therefore one of the first topics to be formally discussed by social psychologists — with interest in the topic dating back to LeBon's (1895/1947) analysis of crowd behaviour.

Since that time the behaviour of a range of collectives — from large-scale social movements through to community-based action groups — has been examined through different theoretical lenses. This has given rise to diverse definitions of collective action (e.g. see Chapter 8 in Klandermans, 1997). However, in social psychological terms, collective action occurs when a person's behaviour is structured by a particular group membership (i.e. so that it is informed by *shared* values, norms and goals) and he or she acts in concert with other group members. Within organizations, this form of action is most commonly associated with the activities of trade unions whose members act collectively, usually to address some grievance with their employers. Like our nurse, they seek improvements to pay and working conditions, more security, greater input, or simply more respect.

An all-encompassing understanding of such action is not possible without a full appreciation of the social context in which it takes place. This must take into account issues of history, politics, economics and culture. For example, it is impossible to understand the 1984-5 British miners' strike without awareness of the history of relations between miners and mine owners, of the political imperatives of major political parties, of the legislative parameters within which the strike took place, or of the communities who were affected by it (e.g. see Samuel, Bloomfield & Boanas, 1986). Yet while these topics fall outside the domain of psychology, social psychologists *can* attempt to provide an account of individuals' understanding of these social arrangements and of how that understanding then contributes to subsequent attitudes and behaviour (Tajfel, 1979; Turner & Bourhis, 1996).

With this goal in mind, this chapter starts by reviewing different theories of collective action (following in the footsteps of excellent reviews by Kelly, 1993; Kelly & Breinlinger, 1996; see also Veenstra & Haslam, 2000). This is followed by an elaboration of the social identity approach, which explores the nature of the relationship between group identification, perceptions of social context and people's willingness to participate in collective action. A central message here is that while it has been customary in social psychology (as in the media and in lay theory), to impugn collective action as a product of the very lowest forms of psychological impulse and drive, it can in fact be seen as one of the clearest expressions of higher-order human sociality.

## An overview of research into collective action

### Primitive instincts

Reflecting on the statement with which this chapter began, it is not hard to imagine that many people would seek to explain the behaviour of the nurse as an irrational, perhaps even pathological, outburst. When dealing with the behaviour of an individual in isolation, this might be a plausible explanation. However, it becomes more problematic when attempting to explain the action of large groups of people.

Faced with this problem, some early researchers argued that the collective action of workers was best understood as a form of collective pathology reflecting a shared regression to pre-intellectual instincts of aggression and anarchy. Such arguments were central to LeBon's (1895/1947) analysis of crowd behaviour in which individuals were seen to lose a sense of personal accountability and submit to the forces of a collective unconscious. This idea was later developed by Allport (1924) as part of an argument which sought to explain the actions of striking workers as evidence of a pre-social 'struggle reflex' (see Reicher, 1987, p. 176). A similar idea underpins more recent studies of deindividuation which, as we noted in Chapter 6, suggest that in collectives individuals lose their sense of self and with it a sense of decency and self-control (e.g. Cannavale, Scarr & Pepitone, 1970; Zimbardo, 1969). In this vein, Weller (1985) explains unrest on picket lines as a situation in which there is:

> Chaos of mob violence and the sway of orators over crowds, when individual judgement is momentarily submerged in shared powerful emotions. (p. 295)

Unflattering as this analysis is, it is surpassed by the brutality of Weller's suggested intervention strategies. These include:

> Shifting attention, impelling a realization of personal identity and values, using even stronger stimuli than that which ignited the crowd (such as gunfire), dividing the opinions of the group and isolating the ringleaders. (p. 300)

Ideas such as these are still quite common in political and media discourse that portrays strikers as senseless animals or crazed political extremists. However, these ideas are rarely endorsed in formal contemporary treatments of industrial protest. This reflects an unwillingness on the part of researchers to commit themselves to the extreme remedies which the analysis logically dictates, together with a dearth of supporting evidence (see McPhail, 1991; Postmes & Spears, 1998; Reicher, 1982, 1987). Nonetheless, the legacy of this approach is apparent in the fact that in most textbooks, when they are discussed, strikes and industrial action are usually identified alongside sabotage and soldiering within a general class of undesirable and irrational organizational behaviours. In effect, then, 'the rabble hypothesis' (Mayo, 1949; see Chapter 1 above) continues to inform this area of organizational theory and industrial protest is seen largely as a nuisance phenomenon that defies clear understanding.

### Individual difference approaches

Individual difference approaches to collective action have generally attempted either to identify the personality profile of individuals who are likely to participate in collective action or to isolate factors that contribute to particular people making decisions of this form. At an early stage in research, Rotter, Seeman and Liverant (1962) suggested that *internal locus of control* — a person's belief that they can control events through their own behaviour — is a key determinant of collective action. Specifically, individuals who believe in their own self-efficacy are considered more likely to take part in collective action than those with an external locus of control, who perceive themselves as having little capacity to change the course of events in the world.

Somewhat akin to locus of control is *political efficacy* — a person's belief that he or she can have an impact on the political process (Fiske, 1987). Some evidence supports the view that this individual difference variable may partly predict collective action (e.g. Parry, Moyser & Day, 1992). However, Andrews (1991) argues that political efficacy cannot be viewed solely as an individual characteristic. She notes, for example, that if a socialist has a strong belief in the power of collective action, he or she may experience high levels of perceived political efficacy, not because this perception is unique to self, but because it is shared with other people as a result of membership in specific organizations. Here, then, political efficacy appears to be more a matter of group-based ideology than of personality. Accordingly, political efficacy and a willingness to participate in collective action might be better understood as an aspect of association and identification with particular *groups* rather than simply as a personality characteristic (Kelly & Breinlinger, 1996).

Another individual difference approach identifies *frustration–aggression* as the primary cause of participation in collective action (particularly by trade unions). Advocates of this view propose that individuals strive to achieve their personal goals and that if these are thwarted their psychological 'equilibrium' is disturbed by the experience of frustration, dissatisfaction, or alienation. Participation in trade union activities is then seen as a vehicle for restoring equilibrium. As outlined by Krech and Crutchfield (1948), this chain of events is as follows:

> It is safe to hazard a guess that most instances of industrial conflict can be characterized as constructive and healthy frustration reactions. That is, specific, consciously identified needs are frustrated. The worker, thus frustrated, recognizes management policies as the barriers intervening between him and his goals and he reacts by direct action against those barriers through striking or other forms of industrial conflict. (p. 547)

However, empirical studies typically yield weak correlations between job satisfaction and trade union participation (Klandermans, 1992; Nicholson, Ursell & Blyton, 1981). Moreover, Klandermans (1986) notes that the link between dissatisfaction and union participation is over-specified as union activities provide only one mechanism for reducing frustration or dissatisfaction in the workplace. If dissatisfaction underpins collective protest (and there are good reasons to suppose that on many occasions it may) it is still unclear why this manifests itself in the *particular* form of behaviour that it does.

In light of these problems, it has been proposed more recently that the extent of a person's *collectivist orientation* may predict their involvement in collective action (Triandis, Bontempo, Villareal, Asai & Lucca, 1988). While few studies have examined this link directly, evidence has been advanced for an indirect association (Smith & Bond, 1993). Because individuals with a collectivist orientation are believed to be more likely to (a) favour their own group over others, (b) show concern for group goals rather than personal goals, and (c) be susceptible to social influence, it is suggested that such individuals will also be more likely to participate in collective action (Kelly & Breinlinger, 1996).

Again though, it can be argued that the notion of a 'collectivistic orientation' as a personality attribute is of questionable utility. Not least, this is because the construct can easily become circular if willingness to participate in collective action is explained by a collectivist orientation but this in turn is defined by a willingness to participate in collective action. However, even when defined in these terms, empirical research suggests that the predictive ability of this individual difference variable is limited (e.g. Kelly & Kelly, 1994; see below).

*Cognitive approaches*

One significant variant on individual difference approaches is provided by Klandermans' (1984) *expectancy value model*. This is an individual decision-making approach that distinguishes between two phases of mobilization underlying participation in collective union-based action: *consensus mobilization* in which prospective action is brought to the attention of members and the union tries to elicit support from them; and *action mobilization* in which the union marshals members into activities so as to achieve its goals. The model claims that in this second phase individuals analyse perceived costs and benefits relating to their goals, social outcomes, and rewards. Their willingness to participate is then the weighted sum of these calculations (Klandermans, 1984, p. 108).

However, Klandermans (1986, 1997, p. 210) himself concedes that the assumption of individual rationality upon which this model is premised is questionable. Similarly, Kelly and Breinlinger (1996) argue that the assumption of rationality is especially strained in cases of protracted disputes. In these, union members often bear the financial and social burden of extreme hardship and are usually fully cognisant of the fact that personal benefits, if gained at all, may be slight (e.g. see Samuel et al., 1986). Indeed, for an individual, the rational action would appear to be to leave the union, let others do the protesting and then reap the benefits of any successes they achieve (individualistic behaviour common in a range of other social dilemmas; see Foddy et al., 1999; Messick, 1973). Again, then, a major limitation of this account is its denial of the *social* aspects of collective action. As Schrager (1985) points out, collective action is not merely an economic decision, instead it is heavily influenced by social and ideological factors.

On the basis of these arguments it seems reasonable to conclude that approaches which neglect social context, or which reduce willingness to participate in collective action to an individual's cost–benefit analysis, may have important limitations. Mindful of this, other researchers have been concerned to understand the social nature of collective action by focusing on the impact of group memberships on people's self-concept and their distinct contribution to attitudes and behaviour in particular settings.

### Relative deprivation

One group-based theory that has been at the forefront of collective action research is *relative deprivation theory* (Gurr, 1970). This focuses on individuals' perceptions of inequality between groups and its impact on cognition and behaviour. In so doing it unpacks some of the relatively underdeveloped ideas put forward by frustration–aggression theorists by attempting to specify the origins of frustration more fully. The theory suggests that people only feel frustrated — and only vent that frustration — when they perceive themselves to be worse off than others with whom they compare themselves. Significantly too, in order for such frustration to be felt, these others must be in some sense comparable with or equivalent to the perceiver — an idea similar to that which underpins equity theory (Thibaut & Walker, 1975; see Chapter 4 above). This argument proposes that people are sensitive not to injustice in the abstract but to *relative injustice*. How happy employees feel about their salary (and their judgements of whether it is high or low) will typically depend on whether it is higher or lower than that of the other people with whom they compare themselves (see Brown, 1978; Chapter 2 above).

Within this theory an important distinction has been made between personal and collective relative deprivation (after Runciman's, 1966, distinction between egoistic and fraternal relative deprivation). The latter refers to the feeling of deprivation experienced by individuals as members of a group and evidence suggests that only this form of deprivation leads to collective responses (Walker & Mann, 1987; Walker & Pettigrew, 1984). Under this analysis, a sense of identification with a group should motivate people into action because they experience discontent when they find that their group is disadvantaged relative to another (Hogg & Abrams, 1988; Kelly & Breinlinger, 1996).

However, as Klandermans (1997) points out, relative deprivation theory tends to take the outcome which is to be explained by the study of collective action too much for granted. He notes that it is much more common for feelings of injustice to be ignored than for them to be acted upon. Given this fact, the real question is not why collective action to redress industrial grievances occurs but why it occurs *so rarely*. A sense of relative deprivation may be a necessary condition for groups to revolt, but it is certainly not sufficient.

Another important issue here is that once it is understood as a group-based collective response rather than the egotistical one originally envisaged by Gurr (1970) and Crosby (1976), relative deprivation theory actually starts to look like a stripped-down version of social identity theory. This is because at core it mirrors a key hypothesis that we discussed in Chapter 2 — namely that group behaviour is often motivated by a need to establish, maintain or restore a positive definition of the social self. Along these lines, Walker and Pettigrew's (1984) influential review argued that relative deprivation theory only has explanatory force when it is focuses on experiences of collective deprivation and is therefore aligned with predictions from social identity theory. This point has been developed by Tougas and Veilleux (1988) who note that collective relative deprivation is conceptually related to social identification because the extent of a person's identification with an aggrieved group strongly influences their perception of disadvantage in the first place (Smith, Spears & Oyen, 1994; Taylor & McGarty, 1999; see Chapter 8). Women, for example, only become aware of their disadvantaged status in the workplace if they perceive themselves in terms of a gender-based social identity (i.e. as 'us women'; Fajak & Haslam, 1998; Skevington & Baker, 1989; see Tougas and Veilleux, 1988, below). Given this, it seems appropriate to ask whether our understanding of collective action could be further enhanced by drawing upon the full suite of hypotheses generated by the social identity approach.

## Social identity and collective action

As we have seen, many attempts to explore the determinants of individual participation in collective action have tended to neglect the contribution that social context and psychologically salient group membership make to shaping both attitudes and behaviour. Nonetheless, largely because the contribution of group membership is close to undeniable, it has been harder for researchers to ignore this factor in this area than in most of the others discussed in previous chapters. Indeed, in seeking to examine the psychology of collective action, social identity principles have figured very prominently (e.g. see Kelly, 1993; Simon, 1998; Wright, 1997).

In this regard it is worth noting that Klandermans' (1997; Klandermans & Oegema, 1992) more recent work on the social psychology of protest attempts to synthesize a number of the above approaches within an eclectic model that accounts for different phases of protest in terms of principles couched at different levels of analysis (see Figure 10.1). Here individual cognitive principles are invoked to account for people's initial perception of grievance and their identification with a group such that 'injustice and agency are beliefs shared by people who have the same social identity and a common enemy' (Klandermans, 1997, p. 208). Group-level principles of socialization are then recruited to account for the processes by which these perceptions are given common meaning and individuals become motivated. Finally, organizational and structural principles are used to explain how people and resources (e.g. time, money, energy) are actually mobilized and barriers to action overcome.

Yet while arguing that these different components of protest must be understood in terms of discrete processes operating at different levels, Klandermans (1997; de Weerd & Klandermans, 1999) also identifies the potential for unitary analysis. This argument is based on observations that:

> Sharedness of beliefs ... [is] the binding element. However, sharedness of belief presupposes a common social identity. Indeed, ... collective identity *is* a key concept in the social psychology of protest. Protest is staged by people who c[o]me to share a continuous identity, who share anger about injustice done to them, and who share the conviction that collectively they can act and exact changes from those whom they hold responsible. ... A social psychology of protest, then, is about how people develop such common social identities. (p. 211)

Consistent with this argument, when we look over the range of factors that Klandermans identifies as contributing to collective action it is possible to see all as flowing from principles that were outlined in Chapter 2 — a point represented schematically in Figure 10.1 below. Thus the reality of conflict, awareness of a common fate and of a common enemy should increase the comparative fit of a shared social self-categorization (Haslam & Turner, 1992; Simon et al., 1995; Wilder & Thompson, 1988). As well as this, participants should be more likely to define themselves in terms of a given social self-categorization to the extent that it has prior meaning and so is accessible to them. For this reason collective action tends to be orchestrated around pre-existing identities — for example, as a member of a union or of a particular interest group (Simon, 1998; Simon et al., 1998). Following social identity theory, other social structural factors should also contribute to group-based self-definition of this form (see Kelly & Breinlinger, 1996; Wright et al., 1990). Specifically, direct collective challenges to a high-status outgroup should be most likely to occur when group boundaries are impermeable and status-based group relations are perceived to be unstable and illegitimate (i.e. insecure; see Figure 2.5a).

When rendered salient by these various factors, social identity should provide workers with a common perspective on reality, and align and render more homogeneous their otherwise unique experiences of injustice and grievance. It should also provide a psychological platform for *new* experiences, as the behaviour of individual group members becomes oriented towards and structured by *emergent* norms that define what is appropriate (prototypical) group action in the prevailing context (Reicher, 1987; see Chapter 6 above). However, as well as this, shared identity should also act as a basis and motivation for mutual

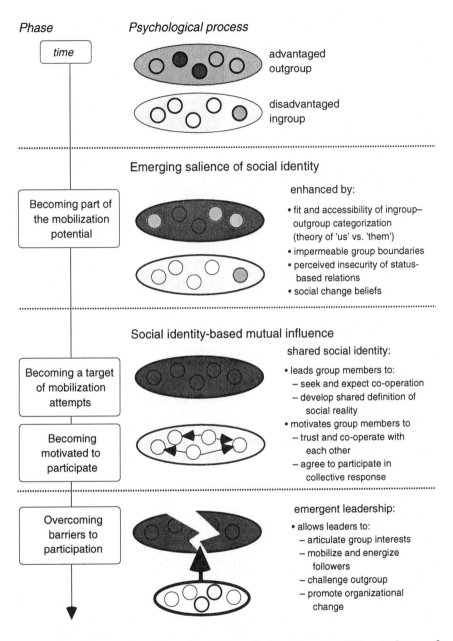

Phase

Psychological process

time

advantaged outgroup

disadvantaged ingroup

Emerging salience of social identity

Becoming part of the mobilization potential

enhanced by:

- fit and accessibility of ingroup–outgroup categorization (theory of 'us' vs. 'them')
- impermeable group boundaries
- perceived insecurity of status-based relations
- social change beliefs

Social identity-based mutual influence

Becoming a target of mobilization attempts

Becoming motivated to participate

shared social identity:

- leads group members to:
  - seek and expect co-operation
  - develop shared definition of social reality
- motivates group members to
  - trust and co-operate with each other
  - agree to participate in collective response

Overcoming barriers to participation

emergent leadership:

- allows leaders to:
  - articulate group interests
  - mobilize and energize followers
  - challenge outgroup
  - promote organizational change

*Figure 10.1* The contribution of social identity processes to different phases of collective action (as identified by Klandermans & Oegema, 1992; see also Simon, 1998)

*Note*: ·············· = barrier to collective action (point at which movement towards collective action can break down) influence, so that social interaction serves to galvanize and consensualize perceptions (Haslam, Turner, Oakes, McGarty & Reynolds, 1998; Turner, 1987a; Wright, 1997). These perceptions should include those that pertain to the potential costs and benefits of any prospective course of action and should contribute to a motivational goal of *collective* self-actualization (along lines discussed in Chapters 4 and 8 above).

Here too, the role and judgements of leaders who represent and are empowered by the group may be critical as they will often have responsibility for decisions of strategy and resource mobilization. Other group members will also play a distributed leadership role in solving the strategic problems of others around them and in persuading waverers of the worth of the cause and of the surmountability of obstacles to participation ('I'll give you a lift', 'Come on, that can wait till later'). In this way, both intellectual and material resources will be mobilized to remove potential barriers to action. Consistent with this idea, Tannenbaum and Kahn (1957) found that union action was highest where both leaders and rank-and-file members felt they had control of, and input into, union activities.

Again though, as we argued in Chapters 3 and 8, leaders will only be in a position to mobilize resources and to motivate and act on behalf of followers to the extent that they have a vision that is perceived to be grounded in what the group *is* and what it needs to do to promote its collective interests. Leaders who are not perceived by followers to reflect the group's interest will be ineffectual, and the same will be true of followers led by unrepresentative leaders (Haslam & Platow, in press; Hollander, 1985).

In this way it is apparent that a collective sense of self grounded in a shared social identity plays an instrumental role in an array of processes that contribute to collective action. Moreover, we can see that the potential for collective action *not* to occur is also considerable. In particular, collective action is precluded when individuals choose to pursue a strategy of individual mobility, when a common identity is not accessible or meaningful, or when formal leaders and representatives are not perceived to represent group interests. In all these cases social and structural barriers to collective action will be perceived, and prove, to be insurmountable.

Looked at as a whole, a core element of this analysis is that industrial protest reflects, and is made possible by, a *redefinition* of self (not a *loss* of self, as originally argued by LeBon, 1895/1947). Indeed, collective action of this form provides one of the clearest examples of depersonalized behaviour based on a highly salient social self-categorization. Moreover, where such action has tended to be seen as poorly targeted, senseless and inchoate (along the lines of 'the rabble hypothesis' against which Mayo, 1949, railed), the social identity approach sees it as a meaningful, collective response to a particular configuration of intergroup relations. This is shown particularly clearly in Reicher's (1982, 1987) studies of crowd behaviour where, far from being indiscriminate, the behaviour of protesters is found to have clear targets and boundaries with both being defined by the specific meaning of the conflict for participants.

A key issue here is one of perspective. The rabble hypothesis reflects the view of *outsiders*, opposed to the actions of strikers with no sensitivity to their social or psychological predicament. The present analysis, on the other hand, attempts to explain and understand the actions of workers in terms of the social realities that they themselves confront. This is not to say that all industrial protest is good or should be actively encouraged. Whether it is good or bad is a completely different matter (see Tannenbaum, 1965). Instead the point is that, as psychologists, it makes little sense to attempt to explain the activities of people with reference to a set of group-based norms, values and goals that is not informing their own actions. This is an argument that we have developed throughout this book (e.g. in Chapters 6 and 9). Thus the nurse's outrage makes no sense if we think of her either as an individual, as a member of a social category that is not salient (e.g. as a woman) or as a member of a social category defined by another comparative context (e.g. within a patient-nurse relationship). However, her behaviour makes much more sense if understood as that of a group member engaged in a struggle with an employer perceived to be uncaring, callous, and indifferent. Here the actions of the man in the car exemplify exactly what nurses are collectively fighting against, and her response — reflecting, and supported by, the views of other group members — is a meaningful contribution to that fight. As Neale (1983) concludes in his own insider's account of the nurses' strike:

> The feeling was there. The solidarity was there. ... We are being attacked as a class. It's a serious matter. We have to fight as a class, in a serious manner. If we don't, we'd better pray our children don't get sick. (p. 107)

## Some empirical tests of the social identity approach

*Social identification and the perception of social injustice*

A key argument in the above analysis is that the *fact* of social injustice is not enough to motivate members of disadvantaged groups to act collectively to improve their lot. Instead, at least two conditions have to be satisfied before the potential for such action exists. First, any injustice has to be internalized and subjectively experienced by those who are victims of it and, second, this experience has to be perceived as something the individual shares with other members of a relevant ingroup rather than something he or she is suffering alone.

As part of a research programme that is highly relevant to the above predictions, Tougas and Veilleux (1988) conducted a study of Canadian women's responses to affirmative action programmes in the workplace. The women, who came from a range of occupational backgrounds, were asked questions related to their identification with other women, their perceptions of inequality, their dissatisfaction with women's situation in the workforce and their attitudes towards gender-based affirmative action. Affirmative action was defined as comprising 'programmes which aim at increasing the percentage of women in the higher levels of the hierarchy as well as in job categories traditionally held by men' (Tougas & Veilleux, 1988, p. 20). As part of an experimental manipulation, the procedures associated with this programme were also described differently in different versions of the questionnaire. In one version, affirmative action was described as a strategy in which women would be given preference over equally qualified men in job appointments; in the other version the policy was described as one which would simply remove discriminatory practices from the workplace. Having obtained responses, the researchers conducted structural modelling in order to identify factors that contributed to positive attitudes towards this programme.

Consistent with a predictive model derived from social identity theory, the authors found that identification with other women and the subjective experience of collective injustice (leading to a sense of dissatisfaction) were major determinants of whether or not women supported the affirmative action programme. Support for the programme was also independently affected by the way in which it was described. Women were more supportive of affirmative action when it was described as involving procedures for removing discrimination than when it was described in terms of procedures which could themselves be seen as discriminatory. Interestingly too, this experimental manipulation also affected respondents' support for the goals of affirmative action, even though these were stated identically in both versions of the questionnaire.

Yet as Smith et al. (1994) observe, although Tougas and Veilleux's study is very instructive, one problem it shares with other work into experiences of collective injustice, is that its design is correlational rather than experimental. Thus while it appears that a salient social identity leads to collective action, the causal link here may be reversed. Indeed, it seems highly likely that collective action does in fact enhance social identity salience as part of an ongoing dynamic. More problematically, though, both phenomena could be caused by a third factor of the form envisaged within other theories of collective action (e.g. a sense of political efficacy).

To rule out possibilities of this form, Smith et al. (1994, Experiment 1) conducted an experimental study in which participants were randomly assigned to conditions where their group membership (as psychology students) was or was not made salient. As well as this, the experimenter told all participants that she was going to have trouble paying them because 'I just got a memo from my adviser in the States yesterday telling me that due to budget problems, the original grant from the United States Education and Science Agency has been cut in half' (Smith et al., 1994, p. 282). As a result, only half of the participants in the study were ostensibly paid: 3 of 11 psychology students and 8 of 11 economics students. Whether participants were themselves one of the three lucky psychology students was varied between conditions along with social identity salience.

Unsurprisingly, participants tended to be more aggrieved when they were not paid than when they were. However, non-paid participants were most likely to report a feeling of injustice in the condition where their social identity was made salient. That is, as predicted by social identity principles, participants' sense of deprivation was greatest when they were attuned to the fact that their loss was shared with other group members.

As well as this, group-primed participants who *did* receive payment reported the lowest sense of deprivation. The authors explain this second effect in terms of self-categorization theory's comparative fit principle in conjunction with identity-management strategies for self-enhancement. That is, they argue that successful members of the low-status group made interpersonal (rather than intergroup) comparisons because these allowed them to them to see themselves as better off (and better) than other ingroup members.

These arguments were supported in a second study which examined the possibility that the relatively positive response of group-primed 'winners' could arise from ignorance of the ingroup's plight. In this study as well as stating how they themselves felt, participants were asked to reflect on the experience of a typical ingroup member. Results on this measure eliminated ignorance of ingroup members' fate as a possible explanation of the effect. Indeed, it seemed that these 'winners' felt good *precisely because* they were aware of how well they had done relative to other ingroup members. As the authors wistfully observe 'the salience of group membership did not encourage personally gratified subjects to challenge the distribution of the pie, it only made their slice of it taste sweeter' (Smith et al., 1994, p. 298).

The results of these studies thus make it clear that social identity salience in the face of collective injustice is not a general spur to collective action. In particular, this is because there is considerable potential for people from low-status groups who 'make good' or 'get lucky' to become particularly committed advocates of the high-status group's ideology of individual mobility (see Gelineau & Merenda, 1981). One reason why such individuals develop conservative convictions of this form is that the ideology of 'opportunity for all' provides a fitting explanation of their own experience as 'self-made' success stories. Token winners are therefore likely to be a major impediment to collective action. The same is true of the overall strategy of tokenism — a point we return to below.

*Social identification as a determinant of willingness to participate in industrial action*

Yet, leaving the issue of tokenism aside for the time being, a fundamental implication of the social identity analysis is that identification with a relevant social category should be a much better predictor of collective action than the range of individual-based variables considered important by other theorists. This hypothesis has been tested by theorists in a range of domains (e.g. Reicher, 1987; Platow & Hunter, in press). However, research into industrial protest has been dominated by the work of Kelly and Kelly (e.g. C. Kelly, 1993; C. Kelly & Breinlinger, 1996; C. Kelly & J. Kelly, 1994; J. Kelly & C. Kelly, 1992).

One particularly telling study involved 350 local government employees who were members of a white-collar trade union in London (Kelly & Kelly, 1994). The study's goal was to identify which of a range of potentially important psychological variables was the best predictor of willingness to engage in union-based collective action. The authors looked at a number of different forms of action with statistical analysis differentiating between two key types: 'easy' (e.g. attending meetings and discussing union activities) and 'difficult' (e.g. standing for election as an official, speaking at meetings).

The results of this study are presented in Table 10.1 below. As is clear from this table, the authors found that identification with the union was the best predictor of both easy and difficult forms of action. Indeed, it was the *only* predictor of the harder forms. The only other general predictor was negative stereotyping of the management outgroup — a measure of the difference between the participants' responses to a number of questions (e.g. 'trade unions have too

*Table 10.1* Predictors of union-based collective action (regression coefficients from Kelly & Kelly, 1994, p. 74)

| | Form of Participation | | |
| --- | --- | --- | --- |
| Predictor | All | Easy | Hard |
| Identification with union | .63* | .54* | .62* |
| Stereotypic views of management | .16* | .19* | .07 |
| Collectivist orientation | .07 | .15* | .07 |
| Collective relative deprivation | .07 | .06 | .07 |
| Egotistical relative deprivation | −.02 | −.02 | −.02 |
| Political efficacy | −.02 | −.01 | −.05 |
| Perceived intergroup conflict | −.05 | −.06 | −.02 |

*Note:* * = significant correlation ($p < .05$)

great a say in the running of the country') and those they expected 'a typical manager' to make (after Allen & Stephenson, 1983). Union members were more willing to participate in union activities to the extent that they differentiated between their own responses and those they considered likely to be produced by a manager.

In contrast, none of the variables associated with the other theoretical approaches reviewed above emerged as significant predictors (collectivist orientation, political self-efficacy, egotistical or collective relative deprivation). Interestingly too, the mere perception of conflict did not predict willingness to participate. Thus, conflict was only related to industrial action where it was an aspect of a *theory* of conflictual intergroup relations — associated with a belief that 'those managers' see the world differently to 'us workers'. This finding is consistent with the argument that conflict has to be internalized — as something in which the collective self is implicated — before it precipitates reaction. In this vein, the authors conclude by painting a picture in which:

> The potential group activist [is] a person who is firmly committed to a 'them and us' representation of intergroup relations, having a strong sense of identification with the ingroup and a clear perception of difference between ingroup and outgroup members, grounded in a general collectivist orientation. (Kelly & Kelly, 1994, p. 78)

Although very important, one of the interesting questions left unanswered by this research is whether the impact of identification is in any way mediated by features of the social context that union members confront. Do high and low identifiers react differently to different organizational circumstances? One question of particular significance is how these group members respond to issues of threat and conflict.

In relation to the presence of threat, it follows from social identity theory that people who identify highly with a group (for whom there is greater potential for threat-induced negative self-esteem in intergroup contexts) should be more inclined to protect their social identity by dealing with any threats collectively. One way in which they may do this is by accentuating intragroup homogeneity thereby emphasizing group solidarity. Low identifiers on the other hand may cope with threats to identity by opting for individualistic strategies. As Doosje et al. (1995) argue, low identifiers may represent their ingroup as being relatively heterogeneous so that they can differentiate themselves, as individuals, from other ingroup members and thus disassociate themselves from the group. Where high identifiers die hard, low identifiers may quietly withdraw.

Direct support for these arguments is provided in a range of empirical studies reported by Doosje et al. (1995), Karasawa (1991), Kelly (1989) and Spears et al. (1997). These indicate that high identifiers not only see their group as more homogeneous but show a propensity to 'stand and fight' in the face of threat. On the other hand, low identifiers emphasize the heterogeneity of the group and demonstrate 'at best indifference' to its future (Ellemers, Spears & Doosje, 1997, p. 625). With regard to collective action, then, it would seem that in situations of conflict or threat, only those who identify highly with the group would strive for unity and 'stand and fight' while low identifiers might be expected to 'bail out' at the first sign of trouble.

In order to investigate this possibility, Veenstra and Haslam (2000) conducted a study examining the willingness of 300 union members to participate in both easy and difficult forms of union activity. The study was conducted in mid-1997 at a time when the newly elected Australian federal government was in the process of introducing a range of policies designed to reform industrial relations and the nature of employer–employee relations. Central to this policy was the introduction of a new Workplace Relations Act which sought to replace the right to union-mediated collective bargaining with individually negotiated contracts.

The study had a survey format, but different versions of a questionnaire drew attention to different features of the prevailing industrial and political landscape. Specifically, union members were asked to indicate their willingness to participate in union activities in response to one of three questionnaires, each of which located these activities within a different frame of reference. In a *control* condition, participants responded without any reference being made to the broader context, as in Kelly and Kelly's (1994) study. A *conflict* condition referred explicitly to the conflict between the Federal government and unions in terms of recent changes to industrial relations legislation. Finally, in a third *conflict + threat* condition, participants were also made aware of the threat which those reforms posed to all union members.

As expected, the results of the study suggested that group identification plays a significant role both in shaping a person's perceptions of their union ingroup and in predisposing them to collective action. Specifically, those who identified more strongly with the union perceived there to be more solidarity within it — a finding that replicates previous research by Doosje et al. (1995), Karasawa (1991) and Kelly (1989). This sense of solidarity was associated with perceptions of greater ingroup homogeneity, a stronger sense of 'us and them', faith in processes of collective bargaining, and a belief that consensus among union members was both more important and more likely (cf. Haslam, 1997; Haslam, Turner, Oakes, McGarty & Reynolds, 1998; Turner, 1991).

Replicating the results of Kelly and Kelly (1994), it was also found that those who identified strongly with the union were more willing to engage in union activities than low identifiers. This willingness also varied as a function of response context, so that respondents were generally more willing to participate when the questionnaire referred to both conflict and threat than they were in other conditions.

Importantly though, as can be seen from Figure 10.2, response context did not have a uniform impact on high and low identifiers. When high identifiers were confronted with information referring to union–government conflict, and regardless of whether or not threat was mentioned, they responded by indicating a greater willingness to participate in collective action — in effect, they were prepared to 'stand and fight' (Ellemers et al., 1997). However, reference to conflict alone had quite the opposite effect on low identifiers. As had previously been found by Doosje et al. (1995) and Ellemers et al. (1997), these participants responded to this situation by showing a marked *de*crease in their willingness to participate in collective action. This is consistent with the view that here they were attempting to psychologically disassociate themselves from the ingroup. However, when the ingroup–outgroup division was specified further by referring not only to intergroup conflict but also to the associated threat that the outgroup posed to the ingroup, there was no evidence of 'bailing out' on the part of these low identifiers.

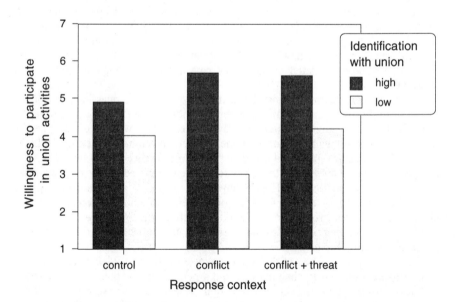

*Figure 10.2*  Union members' willingness to participate in future union activities as a function of identification and response context (from Veenstra & Haslam, 2000)

Clearly a number of factors may have contributed to the relative vigour of low identifiers faced with conflict and threat. First, it may simply have been the case that for these participants 'bailing out' and denying or avoiding the need for action was no longer a viable response to the threat they confronted. As suggested by Wright et al. (1990), low identifiers' expression of some renewed willingness to participate in collective action may here simply have been a by-product of their desire to protect their own personal interests. Low identifiers may stand and fight only when they can no longer run and hide.

On the other hand, taking a less cynical view, this situation may have represented the very set of circumstances which *all* union members recognize as necessitating some form of solidarity-based action (along lines suggested by Fosh, 1993). This view would suggest that low identifiers are strategic in their choice of *which* battles to fight, but still recognize that there are some that need fighting. More formally too, it can be argued that in this condition the salience and self-relevance of a union-based self-categorization became much clearer for all participants (as suggested by the main effect for response context).

But whatever its precise explanation, the pattern revealed in Figure 10.2 is critical as it suggests that collective action does not result from chronic psychological factors, but rather is a meaningful response to subjectively apprehended features of social reality. Because high and low identifiers have a *different* perspective on the social world, each responds to variations in context in a different way. Social identification therefore achieves its effects not because it is an individual difference, but because it is the expression of a person's position in relation to a particular group-based reality (Turner & Oakes, 1997).

Taken as a whole, then, research suggests that willingness to engage in group-based collective action depends both on identification with the group (Kelly & Kelly, 1994) *and* the frame of reference and informational content to which group members are exposed (Veenstra & Haslam, 2000). This is consistent with the view that collective action is underpinned by social identity salience and hence requires a social self-category to be both accessible *and* fitting (Oakes, 1987). Accordingly, we can see that rather than being the over-eager participants in industrial action that committed union members are popularly portrayed to be, their reactions to the social world are highly sensitive to specific features of the social and political reality that they confront at any given point in time. Like all other forms of organizational behaviour, collective action does not emerge or express itself in a vacuum, but is structured by the psychological realities associated with group life and its changeable exigencies.

## The impact of perceived social structure

Having started to integrate issues of identification and social context, we are now in a position to consider the broader role that social structure plays in disposing individuals to collective action. What form does conflict have to take, and in what ways must it be understood, before people are ready to take arms collectively against their troubles?

In presenting the core hypotheses of social identity theory in Chapters 2 and 8, it was argued that individual members of a disadvantaged (e.g. low-status or low-power) group should be more likely to band together and challenge an advantaged outgroup under specific social structural conditions. In particular, this form of action is anticipated when relations between the groups are insecure (in the sense of being unstable and illegitimate) and boundaries between the groups are impermeable (see Figure 2.5a; after Tajfel & Turner, 1979). Moreover, the influence of these factors should be heightened to the extent that individuals are culturally and politically predisposed to a social change belief system, rather than one of social mobility.

Taking these ideas together, we could therefore locate individuals on a continuum in terms of the likelihood of their seeking out and contributing to collective action. A person particularly unlikely to take this course would be someone located within a culture and political environment that encourages people to think about the world as a meritocratic melting-pot in which individuals are constrained only by their imagination and talent, and where this is in fact true. On the other hand, an environment in which people are sensitized to the reality of hardened intergroup boundaries is most likely to dispose someone to collective action.

History, of course, provides many examples of both these extremes. As Kelly and Breinlinger (1996) observe, conservative disciples of Mrs Thatcher and her view that 'there is no such thing as society' are particularly unlikely to strike, while members of the unions with which her government came into conflict — and for whom her vision of 'opportunity for all' appeared to be a flagrant lie — saw little other option. Moreover, it is clear that injunctions for workers to think of themselves, and to be treated, as individuals have been a major contributor to a recent decline in work-based collective protest (Taylor et al., 1987).

Beyond this historical evidence, though, a major empirical programme conducted by Wright, Taylor and colleagues has sought to test social identity principles directly (Taylor et al., 1987; Wright, 1997; Wright et al., 1990; Wright & Taylor, 1998; see also Lalonde & Silverman, 1994; Reynolds et al., in press). Generally speaking, this research has involved manipulating those elements of social structure predicted to impact upon social change beliefs and induce collective behaviour.

In a seminal study of this form, Taylor et al. (1987, Experiment 1) created a situation in which participants were led to believe they were taking part in a study of decision-making ability. The importance of decision-making in the 'real world' was emphasised and participants were told that, 'as in the real world', they would start the experiment in a low-status group of unsophisticated decision makers. Events in the remainder of the study would determine whether they made it into the high-status group of sophisticated decision-makers. The participants then completed a task designed to assess their decision-making ability. In this they had to respond to questions about a stabbing incident that was the centre of a criminal court case. Having done this, they were given feedback from members of the high-status group about their performance and its consequences. All participants were told that they needed a score of 8.5 more on the task to gain entry to the high-status group. To make the prospect of gaining entry into this group even more attractive, they were told that sophisticated decision makers would be entered into a draw with a prize of $100, while those in the unsophisticated group would be in a draw for a meagre $10 prize.

It was here that things started to get interesting because this feedback was in fact bogus and its content depended on the experimental condition to which participants had been randomly assigned. In all conditions participants were told that they had failed to make it into the high-status group. However, the distributive and procedural justice of this decision, and hence its overall legitimacy, varied across four conditions. For half of the participants the distributive basis of the decision to exclude them from the high-status group seemed quite legitimate because they were shown a very good example of the sort of judgements required. However, for the other half the decision seemed unjust because they were given a very poor example of what constituted sophisticated decisions. As well as this, the procedural justice of the decision was manipulated by informing half the participants that the decision had been made on the basis of very strict criteria, and the other half that the judges' criteria were very subjective.

The key measures in which the researchers were interested were how participants would react to this feedback. Given a choice, would they (a) go along with the verdict of the high-status group, (b) ask for an individual retest, (c) make a personal written protest to the high-status group, or (d) solicit the support of other participants to present a petition of protest to the high-status group?

The pattern of participants' preference for these options provided evidence of the role that the perceived illegitimacy of intergroup relations plays in promoting collective action. Here acceptance was the participants' preferred option where the outgroup's actions were distributively and procedurally just. However, collective action was much more popular when the outgroup's response was distributively and procedurally unjust — that is, where relations where perceived to be especially illegitimate. Results of a second experiment also suggested that this desire for collective protest was stronger when participants' perceptions of grievance were heightened by their being close to the cut-off for entry into the high-status group rather than far away.

In subsequent research, Wright et al. (1990) modified this paradigm in an attempt to examine the impact of the permeability of group boundaries on willingness to participate in collective action. The framework for this research was similar to that of Taylor et al.'s (1987) studies, but it involved different manipulations of feedback from the high-status outgroup, and a greater range of response options.

In this study half of the participants were told their score was very *near* to that required for entry to the high-status group, while the other half were told that they had missed out by a large margin. As well as this, participants were given different information about exactly how the scores of the low-status group members had been dealt with. In an *open* condition, participants were simply told that they had not reached the designated score and hence would not be admitted. In a range of *quota* conditions, participants were told that the high-status group had decided to set a quota restricting entry into its ranks to a limited number of low-status group members. Indeed, participants in the near conditions were told that they had actually secured the mark required for entry (they obtained scores of 8.8), but had been excluded from the high-status group on the basis of this quota. No reasons were given for this, in various conditions participants were only told that the high-status group had decided to allow entry to 30 per cent, 2 per cent or 0 per cent of participants who had obtained the required mark. These three quotas thus meant that entry to the high-status group was either reasonably open, virtually closed, or completely closed.

As in Taylor et al.'s (1987) earlier studies, the researchers were interested in how participants would react to this feedback. Here though, the choices were to (a) go along with the verdict of the high-status group, (b) ask for an individual retest, (c) make a personal written protest to the high-status group, (d) ask for a collective retest of all participants, or (e) make a collective written protest to the high-status group. Significantly, participants were told that retests (options (b) and (d)) were approved by the high-status group, but that protests (options (c) and (e)) were frowned upon. The final option (e) was thus a collective response to the high-status group that explicitly challenged its authority. It was an act of collective rebellion.

The responses of participants near and far from the pre-determined cut-off score (8.5) were quite similar, although participants near to the cut-off were more likely to protest and less likely to accept the judges' outcome or ask for a collective retest. However, in line with social identity theory, participants' preference for the five behavioural options, varied significantly as a function of the way in which the sophisticated group appeared to have managed the exercise. As can be seen from Figure 10.3, participants in the more open conditions preferred to accept this outgroup's judgement or ask for an individual re-test (an action approved by the outgroup). However, in the totally closed condition, collective protest was much the preferred option. Significantly though, this

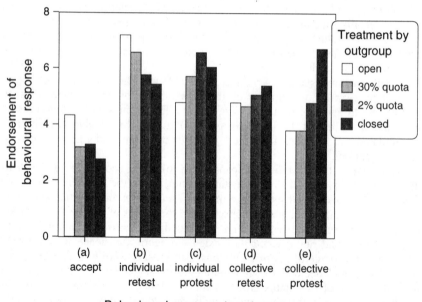

*Figure 10.3* Low-status group members' willingness to engage in different forms of action as a function of their treatment (from Wright et al., 1990)

option was not particularly attractive in any of the other conditions — even in the condition where the possibility of entry into the high-status group was extremely remote (2 per cent). In this virtually closed condition the preferred strategy was one of individual protest. So, in effect, these participants wanted to prosecute their case for unfair treatment individually rather than become involved in class action.

This intriguing pattern of results has since been replicated by Lalonde and Silverman (1994) and Reynolds et al. (in press; see Chapter 8 above). However, Lalonde and Silverman's study extended Wright et al.'s findings by showing that support for collective action under conditions of boundary impermeability also varied as a function of social identity salience. As predicted on the basis of social identity principles, participants whose shared group membership was made salient by the experimenters were more likely to opt for collective action in closed conditions than those whose personal identity had been invoked.

Yet of all the effects to emerge from Wright et al.'s original study, probably the most striking is the very different manner in which participants in the virtually closed (2 per cent quota) and totally closed (0 per cent) conditions reacted. The practical difference between these conditions was negligible, and yet the remotest possibility that they might gain entry into the high-status group was sufficient to deter the participants from collective protest. As Wright and Taylor (1998) observe:

> The implications of this pattern of results are disquieting in the sense that 'tokenism' would appear to be an effective means by which advantaged groups can engage in discriminatory practices with little chance of provoking group-level confrontation. (p. 648)

Accordingly, it is on this issue of tokenism that much of Wright's subsequent work has focused. In the first instance, this has extended his original research by replicating the above patterns in the context of real group memberships. Thus Wright and Taylor (1998, Experiment 1) showed that students who were denied access to a high-status group on the basis of their faculty membership (e.g. because they were management students) were less likely to support collective action in the context of a restrictive quota rather than a completely exclusive one.

As well as this, a second study showed that the opportunity for individuals to interact with other students to discuss their grievances before the quota was imposed did not help to increase their disposition to collective action (Wright & Taylor, 1998, Experiment 2). The design of the study did not allow for a full test of a social identity model (which would have predicted an enhanced willingness to engage in collective action after interaction with other students in a closed condition), but nonetheless this finding is consistent with the argument that interaction-based influence will not contribute to enhanced consensus or group motivation unless individuals' behaviour is grounded in a shared social identity (see Haslam, Turner, Oakes, Reynolds et al., 1998). In the absence of social identification, interaction is unable to provide consensualizing impetus to collective action and so the dulling effects of tokenism thrive.

Some further support for this argument comes from a final series of studies reported by Wright (1997). The first of these showed that participants subjected to tokenistic strategies *could* become more disposed to collective action when alerted to the illegitimacy of those strategies by messages from an ingroup member. In this study a confederate of the experimenter read out the feedback from the high-status judges explaining why the participant had been unsuccessful. In the process he or she referred (or did not refer) to the feedback as 'discrimination' and also indicated (or did not indicate) that he or she was angry. As predicted, collective protest and requests for a collective remark were more likely when the fellow victim labelled the feedback discriminatory and showed anger. As well as this, labelling the feedback discriminatory increased participants' perception that the outgroup was being unjust and the display of anger also heightened perceptions that the conditions of the low-status ingroup could be improved. Predisposition to collective action was also enhanced in a second experiment in which the feedback from the outgroup made it clear that the participants' ingroup as a whole was being discriminated against, rather than just them personally.

Taken as a whole, then, the body of work on responses to various forms of personal and social injustice, is highly consistent with the analysis of collective action that we presented earlier in this chapter (see Figure 10.1). It reinforces the view that individuals have a *propensity* to engage in collective action, but that in contemporary society a number of factors militate against this outcome. In particular, in the context of a widespread faith in the ideology of personal mobility, individuals from disadvantaged groups may resile from collective action whenever they benefit from opportunities for individual-based advancement (as in Smith et al., 1994) or where there is the slightest prospect that they might. Moreover, their faith in individual action is only likely to waver when attempts at social influence are grounded in shared group membership and *explain* their plight as a *collective* injustice.

Although only a small part of this research is directed specifically towards organizational issues (and most has focused on the formative stages of collective action; i.e. the top portions of Figure 10.1), its relevance for the analysis of industrial protest is clear. In the first instance, it serves as a partial explanation of the fact that industrial action is relatively rare (particularly in English-speaking Western countries). As well as this, it also indicates how any inclination to take part in collective action can be dampened by structural arrangements that promise individual mobility but deliver social injustice.

This last point is one of which most organizational élites appear to be well aware. Thus even though *theories* of organizational psychology are largely incompatible with the ideas discussed in this chapter, the *practice* of management typically shows acute sensitivity to them. Indeed, as Warhurst and Thompson (1998) observe (and as we remarked in Chapters 6 and 8), a prominent feature of contemporary managerial practice is an ability to preserve a discontinuity between the *rhetoric* of equality and participatory democracy and the *reality* of social exclusivity and hierarchical control. Moreover, this strategy has proved, and is likely to remain, immensely successful — at least from the perspective of those with an interest in quarantining organizations from major *employee-motivated* structural change.

## Conclusion

The material discussed in this chapter notwithstanding, the most striking feature of organizational research into the psychology of collective action is its conspicuous absence. Indeed, as King and Anderson (1995, p. 177) lament, in recent years organizational psychology has quietly drawn a veil over the topic. Testament to this fact, amongst a representative sample of ten major organizational texts none have index entries for 'collective action' or 'industrial protest', while only four have entries for 'strikes' and three for 'unions'. Of these, the most extensive coverage is provided by Muchinsky (1997, pp. 431-433) and this focuses primarily on the *effects* of strikes (e.g. in terms of lost income and productivity) rather than their *causes*.

Reflecting on this reluctance to study industrial unrest, Gordon and Nurick (1981; see also Huszczo, Wiggins & Currie, 1984) note that there are a number of reasons why studies of union action have proved unpopular amongst organizational psychologists. In the first instance they note that there is a reticence on the part of unions to participate in such research as they tend to view psychology as 'just another tool of the clever manager' (p. 294). Surveying the history of organizational psychology, this view is not particularly difficult to sustain (e.g. see Chapter 1).

Second, Gordon and Nurick (1981) note that most researchers have fairly clear-cut ideas about the role of unions in the workplace which make such research appear unnecessary or unwelcome. For researchers with a human relations orientation who share Mayo's vision of the organization as a harmonious community, the study of union–management conflict is anathema because it either concedes or encourages defeat. Mayo's (1949) social vision for organizations and society prescribed that 'we must have no hatred or bitterness towards anyone' (p. 101) — so what place is there in this vision for people like our nurse on the picket line? On the other hand, the view that such conflict could be a real contributor to organizational behaviour sits uncomfortably with Münsterberg's vision of workers as individuals in an interpersonal melting-pot and with the methodological commitments engendered by that approach. How could the behaviour of our nurse be reconciled with this view, and how could it be predicted on the basis of formal personality-based testing procedures? In light of the intractable problems posed by such questions, Shostak (1964) has characterized relations between unions and these two main brands of organizational psychologists as 'a matter of mutual indifference'.

Third and finally, Gordon and Nurick (1981) observe that even if they were welcome, most organizational psychologists would be reluctant to get too heavily involved in research into collective action, for fear that they would be seen as incipient troublemakers. Certainly any entry into the dirty world of politics, conflict and mutual distrust threatens the view of organizational research as clean-cut and hygienic (Friedlander, 1974). Of course, worse still, interest in collective action might be seen as communicating to managers the view that researchers actually *sided* with the unions and this could have a negative in ʳˑt on prospects for their own advancement and that of their project.

Yet based on some of the issues we have discussed throughout this cʰ seems appropriate to identify two further factors which have contribuᵗ lack of interest. The first is that, at least in Western societies, thᵉ unions in the workplace and the likelihood of collective protest has declined quite sharply in the last two decades. In Britain, for example, between 1979 (the year Margaret Thatcher came to power) and 1998 trade union membership dropped from 12 million to 7 million and there was a corresponding decline in industrial action (an outcome much celebrated by Mrs Thatcher's supporters). Although this change was attributed by the Conservative government to improved working conditions, the reality was that for the majority of workers these declined substantially over this period. Instead, then, the change appeared to be a direct and deliberate result of political and legislative changes that impacted on the social and psychological factors which encourage union-based activity (Fosh, 1993).

More pertinent to the overall purpose of this book, we can also see that declining interest in collective action is *inevitable* given the theoretical and empirical tools available for organizational psychologists to work with. Put simply, if researchers are theoretically wedded to the view that the basis of organizational behaviour is people's psychology *as individuals*, then collective action must be viewed either as a logical impossibility, as a sign of widespread psychopathology, or as a freakish accident. Whichever of these views is preferred, attempting to research the topic makes little sense.

Yet what is striking about the treatment we have offered in this chapter is that in a number of different ways it challenges the widely held view that mass protest is a denial or abnegation of people's basic social psychological make-up. The ideas we have discussed thus draw together many of the ideas and principles discussed in earlier chapters. They suggest that in a range of organizational and other contexts the social identity processes that produce collective action are a valid, valuable and *socially necessary* expression of self. Indeed, when we look at many of the other social phenomena to which the very same analysis applies — for example, the behaviour of supporters at a football match or at an election rally — this point appears remarkably uncontroversial. So we take it for granted that supporters of one particular football team or political party will act in terms of subjectively meaningful group memberships in order to promote with gusto and creativity the interests of those groups in relation to others with whom they are competing. And we see such behaviour as all the more appropriate if those groups have been unfairly treated or disadvantaged.

The fact that these same processes *can and do* occur within work organizations underlines the importance of the topic and of the social identity approach to it. As yet, though, the merits of this approach remain to be fully exploited. In particular, theory in this area would benefit from further research examining how processes of social influence and leadership translate a general willingness to act on behalf of the group (the main dependent variable in most of the research conducted to date) into concerted collective protest.

Of course, the possible benefits of such research are even more apparent if we are prepared to concede that industrial conflict, like group-based activity in general, can have positive as well as negative outcomes. This is a possibility that we have tended to skirt around both in this chapter and in those that have preceded it. However, it can be side-stepped no longer. So, in concluding this book, it is to this and some of the other big questions in organizational psychology that we now return.

**Further Reading**

Although the study of collective action has tended to be neglected within mainstream organizational psychology, there is a surfeit of excellent research informed by the social identity approach. Reading relevant papers by Reicher and either C. or J. Kelly is essential to gain insight into this work, and the review by Klandermans (1997) provides important links with other bodies of research. The creative and engaging experimental studies reported by Ellemers et al. (1997), Smith et al. (1994) and Wright et al. (1990) also serve as an entrée into a really fascinating literature.

Ellemers, N., Spears, R. & Doosje, B. (1997). Sticking together or falling apart: In-group identification as a psychological determinant of group commitment versus individual mobility. *Journal of Personality and Social Psychology, 72*, 617-626.

Kelly, C. & Breinlinger, S. (1996). *The social psychology of collective action: Identity, injustice and gender*. London: Taylor & Francis.

Klandermans, B. (1997). *The social psychology of protest*. Oxford: Blackwell.

Reicher, S. D. (1987). Crowd behaviour as social action. In J. C. Turner, M. A. Hogg, P. J. Oakes, S. D. Reicher & M. S. Wetherell, *Rediscovering the social group: A self-categorization theory* (pp. 171-202). Oxford: Blackwell.

Smith, H. J., Spears, R. & Oyen, M. (1994). 'People like us': The influence of personal deprivation and group membership salience on justice evaluations. *Journal of Experimental Social Psychology, 30*, 277-299.

Wright, S. C., Taylor, D. M. & Moghaddam, F. M. (1990). Responding to membership in a disadvantaged group: From acceptance to collective protest. *Journal of Personality and Social Psychology, 58*, 994-1003.

# 11 The Theory, Practice and Politics of Organizational Psychology: A Case for Organic Pluralism

In Chapter 1 we introduced the key paradigms that have held sway in the organizational field throughout the twentieth century: economic, individual difference, human relations and cognitive. There, and in the chapters that followed, limitations of those paradigms were identified and the case was made for the social identity approach advanced in this book. This case has been founded on the merits of psychological theories that recognize and account for the distinct contribution of groups and group membership to organizational functioning.

In order to make this case clearly we have focused assiduously on issues of *psychological process* and tried to identify and avoid political or moral judgements of particular organizational *products*. This strategy has been justified on grounds that a failure to make this distinction has contributed considerably to prior confusion in the field. For example, where groups have acquired a bad reputation in organizational psychology (e.g. in the study of decision-making, negotiation and productivity), it appears that this may have arisen not so much from their psychological deficiencies as from the fact that their achievements are often at odds with organizational goals perceived to be important and appropriate by *other* groups (or the same group at another time).

Having said that, it is apparent that the analysis we have presented raises a wide range of issues that are not purely psychological. In fact, almost paradoxically, in many instances our attempt to disentangle issues of psychology and politics actually brings political questions to the fore. This is because the social identity approach serves generally to reveal the political dimensions of issues that are customarily concealed within, and explained away by, psychological analysis. For example, if we refuse to dismiss collective under-performance, concurrence-seeking, social conflict and industrial protest as psychological aberrations we must consider anew some difficult questions regarding their role in organizations. Indeed, it can be argued that one of the reasons why prevailing approaches have proved so popular is that by taking the politics of organizations as an unproblematic 'given', they allow researchers and practitioners to ignore these difficult questions altogether.

The goal of this final chapter is therefore to review and integrate arguments presented in previous chapters, but also to consider the broader implications of the approach we have put forward. In this, it attempts to make connections between issues of theory, practice and politics that are *absolutely critical* to the discipline of organizational psychology, but which are all too often avoided or overlooked. The review argues for the theoretical utility of the social identity approach, but also sounds significant notes of caution. At heart, these arise from the fact that issues of organizational psychology can never be divorced from the social and political purposes of organizations. This means that the observations, recommendations and interventions of psychologists can never be made in a value-free, 'objective' vacuum. Instead they are determined by, and contribute to, the political currents of human behaviour.

However, in line with the above comments, one of the principal achievements of the social identity approach is that it helps us to understand the interplay between the political and psychological dimensions of organizational life as these are played out and as we attempt to manage them. In this, it makes psychologists' role as political agents explicit, encouraging us both to acknowledge this role and to reflect upon the uses to which it is, and can be, put.

## The need for sustainable organizational theory

Expressed baldly, the core problem with existing organizational paradigms is that they are unsustainable in key domains where organizational theory needs to prove itself: theoretical, practical, and political. The problems of economic, individual difference, and cognitive approaches are all closely aligned, founded as they are on a common metatheory of *individualism* (Pfeffer, 1997). Because these approaches generally ignore or downplay the contribution of groups to individual psychology, they are ill equipped for examination of the psychological processes that are at work in the broad class of organizational contexts where group membership is the primary determinant of individual behaviour. The practical utility of these approaches is therefore confined to settings in which considerable effort has been made to expurgate the influence of groups and social context. This effort either involves practical interventions designed to ensure that group-based interaction does not occur (as recommended by Taylor, 1911) or standardized methodologies that 'control out' social influences (e.g. personality testing of the form first recommended by Münsterberg, 1913). However, as we have seen throughout this book such attempts at practical and methodological sanitization do violence to both the demands and the realities of organizational life (see also Mayo, 1933, 1949; Steiner, 1972). This is for the very simple reason that *social groups exist in, as, and across organizations and such groups fundamentally transform the psychology of the individual*. Accordingly, any approach that fails to acknowledge the distinct psychology of groups or which places these concerns off-limits confines itself to a very *partial* analysis of organizational behaviour.

This partiality is a dominant feature of contemporary organizational psychology. Importantly too, it extends from a limited model of human psychology to a limited political analysis of organizational behaviour. Thus the practical and theoretical imperatives that compel researchers to view the isolated individual as the principal psychological ingredient of organizations, go hand-in-hand with a view that champions the individual as the source of organizational efficacy and success. Under this view, individuals are typically associated with positive outcomes (e.g. leadership, motivation, industrial harmony), but groups are seen as a source of malady and malaise (e.g. soldiering, loafing, information mismanagement, groupthink, conflict, protest). In this way groups are marginalized as feared and unwanted organizational by-products rather than regarded as in any sense desirable or primary.

A number of practical and ideological imperatives have also contributed to the widespread appeal of these approaches. In the case of the economic and individual difference paradigms, practical and professional dividends are derived from the concreteness and practitioner-sustaining qualities of the products to which they lend themselves (e.g. time-and-motion studies, standardized personality tests). More generally, however, all of these approaches subscribe to, and sustain, the view of organizations as melting pots that are the sum of their individual constituents. Here success and failure are attributed to individual competence and character — a view which conveniently validates managers' own positions and justifies their 'managerial prerogative' or 'right to manage' others. In effect, then, the approach feeds off and contributes to the political status quo. At the same time, by neglecting the group-based determinants of individual psychology, the opportunity and justification for collective challenges to that status quo are denied.

Historically, the principal alternative to this view has been the human relations paradigm (after Mayo, 1933). This is founded upon a critique of individualism and recognition of the discontinuity between individual and group psychology (see also Asch, 1952; Sherif, 1966; Turner et al., 1987). However, the theoretical and practical aspects of this approach are poorly specified and hence its prospects as a viable alternative have always been limited. Moreover, the political vision to which Mayo subscribed — in which group affiliation was seen as a general panacea for organizational ills — was hopelessly naive and lent itself to ridicule and parody. Indeed, this was the thrust of Whyte's (1960) influential text *The Organization Man* in which Mayo's ideas of 'false collectivization' were savagely critiqued (an attack recently updated by Ghoshal & Bartlett, 1997; but for a riposte see McGregor, 1960, pp. 229-231).

Nonetheless, evidence that groups can be a potential source of organizational efficacy has been a significant and enduring legacy of the human relations school (e.g. see Hackman, 1987; Leavitt, 1995). This remains a cloud over organizational theory, promising to rain on individualistic theories that stray too far from the confines of the standardized, asocial (and hence largely fictional) environment on which they are predicated. However, in the absence of a theory to account for the distinctive psychological properties of groups that Mayo identified, organizational psychology has had to make do with an unhappy marriage between psychological and political individualism and social reality. As we noted in Chapter 1, one prominent form in which this manifests itself is in the unrefined transplantation of economic and cognitive principles to the group level, with prescriptions that the group as a whole be understood and managed like the individuals in Taylor's original studies. This leads to a form of 'team-Taylorism' (Baldry et al., 1998) or 'super-Taylorism' (Parker, 1993) in which groups are wooed with the rhetoric of greater recognition, autonomy and reward, only to encounter the hard reality of more control and increased exploitation (Harley, 1999; Kelly & Kelly, 1991; McGregor, 1960, p. 241).

One common way in which this is achieved is through managerial techniques (e.g. just-in-time production systems, total quality management) that place workgroups under constant strain and then rely on group members to exert the necessary pressure to ensure that work still gets done (along lines observed in the original Hawthorne studies; Mayo, 1949, p. 90; see Sewell, 1998; Sewell &

Wilkinson, 1992). In this way, groups become instruments of their own abuse — and extremely effective ones at that. Here, as Parker (1993) notes:

> The assembly line and traditional scientific management methods ... actually [find] a new life in the team concept idea. We call this new production system 'management by stress' in which a new kind of worker empowerment takes place, but only insofar as it conforms to an even more carefully regimented shop-floor regime. Indeed, rather than taking a step toward a new era of industrial democracy, the new participatory management schemes constitute an intensification, not an abandonment, of the essence of classical Taylorism. (p. 250; see also Parker & Slaughter, 1988)

In this new industrial order the supposedly liberating strategy of team-based empowerment thus means simply that the organizational rod is now collectively self-administered. The philosophy that 'lunch is for losers' is peddled not by one's superiors but by one's co-workers. And the result is a particularly insidious form of corporate self-starvation.

Moreover, at a societal level, one of the significant consequences of dominant managerial theory is that the goals of organizations have had to be defined ever-more narrowly in order for the enterprise in which organizational psychologists participate to be construed as successful. Remember that in Taylor's initial research at the Midvale Steel Company, although productivity soared and a few workers were much better off, the overall profitability of the company declined as a result of the negative impact of Taylorism on the majority of the workforce and the community as a whole. The company could only maintain profitability by divesting itself of auxiliary interests (e.g. in retail and housing spheres) for which there was no longer much demand.

The Midvale experience serves as something of a metaphor for contemporary organizational practice. This can be considered remarkably successful when looked at with the relatively narrow focus encouraged by those who argue for the financial bottom line. And, contrary to popular opinion, this success is not a result of dramatic changes in the nature of work over the last few generations. Indeed upon close inspection, many observers doubt whether *the way* employees work has changed very much at all in the last fifty years (see Micklethwait & Wooldridge, 1997; Rees & Rodley, 1995; Thompson & Warhurst, 1998). Reviewing the situation in the United States, Milkman (1998) concludes:

> Although many companies have been spurred to adopt piecemeal reforms, these typically only affect a minority of employees and they often prove to be short-lived. Thus despite the impression of widespread change conveyed by the business press and the academic literature on the subject, only a few firms have radically transformed their work systems, and many have not attempted the most superficial reforms. (p. 37)

And similarly in Britain:

> Despite the bewildering number of change programmes and grand new titles for people and practices, the 'new workplace' is still easily recognizable for the vast majority who too often remain poorly motivated, overworked and undervalued. (Warhurst & Thompson, 1998, p. 19)

What has changed is the *amount* employees work. Most commentators agree
that this has risen dramatically in recent times. So, although they sound
enlightened, what managerialist terms like 'flexibility', 'accountability' and
'rationalization' mean in practice is that under conditions of less job security
and increased fear for their future, people now work longer hours, with fewer
colleagues and under more pressure (e.g. Harley, 1994; Martin, 1997; Rees &
Rodley, 1995; Sennett, 1998). And these changes are in no way confined to
those lower down the organizational pecking-order. Under contemporary
regimes, most managers are every bit as shattered and paranoid as those they
manage (Micklethwait & Wooldridge, 1997, p. 232).

This is a change for which organizational psychologists can take much credit,
and it is a goal towards which many have themselves worked tirelessly.
However, as at the Midvale Steelworks, it is not self-evident that this change has
benefited society as a whole. Certainly, one is entitled to question the
appropriateness of a preoccupation with the economy of production and profit
(that ignores the economy of happiness and fulfilment) and to worry, like Rees
and Rodley (1995), about the human cost of managerialism. When one does, it
is not hard to see that work intensification may be in the interests neither of the
unemployed (who have no work to do) nor of the employed (who have little to
do other than work). The problem is all the more pronounced because society as
a whole contains, and must cater for, people who belong to both groups. So, as
the division between the two broadens (e.g. see Crystal, 1991), the task of
looking after the whole becomes increasingly difficult (Heller, 1998; Milkman,
1998; Stilwell, 1995). It is therefore at this societal level that the unsustain-
ability of the assumptions and goals of existing approaches is most tangible.
And it is this problem that most begs resolution (Giddens, 1999; Saul, 1998).

## The social identity approach as a sustainable organizational paradigm

The primary purpose of this book has been to make the *theoretical* case for the
social identity approach by spelling out and testing its implications for key
organizational topics. In all the areas that have been addressed in the previous
eight chapters it is clear that the approach offers a new and refreshing way to
tackle age-old problems — one that in many instances flies in the face of received
wisdom. In large part this arises from the fact that where prevailing approaches
accord privileged status to the psychology of the individual *as an individual*, the
present approach also points to the productive potential of the individual *as
group member* (Lembke & Wilson, 1998). Thus we have argued that leadership
is not located solely in the leader but in the psychology of the group as a whole;
motivation and commitment are not the preserve of the personally self-actualized
worker but also arise from his or her social ties and loyalties; group decisions
and organizational communication do not pervert individual self-expression but
express the meaning and purpose of the collective self; negotiation to resolve
social differences is not hampered by group interests, instead those interests
allow it to be fruitful and purposive; industrial protest is not an expression of
personal frustration or madness but a shared response to collectively experienced
injustice.

It is also true that in each of these areas a large amount of research remains to be done in order to test and extend social identity and self-categorization principles. Moreover, there is considerable opportunity to use those same principles to enrich our understanding of topics that have not been dealt with extensively in this book. In this regard, a major attraction of the social identity approach is that it provides a range of *theoretical resources* with which to broach new frontiers in the organizational domain rather than a limited collection of off-the-peg prescriptions tailored only to highly circumscribed problems (Turner & Haslam, 2000).

The question that this observation naturally raises is whether the social identity approach is handicapped by a failure to provide a set of tools that can be directly applied by organizational psychologists as they go about their duty. What does the approach offer to compete with the proliferation of questionnaires, inventories and tests that are the stock-in-trade of the profession? One answer is a superior appreciation of the social psychology of organizational life. This is not a trivial consideration, and indeed this is the message that has been promoted most vigorously in previous chapters (along lines recommended by Lewin, 1952, and Back, 1979). However, as well as this, it is clear that there are any number of applied lessons to be gleaned from our treatment of the various topics we have addressed. Table 11.1 identifies some of the more provocative conclusions, but these are only a small sub-sample of those that it is possible to draw.

Yet awareness of the possible applications of the social identity approach leads to an even thornier question. Would organizations function more effectively if they were managed with an awareness of, and with sensitivity to, the principles we have identified? Is this approach any more sustainable at a societal level than the individualistic and human relations perspectives?

The first point to make here is that this book has been about *psychology* in organizations. It does not profess to be a book about politics, social policy, or even how to manage people appropriately. It is far less a book about ethics, morality and human decency. *As psychologists*, then, our primary responsibility is to identify limitations in the psychological theorizing of others and to develop sound theories of our own. As soon as we stray beyond these bounds we are in danger. As intimated above, this problem is particularly apparent in Mayo's (1949) classic text *The Social Problems of an Industrial Civilization* in which brilliant psychological insights were washed away with easily parodied social theory (e.g. Whyte, 1960). Although poor psychology always makes for poor social theory, good psychology can achieve the same end just as well.

This answer may seem like a cop-out, and to some extent it is. This is because, as we have seen throughout this book, psychological theorizing is never wholly divorced from issues of politics (Haslam & McGarty, 1998, in press). Indeed, in large part our psychological theories serve as a clear *reflection* of our political analyses and objectives. So it is no accident that researchers sympathetic to the 'big end of town' formulate psychological theories of leadership that portray leaders as spectacular people who can only be motivated by equally spectacular salaries (Hollander, 1995). It is no accident that a belief in (personal) self-actualization as the core human motivation developed within a North American culture of rampant individualism (Baumeister, 1991). It is no accident that collective action — the one route by which disempowered groups

*Table 11.1* Some practical implications of the social identity approach

| Chapter, Topic | Practical Implication |
| --- | --- |
| 2 General Processes | • in group contexts, the perceptions and behaviour of individual workers will be dictated more by their group membership than by their individuality<br><br>• mutual influence, persuasion, co-operation, and trust all increase to the extent that parties share a salient social identity<br><br>• shared social identity is the basis of a distinct and consensually embraced organizational culture |
| 3 Leadership | • even-handedness will undermine a leader's capacity to demonstrate leadership in many intergroup contexts<br><br>• leaders and followers must define themselves in terms of a shared social identity in order for leadership to emerge<br><br>• pay structures that are perceived to differentiate unfairly between leaders and followers (and which create a sense of 'us' and 'them') will undermine leadership and group productivity |
| 4 Motivation | • loyalty, rule-following and extra-role behaviour increase when employees define themselves in terms of a relevant team or organizational identity<br><br>• (personal) self-actualization is associated with career commitment and personal advancement, not necessarily with advancement towards organizational goals<br><br>• attention to employees' personal costs and benefits makes it harder to achieve substantial collaborative goals |
| 5 Communication | • information-sharing between parties increases if they share a salient social identity<br><br>• barriers to communication increase across self-categorical boundaries<br><br>• enduring social identities lead groups to develop shared and distinctive communication practices |
| 6 Decision-making | • group decisions are likely to be polarized under conditions of intergroup conflict<br><br>• group decisions based on a shared social identity will be associated with enhanced desire for, and achievement of, consensus<br><br>• groups whose members share a strong sense of shared identity are more likely to make courageous decisions |

| 7 Negotiation | • negotiated settlements to social conflict that are based only on personal relationships and understandings will tend to be short-lived |
| | • when their social identity is salient, parties' satisfaction with negotiated outcomes increases if group-based differences have been addressed |
| | • integrative solutions to group differences are more likely to be preceded by conflict than by concession-making |
| 8 Power | • non-contingent treatment of employees (i.e. petty tyranny) increases where those employees are perceived to be an outgroup |
| | • empowerment and power sharing will be increased when parties share a salient social identity |
| | • power use will be interpreted more positively (e.g. as leadership) when it is perceived to be predicated on shared social identification |
| 9 Group Productivity | • individuals in groups will tend to underperform when a relevant social identity is not salient or a group goal is prescribed by an outgroup |
| | • labour will be divided more effectively if group members share a salient social identity |
| | • productivity on a group task will increase to the extent that group goals are congruent with a salient social identity |
| 10 Collective Action | • identification with a group increases an individual's sensitivity to injustices against it |
| | • tokenism reduces the likelihood of collective action |
| | • shared social identification is a necessary pre-condition of collective action |

can re-empower themselves — has been pathologized by those who act on behalf of the powerful (Reicher, 1982).

If this is true of other approaches, it must, of course, be true of the one advocated in this book. So where exactly does the social identity approach stand on all these issues? Is the sub-text of this book that groups are universally virtuous and the psychological route to all forms of organizational enlightenment? The answer to this question is definitely 'No'. As Sennett (1998, pp. 136-148) makes clear, in the wrong hands and working for the wrong purposes, 'we' can be a very dangerous pronoun.

Accordingly, what we have tried to show in the preceding chapters is not that groups are an undeniable force for good, but that, psychologically speaking, *group processes* are just as valid — and just as valid an expression of self — as those of individuals in isolation. Moreover, we have argued that these processes are *necessary* in order for particular forms of organizational behaviour to occur. Leadership, organizational citizenship, communication, persuasion, trust and industrial protest are all contingent upon people being able to define themselves in terms of a shared social identity. To the extent that these things are judged as good and desirable, social identification and the capacity to define the self in depersonalized terms is therefore also good.

But whether or not particular organizational outcomes are seen as good and desirable is generally a matter of *political* not psychological judgement. Most organizational psychologists see leadership as a good thing, which is why they venerate its cognitive and motivational underpinnings; but most see industrial protest as a bad thing, which is why they are happy to malign its psychology. In fact though, the utility of these phenomena can never be judged independently of the purposes towards which they are marshalled. Few people see Albert Speer's leadership of industry in Nazi Germany as a positive thing, and few see the nineteenth-century rising of the Tolpuddle Martyrs against their repressive bosses as bad. Yet both these examples provide clear illustrations of social identity processes in action. This suggests two things. The first is that social identity principles can be (and are routinely) exploited for both progressive and regressive ends. The second is that the interpretation of those ends will itself be a matter of social judgement grounded in the perceiver's own group membership (Handy, 1976, p. 48).

In this way, the implementation of social identity principles — like the practice of organizational psychology as a whole — contributes only to the *political process* through which *competing* sets of shared values and goals are continually tested and refined. But as Oakes et al. (1994, p. 211) caution, this political process provides no guarantee of progress. Organizational evolution is not a process of benign social Darwinism that ensures the survival of the fittest or the best. Rather more mundanely, it is about the survival of those individuals and groups whose status as winners allows them to write organizational history and interpret organizational science in a manner that affirms their fitness and superiority. The fact that winners always *think* they are right — and that their victory proves it — does not *make* them right.

Accordingly, our confidence in the political process derives not from its capacity to weed out inferior ideas or practices but solely from its *potential* to provide social and organizational improvement through ongoing *social correction*. Whether this potential is ever realized is a judgement that organizational theorists of the future will make. What we can be sure of is that if the political process is subverted by bad organizational theory, the ability of organizations to contribute to genuinely democratic goals of justice and service will be limited.

In this book we have argued that individualism *is* bad theory and that it undermines the political process by serving largely to buttress the privileged position of the powerful stakeholders in organizations and society (Deschamps, 1982; Ng, 1980; see Chapter 8 above). At the same time we have argued that the theoretical underpinnings of the social identity approach are much more sound. Moreover, the approach can be used to advance the interests of either the powerful or the powerless and it sees participation in the political aspects of organizational life as inevitable. These arguments may desecrate the pictures of meritocratic and technological orderliness that are painted in most popular portraits of the organizational landscape, but such pictures are (and always have been) chimerical.

If this analysis is accepted, then it follows that in order to be socially sustainable, organizational theory must allow for the possibility *and the psychological validity* of competing social identities and potentially antagonistic group-based action. In the past, such a message has been rejected by both scientific management and human relations theorists alike, because it opens up the door to organizational conflict and unrest. Thus Taylor (1911, p. 96) encouraged 'friendly relations' between managers and employees because this 'rendered labor troubles of any kind or a strike impossible' and in this he was in almost perfect agreement with Mayo (e.g. 1949, p. 110). For this reason, researchers throughout the twentieth century have been united in an enterprise that centres around identifying and encouraging arrangements that *avoid* intra-organizational conflict at all costs (e.g. Bridges, 1986; Edstrom & Galbraith, 1977; Kabanoff, 1985; Pruitt & Carnevale, 1993; see Chapter 7 above). This state-of-play is nicely summarized by Daft (1995):

> The most recent thinking suggests managers should encourage co-operation within the organization. ... This approach increases cohesion, satisfaction, and performance for the organization as a whole. Too severe conflict among departments can lead to disregard and dislike for other groups, seeing other departments as inferior, as the enemy; hence co-operation will decrease. Organizations can manage conflict with techniques such as member rotation or intergroup training. Some organizations are pushing co-operation even further by establishing permanent cross-functional work teams that virtually eliminate boundaries between departments. (p. 472)

The prevailing view is thus that work behaviour should ideally be premised upon a *single* organizational identity and be *interpersonal* rather than intergroup in nature. Significantly though (as we saw in Chapter 7; see Figure 7.3), this can be achieved either by individuating the workforce (so-called *de*categorization; as recommended by followers of Taylor) or by attempting to create all-embracing superordinate identities (*re*categorization; as recommended by followers of Mayo). So, despite the differences in social psychological theory that lead researchers to advocate either of these two strategies, both actually lend themselves to very similar organizational practices (Eggins, 1999; Salaman, 1987). In pursuit of industrial harmony, all roads lead to Rome.

But as we have seen at various junctures throughout this book (especially in Chapter 8), this theoretical championing of individuation under the umbrella of a single organizational identity (albeit with managerially crafted differences between teams — à la team-Taylorism) generally leads, in practice, to the justification and protection of an oppressive consensus in which power, rights, and material resources are concentrated in the hands of those who control the organizational reins. In effect, it is a recipe for a fear-ridden dog-eat-dog world in which employees are encouraged to pursue a strategy of individual mobility but where most (including quite senior managers) ultimately bow down as individual servants (Mills, 1970; Robinson, 1995, pp. 257-258; Saul, 1998). Here workers are seduced, tamed and ultimately zombified by the rhetoric of personal empowerment, at the same time that their capacity to contribute to large-scale innovative organizational projects and genuine social reform — the most empowering process of all — is quietly whittled away.

This reality contrasts very starkly with the promises of personal fulfilment that abound in the popular texts on business and management that one finds prominently displayed in airport bookshops. It is part of the seamy side of enterprise that most people are familiar with but that no-one likes to advertise. And it is the great tragedy of the managerial age. For when social historians of tomorrow look back on the present era it seems likely that they will be struck by Western society's comparative failure — despite unprecedented economic, technological and human resources and unprecedented self-analysis —  to bequeath much of any enduring worth to the future (in the way, for example, of social, educational and cultural infrastructure; Hughes, 1993).

At the same time, though, it is clear that the analysis contained within Daft's (1995) summary is entirely consistent with self-categorization principles. Moreover, the prescription for organizational harmony he delivers also has clear attractions under conditions where our own personal or social goals are aligned with those of the organization or corporation in question. But what if this is not the case? What if the purpose, strategy, products and vision of the organization fail to deliver justice or service? The problem here is that employees can only effectively resist or initiate organizational change when they act as members of meaningfully distinct groups (see Chapter 10 above; also Haunschild et al., 1994; King & Anderson, 1995, pp. 73-75). So when change or inertia are for the worse but avenues to socially meaningful dissent are designed out, there is no mechanism that allows organizational error to be corrected (Veenstra & Haslam, 2000). This is a formula for failure not success.

This being the case, one might well ask what it is that sustains the view that groups and intra-organizational conflict are bad. Politically, it is not hard to see that these are arguments that those at the top of organizational hierarchies might champion quite vigorously, believing them to be in their interests. Intellectually though, one fundamental and extremely effective way in which the same message has been promoted is through the depiction of groups as sources of psychological deficiency and inadequacy. This view is neatly summarized in Buys' (1978) bold assertion that 'humans would do better without groups' (p. 123). This means that even when the productive potential of groups and teams is acknowledged, the view that they subvert the true character and better instincts of their members — and with them the interests of the organization — still lingers. Accordingly, as Leavitt (1995) observes, they 'continue, as in earlier days, to be treated as pests, forever fouling up the beauty of rationally designed individualized organizations, forever forming informally (and irrationally) to harass and outgame the planners' (p. 385).

Yet as we have seen throughout the latter chapters of this book, attempts to deny the psychological validity of group processes are generally unsustainable — even where we ourselves disapprove of the organizational objectives and accomplishments of the particular groups in question. Again, the evidence we have presented suggests that the psychology of group behaviour is *of necessity* no less rational, no less valid and no more biased than that of individuals in isolation (Turner & Oakes, 1997). In many instances, then, anti-group prejudice is simply a manifestation of the twin evils of *psychologization* and *managerialization*. Here, then, researchers attempt to explain away behaviour that they object to as a product of faulty psychology and poor management practice, rather than tackling the social and political dimensions of those objections (a strategy well illustrated by conventional approaches to groupthink; see Chapter 6 above). In this regard, it is always useful to remind ourselves that while every organizational problem has a psychological and managerial *dimension*, not all problems have a psychological or managerial *cause*.

Furthermore, when we examine the social and political aspects of group life, it is clear that the social identity approach also goes against received wisdom by suggesting that in-and-of-itself conflict between groups is not necessarily degrading or destructive (Eggins, 1999; Kelly & Kelly, 1992; Oakes et al., 1994; Stephenson, 1981, 1984; Worchel et al., 1993; see also de Dreu, Harinck & van Vianen, in press; Mitchell et al., 1988). Although it is now less fashionable, this point was readily conceded by social scientists around the middle of the twentieth century — when, in the wake of the Second World War, people were generally much more conscious of the dangers of appeasement and of the need collectively to resist oppression (see Douglas, 1957; Parker, 1993). Thus in a discussion of the merits of union–management conflict, Tannenbaum (1965) followed Coser (1956), Cooley (1918), Kerr (1954), and others in arguing that:

> From a functional or pragmatic standpoint, the distinction between conflict and co-operation is often subtle. Conflict ... can have constructive consequences, just as co-operation can be stultifying. (p. 720)

And even more strongly, Katz (1964a) contended that:

> Organizations without internal conflict are on the way to dissolution. A system with differentiated substructures has conflict built into it by virtue of its differentiated subsystems. If it moves toward complete harmony, it moves toward homogeneity and random distribution of all its elements. Entropy takes over. (p. 114)

Developing this argument, we would suggest that in order to be fully sustainable, any approach to organizational psychology must acknowledge the symbiotic relationship between conflict and co-operation. This involves recognizing that each process has the capacity to correct for the limitations of the other and, more fundamentally, that each is contingent on the other (Coser, 1956; Gamson, 1972; Oakes et al., 1994; Simmel, 1955; Turner, 1985). Thus conflict between groups is made possible by co-operation within them and can be precipitated by demands for co-operation at a higher level (e.g. when two departments resist a merger). By the same token, co-operation between groups can be precipitated by conflict with other groups or conflict at a higher level (e.g. when unions and management unite to resist a takeover or to challenge government policy). Organizations therefore need social conflict for the very same reasons that they need co-operation — to shape and harness the productive potential of the socially structured self. Moreover, because there is no contextually independent 'basic' or 'ideal' self-categorization, there is no optimum level or form of conflict that should be encouraged in the interests of organizational efficacy.

The various strands of the foregoing analysis combine to suggest that the healthiest and most productive organizational philosophy is one of *organic pluralism* that celebrates the ability and right of employees to advance *collectively* their various causes, their various aspirations and their various social identities — not just those of the monolithic organization (along lines suggested in Chapter 7; see also Berry, 1991; Buchanan, 1995; Eggins & Haslam, 1999a; Haslam, Powell et al., 2000; Heller, 1998; Huo et al., 1996; Pollert, 1996). Organizations will always make mistakes and will almost always harbour real differences of perspective, so these identities will often clash. However, the prospect of disagreement and conflict en route to error rectification is much less alarming than the neo-Orwellian landscape outlined by Daft (1995) in which an *organizational monoculture* prevails.

The environmental and biological sciences teach us that monocultures are peculiarly maladaptive. Lacking nutrition and vitality, they hurry only towards their own demise. This is no less true in the organizational sphere. In order for organizations to be sustainable in the very broadest sense — as contributors to, and constituents of, society — the 'right to manage' must therefore be weighed against, and balanced by, rights associated with other predicaments and other social identities. Making room for *real social choice* of this form is something for which management theorists have hitherto shown little enthusiasm (as noted by West, 1996; Williams & O'Reilly, 1998). Their apprehension is understandable, but it may also be misguided. At core, this is because the interwoven arguments developed in previous chapters suggest that the existence of diverse social identities is the source of a range of positive organizational and social outcomes — motivational, intellectual and material. Without them, organizations and society are not only less rich, they are also less viable.


## Prospects for change

In putting forward any new set of ideas, the temptation is always to present them as if they were entirely new. In truth, though, very few of the insights contained in previous chapters are entirely novel, and most find echo in influential critiques of theory and practice provided by other researchers in all the areas we have addressed. However, that said, two distinctive features of the social identity approach are first, that it accounts for a range of organizational phenomena in terms of a limited, clearly articulated, and well-tested set of theoretical principles (as set out in Chapter 2), and second, that in so doing it presents a *unified* analysis of issues that have hitherto been subjected to disparate and largely unconnected theoretical treatments.

Indeed, when looking at research into seemingly disparate topics such as leadership, motivation, negotiation, power and collective action, it is clear that existing analyses have only really been united by an underlying commitment to individualistic metatheory (Pfeffer, 1998). To date, then, organizational theory has tended simply to rally behind the unifying message that groups are a methodological and professional nuisance, and are best swept under the theoretical carpet. Viewed in this light, it is easy to see most of the organizational advances that have been heralded in the latter part of the twentieth century not as feats of iconoclasm but as 'more of the same'. This point was presaged forty years ago by McGregor (1960) when he pointed to the widespread infiltration of Theory X (i.e. Taylorism) into management theory:

> What sometimes appear to be new strategies — decentralization, management by objective, consultative supervision, 'democratic' leadership — are usually but old wine in new bottles because the procedures developed to implement them are derived from the same inadequate assumptions about human nature. Management is constantly becoming disillusioned with the widely touted and expertly merchandised 'new approaches' to the human side of enterprise. The real difficulty is that these approaches are no more than different tactics — programs, procedures, gadgets — within an unchanged strategy based on Theory X. (p. 42; see also Pinder, 1984)

Of course, organizational fashions have come and gone since 1960, so that now decentralization and management by objective have been replaced by practices of incentivation, lean production, total quality management and 360-degree feedback. New regimes have also been introduced in the context of drastic programmes of rationalization, restructuring, de-layering and downsizing. So 'change' is still very much in vogue. Indeed, the manager who does not worship at its altar is liable to slide swiftly down the greasy pole of personal advancement. It is therefore to service the needs of such individuals — and to swiftly cover up the tracks of their failure — that the industry of management and organizational theory has had to become 'peculiarly faddish' in order to satisfy 'a relentless appetite for more fuel — more ideas to process, print, sell and regurgitate' (Micklethwait & Wooldridge, 1997, p. 50; see also Harley, 1999).

Yet, as McGregor (1960) well appreciated, for all the movement and light that the ever-burgeoning management literature appears to generate, the *understanding* of organizational life that informs its theory and practice has not progressed much at all. Politically and intellectually, management science is perhaps the most conservative of all sciences. Reflecting this, a recent survey of the physical and psychological dimensions of the contemporary office environment concludes:

> If we combine office workers' experience of work intensification under Team Taylorism with their daily ordeal at the mercy of a malfunctioning built environment we can see that the total reality does not seem 'modern' at all but almost approximates to a Dickensian sweatshop. (Baldry et al., 1998, p. 182)

It is also a mistake to suppose that this state of affairs will improve when present philosophies are consigned to the industrial archives and new 'breakthrough' approaches (and new gurus) appear to take their place. As editors from *The Economist* poignantly conclude, amidst all the hullabaloo about work practices of the future, the most frightening prospect is just how much they will resemble those of the past (Micklethwait & Wooldridge, 1997, p. 239). For those who are punch-drunk on change — the vast swathe of managers and other workers who are the cannon-fodder for organizational theory — this is a very sobering message.

So is that it? Is this the end of our story? Should we now just resign ourselves to the depressing gap between the rhetoric of theorists and the reality confronted by their victims? No. A central argument of this book is that real advances *can* be made in both organizational theory and the practice that it informs. However, amongst other things, these are conditional upon acceptance of a new metatheory that allows issues of psychology and behaviour in organizations to be appreciated in a new light. Building on an intellectual heritage going back to the interactionism of Asch, Sherif and Lewin and the group dynamics movement of Cartwright, Festinger, Schachter and others, the metatheory that underpins social identity and self-categorization theories offers a realistic prospect for renewal. Based on a full appreciation of the statement with which this book began — that humans are *social* animals — this argues for the necessity of appreciating the capacity for society and psychology to *shape each other*. Such a view recognizes that group membership affects the way people think, but also that people's thinking and behaviour in groups has the capacity to change society (Turner & Oakes, 1986). As we have noted at a number of junctures (e.g. in Chapters 6, 8 and 10), a distinctive contribution of the approach is that by reconceptualizing the psychological underpinnings of collective action it contributes to a *psychology of social change* as an alternative to the psychology of status quo that currently pervades organizational literature (Reicher, 1987; Tajfel, 1981a).

This, of course, begs the last big question of whether change is really of any interest to those who own and control organizations — apart, that is, from change to the terminology and professional paraphernalia that are continually being recycled to create the impression of progress. Do the paymasters of organizational psychologists really want their deeply embedded ways of thinking and operating to be profoundly challenged and fundamentally reformed? Some may, but on reflection it is hard to imagine that psychologists and management theorists in general could have done a much better job if their explicit directive had been to mask the reality of organizational inertia beneath a touted concern for change. That they have done this job so effectively, and in many cases so unwittingly, points in part to the potency of the metatheoretical and political assumptions with which they are currently armed and by which their various treatments are bound. As summarized by Pfeffer (1997), organizational studies 'is trapped by its context and seems almost unconscious of this fact' (p. 202).

Pfeffer (1997) lays much of the blame for this overarching problem on the fact that 'connections among topics and tests of competing perspectives remain all too rare' (p. 202; see also 1998, p. 765). Accordingly, even if it serves no other purpose, one of the major contributions of the social identity approach is to provide an integrated treatment of diverse topics that brings the psychological and political assumptions of organizational theory out into the open and engages them in competitive testing. If we take our identity as scientists seriously, this is work that we should continue. But it is also work that we should relish.

# References

Abrams, D. (1999). *Social and psychological dynamics within and between groups.* Paper presented at the Small Groups Preconference to the Annual Meeting of the Society of Experimental Social Psychology, St Louis, MI, October 14-16.

Abrams, D., Ando, K., & Hinkle, S. (1998). Psychological attachment to the group: Cross-cultural differences in organizational identification and subjective norms as predictors of workers' turnover intentions. *Personality and Social Psychology Bulletin, 24,* 1027-1039.

Abrams, D. & Hogg, M. A. (1987). Language attitudes, frames of reference and social identity: A Scottish dimension. *Journal of Language and Social Psychology, 6,* 201-213.

Abrams, D. & Hogg, M. A. (1990). Social identification, self-categorization, and social influence. *European Review of Social Psychology, 1,* 195-228.

Abrams, D., Wetherell, M. S., Cochrane, S., Hogg, M. A., & Turner, J. C. (1990). Knowing what to think by knowing who you are: A social identity approach to norm formation, conformity and group polarization. *British Journal of Social Psychology, 29,* 97-119.

Adair, J. (1983). *Effective leadership.* Pan: London.

Adams, J. S. (1965). Inequity in social exchange. In L. Berkowitz (Ed.), *Advances in experimental social psychology* (vol. 2, pp. 267-296). New York: Academic Press.

Adorno, T. W., Frenkel-Brunswik, E., Levinson, D. J., & Sanford, R. N. (1950). *The authoritarian personality.* New York: Harper.

Agama, A. (1997). *The communication of information in an organizational setting: The role of self-categorization and perceived group membership.* Unpublished thesis: The Australian National University.

Aldag, R. J. & Fuller, S. R. (1993). Beyond fiasco: a reappraisal of the groupthink phenomenon and a new model of group decision processes. *Psychological Bulletin, 113,* 533-552.

Alderfer, C. P. (1969). An empirical test of a new theory of human needs. *Organizational Behaviour and Human Performance, 4,* 142-175.

Alderfer, C. P. (1972). *Existence, relatedness and growth: Human needs in organizational settings.* New York: Free Press.

Alderfer, C. P. & Smith, K. K. (1982). Studying intergroup relations embedded in organizations. *Administrative Science Quarterly, 27,* 35-65.

Allen, P. T. & Stephenson, G. M. (1983). Intergroup understanding and size of organization. *British Journal of Industrial Relations, 21,* 312-329.

Allport, F. H. (1924). *Social psychology.* New York: Houghton Mifflin.

Allport, F. H. (1962). A structuronomic conception of behavior: Individual and collective. *Journal of Abnormal and Social Psychology, 64,* 3-30.

Allport, G. W. (1954) *The nature of prejudice.* Cambridge, MA: Addison Wesley.

Amir, Y. (1969). Contact hypothesis in ethnic relations. *Psychological Bulletin, 71,* 319-342.

Anastasio, P., Bachman, B., Gaertner, S., & Dovidio, J. (1997). Categorization, recategorization and common ingroup identity. In R. Spears, P. J. Oakes, N. Ellemers, & S. A. Haslam (Eds.), *The social psychology of stereotyping and group life* (pp. 236-256). Oxford: Blackwell.

Andrews, J. D. W. (1967). The achievement motive in two types of organization. *Journal of Personality and Social Psychology, 6,* 163-168.

Andrews, M. (1991). *Lifetimes of commitment: Aging, politics, psychology.* Cambridge: Cambridge University Press.

Argote, L., Insko, C. A., Yovetich, N., & Romero, A. A. (1995). Group learning curves: The effects of turnover and task complexity on group performance. *Journal of Applied Psychology, 25,* 512-529.

Argyle, M. (1953). The relay assembly test room in retrospect. *Occupational Psychology, 27,* 98-103.

Aronson, E. (1997). The theory of cognitive dissonance: The evolution and vicissitudes of an idea. In C. McGarty & S. A. Haslam (Eds.), *The message of social psychology: Perspectives on mind in society* (pp. 20-35). Oxford: Blackwell.

Asch, S. E. (1951). Effects of group pressure upon the modification and distortion of judgements. In H. Guetzkow (Ed.), *Groups, leadership and men* (pp. 177-90). Pittsburgh, PA: Carnegie Press.

Asch, S. E. (1952). *Social psychology.* Engelwood Cliffs: NJ: Prentice Hall.

Ashforth, B. E. (1989). The experience of powerlessness in organizations. *Organizational Behavior and Human Decision Processes, 43,* 207-242.

Ashforth, B. E. (1994). Petty tyranny organizations. *Human Relations, 47,* 755-778.

Ashforth, B. E. & Mael, F. (1989). Social identity theory and the organization. *Academy of Management Review, 14,* 20-39.

Atkinson, J. W. (1964). *An introduction to motivation.* Princeton, NJ: van Nostrand

Atkinson, J. W. & Feather, N. T. (Eds.) (1966). *A theory of achievement motivation.* New York: Wiley.

Bacharach, S. B. & Lawler, E. J. (1980). *Power and politics in organizations.* San Francisco, CA: Jossey-Bass Publishers.

Bachman, B. A. (1993). *An intergroup model of organizational mergers.* Unpublished PhD dissertation: University of Delaware.

Back, K. W. (1979). The small tightrope between sociology and personality. *Journal of Applied Behavioural Science, 15,* 283-294.

Balaam, B. & Haslam, S. A. (1998). A closer look at the role of social influence in the development of attitudes to eating. *Journal of Community and Applied Social Psychology, 8,* 195-212.

Baldry, C., Bain, P., & Taylor, P. (1998). 'Bright satanic offices': Intensification, control and Team Taylorism. In P. Thompson & C. Warhurst (Eds.), *Workplaces of the future* (pp. 163-183). Houndmills: Macmillan.

Bar-Tal, D. (1990). Israeli-Palestinian conflict: A cognitive analysis. *International Journal of Intercultural Relations, 14,* 7-29.

Bar-Tal, D. (1998). Group beliefs as an expression of social identity. In S. Worchel, J. F. Morales, D. Paez, J.-C. Deschamps (Eds.), *Social identity: International perspectives* (pp. 92-113). London: Sage.

Barker, J. & Tomkins, P. (1994). Identification in the self-managing organization. *Human Communication Research, 21,* 223-240.

Barnes, R. M. (1937). *Motion and time study: Design and measurement of work.* New York: Wiley.

Barsalou, L. W. (1987). The instability of graded structure: Implications for the nature of concepts. In U. Neisser (Ed.), *Concepts and conceptual development: Ecological and intellectual factors in categorization.* Cambridge: Cambridge University Press.

Bartlett, E. J. (1911/1972). Academic efficiency. In *Dartmouth College conferences, First Tuck school conference: Addresses and discussions at the conference on scientific management, 12-14 October 1911* (pp. 288-294). Dartmouth, USA: Easton Hive Publishing Company.

Bass, B. M. (1985). *Leadership and performance beyond expectations.* New York: Free Press.

Bass, B. M. (1990). *Stogdill's handbook of leadership: A survey of theory and research* (2nd ed.). New York: Free Press.

Bate, P. (1984). The impact of organizational culture on approaches to organizational problem solving. *Organizational Studies, 5,* 43-66.

Baumeister, R. F. & Leary, M. R. (1995). The need to belong: Desire for interpersonal attachments as a fundamental human motivation. *Psychological Bulletin, 117,* 497-529.

Baumeister, R. F. (1991). *Meanings of life.* New York: Guilford.

Bavelas, A. (1956). Communication patterns in task-oriented groups. In D. Cartwright & A. Zander (Eds.), *Group dynamics: Research and theory* (2nd ed., pp. 493-506). Evanston, IL: Row Peterson.

Bavelas, A. & Barrett, D. (1951). An experimental approach to organizational communication. *Personnel, 27,* 366-371.

Bazerman, M. H., Mannix, E., Sondak, H., & Thompson, L. (1990). Negotiation behaviour and decision processes in dyads, groups and markets. In J. S. Carroll (Ed.), *Applied social psychology and organizational settings* (pp. 13-44). Hillsdale, NJ: Erlbaum.

Beatty, R. W. & Ulrich, D. O. (1991). Re-energizing the mature organization. *Organizational Dynamics, 20,* 16-30.

Becker, T. E. (1992). Foci and bases of commitment: Are they distinctions worth making? *Academy of Management Journal, 35,* 232-244.

Becker, T. E. & Billings, R. S. (1993). Profiles of commitment: An empirical test. *Journal of Organizational Behavior, 14,* 177-190.

Bellman, B. L. (1981). The paradox of secrecy. *Human Studies, 4,* 1-24.

Ben-Yoav, O. & Pruitt, D. G. (1984a). Accountability to constituents: A two-edged sword. *Organizational Behavior and Human Performance, 34,* 283-295.

Ben-Yoav, O. & Pruitt, D. G. (1984b). Resistance to yielding and the expectation of co-operative future interaction in negotiation. *Journal of Experimental Social Psychology, 34,* 323-335.

Berry, J. W. (1984). Cultural relations in plural societies: Alternatives to segregation and their sociopsychological implications. In N. Miller & M. B. Brewer (Eds.), *Groups in contact: The psychology of desegregation* (pp. 11-27). Orlando, FL: Academic Press.

Berry, J. W. (1991). Understanding and managing multiculturalism: Some possible implications of research in Canada. *Psychology and Developing Societies, 3,* 17-49.

Bierstedt, R. (1950). An analysis of social power. *American Sociological Review, 15,* 730-738.

Biko, B. S. (1988). *I write what I like.* London: Penguin (first published in 1978).

Billig, M. (1978). *Fascists: A social psychological view of the National Front.* London: Academic Press.

Billig, M. G. & Tajfel, H. (1973). Social categorization and similarity in intergroup behaviour. *European Journal of Social Psychology, 3,* 27-52.

Binning, J. F., Goldstein, M. A., Garcia, M. F., & Scatteregia, J. H. (1988). Effects of pre-interview impressions on questioning strategies in same- and opposite-sex employment interviews. *Journal of Applied Psychology, 73,* 30-37.

Blackler, F. & Williams, R. (1971). People's motives at work. In P. B. Warr (Ed.), *Psychology at work.* Harmondsworth: Penguin.

Blake, R. R. & Mouton, J. S. (1964). *The managerial grid.* Houston, TX: Gulf.

Blau, P. M. (1964). *Exchange and power in social life.* New York: Wiley.

Borman, W. C. & Motowidlo, S. J. (1997). Task performance and contextual performance: The meaning for personnel selection research. *Human Performance, 10,* 99-109.

Bornman, E. & Mynhardt, J. C. (1992). Social identity and intergroup contact with specific reference to the work situation. *Genetic, Social and General Psychology Monographs, 117*, 439-462.

Bourhis, R. Y. (1991). Organizational communication and accommodation: Toward some conceptual and empirical links. In H. Giles, J. Coupland & N. Coupland (Eds.), *Contexts of accommodation: Developments in applied sociolinguistics. Studies in emotion and social interaction* (pp. 270-303). Cambridge: Cambridge University Press.

Bourhis, R. Y. (1994a). Bilingualism and the language of work: The linguistic work environment survey. *International Journal of the Sociology of Language, 105-106*, 217-266.

Bourhis, R. Y. (1994b). Power, gender, and intergroup discrimination: Some minimal group experiments. In M. P. Zanna & J. M. Olson (Eds.), *The psychology of prejudice: The Ontario symposium* (vol. 7). Hillsdale, NJ: Erlbaum.

Bourhis, R. Y. & Giles, H. (1977). The language of intergroup distinctiveness. In H. Giles (Ed.), *Language, ethnicity and intergroup relations* (pp. 119-135). London: Academic Press.

Bourhis, R. Y. Giles, H. Leyens, J.-P., & Tajfel, H. (1979). Psycholinguistic distinctiveness: Language divergence in Belgium. In H. Giles & R. St Clair (Eds.), *Language and social psychology* (pp. 158-185). Oxford: Blackwell.

Bourhis, R. Y., Roth, S., & MacQueen, G. (1989). Communication in the hospital setting: A survey of medical and everyday language use amongst patients, nurses and doctors. *Social Science and Medicine, 4*, 339-346.

Bourhis, R. Y., Turner, J. C., & Gagnon, A. (1997). Interdependence, social identity and discrimination. In R. Spears, P. J. Oakes, N. Ellemers & S. A. Haslam (Eds.), *The social psychology of stereotyping and group life* (pp. 273-295). Oxford: Blackwell.

Bowers, D. G. & Seashore, S. E. (1966). Predicting organizational effectiveness with a four-factor theory of leadership. *Administrative Science Quarterly, 11*, 238-163.

Branscombe, N. R. (1998). Thinking about one's gender group's privileges or disadvantages: Consequences for well-being in women and men. *British Journal of Social Psychology, 37*, 167-184.

Branscombe, N. R. & Wann D. L. (1994). Collective self-esteem consequences of outgroup derogation when a valued social identity is on trial. *European Journal of Social Psychology, 24*, 641-658.

Braverman, H. (1974). *Labor and monopoly capital.* New York: Monthly Review Press.

Breakwell, G. M. (1983). *Threatened identities.* Chichester: Wiley.

Brehm, J. W. (1966). *A theory of psychological reactance.* New York: Academic Press.

Brewer, M. B. (1979). Ingroup bias in the minimal intergroup situation: A cognitive-motivational analysis. *Psychological Bulletin, 86*, 307-324.

Brewer, M. B. (1981). Ethnocentrism and its role in interpersonal trust. In M. B. Brewer & B. E. Collins (Eds.), *Scientific enquiry in the social sciences.* San Francisco: Jossey Bass.

Brewer, M. B. (1988). A dual process model of impression formation. In T. K. Srull & R. S. Wyer (Eds.), *Advances in social cognition* (vol. 1, pp. 1-36). Hillsdale, NJ: Erlbaum.

Brewer, M. B. (1991). The social self: On being the same and different at the same time. *Personality and Social Psychology Bulletin, 17*, 475-482.

Brewer, M. B. (1995). Managing diversity: The role of social identities. In S. E. Jackson & M. N. Ruderman (Eds.), *Diversity in work teams: Research paradigms for a changing workplace* (pp. 47-68). American Psychological Association: Washington, DC.

Brewer, M. B. & Kramer, R. M. (1985). The psychology of intergroup attitudes and behavior. *Annual Review of Psychology, 36,* 219-243.

Brewer, M. B. & Miller, N. (1984). Beyond the contact hypothesis: Theoretical perspectives on desegregation. In N. Miller & M. B. Brewer (Eds.), *Groups in contact: The psychology of desegregation* (pp. 281-302). Orlando, FL: Academic Press.

Brewer, M. B. & Schneider, S. K. (1990). Social identity and social dilemmas: A double-edged sword. In D. Abrams & M. A. Hogg (Eds.), *Social identity theory: Constructive and critical advances.* London: Harvester-Wheatsheaf.

Brewer, M. B. & Silver, M. (1978). Ingroup bias as a function of task characteristics. *European Journal of Social Psychology, 8,* 393-400.

Brickner, M. A., Harkins, S. G., & Ostrom, T. M. (1986). The effects of personal involvement: Thought-provoking implications for social loafing. *Journal of Personality and Social Psychology, 51,* 763-769.

Bridges, W. (1986). How to manage organizational transitions. *Organizational Dynamics, 15,* 24-33.

Brotherton, C. (1999). *Social psychology and management: Issues for a changing society.* Milton Keynes: Open University Press.

Brown, J. A. C. (1954). *The social psychology of industry.* Harmondsworth: Penguin.

Brown, P. (1999). *Theories, fit and the formation of stereotype content.* Unpublished PhD thesis: The Australian National University.

Brown, R. (1965). *Social psychology.* New York: Free Press.

Brown, R. J. (1978). Divided we fall: Analysis of relations between different sections of a factory workforce. In H. Tajfel (Ed.), *Differentiation between social groups: Studies in the social psychology of intergroup relations* (pp. 395-429). London: Academic Press.

Brown, R. J. (1988). *Group processes: Dynamics within and between groups.* Oxford: Blackwell.

Brown, R. J., Condor, S., Mathews, A., Wade, G., & Williams, J. (1986). Explaining intergroup differentiation in an industrial organization. *Journal of Occupational Psychology, 59,* 273-286.

Brown, R. J. & Turner, J. C. (1981). Interpersonal and intergroup behaviour. In J. C. Turner & H. Giles (Eds.), *Intergroup behaviour* (pp. 33-65). Oxford: Blackwell.

Brown, R. J. & Wade, G. (1987). Superordinate goals and intergroup behaviour: The effects of role ambiguity and status on intergroup attitudes and task performance. *European Journal of Social Psychology, 17,* 131-142.

Brown, S. P. & Leigh, T. W. (1996). A new look at psychological climate and its relationship to job involvement, effort and performance. *Journal of Applied Psychology, 81,* 358-368.

Bruins, J., Ellemers, N., & de Gilder, D. (1999). Power use and status differences as determinants of subordinates' evaluative and behavioural responses in simulated organizations. *European Journal of Social Psychology, 29,* 843-870.

Bruins, J., Platow, M. J., & Ng, S. H. (1995). Distributive and procedural justice in interpersonal and intergroup situations: Issues, solutions and extensions. *Social Justice Research, 8,* 103-121.

Bruins, J. & Wilke, H. A. (1992). Cognitions and behavior in a hierarchy: Mulder's power theory revisited. *European Journal of Social Psychology, 22,* 21-39.

Bruins, J. & Wilke, H. A. (1993). Upward power tendencies in a hierarchy: Power distance theory versus bureaucratic rule. *European Journal of Social Psychology, 23,* 239-254.

Bruner, J. S. (1957). On perceptual readiness. *Psychological Review, 64,* 123-152.

Buchanan, J. (1995). Managing labour in the 1990s. In S. Rees & G. Rodley (Eds.), *The human costs of managerialism: Advocating the recovery of humanity.* Leichhardt, Sydney: Pluto Press.

Burgess, R. L. (1969). Communication networks and behavioural consequences. *Human Relations, 22,* 137-160.

Burns, J. M. (1978). *Leadership.* New York: Harper & Row.

Burnstein, E. (1982). Persuasion as argument processing. In H. Brandstatter, J. H. Davis & G. Stocker-Kreichgauer (Eds.), *Group decision making.* London: Academic Press.

Burnstein, E. & Vinokur, A. (1973). Testing two classes of theories about group-induced shifts in individual choices. *Journal of Personality and Social Psychology, 9,* 123-137.

Burnstein, E. & Vinokur, A. (1975). What a person thinks upon learning he has chosen differently from others: Nice evidence for the persuasive-arguments explanation of choice shifts. *Journal of Experimental Social Psychology, 11,* 412-426.

Burnstein, E. & Vinokur, A. (1977). Persuasive argumentation and social comparison as determinants of attitude polarization. *Journal of Experimental Social Psychology, 13,* 315-332.

Burton, J. (1993). *The social contextual basis of leadership perceptions.* Unpublished thesis: The Australian National University.

Buys, C. J. (1978). Humans would do better without groups. *Personality and Social Psychology Bulletin, 4,* 123-125.

Caddick, B. (1981). Equity theory, social identity and intergroup relations. In L. Wheeler (Ed.), *Review of Personality and Social Psychology* (vol. 1). Beverley Hills, CA: Sage.

Caddick, B. (1982). Perceived illegitimacy and intergroup relations. In H. Tajfel (Ed.), *Social identity and intergroup relations* (pp. 137-54). Cambridge: Cambridge University Press.

Cameron, J. E. (1999). *Three factors are better than one: Analyses and implications of a multidimensional model of social identity.* Paper presented at the 5th meeting of the Society of Australasian Social Psychologists, Coolum, QLD, April 8-11.

Campbell, D. T. (1958). Systematic error on the part of human links in communication systems. *Information and Control, 1,* 334-369.

Campbell, D. T. (1975). On the conflict between biological and social evolution and between psychology and moral tradition. *American Psychologist, 30,* 1103-1126.

Campbell, D. T. & Stanley, J. C. (1966). *Experimental and quasi-experimental designs for research.* Chicago: Rand McNally.

Cannavale, F. J., Scarr, H. A., & Pepitone, A. (1970). Deindividuation in the small group: Some further evidence. *Journal of Personality and Social Psychology, 16,* 141-147.

Cappelli, P. & Sherer, P. D. (1991). The missing role of context in OB: The need for a meso-level approach. *Research in Organizational Behavior, 13,* 55-110.

Carey, A. (1967). The Hawthorne studies: A radical criticism. *American Sociological Review, 32,* 403-410.

Carnevale, P. J. & Pruitt, D. G. (1992). Negotiation and mediation. *Annual Review of Psychology, 43,* 531-582.

Carr, E. (1997). Do the million dollar managers deliver value for money? *The Australian Financial Review,* October 11-12, 28-29.

Cartwright, D. & Zander, A. (Eds.), (1956). *Group dynamics: Research and theory* (2nd ed.). Evanston, IL: Row Peterson.

Cartwright, D. & Zander, A. (1960). Leadership and group performance: Introduction. In D. Cartwright & A. Zander (Eds.), *Group dynamics: Research and theory* (3rd ed., pp. 487-510). Evanston, IL: Row Peterson.

Chell, E. (1993). *The psychology of behaviour in organizations* (2nd ed.). Houndmills: Macmillan.

Cinnirella, M. (1997). Towards a European identity? Interactions between the national and European identities manifested by university students in Britain and Italy. *British Journal of Social Psychology, 36,* 19-31.

Cinnirella, M. (1998). Exploring temporal aspects of social identity: The concept of possible social identities. *European Journal of Social Psychology, 28,* 227-248.

Coch, L. & French, J. R. P. (1948). Overcoming resistance to change. *Human Relations, 1,* 512-533.

Collaros, P. A. & Anderson, L. R. (1969). Effect of perceived expertness upon creativity of members of brainstorming groups. *Journal of Applied Psychology, 53,* 159-163.

Condor, S. G. (1990) Social stereotypes and social identity. In D. Abrams & M. A. Hogg (Eds.), *Social identity theory: Constructive and critical advances* (pp. 230-249). Hemel Hempstead: Harvester Wheatsheaf.

Conger, J. A. & Kanungo, R. N. (1988). The empowerment process: Integrating theory and practice. *Academy of Management Review, 13,* 471-482.

Cooke, M. C. (1911). *Academic and industrial efficiency.* Carnegie Foundation for the Advancement of Learning (Bulletin No. 5).

Cooley, C. H. (1918). *Social process.* New York: Scribners and Sons.

Cooper, J. B. & McGaugh, J. L. (1963). Leadership: Integrating principles of social psychology. In C. A. Gibb (Ed.), *Leadership: Selected readings.* Baltimore: Penguin.

Copley, F. B. (1923). *Frederick W. Taylor.* New York: Harper.

Coser, L. (1956). *The functions of conflict.* Glencoe, IL: Free Press.

Cotton, J. L. & Baron, R. S. (1980). Anonymity, persuasive arguments and choice shifts. *Social Psychology Quarterly, 43,* 391-404.

Cottrell, N. B. (1972). Social facilitation. In C. G. McClintock (Ed.), *Experimental social psychology* (pp. 185-236). New York: Holt, Rinehart & Winston.

Cowherd, D. M. & Levine, D. I. (1992). Product quality and pay equity between lower-level employees and top management: An investigation of distributive justice theory. *Administrative Science Quarterly, 37,* 302-320.

Crockett, H. J., Jr. (1964). Social class, education, and the motivation to achieve in differential occupational mobility. *Sociology Quarterly, 5,* 231-242.

Crockett, H. J. Jr. (1966). The achievement motive and differential occupational mobility in the United States. In J. W. Atkinson & N. Feather (Eds.), *A theory of achievement motivation* (pp. 185-204). New York: Wiley.

Crosby, F. (1976). A model of egoistic relative deprivation. *Psychological Review, 83,* 85-113.

Crystal, G. S. (1991). *In search of excess: The overcompensation of American executives.* New York: Norton.

Daft, R. L. (1995). *Organization theory and design* (5th ed.). Minneapolis: West Publishing Company.

Dahl, R. A. (1957). The concept of power. *Behavioural Science, 2,* 201-215.

Dance, F. E. X. (1970). The 'concept' of communication. *Journal of Communication, 20,* 201-10.

Dando-Collins, S. (1998). *The Penguin book of business wisdom.* Harmondsworth: Penguin.

Dashiell, J. F. (1930). An experimental analysis of some group effects. *Journal of Abnormal Social Psychology, 25,* 190-199.

David, B. & Turner, J. C. (1996). Studies in self-categorization and minority conversion: Is being a member of the outgroup an advantage? *British Journal of Social Psychology, 35,* 179-199.

David, B. & Turner, J. C. (1999). Studies in self-categorization and minority conversion: The ingroup minority in intragroup and intergroup contexts. *British Journal of Social Psychology, 38,* 115-134.

Davis, K. (1981). *Human behavior at work.* New Delhi: McGraw-Hill.

Davison, W. P. (1983). The third-person effect in communication. *Public Opinion Quarterly, 47,* 1-15.

Deal, T. E. & Kennedy, A. A. (1982). *Corporate cultures: The rites and rituals of corporate life.* Harmondsworth:   Penguin.

deCharms, R. (1968). *Personal causation: The internal affective determinants of behavior.* New York: Academic Press.

deCharms, R. & Muir, M. S. (1978). Motivation: Social approaches. *Annual Review of Psychology, 29,* 91-113.

de Dreu, C. K. W. (1995). Coercive power and concession making in bilateral negotiation. *Journal of Conflict Resolution, 39,* 646-670.

de Dreu, C. K. W., Harinck, S., & van Vianen, A. E. M. (in press). Conflict and performance in groups and organizations. In C. L. Cooper & I. T. Robertson (Eds.), *International Review of Industrial and Organizational Psychology.*

de Dreu, C. K. W., Carnevale, P. J. D., Emans, B. J. M., & van de Vliert, E. (1995). Outcome frames in bilateral negotiation: Resistance to concession making and frame adoption. *European Review of Social Psychology, 6,* 97-125.

Deci, E. L. (1975). *Intrinsic motivation.* New York: Plenum Press.

Dépret, E. (1995). *Vicarious feelings of personal control and the social categorization of powerful others.* Unpublished manuscript: University of Grenoble.

Dépret, E. & Fiske, S. T. (1993). Social cognition and power: Some cognitive consequences of social structure as a source of control deprivation. In G. Weary, F. Gleicher & K. Marsh (Eds.), *Control, motivation and social cognition.* New York: Springer Verlag.

Dépret, E. & Fiske, S. T. (1999). Perceiving the powerful: Intriguing individuals versus threatening groups. *Journal of Experimental Social Psychology, 35,* 461-480.

Deschamps, J.-C. (1982). Relations of power between groups. In H. Tajfel (Ed.), *Social identity and intergroup relations.* Cambridge:   Cambridge   University Press.

Deschamps, J.-C. & Brown, R. (1983). Superordinate goals and intergroup conflict. *British Journal of Social Psychology, 22,* 189-195.

Deutsch, M. (1958). Trust and suspicion. *Journal of Conflict Resolution, 2,* 65-279.

Deutsch, M. (1973). *The resolution of conflict: Constructive and destructive processes.* New Haven, CT: Yale University Press.

Deutsch, M. & Gerard, H. B. (1955). A study of normative and informational social influences upon individual judgment. *Journal of Abnormal and Social Psychology, 51,* 629-636.

de Weerd, M. & Klandermans, B.   (1999). Group identification and political protest: Farmers' protest in the Netherlands. *European Journal of Social Psychology, 29,* 1073-1095.

Diehl, M. & Stroebe, W. (1987). Productivity losses in brainstorming groups: Toward the solution of a riddle. *Journal of Personality and Social Psychology, 53,* 497-509.

Diehl, M. & Stroebe, W. (1991). Productivity loss in idea-generating groups: Tracking down the blocking effect. *Journal of Personality and Social Psychology, 61,* 392-403.

Dietz-Uhler, B. (1996). The escalation of commitment in political decision-making groups: A social identity approach. *European Journal of Social Psychology, 26,* 611-629.

Digman, J. M. & Takemoto-Chock, N. K. (1981). Factors in the natural language of personality: Re-analysis and comparison of six major studies. *Behavioural Research, 16,* 149-170.

Doise, W. (1987). Intergroup relations and polarization of individual and collective judgements. *Journal of Personality and Social Psychology, 17,* 136-143.

Doise, W., Csepeli, G., Dann, H. D., Gouge, C., Larsen, K. & Ostell, A. (1972). An experimental investigation into the formation of intergroup representations. *European Journal of Social Psychology, 2,* 202-204.

Dollard, J., Doob, L. W., Miller, N. E., Mowrer, O. H., & Sears, R. R. (1939). *Frustration and aggression.* New Haven, CT: Yale University Press.

Dominguez, C. M. (1991). The glass ceiling and Workforce 2000. *Labor Law Journal, 42,* 715-717.

Donley, R. E. & Winter, D. G. (1970). Measuring the motives of public officials at a distance: An exploratory study. *Behavioural Science, 15,* 227-236.

Donnellon, A. (1996). *Team-talk: The power of language in team dynamics.* Boston, MA: Harvard University Business School Press.

Doosje, B. & Ellemers, N. (1997). Stereotyping under threat: The role of group identification. In R. Spears, P. J. Oakes, N. Ellemers & S. A. Haslam (Eds.), *The social psychology of stereotyping and group life* (pp. 257-272). Oxford: Blackwell.

Doosje, B., Ellemers, N., & Spears, R. (1995). Perceived intragroup variability as a function of group status and identification. *Journal of Experimental Social Psychology, 31,* 410-436.

Doosje, B., Haslam, S. A., Spears, R., Oakes, P. J., & Koomen, W. (1998). The effect of comparative context on central tendency and variability judgements and the evaluation of group characteristics. *European Journal of Social Psychology, 28,* 173-184.

Doosje, B., Spears, R., & Ellemers, N. (in press). The dynamic and determining nature of group identification: Responses to anticipated changes in the status hierarchy. *British Journal of Social Psychology.*

Douglas, A. (1957). The peaceful settlement of industrial intergroup disputes. *Journal of Conflict Resolution, 1,* 69-81.

Dovidio, J. F., Gaertner, S. L., Validzic, A., Matoka, K., Johnson, B., & Frazier, S. (1997). Extending the benefits of recategorization: Evaluations, self-disclosure, and helping. *Journal of Experimental Social Psychology, 33,* 401-420.

Driedger, L. (1976). Ethnic self-identity: A comparison of ingroup evaluations. *Sociometry, 39,* 131-141.

Drucker, P. F. (1986). *The frontiers of management: Where tomorrow's decisions are being shaped today.* New York: J. P. Dutton.

Druckman, D., Broome, B. J., & Korper, S. H. (1988). Value differences and conflict resolution. *Journal of Conflict Resolution, 32,* 489-510.

Druckman, D., Solomon, D., & Zechmeister, K. (1972). Effects of representative role obligations on the process of children's distribution of resources. *Sociometry, 35,* 387-410.

Duck, J. M. (1998). *A leader for all not just for some: Leadership and categorization in organizations.* Paper presented at the La Trobe Conference on the Social Psychology of Leadership, Melbourne, Victoria, 3-4 October.

Duck, J. M. & Fielding, K. S. (1999). Leaders and subgroups: One of us or one of them? *Group Processes and Intergroup Relations, 2,* 203-230.

Duck, J. M., Hogg, M. A., & Terry, D. J. (1995). Me, us and them: Political identification and the third-person effect in the 1993 Australian federal election. *European Journal of Social Psychology, 25,* 195-215.

Duck, J. M., Hogg, M. A. & Terry, D. J. (1997). Perceived self-other differences in persuadability: The effects of interpersonal and group-based similarity. *European Journal of Social Psychology, 27,* 842-862.

Duck, J. M., & Mullin, B.-A. (1997). The perceived impact of the mass media: Reconsidering the third person effect. *European Journal of Social Psychology, 25,* 77-93.

Duck, J. M., Terry, D. J., & Hogg, M. A. (1999). Perceptions of a media campaign: The role of social identity and the changing intergroup context. *Personality and Social Psychology Bulletin, 24*, 3-16.

Dunlop, E. E. (1986). *The war diaries of Weary Dunlop: Java and the Burma-Thailand railway, 1942-1945*. Melbourne: Nelson.

Durham, C. C., Knight, D. & Locke, E. A. (1997). Effects of leader role, team-set goal difficulty, efficacy and tactics on team effectiveness. *Organizational Behavior and Human Decision Processes, 72*, 203-231.

Durkheim, E. (1933). *The division of labour in society*. London: Macmillan.

Dutton, J. E. & Dukerich, J. M. (1991). Keeping an eye on the mirror: The role of image and identity in organizational adaptation. *Academy of Management Journal, 34*, 517-554.

Dutton, J. E., Dukerich, J. M., & Harquail, C. V. (1994). Organizational images and member identification. *Administrative Science Quarterly, 39*, 239-263.

Dweck, C. S. & Leggett, E. L. (1988). A social-cognitive approach to motivation and personality. *Psychological Review, 95*, 256-273.

Dyer, L. & Parker, D. F. (1975). Classifying outcomes in work motivation research: An examination of the intrinsic–extrinsic dichotomy. *Journal of Applied Psychology, 60*, 455-458.

Edstrom, A. & Galbraith, J. (1977). Transfer of managers as a co-ordination and control strategy in multinational organizations. *Administrative Science Quarterly, 22*, 248-263.

Eggins, R. A. (1999). *Social identity and social conflict: Negotiating the path to resolution*. Unpublished PhD thesis: The Australian National University.

Eggins, R. A. & Haslam, S. A. (1998). Social identity processes in negotiation. *Australian Journal of Psychology, 49*, 33-34.

Eggins, R. A. & Haslam, S. A. (1999a). *Social identity and negotiation: Giving voice to the group*. Unpublished manuscript: The Australian National University.

Eggins, R. A. & Haslam, S. A. (1999b). *Social identity and social conflict: When is recategorization effective in negotiation?* Unpublished manuscript: The Australian National University.

Eiser, J. R. & Stroebe, W. (1972). *Categorization and social judgement*. European monographs in social psychology, no. 3; London: Academic Press.

Ellemers, N. (1993). The influence of socio-structural variables on identity enhancement strategies. *European Review of Social Psychology, 4*, 27-57.

Ellemers, N., de Gilder, D., & van den Heuvel, H. (1998). Career-oriented versus team-oriented commitment and behaviour at work. *Journal of Applied Psychology, 83*, 717-730.

Ellemers, N., Doosje, B. J., van Knippenberg, A., & Wilke, H. (1992). Status protection in high status minorities. *European Journal of Social Psychology, 22*, 123-140.

Ellemers, N., Kortekaas, P., & Ouwerkerk, J. (1999). Self-categorization, commitment to the group and group self-esteem as related but distinct aspects of social identity. *European Journal of Social Psychology, 29*, 371-389.

Ellemers, N., Spears, R., & Doosje, B. (1997). Sticking together or falling apart: Ingroup identification as a psychological determinant of group commitment versus individual mobility. *Journal of Personality and Social Psychology, 72*, 617-626.

Ellemers, N. & van Knippenberg, A. (1997). Stereotyping in social context. In R. Spears, P. J. Oakes, N. Ellemers, & S. A. Haslam (Eds.), *The social psychology of stereotyping and group life* (pp. 210-235). Oxford: Blackwell.

Ellemers, N., van Knippenberg, A., De Vries, N. K., & Wilke, H. (1988). Social identification and permeability of group boundaries. *European Journal of Social Psychology, 18*, 497-513.

Ellemers, N., van Knippenberg, A., & Wilke, H. (1990). The influence of permeability of group boundaries and stability of group status on strategies of individual mobility and social change. *British Journal of Social Psychology, 29,* 233-246.

Ellemers, N., van Rijswijk, W., Bruins, J., & de Gilder, D. (1998). Group commitment as a moderator of attributional and behavioural responses to power use. *European Journal of Social Psychology, 28,* 555-573.

Ellemers, N., van Rijswijk, W., Roefs, M., & Simons, C. (1997). Bias in intergroup perceptions: Balancing group identity with social reality. *Personality and Social Psychology Bulletin, 23,* 186-198.

Ellemers, N., Wilke, H., & van Knippenberg, A. (1993). Effects of the legitimacy of low group or individual status on individual and collective identity enhancement strategies. *Journal of Personality and Social Psychology, 64,* 766-778.

Ely, R. J. (1994). The effects of organizational demographics and social identity on relationships among professional women. *Administrative Science Quarterly, 39,* 203-238.

Erez, M. & Somech, A. (1996). Is group productivity loss the rule or the exception? Effects of culture and group-based motivation. *Academy of Management Journal, 6,* 1513-1537.

Fajak, A. & Haslam, S. A. (1998). Gender solidarity in organizational hierarchies. *British Journal of Social Psychology, 37,* 73-94.

Falkenberg, L. (1990). Improving the accuracy of stereotypes within the workplace. *Journal of Management, 16,* 107-118.

Farquhar, H. H. (1924). Positive contributions of scientific management. In E. E. Hunt (Ed.), *Scientific management since Taylor: A collection of authoritative papers.* New York: McGraw-Hill.

Feldman, S. P. (1988). Secrecy, information, and politics: An essay on organizational decision making. *Human Relations, 41,* 73-90.

Fiedler, F. E. (1964). A contingency model of leader effectiveness. In L. Berkowitz (Ed.), *Advances in experimental social psychology* (vol. 1, pp. 149-190). New York: Academic Press.

Fiedler, F. E. (1978). The contingency model and the dynamics of the leadership process. In L. Berkowitz (Ed.), *Advances in Experimental Social Psychology* (vol. 11), Academic Press: New York.

Fiedler, F. E. & Garcia, J. E. (1987). *New approaches to effective leadership.* New York: Wiley.

Fiedler, F. E. & House, R. J. (1994). Leadership theory and research: A report of progress. In C. L. Cooper & I. T. Robertson (Eds.), *Key reviews in managerial psychology* (pp. 97-116). New York: Wiley.

Field, R. H. & House, R. J. (1990). A test of the Vroom–Yetton model using manager and subordinate reports. *Journal of Applied Psychology, 75,* 362-366.

Fielding, K. & Hogg, M. A. (1997). Social identity, self-categorization & leadership: A field study of small interactive groups. *Group Dynamics: Theory, Research and Practice, 1,* 39-51.

Fine, G. A. & Holyfield, L. (1996). Secrecy, trust, and dangerous leisure: Generating group cohesion in voluntary organizations. *Social Psychology Quarterly, 59,* 22-38.

Fisher, S. & Todd, A. D. (Eds.) (1983). *The social organization of doctor–patient communication.* Washington: Centre for Applied Linguistics.

Fiske, S. T. (1987). People's reactions to nuclear war. *American Psychologist, 42,* 207-217.

Fiske, S. T. (1993). Controlling other people: The impact of power on stereotyping. *American Psychologist, 48,* 621-628.

Fiske, S. T., Bersoff, D. N., Borgida, E., Deaux, K., & Heilman, M. E. (1991). Social science research on trial: The use of sex stereotyping research in *Price Waterhouse v. Hopkins. American Psychologist, 46,* 1049-1060.

Fiske, S. T. & Dépret, E. (1996). Control, interdependence and power: Understanding social cognition in its social context. *European Review of Social Psychology, 7,* 31-61.

Fiske, S. T. & Glick, P. (1995). Ambivalence and stereotypes cause sexual harassment: A theory with implications for organizational change. *Journal of Social Issues, 51,* 97-115.

Fiske, S. T. & Neuberg, S. L. (1989). Category-based and individuating processes as a function of information and motivation: Evidence from our laboratory. In D. Bar-Tal, C. F. Graumann, A. W. Kruglanski & W. Stroebe (Eds.), *Stereotyping and prejudice: Changing conceptions* (pp. 83-104). New York: Springer Verlag.

Fiske, S. T. & Taylor, S. E. (1984). *Social cognition.* Reading, MA: Addison Wesley.

Fiske, S. T. & Taylor, S. E. (1991). *Social cognition* (2nd ed.). Reading, MA: Addison Wesley.

Fleishman, E. A. (1953). The description of supervisory behaviour. *Journal of Applied Psychology, 67,* 523-532.

Fleishman, E. A. & Peters, D. A. (1962). Interpersonal values, leadership attitudes, and managerial success. *Personnel Psychology, 15,* 43-56.

Flowers, M. L. (1977). A laboratory test of some implications of Janis's groupthink hypothesis. *Journal of Personality and Social Psychology, 35,* 888-896.

Foddy, M. & Hogg, M. A. (1999). Impact of leaders on resource consumption in social dilemmas: The intergroup context. In M. Foddy, M. Smithson, K. Schneider & M. A. Hogg (Eds.), *Resolving social dilemmas: Dynamic, structural and intergroup aspects* (pp. 309-330). New York: Psychology Press.

Foddy, M., Smithson, M., Schneider, S. K., & Hogg, M. A. (Eds.) (1999). *Resolving social dilemmas: Dynamic, structural and intergroup aspects.* New York: Psychology Press.

Fosh, P. (1993). Membership participation in work-place unionism: The possibility of union renewal. *British Journal of Industrial Relations, 31,* 577-592.

Fox, J. B. & Scott, J. F. (1943). *Absenteeism: Management's problem.* Cambridge, MA: Harvard Business School, Business Research Studies No. 29.

Foy, N. (1994). *Empowering people at work.* Aldershot: Gower.

Fraser, C., Gouge, C., & Billig, M. (1971). Risky shifts, cautious shifts and group polarization. *European Journal of Social Psychology, 1,* 7-29.

French, E. G. (1955). Some characteristics of achievement motivation. *Journal of Experimental Psychology, 50,* 232-236.

French, J. R. P. & Raven, B. (1959). The bases of social power. In D. Cartwright (Ed.), *Studies in social power* (pp. 150-167). Ann Arbor, MI: Institute for Social Research.

Freytag, W. R. (1990). Organizational culture. In K. R. Murphy & F. E. Saal (Eds.), *Psychology in organizations: Integrating science and practice.* Hillsdale, NJ: Erlbaum.

Friedlander, F. (1974). Science, organization and humanism: A commentary on social responsibility. *Personnel Psychology, 27,* 448-453.

Fuller, S. R. & Aldag, R. J. (1998). Organizational Tonypandy: Lessons from a quarter century of the groupthink phenomenon. *Organizational Behaviour and Human Decision Processes, 2/3,* 163-184.

Gaertner, S. L. & Dovidio, J. F. (1999). *From superordinate goals to decategorization, recategorization and mutual differentiation.* Paper presented at the Small Groups Preconference to the Annual Meeting of the Society of Experimental Social Psychology, St Louis, MI, 14-16 October.

Gaertner, S. L., Dovidio, J. F., Anastasio, P. A., Bachman, B. A., & Rust, M. C. (1993). The common ingroup identity model: Recategorization and the reduction of intergroup bias. *European Review of Social Psychology, 4*, 1-25.

Gaertner, S. L., Dovidio, J. F., & Bachman, B. A. (1996). Revisiting the contact hypothesis: The induction of a common ingroup identity. *International Journal of Intercultural Relations, 20*, 271-290.

Gaertner, S. L., Mann, J., Murrell, A., & Dovidio, J. F. (1989). Reducing intergroup bias: The benefits of recategorization. *Journal of Personality and Social Psychology, 57*, 239-249.

Gaertner, S. L., Mann, J., Dovidio, J. F., Murrell, A., & Pomare, M. (1990). How does co-operation reduce intergroup bias? *Journal of Personality and Social Psychology, 59*, 692-704.

Gaertner, S. L., Rust, M. C., Dovidio, J. F., Bachman, B. A., & Anastasio, P. A. (1994). The contact hypothesis: The role of a common ingroup identity on reducing intergroup bias. *Small Group Research, 25*, 224-249.

Gaertner, S. L., Rust, M. C., Dovidio, J. F., Bachman, B. A., & Anastasio, P. A. (1996). The contact hypothesis: The role of a common ingroup identity on reducing intergroup bias among minority and majority group members. In J. Nye & A. Brower (Eds.), *What's social about social cognition? Research on socially shared cognition in small groups* (pp. 230-260). Newbury Park, CA: Sage.

Gallois, C., Callan, V. J., & McKenzie-Palmer, J.-A. (1992). The influence of applicant communication style and interviewer characteristics on hiring decisions. *Journal of Applied Social Psychology, 22*, 1040-1059.

Gamson, W. (1972). The management of discontent. In J. M. Thomas & W. G. Bennis (Eds.), *The management of change and conflict* (pp. 448-478). Harmondsworth: Penguin.

Gandz, J. & Murray, V. R. (1980) The experience of workplace politics. *Academy of Management Journal, 23*, 237-251.

Gardner, R. C. (1993). Stereotypes as consensual beliefs. In M. P. Zanna & J. M. Olson (Eds.), *The psychology of prejudice: The Ontario Symposium* (vol. 7, pp. 1-31). Hillsdale, NJ: Erlbaum.

Geen, R. G. (1989). Alternative conceptions of social facilitation. In P. B. Paulus (Ed.), *The psychology of group influence* (vol. 2, pp. 15-51). Hillsdale, NJ: Erlbaum.

Gelineau, E. P. & Merenda, P. F. (1981). Students' pre-election perceptions of Jimmy Carter and Ronald Reagan. *Perceptual and Motor Skills, 52*, 491-498.

Gemmill, G. & Oakley, J. (1992). Leadership: An alienating social myth? *Human Relations, 45*, 113-129.

George, E. & Chattopadhyay, P. (1999). *One foot in each camp: The dual identification of contract workers.* Paper presented at the 5th meeting of the Society of Australasian Social Psychologists, Coolum, Queensland, 8-11 April.

Ghiloni, B. W. (1987). The velvet ghetto: Women, power and the corporation. In G. W. Domhoff & T. R. Dye (Eds.), *Power elites and organizations* (pp. 21-36). Newbury Park, CA: Sage.

Ghoshal, S. & Bartlett, C. A. (1997). *The individualized corporation: A fundamentally new approach to management.* New York: Harper Collins Business.

Gibb, C. A. (1958). An interactional view of the emergence of leadership. *Australian Journal of Psychology, 10*, 101-10.

Giddens, A. (1999). *Runaway world: The 1999 Reith lectures.* BBC: London.

Gilbert, G. M. (1951). Stereotype persistence and change among college students. *Journal of Abnormal and Social Psychology, 46*, 245-54.

Gilbreth, F. B. (1909). *Bricklaying system.* New York: Harper.

Giles, H., Coupland J., & Coupland, N. (Eds.) (1991) *Contexts of accommodation: Developments in applied sociolinguistics. Studies in emotion and social interaction.* Cambridge: Cambridge University Press.

Giles, H & Farrar, K. (1979). Some behavioural consequences of speech and dress styles. *British Journal of Social and Clinical Psychology, 18,* 209-210.

Giles, H. & Johnson, P. (1981). The role of language in intergroup relations. In J. C. Turner & H. Giles (Eds.), *Intergroup behaviour* (pp. 199-243). Oxford: Blackwell.

Giles, H., Mulac, A., Bradac, J. J., & Johnson, P. (1987). Speech accommodation theory: The first decade and beyond. In C. M. McLaughlin (Ed.), *Communication yearbook* (vol. 10; pp. 13-48). Newbury Park, CA: Sage.

Giles, H., Wilson, P., & Conway, A. (1981). Accent and lexical diversity as determinants of impression formation and employment selection. *Language Sciences, 3,* 92-103.

Gomez-Mejia, L. R. & Wiseman, D. B. (1997). *Compensation, organizational strategy, and firm performance.* Cincinnati, OH: South West Publishing.

Gonzalez, R. & Brown, R. J. (1999). *Maintaining the salience of subgroup and superordinate group identities during intergroup contact.* Paper presented at the Small Groups Preconference to the Annual Meeting of the Society of Experimental Social Psychology, St Louis, MI, 14-16 October.

Goodwin, S. A., Fiske, S. T., & Yzerbyt, V. (1995). *Social judgement in power relationships: A judgement-monitoring perspective.* Poster presented at the American Psychological Association, New York, August.

Gordon, M. E. & Nurick, A. J. (1981). Psychological approaches to the study of unions and union-management relations. *Psychological Bulletin, 90,* 293-306.

Grant, P. (1990). Cognitive theories applied to intergroup conflict. In R. Fisher (Ed.), *The social psychology of intergroup and international conflict resolution* (pp. 39-57). New York: Springer Verlag.

Greene, G. & Reed, C. (1968). *The third man* (filmscript). Lorimer: London.

Grice, H. P. (1975). Logic and conversation. In P. Cole & J. L. Morgan (Eds.), *Syntax and semantics* (vol. 3.): *Speech acts* (pp. 365-372). New York: Seminar Press.

Griesinger, D. W. (1990). The human side of economic organization. *Academy of Management Review, 15,* 478-499.

Grieve, P. G. & Hogg, M. A. (1999). Subjective uncertainty and intergroup discrimination in the minimal group situation. *Personality and Social Psychology Bulletin, 25,* 926-940.

Grint, K. (1997). *Leadership: Classical, contemporary and critical approaches.* Oxford: Oxford University Press.

Grossman, W. & Hoskisson, R. E. (1998). CEO pay at the crossroads of Wall Street and Main: Toward the strategic design of executive compensation. *Academy of Management Executive, 12,* 43-57.

Guerin, B. (1986). Mere presence effects in humans: A review. *Journal of Experimental Social Psychology, 22,* 38-77.

Guimond, S. (2000). Group socialization and prejudice: The social transmission of intergroup attitudes and beliefs. *European Journal of Social Psychology, 30,* 335-354.

Gurr, T. R. (1970). *Why men rebel.* Princeton, NJ: Princeton University Press.

Guzzo, R. A. (Ed.) (1982). *Improving group decision making in organizations: Approaches from theory and research.* New York: Academic Press.

Hackman J. R. (1987). The design of work teams. In J. W. Lorsch (Ed.), *Handbook of organizational behaviour.* Engelwood Cliffs, NJ: Prentice Hall.

Hackman J. R. & Morris, C. G. (1975). Group tasks, group interaction process, and group performance effectiveness. In L. Berkowitz (Ed.), *Advances in Experimental Social Psychology* (vol. 8, pp. 45-99). New York: Academic Press.

Hackman, J. R. & Oldham, G. R. (1976). Motivation through the design of work: Test of a theory. *Organizational Behavior and Human Performance, 16,* 250-279.

Hackman, J. R. & Oldham, G. R. (1980). *Work redesign.* Addison-Wesley: Reading, MA.

Haines, H. & Vaughan, G. M. (1979). Was 1898 a 'great date' in the history of experimental social psychology? *Journal of the History of the Behavioural Sciences, 15,* 323-332.

Hains, S. C., Hogg, M. A., & Duck, J. M. (1997). Self-categorization and leadership: Effects of group prototypicality and leader stereotypicality. *Personality and Social Psychology Bulletin, 23,* 1087-1099.

Hamilton, D. L. (Ed.) (1981). *Cognitive processes in stereotyping and intergroup behaviour.* Hillsdale, NJ: Erlbaum.

Hamilton, D. L., Stroessner, S. J., & Driscoll, D. M. (1994). Social cognition and the study of stereotyping. In Devine, P. G., Hamilton, D. L. & Ostrom, T. M. (Eds.), *Social cognition: Contributions to classic issues in social psychology* (pp. 291-321). New York: Springer Verlag.

Handy, C. B. (1976). *Understanding organizations.* Harmondsworth: Penguin.

Harackiewicz, J. & Larson, J. R. Jr. (1986). Managing motivation: The impact of supervisor feedback on subordinate task interest. *Journal of Personality and Social Psychology, 37,* 1352-1363.

Harackiewicz, J., Manderlink, G., & Sansone, C. (1984). Rewarding pinball wizardry: Effects of evaluation and cue validity on intrinsic interest. *Journal of Personality and Social Psychology, 47,* 287-300.

Harackiewicz, J. & Sansone, C. (1991). Goals and intrinsic motivation: You can get there from here. *Advances in Motivation and Achievement, 7,* 21-49.

Hardin, C. & Higgins, E. T. (1996). Shared reality: How social verification makes the subjective objective. In R. M. Sorrentino & E. T. Higgins (Eds.), *Handbook of motivation and cognition* (vol. 3, pp. 28-84). New York: Guilford.

Hardy, C. & Leiba-O'Sullivan, S. (1998). The power behind empowerment: Implications for research and practice. *Human Relations, 51,* 451-483.

Harkins, S. G. (1987) Social loafing and social facilitation. *Journal of Experimental Social Psychology, 23,* 1-18.

Harkins, S. G. & Jackson, J. M. (1985). The role of evaluation in eliminating social loafing. *Personality and Social Psychology Bulletin, 11,* 575-584.

Harkins, S. G. & Szymanski, K. (1989). Social loafing and group evaluation. *Journal of Personality and Social Psychology, 56,* 934-941.

Harley, B. (1994). Post-Fordist theory, Labour process and flexibility in Australian workplaces. *Labour and Industry, 6,* 107-129.

Harley, B. (1999). The myth of empowerment: Work organization, hierarchy and employee autonomy in contemporary Australian workplaces. *Work, Employment and Society, 13,* 41-66.

Harvey-Jones, J. (1994). *All together now.* London: Heinemann.

Haslam, S. A. (1997). Stereotyping and social influence: Foundations of stereotype consensus. In R. Spears, P. J. Oakes, N. Ellemers & S. A. Haslam (Eds.), *The social psychology of stereotyping and group life* (pp. 119-143). Oxford: Blackwell.

Haslam, S. A. (1998). *Your wish is my command: The role of social identity and self-categorization processes in translating a leader's words into followers' actions.* Paper presented at the La Trobe Conference on the Social Psychology of Leadership, Melbourne, Victoria, 3-4 October.

Haslam, S. A. (1999a). *Studies in social motivation.* Unpublished manuscript: The Australian National University.

Haslam, S. A. (1999b). *Who needs to know? The role of self-categorization in organizational communication.* Paper presented at the 3rd Australian Industrial and Organizational Psychology Conference, Brisbane, Queensland, 26-27 June.

Haslam, S. A. (in press). Social identity, deindividuation and organizational behaviour: The upSIDE to groupthink, communicative consensus-seeking and soldiering. In T. Postmes, R. Spears, M. Lea & S. D. Reicher (Eds.), *SIDE issues centre stage: Recent developments in studies of deindividuation in groups.* Amsterdam: Royal Netherlands Academy of Arts and Sciences.

Haslam, S. A., Brown, P., McGarty, C., & Reynolds, K. J. (1998). *The impact of differential reward on the motivation of leaders and followers.* Unpublished manuscript: The Australian National University.

Haslam, S. A. & McGarty, C. (1998). *Doing psychology: An introduction to research methodology and statistics.* London: Sage.

Haslam, S. A. & McGarty, C. (in press). A hundred years of certitude? Social psychology, the experimental method and the management of scientific uncertainty. *British Journal of Social Psychology.*

Haslam, S. A., McGarty, C., Brown, P. M., Eggins, R. A, Morrison, B. E., & Reynolds, K. J. (1998). Inspecting the emperor's clothes: Evidence that randomly-selected leaders can enhance group performance. *Group Dynamics: Theory, Research and Practice, 2,* 168-184.

Haslam, S. A., McGarty, C., & Reynolds, K. J. (1999). *The role of self-categorization in the interpretation of power use.* Unpublished manuscript: The Australian National University.

Haslam, S. A., McGarty, C., & Turner, J. C. (1996). Salient group memberships and persuasion: The role of social identity in the validation of beliefs. In J. Nye & A. Brower (Eds.), *What's social about social cognition? Research on socially shared cognition in small groups* (pp. 29-56). Newbury Park, CA: Sage.

Haslam, S. A., Oakes, P. J., McGarty, C., Turner, J. C., & Onorato, R. (1995). Contextual shifts in the prototypicality of extreme and moderate outgroup members. *European Journal of Social Psychology, 25,* 509-530.

Haslam, S. A., Oakes, P. J., McGarty, C., Turner, J. C., Reynolds, K. J., & Eggins, R. A. (1996). Stereotyping and social influence: The mediation of stereotype applicability and sharedness by the views of ingroup and outgroup members. *British Journal of Social Psychology, 35,* 369-397.

Haslam, S. A., Oakes, P. J., Reynolds, K. J., & Turner, J. C. (1999). Social identity salience and the emergence of stereotype consensus. *Personality and Social Psychology Bulletin, 25,* 809-818.

Haslam, S. A., Oakes, P. J., Turner, J. C., & McGarty, C. (1995). Social categorization and group homogeneity: Changes in the perceived applicability of stereotype content as a function of comparative context and trait favourableness. *British Journal of Social Psychology, 34,* 139-160.

Haslam, S. A., Oakes, P. J., Turner, J. C., & McGarty, C. (1996). Social identity, self-categorization, and the perceived homogeneity of ingroups and outgroups: The interaction between social motivation and cognition. In R. M. Sorrentino and E. T. Higgins (Eds.), *Handbook of motivation and cognition* (vol. 3, pp. 182-222). New York: Guilford Press.

Haslam, S. A. & Platow, M. J. (2000). *The importance of standing up for us: How support for particular ingroup members translates a leader's vision into followers' actions.* Unpublished manuscript: The Australian National University.

Haslam, S. A. & Platow, M. J. (in press). Your wish is my command: How a leader's vision becomes a follower's task. In M. A. Hogg & D. J. Terry (Eds.), *Social identity processes in organizational contexts.* New York: Taylor & Francis.

Haslam, S. A., Platow, M. J., Turner, J. C., Reynolds, K. J., McGarty, C. Oakes, P. J., Johnson, S., Ryan, M. K., & Veenstra, K. (2000). *Variation in a leader's perceived charisma and perceived agency as a function of organizational outcomes and displayed group membership: A social identity dimension to the romance of leadership.* Unpublished manuscript: The Australian National University.

Haslam, S. A., Powell, C. & Turner, J. C. (2000). Social identity, self-categorization and work motivation: Rethinking the contribution of the group to positive and sustainable organizational outcomes. *Applied Psychology: An International Review*, *49*, 319-339.

Haslam, S. A., Ryan, M. K., Postmes, T., Spears, R., & Smithson, M. (1999). *Rethinking groupthink: Social identity as a basis for commitment to faltering organizational projects*. Unpublished manuscript: The Australian National University.

Haslam, S. A. & Turner, J. C. (1992). Context-dependent variation in social stereotyping 2: The relationship between frame of reference, self-categorization and accentuation. *European Journal of Social Psychology*, *22*, 251-277.

Haslam, S. A. & Turner, J. C. (1995). Context-dependent variation in social stereotyping 3: Extremism as a self-categorical basis for polarized judgement. *European Journal of Social Psychology*, *25*, 341-371.

Haslam, S. A. & Turner, J. C. (1998). Extremism and deviance: Beyond taxonomy and bias. *Social Research*, *65*, 435-448.

Haslam, S. A., Turner, J. C., & Oakes, P. J. (1999). *Contextual variation in leader prototypes*. Unpublished Manuscript: The Australian National University.

Haslam, S. A., Turner, J. C., Oakes, P. J., McGarty, C., & Reynolds, K. J. (1998). The group as a basis for emergent stereotype consensus. *European Review of Social Psychology*, *9*, 203-239.

Haslam, S. A., Turner, J. C., Oakes, P. J., Reynolds, K. J., Eggins, R. A., Nolan, M., & Tweedie, J. (1998). When do stereotypes become really consensual? Investigating the group-based dynamics of the consensualization process. *European Journal of Social Psychology*, *28*, 755-776.

Haunschild, P. R., Moreland, R. L., & Murrell, A. J. (1994). Sources of resistance to mergers between groups. *Journal of Applied Social Psychology*, *24*, 1150-1178.

Heider, F. (1958). *The psychology of interpersonal relations*. New York: Wiley.

Heilman, M. E. (1995). Sex stereotypes and their effects in the workplace: What we know and what we don't know. *Journal of Social Behavior and Personality*, *10*, 3-26.

Heller, F. (1998). Influence at work: A 25-year program of research. *Human Relations*, *51*, 1425-1456.

Hemphill, J. K. (1949). The leader and his group. In C. A. Gibb (Ed.), *Leadership*. Baltimore, ML: Penguin.

Herzberg, F. (1966). *Work and the nature of man*. Cleveland, OH: World Publishing Co.

Herzberg, F. (1968). One more time: How do you motivate employees? *Harvard Business Review*, *46*, 53-62.

Herzberg, F., Mausner, B., & Snyderman, B. (1959). *The motivation to work*. New York: Wiley.

Hewstone, M. (1990). The ultimate attribution error: A review of the literature on intergroup causal attribution. *European Journal of Social Psychology*, *20*, 311-355.

Hewstone, M. & Brown, R. J. (Eds.) (1986). *Contact and conflict in intergroup encounters*. Oxford: Blackwell.

Hewstone, M. & Giles, H. (1986). Social groups and stereotypes in intergroup communication: Review and model of communication breakdown. In W. B. Gudykunst (Ed.), *Intergroup communication* (pp. 10-26). London: Edward Arnold.

Hewstone, M. & Jaspars, J. M. F. (1982). Intergroup relations and attribution processes. In H. Tajfel (Ed.), *Social identity and intergroup relations* (pp. 99-133). Cambridge: Cambridge University Press.

Hewstone, M. & Jaspars, J. M. F. (1984). Social dimensions of attribution. In H. Tajfel (Ed.), *The social dimension* (vol. 2; pp. 379-404). Cambridge: Cambridge University Press.

Hiltz, S. R. & Turoff, M. (1992). *The network nation: Human communication via computer.* Reading MA: Addison-Wesley.

Hinkle, S., Taylor, L. A., Fox-Cardamone, D. L., & Crook, K. F. (1989). Intragroup identification and intergroup differentiation: A multicomponent approach. *British Journal of Social Psychology, 28,* 305-317.

Hobbes, T. (1651/1968). *Leviathan.* Harmondsworth: Penguin.

Hofstede, G., Neuijen, B., Ohayv, D. D., & Sanders, G. (1990). Measuring organizational cultures: A qualitative and quantitative study across twenty cultures. *Administrative Science Quarterly, 35,* 286-316.

Hogg, M. A. (1987). Social identity and group cohesiveness. In J. C. Turner, M. A. Hogg, P. J. Oakes, S. D. Reicher, & M. S. Wetherell *Rediscovering the social group: A self-categorization theory* (pp. 89-116). Oxford: Blackwell.

Hogg, M. A. (1992). *The social psychology of group cohesiveness: From attraction to social identity.* Hemel Hempstead: Harvester Wheatsheaf.

Hogg, M. A. (1996). Intragroup processes, group structure and social identity. In W. P. Robinson (Ed.), *Social groups and identities: The developing legacy of Henri Tajfel* (pp. 65-93). Oxford: Butterworth–Heineman.

Hogg, M. A. & Abrams, D. (1988) *Social identifications: A social psychology of intergroup relations and group processes.* London: Routledge.

Hogg, M. A. & Abrams, D. (1990). Social motivation, self-esteem and social identity. In D. Abrams & M. A. Hogg (Eds.), *Social identity theory: Constructive and critical advances* (pp. 28-47). London: Harvester Wheatsheaf.

Hogg, M. A. & Abrams, D. (1993). Towards a single-process uncertainty-reduction model of social motivation in groups. In M. A. Hogg & D. Abrams (Eds.), *Group motivation: Social psychological perspectives* (pp. 173-90). London: Harvester Wheatsheaf.

Hogg, M. A. & Hains, S. C. (1998). Friendship and group identification: A new look at the role of cohesiveness in groupthink. *European Journal of Social Psychology, 28,* 323-341.

Hogg, M. A., Hains, S. C., & Mason, I. (1998). Identification and leadership in small groups: Salience, frame of reference, and leader stereotypicality effects on leader evaluations. *Journal of Personality and Social Psychology, 75,* 1248-1263.

Hogg, M. A. & Hardie, E. A. (1991). Social attraction, personal attraction and self-categorization: A field study. *Personality and Social Psychology Bulletin, 17,* 175-180.

Hogg, M. A. & Hardie, E. A. (1992). Prototypicality, conformity and depersonalized attraction: A self-categorization analysis of group cohesiveness. *British Journal of Social Psychology, 31,* 41-56.

Hogg, M. A. & Sunderland, J. (1991). Self-esteem and intergroup discrimination in the minimal group paradigm. *British Journal of Social Psychology, 30,* 51-62.

Hogg M. A. & Terry, D. J. (2000). Social identity and self-categorization processes in organizational contexts. *Academy of Management Review, 25,* 121-140.

Hogg M. A. & Terry, D. J. (Eds.) (in press). *Social identity processes in organizations.* New York: Taylor & Francis.

Hogg, M. A. & Turner, J. C. (1985). Interpersonal attraction, social identification and psychological group formation. *European Journal of Social Psychology, 15,* 51-66.

Hogg, M. A. & Turner, J. C. (1987a). Intergroup behaviour, self-stereotyping and the salience of social categories. *British Journal of Social Psychology, 26,* 325-340.

Hogg, M. A. & Turner, J. C. (1987b). Social influence and conformity: A theory of referent informational influence. In W. Doise & S. Moscovici (Eds.), *Current issues in European social psychology* (vol. 2, pp. 139-182). Cambridge: Cambridge University Press.

Hogg, M. A., Turner, J. C., & David, B. (1990). Polarized norms and social frames of reference: A test of the self-categorization theory of group polarization. *Basic and Applied Social Psychology, 11*, 77-100.

Hollander, E. P. (1958). Conformity, status, and idiosyncrasy credit. *Psychological Review, 65*, 117-127.

Hollander, E. P. (1964). *Leaders, groups, and influence.* New York: Oxford University Press.

Hollander, E. P. (1985). Leadership and power. In G. Lindzey & E. Aronson (Eds.), *The handbook of social psychology* (3rd ed., pp. 485-537). New York: Random House.

Hollander, E. P. (1993). Legitimacy, power, and influence: A perspective on relational features of leadership. In M. M. Chemers & R. Ayman (Eds.), *Leadership theory and research: Perspectives and directions* (pp. 29-47). Orlando, FL: Academic Press.

Hollander, E. P. (1995). Organizational leadership and followership. In P. Collett & A. Furnham (Eds.), *Social psychology at work: Essays in honour of Michael Argyle* (pp. 69-87). London: Routledge.

Hollander, E. P. & Julian, J. W. (1970). Studies in leader legitimacy, influence and innovation. In L. Berkowitz (Ed.), *Advances in experimental social psychology* (vol. 2, pp. 485-537). New York: Random House.

Homans, G. C. (1951). *The human group.* London: Routledge & Kegan Paul.

Hopkins, K. M. (1997). Supervisor intervention with troubled workers: A social identity perspective. *Human Relations, 10*, 1215-1238.

Horgan, D. D. & Simeon, R. J. (1990). Mentoring and participation: An application of the Vroom–Yetton model. *Journal of Business and Psychology, 5*, 63-84.

Hornsey, M. J. & Hogg, M. A. (1999). Subgroup differentiation as a response to an overly-inclusive group: A test of optimal distinctiveness theory. *European Journal of Social Psychology, 29*, 543-550.

Hornsey, M. J. & Hogg, M. A. (2000). Subgroup relations: Two experiments comparing subgroup differentiation and common ingroup identity models of prejudice reduction. *Personality and Social Psychology Bulletin, 26*, 242-256.

Horwitz, M. & Berkowitz, N. (1990). Interpersonal and intergroup means of managing social conflict. In S. A. Wheelan & E. A. Pepitone (Eds.), *Advances in Field Theory* (pp. 177-193). Newbury Park, CA: Sage.

Hothersall, D. (1984). *History of psychology.* New York: Random House.

House, R. J. (1971). A path–goal theory of leader effectiveness. *Administrative Science Quarterly, 16*, 321-39.

House, R. J. & Shamir, B. (1993). Toward the integration of transformational, charismatic, and visionary theories. In M. M. Chemers & R. Ayman (Eds.), *Leadership theory and research: Perspectives and directions* (pp. 81-107). Orlando, FL: Academic Press.

Howell, J. P., Dorfman, P. W., & Kerr, S. (1986). Moderator variables in leadership research. *Academy of Management Review, 11*, 88-102.

Hughes, R. (1993). *Culture of complaint: The fraying of America.* Oxford: Oxford University Press.

Hunt, S. D. & Morgan, R. M. (1994). Organizational commitment: One of many commitments or key mediating construct? *Academy of Management Journal, 37*, 1568-1587.

Huo, Y. J., Smith, H. J., Tyler, T. R., & Lind, E. A. (1996). Superordinate identification, subgroup identification, and justice concerns: Is separatism the problem? Is assimilation the answer? *Psychological Science, 7*, 40-45.

Huszczo, G. E., Wiggins, J. G., & Currie, J. S. (1984). The relationship between psychology and organized labour: Past, present and future. *American Psychologist, 39*, 432-440.

Hyman, H. H. (1953). The value systems of different classes: A social psychological contribution to the analysis of stratification. In R. Bendix & S. M. Lipset (Eds.), *Class, status and power*. New York: Free Press of Glencoe.

Ibarra, H. & Andrews, S. B. (1993). Power, social influence and sense making: Effects of network centrality and proximity on employee perceptions. *Administrative Science Quarterly, 38*, 277-303.

Ickes, W. & Gonzalez, R. (1994). 'Social' cognition and *social* cognition: From the subjective to the intersubjective. *Small Group Research, 25*, 294-315.

Ingham, A. G., Levinger, G., Graves, J., & Peckham, V. (1974). The Ringelmann effect: Studies of group size and group performance. *Journal of Experimental Social Psychology, 10*, 371-384.

Jackson, J. M. & Harkins, S. G. (1985). Equity in effort: An explanation of the social loafing effect. *Journal of Personality and Social Psychology, 49*, 1199-1206.

Jackson, J. M. & Williams, K. D. (1985). Social loafing on difficult tasks: Working collectively can improve performance. *Journal of Personality and Social Psychology, 49*, 937-942.

Jackson, J. W. & Smith, E. R. (1999). Conceptualizing social identity: A new framework and evidence for the impact of different dimensions. *Personality and Social Psychology Bulletin, 25*, 120-135.

Jackson, S. E. (1992). Team composition in organizational settings: Issues in managing an increasingly diverse workforce. In S. Worchel, W. Wood & J. A. Simpson (Eds.), *Group processes and productivity* (pp. 136-180). Newbury Park, CA: Sage.

Jackson, S. E., Brett, J. F., Sessa, V. I., Cooper, D. M., Julin, J. A., & Peyronnin, K. (1991). Some differences make a difference: Individual dissimilarity and group heterogeneity as correlates of recruitment, promotions and turnover. *Journal of Applied Psychology, 76*, 675-689.

Jaeger, M. E., Anthony, S., & Rosnow, R. L. (1980). Who hears what from whom and with what effect: A study of rumor. *Personality and Social Psychology Bulletin, 6*, 473-478.

James, K. & Cropanzano, R. (1994). Dispositional group loyalty and individual action for the benefit of an ingroup: Experimental and correlational evidence. *Organizational Behavior and Human Decision Making, 60*, 179-205.

James, K. & Greenberg, J. (1989). Ingroup salience, intergroup comparison and individual performance and self-esteem. *Personality and Social Psychology Bulletin, 15*, 604-616.

Janis, I. L. (1971). Groupthink. *Psychology Today*, November, 43-46, 74-76.

Janis, I. L. (1972). *Victims of groupthink*. Boston: Houghton-Mifflin.

Janis, I. L. (1982). *Groupthink: Psychological studies of policy decisions and fiascoes* (2nd ed.). Boston: Houghton Mifflin.

Janis, I. L. (1989). *Crucial decisions: Leadership in policymaking and crisis management*. New York: Free Press.

Janis, I. L. & Mann, L. (1977). *Decision making: A psychological analysis of conflict, choice and commitment*. New York: Free Press.

Jellison, J. & Arkin, R. (1977). Social comparison of abilities: A self-presentation approach to decision-making in groups. In J. M. Suls & R. L. Miller (Eds.), *Social comparison processes* (pp. 235-257). Washington: Hemisphere.

Jenkins, W. O. (1947). A review of leadership studies with particular reference to military problems. *Psychological Bulletin, 44,* 54-79.

Jetten, J., Spears, R., & Manstead, A. R. (1997). Strength of identification and intergroup differentiation: The influence of group norms. *European Journal of Social Psychology, 27,* 603-609.

Jewell, L. N. (1998). *Contemporary industrial/organizational psychology* (3rd ed.). Pacific Grove, CA: Brooks/Cole Publishing.

Johnson D. W. & Johnson F. P. (1991). *Joining together: Group theory and group skills.* Englewood Cliffs, NJ: Prentice Hall.

Jones, E. E. & Davis, K. E. (1965). From acts to dispositions: The attribution process in person perception. In L. Berkowitz (Ed.), *Advances in experimental social psychology* (vol. 2). New York: Academic Press.

Jones, E. E. & Gerard, H. B. (1967). *Foundations of social psychology.* New York: Wiley.

Jones, E. E. & Nisbett, R. E. (1972). The actor and the observer: divergent perceptions of the causes of behaviour. In E. E. Jones, D. E. Kanouse, H. H. Kelley, R. E. Nisbett, S. Valins & B. Weiner (Eds.), *Attributions: Perceiving the causes of behaviour* (pp. 79-94). Morristown, NJ: General Learning Press.

Jones, E. E. & Sigall, H. (1971). The bogus pipeline: A new paradigm for measuring affect and attitude. *Psychological Bulletin, 76,* 349-364.

Jost, J. T. & Banaji, M. R. (1994). The role of stereotyping in system-justification and the production of false consciousness. *British Journal of Social Psychology, 33,* 1-27.

Judd, C. M. & Park, B. (1993). Definition and assessment of accuracy in social stereotypes. *Psychological Review, 100,* 109-128.

Kabanoff, B. (1985). Potential influence structures as sources of interpersonal conflict in groups and organizations. *Organizational Behaviour and Group Decision Processes, 36,* 113-141.

Kahn, R. L., Wolfe, D. M., Quinn, R. P., Snoek, J. D., & Rosenthal, R. A. (1964). *Organizational stress: Studies in role conflict and ambiguity.* New York: Wiley.

Kahneman, D. & Tversky, A. (1979). Prospect theory: An analysis of decision making under risk. *Econometrica, 47,* 263-291.

Kakar, S. (1970). *Frederick Taylor: A study in personality and innovation.* Cambridge, MA: MIT Press.

Kanfer, R. (1994). Work motivation: New directions in theory and research. In C. L. Cooper & I. T. Robertson (Eds.), *Key reviews in managerial psychology* (pp. 1-53). New York: Wiley.

Kanter, R. (1977). *Men and women of the organization.* New York: Basic Books.

Kanter, R. (1979). Power failure in management circuits. *Harvard Business Review,* July-August, 65-75.

Kaplan, A. (1964). *Conduct of inquiry.* San Francisco: Chandler.

Karasawa, M. (1991). Toward an assessment of social identity: The structure of group identification and its effects on in-group evaluations. *British Journal of Social Psychology, 30,* 293-307.

Karau, S. J. & Williams, K. D. (1993). Social loafing: A meta-analytic review and theoretical integration. *Journal of Personality and Social Psychology, 65,* 681-706.

Karlins, M., Coffman, T. L., & Walters, G. (1969). On the fading of social stereotypes: Studies in three generations of college students. *Journal of Personality and Social Psychology, 13,* 1-16.

Katz, D. (1964a). Approaches to managing conflict. In R. L. Kahn & E. Boulding (Eds.), *Power and conflict in organizations.* London: Tavistock Publications.

Katz, D. (1964b). The motivational basis of organizational behaviour. *Behavioural Science, 9,* 131-146.

Katz, D. & Braly, K. (1933). Racial stereotypes of one hundred college students. *Journal of Abnormal and Social Psychology, 28,* 280-290.

Katz, D. & Kahn, R. L. (1966). *The social psychology of organizations.* New York: Wiley.

Keenan, P. A. & Carnevale, P. J. (1989). Positive effects of within-group co-operation on between group negotiation. *Journal of Applied Social Psychology, 19,* 977-992.

Kelley, H. H. (1967). Attribution theory in social psychology. In D. Levine (Ed.), *Nebraska symposium on motivation.* Lincoln, NE: University of Nebraska Press.

Kelley, H. H. & Thibaut, J. W. (1954). Experimental studies of group problem solving and process. In G. Lindzey (Ed.), *The handbook of social psychology.* Cambridge, MA: Addison-Wesley.

Kelley, H. H. & Thibaut, J. W. (1969). Group problem solving. In G. Lindzey (Ed.), *The handbook of social psychology* (2nd ed.). Cambridge, MA: Addison-Wesley.

Kelly, C. (1989). Political identity and perceived intragroup homogeneity. *British Journal of Social Psychology, 29,* 289-301.

Kelly, C. (1993). Group identification, intergroup perceptions and collective action. *European Review of Social Psychology, 4,* 59-83.

Kelly, C. & Breinlinger, S. (1996). *The social psychology of collective action: Identity, injustice and gender.* London: Taylor & Francis.

Kelly, C. & Kelly, J. (1991). 'Them and us': Social psychology and 'the new industrial relations'. *British Journal of Industrial Relations, 29,* 25-48.

Kelly, C. & Kelly, J. (1994). Who gets involved in collective action? Social psychological determinants of individual participation in trade unions. *Human Relations, 47,* 63-88.

Kelly, J. (1982). *Scientific management, job redesign and work performance.* London: Academic Press.

Kelly, J. & Kelly, C. (1992). Industrial action. In J. F. Hartley & G. M. Stephenson (Eds.), *Employment relations: The psychology of influence and control at work* (pp. 246-268). Oxford: Blackwell.

Kerr, C. (1954). Industrial conflict and its mediation. *American Journal of Sociology, 60,* 230-245.

Kerr, N. L. & Bruun, S. E. (1983). Dispensability of member effort and group motivation losses: Free rider effects. *Journal of Personality and Social Psychology, 44,* 78-94.

Kerr, S. & Jermier, J. M. (1978). Substitutes for leadership: Their meaning and measurement. *Organizational Behavior and Human Performance, 22,* 375-403.

Kiesler, S., Siegel, J., & McGuire, T. (1984). Social psychological aspects of computer-mediated communication. *American Psychologist, 39,* 1123-1134.

Kim, P. H. (1997). When what you know *can* hurt you: A study of experiental effects on group discussion and performance. *Organizational Behavior and Human Decision Processes, 69,* 165-177.

Kinder, D. R. (1986). Presidential character revisited. In R. R. Lau & D. O. Sears (Eds.), *Political cognition: The 19th annual Carnegie symposium on cognition.* Hillsdale, NJ: Erlbaum.

King, N. & Anderson, N. (1995). *Innovation and change in organizations.* London: Routledge.

Kipnis, D. (1972). Does power corrupt? *Journal of Personality and Social Psychology, 24,* 33-41.

Klandermans, B. (1984). Mobilization and participation in trade union action: An expectancy-value approach. *Journal of Occupational Psychology, 57,* 107-120.

Klandermans, B. (1986). Psychology and trade union participation: Joining, acting, quitting. *Journal of Occupational Psychology, 59,* 189-204.

Klandermans, B. (1992). Trade union participation. In J. F. Hartley & G. M. Stephenson (Eds.), *Employment relations: The psychology of influence and control at work* (pp. 184-199). Oxford: Blackwell.

Klandermans, B. (1997). *The social psychology of protest.* Oxford: Blackwell.

Klandermans, B. & Oegema, D. (1992). Potentials, networks, motivations and barriers: Steps toward participation in social movements. *American Sociological Review, 52,* 519-531.

Klemmer, E. T. & Snyder, F. W. (1972). Measurement of time spent communicating. *Journal of Communication, 22,* 142-58.

Kogan, N. & Wallach, M. A. (1964). *Risk taking: A study in cognition and personality.* New York: Holt, Rhinehart & Winston.

Kolb, D. A. & Rubin, I. M. (1991). Mediation from a disciplinary perspective. In M. H. Bazerman, R. J. Lewicki & B. H. Sheppard (Eds.), *Research on negotiation in organizations* (vol. 3). Greenwich, CT: JAI Press.

Kolb, D. A., Rubin, I. M. & McIntyre, J. M. (1979). *Organizational psychology: A book of readings.* New Jersey: Prentice Hall.

Kouzes, J. M. & Posner, B. (1988). *The leadership challenge: How to get things done in organizations.* San Francisco: Jossey-Bass.

Kouzes, J. M. & Posner, B. (1990). The credibility factor: What followers expect from their leaders. *Management Review,* January, 29-33.

Kramer, R. M. (1993). Cooperation and organizational identification. In J. K. Murnigham (Ed.), *Social psychology in organizations: Advances in theory and research* (pp. 244-268). Engelwood Cliffs, NJ: Prentice Hall.

Kramer, R. M. (1998). Revisiting the Bay of Pigs and Vietnam decisions twenty-five years later: How well has the groupthink hypothesis stood the test of time? *Organizational Behaviour and Human Decision Processes, 2/3,* 236-271.

Kramer, R. M. & Brewer, M. B. (1984). Effects of group identity on resource use in a situated commons dilemma. *Journal of Personality and Social Psychology, 46,* 1044-1057.

Kramer, R. M, Brewer, M. B., & Hanna, B. A. (1996). Collective trust and collective action: The decision to trust as a social decision. In R. M. Kramer & T. R. Tyler (Eds.), *Trust in organizations: Frontiers of theory and research* (pp. 357-389). Thousand Oaks, CA: Sage.

Kramer, R. M., Pommerenke, P., & Newton, E. (1993). The social context of negotiation: Effects of social identity and interpersonal accountability on negotiator decision making. *Journal of Conflict Resolution, 37,* 633-654.

Kramer, R. M., Shah, P. P., & Woerner, S. L. (1995). Why ultimatums fail: Social identity and moralistic aggression in coercive bargaining. In R. M. Kramer & D. M. Messick (Eds.), *Negotiation as a social process* (pp. 285-308). Thousand Oaks, CA: Sage.

Krauss, R. M. & Fussell, S. R. (1996). Social psychological models of interpersonal communication. In E. T. Higgins & A. W. Kruglanski (Eds.), *Social psychology: Handbook of basic principles* (pp. 655-701). New York: Guilford Press.

Kravitz, D. & Martin, B. (1986) Ringelmann revisited: Alternative explanations for the social loafing effect. *Personality and Social Psychology Bulletin, 50,* 936-941.

Krech, D. & Crutchfield, R. S. (1948). *Theory and problems of social psychology.* New York: McGraw-Hill.

Kuhn, M. H. & McPartland, T. S. (1954). An experimental investigation of self-attitudes. *American Sociological Review, 19,* 68-76.

Kuna, D. P. (1978). One-sided portrayal of Münsterberg. *American Psychologist, 33,* 700.

Lalonde, R. N. & Silverman, R. A. (1994). Behavioral preferences in response to social injustice: The effects of group permeability and social identity salience. *Journal of Personality and Social Psychology, 66,* 78-85.

Lambert, R. A., Larcker, D. F., & Weigelt, K. (1991). How sensitive is executive compensation to organizational size? *Strategic Management Journal, 12,* 395-402.

Lamm, H. & Myers, D. G. (1978). Group-induced polarization of attitudes and behavior. In L. Berkowitz (Ed.), *Advances in experimental social psychology* (vol. 11, pp. 145-195). New York: Academic Press.

Lamm, H. & Trommsdorff, G. (1973). Group versus individual performance on tasks requiring ideational proficiency (brainstorming). *European Journal of Social Psychology, 3,* 361-387.

Landy, F. J. (1989). *Psychology of work behaviour* (4th ed.). Pacific Grove, CA: Brooks Cole.

Landy, F. J. (1992). Hugo Münsterberg: Victim or visionary? *Journal of Applied Psychology, 77,* 787-802.

Larrick, R. P. & Blount, S. (1995). Social context in tacit bargaining games. In R. D. Kramer & D. M. Messick (Eds.), *Negotiation as a social process* (pp. 268-284). Thousand Oaks, CA: Sage.

Larson, J. R., Jr., Christensen, C., Abbott, A. S., & Franz, T. M. (1996). Diagnosing groups: Charting the flow of information in medical decision-making teams. *Journal of Personality and Social Psychology, 71,* 315-330.

Larson, J. R., Foster-Fishman, P. G. & Keys, C. B. (1994). Discussion of shared and unshared information in decision-making groups. *Journal of Personality and Social Psychology, 67,* 446-461.

Larson, J. R., Lingle, J. H., & Scerbo, M. M. (1984). The impact of performance cues on leader-behavior ratings: The role of selective information availability and probabilistic response bias. *Organizational Behavior and Human Decision Processes, 33,* 323-349.

Latané, B. (1981). The psychology of social impact. *American Psychologist, 36,* 343-356.

Latané, B., Williams, K., & Harkins, S. (1979). Many hands make light work: The causes and consequences of social loafing. *Journal of Personality and Social Psychology, 37,* 822-832.

Latham, G. P., Mitchell, T. R., Dossett, D. L. (1978). Importance of participative goal setting and anticipated rewards on goal difficulty and job performance. *Journal of Applied Psychology, 63,* 163-171.

Lawler, E. E. (1973). *Motivation in work organizations.* Monterey, CA: Brooks Cole.

Lawler, E. E. (1995). Drives, needs and outcomes. In B. M. Staw (Ed.), *Psychological dimensions of organizational behaviour* (2nd ed., pp. 3-26). Englewood Cliffs, NJ: Prentice Hall.

Lawler, E. E., Mohrman, S. A., & Ledford, G. E. (1992). *Employee involvement and total quality management.* San Francisco: Jossey-Bass.

Lazega, E. (1990). Internal politics and the interactive elaboration of information in workgroups: An exploratory study. *Human Relations, 43,* 87-101.

Lea, M. & Spears, R. (1991). Computer-mediated communication, deindividuation and group decision making. *International Journal of Man-Machine Studies, 34,* 283-301.

Leana, C. R. (1985). A partial test of Janis's groupthink model: Effects of group cohesiveness and leader behavior on defective decision making. *Journal of Management, 11,* 5-17.

Leavitt, H. J. (1972). *Managerial psychology* (3rd ed.). Chicago: University of Chicago Press.

Leavitt, H. J. (1995). 'Suppose we took groups seriously ...' In B. M. Staw (Ed.), *Psychological dimensions of organizational behavior* (2nd ed.). Englewood Cliffs, NJ: Prentice Hall.

LeBon, G. (1895, trans. 1947). *The crowd: A study of the popular mind.* London: Ernest Benn.

Lee, C. & Earley, P. (1992). Comparative peer evaluations of organizational behavior theories. *Organization Development Journal, 10,* 37-42.

Lembke, S. & Wilson, M. G. (1998). Putting the 'team' into teamwork: Alternative theoretical contributions for contemporary management practice. *Human Relations, 51,* 927-943.

Lemyre, L. & Smith, P.M. (1985). Intergroup discrimination and self-esteem in the minimal group paradigm. *Journal of Personality and Social Psychology, 49,* 660-670.

Leonard, N. H., Beauvais, L. L., & Scholl, R. W. (1999). Work motivation: The incorporation of self-concept-based processes. *Human Relations, 52,* 969-998.

Lepper, M. R. & Greene, D. (1975). Turning play into work: Effects of adult surveillance and extrinsic rewards: A test of the overjustification hypothesis. *Journal of Personality and Social Psychology, 31,* 479-486.

Lepper, M. R., Greene, D., & Nisbett, R. E. (1973). Undermining children's intrinsic interest with extrinsic reward. A test of the over-justification hypothesis. *Journal of Personality and Social Psychology, 28,* 129-137.

LeVine, R. (1966). *Dreams and deeds: Achievement motivation in Nigeria.* Chicago: University of Chicago Press.

Levine, D. I. & Tyson, L. D. (1990). Participation, productivity, and the firm's environment. In A. S. Binder (Ed.), *Paying for productivity: A look at the evidence* (pp. 183-237). Washington, DC: Brookings.

Levine, J. & Butler, J. (1956). Lecture versus group decision in changing behavior. In D. Cartwright & A. Zander (Eds.), *Group dynamics: Research and theory* (2nd ed., pp. 280-286). Evanston, IL: Row Peterson.

Levine, J. M. & Moreland, R. L. (1991). Culture and socialization in work groups. In L. B. Resnick, J. M. Levine & S. D. Teasley (Eds.), *Perspectives on socially shared cognition* (pp. 257-279). Washington, DC: American Psychological Association.

Levinger, G. & Schneider, D. J. (1969). Test of the 'risk is a value' hypothesis. *Journal of Personality and Social Psychology, 11,* 165-170.

Lewin, K. (1952). *Field theory in social science.* London: Tavistock.

Lewin, K. (1956). Studies in group decision. In D. Cartwright & A. Zander (Eds.), *Group dynamics: Research and theory* (2nd ed., pp. 287-301). Evanston, IL: Row Peterson.

Lewin, K. Lippett, R., & White, R. (1939). Patterns of aggressive behaviour in experimentally created 'social climates'. *Journal of Social Psychology, 10,* 271-99.

Leyens, J.-P, Yzerbyt, V., & Schadron, G. (1994). *Stereotypes and social cognition.* London: Sage.

Liang, D. W., Moreland, R., Argote, L. (1995). Group versus individual training and group performance: The mediating factor of transactive memory. *Personality and Social Psychology Bulletin, 21,* 384-393.

Likert, R. (1961). *New patterns of management.* New York: McGraw Hill.

Lippitt, R., Polansky, N., Redl, F., & Rosen, S. (1956). The dynamics of power. In D. Cartwright & A. Zander (Eds.), *Group dynamics: Research and theory* (2nd ed., pp. 462-482). Evanston, IL: Row Peterson.

Lippitt, R. & White, R. (1943). The 'social climate' of children's groups. In R. G. Barker, J. Kounin, & H. Wright (Eds.), *Child behaviour and development.* New York: McGraw-Hill.

Lippmann, W. (1922). *Public opinion.* New York: Harcourt Brace.

Locke, E. A. (1968). Toward a theory of task motivation and incentives. *Organizational Behavior and Human Performance, 3*, 157-189.

Locke, E. A. (1982). The ideas of Frederick W. Taylor: An evaluation. *Academy of Management Review, 7*, 14-24.

Locke, E. A. & Latham, G. P. (1990). *A theory of goal setting and task performance.* Englewood Cliffs, NJ: Prentice Hall.

Locke, E. A., Shaw, K. N., Saari, L. M., & Latham, G. P. (1981). Goal setting and task performance: 1969-1980. *Psychological Bulletin, 90*, 125-152.

Long, K. & Spears, R. (1997). The self-esteem hypothesis revisited: Differentiation and the disaffected. In R. Spears, P. J. Oakes, N. Ellemers & S. A. Haslam (Eds.), *The social psychology of stereotyping and group life* (pp. 296-317). Oxford: Blackwell.

Lord, R. G., Brown, D. J., & Freiberg, S. J. (1999). Understanding the dynamics of leadership: The role of follower self-concepts in the leader/follower relationship. *Organizational Behavior and Human Decision Processes, 78*, 167-203.

Lord, R. G. Foti, R., & De Vader, C. L. (1984). A test of leadership categorization theory: Internal structure, information processing and leadership perceptions. *Organizational Behaviour and Human Performance, 34*, 343-378.

Lord, R. G. Foti, R., & Phillips, J. S. (1982). A theory of leadership categorization. In J. G. Hunt, V. Sekaran & C. Schriesheim (Eds.), *Leadership: Beyond established views.* Carbondale: South Illinois University Press.

Lord, R. G. & Maher, K. J. (1990). Perceptions of leadership and their implications in organizations. In J. S. Carroll (Ed.), *Applied social psychology and organizational settings.* Hillsdale, NJ: Erlbaum.

Lord, R. G. & Maher, K. J. (1991). *Leadership and information processing: Linking perceptions and performance* (pp. 129-154). London: Unwin Hyman.

Luhtanen, R. & Crocker, J. (1992). A collective self-esteem scale: Self-evaluation of one's social identity. *Personality and Social Psychology Bulletin, 18*, 302-318.

Macan, T. H. & Dipboye, R. L. (1994). The effects of the application on processing of information from the employment interview. *Journal of Applied Social Psychology, 24*, 1291-1314.

McClelland, D. C. (1955). Some social consequences of achievement motivation. In M. R. Jones (Ed.), *Nebraska symposium on motivation.* Lincoln, NB: University of Nebraska Press.

McClelland, D. C. (1961). *The achieving society.* Princeton, NJ: Van Nostrand Co.

McClelland, D. C. (1978). Managing motivation to expand human freedom. *American Psychologist, 33*, 201-10.

McClelland, D. C. (1985). *Motives, personality and society: Selected papers.* New York: Prager.

McClelland, D. C. (1987). *Human motivation.* New York: Cambridge University Press.

McClelland, D. C, Atkinson, J. W., Clark, R. A. & Lowell, E. L. (1976). *The achievement motive.* New York: Irvington.

McClelland, D. C. & Winter, D. G. (1969). *Motivating economic achievement.* New York: Free Press.

McCormack, G. & Nelson, H. (Eds.) (1993) *The Burma–Thailand railway: Memory and history.* Sydney: Allen & Unwin.

McCrae, R. R. & Costa, P. T., Jr (1990). *Personality in adulthood.* New York: Guilford Press.

McGarty, C. (1999a). *Distinguishing social identification from the salience of social categorizations.* Paper presented at the 5th meeting of the Society of Australasian Social Psychologists, Coolum, Queensland, 8-11 April.

McGarty, C. (1999b). *The categorization process in social psychology.* London: Sage.

McGarty, C., Haslam, S. A., Hutchinson, K. J., & Turner, J. C. (1994). The effects of salient group memberships on persuasion. *Small Group Research, 25,* 267-293.

McGarty, C., Reynolds, K. J., Haslam, S. A., Turner, J. C., & Ryan, M. K. (1999). *On the enduring and contextual aspects of social identity: Specifying and testing the inter-relationship between social identification and social identity salience.* Unpublished manuscript: The Australian National University.

McGarty, C. , Taylor, N. & Douglas, K. (in press). Between commitment and compliance: Obligation and the strategic dimension of SIDE. In T. Postmes, R. Spears, M. Lea & S. D. Reicher (Eds.), *SIDE issues centre stage: Recent developments in studies of deindividuation in groups.* Amsterdam: Royal Netherlands Academy of Arts and Sciences.

McGarty, C., Turner, J. C., Hogg, M. A., David, B., & Wetherell, M. S. (1992). Group polarization as conformity to the prototypical group member. *British Journal of Social Psychology, 31,* 1-20.

McGarty, C., Turner, J. C., Oakes, P. J., & Haslam, S. A. (1993). The creation of uncertainty in the influence process: The roles of stimulus information and disagreement with similar others. *European Journal of Social Psychology, 23,* 17-38.

McGregor, D. (1957). The human side of enterprise. In *Adventures in thought and action.* Proceedings of the 5th anniversary of the School of Industrial Management, Massachusetts Institute of Technology.

McGregor, D. (1960). *The human side of enterprise.* New York: McGraw-Hill.

McGregor, D. (1966). *Leadership and motivation.* Cambridge, MA: MIT Press.

Machiavelli, N. (1513/1984). *The prince.* Oxford: Oxford University Press.

Mackie, D. M. (1986). Social identification effects in group polarization. *Journal of Personality and Social Psychology, 50,* 720-728.

Mackie, D. M. & Cooper, J. (1984). Attitude polarization: The effects of group membership. *Journal of Personality and Social Psychology, 46,* 575-585.

Mackie, D. M., Gastardo-Conaco, M. C., & Skelly, J. J. (1992). Knowledge of the advocated position and the processing of ingroup and outgroup persuasive messages. *Personality and Social Psychology Bulletin, 18,* 145-151.

Mackie, D. M., Worth, L. T., & Asuncion, A. G. (1990). Processing of persuasive ingroup messages. *Journal of Personality and Social Psychology, 58,* 812-822.

McLachlan, A. (1986). The effects of two forms of decision reappraisal on the perception of pertinent arguments. *British Journal of Social Psychology, 25,* 129-138.

McPhail, C. (1991). *The myth of the madding crowd.* Hawthorne, NY: Aldine de Gruyter.

Madison, D. L., Allen, R. W., Porter, L. W., Renwick, P. A., & Mayes, B. T. (1980). Organizational politics: An exploration of managers' perceptions. *Human Relations, 33,* 79-100.

Mael, F. A. (1988). *Organizational identification: Construct redefinition and a field application with organizational alumni.* Unpublished doctoral dissertation: Wayne State University, Detroit.

Mael, F. A. & Ashforth, B. E. (1992). Alumni and their alma mater: A partial test of the reformulated model of organizational identification. *Journal of Organizational Behavior, 13,* 103-123.

Mael, F. A. & Ashforth, B. E. (1995). Loyal from day one: Biodata, organizational identification, and turnover among newcomers. *Personnel Psychology, 48,* 309-333.

Mael, F. A. & Tetrick, L. E. (1992). Identifying organizational identification. *Educational and Psychological Measurement, 52,* 813-824.

Maier, N. R. F. (1952). *Principles of human relations.* New York: Wiley.

Maier, N. R. F. (1967). Assets and liabilities in group problem solving: The need for an integrative function. *Psychological Review, 74,* 238-249.

Mann, L. (1974). On being a sore loser: How fans react to their team's failure. *Australian Journal of Psychology, 26,* 37-47.

Mann, R. D. (1959). A review of the relationship between personality and performance in small groups. *Psychological Bulletin, 56,* 241-270.

Manstead, A. S. R. (1997). Situations, belongingness, attitudes and culture: Four lessons learned from social psychology. In C. McGarty & S. A. Haslam (Eds.), *The message of social psychology: Perspectives on mind in society* (pp. 238-251). Oxford: Blackwell.

Martin, P. (1997). *The sickening mind: Brain, behaviour, immunity and disease.* London: Flamingo.

Maslow, A. H. (1943). A theory of motivation. *Psychological Review, 50,* 370-396.

Maslow, A. H. (1972). Management as a psychological experiment. In W. Nord (Ed.), *Concepts and controversy in organizational behaviour.* Pacific Palisades, CA: Goodyear Publishing Co.

Mayo, E. (1924). Revery and industrial fatigue. *Personnel Journal, 3,* 273-281.

Mayo, E. (1933). *The human problems of an industrial civilization.* Cambridge, MA: Macmillan.

Mayo, E. (1949). *The social problems of an industrial civilization.* London: Routledge and Kegan Paul.

Medin, D. L. (1988). Social categorization: Structures, processes and purposes. In T. K. Srull & R. S. Wyer (Eds.), *Advances in social cognition* (vol. 1, pp. 119-126). Hillsdale, NJ: Erlbaum.

Medin, D. L. (1989). Concepts and conceptual structure. *American Psychologist, 44,* 1469-1481.

Medin, D. L., Goldstone, R. L., & Gentner, D. (1993). Respects for similarity. *Psychological Review, 100,* 254-278.

Meindl, J. R. (1993). Reinventing leadership: A radical, social psychological approach. In J. K. Murnigham (Ed.), *Social psychology in organizations: Advances in theory and research* (pp. 89-118). Engelwood Cliffs, NJ: Prentice Hall.

Meindl, J. R. & Ehrlich, S. B. (1987). The romance of leadership and the evaluation of organizational performance. *Academy of Management Journal, 30,* 91-109.

Meindl, J. R., Ehrlich, S. B., & Dukerich, J. M. (1985). The romance of leadership. *Administrative Science Quarterly, 30,* 78-102.

Merkle, J. (1980). *Management and ideology: The legacy of the international scientific management movement.* Berkeley, CA: University of California Press.

Merton, R. K. (1957). *Social theory and social structure.* New York: Free Press.

Messick, D. M. (1973). To join or not to join: An approach to the unionization decision. *Organizational Behavior and Human Performance, 10,* 145-156.

Messick, D. M. & McClintock, C. G. (1968). Motivational bases of choice in experimental games. *Journal of Experimental Social Psychology, 4,* 1-25.

Micklethwait, J. & Wooldridge, A. (1997). *The witch doctors: What the management gurus are saying, why it matters and how to make sense of it.* London: Random House.

Milgram, S. (1963). Behavioral study of obedience. *Journal of Abnormal and Social Psychology, 67,* 371-378.

Milgram, S. (1974). *Obedience to authority.* London: Tavistock.

Milkman, R. (1998). The new American workplace: High road or low road? In P. Thompson & C. Warhurst (Eds.), *Workplaces of the future* (pp. 25-39). Houndmills: Macmillan.

Miller, D. I. & Monge, P. R. (1986). Participation, satisfaction, and productivity: A meta-analytic review. *Academy of Management Journal, 29,* 727-753.

Miller, D. T. & Prentice, D. A. (1994). Collective errors and errors about the collective. *Personality and Social Psychology Bulletin, 20,* 541-550.

Miller, J. G. (1960). Information input, overload and psychopathology. *American Journal of Psychiatry, 116*, 695-704.

Mills, C. W. (1970). *The sociological imagination.* Harmondsworth: Penguin.

Mintzberg, H. (1973). *The nature of managerial work.* New York: Harper & Row.

Mintzberg, H. (1983). *Power in and around organizations.* Englewood Cliffs, NJ: Prentice Hall.

Mitchell, T. R., Dowling, P. J., Kabanoff, B. V., & Larson, J. R. (1988). *People in organizations: An introduction to organizational behaviour in Australia.* Sydney: McGraw-Hill.

Mlicki, P. P. & Ellemers, N. (1996). Being different or being better? National stereotypes and identifications of Polish and Dutch students. *European Journal of Social Psychology, 26*, 97-114.

Moede, W. (1927). Die Richtlinien der Leistungs-Psychologie. *Industrielle Psychotechnik, 4*, 193-207.

Mone, M. A. & McKinley, W. (1993). The uniqueness value and its consequences for organizational studies. *Journal of Management Enquiry, 2*, 284-296.

Montgomery, M. (1986). *An introduction to language and society.* London: Routledge.

Moorhead, G., Ference, R., & Neck, C. P. (1991). Group decision fiascoes continue: Space shuttle challenger and a revised groupthink framework. *Human Relations, 44*, 539-550.

Moreland, R. L. (1999). *Transactive memory within and between work groups and organizations.* Paper presented at the Small Groups Preconference to the Annual Meeting of the Society of Experimental Social Psychology, St Louis, MI, 14-16 October.

Moreland, R. L., Argote, L., & Krishnan, R. (1996). Socially shared cognition at work: Transactive memory and group performance. In J. Nye & A. Brower (Eds.), *What's social about social cognition? Research on socially shared cognition in small groups* (pp. 57-84). Newbury Park, CA: Sage.

Morley, I. E. (1992). Intra-organizational bargaining. In J. F. Hartley & G. M. Stephenson (Eds.), *Employment relations.* Oxford: Blackwell.

Morley, I. E. & Stephenson, G. (1979). *The social psychology of bargaining.* London: Allen & Unwin.

Morrison, B. E. (1998). *Social co-operation: Re-defining the self in self-interest.* Unpublished PhD thesis, The Australian National University.

Moscovici, S. (1984). The phenomenon of social representations. In R. M. Farr & S. Moscovici (Eds.), *Social Representations.* Cambridge: Cambridge University Press.

Moscovici, S. & Zavalloni, M. (1969). The group as a polarizer of attitudes. *Journal of Personality and Social Psychology, 12*, 125-135.

Moskowitz, M. J. (1977). Hugo Münsterberg: A study in the history of applied psychology. *American Psychologist, 32*, 824-42.

Mowday, R. T. (1978). Equity theory predictions of behavior in organizations. In R. M. Steers & L. W. Porter (Eds.), *Motivation and work behavior.* New York: McGraw Hill.

Mowday, R. T., Steers, R. M. & Porter, L. W. (1979). The measurement of organizational commitment. *Journal of Vocational Behaviour, 4*, 224-247.

Mowday, R. T. & Sutton, R. I. (1993). Organizational behaviour: Linking individuals and groups to organizational contexts. *Annual Review of Psychology, 44*, 195-229.

Muchinsky, P. M. (1997). *Psychology applied to work* (5th ed.). Pacific Grove, CA: Brooks/Cole.

Mulder, M. (1977). *The daily power game.* Leiden, The Netherlands: Martinus Nijoff.

Mullen, B., Anthony, T., Salas, E., & Driscoll, J. E. (1994). Group cohesiveness and quality of decision making: An integration of tests of the groupthink hypothesis. *Small Group Research, 25,* 189-204.

Mullen, B., Johnson, C., & Salas, E. (1991). Productivity loss in brainstorming groups: A meta-analytic integration. *Basic and Applied Social Psychology, 12,* 3-24.

Mullen, B. & Riordan, C. A. (1988). Self-serving attributions for performance in naturalistic settings: A meta-analytic review. *Journal of Applied Social Psychology, 18,* 3-22.

Mummendey, A. & Schreiber, H.-J. (1983). Better or just different?: Positive social identity by discrimination against or differentiation from outgroups. *European Journal of Social Psychology, 13,* 389-397.

Mummendey, A. & Schreiber, H.-J. (1984). Different just means better: Some obvious and some hidden pathways to ingroup favouritism. *British Journal of Social Psychology, 23,* 363-368.

Mummendey, A. & Simon, B. (1989). Better or just different? III: The impact of comparison dimension and relative group size upon intergroup discrimination. *British Journal of Social Psychology, 28,* 1-16.

Mummendey, A. & Wenzel, M. (1999). Social discrimination and tolerance in intergroup relations: Reactions to intergroup difference. *Personality and Social Psychology Review, 3,* 158-174.

Münsterberg, H. (1913). *Psychology and industrial efficiency.* Boston: Houghton Mifflin.

Murrell, H. (1976). *Motivation at work.* London: Methuen.

Myers, D. G., Bruggink, J. B., Kersting, R. C., & Schlosser, B. A. (1980). Does learning others' opinions change one's opinions? *Personality and Social Psychology Bulletin, 6,* 253-260.

Myers, D. G. & Lamm, H. (1976). The group polarization phenomenon. *Psychological Bulletin, 83,* 602-627.

Nadler, D. A. & Tushman, M. L. (1990). Beyond the charismatic leader: Leadership and organizational change. *California Management Review, 32,* 77-97.

Naylor, J. C., Pritchard, R. D., & Ilgen, D. R. (1980). *A theory of behaviour in organizations.* New York: Academic Press.

Neale, J. (1983). *Memoirs of a callous picket.* London: Pluto Press.

Neale, M. A. & Bazerman, M. (1991). *Cognition and rationality in negotiation.* New York: The Free Press.

Ng, S. H. (1980). *The social psychology of power.* New York: Academic Press.

Ng, S. H. (1982). Power and intergroup discrimination. In H. Tajfel (Ed.), *Social identity and intergroup relations.* Cambridge: Cambridge University Press.

Ng, S. H. (1996). Power: An essay in honour of Henri Tajfel. *Social groups and identities: The developing legacy of Henri Tajfel* (pp. 191-214). Oxford: Butterworth–Heinemann.

Nicholls, J. G. (1984). Achievement orientation: Conceptions of ability, subjective experience, task choice and performance. *Psychological Review, 91,* 328-346.

Nicholson, N., Ursell, G., & Blyton, P. (1981). *The dynamics of white collar unionism.* London: Academic Press.

Nietzsche, F. (1888/1968). *The will to power* (W. Kaufman trans.). New York: Vintage Books.

Nkomo, S. M. & Cox, T, Jr. (1996). Diverse identities in organizations. In S. R. Clegg, C. Hardy & W. R. Nord (Eds.), *Handbook of organization studies* (pp. 338-356). London: Sage.

Noe, R. A.(1988). Women and mentoring: A review and research agenda. *Academy of Management Review, 13,* 65-78.

Nolan, M., Haslam, S. A., Spears, R., & Oakes, P. J. (1999). An examination of resource-based and fit-based theories of stereotyping under cognitive load and fit. *European Journal of Social Psychology, 29,* 641-664.

Northcraft, G. B, Polzer, J. T., Neale, M. A., & Kramer, R. M. (1995). Diversity, social identity, and performance: Emergent social dynamics in cross-functional teams. In S. E. Jackson & M. N. Ruderman (Eds.), *Diversity in work teams: Research paradigms for a changing workplace* (pp. 69-96). Washington, DC: American Psychological Association.

Nutt, P. C. (1976). Models for decision making in organizations and some contextual variables which stipulate optimal use. *Academy of Management Review, 1,* 94-98.

Nuttin, J. (1984). *Motivation, planning and action.* Hillsdale, NJ: Erlbaum.

Nye, J. L. & Simonetta, L. G. (1996). Followers' perceptions of group leaders. The impact of recognition-based and inference-based processes. In J. Nye & A. Brower (Eds.), *What's social about social cognition? Research on socially shared cognition in small groups* (pp. 124-153). Newbury Park, CA & London: Sage.

Oaker, G. & Brown, R. (1986). Intergroup relations in a hospital setting: A further test of social identity theory. *Human Relations, 39,* 767-778.

Oakes, P. J. (1987). The salience of social categories. In J. C. Turner, M. A. Hogg, P. J. Oakes S. D. Reicher, & M. S. Wetherell, *Rediscovering the social group: A self-categorization theory* (pp. 117-141). Oxford: Blackwell.

Oakes, P. J. (1996). The categorization process. Cognition and the group in the social psychology of stereotyping. In W. P. Robinson (Ed.), *Social groups and identities: Developing the Legacy of Henri Tajfel.* Oxford: Butterworth–Heinemann.

Oakes, P. J. & Haslam, S. A. (in press). *Distortion v. Meaning:* Categorization on trial for incitement to intergroup hatred. In M. Augoustinos & K. Reynolds (Eds.), *Social psychological approaches to prejudice and racism.* London: Sage.

Oakes, P. J., Haslam, S. A., Morrison, B. & Grace, D. (1995). Becoming an ingroup: Re-examining the impact of familiarity on perceptions of group homogeneity. *Social Psychology Quarterly, 58,* 52-61.

Oakes, P. J., Haslam, S. A., & Turner, J. C. (1994). *Stereotyping and social reality.* Oxford: Blackwell.

Oakes, P. J., Haslam, S. A., & Turner, J. C. (1998). The role of prototypicality in group influence and cohesion: Contextual variation in the graded structure of social categories. In S. Worchel, J. F. Morales, D. Paez, J.-C. Deschamps (Eds.), *Social identity: International perspectives* (pp. 75-92). London: Sage.

Oakes, P. J. & Reynolds, K. J. (1997). Asking the accuracy question: Is measurement the answer? In R. Spears, P. J. Oakes, N. Ellemers, & S. A. Haslam (Eds.), *The social psychology of stereotyping and group life* (pp. 51-71). Oxford: Blackwell.

Oakes, P. J. & Turner, J. C. (1980). Social categorization and intergroup behaviour: Does minimal intergroup discrimination make social identity more positive? *European Journal of Social Psychology, 10,* 295-301.

Oakes, P. J. & Turner, J. C. (1990). Is limited information processing capacity the cause of social stereotyping? *European Review of Social Psychology, 1,* 111-135.

Oakes, P. J., Turner, J. C., & Haslam, S. A. (1991). Perceiving people as group members: The role of fit in the salience of social categorizations. *British Journal of Social Psychology, 30,* 125-144.

O'Brien, A. T. & Terry, D. J. (1999). *Intergroup contact and organizational mergers: The role of contact norms and typicality.* Paper presented at the 5th meeting of the Society of Australasian Social Psychologists, Coolum, Queensland, 8-11 April.

Olekalns, M., Smith, P. L., & Walsh, T. (1996). The process of negotiating: Strategy and timing as predictors of outcomes. *Organizational Behavior and Human Decision Processes, 68,* 68-77.

Operario, D., & Fiske, S. T. (1998). Racism equals power plus prejudice. In J. L. Eberhardt and S. T. Fiske (Eds.), *Confronting racism: The problem and the response* (pp. 33-53). Thousand Oaks, CA: Sage.

O'Reilly, C. (1991). Organizational behaviour: Where we've been, where we're going. *Annual Review of Psychology, 42,* 427-458.

O'Reilly, C. & Chatman, J. (1986). Organizational commitment and psychological attachment: The effects of compliance, identification and internalization on prosocial behavior. *Journal of Applied Psychology, 71,* 492-499.

O'Reilly, C. & Chatman, J., & Anderson, J. C. (1987). Message flow and decision making. In F. Jablin, L. L. Putnam, K. H. Roberts & L. W. Porter (Eds.), *Handbook of organizational communication: An interdisciplinary perspective* (pp. 600-623). Newbury Park, CA: Sage.

Organ, D. W. (1978). *The applied psychology of work behavior: A book of readings.* Plano, TX: Business Publications Inc.

Organ, D. W. (1988). *Organizational citizenship behavior: The good soldier syndrome.* Lexington, MA: Lexington.

Organ, D. W. (1990). The motivational basis of citizenship behaviour. In B. M. Staw & L. L. Cummings (Eds.), *Research in Organizational Behavior* (vol. 12, pp. 43-72). Greenwich, CT: JAI Press.

Organ, D. W. (1997). Organizational citizenship behavior: Its construct clean-up time. *Human Performance, 10,* 85-97.

Osborn, A. F. (1953). *Applied imagination.* New York: Scribner.

Ouchi, W. C. (1981). *Theory Z: How American business can meet the Japanese challenge.* Reading, MA: Addison Wesley.

Ouchi, W. C. & Jaeger, A. M. (1978). Type Z organization: Stability in the midst of mobility. *Academy of Management Review, 3,* 305-314.

Ouwerkerk, J. W., Ellemers, N., & de Gilder, D. (1999). Social identification, affective commitment and individual effort on behalf of the group. In N. Ellemers, R. Spears & B. J. Doosje (Eds.), *Social identity: Context, commitment, content* (pp. 184-204). Oxford: Blackwell.

Oyserman, D. & Packer, M. J. (1996). Social cognition and self-concept: A socially contextualized model of identity. In J. Nye & A. Brower (Eds.), *What's social about social cognition? Research on socially shared cognition in small groups* (pp. 174-201). Newbury Park, CA: Sage.

Parker, E. (1997). *Motivation to achieve at work: An individual difference or a response to social reality?* Unpublished thesis: The Australian National University.

Parker, M. (1993). Industrial relations myth and shop floor reality: The team concept in the auto industry. In N. Lichtenstein & J. H. Howell (Eds.), *Industrial democracy in America* (pp. 249-274). Cambridge: Cambridge University Press.

Parker, M. & Slaughter, J. (1988). *Choosing sides: Unions and the team concept.* Boston: South End Press.

Parry, G., Moyser, G., & Day, N. (1992). *Political participation and democracy in Britain.* Cambridge: Cambridge University Press.

Parsons, H. M. (1992). Hawthorne: An early OBM experiment. *Journal of Organizational Behaviour, 12,* 27-43.

Paulus, P. B. (1998). Developing consensus about groupthink after all these years. *Organizational Behaviour and Human Decision Processes, 2/3,* 362-374.

Paulus, P. B. & Dzindolet, M. T. (1993). Social influence processes in brainstorming. *Journal of Personality and Social Psychology, 64,* 575-586.

Pears, I. (1992). The gentleman and the hero: Wellington and Napoleon in the nineteenth century. In R. Porter (Ed.), *Myths of the English* (pp. 216-236). Cambridge: Polity Press.

Perloff, L. S. & Fetzer, B. K. (1986). Self-other judgements and perceived vulnerability to victimization. *Journal of Personality and Social Psychology, 50,* 502-510.

Person, H. S. (1911/1972). Scientific management. In *Dartmouth College conferences, First Tuck school conference: Addresses and discussions at the conference on scientific management, 12-14 October 1911.* Dartmouth, USA: Easton Hive Publishing Company.

Person, H. S. (1929). *Scientific management in American industry.* New York: Harper.

Peters, T. & Waterman, R. H., Jr. (1995). *In search of excellence: Lessons from America's best-run companies* (2nd ed.). London: HarperCollins Business.

Peterson, R. S., Owens, P. D., Tetlock, P. E., Fan, E. T., & Martorana, B. (1998). Group dynamics in top management teams: Groupthink, vigilance and alternative models of organizational failure and success. *Organizational Behaviour and Human Decision Processes, 2/3,* 272-305.

Petty R. E. & Cacioppo, J. T. (1981). *Attitudes and persuasion: classic and contemporary approaches.* Dubuque, IA: W. C. Brown.

Petty R. E. & Cacioppo, J. T. (1986). The elaboration likelihood model of persuasion. In L. Berkowitz (Ed.), *Advances in experimental social psychology* (vol. 19, pp. 123-205). New York: Academic Press.

Pfeffer, J. (1977). The ambiguity of leadership. *Academy of Management Review, 2,* 104-112.

Pfeffer, J. (1981). *Power in organizations.* Boston, MA: Pitman.

Pfeffer, J. (1992). *Managing with power.* Boston, MA: Harvard Business School Press.

Pfeffer, J. (1997). *New directions for organizational theory: Problems and prospects.* New York: Oxford University Press.

Pfeffer, J. (1998). Understanding organizations: Concepts and controversies. In D. Gilbert, S. Fiske & G. Lindzey (Eds.), *The handbook of social psychology* (4th ed., pp. 733-777). New York: Oxford University Press.

Pfeffer, J. & Davis-Blake, A. (1992). Salary dispersion, location in the salary distribution, and turnover among college administrators. *Industrial and Labor Relations Review, 45,* 753-763.

Pfeffer, J. & Langton, N. (1988). The effect of wage dispersion on satisfaction, productivity and working collaboratively: Evidence from college and university faculty. *Administrative Science Quarterly, 38,* 382-407.

Phillips, A. P. & Dipboye, R. L. (1989). Correlational tests of predictions from a process model of the interview. *Journal of Applied Psychology, 74,* 41-52.

Pilegge, A. J., & Holtz, R. (1997). The effects of social identity on the self-set goals and task performance of high and low self-esteem individuals. *Organizational Behavior and Human Decision Processes, 70,* 17-26.

Pillai, R. & Meindl, J. R. (1991). The impact of a performance crisis on attributions of charismatic leadership: A preliminary study. *Best paper proceedings of the 1991 Eastern Academy of Management Meetings.* Hartford, CT.

Pinder, C. C. (1984). *Work motivation: Theory, issues and applications.* Glenview, IL: Scott, Foresman.

Platow, M. J., Durante, M., Williams, N., Garrett, M., Walshe, J., Cincotta, S., Lianos, G., & Barutchu, A. (1999). The contribution of sport fan social identity to the production of prosocial behavior. *Group Dynamics, 3,* 161-169.

Platow, M. J., Hoar, S., Reid, S., Harley, K., & Morrison, D. (1997). Endorsement of distributively fair or unfair leaders in interpersonal and intergroup situations. *European Journal of Social Psychology, 27,* 465-494.

Platow, M. J. & Hunter, J. (in press). Realistic intergroup conflict: Prejudice, power, and protest. In M. Augoustinos & K. J. Reynolds (Eds.), *The psychology of prejudice and racism.* London: Sage.

Platow, M. J., O'Connell, A., Shave, R. & Hanning, P. (1995). Social evaluations of fair and unfair allocators in interpersonal and intergroup situations. *British Journal of Social Psychology*, *34*, 363-381.

Plous, S. (1995) A comparison of strategies for reducing interval overconfidence in group judgments. *Journal of Applied Psychology*, *80*, 443-454.

Pollert, A. (1996). Teamwork on the assembly line: Contradictions and the dynamics of union resilience. In P. Ackers, C. Smith & P. Smith (Eds.), *The new workplace and trade unionism*. London: Routledge.

Porter, L. W. & Roberts, K. (Eds.) (1977). *Communication in organizations*. Harmondsworth: Penguin.

Postmes, T. & Spears, R. (1998). Deindividuation and anti-normative behavior: A meta-analysis. *Psychological Bulletin*, *123*, 238-259.

Postmes, T. & Spears, R. (1999). *Quality of decision making and group norms*. Unpublished manuscript: University of Amsterdam.

Postmes, T., Spears, R., & Lea, M. (1998). Breaching or building social boundaries? SIDE-effects of computer-mediated communication. *Communication Research*, *25*, 689-715.

Pratt, M. G. & Rafaeli, A. (1997). Organizational dress as a symbol of multilayered social identities. *Academy of Management Journal*, *40*, 862-898.

Prentice, D., Miller, D. T., & Lightdale, J. R. (1994). Asymmetries in attachment bonds to groups and their members: distinguishing between common identity and common group bonds. *Personality and Social Psychology Bulletin*, *20*, 484-493.

Preston, M. G. & Heintz, R. K. (1956). Effects of participatory vs. supervisory leadership on group judgement. In D. Cartwright & A. Zander (Eds.), *Group dynamics: Research and theory* (2nd ed., pp. 573-584). Evanston, IL: Row Peterson .

Pritchard, R. D. (1990). *Measuring and improving organizational productivity: A practical guide*. New York: Prager.

Pritchard, R. D. (1992). Organizational productivity. In M. D. Dunnette & L. M. Hough (Eds.), *Handbook of industrial and organizational psychology* (vol. 3, pp. 443-471). Palo Alto, CA: Consulting Psychologists Press.

Pruitt, D. G. & Carnevale, P. J. (1993). *Negotiation in social conflict*. Milton Keynes: Open University Press.

Pruitt, D. G., Carnevale, P. J., Ben-Yoav, O., Nochajki, T. H. & Van Slyck, M. (1983). Incentives for co-operation in integrative bargaining. In R. Tietz (Ed.), *Aspiration levels in bargaining and economic decision making* (pp. 22-34). Berlin: Springer.

Pruitt, D. G., Pierce, R. S., Zubek, J. M., McGillicuddy, N. B., & Welton, G. L. (1993). Determinants of short-term and long-term success in mediation. In S. Worchel & J. A. Simpson (Eds.), *Conflict between people and groups: Causes, processes, and resolutions*. Chicago, IL: Nelson-Hall.

Pruitt, D. G. & Rubin, J. Z. (1986). *Social conflict: Escalation, stalemate and settlement*. New York: McGraw-Hill.

Pruitt, D. G. & Syna, H. (1985). Mismatching the opponent's offers in negotiation. *Journal of Experimental Social Psychology*, *21*, 103-113.

Putnam, L. L., Phillips, N., & Chapman, P. (1996) Metaphors of communication and organization. In S. R. Clegg, C. Hardy & W. R. Nord (Eds.), *Handbook of organization studies* (pp. 375-408). London: Sage.

Putman, W. & Street, R. L., Jr. (1984). The conception and perception of noncontent speech performance: Implications for speech accommodation theory. *International Journal of the Sociology of Language*, *46*, 97-114.

Rabbie, J. M. & Bekkers, F. (1978). Threatened leadership and intergroup competition. *European Journal of Social Psychology*, *8*, 9-20.

Radke, M. & Klisurich, D. (1947). Experiments in changing food habits. *Journal of the American Dietetics Association*, *23*, 403-409.

Ragins, B. R. & Sundstrom, E. (1989). Gender and power in organisations: A longitudinal perspective. *Psychological Bulletin, 105*, 51-88.

Raven, B. H. (1965). Social influence and power. In I. D. Steiner & M. Fishbein (Eds.), *Current studies in social psychology*. New York: Holt, Rinehart & Winston.

Raven, B. H. (1992). A power/interaction model of interpersonal influence: French and Raven thirty years later. *Journal of Social Behavior and Personality, 7*, 217-244.

Raven, B. H. (1998). Groupthink, Bay of Pigs, and Watergate reconsidered. *Organizational Behavior and Human Decision Processes, 2/3*, 352-361.

Raven, B. H. & Rubin, J. Z. (1976). *Social psychology: People in groups*. New York: Wiley.

Rees, S. & Rodley, G. (Eds.) (1995). *The human costs of managerialism: Advocating the recovery of humanity*. Leichhardt, Australia: Pluto.

Reicher, S. D. (1982). The determination of collective action. In H. Tajfel (Ed.), *Social identity and intergroup relations* (pp. 41-84). Cambridge: Cambridge University Press.

Reicher, S. D. (1984). Social influence and the crowd: Attitudinal and behavioral effects of deindividuation in conditions of high and low group salience. *British Journal of Social Psychology, 23*, 341-350.

Reicher, S. D. (1987). Crowd behaviour as social action. In J. C. Turner, M. A. Hogg, P. J. Oakes, S. D. Reicher, & M. S. Wetherell, *Rediscovering the social group: A self-categorization theory* (pp. 171-202). Oxford: Blackwell.

Reicher, S. D. (1996). Social identity and social change: Rethinking the context of social psychology. In P. Robinson (Ed.), *Social groups and identities: Developing the Legacy of Henri Tajfel*. Oxford: Butterworth–Heinemann.

Reicher, S. D. (in press). Social identity definition and enactment: A broadSIDE against irrationalism and relativism. In T. Postmes, R. Spears, M. Lea & S. D. Reicher (Eds.), *SIDE issues centre stage: Recent developments in studies of deindividuation in groups*. Amsterdam: Royal Netherlands Academy of Arts and Sciences.

Reicher, S. D., Drury, J., Hopkins, N. & Stott, C. (in press). A model of crowd prototypes and crowd leadership. In C. Barker (Ed.), *Leadership and social movements*. Manchester: Manchester University Press.

Reicher, S. D. & Hopkins, N. (1996a). Seeking influence through characterising self-categories: An analysis of anti-abortionist rhetoric. *British Journal of Social Psychology, 35*, 297-311.

Reicher, S. D. & Hopkins, N. (1996b). Self-category constructions in political rhetoric: An analysis of Thatcher's and Kinnock's speeches concerning the British Miners' Strike (1984-5). *European Journal of Social Psychology, 26*, 353-372.

Reicher, S. D., Hopkins, N., & Condor, S. (1997). Stereotype construction as a strategy of influence. In R. Spears, P. J. Oakes, N. Ellemers, & S. A. Haslam (Eds.), *The social psychology of stereotyping and group life* (pp. 94-118). Oxford: Blackwell.

Reicher, S. D., Spears, R., & Postmes, T. (1995). A social identity model of deindividuation phenomena. *European Review of Social Psychology, 6*, 161-198.

Reichers, A. E. (1986). Conflict and organizational commitments. *Journal of Applied Psychology, 71*, 508-514.

Reynolds, K. J., & Oakes, P. J. (1999). Understanding the impression formation process: A self-categorization theory perspective. In T. Sugiman, M. Karasawa, J. Lui, & C. Ward (Eds.), *Progress in Asian social psychology: Theoretical and empirical contributions*. (vol. 2, pp. 213-235). Seoul, Korea: Kyoyook-Kwahak-Sa Publishing Company.

Reynolds, K. J. & Oakes, P. J. (2000). Variability in impression formation: Investigating the role of motivation, capacity and the categorization process. *Personality and Social Psychology Bulletin, 26,* 355-373.

Reynolds, K. J., Oakes, P. J., & Haslam, S. A. (1999). To think, feel and act as a collective: The role of intergroup versus intragroup self-other comparisons. *Responses to powerlessness: Stereotyping as an instrument of social conflict.* Paper presented at the Homogeneity and Entitativity Small Group Meeting of the EAESP: Louvain-la-Neuve, Belgium, 4-5 July.

Reynolds, K. J., Oakes, P. J., Haslam, S. A., Nolan, M., & Dolnik, L. (in press). Responses to powerlessness: Stereotypes as an instrument of social conflict. *Group Dynamics: Theory, Research and Practice.*

Reynolds, K. J., Oakes, P. J., Haslam, S. A., Spears, R., & Wegner, R. (1997). Does having power always lead to stereotyping? Investigating cognitive capacity and group-based accounts of the stereotyping process. *Australian Journal of Psychology, 50,* 32.

Reynolds, K. J., Turner, J. C., & Haslam, S. A. (2000). When are we better than them and they worse than us? A closer look at social discrimination in positive and negative domains. *Journal of Personality and Social Psychology, 78,* 64-80.

Ridgeway, C. (1991) The social construction of status value: Gender and other nominal characteristics. *Social Forces, 70,* 367-386.

Ritchie, R. J. & Moses, J. L. (1983). Assessment center correlates of women's advancement into middle-management. *Journal of Applied Psychology, 68,* 227-231.

Robbins, S. P., Millett, B., Cacioppe, R., & Waters-Marsh, T. (1998). *Organizational behaviour.* Sydney: Prentice Hall.

Roberts, K. H., O'Reilly, C. A., Bretton, G. E., & Porter, L. W. (1974). Organizational theory and organizational communication: A communication failure? *Human Relations, 27,* 501-524.

Robinson, P. (1995). Social psychology of work: Towards 2000. In P. Collett & A. Furnham (Eds.), *Social psychology at work: Essays in honour of Michael Argyle* (pp. 254-271). London: Routledge.

Roethlisberger, F. J. & Dickson, W. J. (1939). *Management and the worker: An account of a research program conducted by the Western Electric Company, Hawthorne Works, Chicago.* Cambridge, MA: Harvard University Press.

Rosch, E. (1978). Principles of categorization. In E. Rosch & B. B. Lloyd (Eds.), *Cognition and categorization* (pp. 28-49). Hillsdale, NJ: Erlbaum.

Rosenberg, M. (1965). *Society and the adolescent self-image.* Princeton, NJ: Princeton University Press.

Rosnow, R. L. (1991). Inside rumor: A personal journey. *American Psychologist, 46,* 484-496.

Ross, L. (1977). The intuitive psychologist and his shortcomings. In L. Berkowitz (Ed.), *Advances in Experimental Social Psychology* (vol. 10, pp. 174-220). New York: Academic Press.

Rothbart, M. & Hallmark, W. (1988). Ingroup–outgroup differences in the perceived efficacy of coercion and conciliation in resolving social conflict. *Journal of Personality and Social Psychology, 55,* 248-257.

Rothe, H. F. (1978). Output rates among industrial employees. *Journal of Applied Psychology, 63,* 40-46.

Rotter, J. B., Seeman, M. R., & Liverant, S. (1962). Internal versus external control of reinforcements: A major variable in behavior theory. In W. F. Washburn (Ed.), *Decisions, values and groups* (vol. 2, pp. 473-516). New York: Pergamon.

Rousseau, D. M. (1998). Why workers still identify with organizations. *Journal of Organizational Behavior, 19,* 217-233.

Rubin, J. Z. & Brown, B. (1975). *The social psychology of bargaining and negotiations.* New York: Academic Press.

Ruble, T. L. & Thomas, K. W. (1976). Support for a two-dimensional model of conflict behavior. *Organizational Behaviour and Human Performance, 16,* 143-155.

Runciman, W. G. (1966). *Relative deprivation and social justice.* Berkeley, CA: University of California Press.

Sachdev, I. & Bourhis, R. Y. (1984). Minimal majorities and minorities. *European Journal of Social Psychology, 14,* 35-52.

Sachdev, I. & Bourhis, R. Y. (1985). Social categorization and power differentials in group relations. *European Journal of Social Psychology, 15,* 415-434.

Sachdev, I. & Bourhis, R. Y. (1987). Status differentials and intergroup behaviour. *European Journal of Social Psychology, 17,* 277-293.

Sachdev, I. & Bourhis, R. Y. (1990). Language and social identification. In D. Abrams & M. A. Hogg (Eds.), *Social identity theory: Constructive and critical advances* (pp. 211-229). Hemel Hempstead: Harvester Wheatsheaf.

Sachdev, I. & Bourhis, R.Y. (1991). Power and status differentials in minority and majority group relations. *European Journal of Social Psychology, 21,* 1-24.

Sagie, A. (1995). Employee participation and work outcomes: An end to the dispute? *Academy of Management Review, 20,* 278-280.

Salaman, A. (1987). *Work resistance and control.* London: Longman.

Salancik, G. R. (1977). Commitment and the control of organizational behaviour and belief. In B. Staw & G. Salancik (Eds.), *New directions in organizational behaviour* (pp. 1-54). Chicago: St Clair.

Salancik, G. R. & Pfeffer, J. (1978). A social information processing approach to job attitudes and task design. *Administrative Science Quarterly, 23,* 224-253.

Samuel, R., Bloomfield, B., & Boanas, G. (1986). *The enemy within: Pit villages and the miners' strike of 1984-5.* Oxford: Routledge & Kegan Paul.

Sani. F. & Thomson, L. E. (1999). *We are what we wear: The emergence of consensus in stereotypes of organizational dress.* Unpublished manuscript: University of Dundee.

Sarros, J. C., & Butchatsky, O. (1996). *Leadership: Australia's top CEOs — Finding out what makes them the best.* Sydney: Harper Collins Business.

Saul, J. R. (1998). *The unconscious civilization.* London: Penguin.

Schittekatte, M. & Van Hiel, A. (1996). Effects of partially shared information and awareness of unshared information on information sampling. *Small Group Research, 27,* 431-449.

Schmidt, K. & Haslam, S. A. (1999). *The contribution of shared social identification to the provision, receipt and benefits of social support.* Unpublished manuscript: The Australian National University.

Schneider, B. (1987). The people make the place. *Personnel Psychology, 40,* 437-453.

Schrager, L. S. (1985). Private attitudes and collective action. *American Sociological Review, 50,* 858-9.

Scott, W. D. (1911). *Influencing men in business.* New York: Ronald.

Seashore, S. E. (1954). *Group cohesiveness in the industrial workgroup.* Survey Research Centre: University of Michigan Press.

Semin, G. R. (1997). The relevance of language to social psychology. In C. McGarty & S. A. Haslam (Eds.), *The message of social psychology: Perspectives on mind in society* (pp. 291-304).

Sennett, R. (1998). *The corrosion of character: The personal consequences of work in the new capitalism.* New York: W. W. Norton & Co.

Sewell, G. (1998). The discipline of teams: The control of team-based industrial work through electronic and peer surveillance. *Administrative Science Quarterly, 43,* 397-428.

Sewell, G. & Wilkinson, B. (1992). 'Someone to watch over me': surveillance, discipline and the just-in -time labour process. *Sociology, 26,* 271-289.

Shamir, B. (1991). Meaning, self and motivation in organizations. *Organizational Studies, 12,* 405-24.

Shamir, B., House, R. J., & Arthur, M. B. (1993). The motivational effects of charismatic leadership: A self-concept based theory. *Organizational Science, 4,* 577-594.

Shaw, J. B. & Barrett-Power, E. (1998). The effects of diversity on small work group processes and performance. *Human Relations, 51,* 1307-1325.

Shaw, M. E. (1964). Communication networks. In L. Berkowitz (Ed.), *Advances in Experimental Social Psychology* (vol. 1, pp. 111-147). New York: Academic Press.

Shaw, M. E. (1978). Communication networks fourteen years later. In L. Berkowitz (Ed.), *Group Processes* (pp. 351-261). New York: Academic Press.

Shea, G. P. & Guzzo, R. A. (1987). Groups as human resources. In K. M. Rowland & G. R. Ferris (Eds.), *Research in personnel and human resources management* (vol. 5, pp. 289-322). Greenwich, CT: JAI Press.

Sheppard, H. L. & Belintsky, A. H. (1966). *The job hunt.* Baltimore, MD: Johns Hopkins Press.

Sherif, M. (1936). *The psychology of social norms.* New York: Harper.

Sherif, M. (1956). Experiments in group conflict. *Scientific American, 195,* 54-58.

Sherif, M. (1966). *Group conflict and co-operation: Their social psychology.* London: Routledge and Kegan Paul.

Sherif, M. & Cantril, H. (1947). *The social psychology of ego-involvements, social attitudes and identifications.* New York: Wiley.

Sherif, M. Harvey, O. J., White, B. J., Hood, W. R., & Sherif, C. W. (1961) *Intergroup conflict and co-operation: The Robbers Cave experiment.* Norman, OK: University of Oklahoma.

Sherif, M. & Sherif, C. (1969). *Social psychology.* New York: Harper Row.

Shostak, A. B. (1964). Industrial psychology and the trade unions: A matter of mutual indifference. In G. Fisk (Ed.), *The frontiers of management psychology.* New York: Harper.

Simmel, G. (1955). *Conflict and the web of group affiliations* (trans. K. H. Wolff). New York: Free Press.

Simon, B. (1998). Individuals, groups, and social change: On the relationship between individual and collective self-interpretations and collective action . In C. Sedikides, J. Schopler & C. A. Insko (Eds.), *Intergroup cognition and intergroup behaviour.* Hillsdale, NJ: Erlbaum.

Simon, B., Loewy, M., Sturmer, S., Weber, U., Freytag, P., Habig, C., Kampmeier, C., & Spahlinger, P. (1998). Collective identity and social movement participation. *Journal of Personality and Social Psychology, 74,* 646-658.

Simon, B., Pantaleo, G., & Mummendey, A. (1995). Unique individual or interchangeable group member? The accentuation of intragroup differences versus similarities as an indicator of the individual self versus the collective self. *Journal of Personality and Social Psychology, 69,* 106-119.

Skevington, S. M. (1980). Intergroup relations and social change within a nursing context. *British Journal of Social and Clinical Psychology, 19,* 201-213.

Skevington, S. M. & Baker, D. (Eds.) (1989). *The social identity of women.* London: Sage.

Smith, E. R. & Mackie, D. M. (1997). Integrating the psychological and the social to understand human behavior. In C. McGarty & S. A. Haslam (Eds.), *The message of social psychology: Perspectives on mind in society* (pp. 305-314). Oxford: Blackwell.

Smith, E. R., Murphy, J., & Coats, S. (1999). Attachment to groups: Theory and measurement. *Journal of Personality and Social Psychology, 77,* 94-110.

Smith, H. J., Spears, R. & Oyen, M. (1994). 'People like us': The influence of personal deprivation and group membership salience on justice evaluations. *Journal of Experimental Social Psychology, 30,* 277-299.

Smith, H. J. & Tyler, T. R. (1996). Justice and power: When will justice concerns encourage the disadvantaged to support policies which redistribute economic resources and the disadvantaged to willingly obey the law? *European Journal of Social Psychology, 26,* 171-200.

Smith, H. J. & Tyler, T. R. (1997). Choosing the right pond: The influence of the status of one's group and one's status in that group on self-esteem and group-oriented behaviours. *Journal of Experimental Social Psychology, 33,* 146-170.

Smith, P. & Bond, M. H. (1993). *Social psychology across cultures: Analysis and perspectives.* London: Harvester Wheatsheaf.

Smith, P. M. (1995a). Leadership. In A. S. R. Manstead & M. R. C. Hewstone (Eds.), *The Blackwell encyclopedia of social psychology* (pp. 358-362). Oxford: Blackwell.

Smith, P. M. (1995b). Organizations. In A. S. R. Manstead & M. R. C. Hewstone (Eds.), *The Blackwell encyclopedia of social psychology* (pp. 424-429). Oxford: Blackwell.

Smith, S. (1984). Groupthink and the hostage rescue mission. *British Journal of Political Science, 15,* 117-126.

Smither, R. D. (1992). *The psychology of work and human performance.* New York: HarperCollins.

Smyth, L. F. (1994). Intractable conflicts and the role of identity. *Negotiation Journal, 10,* 311-321.

Snow, C. E. (1927). *A discussion of the relation of illumination intensity to productive efficiency.* The Technical Engineering News, November.

Snyder, M. (1981a). On the self-perpetuating nature of social stereotypes. In D. L. Hamilton (Ed.), *Cognitive processes in stereotyping and intergroup behaviour.* Hillsdale, NJ: Erlbaum.

Snyder, M. (1981b). Seek and ye shall find: Testing hypotheses about other people. In E. T. Higgins, C. P. Herman & M. P. Zanna (Eds.), *Social cognition: The Ontario Symposium* (vol. 1). Hillsdale, NJ: Erlbaum.

Snyder, M. (1984). When belief creates reality. In L. Berkowitz (Ed.), *Advances in experimental social psychology* (vol. 18). New York: Academic Press.

Snyder, M., Campbell, B. H., & Preston, E. (1982). Testing hypotheses about human nature: Assessing the accuracy of social stereotypes. *Social Cognition, 1,* 256-272.

Snyder, M. & Swann, W. B. (1978). Hypothesis-testing processes in social interaction. *Journal of Personality and Social Psychology, 36,* 1202-1212.

Snyder, M., Tanke, E. D. & Berscheid, E. (1977). Social perception and interpersonal behaviour: On the self-fulfilling nature of social stereotypes. *Journal of Personality and Social Psychology, 35,* 656-666.

Snyder, M. & White, P. (1981). Testing hypotheses about other people: Strategies of verification and falsification. *Personality and Social Psychology Bulletin, 7,* 39-43.

Sorrentino, R. N. (1973). An extension of theory of achievement motivation to the study of emergent leadership. *Journal of Personality and Social Psychology, 26,* 356-368.

Sorrentino, R. N. & Field, N. (1986). Emergent leadership over time: The functional value of positive motivation. *Journal of Personality and Social Psychology, 50,* 1091-1099.

Spears, R., Doosje, B., & Ellemers, N. (1997). Self-stereotyping in the face of threats to group status and distinctiveness: The role of group identification. *Personality and Social Psychology Bulletin, 23,* 538-553.

Spears, R. & Haslam, S. A. (1997). Stereotyping and the burden of cognitive load. In R. Spears, P. J. Oakes, N. Ellemers, & S. A. Haslam (Eds.), *The social psychology of stereotyping and group life* (pp. 171-207). Oxford: Blackwell.

Spears, R., Haslam, S. A., & Jansen, R. (1999). The effect of cognitive load on social categorization in the category confusion paradigm. *European Journal of Social Psychology, 29*, 621-640.

Spears, R. & Lea, M. (1992). Social influence and the influence of the social in computer-mediated communication. In M. Lea (Ed.), *Contexts of computer-mediated communication* (pp. 30-65). Hemel Hempstead: Harvester Wheatsheaf.

Spears, R. & Lea, M. (1994). Panacea or panopticon? The hidden power in computer-mediated communication. *Communication Research, 21*, 427-459.

Spears, R., Lea, M., & Lee, S. (1990). Deindividuation and group polarization in computer-mediated communication. *British Journal of Social Psychology, 29*, 121-134.

Spillmann, J. & Spillmann, L. (1993). The rise and fall of Hugo Münsterberg. *Journal of the History of the Behavioural Sciences, 29*, 322-38.

Stagner, R. (1950). Psychological aspects of industrial conflict II: Motivation. *Personnel Psychology, 3*, 1-15.

Stasser, G. (1992). Pooling of unshared information during group discussion. In S. Worchel, W. Wood & J. Simpson (Eds.), *Group process and productivity* (pp. 48-57). Newbury Park, CA: Sage.

Stasser, G. & Stewart, D. (1992). Discovery of hidden profiles by decision-making groups: Solving a problem versus making a judgment. *Journal of Personality and Social Psychology, 63*, 426-434.

Stasser, G., Stewart, D. & Wittenbaum, G. (1995). Expert roles and information sharing during discussion: The importance of knowing who knows what. *Journal of Experimental Social Psychology, 31*, 244-265.

Stasser, G., Taylor, L. A., & Hanna, C. (1989). Information sampling in structured and unstructured discussions of three- and six-person groups. *Journal of Personality and Social Psychology, 57*, 67-78.

Stasser, G. & Titus, W. (1985). Pooling of unshared information in group decision making: Biased information sampling during discussions. *Journal of Personality and Social Psychology, 48*, 1467-1478.

Stasser, G. & Titus, W. (1987). Effects of information load and percentage of shared information on the dissemination of unshared information during group discussion. *Journal of Personality and Social Psychology, 53*, 81-93.

Statt, D. A. (1994). Psychology and the world of work. Basingstoke: Macmillan.

Staw, B. M. (Ed.) (1995). *Psychological dimensions of organizational behaviour* (2nd ed.). Englewood Cliffs, NJ: Prentice Hall.

Steers, R. & Braunstein, D. N. (1976). A behaviorally-based measure of manifest needs in work settings. *Journal of Vocational Behavior, 9*, 251-266.

Stein, M. I. (1982) Creativity, groups, and management. In R. A. Guzzo (Ed.), *Improving group decision making in organizations: Approaches from theory and research* (pp. 127-155). New York: Academic Press.

Steiner, I. D. (1972). *Group process and productivity.* New York: Academic Press.

Steiner, I. D. (1974). Whatever happened to the group in social psychology? *Journal of Experimental Social Psychology, 10*, 94-108.

Stephenson, G. M. (1981). Intergroup bargaining and negotiation. In J. C. Turner & H. Giles (Eds.), *Intergroup behaviour* (pp. 168-198). Oxford: Blackwell.

Stephenson, G. M. (1984). Interpersonal and intergroup dimensions of bargaining and negotiation. In H. Tajfel (Ed.), *The social dimension: European developments in social psychology* (pp. 646-667). Cambridge: Cambridge University Press.

Stephenson, G. M. & Brotherton, C. (1973). The first line supervisor in the British coal industry. *Industrial Relations Journal, 4*, 27-36.

Stephenson, G. M. & Brotherton, C. (1975). Social progression and polarization: A study of discussion and negotiation in groups of mining supervisors. *British Journal of Social and Clinical Psychology, 14*, 241-252.

Stewart, D. D., Billings, R. S., & Stasser, G. (1998). Accountability and the discussion of unshared, critical information in decision-making groups. *Group Dynamics, 2*, 18-23.

Stewart, D. D. & Stasser, G. (1995). Expert role assignment and information sampling during collective recall and decision making. *Journal of Personality and Social Psychology, 69*, 619-628.

Stilwell, F. (1995). Reworking Australia. In S. Rees & G. Rodley (Eds.), *The human costs of managerialism: Advocating the recovery of humanity* (pp. 262-269). Leichhardt, Australia: Pluto.

Stogdill, R. M. (1948). Personality factors associated with leadership: A survey of the literature. *Journal of Psychology, 25*, 35-71.

Stodgill, R. M. (1950). Leadership, membership and organization. *Psychological Bulletin, 47*, 1-14.

Stohl C. & Redding, C. R. (1987). Messages and message exchange processes. In F. Jablin, L. L. Putnam, K. H. Roberts, & L. W. Porter (Eds.), *Handbook of organizational communication: An interdisciplinary perspective* (pp. 451-502). Newbury Park, CA: Sage.

Stoner, J. A. F. (1961). *A comparison of individual and group dimensions involving risk.* Unpublished thesis: School of Industrial Management, Massachusetts Institute of Technology.

Strauss, G. (1977). Managerial practices. In J. R. Hackman & J. L. Suttle (Eds.), *Improving life at work.* Santa Monica, CA: Goodyear.

Street. R. L., Jr. (1984). Speech convergence and speech evaluation in fact-finding interviews. *Human Communication Research, 11*, 139-169.

Stroebe, W. & Diehl, M. (1994). Why groups are less effective than their members: On productivity losses in idea-generating groups. *European Review of Social Psychology, 5*, 271-303.

Stroebe, W., Diehl, M., & Abakoumkin, G. (1992). The illusion of group effectivity. *Personality and Social Psychology Bulletin, 18*, 643-650.

Stumpf, S. A., Zand, D. E. & Freedman, R. D. (1979). Designing groups for judgmental decisions. *Academy of Management Review, 4*, 589-600.

Suedfeld, P. (1988). Authoritarian thinking, groupthink, and decision making under stress: Are simple decisions always worse? *Society, 25*, 25-27.

Sutton, H. & Porter, L. W. (1968). A study of the grapevine in a governmental organization. *Personnel Psychology, 21*, 223-230.

Suzuki, S. (1998). In-group and out-group communication patterns in international organizations: Implications for social identity theory. *Communication Research, 25*, 154-182.

Tajfel, H. (1969). Cognitive aspects of prejudice. *Journal of Social Issues, 25*, 79-97.

Tajfel, H. (1970). Experiments in intergroup discrimination. *Scientific American, 223*, 96-102.

Tajfel, H. (1972). La catégorisation sociale (English trans.). In S. Moscovici (Ed.), *Introduction à la psychologie sociale.* Paris: Larouse.

Tajfel, H. (1974). Social identity and intergroup behaviour. *Social Science Information, 13*, 65-93.

Tajfel, H. (1975). The exit of social mobility and the voice of social change. *Social Change Information, 14*, 101-118.

Tafjel, H. (1978a). Interindividual behaviour and intergroup behaviour. In H. Tajfel (Ed.), *Differentiation between social groups: Studies in the social psychology of intergroup relations* (pp. 27-60). London: Academic Press.

Tajfel, H. (1978b). Social categorization, social identity and social comparison. In H. Tajfel (Ed.), *Differentiation between social groups: Studies in the social psychology of intergroup relations* (pp. 61-76). London: Academic Press.

Tajfel, H. (1978c). The achievement of group differentiation. In H. Tajfel (Ed.), *Differentiation between social groups: Studies in the social psychology of intergroup relations* (pp. 77-98). London: Academic Press.

Tajfel, H. (Ed.) (1978d). *Differentiation between social groups: Studies in the social psychology of intergroup relations.* London: Academic Press.

Tajfel, H. (1979). Individuals and groups in social psychology. *British Journal of Social and Clinical Psychology, 18,* 183-190.

Tajfel, H. (1981a). *Human groups and social categories.* Cambridge: Cambridge University Press.

Tajfel, H. (1981b). Social stereotypes and social groups (pp. 144-167). In J. C. Turner & H. Giles (Eds.), *Intergroup Behaviour.* Oxford: Blackwell.

Tajfel, H. (1982a). Psychological concepts of equity: The present and the future. In P. Fraisse (Ed.), *Psychologie de demain.* Paris: Presses Universitaires de France.

Tajfel, H. (1982b). *Social identity and intergroup relations.* Cambridge: Cambridge University Press.

Tajfel, H., Flament, C., Billig, M. G., & Bundy, R. F. (1971). Social categorization and intergroup behaviour. *European Journal of Social Psychology, 1,* 149-177.

Tajfel, H., Jaspars, J. M. F., & Fraser, C. (1984). The social dimension in European social psychology. In H. Tajfel (Ed.), *The social dimension: European developments in social psychology* (pp. 1-8). Cambridge: Cambridge University Press.

Tajfel, H. & Turner, J. C. (1979). An integrative theory of intergroup conflict. In W. G. Austin & S. Worchel (Eds.), *The social psychology of intergroup relations* (pp. 33-47). Monterey, CA: Brooks/Cole.

Tajfel, H. & Turner, J. C. (1986). The social identity theory of intergroup behaviour. In S. Worchel & W. G. Austin (Eds.), *Psychology of intergroup relations* (2nd ed., pp. 7-24). Chicago: Nelson-Hall.

Tajfel, H. & Wilkes, A. L. (1963). Classification and quantitative judgement. *British Journal of Psychology, 54,* 101-114.

Talbott, S. (1984). *Deadly gambits.* New York: Alfred Knopf.

Tannenbaum, A. S. (1965). Unions. In J. G. March (Ed.), *Handbook of organizations* (pp. 710-763). Chicago: Rand McNally.

Tannenbaum, A. S. (1966). *Social psychology of the work organization.* London: Tavistock.

Tannenbaum, A. S. & Kahn, R. L. (1957). Organizational control structure: A general descriptive technique as applied to four local unions. *Human Relations, 10,* 127-40.

Taylor, D. M., Moghaddam, F., Gamble, I. Z., & Zellerer, E. (1987). Disadvantaged group responses to perceived inequality: From passive acceptance to collective action. *Journal of Social-Psychology, 127,* 259-272.

Taylor, D. W., Berry, P. C., & Block, C. H. (1958). Does group participation when using brainstorming facilitate or inhibit creative thinking? *Administrative Science Quarterly, 3,* 23-47.

Taylor, F. W. (1911). *Principles of scientific management.* New York: Harper.

Taylor, F. W. (1911/1972). Principles of scientific management. In *Dartmouth College conferences, First Tuck school conference: Addresses and discussions at the conference on scientific management, 12-14 October 1911.* Dartmouth, USA: Easton Hive Publishing Company.

Taylor, N. & McGarty, C. (1999). *Does power tell the story? The role of power and group membership in the construal of industrial relations.* Paper presented at the 5th meeting of the Society of Australasian Social Psychologists, Coolum, Queensland, 8-11 April.

Taylor, S. E. (1981). The interface of cognitive and social psychology. In J. Harvey (Ed.), *Cognition, social behaviour and the environment* (pp. 189-211). Hillsdale, NJ: Erlbaum.

Terry, D. J. & Callan, V. J. (1998). Ingroup bias in response to an organizational merger. *Group Dynamics: Theory, Research and Practice, 2*, 67-81.

Terry, D. J., Callan, V. J., & Sartori, G. (1996). Employee adjustment to an organizational merger: Stress, coping and intergroup differences. *Stress Medicine, 12*, 105-122.

Terry, D. J., Carey, C. J., & Callan, V. J. (1997). Employee responses to an organizational merger: Group status, group permeability and identification. *Australian Journal of Psychology, 49*, 48.

Terry, D. J., Neilsen, M., & Perchard, L. (1993). Effects of work stress on psychological well-being and job satisfaction: The stress-buffering role of social support. *Australian Journal of Psychology, 45*, 168-175.

Terry, D. J. & O'Brien, A. T. (1999). *Employee responses to an organizational merger: A social identity perspective.* Paper presented at the 3rd Australian Industrial and Organizational Psychology Conference, Brisbane, Queensland, 25-27 June.

Tetrault, L. A., Schriesheim, C. A., & Neider, L. L. (1988). Leadership training interventions: A review. *Organization Development Journal, 6*, 77-83.

Thelen, H. A. (1949). Group dynamics in instruction: Principles of least group size. *School Review, 57*, 139-148.

Thibaut, J. & Kelley, H. H. (1959). *The social psychology of groups.* New York: Wiley.

Thibaut, J. & Walker, L. (1975). *Procedural justice.* Hillsdale, NJ: Erlbaum.

Thibaut, J. & Walker, L. (1978). A theory of procedure. *California Law Review, 66*, 541-566.

Thierry, H. (1998). Compensating work. In P. J. D. Drenth, H. Thierry & C. J. de Wolff (Eds.), *Handbook of Work and Organizational Psychology* (2nd ed., vol. 4). Hove: Psychology Press.

Thierry, H. (in press). The strategic nature of strategic compensation. *Applied Psychology: An International Review.*

Thomas, K. (1976). Conflict and conflict management. In M. D. Dunette (Ed.), *Handbook of Industrial and Organizational Psychology* (pp. 889-935). Chicago: Rand McNally.

Thompson, P. & McHugh, D. (1995). *Work Organizations: A critical introduction* (2nd ed.). Houndmills: Macmillan.

Thompson, P. & Warhurst, C. (Eds.) (1998). *Workplaces of the future.* Houndmills: Macmillan.

Thompson, V. A. (1961). *Modern organization.* New York: Alfred A. Knopf.

Tindale, R. S., Smith, C. M., Thomas, L. S., Filkins, J., & Sheffey, S. (1996). Shared representations and asymmetric social influence processes in small groups. In E. Witte & J. Davis (Eds.), *Understanding group behavior: Consensual action by small groups* (vol. 1, pp. 81-103). Mahwah, NJ: Lawrence Erlbaum Associates.

Tosi, H. L. Katz, J. P., & Gomez-Mejia, L. R. (1997). Disaggregating the agency contract: The effects of monitoring, incentive alignment, and term in office on agent decision making. *Academy of Management Journal, 40*, 584-602.

Tougas, F. & Veilleux, F. (1988). The influence of identification, collective relative deprivation, and procedure of implementation on women's response to affirmative action: A causal modelling approach. *Canadian Journal of Behavioural Science, 20,* 15-28.

Triandis, H. C. (1990). Cross-cultural studies of individualism and collectivism. In J. Berman (Ed.), *Nebraska symposium on motivation* (pp. 41-133). Lincoln, NB: University of Nebraska Press.

Triandis, H. C. (1994). *Culture and social behavior.* New York: McGraw-Hill.

Triandis, H. C., Bontempo, R., Villareal, M. J., Asai, M., & Lucca, N. (1988). Individualism and collectivism: Cross-cultural perspectives on self-ingroup relationships. *Journal of Personality and Social Psychology, 54,* 323-328.

Triplett, N. (1898). The dynamogenic factors in pacemaking and competition. *American Journal of Psychology, 9,* 507-533.

Trivers, R. L. (1971). The evolution of reciprocal altruism. *Quarterly Review of Biology, 46,* 35-57.

Tsui, A. S. (1984). Multiple-constituency framework of managerial reputational effectiveness. In J. G. Hunt, D. Hosking, C. A. Schrieshiem & R. Stewart (Eds.), *Leaders and managers: International perspectives on managerial behaviour and leadership.* New York: Pergamon Press.

Tsui, A. S. & O'Reilly, C. (1989). Beyond simple demographic effects: The importance of relational demography in superior-subordinate dyads. *Academy of Management Journal, 32,* 402-433.

Turner, J. C. (1975). Social comparison and social identity: Some prospects for intergroup behaviour. *European Journal of Social Psychology, 5,* 5-34.

Turner, J. C. (1981). The experimental social psychology of intergroup behaviour. In J. C. Turner & H. Giles (Eds.), *Intergroup behaviour* (pp. 66-101). Oxford: Blackwell.

Turner, J. C. (1982).Towards a cognitive redefinition of the social group. In H. Tajfel (Ed.), *Social identity and intergroup relations* (pp. 15-40). Cambridge: Cambridge University Press.

Turner, J. C. (1985). Social categorization and the self-concept: A social cognitive theory of group behaviour. In E. J. Lawler (Ed.), *Advances in Group Processes* (vol. 2, pp. 77-122) Greenwich, CT: JAI Press.

Turner, J. C. (1987a). The analysis of social influence. In J. C. Turner, M. A. Hogg, P. J. Oakes, S. D. Reicher & M. S. Wetherell, *Rediscovering the social group: A self-categorization theory* (pp. 68-88). Oxford: Blackwell.

Turner, J. C. (1987b). Introducing the problem: Individual and group. In J. C. Turner, M. A. Hogg, P. J. Oakes, S. D. Reicher & M. S. Wetherell, *Rediscovering the social group: A self-categorization theory* (pp. 1-18). Oxford: Blackwell.

Turner, J. C. (1991). *Social influence.* Milton Keynes: Open University Press.

Turner, J. C. (1996). Henri Tajfel: An introduction. In W. P. Robinson (Ed.), *Social groups and identities: The developing legacy of Henri Tajfel* (pp. 1-23). Oxford: Butterworth–Heinemann.

Turner, J. C. (1998). *Social identity, self-categorization and leadership.* Paper presented at the La Trobe Conference on the Social Psychology of Leadership, Melbourne, Victoria, 3-4 October.

Turner, J. C. (1999). Some current themes in research on social identity and self-categorization theories. In N. Ellemers, R. Spears, & B. Doosje (Eds.), *Social identity: Context, commitment, content* (pp. 6-34). Oxford: Blackwell.

Turner, J. C. & Bourhis, R. Y. (1996). Social identity, interdependence and the social group: A reply to Rabbie et al.. In W. P. Robinson (Ed.), *Social groups and identities: Developing the legacy of Henri Tajfel.* Oxford: Butterworth–Heinemann.

Turner, J. C. & Brown, R. J. (1978). Social status, cognitive alternatives and inter-group relations. In H. Tajfel (Ed.), *Differentiation between social groups: Studies in the social psychology of intergroup relations* (pp. 201-234). London: Academic Press.

Turner, J. C. & Giles, H. (Eds.) (1981). *Intergroup behaviour.* Oxford: Blackwell.

Turner, J. C. & Haslam, S. A. (2000). Social identity, organizations and leadership. In M. E. Turner (Ed.), *Groups at work: Advances in theory and research.* Hillsdale, NJ: Erlbaum.

Turner, J. C., Hogg, M. A., Oakes, P. J., Reicher, S. D., & Wetherell, M. S. (1987). *Rediscovering the social group: A self-categorization theory.* Oxford: Blackwell.

Turner, J. C., Hogg, M. A., Turner, P. J., & Smith, P. M. (1984). Failure and defeat as determinants of group cohesiveness. *British Journal of Social Psychology, 23,* 97-111.

Turner, J. C. & Oakes, P. J. (1986). The significance of the social identity concept for social psychology with reference to individualism, interactionism, and social influence. *British Journal of Social Psychology, 25,* 237-252.

Turner, J. C. & Oakes, P. J. (1989). Self-categorization theory and social influence. In P. B. Paulus (Ed.), *The psychology of group influence* (vol. 2, pp. 233-275). Hillsdale, NJ: Erlbaum.

Turner, J. C. & Oakes, P. J. (1997). The socially structured mind. In C. McGarty & S. A. Haslam (Eds.), *The message of social psychology: Perspectives on mind in society* (pp. 355-373). Oxford: Blackwell.

Turner, J. C., Oakes, P. J., Haslam, S. A., & McGarty, C. A. (1994). Self and collective: Cognition and social context. *Personality and Social Psychology Bulletin, 20,* 454-463.

Turner, J. C. & Onorato, R. (1999). Social identity, personality and the self-concept: A self-categorization perspective. In T. R. Tyler, R. Kramer & O. John (Eds.), *The psychology of the social self.* Hillsdale, NJ: Erlbaum.

Turner, J. C. & Reynolds, K. J. (in press). The social identity perspective in intergroup relations: Theories, themes and controversies. In R. J. Brown & S. Gaertner (Eds.), *Blackwell handbook of social psychology* (vol. 4): *Intergroup processes.* Oxford: Blackwell.

Turner, J. C., Sachdev, I. & Hogg, M. A. (1983). Social categorization, interpersonal attraction and group formation. *British Journal of Social Psychology, 22,* 227-239.

Turner, J. C., Wetherell, M. S., & Hogg, M. A. (1989). Referent informational influence and group polarization. *British Journal of Social Psychology, 28,* 135-147.

Turner, M. E. & Pratkanis, A. R. (1994). Social identity maintenance prescriptions for preventing groupthink: Reducing identity protection and enhancing intellectual conflict. *International Journal of Conflict Management, 5,* 254-270.

Turner, M. E. & Pratkanis, A. R. (1998a). A social identity maintenance model of groupthink. *Organizational Behaviour and Human Decision Processes, 2/3,* 210-235.

Turner, M. E. & Pratkanis, A. R. (Eds.) (1998b). Theoretical perspectives on group-think: A twenty-fifth anniversary appraisal. *Organizational Behaviour and Human Decision Processes, 2/3* (whole issues).

Turner, M. E. & Pratkanis, A. R. (1998c). Twenty-five years of groupthink theory and research: Lessons from an evaluation of the theory. *Organizational Behaviour and Human Decision Processes, 2/3,* 210-235.

Turner, M. E., Pratkanis, A. R., Probasco, P., & Leve, C. (1992). Threat, cohesion, and group effectiveness: Testing a social identity maintenance perspective on group-think. *Journal of Personality and Social Psychology, 63,* 781-796.

Tyler, T. R. (1988). What is procedural justice? *Law and Society Review, 22,* 301-335.

Tyler, T. R. (1989). The psychology of procedural justice: A test of the group-value model. *Journal of Personality and Social Psychology, 57,* 830-838.

Tyler, T. R. (1990). *Why people obey the law.* New Haven: Yale University Press.

Tyler, T. R. (1993). The social psychology of authority. In J. R. Murnighan (Ed.), *Social psychology in organizations: Advances in theory and research* (pp. 141-160). Englewood Cliffs, NJ: Prentice Hall.

Tyler, T. R. (1994). Psychological models of the justice motive: Antecedents of distributive and procedural justice. *Journal of Personality and Social Psychology, 67,* 850-863.

Tyler, T. R. (1997). The psychology of legitimacy: A relational perspective on voluntary deference to authorities. *Personality and Social Psychology Review, 1,* 323-345.

Tyler, T. R. (1998). The psychology of authority relations: A relational perspective on influence and power in groups. In R. M. Kramer & M. A. Neale (Eds.), *Power and influence in organizations* (pp. 251-260). Thousand Oaks, CA: Sage.

Tyler, T. R. (1999a). Why people co-operate with organizations: An identity-based perspective. In B. M. Staw & R. Sutton (Eds.), *Research in organizational behaviour* (vol. 21, pp. 201-246). Greenwich, CT: JAI Press.

Tyler, T. R. (1999b). *Justice in intragroup and intergroup relations.* Paper presented at the Small Groups Preconference to the Annual Meeting of the Society of Experimental Social Psychology, St Louis, MI, 14-16 October.

Tyler, T. R. & Blader, S. (in press). *Co-operation in groups: Procedural justice, social identity and behavioral engagement.* Philadelphia, PA: Psychology Press.

Tyler, T. R. & Degoey, P. (1995). Collective restraint in social dilemmas: Procedural justice and social identification effects on support for authorities. *Journal of Personality and Social Psychology, 69,* 482-497.

Tyler, T. R., Degoey, P., & Smith, H. J. (1996). Understanding why the fairness of group procedures matters: A test of the psychological dynamics of the group-value model. *Journal of Personality and Social Psychology, 70,* 913-930.

Tyler, T. R., Lind, A., Ohbuchi, K.-I., Sugarawa, I., & Huo, Y. J. (1998). Conflict with outsiders: Disputing within and across boundaries. *Personality and Social PsychologyBulletin, 24,* 137-146.

Tyler, T. R., Rasinski, K. A., & Spoddock, N. (1985). Influence of voice on satisfaction with leaders: Exploring the meaning and process of control. *Journal of Personality and Social Psychology, 48,* 72-81.

Uzubalis, M. (1999). *For the good of the organization: The role of social identity salience and influence in employees' performance of organizational citizenship behaviours.* Unpublished thesis: The Australian National University.

Van de Vliert, E. (1990). Positive effects of conflict: A field assessment. *The International Journal of Conflict Management, 1,* 69-80.

Vanderslice, V. J. (1988). Separating leadership from leaders: An assessment of the effect of leader and follower roles in organizations. *Human Relations, 41,* 677-696.

Vanek, J. (Ed.) (1975). *Self-management: Economic liberation of man.* Harmondsworth: Penguin.

van Knippenberg, A. & Ellemers, N. (1990). Social identity and intergroup differentiation processes. *European Review of Social Psychology, 1,* 137-170.

van Knippenberg, A. & van Oers, H. (1984). Social identity and equity concerns in intergroup perceptions. *British Journal of Social Psychology, 23,* 351-361.

van Knippenberg, D. (2000). Work motivation and performance: A social identity perspective. *Applied Psychology: An International Review, 49,* 357-371.

van Knippenberg, D., de Vries, N., & van Knippenberg, A. (1990). Group status, group size and attitude polarization. *European Journal of Social Psychology, 20,* 253-257.

van Knippenberg, D., Lossie, N., & Wilke, H. (1994). Ingroup prototypicality and persuasion: Determinants of heuristic and systematic message processing. *British Journal of Social Psychology, 33,* 289-300.

van Knippenberg, D. & van Knippenberg, B. (1996). *Group member prototypicality and influence exertion.* Paper presented at the 2nd meeting of Australasian Social Psychologists, 2-5 May.

van Knippenberg, D., van Knippenberg, B., Monden, L. & de Lima, F. (1998). *A social categorization perspective on mergers and acquisitions.* Unpublished manuscript: University of Amsterdam.

van Knippenberg, D., & van Schie, E. C. M. (in press). Foci and correlates of organizational identification. *Journal of Occupational and Organizational Psychology.*

van Knippenberg, D. & Wilke, H. (1992). Prototypicality of arguments and conformity to ingroup norms. *European Journal of Social Psychology, 22,* 141-155.

van Leeuwen, E., van Knippenberg, D., & Ellemers, N. (2000). *Preserving identity in times of change: The dynamics of post-merger identification.* Unpublished Manuscript: University of Amsterdam.

van Leeuwen, E., van Knippenberg, D., & Wilke, H. (1999). *Determinants of post-merger identification: A dynamic approach.* Paper presented at the XIIth meeting of the European Association of Experimental Social Psychology, Oxford, 7-11 July.

van Vugt, M. & de Cremer, D. (1999). Leadership in social dilemmas: The effects of group identification on collective actions to provide public goods. *Journal of Personality and Social Psychology, 76,* 587-599.

Veenstra, K. & Haslam, S. A. (2000). Willingness to participate in industrial protest: Exploring social identification in context. *British Journal of Social Psychology, 39,* 153-172.

Veenstra, K. & Haslam, S. A. (2000). *The hidden costs of casualisation: Error rectification and the importance of long-term low identifiers.* Unpublished manuscript: The Australian National University.

Velthouse, B. A. (1990). Creativity and empowerment: A complementary relationship. *Review of Business, 12,* 13-18.

Verkuyten, M. & Hagendoorn, L. (1998) Prejudice and self-categorization: The variable role of authoritarianism and ingroup stereotypes. *Personality and Social Psychology Bulletin, 24,* 99-110.

Viteles, M. S. (1932). *Industrial Psychology.* New York: Norton.

von Cranach, M. (1986). Leadership as a function of group action. In C. F. Graumann & S. Moscovici (Eds.), *Changing conceptions of leadership* (pp. 115-134). New York: Springer Verlag.

Vroom, V. H. (1964). *Work and motivation.* New York: Wiley.

Vroom, V. H. (1969). Industrial social psychology. In G. Lindzey & E. Aronson (Eds.), *The handbook of social psychology* (2nd ed.). Cambridge, MA: Addison-Wesley.

Vroom, V. H. (1974). A new look at managerial decision-making. *Organizational Dynamics, 5,* 66-80.

Vroom, V. H. & Deci, E. L. (1970). *Management and motivation.* Harmondsworth: Penguin.

Vroom, V. H. & Jago, A. G. (1988). Managing participation: A critical dimension of leadership. *Journal of Management Development, 7,* 32-42,

Vroom, V. H. & Yetton, P. W. (1973). *Leadership and decision making.* Pittsburgh: University of Pittsburgh Press.

Walker, I. & Mann, L. (1987). Unemployment, relative deprivation and social protest. *Personality and Social Psychology Bulletin, 13,* 275-283.

Walker, I. & Pettigrew, T. F. (1984). Relative deprivation theory: An overview and conceptual critique. *British Journal of Social Psychology, 23,* 301-310.

Wallace, N. (1998). *Soldiering reassessed: Congruity between self-categorization, task conditions and goals as a determinant of social loafing, labouring and facilitation.* Unpublished thesis: The Australian National University.

Wallach, M. A., Kogan, N., & Bem, D. J. (1962). Group influence on individual risk taking. *Journal of Abnormal and Social Psychology, 65,* 75-86.

Walster, E., Walster, G. W., & Berscheid, E. (1978). *Equity theory and research.* Boston MA: Allyn & Bacon.

Wann, D. L. & Branscombe, N. R. (1990). Die hard and fair-weather fans: Effects of identification on BIRGing and CORFing tendencies. *Journal of Sport and Social Issues, 14,* 103-117.

Wann, D. L. & Branscombe, N. R. (1993). Sport fans: Measuring degree of identification with their team. *International Journal of Sport Psychology, 24,* 1-17.

Warhurst, C. & Thompson, P. (1998). Hands, hearts and minds: Changing workers at the end of the century. In P. Thompson & C. Warhurst (Eds.), *Workplaces of the future* (pp. 1-24). Houndmills: Macmillan.

Waring, S. P. (1991). *Taylorism transformed: Scientific management since 1945.* Chapel Hill: University of North Carolina Press.

Weber, M. (1921). The sociology of charismatic authority. Republished in translation (1946) in H. H. Gerth & C. W. Milles (trans. Eds.), *Max Weber: Essays in sociology* (pp. 245-252). New York: Oxford University Press.

Weber, M. (1947). *The theory of social and economic organization* (A. M. Henderson & T. Parsons trans.). New York: Oxford University Press.

Webster, A. G. (1911/1972). Academic Efficiency. In *Dartmouth College conferences, First Tuck school conference: Addresses and discussions at the conference on scientific management, 12-14 October 1911.* Dartmouth, USA: Easton Hive Publishing Company.

Wegge, J. (1999). *Participation in group goal setting: Some novel findings and a comprehensive theory as a new ending to an old story.* Paper presented at the 4th International Work Motivation conference. Sydney, 22-24 June.

Wegge, J. (in press). Participation in group goal setting. *Applied Psychology: An International Review.*

Wegner, D. M. (1987). 'Transactive memory': A contemporary analysis of the group mind. In B. Mullen & G. R. Goethals (Eds.), *Theories of group behavior* (pp. 185-208). New York: Springer Verlag.

Weick, K. E. (1985). The significance of corporate culture. In J. P. Frost, L. F. Moore, M. Reise Louis, C. C. Lundburg & J. Martin (Eds.), *Organizational culture* (pp. 381-389). Beverley Hills, CA: Sage.

Weick, K. E. & Roberts, K. H. (1993). Collective mind in organizations: Heedful interrelating on flight decks. *Administrative Science Quarterly, 38,* 357-381.

Weiss, H. M. & Adler, S. (1984). Personality and organizational behaviour. In B. M. Staw & L. L. Cummings (Eds.), *Research in organizational behaviour* (pp. 1-50). Greenwich, CT: JAI Press.

Weller, M. P. I. (1985). Crowds, mobs and riots. *Medical Science Law, 25,* 295-303.

West, M. A. (Ed.) (1996). *Handbook of work group psychology.* New York: Wiley.

Wetherell, M. S. (1987). Social identity and group polarization. In J. C. Turner, M. A. Hogg, P. J. Oakes, S. D. Reicher, & M. S. Wetherell *Rediscovering the social group: A self-categorization theory* (pp. 142-170). Oxford: Blackwell.

Wharton, A. S. (1992). The social construction of gender and race in organizations: A social identity and group mobilization perspective. *Research in the Sociology of Organizations, 10,* 55-84.

White, R. & Lippitt, R. (1956). Leader behaviour and member reaction in three 'social climates'. In D. Cartwright & A. Zander (Eds.), *Group dynamics: Research and theory* (2nd ed., pp. 585-611). Evanston, IL: Row Peterson.

Whyte, G. (1989). Groupthink reconsidered. *Academy of Management Review, 14,* 40-56.

Whyte, G. (1993). Escalating commitment in individual and group decision making: A prospect theory approach. *Organizational Behavior and Human Decision Processes, 54,* 430-455.

Whyte, W. H. (1960). *The organization man.* Harmondsworth: Penguin.

Wiemann, J. M. & Giles, H. (1996). Communication in interpersonal and social relationships. In M. Hewstone, W. Stroebe, & G. M. Stephenson (Eds.), *Introduction to social psychology: A European perspective* (2nd ed., pp. 316-344). Oxford: Blackwell.

Wilder, D. A. (1977). Perception of groups, size of opposition and social influence. *Journal of Experimental Social Psychology, 13,* 253-268.

Wilder, D. A. (1984). Predictions of belief homogeneity and similarity following social categorization. *British Journal of Social Psychology, 23,* 323-333.

Wilder, D. A. (1990). Some determinants of the persuasive power of ingroups and outgroups: Organization of information and attribution of independence. *Journal of Personality and Social Psychology, 59,* 1202-1213.

Wilder, D. A. & Thompson, J. E. (1988). Assimilation and contrast effects in the judgements of groups. *Journal of Personality and Social Psychology, 54,* 62-73.

Wilensky, H. L. (1967). The failure of intelligence: Knowledge and policy in government and industry. *Proceedings of the Nineteenth Annual Winter Meeting of the Industrial Relations Research Association.* Reprinted in L. W. Porter & K. Roberts (Eds.), *Communication in organizations* (pp. 118-131). Harmondsworth: Penguin.

Wilhelm, D. (1966). Priorities for effective development. In J. D. Montgomery & A. Smithies (Eds.), *Public policy* (vol. 15, pp. 304-22). Cambridge MA: Harvard University Press.

Willemyns, M., Gallois, C., & Callan, V. J. (in press). Accommodating power in supervisor-supervisee communication: A content analysis. *Australian Journal of Communication.*

Willemyns, M., Gallois, C, Callan, V. J., & Pittam, J. (1997). Accent accommodation in the job interview: Impact of interviewer accent and gender. *Journal of Language and Social Psychology, 16,* 3-22.

Williams, K., Harkins, S., & Latané, B. (1981). Identifiability as a deterrent to social loafing: two cheering experiments. *Journal of Personality and Social Psychology, 40,* 303-311.

Williams, K., Karau, S., & Bourgeois, M. (1991). Working on collective tasks: Social loafing and social compensation. In M. A. Hogg & D. Abrams (Eds.), *Group motivation: Social psychological perspectives* (pp. 130-148). London: Harvester Wheatsheaf.

Williams, K. Y. & O'Reilly, C. A. (1998). Demography and diversity in organizations: A review of 40 years of research. *Research in Organizational Behavior, 20,* 77-140.

Winquist, J. R. & Larson, J. R., Jr. (1998). Information pooling: When it impacts group decision making. *Journal of Personality & Social Psychology, 74,* 371-377.

Wittenbaum, G. M. & Stasser, G. (1996). Management of information in small groups. In J. L. Nye & A. M. Brower (Eds.), *What's social about social cognition? Research on socially shared cognition in small groups* (pp. 3-28). Thousand Oaks, CA: Sage.

Worchel, S. (1994). You can go home again: Returning group research to the group context with an eye on developmental issues. *Small Group Research, 25,* 205-223.

Worchel, S. (1998). A developmental view of the search for group identity. In S. Worchel, J. F. Morales, D. Paez, J.-C. Deschamps (Eds.), *Social identity: International perspectives* (pp. 53-74). London: Sage.

Worchel, S., Coutant-Sassic, D., & Grossman, M. (1992). A developmental approach to group dynamics: A model and illustrative research. In S. Worchel, W. Wood & J. A. Simpson (Eds.), *Group processes and productivity* (pp. 181-202). Newbury Park, CA: Sage.

Worchel, S., Coutant-Sassic, D., & Wong, F. (1993). Toward a more balanced view of conflict: There is a positive side. In S. Worchel & J. A. Simpson (Eds.), *Conflict between people and groups* (pp. 73-89). Chicago: Nelson Hall.

Worchel, S., Rothgerber, H., Day, A., Hart, D. & Butemeyer, J. (1998). Social identity and individual productivity within groups. *British Journal of Social Psychology, 37,* 389-413.

Wright, S. C. (1997). Ambiguity, social influence, and collective action: Generating collective protest in response to tokenism. *Personality and Social Psychology Bulletin, 23,* 1277-1290.

Wright, S. C. & Taylor, D. M. (1998). Responding to tokenism: Individual action in the face of collective injustice. *European Journal of Social Psychology, 28,* 647-667.

Wright, S. C., Taylor, D. M., & Moghaddam, F. M. (1990). Responding to membership in a disadvantaged group: From acceptance to collective protest. *Journal of Personality and Social Psychology, 58,* 994-1003.

Yukl, G. A. (1981). *Leadership in organizations.* Engelwood Cliffs, NJ: Prentice Hall.

Zajonc, R. B. (1965). Social facilitation. *Science, 149,* 269-274.

Zajonc, R. B., Heingartner, A., & Herman, E. M. (1969). Social enhancement and impairment of performance in the cockroach. *Journal of Personality and Social Psychology, 13,* 82-92.

Zander, A. (1971). *Motives and goals in groups.* New York: Academic Press.

Zander, A. (1985). *The purposes of groups and organizations.* San Francisco: Jossey-Bass.

Zander, A. (1997). *Groups at work.* San Francisco: Jossey-Bass.

Zimbardo, P. (1969). The human choice: Individuation, reason and order versus deindividuation, impulse and chaos. In W. J. Arnold & D. Levine (Eds.), *Nebraska symposium on motivation* (vol. 17). Lincoln, NB: University of Nebraska Press.

Zurcher, L. A. (1965). The sailor aboard ship: A study of role behaviour in a total institution. *Social Forces, 43,* 389-400.

# Appendix 1

# Measures of Social and Organizational Identification

Over the past fifteen or so years, researchers have developed a range of different measures of social and organizational identification. As with all psychological measures, the relative utility of each is a major topic of debate (e.g. see Ashforth & Mael, 1989; Cameron, 1999; Hinkle, Taylor, Fox-Cardamone & Crook, 1989; Jackson & Smith, 1999; Smith et al., 1999). This appendix presents some of the most commonly used measures, many of which are integral to the research discussed in the various chapters of this book. Table A1.1 also provides a summary of the relative merits of each measure.

When deciding which scale to use in any piece of research, a key issue is whether to opt for a global measure of social identification (which treats social identity as a unitary construct) or to employ a measure that incorporates discrete

*Table A1.1* Summary of the features and merits of different measures of social and organizational identification

| Feature | Global measures | | | | Multi-component measures | | |
|---|---|---|---|---|---|---|---|
| | Brown et al. (1986) | Mael & Ashforth (1988) | Doosje et al. (1995) | Haslam et al. (1999) | Hinkle et al. (1989) | Karasawa (1991) | Ellemers et al. (1999) |
| Number of items | 10 | 6 | 4 | 1 | 7 | 7 | 10 |
| High inter-item reliability | | ✓ | ✓ | n/a | within sub-scales | within sub-scales | within sub-scales |
| Encompasses multiple components of identity | ✓ | | ✓ | | ✓ | ✓ | ✓ |
| Differentiates between sub-components of identification | | | | | ✓ | ✓ | ✓ |
| Suitable for real groups | ✓ | ✓ | ✓ | ✓ | | ✓ | ✓ |
| Suitable for ad hoc groups | | | ✓ | ✓ | ✓ | | ✓ |
| Suitable as a measure of social identity salience | | | ✓ | ✓ | | | |

sub-scales (each measuring different sub-components of the construct — e.g. a person's emotional attachment to a group as distinct from his or her awareness of group membership). In making this choice, most researchers agree that a measure's appropriateness depends on the theoretical and empirical question that is being addressed and that no one scale is appropriate for all research settings. In particular, global measures are often more appropriate when comparing the relative merit of different theories or approaches (e.g. in Kelly & Kelly's, 1994, comparison of different models of industrial protest; see Chapter 10 above), but multi-component scales may be more appropriate when investigating fine-grained issues that hone in on specific social identity mechanisms (e.g. Ouwerkerk et al.'s, 1999, study of work motivation; see Chapter 4 above). By the same token, multi-item scales are preferable when identification is a key dependent variable and is being compared across a range of contexts (to which a subset of items may be particularly sensitive; e.g. Tyler, 1999a), while shorter scales may be preferred if social identification is not the primary focus of investigation (e.g. where a measure is used as a check to establish whether attempts to manipulate social identity salience have been successful; as in Haslam, Oakes et al., 1999).

In this regard it is worth noting that some scales can be used to measure *both* social identification and social identity salience. As suggested in Chapter 2 and Figure A1.1, these process-based states are dynamically interrelated so that each feeds into the other (Doosje, Spears & Ellemers, in press; McGarty, 1999b, 1999b; McGarty, Reynolds, Haslam, Turner & Ryan, 1999; Turner, 1999; Turner et al., 1987). However, social identification reflects a person's relatively enduring identification with a group or organization (i.e. their pre-existing *readiness* to use a social category to define themselves) while social

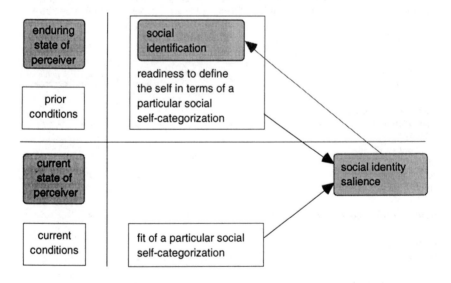

*Figure A1.1* The interrelationship between social identification and social identity salience (after McGarty et al., 1999)

identity salience also reflects their current reaction to a specific set of contextual conditions (i.e. perceiver readiness in interaction with the *fit* of a particular self-categorization; Oakes, 1987). In this way current and prior conditions contribute to the current state of the perceiver which in turn contributes to his or her long-term state. This long-term state then becomes one of the prior conditions that contributes to the perceiver's current state at some time in the future.

## Global measures of identification

### Brown et al.'s (1986) ten-item measure

This was the first measure of social identification to be developed and was modelled on a measure of ethnic identification devised by Driedger (1976). Brown et al.'s original research was conducted in an organizational setting and examined English paper mill workers' identification with the particular departments in which they worked. In that setting it yielded a Cronbach's alpha of .71.

*Note*: Items are presented in random order; * = reverse scored

1. I am a person who considers [Group X] important

         never      seldom      sometimes      often      very often

2. I am a person who identifies with [Group X]

         never      seldom      sometimes      often      very often

3. I am a person who feels strong ties with [Group X]

         never      seldom      sometimes      often      very often

4. I am a person who is glad to belong to [Group X]

         never      seldom      sometimes      often      very often

5. I am a person who sees myself as belonging to [Group X]

         never      seldom      sometimes      often      very often

*6. I am a person who makes excuses for belonging to [Group X]

         never      seldom      sometimes      often      very often

*7. I am a person who tries to hide belonging to [Group X]

         never      seldom      sometimes      often      very often

*8. I am a person who feels held back by [Group X]

         never      seldom      sometimes      often      very often

*9. I am a person who is annoyed to say I'm a member of [Group X]

  never       seldom      sometimes       often       very often

*10. I am a person who criticizes [Group X]

  never       seldom      sometimes       often       very often

## Mael and Ashforth's (1992) six-item measure

Based on Mael's (1988) doctoral work, this is one of the most widely used measures of organizational identification — largely because it is easy to administer and is associated with the pioneering paper by Ashforth and Mael (1989). Inter-item reliability is very high (Cronbach's alpha is generally greater than .80; see Mael & Ashforth, 1992, p. 110), but the scale can be criticized for focusing on the affective aspects of identification at the expense of the cognitive.

1. When someone criticizes [Organization X], it feels like a personal insult

    strongly disagree    1    2    3    4    5    strongly agree

2. I am very interested in what others think about [Organization X]

    strongly disagree    1    2    3    4    5    strongly agree

3. When I talk about [Organization X], I usually say 'we' rather than 'they'

    strongly disagree    1    2    3    4    5    strongly agree

4. [Organization X]'s successes are my successes

    strongly disagree    1    2    3    4    5    strongly agree

5. When someone praises [Organization X], it feels like a personal compliment

    strongly disagree    1    2    3    4    5    strongly agree

6. If a story in the media criticized [Organization X], I would feel embarrassed

    strongly disagree    1    2    3    4    5    strongly agree

## Doosje et al.'s (1995) four-item measure

This very basic scale was first used to measure the identification of Dutch students with the category 'psychology student' where it yielded a Cronbach's alpha of .83. Like most other measures, it can easily be adapted for an organizational setting by substituting the name of the relevant organization. The global and succinct nature of the scale make it suitable as a measure of both social identification and social identity salience.

1. I see myself as a [member of Group X]

    do not agree at all   1   2   3   4   5   6   7   agree completely

2. I am pleased to be a [member of Group X]

    do not agree at all   1   2   3   4   5   6   7   agree completely

3. I feel strong ties with [members of Group X]

    do not agree at all   1   2   3   4   5   6   7   agree completely

4. I identify with other [members of Group X]

    do not agree at all   1   2   3   4   5   6   7   agree completely

## *Haslam, Oakes et al.'s (1999) single-item measure*

This measure was initially used by Haslam, Oakes et al. (1999) as a manipulation check to establish the efficacy of attempts to experimentally manipulate social identity salience. In that context it was intended to be minimally invasive and as non-reactive as possible, so as not to interfere with measures relating to the *consequences* of social identity salience (e.g. ingroup–outgroup stereotyping). However, subsequent research has indicated that this item is highly correlated with other global measures of social and organizational identification (e.g. Doosje et al., 1995; Mael, 1988).

- Being a member of [Group X] is important to me

    do not agree at all   1   2   3   4   5   6   7   agree completely

## Multi-component measures of identification

### *Hinkle et al.'s (1989) three-component measure*

Hinkle et al.'s measure was devised as an adaptation of Brown et al.'s (1986) group identification measure and initially designed for use with ad hoc laboratory groups (e.g. as in Tajfel et al., 1971). The complete scale yielded a Cronbach's alpha of .85, but the authors argued for the utility of distinct sub-scales in light of evidence that these were differentially associated with particular forms of intergroup behaviour.

*Note:* * = reverse scored

*Emotional identification sub-scale*

1. I identify with [Group X]

    strongly disagree   1   2   3   4   5   6   7   8   9   strongly agree

2.  I think [Group X] worked together well

    strongly disagree    1   2   3   4   5   6   7   8   9    strongly agree

3.  I am glad to belong to [Group X]

    strongly disagree    1   2   3   4   5   6   7   8   9    strongly agree

*Individual/group opposition sub-scale*

*1.  I feel uneasy with [Group X]

    strongly disagree    1   2   3   4   5   6   7   8   9    strongly agree

*2.  I feel held back by [Group X]

    strongly disagree    1   2   3   4   5   6   7   8   9    strongly agree

*Cognitive aspects of identification sub-scale*

*1.  I do not consider [Group X] to be important

    strongly disagree    1   2   3   4   5   6   7   8   9    strongly agree

2.  I feel strong ties to [Group X]

    strongly disagree    1   2   3   4   5   6   7   8   9    strongly agree

## Karasawa's (1991) two-component measure

This measure was initially used to examine Japanese school students' identification with their school. In this context Karasawa sought to differentiate between students' identification with the school as a whole and their identification with other students — a distinction that is likely to be relevant in a range of organizational contexts (see also Prentice, Miller & Lightdale, 1994). Following Hinkle et al. (1989), Karasawa also hypothesized that identification with the school would have separate cognitive and affective components, but he found no evidence to support this distinction in either of two studies. This particular measure was used in Karasawa's second study.

*Identification with group sub-scale*

1.  Would you think it was accurate if you were described as a typical [member of Group X]?

    extremely inaccurate    −3   −2   −1   0   1   2   3    extremely accurate

2.  How often do you acknowledge the fact that you are a [member of Group X]?

    never    −3   −2   −1   0   1   2   3    extremely often

3. Would you feel good if you were described as a typical [member of Group X]?

not at all    −3   −2   −1   0   1   2   3    extremely

4. How often do you refer to [Group X] when you introduce yourself?

never    −3   −2   −1   0   1   2   3    extremely often

5. To what extent do you feel attachment to [Group X]?

not at all    −3   −2   −1   0   1   2   3    extremely

*Identification with group members sub-scale*

1. Are there many [members of Group X] who have influenced your thoughts and behaviours?

none    −3   −2   −1   0   1   2   3    very many

2. Where do most of your best friends come from, [Group X] or not?

most not from this group    −3   −2   −1   0   1   2   3    most from this group

*Ellemers et al.'s (1999) three-component measure*

Ellemers and her colleagues devised this measure in order to differentiate between the three components of social identification implicit in Tajfel's (1972) original definition of social identity as 'the individual's *knowledge* that he [or she] belongs to certain groups together with some *emotional* and *value* significance to him [or her] of the group membership' (p. 31, emphasis added; see also Cameron, 1999, and Chapter 2 above). These components are (a) cognitive (a person's knowledge or awareness of a particular social self-categorization), (b) emotional (a person's feeling of affective commitment to the group), and (c) evaluative (a person's sense of group-based self-esteem). Ellemers et al.'s research supported the distinction between these components, and, as in Hinkle et al.'s (1989) earlier study, it suggested that each was differentially associated with particular forms of social behaviour. This research was conducted with university students who either assigned themselves or were experimentally assigned to minimal groups (as deductive or inductive thinkers).

*Note:* * = reverse scored

*Social self-categorization sub-scale*

1. I identify with [other members of Group X]

not at all    1   2   3   4   5   6   7    very much

2. I am like [other members of Group X]

not at all    1   2   3   4   5   6   7    very much

3.  [Group X] is a reflection of who I am

not at all     1    2    3    4    5    6    7    very much

## Group commitment sub-scale

1.  I would like to continue working with [Group X]

not at all     1    2    3    4    5    6    7    very much

*2.  I dislike being a member of [Group X]

not at all     1    2    3    4    5    6    7    very much

*3.  I would rather belong to [Group Y]

not at all     1    2    3    4    5    6    7    very much

## Group self-esteem sub-scale

*1.  I think [Group X] has little to be proud of

not at all     1    2    3    4    5    6    7    very much

2.  I feel good about [Group X]

not at all     1    2    3    4    5    6    7    very much

*3.  I have little respect for [Group X]

not at all     1    2    3    4    5    6    7    very much

*4.  I would rather not tell that I belong to [Group X]

not at all     1    2    3    4    5    6    7    very much

# Appendix 2

## Manipulations of Social and Organizational Identification

In order for researchers to conduct experimental investigations of social identity principles, it has been necessary for them not only to develop ways of *measuring* social identification (along lines suggested in Appendix 1) but also to devise methods for effectively *manipulating* it. In line with the analysis of social identity salience presented in Chapter 2 (Oakes, 1987; Turner, 1985; see also Figure A1.1), most of the strategies for doing this have involved manipulations of either perceivers' readiness to define themselves in terms of a particular social category (i.e. the *accessibility* of a social identity) or the comparative or normative *fit* of a particular social category.

This appendix presents details of a sample of different manipulations in order to provide some indication of the variety of available options. As with measures of social identification, no one manipulation is appropriate for all settings and most have to be adapted to the circumstances of a particular experiment and to the content of the particular identity that is being manipulated. Exactly which manipulation a researcher chooses to use will also depend on factors such as the nature of the identity to be manipulated (e.g. real or minimal), the research setting (e.g. laboratory- or field-based), and the response format (e.g. multi-phase or one-shot). Table A2.1 also provides a summary of the relative merits of each manipulation.

### Accessibility-based manipulations of social identity salience

Accessibility-based manipulations of social identity salience generally involve attempts to increase or decrease participants' awareness of their membership a particular group. Along these lines, basic strategies include (a) assigning only some participants to groups (e.g. Grieve & Hogg, 1999), (b) making some participants wear group-relevant uniform (e.g. badges and team dress; Gaertner et al., 1989; Worchel et al., 1998), or (c) decorating some participants' response environment with group-relevant regalia (e.g. posters and banners; James & Greenberg, 1989). James and Greenberg's (1989) anagram-solving task represents another interesting variation on such techniques. As discussed in Chapter 9, this requires participants in a high-salience condition to solve an anagram of the group's name [e.g. LDCITASW = WILDCATS] and those in a low-salience condition to solve a semantically related but irrelevant anagram [e.g. VREESBA = BEAVERS].

*Table A2.1* Summary of the features and merits of different manipulations of social and organizational identification

| Feature | Accessibility-based | | | | Normative fit-based | | Comparative fit-based | |
|---|---|---|---|---|---|---|---|---|
| | McGarty et al. (1994) | Doosje et al. (1995) | Verkuyten & Hagendoorn (1998) | Haslam et al. (1999) | Jetten et al. (1997) | Ellemers et al. (1999) | Kramer & Brewer (1984) | Uzubalis (1999) |
| Easy to administer | ✓ | | ✓ | ✓ | ✓ | ✓ | ✓ | ✓ |
| Introduces no major confounds | ✓ | ✓ | | ✓ | | ✓ | | |
| Suitable for real groups | ✓ | | ✓ | ✓ | ✓ | | ✓ | ✓ |
| Suitable for ad hoc groups | | ✓ | | | | ✓ | ✓ | |
| Strong and robust | | ✓ | ✓ | | | ✓ | ✓ | |
| Can be administered in conjunction with key dependent variables | ✓ | | ✓ | ✓ | ✓ | | ✓ | ✓ |

## McGarty et al.'s (1994) 'public commitment' manipulation

McGarty et al. (1994) manipulated social identity salience by asking participants in a high salience condition either (a) to state publicly their support for actions endorsed by members of an ingroup (Group X; in McGarty et al.'s study a group that wanted to improve road safety) or (b) to state publicly their rejection of actions endorsed by members of an outgroup (Group Y; in McGarty et al.'s study a group that wanted to ban alcohol consumption). To do this, participants responded to questions of the following form:

> Yes, I am in favour of [actions endorsed by Group X]  ❏
>
> No, I am not in favour of [actions endorsed by Group X]  ❏
>
> or
>
> Yes, I am in favour of [actions endorsed by Group Y]  ❏
>
> No, I am not in favour of [actions endorsed by Group Y]  ❏

Participants in the low salience condition were not required to complete this task. Although this manipulation is not particularly strong (and its effects are likely to wear off quite quickly), findings from McGarty et al.'s (1994) study indicate that it can be quite effective (see Chapter 5 above).

*Doosje et al.'s (1995) 'bogus pipeline' manipulation*

One of the most ingenious and elaborate manipulations of social identity salience was devised by Doosje et al. (1995). This was modelled on famous studies in which participants are led to believe that an experimenter has direct access to their thoughts and feelings via a 'bogus pipeline' (Jones & Sigall, 1971). The first phase of the Doosje et al.'s procedure involved participants responding on a computer to questions that had supposedly assessed their problem-solving style as *deductive* or *inductive* thinkers. However, before they completed this, three electrodes had been attached to one of the participants' hands and they were told that these would measure their galvanic skin response (GSR) as they responded. Participants were then given additional tasks which required them to select association words or numbers from lists that matched a key word or number (e.g. which word is most strongly associated with the key word 'house'? — 'number', 'street', 'flat' or 'room'). Finally, they were asked to respond to additional questions and were told that on the basis of their responses and GSR feedback the computer would be able to establish how strongly they identified with their group. These questions related directly or indirectly to group membership and social contact (e.g. 'Relationships with other people are very important to me' and 'Sometimes I feel lonely').

When they had completed these tasks, participants were told which group the computer had assigned them to and were also given an identification score. The average score was said to be 40. Participants in the high identification condition were given a score of 53 and those in the low identification condition a score of 27. Results on a manipulation check indicated that this was an extremely effective manipulation ($n = 101$, $F = 136.4$, $p < .001$). Obviously though, this procedure can only be attempted in a laboratory environment and is best suited to minimal identities.

*Verkuyten and Hagendoorn's (1998) 'self-esteem' manipulation*

This measure was originally devised to manipulate the salience of national identity but it can easily be adapted to an organizational (or other) context by changing the wording of the rubric and items in the social identity salience condition (e.g. to 'When did you start working with [Organization X]?', 'What is the main business of [Organization X]?', 'What is [Organization X]'s full name?). The final seven items in the social identity salience condition are based on items in Luhtanen and Crocker's (1982) collective self-esteem scale and Rosenberg's ethnic identification scale, and those in the personal identity salience condition are taken from Rosenberg's (1965) personal self-esteem scale. Responses on the manipulation check in Verkuyten and Hagendoorn's (1998) study indicated that the procedure was very effective ($n = 99$, $t = 3.14$, $p < .01$).

*Social identity instructions:*

People belong to all kinds of groups, such as sports clubs, political parties, religious groups and also to a nation. These groups differ from each other and can also compare themselves with others. One sports club can compare itself with another, one political party with another, one nation with another.

1. In which country were you born?  ...........................

2. What language do you speak? ...........................

3. What nationality is your passport? ...........................

Indicate your agreement with the following items by circling one number on each scale:

4.  I feel good about being [a member of Group X]

      do not agree at all    1    2    3    4    5    6    7    agree completely

5.  I often regret that I am [a member of Group X]

      do not agree at all    1    2    3    4    5    6    7    agree completely

6.  In general, I am glad to be [a member of Group X]

      do not agree at all    1    2    3    4    5    6    7    agree completely

7.  Overall, I often do not like being [a member of Group X]

      do not agree at all    1    2    3    4    5    6    7    agree completely

8.  Being [a member of Group X] is important for me

      do not agree at all    1    2    3    4    5    6    7    agree completely

9.  If someone says something bad about [Group X] they say something bad about me

      do not agree at all    1    2    3    4    5    6    7    agree completely

10. If I could be born again, I would want to be [a member of Group X] again

      do not agree at all    1    2    3    4    5    6    7    agree completely

*Personal identity instructions:*

People differ from each other in all kinds of ways, and every person is a unique individual.  One person loves music and another likes to go for a walk, and another person likes to read whereas another likes to go out.  How do you differ from other people?

1. What are your hobbies? ...........................

2. In what year were you born? _ _ _ _

3. Are you concerned with your general appearance? ........

Indicate your agreement with the following items by circling one number on each scale:

4. On the whole I am satisfied with myself

      do not agree at all   1   2   3   4   5   6   7   agree completely

5. At times I think I am no good at all

      do not agree at all   1   2   3   4   5   6   7   agree completely

6. I feel I do not have much to be proud of

      do not agree at all   1   2   3   4   5   6   7   agree completely

7. I take a positive attitude towards myself

      do not agree at all   1   2   3   4   5   6   7   agree completely

8. I certainly feel useless at times

      do not agree at all   1   2   3   4   5   6   7   agree completely

9. All in all, I am inclined to feel that I am a failure

      do not agree at all   1   2   3   4   5   6   7   agree completely

10. I wish I could have more respect for myself

      do not agree at all   1   2   3   4   5   6   7   agree completely

## *Haslam et al.'s (1999) 'three things' manipulation*

Along the lines of Verkuyten and Hagendoorn's (1998) manipulation, Haslam, Oakes et al. (1999) devised a simple procedure that involves participants' reflecting on things they do often, rarely, well and badly. One advantage of this manipulation is that participants make compatible responses in both conditions, and so the procedure does not introduce manipulation-specific confounds (e.g. as might occur if responding to one set of questions was more likely to elevate self-esteem than responding to another set; Campbell and Stanley, 1966). The manipulation is slightly weaker as a result, but Haslam, Oakes et al. found that it was still effective ($n = 132$, $t = 2.83$, $p < .01$).

### *Social identity instructions:*

1. List up to three things that you and most other [members of Group X] do relatively often

      i) ............................... ii) ............................... iii) ...............................

2. List up to three things that you and most other [members of Group X] do relatively rarely

      i) ............................... ii) ............................... iii) ...............................

3. List up to three things that you and most other [members of Group X] generally do well

   i) ................................. ii) ................................. iii) .................................

4. List up to three things that you and most other [members of Group X] generally do badly

   i) ................................. ii) ................................. iii) .................................

*Personal identity instructions:*

1. List up to three things that you personally do relatively often

   i) ................................. ii) ................................. iii) .................................

2. List up to three things that you personally do relatively rarely

   i) ................................. ii) ................................. iii) .................................

3. List up to three things that you generally do well

   i) ................................. ii) ................................. iii) .................................

4. List up to three things that you generally do badly

   i) ................................. ii) ................................. iii) .................................

## Normative fit-based manipulations of social identity salience

The general goal of manipulations which invoke normative fit principles is to vary social identity salience by making a particular group membership more or less consistent with a perceiver's expectations about the self. This is typically achieved by describing the group more positively in one condition than another, or leading participants to believe that they have a direct rather than an indirect role in their assignment to the group.

### Jetten et al.'s (1997) 'linguistic framing' manipulation

The manipulation developed by Jetten, Spears and Manstead (1997) asks participants to indicate their agreement or disagreement with six positive and six negative statements. It achieves its effects by making respondents feel positively about a particular group membership in the high-salience condition (which is normatively fitting with a positive social self-definition) and negatively (or neutrally) about that group in low-salience conditions (which is less fitting). Jetten et al. (1997) used this procedure to manipulate students' identification with their academic discipline (psychology) and responses on key dependent measures indicated that it was quite effective. However, one of the procedure's limitations is that in the process of manipulating social identity salience it may also impact upon participants' self-esteem or mood and so these factors may contribute to any effects that are ultimately observed on key dependent measures.

*High-salience instructions:*

*Negative Things About [Organization X]*

|  | Agree | Disagree |
|---|---|---|
| 1. I feel no real affiliation with [Organization X]. | ❏ | ❏ |
| 2. The facilities at [Organization X] are not as modern as the facilities at other similar organizations. | ❏ | ❏ |
| 3. There is no sense of community spirit at [Organization X]. | ❏ | ❏ |
| 4. Considering everything, [Organization X] has a lower prestige compared to other similar organizations. | ❏ | ❏ |
| 5. The relaxed atmosphere at [Organization X] does not promote dedication to work. | ❏ | ❏ |
| 6. The diversity of the [Organization X] community means that it can never really be a united body. | ❏ | ❏ |

• How many times did you tick 'Agree' to these negative things?                     ........

*Positive Things About [Organization X]*

|  | Agree | Disagree |
|---|---|---|
| 1. Members of [Organization X] are more friendly and sociable than members of other similar organizations. | ❏ | ❏ |
| 2. The standard of work at [Organization X] is generally high. | ❏ | ❏ |
| 3. [Organization X] has a welcoming atmosphere. | ❏ | ❏ |
| 4. [Organization X] offers many activities in which members can become involved. | ❏ | ❏ |
| 5. In general, I like working at [Organization X]. | ❏ | ❏ |
| 6. Members of [Organization X] are intelligent. | ❏ | ❏ |

• How many times did you tick 'Agree' to these positive things?                     ........

*Low-salience instructions:*

*Positive Things About [Organization X]*

|  | Agree | Disagree |
|---|---|---|
| 1. I identify very strongly with [Organization X]. | ❏ | ❏ |
| 2. It is essential for me that my friends are from [Organization X]. | ❏ | ❏ |
| 3. I only want to join in [Organization X] activities. | ❏ | ❏ |
| 4. I wouldn't be able to work at any other organization. | ❏ | ❏ |
| 5. A feeling of solidarity with other members of [Organization X] is most important to me | ❏ | ❏ |
| 6. I don't understand people wanting to work in other organizations. | ❏ | ❏ |

• How many times did you tick 'Agree' to these positive things?                    ........

*Negative Things About [Organization X]*

|  | Agree | Disagree |
|---|---|---|
| 1. When you really think about it, [name of higher status organization] has a higher status in the community than [Organization X]. | ❏ | ❏ |
| 2. I think it is important to have friends outside [Organization X]. | ❏ | ❏ |
| 3. When I first came to [Organization X] I sometimes felt lost. | ❏ | ❏ |
| 4. I would have considered working at other organizations not just [Organization X]. | ❏ | ❏ |
| 5. Sometimes the people at [Organization X] are more interested in controversy than people's needs. | ❏ | ❏ |
| 6. There are some things I don't like about [Organization X]. | ❏ | ❏ |

• How many times did you tick 'Agree' to these negative things?                    ........

*Ellemers et al.'s (1999) 'self-assignment' manipulation*

Ellemers et al. (1999) conducted a minimal group study in which participants were assigned to one of two minimal groups whose members were said to have either an inductive or deductive problem solving style (as in Doosje et al., 1995). In the low-salience condition participants were *assigned by the experimenter* to one of these groups, supposedly on the basis of their responses to a preliminary questionnaire in which they had to state their agreement with statements such as 'I usually see more than one possible solution for problems I am faced with' and 'I sometimes have difficulty seeing things from a broader perspective'. In the high-salience condition participants were given a definition of the two problem solving styles and *assigned themselves* to the group that they thought they belonged to. This manipulation impacted on an aggregate measure of identification (combining the three scales of self-categorization, commitment, and self-esteem; see Appendix 1 above), but this effect was mainly attributable to differences on the commitment sub-scale ($n = 119$, $F = 11.45$, $p < .001$).

## Comparative fit-based manipulations of social identity salience

One of the most tried and tested methods of increasing social identity salience is to invoke intergroup comparison. This can be achieved in any number of ways: for example (a) by exposing participants to an outgroup before they complete a given task (e.g. Haslam, Oakes, Turner & McGarty, 1995; Platow, O'Connell, Shave & Hanning, 1995), (b) by suggesting an ingroup is under threat from an outgroup (e.g. Spears et al., 1997) or (c) by providing a cover story which suggests that a study involves intergroup competition (e.g. Kramer & Brewer, 1984; van Vugt & de Cremer, 1999). Although such manipulations are generally very powerful, one of their problems is that they are relatively indirect and can introduce confounds (e.g. by increasing hostility, fear, competitiveness or demands on attention).

### *Kramer and Brewer's (1984) 'intergroup comparison' manipulation*

In their study of social dilemmas, Kramer and Brewer (1984) told students at the University of Santa Barbara that they were taking part in research that was also being conducted with elderly residents of the Santa Barbara. To manipulate social identity salience, participants in a high salience condition were told that the aim of the study was explicitly to compare the performance of young and old people, while those in the low salience condition were simply told that the research was interested in the performance of Santa Barbara residents in general. Van Vugt and de Cremer (1999) used a similar procedure in two subsequent experiments and responses on a single-item manipulation check ('How much do you identify with your group?') indicated that this was very successful (Experiment 1: $n = 96$, $F = 6.14$, $p < .01$; Experiment 2: $n = 93$, $F = 21.16$, $p < .001$).

### *Uzubalis's (1999) 'major competitor' manipulation*

In a study that examined the impact of comparative context on reactions to power use (Uzubalis, 1999; see Chapter 8 above) manipulated social identity salience by asking participants in a high salience (intergroup) condition to respond to a series of questions that compared their own organization to its major competitor.  Participants in the low salience (intragroup) condition were not given these questions.  The questions were as follows:

1. List three main competitors of [Organization X]

   i) ................................ ii) ................................ iii) ..............................

2. Of these which is [Organization X]'s major competitor? ................................

3. In relation to the major competitor:

   • Which organization has more future potential? (tick one box)

      [Organization X] ❏     Major competitor ❏

   • Which organization has the better reputation for customer service?

      [Organization X] ❏     Major competitor ❏

   • Which organization is the more prestigious in the mind of the general public?

      [Organization X] ❏     Major competitor ❏

   • All things considered, which organization are you more committed to?

      [Organization X] ❏     Major competitor ❏

   • All things considered, which organization do you value more?

      [Organization X] ❏     Major competitor ❏

# Appendix 3

## Glossary of Social Identity and Self-categorization Terms

This glossary contains short definitions of some of the social psychological terms that are central to social identity and self-categorization theories. For examples of common usage, refer to the subject index.

Note that here, and in the appendices that follow, where terms refer to a process they usually also refer to the *outcome* of that process. Convergence, for example, is a process of behavioural accommodation but it is also what is achieved as a result of that process.

**accessibility** A principle of category salience which suggests that a given category is more likely to become salient to the extent that it has prior meaning and significance for a perceiver.

**approval-seeking outgroup violation** Unfair or aggressive treatment of an outgroup by a leader (or other group member) that is intended to increase approval for him or her within an ingroup.

**comparative fit** A principle of category fit which suggests that a given category is more likely to become salient to the extent that the differences between members of that category are perceived to be smaller than the differences between members of that category and comparison others.

**convergence** A process of accommodation whereby a person's language-related or other behaviour becomes more similar to the behaviours perceived to be characteristic of another person or group with whom they are interacting.

**depersonalization** The process of self-stereotyping through which the self comes to be perceived as categorically interchangeable with other ingroup members.

**divergence** A process of accommodation whereby a person's language-related or other behaviour becomes more different from the behaviours perceived to be characteristic of another person or group with whom they are interacting.

**fit** A principle of category salience which suggests that a given category is more likely to become salient to the extent that the pattern of similarities and differences between category members defines that category as meaningfully different from one or more other categories.

**functional antagonism** The assumption that as the salience of one level of self-categorization increases that of other levels decreases.

**impermeable group boundaries** Conditions that prevail when it is perceived to be impossible to move from one particular group into another.

**ingroup** A group that is perceived to be self-defining in a particular context (i.e. a social self-category).

**ingroup violation** Unfair or aggressive treatment of an ingroup that is counter-normative and likely to be disapproved of by its members.

**level of abstraction**  The degree of inclusiveness associated with a particular categorization. Categories defined at a higher level of abstraction are more inclusive.

**mechanical social identity**  An internalized group-based self-definition whose content recognizes similarity amongst group members (e.g. role interchange-ability).

**meta-contrast**  A principle of categorization which suggests (a) that a given category is more likely to become salient to the extent that the differences between members of that category are perceived to be smaller than the differences between members of that category and salient others (i.e. where there is comparative fit) and (b) that a given category member is more likely to be seen as representative of a given category to the extent that he or she is perceived to be less different to other category members than to members of other salient categories.

**minimal group**  A group or social category that has no prior meaning for a perceiver.

**minimal group paradigm**  An experimental strategy which involves assigning individuals to groups that have no prior meaning for them (after Tajfel et al., 1971).

**normative fit**  A principle of category fit which suggests that a given category is more likely to become salient to the extent that the pattern of observed content-related similarities and differences between category members is consistent with the perceiver's prior expectations.

**organic social identity**  An internalized group-based self-definition whose content recognizes complementary differences between group members (e.g. role differentiation or individual specialization).

**organizational identification**  A relatively enduring state that reflects an individual's willingness to define him- or herself as a member of a particular organization.

**outgroup**  A group that is perceived to be *non*self-defining in a particular context (i.e. a social nonself-category).

**outgroup violation**  Unfair or aggressive treatment of an outgroup that is normative and likely to be approved of by an ingroup.

**perceiver readiness**  A principle of category salience which suggests that a given category is more likely to become salient to the extent that a perceiver is psychologically predisposed to use it as a basis for perception or action (e.g. because it has prior meaning and significance).

**permeable group boundaries**  Conditions that prevail when it is perceived to be possible to move from one particular group into another.

**personal identity**  An individual's knowledge that he or she is different from other people (group members) together with some emotional and value significance to him or her of this sense of individuality.

**positive distinctiveness**  A condition in which an ingroup is defined more positively than a comparison outgroup on some self-valued dimension.

**prototypicality**  The extent to which a given category member is representative of the category as a whole. This is partly determined by principles of normative and comparative fit.

**psychological group**  A group that is psychologically real for a perceiver in a particular context because it contributes to his or her social identity.

**reference group** A group to which an individual belongs but which does not necessarily contribute to his or her social identity (e.g. because it has no emotional or value significance).

**referent informational influence** The self-categorization process that leads individuals to define themselves in terms of a particular group membership and then to seek out and act in terms of relevant group norms.

**self-categorization** The process of perceiving the self as an interchangeable member of a category that is defined at a particular level of abstraction (e.g. personal, social or human).

**self-categorization theory** An explanatory framework developed by Turner and colleagues in the 1980s that focuses on the role of social categorization processes in group formation and behaviour (see Turner, 1985; Turner et al., 1987).

**social change** A strategy for self-enhancement that involves collective defence or rejection of existing intergroup relations.

**social change belief system** A set of beliefs associated with the salience of a particular social identity that leads people to pursue self-enhancement by collectively defending or rejecting the status quo.

**social creativity** A strategy for self-enhancement that involves collective redefinition of the content and meaning of existing intergroup relations.

**social identification** A relatively enduring state that reflects an individual's readiness to define him- or herself as a member of a particular social group.

**social identity** An individual's knowledge that he or she belongs to certain groups together with some emotional and value significance to him or her of the group membership (Tajfel, 1972, p. 31).

**social identity approach** A psychological metatheory that encompasses the principles and assumptions articulated within social identity and self-categorization theories.

**social identity salience** The process that leads individuals to define themselves and act in terms of a given social identity in a particular context.

**social identity theory** An explanatory framework developed by Tajfel and Turner in the 1970s that focuses on the psychological underpinnings of intergroup relations and social conflict (see Tajfel, 1978; Tajfel & Turner, 1979).

**social mobility** A strategy for self-enhancement that involves accepting existing intergroup relations and striving for personal advancement within them.

**social mobility belief system** A set of beliefs associated with the salience of people's personal identities that leads them to pursue self-enhancement individually by accepting the status quo and striving for personal advancement.

**speech accommodation** The process underpinning convergent or divergent changes in a person's language-related behaviour that serves to reflect identity-based relations between communicators.

**speech accommodation theory** An explanatory framework developed by Giles and colleagues in the 1970s that focuses on the psychological underpinnings of speech accommodation (see Giles & Johnson, 1981).

# Appendix 4

# Glossary of Social Psychological Terms

This glossary provides short definitions of some of the social psychological terms that relate to the various topics addressed in this book (excluding those already defined in Appendix 3). For examples of common usage, refer to the subject index.

**categorization**  The process of perceiving two or more things to be similar to or different from each other as a function of properties they are perceived to share or not share in a particular context.

**coercion**  The process of attempting to influence another parties' behaviour through the use of power alone.

**cognitive miser approach**  A framework for studying social cognition which suggests that thought processes are constrained by people's limited information-processing capacity and an associated need to conserve cognitive resources.

**cohesion**  A group characteristic that reflects a high degree of psychological alignment amongst its members and enables them to act in concert as a group.

**collecitve action**  Behaviour which is determined by a person's membership of a social group and which is performed in concert with other members of that group.

**communication**  The process of transferring information and meaning between two or more people.

**consistency seeker approach**  A framework for studying social cognition which suggests that people strive to manage and make sense of their various cognitions (especially attitudes and beliefs) by making them mutually consistent.

**deindividuation**  The process that leads people to lose a sense of themselves as accountable individuals and as a result engage in deviant and antisocial behaviour.

**distributive justice**  The provision of fair outcomes (e.g. rewards and penalties).

**equity theory**  A theory of social behaviour which suggests that people seek equality between individuals in the ratio of their inputs to outputs.

**extrinsic motivation**  Motivation based on features of the task environment that are external to the individual (e.g. reward or punishment).

**free-riding**  The process whereby individuals make a strategic decision to reduce their contribution to a group task (e.g. because the contribution is perceived to be unimportant or redundant).

**group consensualization**  The process that leads to individuals' attitudes (and behaviour) becoming more consensual after group interaction.

**group polarization** The process that leads to individuals' attitudes (and behaviour) becoming more extreme after group interaction.

**groupthink** A process of excessive concurrence-seeking that leads members of small cohesive groups to maintain esprit de corps by unconsciously developing a number of shared illusions and related norms that interfere with critical thinking and reality testing (Janis, 1982, p. 35).

**Hawthorne effect** A threat to the validity of research posed by people's awareness that they are being studied. As a result of this awareness, findings reflect the *fact* that research is being conducted, rather than the nature of researchers' manipulations.

**individual difference approach** An approach to the study of social behaviour based on an appreciation of the differences between individuals (e.g. in personality, motivation, cognitive style).

**informational influence** The process whereby attitudes and behaviour are shaped and changed as a result of exposure to relevant information.

**intrinsic motivation** Motivation based on features of the task environment that are internal to the individual (e.g. personal goals).

**leadership** The process of influencing others in a manner that enhances their contribution to the realization of group goals.

**naive scientist approach** A framework for studying social cognition which suggests that thought processes (especially processes of attribution) are the product of rational attempts to make inferences on the basis of multiple sources of information in the environment.

**need for achievement (*n*Ach)** An individual difference in people's motivation to pursue personal goals.

**need for affiliation (*n*Aff)** An individual difference in people's motivation to achieve and maintain rewarding interpersonal relationships with others.

**need for power (*n*Pow)** An individual difference in people's motivation to assume and maintain control over others' circumstances and behaviour.

**norms** Attitudes and behaviours that are shared by members of a particular group. These serve to define the group and to guide its members thoughts, feelings and behaviour.

**persuasive arguments theory** A theory which asserts that social influence occurs as a result of people's exposure to information that they perceive to be relevant, novel and valid.

**pluralistic ignorance** A state that arises when individuals understand the actions of other people that are similar to their own to be the product of a different cause.

**power** The process that results in a person or group having (or being perceived to have) control over the behaviour and circumstances of others by virtue of the reward- and punishment-related resources at their disposal.

**power distance** The perceived discrepancy in the power of two or more people or groups.

**procedural justice** The provision of fair processes for delivering outcomes (e.g. rewards and penalties).

**psychologization** The process of seeking to explain social phenomena as a consequence of psychological functioning. This leads to the view that all social problems (e.g. prejudice, conflict, depression) are psychological problems and can be rectified by appropriate psychological intervention.

**relative deprivation** The process that leads individuals or groups to perceive themselves to be disadvantaged as a result of comparison with relevant others.

**relative deprivation theory** A theory of social behaviour which suggests that perceptions of relative deprivation motivate individuals to engage in certain forms of compensatory behaviour (e.g. industrial action).

**social categorization** The process of perceiving two or more people (or things associated with them — e.g. attitude statements) to be similar to or different from each other in a particular context.

**social cognition** Either (a) mental processes associated with the processing of information about people, (b) mental processes that are associated with, or affected by, social influence, or (c) the study of (a) or (b).

**social comparison** The process of comparing oneself (or one's group) with others that are perceived to be similar in relevant respects in order to gain information about one's opinions and abilities.

**social comparison theory** A theory of social behaviour developed by Festinger in the 1960s which suggests that people evaluate themselves and their abilities through processes of social comparison.

**social compensation** The process that leads members of groups to work harder in order to compensate for the perceived deficiencies of other group members.

**social exchange theory** A theory of social behaviour which suggests that individuals are sensitive to the costs and benefits of particular actions (e.g. improved productivity, industrial protest) and that their behaviour is governed by these perceptions.

**social facilitation** The process that leads to individual performance on a task being enhanced by the co-presence of others.

**social impact theory** A theory developed by Latané and colleagues in the 1980s which asserts that social influence depends on the strength, immediacy and number of the social sources (people and things associated with them) that impact upon a person.

**social influence** The process through which people shape and change the attitudes and behaviour of others.

**social labouring** The process that leads to individual performance on a task being enhanced as a result of working in a group.

**social loafing** The process that leads to individual performance on a task being diminished as a result of working in a group.

**social psychology** Either the study of psychological processes (e.g. thinking and feeling) associated with social interaction, or those processes themselves (as in 'the social psychology of leadership').

**socially shared cognition** Mental processes that are common to different individuals (e.g. as a result of social influence) and that are assumed to underpin various forms of co-ordinated social behaviour (e.g. communication, division of labour).

**stereotype** A cognitive representation of a group (typically in terms of traits and attributes) that is shared by members of that group or by members of another group.

**stereotyping** The process of perceiving people in terms of their group membership rather than as individuals.

**transactive memory**  A process of encoding, storing and retrieving information by group members that relies upon the capacity for different individuals to perform complementary tasks.

**transactive memory system**  The socially shared body of knowledge that results from transactive memory processes.

# Appendix 5

# Glossary of Organizational Terms

This glossary provides short definitions of some of the organizational terms that relate to the various topics addressed in this book (excluding those already defined in Appendix 4). For examples of common usage, refer to the subject index.

**bargaining** A process through which individuals or groups with a conflict of interests attempt to achieve outcomes that are acceptable to all parties.

**bargaining zone** The set of outcomes to a bargaining process in which all parties achieve more than they consider minimally acceptable.

**brainstorming** An idea-generating process which involves group members contributing and developing ideas in an uncritical setting.

**bridging** A negotiation strategy in which parties move towards integrative solutions that provide each party with outcomes that it gives more priority to than the other party.

**bureaucratic control** The process of attempting to manage organizational behaviour and bring about desired outcomes through administrative and other formal strategies.

**bureaupathy** Dysfunctional organizational behaviour that is associated with displays of petty tyranny and is generally assumed to reflect an underlying personality disorder.

**career commitment** A psychological state that reflects a person's willingness to engage in behaviour that enhances their personal career prospects and goals.

**charismatic leadership** A capacity to influence group members to contribute to group goals that is seen to derive from distinctive qualities that are inherent in a leader's personality.

**consideration** Supervisory behaviour characterized by concern for the well-being of subordinates.

**contextual performance** Forms of organizational behaviour that do not represent core organizational activity, but which enhance the organizational environment as a whole.

**contingency theories** A class of organizational theories that explain behaviour as the product of the interaction between an individual's personality and features of the organizational environment in which they operate.

**delphi group** A decision-making unit in which individuals respond privately to questionnaires and to feedback about the responses of the group as a whole before an executive decision is made.

**economic approach** An approach to organizational theory which asserts that individuals' behaviour is motivated by economic principles of profit and loss (e.g. the prospect of material gain).

**effectiveness** A measure of behavioural output relative to goals.

**efficiency** A measure of behavioural output relative to input.

**empowerment** The process of devolving power and authority to individuals or groups that were previously powerless.

**gain frame** A mental state in which a person is more aware of the gains and benefits associated with a particular event (e.g. the outcome of negotiation) than of the losses and costs.

**gainsharing** The policy of sharing the profits that flow from increased organizational productivity amongst the workers that contributed to it.

**glass ceiling** An informal organizational or professional barrier that denies members of disadvantaged groups access to high status positions.

**goal-setting theory** A theory of social behaviour which suggests that motivation is enhanced by providing workers with clearly defined goals.

**human relations approach** An approach to organizational theory and practice which suggests that work behaviour is shaped by individuals' membership in work groups and needs to be sensitive to the norms of those groups and the status and power relations between them.

**human resource management (HRM)** The professional practice of organizational science as applied to manage the behaviour of people in the workplace.

**incentivation** The process of seeking to motivate employees by providing them with personal incentives.

**initiation of structure** Supervisory behaviour that enhances performance by clarifying subordinates' roles, goals and tasks.

**integrative potential** The scope for negotiation to produce an integrative solution as dictated by the size of negotiators' bargaining zone.

**integrative (win–win) solution** An outcome to a negotiation or bargaining process in which all parties achieve more than they consider minimally acceptable.

**just-in-time production systems (JIT)** Methods for organizing the work environment (e.g. managing stock, hiring personnel) which aim to ensure that at any point in time no more resources are available than absolutely necessary.

**leader style** The means by which a leader attempts to influence followers to contribute to group goals. A distinction is typically made between styles that focus on the task and those that focus on relationships between group members.

**lean production** A system of organizational practices which marry reductions in workforce size with increases in work intensification.

**least preferred co-worker (LPC)** A construct central to Fiedler's (e.g. 1964) contingency theory of leadership which is used to identify people with different leader styles. Depending on how positively they rate their least preferred co-worker, the construct differentiates between individuals who are task-oriented (low LPC) and those who are relationship-oriented (high LPC).

**log-rolling** A negotiation strategy in which parties move towards integrative solutions through concessions that are of minimal value to themselves but of considerable value to the other party.

**loss frame** A mental state in which a person is more aware of the losses and costs associated with a particular event (e.g. the outcome of negotiation) than of the gains and benefits.

**management-by-stress (MBS)** Methods for organizing the work environment (e.g. pacing production, hiring personnel) which aim to ensure that at any point in time all workers are stretched (and stretching each other) to capacity.

**managerialization** The process of seeking to explain organizational phenomena as the consequence of management action. This leads to the view that all organizational problems are management problems and can be rectified by appropriate managerial intervention.

**mechanical solidarity** Group cohesion based on group members' performance of similar tasks that serve similar functions.

**mediation** A process of conflict resolution in which individuals or groups interact via, or in collaboration with, a third party in an attempt to resolve their differences.

**negotiation** A process through which individuals or groups with a conflict of interests attempt to achieve outcomes that resolve their differences and are acceptable to all parties.

**nominal group** A decision-making unit in which people develop ideas alone, present and discuss them as a group, and then evaluate them individually.

**open systems approach** An approach to organizational theory and practice which builds upon human relations theory by suggesting that work behaviour is shaped by the flexible system of relations between social groups that exist within and outside an organization.

**organic pluralism** An approach to organizational theory and practice (proposed in Chapter 11 above) which argues that any superordinate organizational identity should recognize, accommodate and encourage subgroup identities that reflect the self-determined interests and aspirations of employees.

**organic solidarity** Group cohesion based on group members' performance of complementary tasks that serve complementary functions.

**organizational change** Change in the circumstances, activities or policies of an organization that is usually initiated by senior management but which affects all members of the organization.

**organizational citizenship** Altruistic or conscientious organizational behaviour that enhances the organizational environment as a whole but which is not explicitly demanded or task-related.

**organizational commitment** A psychological state that reflects a person's willingness to engage in behaviour that enhances the prospects and goals of an organization.

**organizational culture** The constellation of roles, norms and values within any particular organization that serves to create shared meaning for its members.

**organizational science** A generic name for the output from all those academic disciplines that address the psychology and behaviour of people in the workplace.

**organizations** Social systems that co-ordinate people's behaviour by means of roles, norms and values. This co-ordination allows for the achievement of goals that individuals could not achieve on their own.

**performance** A measure of either (a) behavioural output or (b) behavioural output relative to expectations.

**petty tyranny** A regime of management characterized by (a) arbitrariness and self-aggrandizement, (b) belittling of subordinates, (c) lack of consideration for others, (d) a forcing style of conflict resolution, (e) discouraging initiative and (f) non-contingent punishment.

**productivity** A measure of either (a) behavioural output relative to goals (effectiveness) or (b) behavioural output relative to input (efficiency).

**quality circle** A group of employees that meets regularly, frequently and on a voluntary basis to discuss the quality of their work. The group typically has no power to implement ideas or decisions.

**scientific management** An approach to organizational theory and practice which seeks to replace 'rules of thumb' with flexible prescriptions for work behaviour based on rigorous analysis of the total work situation and identification of 'the one best way' for an individual to perform a given task. The approach emphasizes the contribution of efficiency, uniformity and hierarchical authority to positive organizational outcomes.

**soldiering** The process that leads to individual performance on a task being diminished as a result of a collective strategy on the part of group members.

**Taylorism** A name commonly given to the organizational philosophy and practices of scientific management as developed by Frederick Taylor at the start of the twentieth century.

**team-talk** Styles of speech and language use that are characteristic of cohesive work-groups (e.g. including mentions of 'we', 'us' and 'ours', rather than 'I', 'me' or 'mine').

**team-Taylorism** Organizational practice in which the principles of scientific management are applied to the management of workteams. This is generally associated with increased work intensification.

**Theory X** A hypothetical theory of work motivation (akin to that which is implicit in Taylorism) derived from assumptions that workers are inherently under-motivated and will only work hard if coerced into doing so (e.g. through reward and punishment).

**Theory Y** A hypothetical theory of work motivation derived from assumptions that workers are inherently motivated and will work hard without needing to be coerced.

**Theory Z** A hypothetical theory of work motivation derived from a hybrid set of Theory X and Theory Y assumptions.

**360-degree feedback** A method of providing individuals with information about their performance that involves obtaining feedback from multiple co-workers (e.g. supervisors, subordinates, peers). It is used to monitor performance and leadership and to guide planning.

**tokenism** The strategy of allowing a small proportion of members from a low-status group to gain membership of a high-status group. This reduces the likelihood of the low-status group engaging in collective action in order to change status relations.

**total quality management** A set of organizational practices which place responsibility for the quality of output in the hands of workers rather than management.

**work intensification** The process by which labour is extracted with increasing efficiency from a workforce.

# Author Index

# Subject Index

*Note*: ❸ ❹ ❺ = terms defined in Appendices 3, 4 and 5
Numbers in **bold** refer to glossary definitions

Indices compiled by Kristine Veenstra